*In appreciation and gratitude to
those who in mathematics and life have been
our students and our teachers,
especially those who at various times
have been both.*

Robert J. Hill
Thomas A. Keagy

Elementary Linear Algebra with *DERIVE*®

An integrated text

Chartwell-Bratt Studentlitteratur

We would like to thank the personnel of Soft Warehouse for their help whenever we had problems, especially Al Rich and David Stoutemyer.

Derive is a registered trademark of Soft Warehouse, Inc. Honolulu, Hawaii

British Library Cataloguing in Publication Data
A catalogue record for this book is available from the British Library

Chartwell-Bratt (Publishing and Training) Ltd
ISBN 0-86238-403-6

Printed in Sweden
Studentlitteratur, Lund
ISBN 91-44-60781-4

Printing: 1 2 3 4 5 6 7 8 9 10 | 1999 98 97 96 95

PREFACE

This book provides a complete introduction to elementary linear algebra. Some of the topics covered require a background in calculus, but the most important gain from completing a standard one year calculus sequence prior to studying this material is an increased level of mathematical maturity rather than the ability to perform specific calculus techniques. This maturity level is not required for most of the computational work covered in the text - material such as systems of linear equations, which are also discussed in lower level algebra classes. Instead, maturity is required to comprehend the theoretical aspects of the material. For many students, linear algebra is the first mathematics course which has a significant theoretical component. This text seeks to find a balance between theory and application which maintains the integrity of the presentation while at the same time progresses through the material at a pace which allows coverage of interesting and useful applications. Proofs for all but a very small number of theorems are provided in the text. These proofs are accessible to students new to abstract mathematics and should be included in their study since they provide valuable insight into the examples and applications which follow.

Throughout this text the symbolic computer software system *Derive*® is used to illustrate numeric examples which reinforce and explain the theoretical underpinnings of the material. Without this tool the computational requirements present a barrier to learning. Without the computational examples, the theory becomes an empty shell without meaning. Concepts can be illustrated immediately in this environment, without the distraction of learning cumbersome calculation techniques that too frequently frustrate the first time learner. An early example of how the computer software provides the student an easy entree into a topic which can quickly become entwined in computational details which distract the focus of a student is found in determining the inverse of a matrix. On this topic, and many others which follow, an explanation is provided which allows the reader to understand the computations which take place in the background, but the computer facilitates these calculations in a way that promotes an understanding of the theory.

Throughout the text examples of the underlying theory are provided, in most cases with computations illustrated in *Derive* statements. The student is encouraged to duplicate these examples, many of which have missing steps to conserve space and help the narrative of the book flow more smoothly. Sufficient details of the examples are provided to give the reader the major landmarks on the road to the solution, and, as in all mathematics, the material only comes alive when the reader is actively involved in doing the mathematics rather than reading about it. Traditionally, students have been told to read a mathematics text with paper and pencil in hand. The key role of technology in this text requires another important tool for complete understanding: the computer.

With all the emphasis on the use of a symbolic computer software system in this presentation, it is important to note that the focus remains on the mathematics rather than the software system itself. Enough guidance is provided in the text for a first time user of *Derive* to feel comfortable emulating text examples. The software is a simple menu driven system, and the learning curve is so gentle that soon the student will be experimenting with new examples of his or her own design. Although an effort has been made to use efficient command sequences to solve text examples, the emphasis has been placed on presenting examples in a straightforward logical presentation that emulates hand calculations. Experienced *Derive* users will therefore no doubt find shortcuts to simplify some of these routines.

As a final comment about the philosophy behind this presentation, we note that relief from the burden of computation not only allows for expanded content coverage, it also promotes a higher level of learning. Questions about how the results of an example might differ based on some proposed change in the initial conditions are easily answered. With some encouragement from the instructor, students quickly learn to translate their curiosity into modified examples that will answer their questions. The software makes it easy to experiment and places a premium on students' ability to interpret and explain their results.

This book contains more than enough material for a half year introductory course in linear algebra. Although the temptation may be to present the material at an even pace, we recommend a more rapid coverage of the early material, especially the first chapter. Students who are not familiar with *Derive* will require an introduction to the system, but that presentation should be limited since students find the software interesting in its own right and easy to learn by experimenting with the menu driven program using the help screens provided. Chapter IV, Determinants, also contains topics which can be covered in a minimal amount of time. Although determinants are used in subsequent sections, the necessary portion of this material can be summarized in approximately one lecture unit. If this plan is followed, some of the more interesting applications contained in Chapter VII can be covered in enough detail to provide insight into the broad range of potential uses of linear algebra. Of the application sections, only Section 7.1, least squares approximation, can be studied after completing systems of equations in Chapter I. The remaining application sections require material in the matrix analysis sections contained in Chapter VI.

As in any undertaking of this nature, we owe a debt of gratitude to many individuals who supported and encouraged us through the entire process. Philip Yorke, our editor at Chartwell-Bratt, had enough confidence in us to initiate this project and the stamina to see it through to its completion. Our colleagues in the Department of Mathematics and Computer Science at Duquesne University provided an environment that encouraged us to be creative. Among them, we owe special thanks to two individuals in particular: Kathleen Taylor, who taught from a very early version of the text and provided us with many helpful comments and suggestions which improved the presentation, and Bret Larget, who made significant contributions to Section 7.3 on Markov processes. We salute the students who found themselves in courses where this text was pilot tested. Their patience and many helpful comments were greatly appreciated. Two colleagues from Kent State University, John Fridy and Richard Brown, made several helpful suggestions which improved the matrix analysis sections in Chapter VI. Of course, we also thank our reviewers for their many contributions, and note that without the clerical assistance of Josie Stanton and Jerry Shoemaker we would still be buried under a sea of paper. Finally, on a very personal level, we acknowledge the support, understanding, and love of our families and friends. Without them we could have never completed this project. To all who contributed to this effort, we extend a sincere thank you.

CONTENTS

CHAPTER I
DERIVE® AND MATRICES

The presentation of linear algebra given in this textbook relies heavily on the use of the Derive® symbolic computer software system. After a short introduction to the program, the concept of a matrix is introduced, and an algebraic structure is defined for sets of matrices. Finally, matrices are used in an application which results in an efficient method to solve systems of linear equations.

1. INTRODUCTION TO *DERIVE*®

The *Derive* symbolic computer software system has features that perform all the basic tasks presented in a standard algebra-trigonometry-calculus course sequence. In this text we will use the program to simplify the tedious calculations that can distract the learner and discourage the user of linear algebra. Although this first section is devoted to *Derive*, it is unique in the sense that all of the remaining sections of the text use the package as a tool to aid our study rather than have it serve as the object of our study. Since the mathematics presented in this section is not new to linear algebra, the reader who is familiar with the *Derive* program should immediately turn to Section 1.2 to begin the study of linear algebra.

The purpose of this introductory section is to provide enough information about some of the basic commands of *Derive* to allow the reader to begin using the software as quickly as possible, bridging the gap between students who have studied calculus using *Derive* and those who have had no exposure to the software. Basic information required to use the package to study linear algebra is provided in the text. Complete explanations of features are contained in the *Derive User Manual*, and the reader is encouraged to refer to this document if questions arise.

When the *Derive* program is started the initial screen appears as on the next page. Note that each of the choices in the command list has one capital letter. A command can be selected either by typing its corresponding capital letter (which in this text is indicated by bold printed capital letter) or by moving the highlight feature using the Tab key (to move forward in the list) or the Shift-Tab key combination (to move backward in the list) until the desired command is highlighted and then pressing the Enter key.

```
                         D E R I V E
                  A Mathematical Assistant

                        Version 3.03


              Copyright (C) 1988 through 1994 by
                    Soft Warehouse, Inc.
                3660 Waialae Avenue, Suite 304
              Honolulu, Hawaii, 96816-3236, USA

Please do not make illegal copies of DERIVE!  This software is not shareware or
freeware.  It is not to be published on bulletin boards or distributed by any
other means without written permission from Soft Warehouse, Inc.

For technical support or if you know of any person or company distributing
DERIVE as shareware or freeware, please write us at the above address or send a
fax to (808) 735-1105.

                       Press H for help
```

```
COMMAND: Author Build Calculus Declare Expand Factor Help Jump solve Manage
         Options Plot Quit Remove Simplify Transfer Unremove moVe Window approX
Enter option
                                    Free:100%                   Derive Algebra
```

EXAMPLE 1.1 The expression $x^3 - 7x - 6$ can be entered into *Derive* by selecting the **A**uthor command and typing *x*^3-7*x*-6 followed by the Enter key. The expression can then be factored by selecting the command **F**actor followed by the command **R**ational. The results of these two steps appear on the *Derive* screen as follows:

```
         3
1:      x  - 7 x - 6

2:     (x - 3) (x + 1) (x + 2)
```

Note that *Derive* numbers expressions, and these numbers will appear in examples illustrated in this text using the software system. To move from expression to expression use the up and down arrow keys. Unwanted expressions can be deleted from the list using the **R**emove command. To find the derivative of statement #1, highlight the statement, choose the **C**alculus command, then select **D**ifferentiate, choose the order, and confirm the variable. These steps yield statement #3 which is evaluated as statement #4 by selecting the **S**implify command.

$$3: \quad \frac{d}{dx}(x^3 - 7x - 6)$$

$$4: \quad 3x^2 - 7$$

To find the antiderivative of statement #1, highlight the statement, choose the **C**alculus command, then select **I**ntegrate, and confirm the variable. *Derive* will ask for the limits of integration. To find the antiderivative press Enter to continue with the integration without limits. This will yield statement #5. Use the **S**implify or **E**xpand command to evaluate the expression.

$$5: \quad \int (x^3 - 7x - 6)\, dx$$

$$6: \quad \frac{x^4}{4} - \frac{7x^2}{2} - 6x$$

To divide statement #1 by $x-3$, choose the **A**uthor command and enter #1/(*x*-3) to generate statement #7 on the screen. To perform the indicated operation choose the **S**implify or **E**xpand command. The result is given in statement #8.

$$7: \quad \frac{x^3 - 7x - 6}{x - 3}$$

$$8: \quad x^2 + 3x + 2$$

To evaluate statement #1 at $x = 5$, highlight statement #1, select the **M**anage command, choose the **S**ubstitute option, replace *x* with 5, and press Enter. Statement #9 will appear on the screen. To evaluate this expression choose the **S**implify or **E**xpand command.

$$9: \quad 5^3 - 7\,5 - 6$$

$$10: \quad 84$$

EXAMPLE 1.2 A very useful feature of *Derive* is its ability to use functional notation. Given

$$f(x) = \frac{x^2 + 3x + 1}{x - 2} \quad \text{and} \quad g(x) = x + \frac{1}{x}$$

we can enter the two expressions on the right side of the = using the **A**uthor command as in Example 1.1. [Note that statement #1 is entered as (*x*^2+3*x*+1)/(*x*-2).]

$$1: \quad \frac{x^2 + 3x + 1}{x - 2}$$

$$2: \quad x + \frac{1}{x}$$

Next, we use the **D**eclare command and select the **F**unction option. For the name of the function type *f*, and finally for the value of the function type #1. This procedure can be repeated to obtain the second function. The *Derive* screen will appear as follows:

$$3: \quad F(x) := \frac{x^2 + 3x + 1}{x - 2}$$

$$4: \quad G(x) := x + \frac{1}{x}$$

EXAMPLE 1.3 Once a function is defined as in Example 1.2, we can evaluate it at specific values and find expressions to represent more complicated situations such as compositions and functions evaluated at an expression. For example, to find $f(3)$, use the **A**uthor command to enter *f*(3) and the **S**implify command to evaluate statement #5.

5: F(3)

6: 19

(Note that the default setting for *Derive* does not distinguish between capital and lower case letters. To distinguish between the two, use the **O**ptions - **I**nput command sequence. Also, if a string of statements in *Derive* has two different definitions for a function with the same name, the most recent declaration overrides the first.)

To find $f(g(x))$, use the **A**uthor command to enter *f*(*g*(x)) and the **S**implify command to obtain statement #8:

```
7:   F(G(x))
```

$$8: \quad \frac{x^4 + 3x^3 + 3x^2 + 3x + 1}{x(x^2 - 2x + 1)}$$

To find $\dfrac{f(x+h)-f(x)}{h}$, use the **A**uthor command to enter (*f*(*x*+*h*)-*f*(*x*))/*h* and the **S**implify command to obtain statement #10:

$$9: \quad \frac{F(x + h) - F(x)}{h}$$

$$10: \quad \frac{x^2 + x(h - 4) - 2h - 7}{(x - 2)(x + h - 2)}$$

EXAMPLE 1.4 Given $f(x) = 3x^3 + x + 1$, we can find the equation of the tangent line at the point $(p, f(p))$. First, the function is entered using the **D**eclare and **F**unction command sequence, entering *f* for the name of the function and 3*x*^3+*x*+1 for the value of the function.

$$1: \quad F(x) := 3x^3 + x + 1$$

To obtain the slope, we differentiate this expression by choosing the **C**alculus and **D**ifferentiate command sequence and highlighting statement #1 when prompted for the expression to be differentiated. After **S**implifying this expression, we can define a new function *fp* which represents the derivative of *f*.

2: $\frac{d}{dx}(F(x) := 3x^3 + x + 1)$

3: $9x^2 + 1$

4: $FP(x) := 9x^2 + 1$

We may now enter the equation of the line at $(p, f(p))$ using the **A**uthor command. The expressions for *f(p)* and *fp(p)* can then be substituted into statement #5 by using the **S**implify command, and statement #6 can be solved for *y* using the so**L**ve command.

5: $y - F(p) = FP(p)(x - p)$

6: $y - 3p^3 - p - 1 = (x - p)(9p^2 + 1)$

7: $y = x(9p^2 + 1) - 6p^3 + 1$

To find the equation of the tangent line at $(2, f(2))$, use the **M**anage command followed by the **S**ubstitute command to let $p = 2$ in statement #7. Since the statement has three variables, a prompt is provided for each. Press Enter when prompted for x and for y and overtype with a 2 when prompted for p. To evaluate statement #8, use the **S**implify command.

8: $y = x(9\ 2^2 + 1) - 6\ 2^3 + 1$

9: $y = 37x - 47$

Derive provides many curve sketching options that are helpful in working with functions of this type. The reader is referred to the *Derive User Manual* for details on this subject.

In calculus we learned about vectors and vector valued functions. *Derive* provides an easy means of handling vectors through the use of the **D**eclare command when it is followed by the vecto**R** option. *Derive* provides a prompt for a number representing the dimension of the desired vector. Typically vectors studied in calculus were either two or three dimensional. In this section we will use $[p,q,r]$ to denote a vector whose x,y,z components are p,q and r respectively.

EXAMPLE 1.5 The magnitude of the sum of the vectors [1,2,5] and [2,-3,6] can be found by first declaring them as described above, followed by calculating the sum by **A**uthoring the expression #1+#2, and, finally, **S**implifying the resulting expression.

```
1:   [1, 2, 5]

2:   [2, -3, 6]

3:   [1, 2, 5] + [2, -3, 6]

4:   [3, -1, 11]
```

To find the magnitude of the vector in statement #4 we use the **A**uthor command to enter abs(#4), resulting in statement #5. Statement #6 is obtained by using the **S**implify command.

```
5:   |[3, -1, 11]|

6:   √131
```

EXAMPLE 1.6 *Derive* can also be used to find the scalar (dot) and cross products of vectors such as those defined in Example 1.5. The scalar product can be obtained by using the **A**uthor command to enter #1.#2, and the cross product can be obtained by entering cross(#1,#2). Each operation is computed by using either the **S**implify or the **E**xecute command.

```
7:   [1, 2, 5] · [2, -3, 6]

8:   26

9:   CROSS([1, 2, 5], [2, -3, 6])

10:  [27, 4, -7]
```

EXAMPLE 1.7 Recall that two vectors are orthogonal (perpendicular) whenever their scalar product is zero. The cross product of two vectors is always orthogonal to both of the vectors. This property can be illustrated using *Derive* and the vectors defined in Example 1.4.

```
11:  [1, 2, 5] · [27, 4, -7]

12:  0

13:  [2, -3, 6] · [27, 4, -7]

14:  0
```

EXAMPLE 1.8 The vector equation for the line passing through the two points (1,3,2) and (4,-1,2) can be found by first entering the points into *Derive* as vectors from the origin. The difference of these vectors gives a vector from one point to the other which is in the direction of the line. Hence

```
1:   [1, 3, 2]

2:   [4, -1, 2]

3:   [4, -1, 2] - [1, 3, 2]

4:   [3, -4, 0]

5:   [1, 3, 2] + t [3, -4, 0]
```

where statement #5 is the vector equation for the line.

This section has provided a very brief introduction to some of the features of *Derive* which have application in a typical calculus course sequence. As we proceed through the text you will become more familiar with the commands. The best way to learn a new software package is to use it frequently. The *Derive User Manual* and help screens will provide assistance when questions arise.

2. MATRICES AND THE ALGEBRA OF MATRICES

Often is it is convenient to arrange information in a table format. In mathematics such a rectangular array is called a matrix. The dimension of a matrix is determined by its number of rows (horizontal) and columns (vertical) with a matrix having m rows and n columns said to have dimension $m \times n$. Matrices are denoted by boldface capital letters

$\mathbf{A},\mathbf{B},\mathbf{C},\cdots$etc. If $m = n$, the matrix is said to be a square matrix of order n or simply a matrix of order n. Some examples of matrices are

$$\mathbf{A} = \begin{bmatrix} 1 & 0 & 3 \\ -2 & 1 & 4 \\ 3 & 2 & 1 \end{bmatrix},$$

a square matrix of order 3, and

$$\mathbf{B} = \begin{bmatrix} 1 & 2 & 3 \\ 1 & 0 & 2 \end{bmatrix},$$

a 2×3 matrix (2 rows and 3 columns).

The element in row i and column j of the matrix $\mathbf{A}$ is represented by a_{ij}. The order of the subscripts is important: the first represents the row number, and the second represents the column number of the entry. For example, in the matrix $\mathbf{A}$ above, the element a_{32} is 2. Frequently the notation

$$\mathbf{A} = (a_{ij}) \quad i = 1,2,\cdots,m; \quad j = 1,2,\cdots,n$$

will be used to denote an $m \times n$ matrix with elements a_{ij}. Sometimes, especially when a complicated product or sum is involved, the element in row i and column j of a matrix $\mathbf{A}$ is noted by $(\mathbf{A})_{ij}$.

Derive has a special feature to input matrices. The user first selects the command **D**eclare followed by the command **M**atrix. The program then prompts for the number of rows and, after pressing the tab key, the number of columns. After accepting the dimension of the matrix by pressing the enter key, elements of the matrix are inserted row by row with zeroes inserted by the program as default values for any elements skipped. Each entry is accepted by pressing the enter key. The matrix **B** above entered in this fashion would appear on the *Derive* screen as follows:

$$1: \quad \begin{bmatrix} 1 & 2 & 3 \\ 1 & 0 & 2 \end{bmatrix}$$

Matrices can be combined using operations which are reminiscent of the familiar addition and multiplication operations for real numbers and operations which alter a matrix by systematically changing its elements or dimension. Before defining these operations we first state what it means for two matrices to be equal.

DEFINITION 2.1 (Equality of Matrices) Two matrices are said to be equal if they have the same dimension and their corresponding elements are all equal. More formally, **A** and **B** are equal if both are $m \times n$ matrices satisfying $a_{ij} = b_{ij}$ for all i and j. In this case we write **A** = **B**.

DEFINITION 2.2 (Addition of Matrices) The sum of two matrices with the same dimension is found by adding corresponding entries. If $\mathbf{A} = (a_{ij})$ and $\mathbf{B} = (b_{ij})$, $i = 1,2,\cdots,m;\ j = 1,2,\cdots n$, then

$$\mathbf{A} + \mathbf{B} = (a_{ij} + b_{ij}).$$

EXAMPLE 2.1 The sum of the two 3×3 matrices

$$\mathbf{A} = \begin{bmatrix} 1 & 2 & 3 \\ 0 & -1 & 2 \\ -1 & 2 & 4 \end{bmatrix} \text{ and } \mathbf{B} = \begin{bmatrix} 2 & 2 & 2 \\ 1 & 3 & 0 \\ 4 & -2 & -4 \end{bmatrix}.$$

is found by adding the corresponding entries as follows:

$$\mathbf{A} + \mathbf{B} = \begin{bmatrix} 1+2 & 2+2 & 3+2 \\ 0+1 & -1+3 & 2+0 \\ -1+4 & 2-2 & 4-4 \end{bmatrix} = \begin{bmatrix} 3 & 4 & 5 \\ 1 & 2 & 2 \\ 3 & 0 & 0 \end{bmatrix}.$$

To perform the addition in *Derive*, first **D**eclare the two **M**atrices, then **A**uthor the sum to obtain an expression for the sum, and finally **S**implify the sum for the desired result. (Note that *Derive* recognizes the fact that matrix addition is only defined for matrices with the same dimension by repeating the addition expression when a **S**implify command is requested by mistake.) For the above example, the resulting *Derive* screen appears as follows:

1: $\begin{bmatrix} 1 & 2 & 3 \\ 0 & -1 & 2 \\ -1 & 2 & 4 \end{bmatrix}$

2: $\begin{bmatrix} 2 & 2 & 2 \\ 1 & 3 & 0 \\ 4 & -2 & -4 \end{bmatrix}$

3: $\begin{bmatrix} 1 & 2 & 3 \\ 0 & -1 & 2 \\ -1 & 2 & 4 \end{bmatrix} + \begin{bmatrix} 2 & 2 & 2 \\ 1 & 3 & 0 \\ 4 & -2 & -4 \end{bmatrix}$

4: $\begin{bmatrix} 3 & 4 & 5 \\ 1 & 2 & 2 \\ 3 & 0 & 0 \end{bmatrix}$

where statement #3 is the result of **A**uthoring the expression #1+#2 and statement #4 is the result of **S**implifying statement #3.

Since matrix addition is defined in terms of element by element addition of real numbers, the familiar commutative and associative properties hold for the operation.

THEOREM 2.1 If **A**, **B**, and **C** are matrices with equal dimension, then matrix addition is commutative

$$\mathbf{A} + \mathbf{B} = \mathbf{B} + \mathbf{A}$$

and matrix addition is associative

$$\mathbf{A} + (\mathbf{B} + \mathbf{C}) = (\mathbf{A} + \mathbf{B}) + \mathbf{C} = \mathbf{A} + \mathbf{B} + \mathbf{C}.$$

PROOF: The proof of the commutative property is provided. The proof of the associative property is left as an exercise.

Let $\mathbf{A} = (a_{ij})$, and $\mathbf{B} = (b_{ij})$ where i = 1,2,···,m; j = 1,2,···,n. Then

$$\mathbf{A} + \mathbf{B} = (a_{ij} + b_{ij}) = (b_{ij} + a_{ij}) = \mathbf{B} + \mathbf{A}$$

since a_{ij} and b_{ij} are real numbers, and addition of real numbers is commutative.

EXAMPLE 2.2 If $\mathbf{A} = \begin{bmatrix} 1 & 2 \\ 3 & 4 \end{bmatrix}$, $\mathbf{B} = \begin{bmatrix} -1 & 2 \\ 0 & 3 \end{bmatrix}$, and $\mathbf{C} = \begin{bmatrix} 3 & -4 \\ -2 & 1 \end{bmatrix}$, then

$$\mathbf{A} + \mathbf{B} = \begin{bmatrix} 0 & 4 \\ 3 & 7 \end{bmatrix} = \mathbf{B} + \mathbf{A}$$

and

$$\begin{aligned} \mathbf{A} + (\mathbf{B} + \mathbf{C}) &= \begin{bmatrix} 1 & 2 \\ 3 & 4 \end{bmatrix} + \left(\begin{bmatrix} -1 & 2 \\ 0 & 3 \end{bmatrix} + \begin{bmatrix} 3 & -4 \\ -2 & 1 \end{bmatrix} \right) \\ &= \begin{bmatrix} 1 & 2 \\ 3 & 4 \end{bmatrix} + \begin{bmatrix} 2 & -2 \\ -2 & 4 \end{bmatrix} \\ &= \begin{bmatrix} 3 & 0 \\ 1 & 8 \end{bmatrix} \\ &= \begin{bmatrix} 0 & 4 \\ 3 & 7 \end{bmatrix} + \begin{bmatrix} 3 & -4 \\ -2 & 1 \end{bmatrix} \\ &= \left(\begin{bmatrix} 1 & 2 \\ 3 & 4 \end{bmatrix} + \begin{bmatrix} -1 & 2 \\ 0 & 3 \end{bmatrix} \right) + \begin{bmatrix} 3 & -4 \\ -2 & 1 \end{bmatrix} \\ &= (\mathbf{A} + \mathbf{B}) + \mathbf{C}. \end{aligned}$$

Given the set of all matrices of any particular dimension along with the addition operation we have an algebraic system that appears to behave in the same manner as more familiar systems such as the real numbers. In fact two additional familiar properties also hold. If we define **0** to be the matrix having the same dimension as **A** with all elements equal to zero and $-\mathbf{A}$ to be the matrix with entries $-a_{ij}$, then **0** is the *additive identity* of the system (**A** + **0** = **A** for each matrix **A**), and -**A** is the *additive* *inverse* of **A** (**A** + -**A** = **0** for each matrix **A**). We leave it for the exercises to show that the additive identity and inverse are unique.

It might seem natural to define a multiplication operation for matrices at this point (and in fact such an operation exists and is defined in the next section) in an effort to further emphasize similarities between our algebraic structure for matrices and more familiar algebraic systems. Instead, we choose to define two operations which begin to distinguish the algebraic structure of sets of matrices from the algebraic structure of other systems. The first of these provides a means of expressing multiples of matrices.

DEFINITION 2.3 (Matrix Scalar Multiplication) A matrix may be multiplied by a scalar quantity (a real number or a symbol representing a real number) by multiplying each element of the matrix by the scalar. If $\mathbf{A} = (a_{ij})$, i = 1,2,⋯,m; j = 1,2,⋯,n, and α is a real number, then $\alpha \mathbf{A} = (\alpha a_{ij})$, i = 1,2,⋯,m; j = 1,2,⋯,n.

EXAMPLE 2.3 If $\mathbf{A} = \begin{bmatrix} 1 & -1 \\ -2 & 3 \end{bmatrix}$, then $-3\mathbf{A} = \begin{bmatrix} -3 & 3 \\ 6 & -9 \end{bmatrix}$. This operation would appear on a *Derive* screen as follows:

```
        [  1  -1 ]
1:      [        ]
        [ -2   3 ]

           [  1  -1 ]
2:    - 3  [        ]
           [ -2   3 ]

        [ -3   3 ]
3:      [        ]
        [  6  -9 ]
```

where statement #1 is the result of the **D**eclare and **M**atrix commands, statement #2 is obtained by **A**uthoring -3 #1 (or -3∗#1), and statement #3 is obtained by **S**implifying statement #2.

Since matrix scalar multiplication does not involve the combination of two elements from a common set (for example two matrices, or two real numbers), it is impossible to discuss whether the operation is commutative or associative in the same sense that we viewed matrix addition in Theorem 2.1 above. But the following theorem provides some insight into rules that can be used to simplify expressions involving matrix scalar multiplication.

THEOREM 2.2 If **A** and **B** are matrices and α and β are scalars (real numbers), then the following properties hold:

i.) $(\alpha + \beta)\,\mathbf{A} = \alpha\mathbf{A} + \beta\mathbf{A}$

ii.) $\alpha(\mathbf{A} + \mathbf{B}) = \alpha\mathbf{A} + \alpha\mathbf{B}$

iii.) $\alpha(\beta\mathbf{A}) = (\alpha\beta)\mathbf{A}$

iv.) $1\mathbf{A} = \mathbf{A}$

v.) $0\mathbf{A} = \mathbf{0}$

PROOF: The proof of the first property is provided as a model. The proofs of the remaining properties are left as an exercise. Let $\mathbf{A}=(a_{ij})$, i = 1,2,···,m; j = 1,2,···,n. Then

$$(\alpha+\beta)\mathbf{A} = (\alpha+\beta)(a_{ij}) = ((\alpha+\beta)a_{ij}) = (\alpha a_{ij} + \beta a_{ij}) = (\alpha a_{ij}) + (\beta a_{ij}) = \alpha\mathbf{A} + \beta\mathbf{A}$$

where the second and fifth equalities hold by the definition of scalar multiplication, the third equality follows from the fact that real number multiplication distributes over addition, and the fourth equality holds by the definition of matrix addition.

Matrix addition provides a way to combine two matrices to obtain a third matrix. Scalar multiplication provides a way to combine a matrix and a scalar, which for us will be either a real number or an expression representing a real number, to obtain a matrix. A third matrix operation, the transpose of a matrix, provides a way to rearrange the elements of a matrix, resulting in a new matrix with exactly the same elements, but having them arranged in a different order.

DEFINITION 2.4 (Transpose of a Matrix) The transpose of an $m{\times}n$ matrix is obtained by interchanging the rows and columns of the matrix, yielding an $n \times m$ matrix. If $\mathbf{A} = (a_{ij})$, then the transpose of **A**, noted by $\mathbf{A}^{\mathrm{T}}$, is defined to be $\mathbf{A}^{\mathrm{T}} = (a_{ji})$.

EXAMPLE 2.4 If $\mathbf{A} = \begin{bmatrix} 1 & 1 & 1 \\ 2 & 2 & 2 \end{bmatrix}$, then the transpose of **A** can be obtained by merely interchanging the rows and columns **A** yielding: $\mathbf{A}^{\mathrm{T}} = \begin{bmatrix} 1 & 2 \\ 1 & 2 \\ 1 & 2 \end{bmatrix}$. *Derive* can also be used to find $\mathbf{A}^{\mathrm{T}}$. Once the matrix **A** is declared, an expression is **A**uthored by listing the line number of the matrix followed by the back-accent symbol. For example, if $\mathbf{A} = \begin{bmatrix} 11 & 12 \\ 21 & 22 \end{bmatrix}$, then the *Derive* screen would appear as follows:

$$1: \quad \begin{bmatrix} 11 & 12 \\ 21 & 22 \end{bmatrix}$$

$$2: \quad \begin{bmatrix} 11 & 12 \\ 21 & 22 \end{bmatrix}`$$

$$3: \quad \begin{bmatrix} 11 & 21 \\ 12 & 22 \end{bmatrix}$$

where statement #3, which provides $\mathbf{A}^{\mathrm{T}}$, is obtained by **S**implifying statement #2.

Finally, we list two properties of the transpose of a matrix which will assist in simplifying expressions involving the sum of two matrices or the scalar multiple of a matrix.

THEOREM 2.3 If **A** and **B** are matrices with equal dimension, then

i.) $(\mathbf{A} + \mathbf{B})^{\mathrm{T}} = \mathbf{A}^{\mathrm{T}} + \mathbf{B}^{\mathrm{T}}$, and

ii.) $(\alpha\mathbf{A})^{\mathrm{T}} = \alpha\mathbf{A}^{\mathrm{T}}$.

iii.) $(\mathbf{A}^{\mathrm{T}})^{\mathrm{T}} = \mathbf{A}$

PROOF: The proof of property ii.) is provided as a model. The proofs of the other two properties are left as an exercise. Let $\mathbf{A} = (a_{ij})$, $i = 1,2,\cdots,m$; $j = 1,2,\cdots,n$. Then

$$(\alpha\mathbf{A})^{T} = \left(\alpha(a_{ij})\right)^{T} = (\alpha a_{ij})^{T} = (\alpha a_{ji}) = \alpha(a_{ji}) = \alpha\mathbf{A}^{T},$$

where the second and fourth equalities hold by definition of scalar multiplication and the third and fifth equalities hold by definition of the transpose of a matrix.

EXERCISES

1. Let $\mathbf{A} = \begin{bmatrix} 1 & 2 \\ 3 & 4 \end{bmatrix}$ and $\mathbf{B} = \begin{bmatrix} -1 & 0 \\ -1 & 4 \end{bmatrix}$. By hand and by using *Derive* find:

   a) $\mathbf{A} + \mathbf{B}$ b) $\mathbf{A} - \mathbf{B}$
   c) $3\mathbf{A} + 2\mathbf{B}$
   d) $3\mathbf{A}^{T} - 2\mathbf{B} + \mathbf{B}^{T}$
   e) The additive inverse of **A**
   f) The additive inverse of **B**
   g) The additive inverse of $\mathbf{A} + \mathbf{B}$
   h) The additive inverse of 3**A**

2. Based on your observations from Exercise 1 above, state rules for each of the following expressions that follow the patterns in Theorems 2.2 and 2.3:

   a) $-(\mathbf{A} + \mathbf{B}) =$ b) $-(\alpha\mathbf{A}) =$
   c) $-\mathbf{A}^{T} =$
   d) Test your rules for these three expressions by evaluating each side of the equality using *Derive* given $\alpha = -5$,

   $\mathbf{A} = \begin{bmatrix} 3 & -2 & 6 & 2 \\ 0 & -1 & -7 & 8 \end{bmatrix}$ and $\mathbf{B} = \begin{bmatrix} 3 & -5 & -7 & 0 \\ 4 & 1 & 5 & -9 \end{bmatrix}$.

3. Find a matrix **X** such that $\begin{bmatrix} 2 & 3 & 1 \\ 1 & 0 & -1 \end{bmatrix} + \mathbf{X} = \begin{bmatrix} 2 & 0 & 0 \\ 3 & 4 & 5 \end{bmatrix}$.

4. Find $\begin{bmatrix} 1 & 2 \\ 3 & 4 \end{bmatrix}^{T} + \begin{bmatrix} 1 & 2 \\ 3 & 4 \end{bmatrix}$.

5. Does the sum $\begin{bmatrix} 1 & 2 & 3 \\ -1 & 2 & 0 \end{bmatrix}^{T} + \begin{bmatrix} 1 & 0 & 0 \\ -1 & 0 & 3 \end{bmatrix}$ exist? Give reasons for your answer. Perform this addition with *Derive* and explain the result.

6. Find $\left(2\mathbf{A}^{\mathrm{T}}+3\mathbf{B}^{\mathrm{T}}\right)^{\mathrm{T}}$ where $\mathbf{A}=\begin{bmatrix}1 & 0\\ 2 & 4\end{bmatrix}$ and $\mathbf{B}=\begin{bmatrix}-1 & 2\\ 1 & 1\end{bmatrix}$.

7. Given that given that **A**, **B**, and **C** are matrices of equal dimension prove the associative property for matrix addition (the second property listed in Theorem 2.1).

8. Prove properties ii) - v) of Theorem 2.2.

9. Prove properties i) and iii) of Theorem 2.3.

10. Prove -**A** = -1**A**.

11. The additive identity of a system of matrices of the same dimension is unique.

12. Let **A** be a matrix in a system of matrices of the same dimension. The additive inverse of **A** is unique.

3. MULTIPLICATION OF MATRICES

In Section 1.2 we defined three operations on sets of matrices. Included among these was matrix addition which is performed by taking the sum of corresponding entries of the two matrices being added. In this section our definition of matrix multiplication is motivated by a desire to represent a system of linear equations in the matrix form $\mathbf{Ax} = \mathbf{b}$. In particular, if we examine a typical system of three linear equations in three unknowns such as

$$\begin{aligned} 3x - 4y + z &= 13 \\ -2x + y - 3z &= 7 \\ x - y + 17z &= -2 \end{aligned}$$

then after a first glance at the unknowns to make certain they are all listed in the same order on the same side of the equation, we quickly begin to focus on the coefficients and constants in the systems. These are the numbers that will determine the solution, and the particular variables used to express the system are of no importance in obtaining this solution.

Thus, it is natural to separate the coefficients from the variables (in much the same way we would to express a single equation in one unknown such as $2x = 14$) and write a matrix equation for the system of equations:

$$\begin{bmatrix} 3 & -4 & 1 \\ -2 & 1 & -3 \\ 1 & -1 & 17 \end{bmatrix} \begin{bmatrix} x \\ y \\ z \end{bmatrix} = \begin{bmatrix} 13 \\ 7 \\ -2 \end{bmatrix}.$$

Given this equation, our definition for matrix multiplication follows quickly. Since the matrix product on the left side of the equation must equal the matrix on the right side of the equation, we multiply the coefficients in a particular row, term by term, times the corresponding unknowns. The sum of these products equals the constant on the corresponding row of the matrix on the right side of the equation. From this we note that matrix multiplication is only possible when first matrix in the product has the same number of columns (coefficients) as the second matrix has rows (unknowns).

The concept of matrix multiplication can be generalized so that **AB** is defined as long as the number of columns of **A** equals the number of rows of **B**. The number of rows of **A** and the number of columns of **B** are not subject to any restrictions, but these numbers do determine the dimension of the product. As we will learn in this and subsequent sections, matrix multiplication under this definition is useful in solving a large number of applied problems, including systems of linear equations, even though it does not satisfy all of the properties we might expect of a binary operation in an algebraic system.

DEFINITION 3.1 (Matrix Multiplication) The product of the matrix **A** and the matrix **B** is the matrix **C** with elements $(\mathbf{AB})_{ij} = c_{ij}$ obtained by summing the product of the corresponding elements from row i of **A** and column j of **B**. If

$$\mathbf{A} = (a_{ik}) \ i = 1,2,\cdots,m; \ k = 1,2,\cdots,p \text{ and}$$
$$\mathbf{B} = (b_{kj}) \ k = 1,2,\cdots,p; \ j = 1,2,\cdots,n,$$

then the ij element of the product of **A** and **B** is defined to be

$$(\mathbf{AB})_{ij} = c_{ij} = \sum_{k=1}^{p} a_{ik} b_{kj}$$

for $i = 1, 2, \cdots, m$; $j = 1, 2, \cdots, n$.

It follows that the product of two matrices is not always defined, and when it is defined, the result may or may not be the same dimension as either of the two matrices being multiplied. In general a product which is defined appears as follows:

$$\underset{m \times p}{\mathbf{A}} \cdot \underset{p \times n}{\mathbf{B}} = \underset{m \times n}{\mathbf{C}}.$$

Thus, for example,

$$\underset{3 \times 2}{\mathbf{A}} \cdot \underset{2 \times 4}{\mathbf{B}} = \underset{3 \times 4}{\mathbf{C}} \quad \text{but} \quad \underset{3 \times 2}{\mathbf{A}} \cdot \underset{5 \times 4}{\mathbf{B}} \quad \text{is not defined.}$$

EXAMPLE 3.1 If $\mathbf{A} = \begin{bmatrix} k & l \\ m & n \\ o & p \end{bmatrix}$ and $\mathbf{B} = \begin{bmatrix} r & s \\ t & u \end{bmatrix}$, then the product of **A** and **B** is the 3×2 matrix **C** given by

$$\mathbf{C} = \begin{bmatrix} kr + lt & ks + lu \\ mr + nt & ms + nu \\ or + pt & os + pu \end{bmatrix}.$$

EXAMPLE 3.2 If $\mathbf{A} = \begin{bmatrix} 1 & -2 & 0 \\ 3 & -3 & 2 \\ 1 & 0 & -1 \end{bmatrix}$ and $\mathbf{B} = \begin{bmatrix} 1 & 0 & 0 & -1 \\ 3 & 2 & -2 & 2 \\ 3 & -2 & -1 & 4 \end{bmatrix}$,

then the matrix product is

$$\mathbf{AB} = \begin{bmatrix} -5 & -4 & 4 & -5 \\ 0 & -10 & 4 & -1 \\ -2 & 2 & 1 & -5 \end{bmatrix}.$$

EXAMPLE 3.3 Matrix multiplication is not always commutative; in fact, the existence of **AB** does not even imply the existence of **BA**. For instance, in Example 3.2 the product **AB** is defined, but the product **BA** is not defined since **B** has four columns and **A** has three rows. If both **AB** and **BA** are defined, they may not be equal, or even have the same dimension. For example, if **A** has dimension 2×3 and **B** has dimension 3×2, then **AB** has dimension 2×2 and **BA** has dimension 3×3; hence they are not equal. Sets of square matrices (such as the set of all 2×2 matrices) are closed under matrix multiplication (that is matrix multiplication is always defined for any two elements of the set). But it is still not always true that **AB** = **BA**. For example, if

$$\mathbf{A} = \begin{bmatrix} 1 & 0 \\ 0 & 0 \end{bmatrix} \text{ and } \mathbf{B} = \begin{bmatrix} 0 & 1 \\ 0 & 0 \end{bmatrix},$$

then

$$\mathbf{AB} = \begin{bmatrix} 0 & 1 \\ 0 & 0 \end{bmatrix} \text{ and } \mathbf{BA} = \begin{bmatrix} 0 & 0 \\ 0 & 0 \end{bmatrix}.$$

EXAMPLE 3.4 As with the three operations defined in Section 1.2, (matrix addition, scalar multiplication, and transposition), matrix multiplication can be performed easily using *Derive*. First, **A** and **B** are declared using the **D**eclare and **M**atrix commands. The expression **A·B** is then **A**uthored with the multiplication symbol generated by entering the symbol for a period. The result of the product is then found by using the **S**implify command. After declaring a 2×2 matrix and a 2×3 matrix, the product appears on the *Derive* screen as follows:

$$3: \quad \begin{bmatrix} 3 & -1 \\ 2 & 0 \end{bmatrix} \cdot \begin{bmatrix} 1 & 2 & 2 \\ 3 & 4 & 5 \end{bmatrix}$$

$$4: \quad \begin{bmatrix} 0 & 2 & 1 \\ 2 & 4 & 4 \end{bmatrix}$$

where statement #4 is the result of **S**implifying statement #3. If *Derive* is asked to multiply two matrices for which the product is not defined, the result of the **S**implify command is to repeat the product statement:

$$5: \quad \begin{bmatrix} 1 & 2 & 2 \\ 3 & 4 & 5 \end{bmatrix} \cdot \begin{bmatrix} 3 & -1 \\ 2 & 0 \end{bmatrix}$$

$$6: \quad \begin{bmatrix} 1 & 2 & 2 \\ 3 & 4 & 5 \end{bmatrix} \cdot \begin{bmatrix} 3 & -1 \\ 2 & 0 \end{bmatrix}$$

where statement #6 is the result of Simplifying statement #5.

Although the commutative property does not hold for matrix multiplication, the following two theorems show that both the associative property for matrix multiplication and the distributive property of matrix multiplication over matrix addition (for both right and left multiplication) hold as expected. Thus, although we are missing the commutative property, matrix multiplication does behave in much the same manner as operations in other more familiar algebraic systems such as the real numbers.

THEOREM 3.1 (Associative Property for Matrix Multiplication) If the dimensions of the matrices **A**, **B**, and **C** are such that the product **(AB)C** is defined, then the product **A(BC)** is defined, and the two products are equal.

PROOF: If **(AB)C** is defined, then **A** has the same number of columns as **B** has rows, and **C** has the same number of rows as **AB** has columns (which is the same as the number of columns of **B**). Thus let **A** be a matrix with dimension $m \times n$, **B** be a matrix with dimension $n \times p$ (hence **AB** has dimension $m \times p$), and **C** be a matrix with dimension $p \times q$. Both of the products **(AB)C** and **A(BC)** exist and have dimension $m \times q$. The ij entry of **(AB)C** is formed by summing the products of the corresponding entries of the ith row of **AB** and the jth column of **C**. To find the kth entry in the ith row of **AB**, the products of the corresponding entries of the ith row of **A** and the kth column of **B** are summed. Thus

$$(\mathbf{AB})_{ik} = \sum_{l=1}^{n} a_{il} b_{lk}$$

and

$$((\mathbf{AB})\mathbf{C})_{ij} = \sum_{k=1}^{p} (\mathbf{AB})_{ik} c_{kj}$$

$$= \sum_{k=1}^{p} \left(\sum_{l=1}^{n} a_{il} b_{lk} \right) c_{kj}.$$

Similarly, to find the ij entry of **A(BC)**:

$$(\mathbf{BC})_{lj} = \sum b_{lk} c_{kj}$$

and

$$(\mathbf{A}(\mathbf{BC}))_{ij} = \sum_{l=1}^{n} a_{il} (\mathbf{BC})_{lj}$$

$$= \sum_{l=1}^{n} a_{il} \left(\sum_{k=1}^{p} b_{lk} c_{kj} \right).$$

These representations for $((\mathbf{AB})\mathbf{C})_{ij}$ and $(\mathbf{A}(\mathbf{BC}))_{ij}$ differ only in the order of summation, but each of the summations is finite; therefore, the order can be interchanged by repeated use of the associative and distributive properties for the real numbers, and the proof is complete.

THEOREM 3.2 (Distributive Property of Matrix Multiplication over Matrix Addition) If **A**, **B**, and **C** are matrices such that either **A(B + C)** or **AB + AC** is defined, then both expressions are defined and the two expressions are equal. Similarly, if either of **(A + B)C** or **AC + BC** is defined, then both are defined and are equal.

PROOF: The proof is left as an exercise.

THEOREM 3.3 If the product **AB** is defined and k is a scalar, then

$$k(\mathbf{AB}) = (k\mathbf{A})\mathbf{B} = \mathbf{A}(k\mathbf{B}).$$

PROOF: The proof is left as an exercise.

THEOREM 3.4 If the product **AB** is defined, then $\mathbf{B}^{\mathrm{T}}\mathbf{A}^{\mathrm{T}}$ is defined and equals $(\mathbf{AB})^{\mathrm{T}}$.

PROOF: Let **A** be a $m\times p$ matrix and **B** be a $p\times n$ matrix so that **AB** is defined. Then $\mathbf{B}^T$ is a $n\times p$ matrix, $\mathbf{A}^T$ is a $p\times m$ matrix, and it follows that the product $\mathbf{B}^T\mathbf{A}^T$ is defined. Row i of $\mathbf{B}^T$ consists of the elements $b_{1i}, b_{2i}, \ldots, b_{pi}$ from column i of **B**. Column j of $\mathbf{A}^T$ consists of the elements $a_{j1}, a_{j2}, \ldots, a_{jp}$ from row j of **A**. Therefore, the element in row i, column j of $\mathbf{B}^T\mathbf{A}^T$ is $\sum_{k=1}^{p} b_{ki}a_{jk} = \sum_{k=1}^{p} a_{jk}b_{ki}$. But $\mathbf{AB} = \left(\sum_{k=1}^{p} a_{ik}b_{kj}\right)$, and the element in row i and column j of $(\mathbf{AB})^T$ is the element in row j and column i of **AB**. Thus $(\mathbf{AB})^T = \left(\sum_{k=1}^{p} a_{jk}b_{ki}\right)$, and the proof is complete.

EXAMPLE 3.5 Given $\mathbf{A} = \begin{bmatrix} 1 & 3 & -1 \\ 0 & 2 & 4 \end{bmatrix}$ and $\mathbf{B} = \begin{bmatrix} 1 & 0 & 0 & -1 \\ 2 & 2 & 3 & 1 \\ 1 & 1 & -1 & 4 \end{bmatrix}$,

we can compute $(\mathbf{AB})^T$ and $\mathbf{B}^T\mathbf{A}^T$ using *Derive* as follows:

$$3:\quad \begin{bmatrix} 1 & 0 & 0 & -1 \\ 2 & 2 & 3 & 1 \\ 1 & 1 & -1 & 4 \end{bmatrix}' \cdot \begin{bmatrix} 1 & 3 & -1 \\ 0 & 2 & 4 \end{bmatrix}'$$

$$4:\quad \begin{bmatrix} 6 & 8 \\ 5 & 8 \\ 10 & 2 \\ -2 & 18 \end{bmatrix}$$

$$5:\quad \left[\begin{bmatrix} 1 & 3 & -1 \\ 0 & 2 & 4 \end{bmatrix} \cdot \begin{bmatrix} 1 & 0 & 0 & -1 \\ 2 & 2 & 3 & 1 \\ 1 & 1 & -1 & 4 \end{bmatrix}\right]'$$

$$6:\quad \begin{bmatrix} 6 & 8 \\ 5 & 8 \\ 10 & 2 \\ -2 & 18 \end{bmatrix}$$

where statement #4 represents $\mathbf{B}^T\mathbf{A}^T$, and statement #6 represents $(\mathbf{AB})^T$.

In some cases it is more convenient to use a slightly different notation for matrix multiplication. Let **A** be an $n \times m$ matrix and **B** be a $m \times p$ matrix. We can represent the columns of **B** by $\mathbf{b}_1, \mathbf{b}_2, \cdots, \mathbf{b}_p$, so that $\mathbf{B} = [\mathbf{b}_1, \mathbf{b}_2, \cdots, \mathbf{b}_p]$. We can then write our usual matrix multiplication as the column by column products: $\mathbf{AB} = [\mathbf{Ab}_1, \mathbf{Ab}_2, \cdots, \mathbf{Ab}_p]$. The proof of this equivalence is left as an exercise.

If **A** is a square matrix of order n, it is easy to see that $\mathbf{A}^2 = \mathbf{AA}$ is defined, as is $\mathbf{A}^k$ for any integer k, where $\mathbf{A}^k = \mathbf{AA}^{k-1}$ for $k = 2,3,\cdots$. In the following example we evaluate powers of **A** using *Derive*.

EXAMPLE 3.6 If $\mathbf{A} = \begin{bmatrix} 1 & 2 \\ -1 & 0 \end{bmatrix}$, we can compute $\mathbf{A}^2$, $\mathbf{A}^3$, and $\mathbf{A}^{10}$ with *Derive* using exponentiation generated using the ^ symbol in an Author command. The *Derive* screen that generates $\mathbf{A}^2$, $\mathbf{A}^3$, and $\mathbf{A}^{10}$ is provided below with the desired results in statements #3, #5, and #7 respectively.

$$1: \quad \begin{bmatrix} 1 & 2 \\ -1 & 0 \end{bmatrix}$$

$$2: \quad \begin{bmatrix} 1 & 2 \\ -1 & 0 \end{bmatrix}^2$$

$$3: \quad \begin{bmatrix} -1 & 2 \\ -1 & -2 \end{bmatrix}$$

$$4: \quad \begin{bmatrix} 1 & 2 \\ -1 & 0 \end{bmatrix}^3$$

$$5: \quad \begin{bmatrix} -3 & -2 \\ 1 & -2 \end{bmatrix}$$

$$6: \quad \begin{bmatrix} 1 & 2 \\ -1 & 0 \end{bmatrix}^{10}$$

$$7: \quad \begin{bmatrix} 23 & -22 \\ 11 & 34 \end{bmatrix}$$

EXAMPLE 3.7 For the matrix **A** in Example 3.6 we can compute $\mathbf{A}^4 - 2\mathbf{A}^2 + 3\mathbf{A}$ by using a feature provided by *Derive* which permits the substitution of a matrix for a scalar. First, the matrix **A** is **D**eclared and the polynomial $x^4 - 2x^2 + 3x$ is **A**uthored, then the **M**anage command is used to select the polynomial (expression #2 in the *Derive* screen below), and the **S**ubstitute command is used to select the matrix (expression #1 below) which will replace x in the polynomial. Finally, the **S**implify command is used to evaluate expression #3. The *Derive* screen which shows each of these steps follows:

$$1: \quad \begin{bmatrix} 1 & 2 \\ -1 & 0 \end{bmatrix}$$

$$2: \quad x^4 - 2x^2 + 3x$$

$$3: \quad \begin{bmatrix} 1 & 2 \\ -1 & 0 \end{bmatrix}^4 - 2\begin{bmatrix} 1 & 2 \\ -1 & 0 \end{bmatrix}^2 + 3\begin{bmatrix} 1 & 2 \\ -1 & 0 \end{bmatrix}$$

$$4: \quad \begin{bmatrix} 4 & -4 \\ 2 & 6 \end{bmatrix}$$

EXERCISES

1. Multiply if possible:

a) $\begin{bmatrix} 1 & 1 \\ 1 & 0 \\ -1 & 1 \\ 2 & 2 \end{bmatrix}\begin{bmatrix} 1 & 2 & 2 & 0 & 1 \\ 2 & -1 & 1 & 2 & 1 \end{bmatrix}$

b) $\begin{bmatrix} 1 & -2 \\ 3 & 0 \end{bmatrix}\begin{bmatrix} 4 & 0 & 5 \\ 1 & -2 & -3 \end{bmatrix}$

c) $\begin{bmatrix} 2 \\ 1 \\ -3 \end{bmatrix}\begin{bmatrix} 1 & -2 & 0 \\ 0 & 4 & -1 \\ 2 & 2 & 1 \end{bmatrix}$

d) $\begin{bmatrix} 3 & 7 & -4 & 3 \\ 1 & 2 & -2 & -1 \\ 1 & 1 & 3 & 0 \\ 2 & -5 & 0 & 1 \end{bmatrix}\begin{bmatrix} 3 \\ -1 \\ 0 \\ 2 \end{bmatrix}$

e) **AB** where

$$\mathbf{A} = \begin{bmatrix} 3 & 1 & -4 & 0 \\ 0 & 0 & 2 & -3 \\ 0 & 3 & 6 & 0 \end{bmatrix}$$

and $\mathbf{B} = \begin{bmatrix} 1 & 1 & -1 \\ 9 & 0 & 5 \\ 3 & -2 & 0 \end{bmatrix}$.

f) **AB** where

$\mathbf{A} = \begin{bmatrix} 0 & 7 & -2 \\ 5 & 2 & 0 \end{bmatrix}$ and

$$\mathbf{B} = \begin{bmatrix} 0 & 1 & 1 & -8 & 4 \\ 6 & -6 & 3 & 2 & 0 \\ 0 & 4 & 0 & -9 & 3 \end{bmatrix}.$$

2. Multiply $\begin{bmatrix} 1 & 2 & 3 \\ 2 & -1 & 2 \\ 2 & 3 & 1 \end{bmatrix}\begin{bmatrix} x \\ y \\ z \end{bmatrix}$.

3. If $\mathbf{A} = \begin{bmatrix} 1 & 0 \\ 1 & -1 \end{bmatrix}$, compute $\mathbf{A}^5 - \mathbf{A}^3$.

4. If $\mathbf{A} = \begin{bmatrix} 1 & 0 \\ 2 & 2 \\ 0 & 1 \end{bmatrix}$ and $\mathbf{B} = \begin{bmatrix} 0 & 0 & 1 & 1 \\ 2 & 1 & 0 & 2 \end{bmatrix}$, compute $(\mathbf{AB})^{\mathrm{T}}$, $\mathbf{A}^{\mathrm{T}}\mathbf{B}^{\mathrm{T}}$, and $\mathbf{B}^{\mathrm{T}}\mathbf{A}^{\mathrm{T}}$.

5. Express $(\mathbf{ABC})^{\mathrm{T}}$ as the product of transposes. [Since the associative property holds for matrix multiplication, we sometimes write the product of three matrices without any grouping signs. Such a product can therefore be interpreted as either being (**AB**)**C** or **A**(**BC**).]

6. Let **A** be an $n \times m$ matrix and **B** be an $m \times p$ matrix. The columns of **B** can be represented by $\mathbf{b}_1, \mathbf{b}_2, \cdots, \mathbf{b}_p$ so that $\mathbf{B} = [\mathbf{b}_1, \mathbf{b}_2, \cdots, \mathbf{b}_p]$. Show our usual matrix multiplication can be represented by the column by column products: $\mathbf{AB} = [\mathbf{Ab}_1, \mathbf{Ab}_2, \cdots, \mathbf{Ab}_p]$.

7. Prove if **A** is a square matrix, then $\mathbf{AA}^k = \mathbf{A}^k\mathbf{A}$ for $k = 1, 2, 3, \ldots$.

8. Prove Theorem 3.2.

9. Prove Theorem 3.3.

10. Let **A** be a square matrix of order n defined by

$$a_{ij} = \begin{cases} 1 \text{ if } j = i + 1 \\ 0 \text{ otherwise} \end{cases}$$

for $i, j = 1, 2, \ldots, n$. Row i of $\mathbf{A}^k$, $i, k \le n$ has $i + k$ leading zeros before the leading 1; hence, $\mathbf{A}^n = \mathbf{0}$.

4. INVERSE OF A SQUARE MATRIX

In Section 1.2 the concepts of the additive identity matrix and the additive inverse matrix were introduced. The multiplicative identity and the multiplicative inverse are also very important in the theory and applications of matrices. In fact, references to the multiplicative identity and inverse are so frequent that when the terms "identity" and "inverse" are used alone without reference to a particular operation, they are assumed to refer to the "multiplicative identity" and "multiplicative inverse." References to the additive identity matrix and additive inverse matrix require the word "additive" unless the context makes it very clear.

DEFINITION 4.1 (Multiplicative Identity Matrix) The identity matrix of order n is the square matrix $\mathbf{I}$ (or in some cases where the order is to be emphasized as $\mathbf{I}_n$) of order n satisfying $\mathbf{AI} = \mathbf{IA} = \mathbf{A}$ for every square matrix $\mathbf{A}$ of order n. The identity has 1's on the main diagonal (top leftmost corner to bottom rightmost corner) and 0's elsewhere.

$$\mathbf{I}_n = \left[\partial_{ij}\right] = \begin{cases} 0 & i \neq j \\ 1 & i = j \end{cases} \quad i, j = 1, 2, \cdots, n$$

where ∂_{ij} is called the Kronecker delta function.

EXAMPLE 4.1 The identity matrix of order 4 is

$$\mathbf{I}_4 = \begin{bmatrix} 1 & 0 & 0 & 0 \\ 0 & 1 & 0 & 0 \\ 0 & 0 & 1 & 0 \\ 0 & 0 & 0 & 1 \end{bmatrix}.$$

EXAMPLE 4.2 The definition for the identity matrix only applies to square matrices $\mathbf{A}$. If $\mathbf{A}$ is not square, for example if $\mathbf{A}$ has dimension 2×3, then there is no square matrix that will commute with $\mathbf{A}$, and hence no matrix $\mathbf{I}$ that would satisfy $\mathbf{AI} = \mathbf{IA} = \mathbf{A}$. In this case $\mathbf{I}$ would have to have three rows for $\mathbf{AI}$ to be defined and two columns for $\mathbf{IA}$ to be defined. It would follow that $\mathbf{I}$ would have dimension 3×2 in order to commute with **A**. It is true that we could define the concepts of a "right multiplicative identity" and a "left multiplicative identity," since in this case $\mathbf{AI}_3 = \mathbf{A}$ and $\mathbf{I}_2\mathbf{A} = \mathbf{A}$. The following *Derive* example illustrates:

$$4: \quad \begin{bmatrix} 1 & 2 & 3 \\ 4 & 5 & 6 \end{bmatrix} \cdot \begin{bmatrix} 1 & 0 & 0 \\ 0 & 1 & 0 \\ 0 & 0 & 1 \end{bmatrix}$$

$$5: \quad \begin{bmatrix} 1 & 2 & 3 \\ 4 & 5 & 6 \end{bmatrix}$$

$$6: \quad \begin{bmatrix} 1 & 0 \\ 0 & 1 \end{bmatrix} \cdot \begin{bmatrix} 1 & 2 & 3 \\ 4 & 5 & 6 \end{bmatrix}$$

$$7: \quad \begin{bmatrix} 1 & 2 & 3 \\ 4 & 5 & 6 \end{bmatrix}$$

The question of whether every element in a particular system has an inverse with respect to a particular operation is very important. The steps necessary to solve a simple equation in the real number system such as $2x + 3 = 1$ require the existence of an additive inverse for 3 and a multiplicative inverse for 2. Inverses with respect to matrix addition and multiplication are equally important.

Since the additive identity can be of any dimension (square or not), every matrix has an additive inverse. But the multiplicative identity **I** is required to be square, and the multiplicative inverse $\mathbf{A}^{-1}$ of a matrix **A** must commute with **A**. Thus if **A** has dimension $p \times q$ and $\mathbf{A}^{-1}$ has dimension $m \times n$, then the existence of $\mathbf{AA}^{-1}$ implies that $q = m$, the existence of $\mathbf{A}^{-1}\mathbf{A}$ implies that $n = p$, and the fact $\mathbf{AA}^{-1} = \mathbf{A}^{-1}\mathbf{A}$ implies $p = m$ and $n = q$. It follows that $p = q = m = n$, and **A** and $\mathbf{A}^{-1}$ are both square matrices of the same order. As we will soon see, the set of matrices that have multiplicative inverses is even more restrictive than the set of square matrices, since it is not even true that every square matrix has a multiplicative inverse.

DEFINITION 4.2 (Multiplicative Inverse of a Matrix, Invertible, Singular) The (multiplicative) inverse of a matrix **A** is defined to be a matrix **B** such that $\mathbf{AB} = \mathbf{BA} = \mathbf{I}$. The matrix **B** will be denoted by $\mathbf{A}^{-1}$. When $\mathbf{A}^{-1}$ does not exist, **A** is said to be singular. When $\mathbf{A}^{-1}$ does exist, **A** is said to be invertible or non-singular.

Invertible matrices play a very important role in the study of linear algebra. Next, we establish a series of results that will help us understand and use the power they provide.

PROPOSITION 4.1 If **A** is invertible, then **A** and $\mathbf{A}^{-1}$ are square matrices of the same order.

PROOF: The proof is left as an exercise.

PROPOSITION 4.2 The inverse of a matrix **A** is unique.

PROOF: Assume **A** has two different inverses say **B** and **C**. Since **B** is an inverse $\mathbf{AB} = \mathbf{I}$. Multiplying both sides of this equation on the left by **C** we obtain $\mathbf{CAB} = \mathbf{CI} = \mathbf{C}$. Since $\mathbf{CA} = \mathbf{I}$, we have $\mathbf{B} = \mathbf{IB} = \mathbf{CAB} = \mathbf{CI} = \mathbf{C}$. This contradicts the assumption that **B** and **C** are different.

PROPOSITION 4.3 If **A** is invertible, then $\mathbf{A}^{-1}$ is invertible and $\left(\mathbf{A}^{-1}\right)^{-1} = \mathbf{A}$.

PROOF: Since **A** is invertible, we can substitute $\mathbf{A}^{-1}$ for **B** in Definition 4.2 giving us $\mathbf{AA}^{-1} = \mathbf{A}^{-1}\mathbf{A} = \mathbf{I}$. It follows immediately that $\mathbf{A}^{-1}$ is invertible and $\left(\mathbf{A}^{-1}\right)^{-1} = \mathbf{A}$.

PROPOSITION 4.4 If **A** and **B** are two invertible square matrices of the same order, then **AB** is invertible and $(\mathbf{AB})^{-1} = \mathbf{B}^{-1}\mathbf{A}^{-1}$.

PROOF: Since **B** is invertible, $\mathbf{BB}^{-1} = \mathbf{I}$. Multiplying on the left by **A** yields $\mathbf{A}\left(\mathbf{BB}^{-1}\right) = \mathbf{AI} = \mathbf{A}$. Multiplying this equation on the right by $\mathbf{A}^{-1}$ yields $\mathbf{A}\left(\mathbf{BB}^{-1}\right)\mathbf{A}^{-1} = \mathbf{AA}^{-1} = \mathbf{I}$. But in Section 4.3 we established that matrix multiplication for square matrices of the same order is associative; therefore, $(\mathbf{AB})(\mathbf{B}^{-1}\mathbf{A}^{-1}) = \mathbf{I}$. By a similar argument, $(\mathbf{B}^{-1}\mathbf{A}^{-1})(\mathbf{AB}) = \mathbf{I}$ and by definition $(\mathbf{AB})^{-1} = \mathbf{B}^{-1}\mathbf{A}^{-1}$.

EXAMPLE 4.3 *Derive* can be used to compute the inverse of a nonsingular matrix such as $\begin{bmatrix} 1 & 1 & 1 \\ 2 & 3 & 3 \\ 2 & 5 & 6 \end{bmatrix}$:

$$2: \quad \begin{bmatrix} 1 & 1 & 1 \\ 2 & 3 & 3 \\ 2 & 5 & 6 \end{bmatrix}^{-1}$$

$$3: \quad \begin{bmatrix} 3 & -1 & 0 \\ -6 & 4 & -1 \\ 4 & -3 & 1 \end{bmatrix}$$

Here statement #1 was used to enter the matrix with the **D**eclare-**M**atrix command sequence. Statement #2 was generated by **A**uthoring the expression #1^-1. The inverse was then calculated automatically by *Derive* in statement #3 by using the **S**implify command.

EXAMPLE 4.4 If a matrix is singular, *Derive* will not return an inverse. For example:

$$2: \quad \begin{bmatrix} 1 & 2 & 3 \\ 4 & 5 & 6 \\ 7 & 8 & 9 \end{bmatrix}^{-1}$$

$$3: \quad \begin{bmatrix} 1 & 2 & 3 \\ 4 & 5 & 6 \\ 7 & 8 & 9 \end{bmatrix}^{-1}$$

Here again, statement #1 was used to input of the matrix using the **D**eclare-**M**atrix command sequence. Statement #2 was formed by **A**uthoring #1^-1, and statement #3 is the **S**implification of statement #2. Notice that *Derive* did not return an inverse but simply repeated statement #2. We will learn more in later sections about why some square matrices do not have an inverse, but it is sufficient to state at this point that the reasons are related to why some systems of n equations in n unknowns do not have unique solution sets. The following example provides some insight into how these two seemingly different concepts are tied together.

EXAMPLE 4.5 In Section 1.3 we showed how to write a system of linear equations as an matrix equation involving matrix multiplication. The inverse of a matrix can be used to solve such a matrix equation for the unknowns. For example,

$$\begin{bmatrix} 1 & 3 & 1 \\ 2 & 2 & 3 \\ 2 & 5 & 3 \end{bmatrix} \begin{bmatrix} x \\ y \\ z \end{bmatrix} = \begin{bmatrix} 2 \\ 3 \\ 1 \end{bmatrix}$$

can be solved for x, y, and z using the inverse of the coefficient matrix in a similar manner to how the multiplicative inverse can be used to solve a simple real valued algebraic equation such as $2x = 14$. In this basic example, both sides of the equation are multiplied by the multiplicative inverse of the coefficient 2, yielding $x = 7$. To solve the above system of equations written in matrix notation, we multiply both sides of the matrix equation by the inverse of the coefficient matrix. The result appears on a *Derive* screen as follows:

4: $$\begin{bmatrix} 1 & 3 & 1 \\ 2 & 2 & 3 \\ 2 & 5 & 3 \end{bmatrix} \cdot \begin{bmatrix} x \\ y \\ z \end{bmatrix} = \begin{bmatrix} 2 \\ 3 \\ 1 \end{bmatrix}$$

5: $$\begin{bmatrix} 1 & 3 & 1 \\ 2 & 2 & 3 \\ 2 & 5 & 3 \end{bmatrix}^{-1} \cdot \begin{bmatrix} 1 & 3 & 1 \\ 2 & 2 & 3 \\ 2 & 5 & 3 \end{bmatrix} \cdot \begin{bmatrix} x \\ y \\ z \end{bmatrix} = \begin{bmatrix} 1 & 3 & 1 \\ 2 & 2 & 3 \\ 2 & 5 & 3 \end{bmatrix}^{-1} \cdot \begin{bmatrix} 2 \\ 3 \\ 1 \end{bmatrix}$$

6: $$\begin{bmatrix} x = \dfrac{23}{3} \\ y = -\dfrac{2}{3} \\ z = -\dfrac{11}{3} \end{bmatrix}$$

Statements #1, #2, and #3 were used to input the matrices used in statement #4. The command generating statement #5 can be **A**uthored by the expression #1^−1.#1.#2=#1^−1.#3. Statement #6 is the **S**implification of statement #5.

EXERCISES

1. Use *Derive* to find the inverse (if it exists) of the following matrices:

a) $\begin{bmatrix} 0 & 0 \\ 1 & 0 \end{bmatrix}$ b) $\begin{bmatrix} 3 & -1 \\ -6 & 2 \end{bmatrix}$

c) $\begin{bmatrix} 5 & -3 \\ 2 & 2 \end{bmatrix}$ d) $\begin{bmatrix} 2 & -1 & 1 \\ 1 & 2 & 1 \\ 3 & 1 & 2 \end{bmatrix}$

e) $\begin{bmatrix} 4 & 1 & -1 \\ 2 & 2 & 0 \\ 3 & 1 & -2 \end{bmatrix}$

f) $\begin{bmatrix} -1 & 3 & 2 \\ 0 & 1 & 1 \\ 2 & -2 & 0 \end{bmatrix}$

g) $\begin{bmatrix} -2 & 3 & -1 \\ 7 & 7 & 7 \\ 0 & -2 & 9 \end{bmatrix}$

h) $\begin{bmatrix} 1 & 3 & -2 & 4 \\ 1 & 1 & 0 & 9 \\ 6 & 1 & 1 & 0 \\ -2 & 4 & 7 & -6 \end{bmatrix}$

i) $\begin{bmatrix} 5 & -3 & 2 & 6 & 1 \\ 1 & 1 & 0 & 6 & -4 \\ 2 & 3 & 2 & 4 & 7 \\ 1 & 1 & 1 & 0 & 8 \\ 3 & 4 & 2 & 2 & -1 \end{bmatrix}$

. Use *Derive* to find $(\mathbf{AB})^{-1}$ and $\mathbf{B}^{-1}\mathbf{A}^{-1}$and verify that the results are the same, given:

$\mathbf{A} = \begin{bmatrix} 1 & 2 \\ 1 & 3 \end{bmatrix}$ and $\mathbf{B} = \begin{bmatrix} 1 & 4 \\ 0 & 3 \end{bmatrix}$

3. If $\mathbf{A} = \begin{bmatrix} 1 & 1 & 2 \\ 2 & 3 & 3 \\ 1 & 2 & 3 \end{bmatrix}$, verify that $(\mathbf{A}^{T})^{-1} = (\mathbf{A}^{-1})^{T}$.

4. Solve:

$$\begin{bmatrix} 0 & 1 & 1 \\ 0 & 2 & 3 \\ 1 & 2 & 3 \end{bmatrix}\mathbf{X} = \begin{bmatrix} 1 & 2 & 3 \\ 2 & 3 & 4 \\ 3 & 4 & 5 \end{bmatrix}.$$

5. If $\mathbf{A} = \begin{bmatrix} 1 & 1 & 0 \\ 1 & 1 & 3 \\ 2 & 3 & 4 \end{bmatrix}$, compute $(\mathbf{A}^{-1})^{-1}$ and verify that the result is **A**.

6. Prove Proposition 4.1.

7. Prove:

   i.) If **A** is any $m \times n$ matrix, then $\mathbf{AI}_n = \mathbf{A}$.

ii.) If **B** is any $n \times k$ matrix, then $\mathbf{I}_n \mathbf{B} = \mathbf{B}$.

8. Write the following system of equations as a matrix equation and solve using the inverse of the coefficient matrix:

$$\begin{aligned} 2x - 5y + z &= -1 \\ 3x \quad\quad + 5z &= -1 \\ x + 2y - z &= 9 \end{aligned}$$

5. ELEMENTARY MATRICES

In Section 1.4 we learned how to represent a system of linear equations by a matrix equation. We also saw that such a system can be solved by multiplying both sides of the equation by the inverse of the coefficient matrix if the inverse exists. *Derive* computes the inverse quickly, but immediately employing such a technique provides little insight into why the coefficient matrix does or does not have an inverse and as a result why the system does or does not have a unique solution.

In elementary algebra courses systems of linear equations are solved using a technique known as the addition-subtraction or elimination method. For a simple system such as

$$\begin{aligned} 2x - 3y &= 1 \\ x + 4y &= 6 \end{aligned}$$

we would first multiply all terms in the second equation by -2 and add the result to the first equation. This result, $-11y = -11$, would then be multiplied by -1/11 to yield $y = 1$. This value could then be substituted into the first equation to yield $x = 2$. In this section we study a matrix equivalent to these steps: multiplying the matrix equation representing the system by special matrices (called elementary matrices) that effectively perform these same steps. For example

$$\begin{bmatrix} 1 & 0 \\ 0 & -2 \end{bmatrix} \begin{bmatrix} 2 & -3 \\ 1 & 4 \end{bmatrix} \begin{bmatrix} x \\ y \end{bmatrix} = \begin{bmatrix} 1 & 0 \\ 0 & -2 \end{bmatrix} \begin{bmatrix} 1 \\ 6 \end{bmatrix}$$

multiplies each term of the second equation by -2, yielding

$$\begin{bmatrix} 2 & -3 \\ -2 & -8 \end{bmatrix}\begin{bmatrix} x \\ y \end{bmatrix} = \begin{bmatrix} 1 \\ -12 \end{bmatrix} \quad \text{or} \quad \begin{matrix} 2x - 3y = 1 \\ -2x - 8y = -12 \end{matrix}.$$

Similarly,

$$\begin{bmatrix} 1 & 0 \\ 1 & 1 \end{bmatrix}\begin{bmatrix} 2 & -3 \\ -2 & -8 \end{bmatrix}\begin{bmatrix} x \\ y \end{bmatrix} = \begin{bmatrix} 1 & 0 \\ 1 & 1 \end{bmatrix}\begin{bmatrix} 1 \\ -12 \end{bmatrix}$$

adds the first equation to the new second equation with the result replacing the second equation, yielding

$$\begin{bmatrix} 2 & -3 \\ 0 & -11 \end{bmatrix}\begin{bmatrix} x \\ y \end{bmatrix} = \begin{bmatrix} 1 \\ -11 \end{bmatrix} \quad \text{or} \quad \begin{matrix} 2x - 3y = 1 \\ -11y = -11 \end{matrix}.$$

And, finally,

$$\begin{bmatrix} 1 & 0 \\ 0 & -1/11 \end{bmatrix}\begin{bmatrix} 2 & -3 \\ 0 & -11 \end{bmatrix}\begin{bmatrix} x \\ y \end{bmatrix} = \begin{bmatrix} 1 & 0 \\ 0 & -1/11 \end{bmatrix}\begin{bmatrix} 1 \\ -11 \end{bmatrix}$$

multiplies the new second equation by -1/11, yielding

$$\begin{bmatrix} 2 & -3 \\ 0 & 1 \end{bmatrix}\begin{bmatrix} x \\ y \end{bmatrix} = \begin{bmatrix} 1 \\ 1 \end{bmatrix} \quad \text{or} \quad \begin{matrix} 2x - 3y = 1 \\ y = 1 \end{matrix}.$$

This new system of equations is equivalent to our original system in the sense that it has the same solution set. The three matrices we have used to multiply by the new matrix equations are all examples of elementary matrices. Each can be thought of as a modification of the identity matrix in the following sense.

DEFINITION 5.1 (Elementary Matrices) The square matrix **E** is an elementary matrix if it can be obtained from the identity matrix of the same order by performing one or more of the following elementary operations:

1. Interchange two rows or columns.
2. Add a scalar multiple of one row or column to another row or column.
3. Multiply one row or column by a scalar.

We have already seen that not every square matrix is invertible. The following theorem guarantees that all elementary matrices are invertible. It follows that the set of all invertible matrices can therefore be characterized in terms elementary matrices.

THEOREM 5.1 Every elementary matrix is invertible.

PROOF: The proof is left as an exercise.

THEOREM 5.2 Let **A** be a square matrix of order n. If there exists an elementary matrix **E** of order n such that **EA** = **I**, then **A** is invertible.

PROOF: Since **E** is invertible by Theorem 5.1, $\mathbf{E}^{-1}$ exists and $\mathbf{E}^{-1}(\mathbf{EA}) = \mathbf{E}^{-1}\mathbf{I}$. It follows that $\mathbf{A} = \mathbf{E}^{-1}$; hence, $\mathbf{A}^{-1} = \left(\mathbf{E}^{-1}\right)^{-1} = \mathbf{E}$ by Proposition 4.3, and the proof is complete.

EXAMPLE 5.1 The elementary matrix

$$\begin{bmatrix} 1 & 0 & 0 & 0 \\ 0 & 0 & 1 & 0 \\ 0 & 1 & 0 & 0 \\ 0 & 0 & 0 & 1 \end{bmatrix}$$

is obtained by interchanging row 2 and 3 of the identity matrix. Its inverse is also obtained by interchanging row 2 and row 3 of the identity matrix. In other words, this elementary matrix is its own inverse as seen by the fact that

$$\begin{bmatrix} 1 & 0 & 0 & 0 \\ 0 & 0 & 1 & 0 \\ 0 & 1 & 0 & 0 \\ 0 & 0 & 0 & 1 \end{bmatrix}\begin{bmatrix} 1 & 0 & 0 & 0 \\ 0 & 0 & 1 & 0 \\ 0 & 1 & 0 & 0 \\ 0 & 0 & 0 & 1 \end{bmatrix} = \begin{bmatrix} 1 & 0 & 0 & 0 \\ 0 & 1 & 0 & 0 \\ 0 & 0 & 1 & 0 \\ 0 & 0 & 0 & 1 \end{bmatrix}.$$

EXAMPLE 5.2 The elementary matrix

$$\begin{bmatrix} 1 & 0 & 0 \\ 1 & 1 & 0 \\ 0 & 0 & 1 \end{bmatrix}$$

is obtained by adding row 1 to row 2 of the identity matrix. Its inverse is obtained by subtracting row 1 from row 2 of the identity matrix:

$$\begin{bmatrix} 1 & 0 & 0 \\ -1 & 1 & 0 \\ 0 & 0 & 1 \end{bmatrix}.$$

That this is the inverse is verified by

$$\begin{bmatrix} 1 & 0 & 0 \\ 1 & 1 & 0 \\ 0 & 0 & 1 \end{bmatrix}\begin{bmatrix} 1 & 0 & 0 \\ -1 & 1 & 0 \\ 0 & 0 & 1 \end{bmatrix} = \begin{bmatrix} 1 & 0 & 0 \\ -1 & 1 & 0 \\ 0 & 0 & 1 \end{bmatrix}\begin{bmatrix} 1 & 0 & 0 \\ 1 & 1 & 0 \\ 0 & 0 & 1 \end{bmatrix} = \begin{bmatrix} 1 & 0 & 0 \\ 0 & 1 & 0 \\ 0 & 0 & 1 \end{bmatrix}.$$

EXAMPLE 5.3 The elementary matrix $\begin{bmatrix} 5 & 0 \\ 0 & 1 \end{bmatrix}$ is obtained from the identity matrix by multiplying row 1 by 5. Its inverse is obtained by multiplying row 1 of the identity by 1/5: $\begin{bmatrix} \frac{1}{5} & 0 \\ 0 & 1 \end{bmatrix}$.

To check this result note that

$$\begin{bmatrix} 5 & 0 \\ 0 & 1 \end{bmatrix}\begin{bmatrix} \frac{1}{5} & 0 \\ 0 & 1 \end{bmatrix} = \begin{bmatrix} \frac{1}{5} & 0 \\ 0 & 1 \end{bmatrix}\begin{bmatrix} 5 & 0 \\ 0 & 1 \end{bmatrix} = \begin{bmatrix} 1 & 0 \\ 0 & 1 \end{bmatrix}.$$

Elementary operations may be performed on any matrix by multiplying it by the appropriate elementary matrix. To generate row operations on a matrix **A,** we multiply on the left by the corresponding elementary row matrix. To generate column operations on **A**, we multiply on the right by the corresponding elementary column matrix. In the examples which follow we examine some basic row operations. Column operations follow similarly.

EXAMPLE 5.4 If a matrix is multiplied on the left by an elementary matrix formed by interchanging rows i and j of the identity matrix, then the result is that rows i and j of the original matrix are interchanged. Thus rows 2 and 3 of

$$\mathbf{A} = \begin{bmatrix} 1 & 1 & 1 & 1 & 1 \\ 2 & 2 & 2 & 2 & 2 \\ 3 & 3 & 3 & 3 & 3 \end{bmatrix}$$

can be interchanged by multiplying $\mathbf{A}$ by the elementary matrix resulting from interchanging rows 2 and 3 of the identity matrix.

$$\begin{bmatrix} 1 & 0 & 0 \\ 0 & 0 & 1 \\ 0 & 1 & 0 \end{bmatrix}\begin{bmatrix} 1 & 1 & 1 & 1 & 1 \\ 2 & 2 & 2 & 2 & 2 \\ 3 & 3 & 3 & 3 & 3 \end{bmatrix} = \begin{bmatrix} 1 & 1 & 1 & 1 & 1 \\ 3 & 3 & 3 & 3 & 3 \\ 2 & 2 & 2 & 2 & 2 \end{bmatrix}$$

EXAMPLE 5.5 If a matrix is multiplied on the left by an elementary matrix formed by adding row i to row j of the identity matrix, then row i is added to row j of the original matrix. Thus row 1 of the matrix

$$\begin{bmatrix} 1 & 2 & 1 \\ 2 & 3 & 4 \\ 1 & 3 & 6 \end{bmatrix}$$

can be added to row 3 by multiplying by the appropriate elementary matrix.

$$\begin{bmatrix} 1 & 0 & 0 \\ 0 & 1 & 0 \\ 1 & 0 & 1 \end{bmatrix}\begin{bmatrix} 1 & 2 & 1 \\ 2 & 3 & 4 \\ 1 & 3 & 6 \end{bmatrix} = \begin{bmatrix} 1 & 2 & 1 \\ 2 & 3 & 4 \\ 2 & 5 & 7 \end{bmatrix}$$

EXAMPLE 5.6 If a matrix is multiplied on the left by an elementary matrix formed by multiplying row i of the identity matrix by a constant, then row i of the original matrix is multiplied by this constant. For the matrix of Example 5.6, multiply 5 times the third row by multiplying by the appropriate elementary matrix.

$$\begin{bmatrix}1 & 0 & 0\\0 & 1 & 0\\0 & 0 & 5\end{bmatrix}\begin{bmatrix}1 & 2 & 1\\2 & 3 & 4\\1 & 3 & 6\end{bmatrix}=\begin{bmatrix}1 & 2 & 1\\2 & 3 & 4\\5 & 15 & 30\end{bmatrix}$$

In later sections it will be useful to transform a matrix, which in many cases represents the coefficients and constants in a system of equations, into another equivalent matrix that is more convenient to handle. The following example provides a guide in performing these operations.

EXAMPLE 5.7 Given the matrix

$$\mathbf{A}=\begin{bmatrix}2 & 3 & 1 & 2\\1 & 3 & 4 & 2\\3 & 2 & 5 & 3\end{bmatrix},$$

we seek a series of elementary matrices that will transform **A** into

$$\begin{bmatrix}1 & \frac{3}{2} & \frac{1}{2} & 1\\0 & 1 & \frac{7}{3} & \frac{2}{3}\\0 & 0 & 1 & \frac{5}{28}\end{bmatrix}$$

using matrix multiplication. Our first goal is to transform the first column from [2 1 3] into [1 0 0]. We can accomplish this by declaring a series of elementary matrices that will (1) multiply the first row of **A** by 1/2, (2) add the negative of the new first row of **A** to the second row of **A**, and (3) add -3 times the new first row of **A** to the third row of **A**. The resultant matrix multiplication is shown below as it appears on the *Derive* screen:

$$5: \begin{bmatrix}1 & 0 & 0\\0 & 1 & 0\\-3 & 0 & 1\end{bmatrix}\cdot\begin{bmatrix}1 & 0 & 0\\-1 & 1 & 0\\0 & 0 & 1\end{bmatrix}\cdot\begin{bmatrix}\frac{1}{2} & 0 & 0\\0 & 1 & 0\\0 & 0 & 1\end{bmatrix}\cdot\begin{bmatrix}2 & 3 & 1 & 2\\1 & 3 & 4 & 2\\3 & 2 & 5 & 3\end{bmatrix}$$

$$6: \begin{bmatrix} 1 & \frac{3}{2} & \frac{1}{2} & 1 \\ 0 & \frac{3}{2} & \frac{7}{2} & 1 \\ 0 & -\frac{5}{2} & \frac{7}{2} & 0 \end{bmatrix}$$

Next, this result is multiplied by an elementary matrix which multiplies each element of the second row of statement #6 by 2/3, transforming the element in the second row and second column into a 1. Finally, that result is multiplied by an elementary matrix which adds 5/2 times this new second row to the third row of statement #6, transforming the element in the third row and second column into a 0. The resulting matrix multiplication appears on the *Derive* screen as follows:

$$9: \begin{bmatrix} 1 & 0 & 0 \\ 0 & 1 & 0 \\ 0 & \frac{5}{2} & 1 \end{bmatrix} \cdot \begin{bmatrix} 1 & 0 & 0 \\ 0 & \frac{2}{3} & 0 \\ 0 & 0 & 1 \end{bmatrix} \cdot \begin{bmatrix} 1 & \frac{3}{2} & \frac{1}{2} & 1 \\ 0 & \frac{3}{2} & \frac{7}{2} & 1 \\ 0 & -\frac{5}{2} & \frac{7}{2} & 0 \end{bmatrix}$$

$$10: \begin{bmatrix} 1 & \frac{3}{2} & \frac{1}{2} & 1 \\ 0 & 1 & \frac{7}{3} & \frac{2}{3} \\ 0 & 0 & \frac{28}{3} & \frac{5}{3} \end{bmatrix}$$

Our desired result can now be found by multiplying statement #10 by an elementary matrix which multiplies each term in the last row by 3/28, transforming the element in the third row and third column into a 1.

$$12: \begin{bmatrix} 1 & 0 & 0 \\ 0 & 1 & 0 \\ 0 & 0 & \frac{3}{28} \end{bmatrix} \cdot \begin{bmatrix} 1 & \frac{3}{2} & \frac{1}{2} & 1 \\ 0 & 1 & \frac{7}{3} & \frac{2}{3} \\ 0 & 0 & \frac{28}{3} & \frac{5}{3} \end{bmatrix}$$

$$13: \begin{bmatrix} 1 & \frac{3}{2} & \frac{1}{2} & 1 \\ 0 & 1 & \frac{7}{3} & \frac{2}{3} \\ 0 & 0 & 1 & \frac{5}{28} \end{bmatrix}$$

EXERCISES

1. Multiply: $\begin{bmatrix} 1 & 0 & 0 \\ -1 & 1 & 0 \\ -3 & 0 & 1 \end{bmatrix}\begin{bmatrix} 1 & 3 & 3 \\ 1 & 2 & 3 \\ 3 & 1 & 2 \end{bmatrix}$. What do you notice about the first column of the result? Decompose the elementary matrix $\begin{bmatrix} 1 & 0 & 0 \\ -1 & 1 & 0 \\ -3 & 0 & 1 \end{bmatrix}$ into the product of two elementary matrices.

2. Find the inverse of the product of the elementary matrices in Exercise 1.

3. Find **E** and the inverse of **E** where **E** is the product of elementary matrices and $\mathbf{E}\begin{bmatrix} 2 & 3 & 5 \\ 5 & 3 & 6 \\ -1 & 0 & 2 \end{bmatrix} = \begin{bmatrix} 5 & 3 & 6 \\ -1 & 0 & 2 \\ 2 & 3 & 5 \end{bmatrix}$.

4. If $\mathbf{E}\begin{bmatrix} 1 & 2 \\ 1 & 4 \end{bmatrix} = \begin{bmatrix} 1 & 2 \\ 0 & x \end{bmatrix}$, find the elementary matrix **E** and the scalar x. Also, find $\mathbf{E}^{-1}$.

5. If $\begin{bmatrix} 1 & 1 & 3 \\ 2 & 3 & 4 \\ 6 & 0 & 1 \end{bmatrix}\mathbf{E} = \begin{bmatrix} 3 & 1 & 1 \\ 4 & 2 & 3 \\ 1 & 6 & 0 \end{bmatrix}$, find **E** and its inverse.

6. The matrix $\mathbf{L} = (l_{ij})$ is lower triangular if $l_{ij} = 0$ if $i < j$. The matrix $\mathbf{U} = (u_{ij})$ is upper

triangular if $u_{ij} = 0$ if $i > j$.

Factor

$$\mathbf{A} = \begin{bmatrix} 2 & 4 & 6 & 2 \\ 1 & 5 & 3 & 4 \\ 0 & 1 & 1 & 4 \\ 2 & 5 & 6 & 5 \end{bmatrix} \text{ into the}$$

product of a lower triangular matrix **L** and an upper triangular matrix **U**. Hint:

a) Use a sequence of lower triangular elementary matrices to reduce **A** to an upper triangular matrix $\mathbf{E}_k \cdots \mathbf{E}_2\mathbf{E}_1\mathbf{A} = \mathbf{U}$.
b) Find the inverses of these elementary matrices and write $\mathbf{A} = \mathbf{E}_1^{-1}\mathbf{E}_2^{-1} \cdots \mathbf{E}_{k-1}^{-1}\mathbf{E}_k^{-1}\mathbf{U}$.
c) Show if $\mathbf{E}_p$ is lower triangular, then $\mathbf{E}_p^{-1}$ is lower triangular.
d) Prove that the product of two lower triangular matrices is lower triangular.
e) For the matrix **A** given above, write **LU** = **A** as follows:

$$\begin{bmatrix} 2 & 0 & 0 & 0 \\ 1 & 2 & 0 & 0 \\ 0 & 1 & 1 & 0 \\ 0 & 1 & 0 & 1 \end{bmatrix}\begin{bmatrix} 1 & 2 & 3 & 1 \\ 0 & 1 & 0 & 1 \\ 0 & 0 & 1 & 3 \\ 0 & 0 & 0 & 1 \end{bmatrix} = \begin{bmatrix} 2 & 4 & 6 & 2 \\ 1 & 5 & 3 & 4 \\ 0 & 1 & 1 & 4 \\ 2 & 5 & 6 & 5 \end{bmatrix}$$

7. Factor the following matrix into a decomposition **LU** = **A**:

$$\mathbf{A} = \begin{bmatrix} 3 & 6 & 12 & 9 \\ 1 & 4 & 4 & 9 \\ 4 & 10 & 18 & 24 \\ 0 & 0 & 1 & 4 \end{bmatrix}.$$

8. Use the following outline to prove that every 3×3 elementary matrix is invertible:

a) Prove if **E** is an elementary matrix obtained by interchanging two rows (columns) of **I**, then $\mathbf{E}^{-1} = \mathbf{E}$.
b) Prove if **E** is an elementary matrix obtained by adding a non-zero scalar multiple α times a row (column) of **I** to another row (column) of **I**, then $\mathbf{E}^{-1}$ is found by multiplying -α times the same row (column) of **I**.
c) Prove if **E** is an elementary matrix obtained by multiplying a non-zero scalar α times a row (column) of **I**, then $\mathbf{E}^{-1}$ is the matrix obtained by multiplying $1/\alpha$, $\alpha \neq 0$, times the same row (column) of **I**.
d) The product of two invertible matrices is an invertible matrix. (Hint: see Proposition 4.4.)

6. LINEAR SYSTEMS OF EQUATIONS

Linear equations, particularly systems of linear equations, play a very important role in the study of linear algebra. We have already used the concept to motivate our definition for matrix multiplication, and we have seen how this definition leads to a method of solving systems of linear equations using the inverse of the coefficient matrix. In this section we formalize some of the ideas that have been suggested in previous sections. In particular, we will examine systems of linear equations, the matrix equation that represents such a system, and equivalent systems of linear equations. Formal consideration of these concepts leads us to an efficient method for solving systems of linear equations that will be used extensively throughout the remainder of this book.

DEFINITION 6.1 (Linear Equation; System of Linear Equations) A linear equation is an equation of the form $a_1x_1 + a_2x_2 + \cdots + a_nx_n = b$, where $a_1, \cdots, a_n$ and b are constants and $x_1, \cdots, x_n$ are unknowns. The constants $a_1, \cdots, a_n$ are said to be the coefficients of the unknowns $x_1, \cdots, x_n$. In general, a system of m linear equations in n unknowns will appear as

$$\begin{array}{cccc} a_{11}x_1 + a_{12}x_2 + \cdots + a_{1n}x_n = b_1 \\ a_{21}x_1 + a_{22}x_2 + \cdots + a_{2n}x_n = b_2 \\ \vdots \quad\quad \vdots \quad\quad\quad\quad \vdots \quad\quad \vdots \\ a_{m1}x_1 + a_{m2}x_2 + \cdots + a_{mn}x_n = b_m \end{array}$$

where the unknowns are $x_1, x_2, \cdots, x_n$, and the constants a_{ij}, $i = 1,2,\ldots,m$; $j = 1,2,\ldots,n$ are the coefficients.

DEFINITION 6.2 (Coefficient Matrix of a System of Linear Equations) The coefficient matrix of a system of m linear equations in n unknowns is the $m \times n$ matrix

$$\mathbf{A} = \begin{bmatrix} a_{11} & a_{12} & \cdots & a_{1n} \\ a_{21} & a_{22} & \cdots & a_{2n} \\ \vdots & \vdots & & \vdots \\ a_{m1} & a_{m2} & \cdots & a_{mn} \end{bmatrix}.$$

With this notation the system of equations may be written as $\mathbf{Ax} = \mathbf{b}$, or

$$\begin{bmatrix} a_{11} & a_{12} & \cdots & a_{1n} \\ a_{21} & a_{22} & \cdots & a_{2n} \\ \vdots & \vdots & & \vdots \\ a_{m1} & a_{m2} & \cdots & a_{mn} \end{bmatrix} \begin{bmatrix} x_1 \\ x_2 \\ \vdots \\ x_n \end{bmatrix} = \begin{bmatrix} b_1 \\ b_2 \\ \vdots \\ b_m \end{bmatrix}.$$

EXAMPLE 6.1 The system of equations

$$\begin{aligned} 2x_1 + 3x_2 - x_3 &= 4 \\ 3x_1 + x_2 - x_3 &= 5 \\ 5x_1 - 2x_2 + 2x_3 &= 2 \end{aligned}$$

written in matrix form is

$$\begin{bmatrix} 2 & 3 & -1 \\ 3 & 1 & -1 \\ 5 & -2 & 2 \end{bmatrix} \begin{bmatrix} x_1 \\ x_2 \\ x_3 \end{bmatrix} = \begin{bmatrix} 4 \\ 5 \\ 2 \end{bmatrix}.$$

Systems of linear equations may also be written in a shorthand form, called an "augmented matrix," that omits the symbols for the unknowns.

DEFINITION 6.3 (Augmented Matrix) The augmented matrix of a system of m equations in n unknowns is defined to be the $m \times (n+1)$ matrix

$$\begin{bmatrix} a_{11} & a_{12} & \cdots & a_{1n} & b_1 \\ a_{21} & a_{22} & \cdots & a_{2n} & b_2 \\ \vdots & \vdots & & \vdots & \vdots \\ a_{m1} & a_{m2} & \cdots & a_{mn} & b_m \end{bmatrix},$$

which is formed by supplementing the coefficient matrix on the right with an extra column consisting of the constants $b_1, \cdots, b_m$.

EXAMPLE 6.2 The system of equations in Example 6.1 written as an augmented matrix is

$$\begin{bmatrix} 2 & 3 & -1 & 4 \\ 3 & 1 & -1 & 5 \\ 5 & -2 & 2 & 2 \end{bmatrix}.$$

DEFINITION 6.4 (Solution of a System of Equations) A solution of a system of linear equations is any set of numbers $\{x_1, x_2, \cdots, x_n\}$ that satisfies the system.

EXAMPLE 6.3 Using *Derive* we can easily verify that $x_1 = 12/11$, $x_2 = 1/22$, and $x_3 = -37/22$ is a solution of the system of equations in Example 6.1:

$$3: \quad \begin{bmatrix} 2 & 3 & -1 \\ 3 & 1 & -1 \\ 5 & -2 & 2 \end{bmatrix} \cdot \begin{bmatrix} \frac{12}{11} \\ \frac{1}{22} \\ -\frac{37}{22} \end{bmatrix}$$

$$4: \quad \begin{bmatrix} 4 \\ 5 \\ 2 \end{bmatrix}$$

The coefficient matrix and a column matrix containing our proposed solution set were entered as statements #1 and #2 prior to what appears above. Their product is indicated in statement #3. The result of this multiplication, which is shown in statement #4, was found by Simplifying statement #3. Since statement #4 contains the constants in our original system of equations, the values in the second matrix in statement #3 satisfy the system of Example 6.1.

In Section 1.5 we learned that we can multiply the augmented matrix representation of a system of linear equations by a series of elementary matrices to obtain a matrix with the same dimension as the augmented matrix. Since elementary matrices are invertible (by Theorem 5.1), the following definition and theorem show that multiplying by a series of elementary matrices always yields an augmented matrix representing a system of equations that has the same solutions as the original system of equations. We will use this fact to modify the augmented matrix of any system that has no apparent solution into an augmented matrix for a system with obvious solutions.

DEFINITION 6.5 (Equivalent Systems of Equations) Two systems of linear equations are said to be equivalent if they have the same solution.

THEOREM 6.1 If a system of equations $\mathbf{Ax} = \mathbf{b}$ is multiplied by an invertible matrix $\mathbf{C}$ to obtain $\mathbf{CAx} = \mathbf{Cb}$, then the new system is equivalent to $\mathbf{Ax} = \mathbf{b}$.

PROOF If $\mathbf{w}$ is any solution of the system $\mathbf{Ax} = \mathbf{b}$, then $\mathbf{CAw} = \mathbf{C}(\mathbf{Aw}) = \mathbf{Cb}$, and $\mathbf{w}$ is also a solution of $\mathbf{CAx} = \mathbf{Cb}$. On the other hand, if $\mathbf{w}$ is any solution of the system $\mathbf{CAx} = \mathbf{Cb}$, then since $\mathbf{C}$ is invertible, $\mathbf{C}^{-1}$ exists, and both sides of $\mathbf{CAx} = \mathbf{Cb}$ can be multiplied on the left by $\mathbf{C}^{-1}$ to obtain $\mathbf{C}^{-1}\mathbf{CAw} = \mathbf{C}^{-1}\mathbf{Cb}$. Thus $\mathbf{Aw} = \mathbf{b}$, and $\mathbf{w}$ is a solution to $\mathbf{Ax} = \mathbf{b}$.

The system $\mathbf{CAx} = \mathbf{Cb}$ can be represented in augmented form by multiplying the augmented matrix of $\mathbf{Ax} = \mathbf{b}$ by $\mathbf{C}$. This result can be used to find the solution of a system of equations.

EXAMPLE 6.4 To solve the system of equations

$$\begin{aligned} x + 2y &= 3 \\ 2x + 3y &= 4 \end{aligned},$$

we first write the augmented matrix of the system $\mathbf{Ax} = \mathbf{b}$. Next, we multiply this augmented matrix by an invertible matrix which will result in a system which is easier to solve. For this example we choose an elementary matrix which will subtract twice row 1 from row 2. This elementary matrix is then multiplied by the augmented matrix of $\mathbf{Ax} = \mathbf{b}$

(statement #3) to yield the augmented matrix of a new system (statement #4) having zero in the second row, first column entry.

$$3: \quad \begin{bmatrix} 1 & 0 \\ -2 & 1 \end{bmatrix} \cdot \begin{bmatrix} 1 & 2 & 3 \\ 2 & 3 & 4 \end{bmatrix}$$

$$4: \quad \begin{bmatrix} 1 & 2 & 3 \\ 0 & -1 & -2 \end{bmatrix}$$

The augmented matrix in statement #4 represents the system

$$\begin{aligned} x + 2y &= 3 \\ -y &= -2 \end{aligned}.$$

We readily see that the second of these equations has $y = 2$ for a solution and substitute this value into the first equation to obtain $x = -1$. By Theorem 6.1 the system in statement #1 is equivalent to the system in statement #4; therefore, $x = -1$ and $y = 2$ are solutions to both systems.

EXAMPLE 6.5 To solve the system

$$\begin{aligned} x + y + z &= 6 \\ 2x + 3y + 7z &= 18 \\ 2x + 5y + 14z &= 32 \end{aligned}$$

we first find an elementary matrix that is itself the product of two elementary matrices:

$$\begin{bmatrix} 1 & 0 & 0 \\ -2 & 1 & 0 \\ 0 & 0 & 1 \end{bmatrix} \begin{bmatrix} 1 & 0 & 0 \\ 0 & 1 & 0 \\ -2 & 0 & 1 \end{bmatrix} = \begin{bmatrix} 1 & 0 & 0 \\ -2 & 1 & 0 \\ -2 & 0 & 1 \end{bmatrix}.$$

The first of these matrices, when multiplied by the augmented matrix for the system of equations generates an equivalent system of equations with a zero in the first entry of the second row of its augmented matrix. The second matrix generates an equivalent system of equations represented by an augmented matrix with a zero entry in the first entry of the third row.

This elementary matrix is multiplied by the augmented matrix for the system to produce an augmented matrix for an equivalent system:

$$3:\quad \begin{bmatrix} 1 & 0 & 0 \\ -2 & 1 & 0 \\ -2 & 0 & 1 \end{bmatrix} \cdot \begin{bmatrix} 1 & 1 & 2 & 6 \\ 2 & 3 & 7 & 18 \\ 2 & 5 & 14 & 32 \end{bmatrix}$$

$$4:\quad \begin{bmatrix} 1 & 1 & 2 & 6 \\ 0 & 1 & 3 & 6 \\ 0 & 3 & 10 & 20 \end{bmatrix}$$

Next, we find an elementary matrix which when multiplied by the augmented matrix in statement #4 generates a zero entry in the third row of the second column.

$$6:\quad \begin{bmatrix} 1 & 0 & 0 \\ 0 & 1 & 0 \\ 0 & -3 & 1 \end{bmatrix} \cdot \begin{bmatrix} 1 & 1 & 2 & 6 \\ 0 & 1 & 3 & 6 \\ 0 & 3 & 10 & 20 \end{bmatrix}$$

$$7:\quad \begin{bmatrix} 1 & 1 & 2 & 6 \\ 0 & 1 & 3 & 6 \\ 0 & 0 & 1 & 2 \end{bmatrix}$$

Statement #7 represents the augmented matrix of the following system which, by Theorem 6.1, is equivalent to the original system:

$$\begin{aligned} x + y + 2z &= 6 \\ y + 3z &= 6 \\ z &= 2 \end{aligned}$$

From this equivalent system we readily obtain the solution $x = 2$, $y = 0$, and $z = 2$ by first substituting $z = 2$ into the second equation and solving for y, and then substituting $z = 2$ and $y = 0$ into the first equation and solving for x.

The final process of solving the reduced equivalent system of equations employed in the above example is known as "back substitution." The process of obtaining an equivalent system of equations may be carried out to a point that requires little or no back substitution by multiplying by elementary matrices on the left to affect further changes. The next example will serve to illustrate that not all systems have a solution.

EXAMPLE 6.6 We consider the system of equations

$$x+2y+3z=1$$
$$2x+3y+4z=2$$
$$3x+4y+5z=7$$

by first declaring the augmented matrix in *Derive* and then multiplying by the appropriate elementary matrix to obtain an equivalent system with zeros in the first entry of the second and third rows:

$$3: \begin{bmatrix} 1 & 0 & 0 \\ -2 & 1 & 0 \\ -3 & 0 & 1 \end{bmatrix} \cdot \begin{bmatrix} 1 & 2 & 3 & 1 \\ 2 & 3 & 4 & 2 \\ 3 & 4 & 5 & 7 \end{bmatrix}$$

$$4: \begin{bmatrix} 1 & 2 & 3 & 1 \\ 0 & -1 & -2 & 0 \\ 0 & -2 & -4 & 4 \end{bmatrix}$$

Next, we further simplify the system represented by multiplying by elementary matrices that will generate a one in the second entry of the second row

$$6: \begin{bmatrix} 1 & 0 & 0 \\ 0 & -1 & 0 \\ 0 & 0 & 1 \end{bmatrix} \cdot \begin{bmatrix} 1 & 2 & 3 & 1 \\ 0 & -1 & -2 & 0 \\ 0 & -2 & -4 & 4 \end{bmatrix}$$

$$7: \begin{bmatrix} 1 & 2 & 3 & 1 \\ 0 & 1 & 2 & 0 \\ 0 & -2 & -4 & 4 \end{bmatrix}$$

and then a zero in the second entry of the third row

$$9: \quad \begin{bmatrix} 1 & 0 & 0 \\ 0 & 1 & 0 \\ 0 & 2 & 1 \end{bmatrix} \cdot \begin{bmatrix} 1 & 2 & 3 & 1 \\ 0 & 1 & 2 & 0 \\ 0 & -2 & -4 & 4 \end{bmatrix}$$

$$10: \quad \begin{bmatrix} 1 & 2 & 3 & 1 \\ 0 & 1 & 2 & 0 \\ 0 & 0 & 0 & 4 \end{bmatrix}$$

The last row of statement #10 represents the equation

$$0x + 0y + 0z = 4$$

which can not be true for any choice of x, y, and z. It follows that the original system of equations also has no solution.

Next, we develop a method to find the inverse of a square matrix that utilizes what we have learned about systems of equations. In Section 1.3 we defined the inverse of a matrix **A** as the matrix **B** satisfying the equation $\mathbf{AB} = \mathbf{BA} = \mathbf{I}$. If we let $\mathbf{I} = [\mathbf{e}_1, \mathbf{e}_2, \cdots, \mathbf{e}_n]$, where $\mathbf{e}_j$ is the $n \times 1$ column matrix with 1 in the jth row and 0's elsewhere, and $\mathbf{B} = [\mathbf{b}_1, \mathbf{b}_2, \cdots, \mathbf{b}_n]$, then $\mathbf{AB} = \mathbf{I}$ can be written as

$$\mathbf{A}[\mathbf{b}_1, \mathbf{b}_2, \cdots, \mathbf{b}_n] = [\mathbf{e}_1, \mathbf{e}_2, \cdots, \mathbf{e}_n]$$

or

$$[\mathbf{Ab}_1, \mathbf{Ab}_2, \cdots, \mathbf{Ab}_n] = [\mathbf{e}_1, \mathbf{e}_2, \cdots, \mathbf{e}_n].$$

Thus finding **B** is equivalent to finding the n solutions of n systems of equations

$$\mathbf{Ab}_j = \mathbf{e}_j \quad j = 1, 2, \cdots, n.$$

Since each of these n systems has the same coefficient matrix **A**, the reduction process for the augmented matrix will always be the same. It is therefore convenient to write a special form of the augmented matrix of the original system $[\mathbf{A}, \mathbf{e}_1, \mathbf{e}_2, \cdots, \mathbf{e}_n]$, which can be interpreted as an $n \times (2n)$ matrix with the first n columns being the columns of **A** and the last n columns being $\mathbf{e}_1, \mathbf{e}_2, \ldots, \mathbf{e}_n$ respectively. (In order to show that this same **B** satisfies the equation **BA** = **I** we require some results of Section 4.2.)

EXAMPLE 6.7 To find the inverse of

$$\mathbf{A} = \begin{bmatrix} 1 & 1 & 1 \\ 2 & 3 & 4 \\ 2 & 5 & 9 \end{bmatrix}.$$

we first enter the augmented matrix [**A**, **I**] of the system into *Derive* and reduce it using elementary matrices to $[\mathbf{I}, \mathbf{B}]$. Our first step in this process is to reduce the first column of **A** to $\begin{bmatrix} 1 & 0 & 0 \end{bmatrix}$. We can accomplish this in one step by multiplying **A** times the elementary matrix that leaves the first row unchanged, replaces the second row with the sum of -2 times the first row of **A** and the second row of **A**, and replaces the third row of **A** with the sum of -2 times the first row of **A** and the third row of **A**. The *Derive* screen appears as follows:

$$3: \quad \begin{bmatrix} 1 & 0 & 0 \\ -2 & 1 & 0 \\ -2 & 0 & 1 \end{bmatrix} \cdot \begin{bmatrix} 1 & 1 & 1 & 1 & 0 & 0 \\ 2 & 3 & 4 & 0 & 1 & 0 \\ 2 & 5 & 9 & 0 & 0 & 1 \end{bmatrix}$$

$$4: \quad \begin{bmatrix} 1 & 1 & 1 & 1 & 0 & 0 \\ 0 & 1 & 2 & -2 & 1 & 0 \\ 0 & 3 & 7 & -2 & 0 & 1 \end{bmatrix}$$

Next, we complete the process of converting **A** to a lower triangular matrix by multiplying the matrix in statement #4 by the elementary matrix that leaves the first and second rows unchanged and replaces the third row with the sum of -3 times the second row and the third row.

$$6: \quad \begin{bmatrix} 1 & 0 & 0 \\ 0 & 1 & 0 \\ 0 & -3 & 1 \end{bmatrix} \cdot \begin{bmatrix} 1 & 1 & 1 & 1 & 0 & 0 \\ 0 & 1 & 2 & -2 & 1 & 0 \\ 0 & 3 & 7 & -2 & 0 & 1 \end{bmatrix}$$

$$7: \begin{bmatrix} 1 & 1 & 1 & 1 & 0 & 0 \\ 0 & 1 & 2 & -2 & 1 & 0 \\ 0 & 0 & 1 & 4 & -3 & 1 \end{bmatrix}$$

Our next step is to begin the back substitution process by first converting the third column to the form $\begin{bmatrix} 0 & 0 & 1 \end{bmatrix}$. We accomplish this by multiplying the matrix of statement #7 by the elementary matrix which leaves the third row unchanged, replaces the second row with the sum of -2 times the third row and the second row, and replaces the first row with the sum of -1 times the third row and the first row.

$$9: \begin{bmatrix} 1 & 0 & -1 \\ 0 & 1 & -2 \\ 0 & 0 & 1 \end{bmatrix} \cdot \begin{bmatrix} 1 & 1 & 1 & 1 & 0 & 0 \\ 0 & 1 & 2 & -2 & 1 & 0 \\ 0 & 0 & 1 & 4 & -3 & 1 \end{bmatrix}$$

$$10: \begin{bmatrix} 1 & 1 & 0 & -3 & 3 & -1 \\ 0 & 1 & 0 & -10 & 7 & -2 \\ 0 & 0 & 1 & 4 & -3 & 1 \end{bmatrix}$$

Finally, we complete the back substitution process by converting the second row of the matrix in statement #10 to the form $\begin{bmatrix} 0 & 1 & 0 \end{bmatrix}$. We accomplish this by multiplying the matrix in statement #10 by the elementary matrix which leaves the second and third rows unchanged and replaces the first row with the sum of -1 times the second row and the first row.

$$12: \begin{bmatrix} 1 & -1 & 0 \\ 0 & 1 & 0 \\ 0 & 0 & 1 \end{bmatrix} \cdot \begin{bmatrix} 1 & 1 & 0 & -3 & 3 & -1 \\ 0 & 1 & 0 & -10 & 7 & -2 \\ 0 & 0 & 1 & 4 & -3 & 1 \end{bmatrix}$$

$$13: \begin{bmatrix} 1 & 0 & 0 & 7 & -4 & 1 \\ 0 & 1 & 0 & -10 & 7 & -2 \\ 0 & 0 & 1 & 4 & -3 & 1 \end{bmatrix}$$

We note that the three rightmost columns of statement #13 constitute the inverse of **A**, which can be verified by multiplying on the right and left respectively by **A** to obtain **I**.

EXAMPLE 6.8 The argument preceding Example 6.6 shows that every invertible matrix **A** can be considered as a coefficient matrix of the system of equations **AX** = **I**, which can be reduced using elementary matrices to an equivalent system **IX** = **B**. The solution **B** of this latter system is necessarily equal to the inverse of **A**. It follows that this reduction method can be used to prove that a matrix **A** is not invertible if the system **IX** = **B** has no solution. We consider the matrix $\mathbf{A} = \begin{bmatrix} 1 & 2 \\ 3 & 6 \end{bmatrix}$ and proceed as in the previous example attempting to reduce the augmented matrix [**A**, **I**]:

$$3: \quad \begin{bmatrix} 1 & 0 \\ -3 & 1 \end{bmatrix} \cdot \begin{bmatrix} 1 & 2 & 1 & 0 \\ 3 & 6 & 0 & 1 \end{bmatrix}$$

$$4: \quad \begin{bmatrix} 1 & 2 & 1 & 0 \\ 0 & 0 & -3 & 1 \end{bmatrix}$$

Examination of the second row of statement #4 leads to the conclusion that it is impossible to reduce the original system to the form **IX** = **B**, and in fact we have a system of equations equivalent to our original system that includes $0x + 0y = -3$, which is impossible. It follows that **A** is not invertible.

EXERCISES

1. Write each system as an augmented matrix and find the solution if possible using *Derive*.

   a) $\begin{Bmatrix} x+2y=2 \\ 3x+4y=2 \end{Bmatrix}$

   b) $\begin{Bmatrix} 3x+2y=4 \\ 2x+2y=2 \end{Bmatrix}$

   c) $\begin{Bmatrix} x+2y=1 \\ 2x+4y=4 \end{Bmatrix}$

2. Write each system as an augmented matrix and find the solution if possible using elementary matrices and *Derive*.

a) $\begin{Bmatrix} x+y+2z=4 \\ 5x+6y+12z=3 \\ 5x+3y+7z=11 \end{Bmatrix}$

b) $\begin{Bmatrix} 6x+9y+12z=6 \\ 11x+15y+19z=16 \\ 3x+4y+5z=6 \end{Bmatrix}$

c) $\begin{Bmatrix} 7x+3y+4z=4 \\ 12x+7y+12z=12 \\ 3x+2y+4z=4 \end{Bmatrix}$

[Hint: Notice that all three systems have the same left hand side. See if you can find all three solutions at the same time.]

3. Write each augmented matrix as a system of equations and find the solution if possible using elementary matrices and *Derive*.

a) $\begin{bmatrix} 1 & 2 & 4 \\ 3 & 4 & 5 \end{bmatrix}$

b) $\begin{bmatrix} 1 & 3 & 5 & 7 \\ 2 & 4 & 6 & 8 \\ 3 & 5 & 7 & 9 \end{bmatrix}$

c) $\begin{bmatrix} 1 & 1 & 2 & 3 \\ 2 & 2 & 3 & 5 \\ 3 & 3 & 4 & 8 \end{bmatrix}$

4. Find the solutions of the following systems of equations

a) $\begin{Bmatrix} 2x+3y=2 \\ 4x+y=8 \end{Bmatrix}$

b) $\begin{Bmatrix} 2x+3y=1 \\ 4x+y=2 \end{Bmatrix}$

c) $\begin{Bmatrix} 2x+3y=4 \\ 4x+y=7 \end{Bmatrix}$

5. Find the inverses of the following matrices by setting up [**A**, **I**] and using elementary matrices reduce it to [**I**, **B**]. Check your result by using the *Derive* matrix inverse command.

a) $\begin{bmatrix} 1 & 1 \\ 2 & 3 \end{bmatrix}$ b) $\begin{bmatrix} 14 & 18 & 5 \\ 3 & 4 & 1 \\ 2 & 3 & 1 \end{bmatrix}$

c) $\begin{bmatrix} 2 & 5 & 6 \\ 6 & 7 & 3 \\ 3 & 3 & 3 \end{bmatrix}$

6. Show that the following matrix is singular:

$$\begin{bmatrix} 1 & 2 & 3 & 4 \\ 1 & 2 & 3 & 4 \\ 3 & 4 & 6 & 2 \\ 4 & -1 & 3 & 0 \end{bmatrix}$$

7. The system $\begin{bmatrix} 1 & 2 \\ 3 & 5 \end{bmatrix}\begin{bmatrix} x \\ y \end{bmatrix} = \begin{bmatrix} 3 \\ 6 \end{bmatrix}$ has the solution $x = -3$ and $y = 3$. If the system is multiplied by $\begin{bmatrix} 1 & 0 \\ 1 & 1 \end{bmatrix}$, does the solution change? Is the same true if the system is multiplied by a singular matrix?

8. For the matrix **A** of Exercise 6 in Section 1.5, solve $\mathbf{Ax} = \mathbf{r}$ where $\mathbf{r} = \begin{bmatrix} 2 & 2 & 1 & 3 \end{bmatrix}^T$ as follows:
   a) Factor the system as $\mathbf{LUx} = \mathbf{r}$.
   b) Write $\mathbf{Ux} = \mathbf{z}$ and solve $\mathbf{Lz} = \mathbf{r}$. (Since **L** is lower triangular, use simple forward substitution to find **z**.)
   c) Solve $\mathbf{Ux} = \mathbf{z}$. (Since **U** is upper triangular, use back substitution.)

9. For the matrix **A** in Exercise 7 of Section 1.5, solve $\mathbf{Ax} = \mathbf{r}$, where $\mathbf{r} = \begin{bmatrix} 1 & 2 & 1 & 2 \end{bmatrix}^T$.

7. ROW ECHELON FORM

When solving a system of linear equations using the matrix methods of Section 1.6, we reduced the augmented matrix representation of the system to an equivalent system that is easier to solve. In our earlier examples (such as Example 6.5) the new system required back substitution to achieve a complete solution. Later in Section 1.6, when we were using these same matrix methods to find the inverse of a matrix **A** (Example 6.6), we continued the reduction of the augmented matrix $[\mathbf{A}, \mathbf{I}]$ until we obtained the equivalent system $[\mathbf{I}, \mathbf{B}]$. By carrying out the reduction until the identity **I** appeared where the matrix **A** first appeared, we in effect incorporated the back substitution procedure into the reduction process. When an augmented matrix is reduced in this manner, the result is said to be in row echelon form. The following definition accommodates augmented matrices that represent systems of linear equations with unique solutions, multiple solutions, and no solution.

DEFINITION 7.1 (Row Echelon Form) A matrix is said to be in row echelon form if it has the following properties:

1. If row k consists of all zeros and $l > k$, then row l consists of all zeros.
2. The leading nonzero element in each row is the only nonzero element in that column.
3. The leading nonzero element in each row is a 1.

4. If $p < q$ and row p and row q have nonzero elements, the leading nonzero element in row p occurs to the left of the leading nonzero element in row q.

EXAMPLE 7.1 The matrix methods of Section 1.6, in which we multiplied a matrix by a series of elementary matrices, can be used to achieve row echelon form, but *Derive* can immediately achieve the same result by Authoring the command ROW_REDUCE:

$$2: \quad \text{ROW\_REDUCE}\begin{bmatrix} 1 & 2 & 3 & 4 & 2 \\ 3 & 4 & 3 & 2 & 0 \\ 2 & 2 & 3 & 4 & 4 \end{bmatrix}$$

$$3: \quad \begin{bmatrix} 1 & 0 & 0 & 0 & 2 \\ 0 & 1 & 0 & -1 & -3 \\ 0 & 0 & 1 & 2 & 2 \end{bmatrix}$$

The definition of row echelon form does not require the matrix being reduced to represent a system of linear equations, but any matrix being reduced can be assumed to be a representation of such a system. Thus the above reduction would correspond to solving the two systems of equations

$$\begin{aligned} x + 2y + 3z &= 4 \\ 3x + 4y + 3z &= 2 \\ 2x + 2y + 3z &= 4 \end{aligned} \qquad \text{and} \qquad \begin{aligned} x + 2y + 3z &= 2 \\ 3x + 4y + 3z &= 0 \\ 2x + 2y + 3z &= 4 \end{aligned}$$

in one application of row reduction. Any time two systems of equations have the same coefficient matrix this type of shortcut can be used to solve the two systems simultaneously with a single row reduction operation.

Although we usually think of a system of equations as having the same number of unknowns as it has equations, this is only one of three types of situations which can arise when solving systems of equations.

1. The number of unknowns can equal the number of equations.
2. The number of unknowns can be less than the number of equations. (Such a system is said to be "overdetermined.")

3. The number of unknowns can be greater than the number of equations. (Such a system is said to be "underdetermined.")

When the number of unknowns is equal to the number of equations, the system may or may not have a solution, and if a solution does exist, it may be unique, or it may contain one or more parameters. These possibilities are demonstrated in Example 7.2.

EXAMPLE 7.2 Two lines in a plane either intersect at one, none, or an infinite number of points. Consider the following pairs of linear equations which have for their graphs straight lines.

a) The pair of equations $\begin{Bmatrix} 2x+y=3 \\ x-2y=4 \end{Bmatrix}$ when solved using the ROW_REDUCE command in *Derive* appear as follows:

$$4: \quad \text{ROW\_REDUCE} \begin{bmatrix} 2 & 1 & 3 \\ 1 & -2 & 4 \end{bmatrix}$$

$$5: \quad \begin{bmatrix} 1 & 0 & 2 \\ 0 & 1 & -1 \end{bmatrix}$$

The unique solution for the system read from statement #5 is $x=2$ and $y=-1$, and the lines meet at exactly one point.

b) The pair of equations $\begin{Bmatrix} -2x+y=3 \\ -2x+y=5 \end{Bmatrix}$ when solved using the ROW_REDUCE command in *Derive* appear as follows:

$$6: \quad \text{ROW\_REDUCE} \begin{bmatrix} -2 & 1 & 3 \\ -2 & 1 & 5 \end{bmatrix}$$

$$7: \quad \begin{bmatrix} 1 & -\frac{1}{2} & 0 \\ 0 & 0 & 1 \end{bmatrix}$$

There is no solution for this new system since no x and y exist satisfying the equation $0x+0y=1$ represented in the last row of statement #7. It follows that the two lines represented by the original system of equations are parallel and have no point in common.

c) The pair of equations $\begin{Bmatrix} 3x+4y=1 \\ 6x+8y=2 \end{Bmatrix}$ when solved using the ROW_REDUCE command in *Derive* appear as follows:

$$8: \quad \text{ROW\_REDUCE} \begin{bmatrix} 3 & 4 & 1 \\ 6 & 8 & 2 \end{bmatrix}$$

$$9: \quad \begin{bmatrix} 1 & \frac{4}{3} & \frac{1}{3} \\ 0 & 0 & 0 \end{bmatrix}$$

The equation represented in the last row of statement #9 implies that $0x + 0y = 0$, which places no restrictions on x or y. In this situation it is possible to assign one of the variables the value of an arbitrary parameter such as $y = \alpha$. From the first row of statement #9

$$x + \frac{4}{3}\alpha = \frac{1}{3} \qquad \text{or} \qquad x = \frac{1}{3} - \frac{4}{3}\alpha;$$

therefore, x can also assume an infinite number of values. It follows that these equations are two representations of the same line.

EXAMPLE 7.3 Some systems of equations require more than one parameter to be assigned in the manner of the above example. For example, the system

$$\begin{aligned} 3x_1 + 2x_2 + x_3 + 3x_4 &= 4 \\ x_1 + x_2 + 2x_3 + 4x_4 &= 3 \\ 4x_1 + 3x_2 + 3x_3 + 4x_4 &= 7 \\ 7x_1 + 5x_2 + 4x_3 + 7x_4 &= 11 \end{aligned}$$

can be reduced to row echelon form using the ROW_REDUCE command in *Derive* as follows:

$$2: \quad \text{ROW\_REDUCE}\begin{bmatrix} 3 & 2 & 1 & 3 & 4 \\ 1 & 1 & 2 & 1 & 3 \\ 4 & 3 & 3 & 4 & 7 \\ 7 & 5 & 4 & 7 & 11 \end{bmatrix}$$

$$3: \quad \begin{bmatrix} 1 & 0 & -3 & 1 & -2 \\ 0 & 1 & 5 & 0 & 5 \\ 0 & 0 & 0 & 0 & 0 \\ 0 & 0 & 0 & 0 & 0 \end{bmatrix}$$

Since the last two rows of the row echelon form of the augmented matrix are all zeros, we assign two arbitrary parameters to the solution: $x_4 = \alpha$ and $x_3 = \beta$. The two equations represented by rows 1 and 2 of statement #3 then reduce to

$$x_1 - 3\beta + \alpha = -2 \quad \text{and} \quad x_2 + 5\beta = 5,$$

and finally

$$x_1 = -2 + 3\beta - \alpha \quad \text{and} \quad x_2 = 5 - 5\beta.$$

It follows that the system has an infinite number of solutions.

EXAMPLE 7.4 The two systems of equations

$$\begin{aligned} x + y &= 4 \\ x + 2y &= 3 \\ 2x + 3y &= 6 \end{aligned} \qquad \text{and} \qquad \begin{aligned} x + y &= 4 \\ x + 2y &= 3 \\ 2x + 3y &= 7 \end{aligned}$$

illustrate overdetermined systems that can be solved simultaneously by augmenting the common coefficient matrix with both sets of constants.

$$2: \quad \text{ROW\_REDUCE}\begin{bmatrix} 1 & 1 & 4 & 4 \\ 1 & 2 & 3 & 3 \\ 2 & 3 & 6 & 7 \end{bmatrix}$$

$$3: \quad \begin{bmatrix} 1 & 0 & 0 & 5 \\ 0 & 1 & 0 & -1 \\ 0 & 0 & 1 & 0 \end{bmatrix}$$

The first system has no solution, since the third equation of the system reduces to $0x + 0y = 1$. The third equation of the second system (represented by the first, second, and fourth entries of the last row) reduces to $0x + 0y = 1$. This places no restrictions on values for x and y. We therefore use the first, second, and fourth entries of the first two rows to obtain the unique solution: $x = 5$ and $y = -1$.

EXAMPLE 7.5 The system

$$\begin{aligned} x + y &= 3 \\ 2x + 4y &= 6 \\ 3x + 6y &= 9 \end{aligned}$$

is also overdetermined, but the following reduction shows it has an infinite number of solutions:

```
                        [ 1  2  3 ]
2:      ROW_REDUCE      [ 2  4  6 ]
                        [ 3  6  9 ]

        [ 1  2  3 ]
3:      [ 0  0  0 ]
        [ 0  0  0 ]
```

By assigning an arbitrary parameter α to y, we can reduce the equation $x + 2\alpha = 3$ represented by the first row of statement #3 to find the corresponding values of x: $x = 3 - 2\alpha$.

One way to visualize an underdetermined system of equations is to supplement the system with additional equations having zero coefficients and zero constants (which place no additional restrictions on the unknowns) until there as many equations as there are unknowns. The system can then have multiple solutions or no solution.

EXAMPLE 7.6 The system

$$\begin{aligned} 2x + 3y + 2z &= 3 \\ x - y &= 2 \end{aligned}$$

can be supplemented with one additional equation with zero coefficients and a zero constant term:

$$2: \quad \text{ROW\_REDUCE}\begin{bmatrix} 2 & 3 & 2 & 3 \\ 1 & -1 & 0 & 2 \\ 0 & 0 & 0 & 0 \end{bmatrix}$$

$$3: \quad \begin{bmatrix} 1 & 0 & \frac{2}{5} & \frac{9}{5} \\ 0 & 1 & \frac{2}{5} & -\frac{1}{5} \\ 0 & 0 & 0 & 0 \end{bmatrix}$$

Since the third row of the matrix in row echelon form does not have a 1 in the third column, we assign an arbitrary value α to z. From the second row we obtain

$$y+\frac{2}{5}\alpha=-\frac{1}{5}, \quad \text{and} \quad y=-\frac{1}{5}-\frac{2}{5}\alpha.$$

The first row yields the equation

$$x+\frac{2}{5}\alpha=\frac{9}{5}, \quad \text{and} \quad x=\frac{9}{5}-\frac{2}{5}\alpha.$$

EXAMPLE 7.7 The equation of the line of intersection of the two planes

$$x+3y+2z=3$$
$$x+2y-z=5$$

can be found by solving the system supplemented with an additional equation with zero coefficients and a zero constant term.

```
2:    ROW_REDUCE [ 1  3   2  3 ]
                 [ 1  2  -1  5 ]
                 [ 0  0   0  0 ]
     [ 1  0  -7   9 ]
3:   [ 0  1   3  -2 ]
     [ 0  0   0   0 ]
```

We assign the parameter α to the value of z and obtain the three equations $z = \alpha$, $y = -2 - 3\alpha$, and $x = 9 + 7\alpha$. Thus, by solving each of these equations for α, we obtain the equation of the line in symmetric form:

$$\frac{x-9}{7} = -\frac{y+2}{3} = z.$$

EXERCISES

1. Solve the following systems of equations if possible. If there is no solution, state why.

a) $\begin{cases} 2x + 3y = 2 \\ x + 2y = 1 \end{cases}$

b) $\begin{cases} x + 3y = 1 \\ 2x + 6y = 3 \end{cases}$

c) $\begin{cases} x - y = 2 \\ -2x + 2y = -4 \end{cases}$

d) $\begin{cases} x + y + z = 3 \\ x + 2y - z = 2 \\ y + z = 5 \end{cases}$

e) $\begin{cases} x - y - z = 2 \\ 2x + y - z = 3 \\ 3x - 2z = 5 \end{cases}$

f) $\begin{cases} x + 2y + z = 1 \\ 3x + 3y + 4z = 4 \\ 2x + y + 3z = 2 \end{cases}$

g) $\begin{cases} x + y + z + w = 2 \\ y + z + w = 3 \\ x + z + w = 4 \\ x + y + z = 5 \end{cases}$

h) $\begin{cases} 5x + 8y + 7z + 4w = 1 \\ 5x + 8y + 7z + 4w = 2 \\ 8x + 5y + z = 0 \\ 2x + 5y + 3z + w = 3 \end{cases}$

i) $\begin{cases} 2x - 3y = 1 \\ 4x + 5y = 2 \\ x - y = 7 \end{cases}$

j) $\begin{cases} 3x - 4y + z = 5 \\ x - 7y + 3z = 6 \end{cases}$

k) $\begin{cases} 2x - y + w = 8 \\ y - 4w = -3 \end{cases}$

1) $\begin{Bmatrix} -3x - z = 5 \\ 2x + 3z = -1 \\ x + y - z = 6 \\ -y + 3z = -2 \end{Bmatrix}$

2. Place the matrix $\begin{bmatrix} 1 & 2 & 1 & 1 \\ 1 & 3 & 1 & 3 \\ 1 & 4 & 2 & 1 \end{bmatrix}$ in row echelon form by using elementary matrices and check your result using the *Derive* ROW_REDUCE command.

3. Solve the two systems of equations at the same time.

   a) $\begin{Bmatrix} x + 2y = 3 \\ 3x + y = 1 \end{Bmatrix}$

   b) $\begin{Bmatrix} x + 2y = 8 \\ 3x + y = 1 \end{Bmatrix}$

4. Find ξ so that the system $\begin{Bmatrix} x + 3y = \xi \\ 4x + 12y = 4 \end{Bmatrix}$ will have a solution. In this case what is the solution?

5. The two planes
$$\begin{Bmatrix} x + 2y + 3z = 4 \\ 3x + 2y + z = 8 \end{Bmatrix}$$
intersect in a line. Find the equation of the line and prove the line lies in both planes.

6. Show that the two planes
$$\begin{Bmatrix} x + y + 2z = 5 \\ -2x - 2y - 4z = 11 \end{Bmatrix}$$
are parallel by showing they have no points in common.

7. Show that the three planes
$$\begin{Bmatrix} -8x + 2y + z + 5 = 0 \\ -6x - 3y + 3z + 6 = 0 \\ -2x + y + 1 = 0 \end{Bmatrix}$$
intersect in a common line and find its equation.

8. Show the two planes are parallel:
$$\begin{Bmatrix} 2x + y - 3z = 5 \\ 4x + 2y - 6z = 11 \end{Bmatrix}.$$

9. Show that the three planes intersect in a common point:
$$\begin{Bmatrix} x + 2y + 3z + 6 = 0 \\ 2x - y + 5z + 2 = 0 \\ 3x - 2y - z + 1 = 0 \end{Bmatrix}.$$

10. The following matrix
$$\begin{bmatrix} 1 & 2 & 0 & 0 & 0 & 0 & 1 & 2 \\ 0 & 0 & 1 & 0 & 1 & 0 & 0 & 1 \\ 0 & 0 & 0 & 1 & 2 & 0 & 3 & 1 \\ 0 & 0 & 0 & 0 & 0 & 1 & 2 & 1 \end{bmatrix}$$
represents a system of equations in 7 unknowns. Find the general solution and show a particular solution is $[x_1, x_2, x_3, x_4, x_5, x_6, x_7] = [-1, 1, -1, -6, 2, -1, 1]$.

CHAPTER II
VECTOR SPACES

In calculus the concept of a vector is introduced to represent physical quantities with both direction and magnitude. Examples include force and the motion of a particle, but the discussion is limited to objects which can be interpreted geometrically in terms of either two or three dimensional vectors. The purpose of this chapter is to generalize the concept of a vector and place it in an abstract setting that will make the study of such objects easier and more complete. Various combinations of vectors will be classified to provide characterizations of special sets called vector "spaces."

1. VECTOR SPACES

Much of mathematics takes place in the context of some abstract "space." In general, a space is simply a set of objects with a structure defining the interrelation of objects in the space. The set of real numbers with the usual definition for addition and multiplication is a simple example. Another example which we studied in calculus is the set of ordered triples $\{[a,b,c]:a,b,c \in R\}$. These triples, along with definitions for addition and scalar multiplication, formed a space that corresponded to the set of all three dimensional geometric vectors. Our definition of a vector space will place conditions on the operations addition and scalar multiplication to ensure that elements of the space are interrelated in an orderly manner. Since these rules are guided to some extent by the behavior of our three dimensional geometric vectors, it will be no surprise to see that the set of ordered triples with the usual definitions of addition and scalar multiplication satisfies the definition of a vector space. But the definition of a vector space which follows is also sufficiently abstract to include other mathematical objects such as functions and matrices.

DEFINITION 1.1 (Vector Space) A vector space V consists of a nonempty set of objects called vectors $(\mathbf{x},\mathbf{y},\mathbf{z},\cdots)$ together with a definition of addition of elements of V (denoted by $\mathbf{x} + \mathbf{y}$) and a field F of numbers called scalars $(a,b,c,\cdots)$ along with a definition for multiplying the elements of V by a scalar from F (denoted by $a\mathbf{x}$). The operations of vector addition and scalar multiplication must satisfy the conditions of closure:

If $\mathbf{x},\mathbf{y} \in V$, then $\mathbf{x}+\mathbf{y} \in V$, and if $a \in F$, then $a\mathbf{x} \in V$.

The operations of addition and scalar multiplication must also satisfy the following eight properties or axioms:

1. $\mathbf{x}+\mathbf{y}=\mathbf{y}+\mathbf{x}$.
2. $(\mathbf{x}+\mathbf{y})+\mathbf{z}=\mathbf{x}+(\mathbf{y}+\mathbf{z})$.
3. There exists an element $\mathbf{0}$ in V such that $\mathbf{0}+\mathbf{x}=\mathbf{x}$ for all $\mathbf{x}$ in V.
4. For each vector $\mathbf{x}$ in V there exists an additive inverse $-\mathbf{x}$ such that $\mathbf{x}+(-\mathbf{x})=\mathbf{0}$.
5. $(ab)\mathbf{x}=a(b\mathbf{x})$.
6. $(a+b)\mathbf{x}=a\mathbf{x}+b\mathbf{x}$.
7. $a(\mathbf{x}+\mathbf{y})=a\mathbf{x}+a\mathbf{y}$.
8. $1\mathbf{x}=\mathbf{x}$ for every $\mathbf{x}$ in V.

It is important to note that a complete specification of a vector space requires listing the set of vectors and the scalar field and defining the operations addition and scalar multiplication. [In general, a field is a set with two operations (such as multiplication and addition) defined in such a way that multiplication distributes over addition and both operations satisfy the closure, commutative, associative, identity, and inverse properties.] Normally in this text we will consider only vector spaces over the field of real numbers, and when the scalar field is not explicitly defined, it may be assumed to be the set of real numbers. Specification of rules for addition of vectors and multiplication by a scalar can also be confusing at times. Most sets of objects we will use as vectors in a vector space have already been introduced in some previous setting, and most were introduced in conjunction with operations that satisfy the above restrictions for addition and scalar multiplication. Sometimes we will choose to use these previously defined operations (and refer to them as the "usual" operations), and sometimes we will define a new operation. If there is no specific definition of either addition or scalar multiplication provided for a particular set of objects, the usual operation is assumed.

EXAMPLE 1.1 Consider the set of real number triples with representative elements $\mathbf{x} = [x_1, x_2, x_3]$ and $\mathbf{y} = [y_1, y_2, y_3]$. Let vector addition of two triples be defined by $\mathbf{x}+\mathbf{y} = [x_1 + y_1, x_2 + y_2, x_3 + y_3]$ (the "usual" definition), and scalar multiplication of elements from the field of real numbers times an ordered triple be defined by $\alpha\mathbf{x} = [\alpha x_1, \alpha x_2, \alpha x_3]$ (the "usual" definition). We claim this set, denoted by R^3, satisfies all the properties of a vector space.

First, since R is closed under both addition and multiplication, it follows that R^3 is closed under both vector addition and scalar multiplication. Next, we show that the eight axioms included in the definition are satisfied:

1. Vector addition is commutative since addition in R is commutative:

$$\begin{aligned}\mathbf{x}+\mathbf{y} &= [x_1 + y_1, x_2 + y_2, x_3 + y_3]\\ &= [y_1 + x_1, y_2 + x_2, y_3 + x_3]\\ &= \mathbf{y}+\mathbf{x}\end{aligned}$$

2. Vector addition is associative since addition in R is associative:

$$\begin{aligned}(\mathbf{x}+\mathbf{y})+\mathbf{z} &= [(x_1 + y_1)+z_1, (x_2 + y_2)+z_2, (x_3 + y_3)+z_3]\\ &= [x_1 + (y_1 + z_1), x_2 + (y_2 + z_2), x_3 + (y_3 + z_3)]\\ &= \mathbf{x}+(\mathbf{y}+\mathbf{z})\end{aligned}$$

3. There exists a zero element in the set of triples, namely $\mathbf{0}$ = [0,0,0]:

$$\begin{aligned}\mathbf{x}+\mathbf{0} &= [x_1 + 0, x_2 + 0, +x_3 + 0]\\ &= [x_1, x_2, x_3]\\ &= \mathbf{x}\end{aligned}$$

4. The additive inverse -**x** of every vector **x** exists, and $-\mathbf{x}=[-x_1,-x_2,-x_3]$:

$$\begin{aligned}\mathbf{x}+(-\mathbf{x})&=[x_1+(-x_1),x_2+(-x_2),x_3+(-x_3)]\\&=[0,0,0]\\&=\mathbf{0}\end{aligned}$$

5. Multiplication by a scalar is associative in the sense that $(ab)\mathbf{x}=a(b\mathbf{x})$:

$$\begin{aligned}(ab)\mathbf{x}&=[abx_1,abx_2,abx_3]\\&=a[bx_1,bx_2,bx_3]\\&=a(b\mathbf{x})\end{aligned}$$

6. Multiplication by the sum of scalars distributes in the sense that $(a+b)\mathbf{x}=a\mathbf{x}+b\mathbf{x}$:

$$\begin{aligned}(a+b)\mathbf{x}&=[(a+b)x_1,(a+b)x_2,(a+b)x_3]\\&=[ax_1,ax_2,ax_3]+[bx_1,bx_2,bx_3]\\&=a\mathbf{x}+b\mathbf{x}\end{aligned}$$

7. Scalar multiplication distributes over a vector sum, that is $a(\mathbf{x}+\mathbf{y})=a\mathbf{x}+a\mathbf{y}$:

$$\begin{aligned}a(\mathbf{x}+\mathbf{y})&=[a(x_1+y_1),a(x_2+y_2),a(x_3+y_3)]\\&=[ax_1,ax_2,ax_3]+[ay_1,ay_2,ay_3]\\&=a\mathbf{x}+b\mathbf{y}\end{aligned}$$

8. Multiplication by the scalar identity does not alter the vector:

$$\begin{aligned}1\mathbf{x}&=[1x_1,1x_2,1x_3]\\&=[x_1,x_2,x_3]\\&=\mathbf{x}\end{aligned}$$

Since R^3 satisfies all the axioms of Definition 1.1, it is a vector space over R, the field of real numbers. (The same set of arguments would have also shown that R^3 is a vector space over C, the field of complex numbers.)

Generally, we will simply refer to this vector space as R^3, omitting the reference to the field of numbers.

By a similar argument, R^n is a vector space over R (or C) for each n, where R^n is the set of n-tuples of real numbers with vector addition and scalar multiplication defined as follows:

$$\mathbf{x}+\mathbf{y}=\left[x_1+y_1,x_2+y_2,\cdots,x_n+y_n\right]$$
$$\alpha\mathbf{x}=\left[ax_1,ax_2,\cdots,ax_n\right].$$

The proof of this fact, which may be modeled after the demonstration that R^3 is a vector space, is left as an exercise.

Any set of axioms is expected to satisfy the properties of consistency (no axiom contradicts another axiom) and independence (no axiom can be proved given the remaining axioms). The set of axioms defining a vector space can be shown to satisfy these two properties. We have already shown that R^3 satisfies all eight axioms; therefore, the set of axioms must be consistent. To demonstrate the independence of a particular axiom, we construct an example which does not satisfy that axiom but does satisfy the remaining seven axioms. For example, a system that demonstrates the independence of the eighth axiom in Definition 1.1 is the set of number pairs $\mathbf{x} = [x_1, x_2]$ with addition defined as

$$\mathbf{x}+\mathbf{y}=\left[x_1+y_1,x_2+y_2\right]$$

and scalar multiplication defined as

$$\alpha\mathbf{x}=\left[ax_1,0\right].$$

This system satisfies the first seven axioms but not the eighth axiom since $1\mathbf{x}=\left[x_1,0\right]\neq\mathbf{x}$. The proof of the independence of the remaining seven axioms is left as an exercise.

EXAMPLE 1.2 Let P^n be the set of polynomials with real coefficients of degree less than or equal to n. A typical element of P^n is

$$p(x)=\sum_{i=0}^{n}a_i x^i.$$

Define the operations of vector addition and multiplication by the scalar c in the usual way as follows:

$$\text{if } q(x)=\sum_{i=0}^{n} b_i x^i, \quad \text{then} \quad p(x)+q(x)=\sum_{i=0}^{n}(a_i+b_i)x^i\,,$$

$$\text{and } cp(x)=\sum_{i=0}^{n} ca_i x^i.$$

With this set of definitions, if we assign $-p(x)=\sum_{i=0}^{n}-a_i x^i$ and $0(x)=\sum_{i=0}^{n}0x^i$, then all eight axioms for a vector space are satisfied, and P^n is a vector space.

EXAMPLE 1.3 The set F of real valued functions with at most one discontinuity on [-1,1] is not a vector space if the sum of f and g is defined as $(f+g)(x)=f(x)+g(x)$, and multiplication by a scalar is defined by $(af)(x)=af(x)$. Let

$$f(x)=\begin{cases}0 & -1\le x\le 0\\ 1 & 0<x\le 1\end{cases} \quad \text{and} \quad g(x)=\begin{cases}0 & -1\le x\le -0.5\\ 1 & -0.5<x\le 1\end{cases}.$$

The sum of these two functions is $h(x)=f(x)+g(x)$, where

$$h(x)=\begin{cases}0 & -1\le x\le -0.5\\ 1 & -0.5<x\le 0\,.\\ 2 & 0<x\le 1\end{cases}$$

Since $h(x)$ has two discontinuities on $[-1,1]$, it is not a member of F; therefore, the set is not closed with respect to vector addition and the structure is not a vector space.

EXAMPLE 1.4 In Definitions 2.2 and 2.3 of Section 1.2 we defined matrix addition and scalar multiplication. If we define $M_{m\times n}$ to be the set of all $m\times n$ matrices with real elements, then $M_{m\times n}$ is a vector space over R since it is closed under vector addition and scalar multiplication and satisfies the eight axioms of Definition 1.1. For this space $\mathbf{0} = \left[0_{ij}\right]$ acts as an additive identity, and $-1\mathbf{A}$ acts as the additive inverse of any $m \times n$ matrix **A**.

EXAMPLE 1.5 To determine if the set of all 2×2 matrices that commute with

$$\mathbf{M} = \begin{bmatrix} 1 & 1 \\ 2 & 2 \end{bmatrix}$$

together with the usual definition of matrix addition and multiplication by a scalar forms a vector space over *R*, we first use *Derive* to find a parametric representation of the set of all matrices that commute with **M**. This is accomplished by entering **M** into *Derive* along with the most general matrix that commutes with **M**:

$$3: \quad \begin{bmatrix} 1 & 1 \\ 2 & 2 \end{bmatrix} \cdot \begin{bmatrix} a & b \\ c & d \end{bmatrix} = \begin{bmatrix} a & b \\ c & d \end{bmatrix} \cdot \begin{bmatrix} 1 & 1 \\ 2 & 2 \end{bmatrix}$$

$$4: \quad \begin{bmatrix} a + c = a + 2 b & b + d = a + 2 b \\ 2 a + 2 c = c + 2 d & 2 b + 2 d = c + 2 d \end{bmatrix}$$

where statement #4 is obtained by **S**implifying statement #3. Next, we collect the terms involving *a*, *b*, *c*, and *d* on the left side of each of the four equations of statement #4 and **D**eclare the 4×5 augmented **M**atrix (in statement #5, which is not shown) that represents the system of four equations in four unknowns. This augmented matrix can then be reduced as follows:

$$6: \quad \text{ROW\_REDUCE} \begin{bmatrix} 0 & -2 & 1 & 0 & 0 \\ 1 & 1 & 0 & -1 & 0 \\ 2 & 0 & 1 & -2 & 0 \\ 0 & -2 & 1 & 0 & 0 \end{bmatrix}$$

$$7: \begin{bmatrix} 1 & 0 & \frac{1}{2} & -1 & 0 \\ 0 & 1 & -\frac{1}{2} & 0 & 0 \\ 0 & 0 & 0 & 0 & 0 \\ 0 & 0 & 0 & 0 & 0 \end{bmatrix}$$

The last two rows of this system consist of all zeros and thus the system is underdetermined requiring two parameters, which we will call p and q. By setting $d = p$ and $c = q$, we can use the first two equations in statement #7 to find values for b and a. The resulting matrix

$$\begin{bmatrix} a & b \\ c & d \end{bmatrix} = \begin{bmatrix} p - \frac{1}{2}q & \frac{1}{2}q \\ q & p \end{bmatrix},$$

which has been constructed to commute with **M**, can be checked by multiplying

$$9: \begin{bmatrix} 1 & 1 \\ 2 & 2 \end{bmatrix} \cdot \begin{bmatrix} p - \frac{1}{2}q & \frac{1}{2}q \\ q & p \end{bmatrix}$$

$$10: \begin{bmatrix} p + \frac{q}{2} & p + \frac{q}{2} \\ 2p + q & 2p + q \end{bmatrix}$$

and

$$11: \begin{bmatrix} p - \frac{1}{2}q & \frac{1}{2}q \\ q & p \end{bmatrix} \cdot \begin{bmatrix} 1 & 1 \\ 2 & 2 \end{bmatrix}$$

$$12: \begin{bmatrix} p + \frac{q}{2} & p + \frac{q}{2} \\ 2p + q & 2p + q \end{bmatrix}$$

The demonstration that the set of matrices which commute with **M** is closed under vector addition and multiplication by a scalar is left for an exercise. The **0** matrix commutes with **M** and acts as the additive identity. If **A** is a matrix that commutes with **M**, then -1**A** commutes with **M** and acts as the additive inverse of **A**. Other axioms from Definition 1.1 follow similarly.

Additive identities and additive inverses play especially important roles in understanding the behavior of a particular vector space. The following two theorems provide some guidance in identifying them.

THEOREM 1.1 If V is a vector space and $\mathbf{x}$ is an element of V then $0\mathbf{x} = \mathbf{0}$.

PROOF: Using the fact that 0 is the additive identity in the set of real numbers and Axiom 6 of Definition 1.1:

$$0\mathbf{x} = (0+0)\mathbf{x} = 0\mathbf{x} + 0\mathbf{x}.$$

Thus

$$\begin{aligned}\mathbf{0} &= 0\mathbf{x} + (-(0\mathbf{x}))\\ &= (0\mathbf{x} + 0\mathbf{x}) + (-(0\mathbf{x}))\\ &= 0\mathbf{x} + (0\mathbf{x} + (-(0\mathbf{x})))\\ &= 0\mathbf{x} + \mathbf{0}\\ &= 0\mathbf{x}\end{aligned}$$

THEOREM 1.2 If V is a vector space and $\mathbf{x}$ is any element of V then $-1\mathbf{x} = -\mathbf{x}$

PROOF: Using Theorem 1.1 and Axiom 8 of Definition 1.1:

$$\begin{aligned}-\mathbf{x} &= -\mathbf{x} + 0\mathbf{x}\\ &= -\mathbf{x} + (1-1)\mathbf{x}\\ &= -\mathbf{x} + (\mathbf{x} - 1\mathbf{x})\\ &= (-\mathbf{x} + \mathbf{x}) - 1\mathbf{x}\\ &= \mathbf{0} - 1\mathbf{x}\\ &= -1\mathbf{x}\end{aligned}$$

The following two theorems demonstrate that any vector that behaves like the additive identity or an additive inverse (such as $0\mathbf{x}$ or $-1\mathbf{x}$ above) are **0** and **-x** respectively.

THEOREM 1.3 If V is a vector space then the **0** element is unique.

PROOF: If **u** and **v** are two vectors which can both act a zero elements, then $\mathbf{v} = \mathbf{u} + \mathbf{v} = \mathbf{v} + \mathbf{u} = \mathbf{v}$, and $\mathbf{u} = \mathbf{v}$.

THEOREM 1.4 If V is a vector space and **x** is an element of V, then the additive inverse of **x** is unique.

PROOF: Assume the additive inverse is not unique, and let **u** and **v** be additive inverses of **x**. Then

$$\mathbf{x} + \mathbf{u} = \mathbf{0} \qquad \mathbf{x} + \mathbf{v} = \mathbf{0}$$

and

$$\mathbf{x} + \mathbf{u} = \mathbf{x} + \mathbf{v}.$$

Next, we add **u** to both sides of this equation and use the associative, commutative, and identity properties of a vector space to achieve our desired result.

$$\mathbf{u} + (\mathbf{x} + \mathbf{u}) = \mathbf{u} + (\mathbf{x} + \mathbf{v})$$
$$\mathbf{u} + (\mathbf{x} + \mathbf{u}) = \mathbf{v} + (\mathbf{x} + \mathbf{u})$$
$$\mathbf{u} + \mathbf{0} = \mathbf{v} + \mathbf{0}$$
$$\mathbf{u} = \mathbf{v}$$

We leave the proofs of the following results as exercises.

THEOREM 1.5 If V is a vector space, then

i.) If $c\mathbf{x} = \mathbf{0}$, then either $c = 0$ or $\mathbf{x} = \mathbf{0}$. (Note: In mathematics the word "or" always has an inclusive meaning unless otherwise noted. Therefore, in this case the possibility is open for both $c = 0$ and $\mathbf{x} = \mathbf{0}$.)

ii.) If $\mathbf{x} + \mathbf{y} = \mathbf{x} + \mathbf{z}$, then $\mathbf{y} = \mathbf{z}$.

EXERCISES

1. Show that the following sets along with the given definition of addition and multiplication are vector spaces.

   a) The set of 3×4 matrices where addition and scalar multiplication follow the usual rules.

   b) The set of ordered pairs of real numbers (x_1, x_2) with addition and multiplication and by a scalar defined by $(x_1, x_2)+(y_1, y_2) = (x_1 + y_1, x_2 + y_2)$ and $c(x_1, x_2) = (cx_1, cx_2)$.

   c) The set of 2×2 matrices with the sum of the diagonal elements equal to zero and the usual rules of matrix addition and scalar multiplication. (The sum of the diagonal elements of the $n\times n$ matrix **A** is called the trace of the matrix and is noted as TR(**A**)).

   d) The set of continuous functions on the closed interval $[a, b]$ with addition and multiplication by a scalar defined as $(f+g)(x) = f(x)+g(x)$ and $(cf)(x) = cf(x)$.

   e) The set of real numbers with the usual rules for addition and multiplication of real numbers.

2. Show that the following sets with the given rules for addition and multiplication by a scalar are not vector spaces.

   a) The set of 2×3 matrices with non-negative entries with the usual rules of addition and scalar multiplication.

   b) The set M of $n\times n$ matrices **A** with $\text{TR}(\mathbf{A}) = 1$ (see problem 1-c) along with the usual rules for adding matrices and scalar multiplication.

   c) The set of ordered pairs of real numbers (x_1, x_2) with addition and multiplication by a scalar defined by $(x_1, x_2)+(y_1, y_2) = (x_1 + y_1, x_2 + y_2)$ and $c(x_1, x_2) = (cx_1, -cx_2)$.

   d) The set of $n\times n$ non-singular matrices with the usual rules of matrix addition and multiplication by a scalar.

3. Determine if the set V consisting of pairs of real numbers with addition and multiplication by a scalar defined by the following rules is a vector space: $(x_1, x_2) + (y_1, y_2) = (x_1 + 2y_1, 2x_2 + y_2)$ $c(x_1, x_2) = (cx_1, cx_2)$.

4. Consider the set of ordered pairs of real numbers with the usual definition of vector addition and multiplication by a scalar defined by

$$c[x_1, x_2] = [cx_2, cx_1].$$

Show that this system is not a vector space since the eighth axiom of Definition 1.1 is violated. Does this example provide an alternate proof of the argument provided in this section that the eighth axiom is independent? Why or why not?

5. Let S be the set of 2×2 matrices that commute with $\mathbf{T} = \begin{bmatrix} 0 & 1 \\ 1 & 0 \end{bmatrix}$ with the usual rules for addition and scalar multiplication. Is S a vector space?

6. Let K be the set of all 2×3 matrices that commute with $\mathbf{T} = \begin{bmatrix} 1 & 2 & 3 \\ 2 & 3 & 4 \end{bmatrix}$. Is K a vector space given the usual rules of addition and multiplication by a scalar?

7. Let M be the set of all matrices $\mathbf{A}$ such that $\mathbf{AT} = \mathbf{T}^{\mathrm{T}}\mathbf{A}^{\mathrm{T}}$, where $\mathbf{T}$ is defined in Exercise 5 and $\mathbf{A}$ is a 3×2 matrix. Is M a vector space under the usual rules of matrix algebra? Is the matrix $\mathbf{B} = \begin{bmatrix} 1 & 7 \\ 6 & 1 \end{bmatrix}$ a vector of the set M?

8. Let X be the set of all 3×1 matrices that satisfy the equation $\begin{bmatrix} 1 & 1 & 2 \\ 2 & 3 & 4 \\ 0 & 1 & 0 \end{bmatrix}\begin{bmatrix} x_1 \\ x_2 \\ x_3 \end{bmatrix} = \begin{bmatrix} 0 \\ 0 \\ 0 \end{bmatrix}$. Does X, with the usual rules of matrix algebra, form a vector space?

9. Let Y be the set of all 3×1 matrices that satisfy the equation

$$\begin{bmatrix} 1 & 1 & 2 \\ 2 & 3 & 4 \\ 0 & 1 & 0 \end{bmatrix}\begin{bmatrix} y_1 \\ y_2 \\ y_3 \end{bmatrix} = \begin{bmatrix} 1 \\ 1 \\ 1 \end{bmatrix}.$$

Does the set Y with the usual rules of matrix algebra form a vector space?

10. Let M be the set of 2×2 matrices with addition defined as usual but with multiplication by a scalar defined as follows:

$c\mathbf{A} = \mathbf{0}$ if $c = 0$,

$$c\mathbf{A} \begin{bmatrix} ca_{11} & c^2a_{12} \\ \frac{1}{c}a_{21} & \frac{1}{c^2}a_{22} \end{bmatrix}$$

if $c \neq 0$. Is M a vector space?

11. Does the set of lines $y = mx + b$ form a vector space if addition and multiplication by a scalar are defined as follows: If $y_1 = m_1x + b_1$ and $y_2 = m_2x + b_2$ are two members of the set of lines, then $y_1 + y_2 = (m_1 + m_2)x + b_1 + b_2$ and $cy_1 = cm_1x + cb_1$.

12. Let S be the set of all infinite sequences of real numbers with the addition of two sequences $\mathbf{x} = (x_1, x_2, x_3, \ldots)$ and $\mathbf{y} = (x_1, x_2, x_3, \ldots)$ and multiplication by a scalar defined as follows: $\mathbf{x} + \mathbf{y} = (x_1 + y_1, x_2 + y_2, x_3 + y_3, \ldots)$, $c\mathbf{x} = (cx_1, cx_2, cx_3, \ldots)$. Is S a vector space?

13. Let S be the set of all convergent infinite series with addition and multiplication by a scalar defined as follows: $\sum\limits_n x_n + \sum\limits_n y_n = \sum\limits_n (x_n + y_n)$ and $c\sum\limits_n x_n = \sum\limits_n cx_n$. Is S a vector space?

14. Let F be the set of all functions on $[0,1]$ that are discontinuous at 1/2 (only). Is F a vector space if vector addition and scalar multiplication are as defined in Example 1.3?

15. Prove Theorem 1.5.

16. Prove that the first seven axioms of Definition 1.1 are independent. (For each axiom, find an example of a vector space that satisfies all other axioms except that particular one.

2. SUBSPACES

In Section 2.1 we saw that the concept of a vector space is, at least in part, motivated by the two and three dimensional geometric vectors we considered in calculus. Upon careful examination of these two important vector spaces we see that by setting one of the three components, such as the third or z component, equal to zero, the resulting subset of three dimensional vectors behaves exactly as the set of two dimensional vectors. The question arises as to what other subsets of the set of three dimensional vectors (or any other vector space) possess all the requirements to be a vector space: addition and scalar multiplication are closed and the eight axioms of Definition 1.1 are satisfied. We call such a subset a "subspace" of the original vector space.

DEFINITION 2.1 (Subspace of a Vector Space) A nonempty subset W of a vector space V over a field F is said to be a subspace of V over F with the inherited operations of addition and multiplication by a scalar if W is itself a vector space.

Every vector space V has a trivial subspace $\{\mathbf{0}\}$, where $\mathbf{0}$ is the zero vector of V. This subspace is called the zero subspace of V. Every vector space V is also a subspace of itself.

THEOREM 2.1 If W is a subspace of V, then the $\mathbf{0}$ of V is the $\mathbf{0}$ of W.

PROOF: If $\mathbf{0}'$ is the zero element of W, then for each $\mathbf{x} \in W$, $\mathbf{x} + \mathbf{0}' = \mathbf{x}$. But $\mathbf{x}, \mathbf{0}' \in V$; thus, $\mathbf{x} + \mathbf{0}' = \mathbf{x} = \mathbf{x} + \mathbf{0}$ in V. By adding $-\mathbf{x}$ to both sides of this equation, we obtain $\mathbf{0}' = \mathbf{0}$.

It remains cumbersome to prove that a particular subset of a vector space V is in fact a subspace of V since we must not only prove the operations addition and scalar multiplication are closed but also that all eight axioms of Definition 1.1 are valid for the subset. The following theorem provides a shortcut: closure for both addition and scalar multiplication must be proved, but the only axiom which must be demonstrated is the one requiring the subset to contain the additive identity. The other axioms are inherited in a natural way from the vector space itself.

THEOREM 2.2 Let V be a vector space over F, and let $W \subseteq V$. W is a subspace of V if and only if the elements of W satisfy the following three conditions:

i.) The $\mathbf{0}$ of V is an element of W.
ii.) If $\mathbf{x}, \mathbf{y} \in W$, then $\mathbf{x} + \mathbf{y} \in W$.
iii.) If $\mathbf{x} \in W$ and $a \in F$, then $a\mathbf{x} \in W$.

PROOF: Let W be a subspace of V. The first property follows immediately from Theorem 2.1. By the definition of subspace, W is closed with respect to addition and multiplication by a scalar so the last two properties hold.

If the three conditions hold, then for each $\mathbf{x} \in W$, $-1\mathbf{x} \in W$. But $-\mathbf{x} = -1\mathbf{x}$ by Theorem 1.2; therefore, the additive inverse of each $\mathbf{x} \in W$ is also an element of W. The other seven axioms required for W to be a vector space follow immediately from the fact that V is a vector space, and the proof is complete.

EXAMPLE 2.1 Let W be the subset of $M_{3\times 3}$ containing all 3×3 matrices with a third column consisting of all zeros. If the operations of addition and scalar multiplication are defined in the usual way, then W is a subspace of $M_{3\times 3}$ since the sum of any two matrices with zero elements in the third column will itself have a third column consisting of zeros, any scalar product of an element of W has a third column consisting of zeros, and the zero 3×3 matrix has zeros in its third column.

EXAMPLE 2.2 Let $W \subset R^3$ satisfying $W = \{[x, 2x, t]\colon x, t \in R\}$ and assume the usual operations for addition and scalar multiplication on R^3. The sum of two vectors of W is in W since $[a, 2a, b] + [c, 2c, d] = [a+c, 2(a+c), b+d]$. The product of a scalar times a vector in W is in W since $a[x, 2x, t] = [ax, 2ax, at]$. The zero of R^3 is in W since we can set both $x = 0$ and $t = 0$. Thus, W is a subspace of R^3.

DEFINITION 2.2 (Symmetric Matrix) A square matrix $\mathbf{A}$ is said to be symmetric if $\mathbf{A} = \mathbf{A}^{\mathrm{T}}$.

EXAMPLE 2.3 Consider the set S of symmetric 3×3 matrices as a subset of $M_{3\times 3}$ with the usual operations for addition and scalar multiplication. The sum of two symmetric matrices is symmetric by Theorem 2.3 i.) of Section 1.2 since

$$(\mathbf{A}+\mathbf{B}) = (\mathbf{A}^{\mathrm{T}}+\mathbf{B}^{\mathrm{T}}) = (\mathbf{A}+\mathbf{B})^{\mathrm{T}}.$$

Similarly, and the product of a scalar times a symmetric matrix is a symmetric matrix by Theorem 2.3 ii.) of Section 1.2 since

$$a\mathbf{A} = a\mathbf{A}^{\mathrm{T}} = (a\mathbf{A})^{\mathrm{T}}.$$

Also, the zero matrix is symmetric; therefore, it follows from Theorem 2.2 that S is a subspace of M.

EXAMPLE 2.4 Consider the set S of all solutions of

$$\begin{bmatrix} 4 & 4 & 2 \\ 3 & 4 & 2 \\ 1 & 2 & 1 \end{bmatrix} \begin{bmatrix} x_1 \\ x_2 \\ x_3 \end{bmatrix} = \begin{bmatrix} 0 \\ 0 \\ 0 \end{bmatrix}$$

as a subset of the vector space of all 3×1 matrices with the usual definitions for vector addition and multiplication by a scalar. We can use *Derive* to solve the system by reducing the augmented matrix to row echelon form:

$$2: \quad \text{ROW\_REDUCE} \begin{bmatrix} 4 & 4 & 2 & 0 \\ 3 & 4 & 2 & 0 \\ 1 & 2 & 1 & 0 \end{bmatrix}$$

$$3: \quad \begin{bmatrix} 1 & 0 & 0 & 0 \\ 0 & 1 & \frac{1}{2} & 0 \\ 0 & 0 & 0 & 0 \end{bmatrix}$$

Since the third row of the reduced matrix is all zeros, the general solution for the system is

$$4: \quad \begin{bmatrix} 0 \\ -\frac{1}{2} c \\ c \end{bmatrix}$$

where c is an arbitrary parameter. The sum of two vectors of the type described in statement #4 is also a solution of the system as demonstrated by

$$7: \quad \begin{bmatrix} 4 & 4 & 2 \\ 3 & 4 & 2 \\ 1 & 2 & 1 \end{bmatrix} \cdot \left[\begin{bmatrix} 0 \\ -\frac{1}{2} c \\ c \end{bmatrix} + \begin{bmatrix} 0 \\ -\frac{1}{2} b \\ b \end{bmatrix} \right]$$

$$8: \quad \begin{bmatrix} 0 \\ 0 \\ 0 \end{bmatrix}$$

where statement #8 is obtained by simplifying statement #7. Similarly, a scalar multiple of any solution is itself a solution as demonstrated by

$$9: \quad \begin{bmatrix} 4 & 4 & 2 \\ 3 & 4 & 2 \\ 1 & 2 & 1 \end{bmatrix} \cdot a \begin{bmatrix} 0 \\ -\frac{1}{2} c \\ c \end{bmatrix}$$

$$10: \quad \begin{bmatrix} 0 \\ 0 \\ 0 \end{bmatrix}$$

The zero vector can be written in the form of statement #4 by setting $c = 0$. It therefore follows from Theorem 2.2 that the set of solutions is a subspace of the space of 3×1 matrices.

EXAMPLE 2.5 Let $S = \left\{ \mathbf{A} \in M_{m\times n} : \sum_{i=1}^{m} \sum_{j=1}^{n} a_{ij} = 0 \right\}$, where $M_{m\times n}$ is the set of $m \times n$ matrices. Consider S as a possible subspace of the vector space $M_{m\times n}$. First, we must show that S is closed with respect to addition and multiplication by a scalar. If **A** and **B** are two members of S, then the sum of the elements of **A** + **B** is

$$\sum_{i=1}^{m} \sum_{j=1}^{n} \left(a_{ij} + b_{ij}\right) = \sum_{i=1}^{m} \sum_{j=1}^{n} a_{ij} + \sum_{i=1}^{m} \sum_{j=1}^{n} b_{ij} = 0 + 0 = 0,$$

and the sum of the elements of $c\mathbf{A}$ is

$$\sum_{i=1}^{m}\sum_{j=1}^{n} ca_{ij} = c\sum_{i=1}^{m}\sum_{j=1}^{n} a_{ij} = c0 = 0.$$

Hence, S is closed under vector addition and multiplication by a scalar. Clearly the zero matrix is a member of S; therefore, by Theorem 2.2, S is a subspace of $M_{m\times n}$.

EXAMPLE 2.6 To determine if the set of all 2×2 matrices that commute with

$$\mathbf{T} = \begin{bmatrix} 0 & 1 \\ 1 & 0 \end{bmatrix}$$

form a subspace of the space $M_{2\times 2}$, we first utilize *Derive* to find the most general matrix that commutes with $\mathbf{T}$:

3: $\begin{bmatrix} 0 & 1 \\ 1 & 0 \end{bmatrix} \cdot \begin{bmatrix} a & b \\ c & d \end{bmatrix} - \begin{bmatrix} a & b \\ c & d \end{bmatrix} \cdot \begin{bmatrix} 0 & 1 \\ 1 & 0 \end{bmatrix}$

4: $\begin{bmatrix} c - b & d - a \\ a - d & b - c \end{bmatrix}$

Next, we set statement #4 equal to the zero matrix and obtain four equations in four unknowns which can be written as an augmented matrix and reduced to row echelon form:

6: ROW_REDUCE $\begin{bmatrix} 0 & -1 & 1 & 0 & 0 \\ -1 & 0 & 0 & 1 & 0 \\ 1 & 0 & 0 & -1 & 0 \\ 0 & 1 & -1 & 0 & 0 \end{bmatrix}$

7: $\begin{bmatrix} 1 & 0 & 0 & -1 & 0 \\ 0 & 1 & -1 & 0 & 0 \\ 0 & 0 & 0 & 0 & 0 \\ 0 & 0 & 0 & 0 & 0 \end{bmatrix}$

This leads to the conclusion that $a = d$ and $b = c$, and the most general matrix that commutes with **T** has the form

$$\begin{bmatrix} d & c \\ c & d \end{bmatrix},$$

where c and d are arbitrary. It is a simple exercise to show the set of matrices satisfying this form is closed with respect to vector addition and multiplication by a scalar. Also, the zero matrix is of this type since c and d can both be set equal to zero; therefore, by Theorem 2.2, S is a subspace of $M_{2\times 2}$.

EXAMPLE 2.7 In Exercise 1d) of Section 2.1 we showed that F^{C}, the set of all continuous functions on $[-1,1]$, is a vector space. Now let S be the subset of F^{C} such that $S = \{f : f \in F^{C}, f(0) = 0\}$, and consider S as a possible subspace of F^{C}. Addition is closed on S since if $f, g \in S$, then $(f+g)(0) = f(0) + g(0) = 0$ and $(f+g) \in S$. Similarly, $(af)(0) = a(f(0)) = 0$, and $af \in S$. Also, the zero function is in S since $0(0) = 0$, and it follows from Theorem 2.2 that S is a subspace of F^{C}.

EXAMPLE 2.8 The set of polynomials P^3 of degree less than or equal to 3 is a subspace of P^n for every $n \geq 3$. This follows from the fact that the sum of two polynomials of degree less than or equal to three is a polynomial of degree less than or equal to three, and the product of a scalar and an element of P^3 is an element of P^3. The zero polynomial is an element of P^3 and acts as the zero element of P^3. Thus, by Theorem 2.2, P^3 is a subspace of P^n.

EXAMPLE 2.9 Consider the set K of all matrices **A** such that $\mathbf{AB} = \mathbf{B}^{\mathrm{T}}\mathbf{A}^{\mathrm{T}}$ where

$$\mathbf{B} = \begin{bmatrix} 1 & 1 & 0 \\ 0 & 1 & 1 \end{bmatrix}.$$

Since **B** is a 2×3 matrix, K is a subset of the vector space $M_{3\times 2}$. We will use *Derive* to find the most general representation for the matrix **A**.

$$3: \quad \begin{bmatrix} a & b \\ c & d \\ e & f \end{bmatrix} \cdot \begin{bmatrix} 1 & 1 & 0 \\ 0 & 1 & 1 \end{bmatrix} - \begin{bmatrix} 1 & 1 & 0 \\ 0 & 1 & 1 \end{bmatrix}' \cdot \begin{bmatrix} a & b \\ c & d \\ e & f \end{bmatrix}'$$

$$4: \quad \begin{bmatrix} 0 & a + b - c & b - e \\ -a - b + c & 0 & d - e - f \\ e - b & -d + e + f & 0 \end{bmatrix}$$

Next, we set the matrix in statement #4 equal to zero to generate a system of equations in the unknowns a, b, c, d, e, and f. Of the nine possible equations, the three formed by equating elements on the main diagonal have the form $0 = 0$, and the remaining six can be reduced to only three equations since the ij element of the matrix is the negative of the ji element. By reducing the resulting augmented matrix to row echelon form we obtain:

$$6: \quad \text{ROW\_REDUCE} \begin{bmatrix} 1 & 1 & -1 & 0 & 0 & 0 & 0 \\ 0 & 1 & 0 & 0 & -1 & 0 & 0 \\ 0 & 0 & 0 & 1 & -1 & -1 & 0 \end{bmatrix}$$

$$7: \quad \begin{bmatrix} 1 & 0 & -1 & 0 & 1 & 0 & 0 \\ 0 & 1 & 0 & 0 & -1 & 0 & 0 \\ 0 & 0 & 0 & 1 & -1 & -1 & 0 \end{bmatrix}$$

Next, we assign c, f, and e parametric values and solve the three equations represented by the rows of statement #7 for $a = c - e$, $b = e$, and $d = e + f$. Thus

$$\mathbf{A} = \begin{bmatrix} c - e & e \\ c & e + f \\ e & f \end{bmatrix}.$$

It is a simple exercise to show the set of matrices of this form is closed with respect to vector addition and multiplication by a scalar, and the zero matrix can be written in this form by setting $c, e, f = 0$; therefore, K is a subspace of $M_{3\times 2}$ by Theorem 2.2.

DEFINITION 2.3 (Trace of a Matrix) The trace of the $n\times n$ matrix **A** is the sum of the elements on the main diagonal.

$$\text{TR}(\mathbf{A}) = a_{11} + a_{22} + \ldots + a_{nn}$$

EXAMPLE 2.10 Consider the set T of matrices $\begin{bmatrix} x & y & z \end{bmatrix}$ that satisfy the following property as a subset of $M_{1\times 3}$:

$$\text{TR}\left(\begin{bmatrix} 1 \\ 1 \\ 1 \end{bmatrix}\begin{bmatrix} x & y & z \end{bmatrix}\right) = 0$$

First, we enter this expression into *Derive* to obtain

```
3:    TRACE([[1], [1], [1]] · [ x  y  z ]) = 0

4:    x + y + z = 0

5:    x = -y - z
```

Statement #4 is obtained by Simplifying statement #3, and statement #5 results from Solving statement #4 for x. If we assign parametric values to y and z, the general solution for $\begin{bmatrix} x & y & z \end{bmatrix}$ becomes $\begin{bmatrix} -y-z & y & z \end{bmatrix}$. The set of vectors of this form are closed with respect to vector addition and scalar multiplication, and the zero matrix is included in the set by setting $y = z = 0$; therefore, T satisfies the properties of a subspace of $M_{1\times 3}$ by Theorem 2.2.

EXERCISES

1. Show that the following subsets of the indicated vector spaces are subspaces:

   a) The set of $n\times n$ matrices $\{\mathbf{A}: \text{TR}(\mathbf{A}) = 0\}$ is a subspace of $M_{n\times n}$.

b) The set P^n of polynomials of degree n or less is a subspace of the space of continuous functions on $[-1,1]$.

c) The set $\{[x_1, x_2, x_3]:$ $x_1 + x_2 = 0,\ x_1 + x_3 = 0,$ $x_2 + x_3 = 0\}$ is a subspace of R^3.

d) The set $\{[x_1, x_2, x_3]:$ $3x_1 + 2x_2 + x_3 = 0\}$ is a subspace of R^3.

e) The set of all 2×2 matrices that commute with $\begin{bmatrix} 1 & 2 \\ 2 & 4 \end{bmatrix}$ is a subspace of $M_{2\times 2}$.

f) The set of all continuous functions that pass through the point (2,0) is a subspace of the set of all continuous functions.

2. Show the following subsets of the indicated spaces are not subspaces:
   a) The set of all $n \times n$ matrices $\{\mathbf{A}\text{: TR}(\mathbf{A}) = 1\}$ is not a subspace of $M_{n\times n}$.
   b) The set of all vectors $\{[x_1, x_2, x_3] : x_1 + x_2 = 1,$ $x_1 + x_3 = 1,\ x_2 + x_3 = 1\}$ is not a subspace of R^3.
   c) The set of all vectors $\{[x_1, x_2, x_3]: 3x_1 + 2x_2 + x_3 = 1\}$ is not a subspace of R^3.
   d) The set of all continuous functions that pass through the point (2,1) is a subspace of the set of all continuous functions.

3. Let $\mathbf{x}$ and $\mathbf{y}$ be two vectors in a vector space V, show that the set $\{a\mathbf{x} + b\mathbf{y} : a, b \in R\}$ is a subspace of V.

4. Let S be the subset of R^3 satisfying

$$[x_1, x_2, x_3]\begin{bmatrix} 1 \\ 2 \\ 3 \end{bmatrix} = [0].$$

Show S is a subspace of R^3.

5. Let A and B be subspaces of the vector space V. Show that $A \cap B$ is a subspace of V. Show also that if W is any other subspace contained in both A and B that $W \subset A \cap B$, that is $A \cap B$ is the largest subset contained in both A and B.

6. Let W be a subspace of the vector space V. Show that for each $\mathbf{x} \in W$, the additive inverse of $\mathbf{x}$ in W is the same vector as the additive inverse of $\mathbf{x}$ in V.

7. Prove that a nonempty subset W of a vector space V is a subspace of V if and only if W is closed with respect to addition and scalar multiplication.

3. LINEAR INDEPENDENCE AND DEPENDENCE

In a two dimensional coordinate system we express the equation of a line in standard form as $ax + by = c$, where the left hand side of the equation expresses linear combinations of the variables x and y. In linear algebra we are interested in similar combinations, only we replace the variables with vectors from a vector space V. Since V is closed with respect to multiplication by a scalar and vector addition, these expressions always result in a vector which is also in V. We begin this section by formally stating what is meant by such a combination of vectors.

DEFINITION 3.1 (Linear Combination) Let V be a vector space, $\mathbf{x}_1, \mathbf{x}_2, \cdots, \mathbf{x}_k \in V$, and $a_1, a_2, \cdots, a_k$ be elements of the scalar field for V. Then

$$a_1\mathbf{x}_1 + a_2\mathbf{x}_2 + \cdots + a_k\mathbf{x}_k$$

is said to be a linear combination of the vectors .

EXAMPLE 3.1 The polynomial $p(x) = x^3 + 2x^2 + 3x - 4$ is a linear combination of the four vectors $\{x^3, x^2, x, 1\}$ from P^3 where $a_1 = 1$, $a_2 = 2$, $a_3 = 3$, and $a_4 = -4$. Although it is less clear, we can also show that $p(x)$ is a linear combination of the four polynomials $\mathbf{B}$ = $\{2x^3 + 2, x^3 + x^2 + 1, x^2 + 2x, x + 1\}$ from P^3. First, we use *Derive* to write a generic version of any linear combination of elements from **B**:

```
                3                3    2              2
1:    a (2 x   + 2) + b (x    + x   + 1) + c (x   + 2 x) + d (x + 1)
```

Next, we **Simplify** statement #1:

```
       3               2
2:    x   (2 a + b) + x   (b + c) + x (2 c + d) + 2 a + b + d
```

Since we are searching for values of a, b, c, and d that will yield the polynomial $x^3 + 2x^2 + 3x - 4$, we equate coefficients and obtain four equations represented by the an augmented matrix which can be reduced to row echelon form:

$$4: \quad \text{ROW\_REDUCE}\begin{bmatrix} 2 & 1 & 0 & 0 & 1 \\ 0 & 1 & 1 & 0 & 2 \\ 0 & 0 & 2 & 1 & 3 \\ 2 & 1 & 0 & 1 & -4 \end{bmatrix}$$

$$5: \quad \begin{bmatrix} 1 & 0 & 0 & 0 & \frac{3}{2} \\ 0 & 1 & 0 & 0 & -2 \\ 0 & 0 & 1 & 0 & 4 \\ 0 & 0 & 0 & 1 & -5 \end{bmatrix}$$

with the result that $a = 3/2$, $b = -2$, $c = 4$, and $d = -5$.

EXAMPLE 3.2 We can express the vector $\begin{bmatrix} 1 \\ 4 \end{bmatrix}$ as a linear combination of the vectors

$$\left\{ \begin{bmatrix} 1 \\ 1 \end{bmatrix}, \begin{bmatrix} 1 \\ 2 \end{bmatrix}, \begin{bmatrix} 2 \\ 1 \end{bmatrix} \right\}.$$

Again we use *Derive*, and after **D**eclaring the four **M**atrices in our first four statements, we **A**uthor the matrix equation listed in statement #5 below. Statement #6 is obtained by **S**implifying statement #5.

$$5: \quad a \begin{bmatrix} 1 \\ 1 \end{bmatrix} + b \begin{bmatrix} 1 \\ 2 \end{bmatrix} + c \begin{bmatrix} 2 \\ 1 \end{bmatrix} = \begin{bmatrix} 1 \\ 4 \end{bmatrix}$$

$$6: \quad \begin{bmatrix} a + b + 2\,c = 1 \\ a + 2\,b + c = 4 \end{bmatrix}$$

Next, the augmented matrix of the system of two equations in three unknowns represented in statement #6 is **D**eclared in statement #7, and the ROW_REDUCE command used in statement #8 is **S**implified in statement #9.

8: ROW_REDUCE $\begin{bmatrix} 1 & 1 & 2 & 1 \\ 1 & 2 & 1 & 4 \end{bmatrix}$

9: $\begin{bmatrix} 1 & 0 & 3 & -2 \\ 0 & 1 & -1 & 3 \end{bmatrix}$

Since this is an underdetermined system of equations, the variable c can be assigned an arbitrary value which leads to the solution $b = 3 + c$ and $a = -2 - 3c$.

EXAMPLE 3.3 We can attempt to express $\begin{bmatrix} 1 & 0 \\ 1 & 2 \end{bmatrix}$ as a linear combination of the two vectors

$$\left\{ \begin{bmatrix} 1 & 0 \\ 1 & 1 \end{bmatrix}, \begin{bmatrix} 1 & 2 \\ 1 & 1 \end{bmatrix} \right\}$$

from $M_{2\times2}$ by using *Derive* to write a general form of the linear combination and Simplifying the result:

4: $a \begin{bmatrix} 1 & 0 \\ 1 & 1 \end{bmatrix} + b \begin{bmatrix} 1 & 2 \\ 1 & 1 \end{bmatrix} = \begin{bmatrix} 1 & 0 \\ 1 & 2 \end{bmatrix}$

5: $\begin{bmatrix} a + b = 1 & 2 b = 0 \\ a + b = 1 & a + b = 2 \end{bmatrix}$

This yields four equations in two unknowns which is an overdetermined system and may or may not have a solution. Reduction of the augmented matrix for this system yields

7: ROW_REDUCE $\begin{bmatrix} 1 & 1 & 1 \\ 0 & 2 & 0 \\ 1 & 1 & 1 \\ 1 & 1 & 2 \end{bmatrix}$

$$8: \begin{bmatrix} 1 & 0 & 0 \\ 0 & 1 & 0 \\ 0 & 0 & 1 \\ 0 & 0 & 0 \end{bmatrix}$$

but the third line of the matrix in statement #8 represents the equation $0a + 0b = 1$, which is not possible. Thus, the given matrix cannot be expressed as a linear combination of the two matrices.

The three examples provided thus far in this section provide illustrations of concepts that are important in classifying sets of vectors. In both Examples 3.1 and 3.2 we showed that a given vector can be expressed as a linear combination of vectors from a given set, and thus we say that it is "linearly dependent" on that set. The vector given in Example 3.3 cannot be expressed as a linear combination of the two vectors provided, and thus it is "linearly independent" of the set. Next, we formalize this concept with a definition.

DEFINITION 3.2 (Linearly Independent and Linearly Dependent) The set of vectors $\{\mathbf{x}_1, \mathbf{x}_2, \cdots, \mathbf{x}_n\}$ is said to be linearly independent if

$$a_1\mathbf{x}_1 + a_2\mathbf{x}_2 + \cdots + a_n\mathbf{x}_n = \mathbf{0}$$

implies $a_1 = a_2 = \cdots = a_n = 0$. A set of vectors that is not linearly independent is said to be linearly dependent.

EXAMPLE 3.4 The set of polynomials $\{x^3, x^2, x, 1\}$ is linearly independent. To illustrate this we consider linear combinations of the form $ax^3 + bx^2 + cx + d = 0$. Since the right hand side is a representation for the zero polynomial which has all of its coefficients equal to 0, and since polynomials are equal if and only if the coefficients are equal, we have $a = 0$, $b = 0$, $c = 0$, and $d = 0$. Hence, the set of polynomials is linearly independent.

EXAMPLE 3.5 We can show that the set of polynomials

$$\{x^3 - x + 2,\ x^3 + x^2 + x,\ x + 1,\ x^2 + x\}$$

is linearly independent by first writing in general form a linear combination of the four polynomials in our set and setting this expression equal to zero as indicated in statement #5 below. Next, we use *Derive* to Simplify this equation in statement #6.

$$5:\quad a\,(x^3 - x + 2) + b\,(x^3 + x^2 + x) + c\,(x + 1) + d\,(x^2 + x) = 0$$

$$6:\quad x^3\,(a + b) + x^2\,(b + d) - x\,(a - b - c - d) + 2\,a + c = 0$$

The four coefficients are then set equal to zero and an augmented matrix is Authored representing four equations in four unknowns. The commands ROW_REDUCE and Simplify can then be used to establish $a = 0$, $b = 0$, $c = 0$, and $d = 0$, proving that the set is linearly independent.

$$8:\quad \text{ROW\_REDUCE}\begin{bmatrix} 1 & 1 & 0 & 0 & 0 \\ 0 & 1 & 0 & 1 & 0 \\ -1 & 1 & 1 & 1 & 0 \\ 2 & 0 & 1 & 0 & 0 \end{bmatrix}$$

$$9:\quad \begin{bmatrix} 1 & 0 & 0 & 0 & 0 \\ 0 & 1 & 0 & 0 & 0 \\ 0 & 0 & 1 & 0 & 0 \\ 0 & 0 & 0 & 1 & 0 \end{bmatrix}$$

EXAMPLE 3.6 The set of vectors

$$\left\{ \begin{bmatrix} 1 \\ 1 \\ 0 \end{bmatrix}, \begin{bmatrix} 1 \\ 3 \\ 2 \end{bmatrix}, \begin{bmatrix} 3 \\ 7 \\ 4 \end{bmatrix} \right\}$$

in $\mathbf{R}^3$ is linearly dependent. Following the pattern of the above examples, we first write a general form of linear combinations of these three vectors and set it equal to zero. Then, using *Derive*, the equation is **S**implified.

$$5: \quad a \begin{bmatrix} 1 \\ 1 \\ 0 \end{bmatrix} + b \begin{bmatrix} 1 \\ 3 \\ 2 \end{bmatrix} + c \begin{bmatrix} 3 \\ 7 \\ 4 \end{bmatrix} = \begin{bmatrix} 0 \\ 0 \\ 0 \end{bmatrix}$$

$$6: \quad \begin{bmatrix} a + b + 3\ c = 0 \\ a + 3\ b + 7\ c = 0 \\ 2\ b + 4\ c = 0 \end{bmatrix}$$

After **A**uthoring an augmented matrix representing the three equations in statement #6, the ROW_REDUCE and **S**implify commands are used to solve the system.

$$8: \quad \text{ROW\_REDUCE} \begin{bmatrix} 1 & 1 & 3 & 0 \\ 1 & 3 & 7 & 0 \\ 0 & 2 & 4 & 0 \end{bmatrix}$$

$$9: \quad \begin{bmatrix} 1 & 0 & 1 & 0 \\ 0 & 1 & 2 & 0 \\ 0 & 0 & 0 & 0 \end{bmatrix}$$

Since the third row matrix elements in statement #9 are all zero, the system has non-trivial (non-zero) solutions, and the set of vectors provided is linearly dependent.

EXAMPLE 3.7 If $S = \{x+1, x+2\}$ and $T = \{x+1, x+2, x+3\}$, then S is linearly independent, and T is linearly dependent.

$$1: \quad a\ (x + 1) + b\ (x + 2) = 0$$

$$2: \quad x\ (a + b) + a + 2\ b = 0$$

$$4: \quad \text{ROW\_REDUCE} \begin{bmatrix} 1 & 1 & 0 \\ 1 & 2 & 0 \end{bmatrix}$$

5: $\begin{bmatrix} 1 & 0 & 0 \\ 0 & 1 & 0 \end{bmatrix}$

Following the same pattern as the examples above, we have used *Derive* to write a general form of linear combinations of the vectors from S and set the expression equal to zero; re-organized the equation; and solved the system of equations obtained by setting the coefficients of statement #2 equal to zero. The solution provided in statement #5 establishes the linear independence of the set of vectors in S.

```
6:   a (x + 1) + b (x + 2) + c (x + 3) = 0

7:   x (a + b + c) + a + 2 b + 3 c = 0
```

9: ROW_REDUCE $\begin{bmatrix} 1 & 1 & 1 & 0 \\ 1 & 2 & 3 & 0 \end{bmatrix}$

10: $\begin{bmatrix} 1 & 0 & -1 & 0 \\ 0 & 1 & 2 & 0 \end{bmatrix}$

When the same steps are followed for the vectors in the set T, the solution provided in statement #10 indicates the existence of non-trivial (non-zero) solutions. This establishes the fact that T is linearly dependent.

THEOREM 3.1 The $n\times n$ matrix **A** is invertible if and only if the columns of **A**, taken as vectors in R^n, are linearly independent.

PROOF: We prove the sufficient portion of the theorem here. The necessary portion is left for an exercise in the next section.

If **A** is invertible and $\mathbf{Ax} = \mathbf{0}$, then $\mathbf{A}^{-1}\mathbf{Ax} = \mathbf{A}^{-1}\mathbf{0}$; hence, $\mathbf{x} = \mathbf{0}$.

EXERCISES

1. Show the following sets are linearly independent (consider the functions on $[0,1]$):

a) $\left\{\begin{bmatrix} 1 & 0 \\ 0 & 1 \end{bmatrix}, \begin{bmatrix} 0 & 1 \\ 0 & 1 \end{bmatrix}, \begin{bmatrix} 0 & 0 \\ 1 & 1 \end{bmatrix}\right\}$

b) $\left\{x^2 + x,\ x + 1,\ x^2 + 1\right\}$

c) $\left\{e^x,\ e^{2x}\right\}$

d) {sin x, cos x} Hint: Differentiate to obtain an additional equation.

2. Show if **x** and **y** are linearly independent then **x**+**y** and **x**-**y** are linearly independent.

3. Let $\{\mathbf{x}_1, \mathbf{x}_2, \cdots, \mathbf{x}_n\}$ be a set of vectors in R^n, and let the dot product be defined in the usual way. Show that if $\mathbf{x}_i \cdot \mathbf{x}_j = 0$ for $i \neq j$ that the vectors are linearly independent.

4. Let **x** and **y** be linearly independent vectors of R^3, and let **A** be a non-singular 3×3 matrix. Show that **Ax** and **Ay** are linearly independent.

5. Express $x^3 + 2x^2 + 3x + 4$ as a linear combination of $\{x^3 + x^2, x, x^2 + x, 1\}$ if possible. Is this representation unique?

6. Express $\begin{bmatrix} 1 & 2 \\ 3 & 4 \end{bmatrix}$ as a linear combination of $\left\{\begin{bmatrix} 1 & 0 \\ 0 & 0 \end{bmatrix}, \begin{bmatrix} 0 & 1 \\ 0 & 0 \end{bmatrix}, \begin{bmatrix} 0 & 0 \\ 1 & 0 \end{bmatrix}, \begin{bmatrix} 0 & 0 \\ 0 & 1 \end{bmatrix}, \begin{bmatrix} 1 & 1 \\ 1 & 1 \end{bmatrix}\right\}$. Is the representation unique?

4. SPANNING SETS OF VECTORS

Linear combinations of vectors such as those studied in Section 2.3 often occur in a very natural manner. The most familiar example involves representing all the two dimensional vectors in the plane by specifying horizontal and vertical components. Since the vector [1,0] represents a horizontal vector and [0,1] represents a vertical vector, any two dimensional vector $[a,b]$ can be represented in the form $a[1,0] + b[0,1]$, with horizontal component a and vertical component b.

A second example that requires finding the set of all linear combinations of a particular set of vectors arises when we wish to represent all the solutions of an underdetermined system of equations such as

$$x_1 + x_2 + x_3 = 0$$
$$x_1 + x_4 = 0.$$

We can proceed with the assistance of *Derive* by first **D**eclaring an augmented matrix representation for the system and then reducing the resulting matrix to row echelon form:

```
2:    ROW_REDUCE [ 1  1  1  0  0 ]
                 [ 1  0  0  1  0 ]

3:    [ 1  0  0   1  0 ]
      [ 0  1  1  -1  0 ]
```

From this result we can obtain the solutions $x_1 = -b$, $x_2 = -a + b$, $x_3 = a$, and $x_4 = b$ where a and b are arbitrary. This solution, in turn, can be expressed in vector form as the linear combination:

$$\begin{bmatrix} x_1 \\ x_2 \\ x_3 \\ x_4 \end{bmatrix} = a\begin{bmatrix} 0 \\ -1 \\ 1 \\ 0 \end{bmatrix} + \text{b}\begin{bmatrix} -1 \\ 1 \\ 0 \\ 1 \end{bmatrix}.$$

Since both a and b are arbitrary, the set of solution vectors for our system of equations is the set of all linear combinations of the vectors

$$\left\{\begin{bmatrix} 0 \\ -1 \\ 1 \\ 0 \end{bmatrix}, \begin{bmatrix} -1 \\ 1 \\ 0 \\ 1 \end{bmatrix}\right\}.$$

These examples, which emphasize the importance of being able to discuss the set of all linear combinations of a set of vectors, lead to the following definition:

DEFINITION 4.1 (Vectors Spanned by a Set) Let V be a vector space over the field F and $S = \{\mathbf{x}_1, \mathbf{x}_2, \cdots, \mathbf{x}_k\} \subseteq V$. The set of vectors spanned by S, noted as $\text{SPAN}(S)$, consists of all the possible linear combinations

$$a_1\mathbf{x}_1 + a_2\mathbf{x}_2 + \cdots + a_k\mathbf{x}_k,$$

where $a_1, a_2, \cdots, a_k \in F$.

EXAMPLE 4.1 We can use *Derive* to determine if a vector is in the span of a particular set. For example, if $\mathbf{x} = [2 \quad 2 \quad 2]^{\text{T}}$ and

$$S = \left\{ \begin{bmatrix} 1 \\ 3 \\ 0 \end{bmatrix}, \begin{bmatrix} 0 \\ 0 \\ 1 \end{bmatrix}, \begin{bmatrix} 1 \\ 3 \\ 1 \end{bmatrix} \right\},$$

we can write the vector equation expressing **x** as a linear combination of elements of S and then Simplify the equation as follows:

$$5: \quad a \begin{bmatrix} 1 \\ 3 \\ 0 \end{bmatrix} + b \begin{bmatrix} 0 \\ 0 \\ 1 \end{bmatrix} + c \begin{bmatrix} 1 \\ 3 \\ 1 \end{bmatrix} = \begin{bmatrix} 2 \\ 2 \\ 2 \end{bmatrix}$$

$$6: \quad \begin{bmatrix} a + c = 2 \\ 3a + 3c = 2 \\ b + c = 2 \end{bmatrix}$$

Next, we find the row echelon form of the augmented matrix representing the system of equations listed in statement #6:

$$8: \quad \text{ROW\_REDUCE} \begin{bmatrix} 1 & 0 & 1 & 2 \\ 3 & 0 & 3 & 2 \\ 0 & 1 & 1 & 2 \end{bmatrix}$$

$$9: \quad \begin{bmatrix} 1 & 0 & 1 & 0 \\ 0 & 1 & 1 & 0 \\ 0 & 0 & 0 & 1 \end{bmatrix}$$

From the last row of the matrix in statement #9, we obtain the absurdity $0a + 0b + 0c = 1$, and it follows that the system has no solution, and thus the vector **x** cannot be expressed as a linear combination of the vectors of S.

THEOREM 4.2 If $S = \{\mathbf{x}_1, \mathbf{x}_2, \cdots, \mathbf{x}_k\}$ is a nonempty subset of a vector space V, then SPAN(S) is a subspace of V.

PROOF: The **0** of V is in SPAN(S) since $0\mathbf{x}_1 + 0\mathbf{x}_2 + \cdots + 0\mathbf{x}_k = \mathbf{0}$. If $\mathbf{u}, \mathbf{v} \in \text{SPAN}(S)$, then there exist scalars $a_1, \cdots, a_k$ and $b_1, \cdots, b_k$ such that $\mathbf{u} = a_1\mathbf{x}_1 + \cdots + a_k\mathbf{x}_k$ and $\mathbf{v} = b_1\mathbf{x}_1 + \cdots + b_k\mathbf{x}_k$. Thus

$$\begin{aligned}\mathbf{u}+\mathbf{v} &= (a_1\mathbf{x}_1+\cdots+a_k\mathbf{x}_k)+(b_1\mathbf{x}_1+\cdots+b_k\mathbf{x}_k)\\ &= (a_1+b_1)\mathbf{x}_1+\cdots+(a_k+b_k)\mathbf{x}_k \in \text{SPAN}(S)\end{aligned}$$

and

$$c\mathbf{u}=ca_1\mathbf{x}_1+\cdots+ca_k\mathbf{x}_k \in \text{SPAN}(S);$$

therefore, by Theorem 2.2, SPAN(S) is a subspace of V.

EXAMPLE 4.2 To show the vector space $M_{2\times2}$ of all 2×2 matrices is spanned by

$$S=\left\{\begin{bmatrix}0&1\\1&1\end{bmatrix},\begin{bmatrix}1&0\\1&1\end{bmatrix},\begin{bmatrix}1&1\\0&1\end{bmatrix},\begin{bmatrix}1&1\\1&0\end{bmatrix}\right\},$$

we first Author a general expression for linear combinations of elements of S and set the expression equal to a matrix representing an arbitrary element of $M_{2\times2}$.

6: $a\begin{bmatrix}0&1\\1&1\end{bmatrix}+b\begin{bmatrix}1&0\\1&1\end{bmatrix}+c\begin{bmatrix}1&1\\0&1\end{bmatrix}+d\begin{bmatrix}1&1\\1&0\end{bmatrix}=\begin{bmatrix}p&q\\r&s\end{bmatrix}$

7: $\begin{bmatrix}b+c+d=p & a+c+d=q\\ a+b+d=r & a+b+c=s\end{bmatrix}$

The Simplified version of this equation (statement #7) leads to an augmented matrix representing a system of four equations in four unknowns which yields unique solutions for a, b, c, and d.

9: ROW_REDUCE $\begin{bmatrix}0&1&1&1&p\\1&0&1&1&q\\1&1&0&1&r\\1&1&1&0&s\end{bmatrix}$

$$10: \begin{bmatrix} 1 & 0 & 0 & 0 & -\frac{2p-q-r-s}{3} \\ 0 & 1 & 0 & 0 & \frac{p-2q+r+s}{3} \\ 0 & 0 & 1 & 0 & \frac{p+q-2r+s}{3} \\ 0 & 0 & 0 & 1 & \frac{p+q+r-2s}{3} \end{bmatrix}$$

It follows that each element of $M_{2\times 2}$ can be represented as a linear combination of elements of S, and S spans $M_{2\times 2}$.

EXAMPLE 4.3 The subspace SPAN(S), where $S = \{x^2 + x, x + 1, x^2 + 1\}$, is the set of all polynomials

$$a(x^2 + x) + b(x + 1) + c(x^2 + 1)$$

or

$$(a + c)x^2 + (a + b)x + (b + c),$$

where a, b, and c are arbitrary. We note, for example, that $2x^2 + 2x + 2 \in \text{SPAN}(S)$ since the system of equations

$$\begin{aligned} a + c &= 2 \\ a + b &= 2 \\ b + c &= 2 \end{aligned}$$

has the solution $a = b = c = 1$. In fact, any polynomial $ux^2 + vx + w \in P^3$ is in the SPAN(S) since

$$5: \quad \text{ROW\_REDUCE} \begin{bmatrix} 1 & 0 & 1 & u \\ 1 & 1 & 0 & v \\ 0 & 1 & 1 & w \end{bmatrix}$$

$$6: \quad \begin{bmatrix} 1 & 0 & 0 & \dfrac{u+v-w}{2} \\ 0 & 1 & 0 & -\dfrac{u-v-w}{2} \\ 0 & 0 & 1 & \dfrac{u-v+w}{2} \end{bmatrix}.$$

EXAMPLE 4.4 We can show that

$$S = \left\{ \begin{bmatrix} 1 \\ 0 \\ 2 \end{bmatrix}, \begin{bmatrix} 2 \\ 1 \\ 6 \end{bmatrix}, \begin{bmatrix} 0 \\ 1 \\ 2 \end{bmatrix} \right\} \text{ and } T = \left\{ \begin{bmatrix} 1 \\ 1 \\ 4 \end{bmatrix}, \begin{bmatrix} 0 \\ 2 \\ 4 \end{bmatrix} \right\}$$

span the same subspace of R^3 by first representing an arbitrary vector in SPAN(S) by

$$6: \quad a \begin{bmatrix} 1 \\ 0 \\ 2 \end{bmatrix} + b \begin{bmatrix} 2 \\ 1 \\ 6 \end{bmatrix} + c \begin{bmatrix} 0 \\ 1 \\ 2 \end{bmatrix}$$

$$7: \quad \begin{bmatrix} a + 2b \\ b + c \\ 2a + 6b + 2c \end{bmatrix}$$

and an arbitrary vector in SPAN(T) by

$$8: \quad d \begin{bmatrix} 1 \\ 1 \\ 4 \end{bmatrix} + e \begin{bmatrix} 0 \\ 2 \\ 4 \end{bmatrix}$$

$$9: \quad \begin{bmatrix} d \\ d + 2e \\ 4d + 4e \end{bmatrix}$$

The question is then reduced to whether given values for d and e there exist values for a, b, and c which would make statement #6 equal to statement #9 [in which case, each element in SPAN(T) is also in SPAN(S)] and, conversely, whether given values for a, b, and c there exist values d and e which would make statement #8 equal to statement #7 [in which case, each element in SPAN(S) is also in SPAN(T)].

To determine the answer to the first of these two questions, we assume the existence of a vector written in the form of statement #8 and use *Derive* to **D**eclare an augmented matrix to represent the system of three equations in the three unknowns a, b, and c determined by setting corresponding elements of the vectors in statements #7 and #9 equal to each other. This augmented matrix can then be reduced to row echelon form as follows:

$$11:\quad \text{ROW\_REDUCE}\begin{bmatrix} 1 & 2 & 0 & d \\ 0 & 1 & 1 & d+2e \\ 2 & 6 & 2 & 4d+4e \end{bmatrix}$$

$$12:\quad \begin{bmatrix} 1 & 0 & -2 & -d-4e \\ 0 & 1 & 1 & d+2e \\ 0 & 0 & 0 & 0 \end{bmatrix}$$

From statement #12 we see the value of c in terms of d and e is arbitrary, while $b = d + 2e - c$ and $a = -d - 4e + 2c$, and these three values can be substituted into statement #6. To verify our results, we again use *Derive*:

$$12:\quad (-d - 4e + 2c)\begin{bmatrix} 1 \\ 0 \\ 2 \end{bmatrix} + (d + 2e - c)\begin{bmatrix} 2 \\ 1 \\ 6 \end{bmatrix} + c\begin{bmatrix} 0 \\ 1 \\ 2 \end{bmatrix}$$

$$13:\quad \begin{bmatrix} d \\ d+2e \\ 4d+4e \end{bmatrix}$$

Thus every vector of the form represented in statement #8 can also be represented in the form of statement #6, and SPAN(T) $\subseteq$ SPAN(S).

The second of our two questions can be answered in a similar fashion. Assuming the existence of a vector written in the form of statement #8, we declare an augmented matrix representing three equations in the two unknowns *d* and *e* determined by setting corresponding elements of the two vectors in statements #9 and #7 equal to each other. As above, this augmented matrix can then be reduced to row echelon form using *Derive*:

$$15:\quad \text{ROW\_REDUCE}\begin{bmatrix} 1 & 0 & a + 2b \\ 1 & 2 & b + c \\ 4 & 4 & 2a + 6b + 2c \end{bmatrix}$$

$$16:\quad \begin{bmatrix} 1 & 0 & a + 2b \\ 0 & 1 & -\dfrac{a + b - c}{2} \\ 0 & 0 & 0 \end{bmatrix}$$

From statement #16 we see the value of *e* in terms of *a*, *b* and *c* is -(*a*+*b*-*c*)/2 while *d* = (*a* + 2*b*). These two values can be substituted into statement #8. To verify our results, we again use *Derive*:

$$17:\quad (a + 2b)\begin{bmatrix} 1 \\ 1 \\ 4 \end{bmatrix} + \left[-\frac{a + b - c}{2}\right]\begin{bmatrix} 0 \\ 2 \\ 4 \end{bmatrix}$$

$$18:\quad \begin{bmatrix} a + 2b \\ b + c \\ 2(a + 3b + c) \end{bmatrix}$$

$$19:\quad \begin{bmatrix} a + 2b \\ b + c \\ 2a + 6b + 2c \end{bmatrix}$$

Thus, every vector of the form represented in statement #6 can also be represented in the form of statement #8, and $\text{SPAN}(S) \subseteq \text{SPAN}(T)$.

By combining the two parts of this example we have established $\text{SPAN}(S) = \text{SPAN}(T)$.

EXERCISES

1. Is $\begin{bmatrix} 1 & 2 \\ 1 & 3 \end{bmatrix} \in \text{SPAN}\left\{\begin{bmatrix} 1 & 1 \\ 1 & 1 \end{bmatrix}, \begin{bmatrix} 1 & 2 \\ 1 & 3 \end{bmatrix}\right\}$?

2. Is $\begin{bmatrix} 1 & 2 \\ 1 & 3 \end{bmatrix} \in \text{SPAN}\left\{\begin{bmatrix} 2 & 1 \\ 1 & 1 \end{bmatrix}, \begin{bmatrix} 2 & 2 \\ 1 & 1 \end{bmatrix}, \begin{bmatrix} 2 & 2 \\ 2 & 1 \end{bmatrix}, \begin{bmatrix} 2 & 2 \\ 2 & 2 \end{bmatrix}\right\}$?

3. Is $x^3 + 2x + 1 \in \text{SPAN}\left\{x^3 + 1, x^2 + 1, x + 1, x^3 + x^2 + x + 1\right\}$?

4. Is $\begin{bmatrix} 1 \\ 2 \\ 1 \end{bmatrix} \in \text{SPAN}\left\{\begin{bmatrix} 1 \\ 3 \\ 2 \end{bmatrix}, \begin{bmatrix} 0 \\ 0 \\ 1 \end{bmatrix}\right\}$?

5. Show that $\mathbf{R}^2$ is spanned by $\left\{\begin{bmatrix} \pi \\ e \end{bmatrix}, \begin{bmatrix} 1 \\ 1 \end{bmatrix}\right\}$.

6. Show that the subspace of $\mathbf{M}_{2\times 2}$ defined by $\left\{\mathbf{A} : \mathbf{A} \in \mathbf{M}_{2\times 2}, \text{Tr}(\mathbf{A}) = 0\right\}$ is spanned by $\left\{\begin{bmatrix} 1 & 0 \\ 0 & -1 \end{bmatrix}, \begin{bmatrix} 0 & 1 \\ 0 & 0 \end{bmatrix}, \begin{bmatrix} 0 & 0 \\ 1 & 0 \end{bmatrix}\right\}$.

7. The matrix $\mathbf{A}$ is said to be symmetric if $a_{ij} = a_{ji}$ for all i and j. Show that the set S of all 2×2 symmetric matrices is a subspace of $\mathbf{M}_{2\times 2}$. Furthermore, show that S is spanned by $\left\{\begin{bmatrix} 1 & 0 \\ 0 & 0 \end{bmatrix}, \begin{bmatrix} 0 & 1 \\ 1 & 0 \end{bmatrix}, \begin{bmatrix} 0 & 0 \\ 0 & 1 \end{bmatrix}\right\}$.

8. Characterize an arbitrary vector in $\text{SPAN}\left\{\begin{bmatrix} 1 \\ 1 \\ 0 \end{bmatrix}, \begin{bmatrix} 1 \\ 0 \\ 0 \end{bmatrix}, \begin{bmatrix} 2 \\ 2 \\ 0 \end{bmatrix}\right\}$.

9. Characterize the subspace of P^2 spanned by $S = \left\{x^2 + 1, x + 1\right\}$. Find two second degree polynomials one contained in $\text{SPAN}(S)$ and one not contained in $\text{SPAN}(S)$.

10. Show that $S = \left\{\begin{bmatrix} 1 & 0 \\ 0 & 0 \end{bmatrix}, \begin{bmatrix} 0 & 1 \\ 1 & 0 \end{bmatrix}, \begin{bmatrix} 0 & 0 \\ 0 & 1 \end{bmatrix}\right\}$ and

$$T = \left\{ \begin{bmatrix} 1 & 1 \\ 1 & 0 \end{bmatrix}, \begin{bmatrix} 0 & 1 \\ 1 & 1 \end{bmatrix}, \begin{bmatrix} 1 & 2 \\ 2 & 1 \end{bmatrix} \right\}$$

span the same subspace of $\mathbf{M}_{2\times 2}$.

11. Let S be a linearly independent set of vectors in a vector space **V**. Prove that every $\mathbf{x} \in$ SPAN(S) can be represented uniquely as a linear combination of elements of S.

5. BASIS AND DIMENSION

In Section 2.4 we considered linear combinations of vectors taken from a subset S of a vector space V. We proved that the SPAN(S), the set of all linear combinations of vectors taken from S, is always a subspace of V and in some cases is V itself. Our basic example was $S = \left\{ \begin{bmatrix} 1 \\ 0 \end{bmatrix}, \begin{bmatrix} 0 \\ 1 \end{bmatrix} \right\}$, a subset of R^2. Any arbitrary element $\begin{bmatrix} u \\ v \end{bmatrix}$ of R^2 can be written as a linear combination of the two vectors in S in the following way:

$$u\begin{bmatrix} 1 \\ 0 \end{bmatrix} + v\begin{bmatrix} 0 \\ 1 \end{bmatrix} = \begin{bmatrix} u \\ v \end{bmatrix}.$$

But S is not the only subset of R^2 with a span equal to all of R^2. If $T = \left\{ \begin{bmatrix} 1 \\ 2 \end{bmatrix}, \begin{bmatrix} 1 \\ 3 \end{bmatrix}, \begin{bmatrix} 1 \\ 4 \end{bmatrix} \right\}$, then SPAN($T$) = R^2 since for every arbitrary $\begin{bmatrix} u \\ v \end{bmatrix}$ of R^2:

$$(3u - v + c)\begin{bmatrix} 1 \\ 2 \end{bmatrix} + (-2u + v - 2c)\begin{bmatrix} 1 \\ 3 \end{bmatrix} + c\begin{bmatrix} 1 \\ 4 \end{bmatrix} = \begin{bmatrix} u \\ v \end{bmatrix}$$

where c is arbitrary. In the case of SPAN(S) we are able to write any vector from R^2 uniquely since S is linearly independent. In the case of SPAN(T) the representation is not unique since T is linearly dependent. This leads us to the following definition.

DEFINITION 5.1 (Basis of a Vector Space) A subset β of a vector space V is a basis for V if β is a linearly independent set with SPAN(β) = V.

We note that every linearly independent subset of a vector space V that spans all of V is a basis for V, and every linearly independent subset of a vector space V is a basis for the subspace it spans.

EXAMPLE 5.1 Some bases for particular vector spaces are used so frequently that they have become known as the "standard" basis (denoted by the letter σ) for that space. Included in that category are the following:

a) $\left\{\begin{bmatrix}1\\0\end{bmatrix}, \begin{bmatrix}0\\1\end{bmatrix}\right\}$ is the standard basis for R^2. [Similar bases may be defined for any space R^n.]

b) $\{x^n, x^{n-1}, \cdots, x, 1\}$ is the standard basis for P^n, the polynomials of degree n or less.

c) $\left\{\begin{bmatrix}1 & 0\\0 & 0\end{bmatrix}, \begin{bmatrix}0 & 1\\0 & 0\end{bmatrix}, \begin{bmatrix}0 & 0\\1 & 0\end{bmatrix}, \begin{bmatrix}0 & 0\\0 & 1\end{bmatrix}\right\}$ is the standard basis for $M_{2\times 2}$. [Similar standard bases may be defined for any space $M_{m\times n}$.]

EXAMPLE 5.2 In Example 2.4 we showed that the set of solutions of the matrix equation

$$\begin{bmatrix}4 & 4 & 2\\3 & 4 & 2\\1 & 2 & 1\end{bmatrix}\begin{bmatrix}x_1\\x_2\\x_3\end{bmatrix} = \begin{bmatrix}0\\0\\0\end{bmatrix}$$

form a subspace of R^3 with the general solution taking the form $\begin{bmatrix}0 & -c/2 & c\end{bmatrix}^T$. It follows that $\left\{\begin{bmatrix}0 & -1/2 & 1\end{bmatrix}^T\right\}$ is a basis of the subspace since all solutions can be written in the form $c\begin{bmatrix}0 & -1/2 & 1\end{bmatrix}^T$.

EXAMPLE 5.3 The set $\gamma = \left\{ \begin{bmatrix} 1 & 0 \\ 0 & 0 \end{bmatrix}, \begin{bmatrix} 0 & 1 \\ 1 & 0 \end{bmatrix}, \begin{bmatrix} 0 & 0 \\ 0 & 1 \end{bmatrix} \right\}$ is a basis for the space V of symmetric 2×2 matrices. In order to show γ is a linearly independent set of vectors, note that the only solution for

$$a\begin{bmatrix} 1 & 0 \\ 0 & 0 \end{bmatrix} + b\begin{bmatrix} 0 & 1 \\ 1 & 0 \end{bmatrix} + c\begin{bmatrix} 0 & 0 \\ 0 & 1 \end{bmatrix} = \begin{bmatrix} 0 & 0 \\ 0 & 0 \end{bmatrix}$$

$$\begin{bmatrix} a & b \\ b & c \end{bmatrix} = \begin{bmatrix} 0 & 0 \\ 0 & 0 \end{bmatrix}$$

is $a = b = c = 0$. To show γ spans the space of 2×2 symmetric matrices, let $\begin{bmatrix} u & v \\ v & w \end{bmatrix}$ be an arbitrary element of V and write

$$u\begin{bmatrix} 1 & 0 \\ 0 & 0 \end{bmatrix} + v\begin{bmatrix} 0 & 1 \\ 1 & 0 \end{bmatrix} + w\begin{bmatrix} 0 & 0 \\ 0 & 1 \end{bmatrix} = \begin{bmatrix} u & v \\ v & w \end{bmatrix}.$$

The basis for a vector space is not necessarily unique. In Example 5.1 we stated that the standard basis for the set of polynomials of degree 1 is $\sigma = \{x, 1\}$. Yet recall in Example 3.7 the set $\kappa = \{x+1, x+2\}$ was shown to be linearly independent. Since $(x+2) - (x+1) = 1$ and $2(x+1) - 1(x+2) = x$, $\sigma \subseteq$ SPAN(κ) and κ is also a basis for P^1 [see Exercise 12 at the end of this section]. The fact that both σ and κ have two elements is not just a coincidence. In fact, it follows immediately from Theorem 5.2 below that all bases of a particular vector space V necessarily have the same number of elements, and, therefore, it is not surprising that in Example 3.7 we showed that the set of vectors $\{x+1, x+2, x+3\}$ is linearly dependent and thus not a basis. Although a basis for a vector space is not unique, the following theorem shows that the representation of a particular vector as a linear combination of vectors from a basis is necessarily unique for any given basis.

THEOREM 5.1 If β is a basis for the vector space $\mathbf{V}$, then every vector $\mathbf{v} \in \mathbf{V}$ can be written as a unique combination of elements of $\mathbf{V}$.

PROOF: Suppose $\mathbf{v}$ can be written as both $\mathbf{v} = a_1\mathbf{s}_1 + \ldots + a_n\mathbf{s}_n$ and $\mathbf{v} = b_1\mathbf{s}_1 + \ldots + b_n\mathbf{s}_n$, where $\beta = \{\mathbf{s}_1, \ldots, \mathbf{s}_n\}$ is a basis for $\mathbf{V}$. Then

$$\mathbf{0} = \mathbf{v} - \mathbf{v} = (a_1 - b_1)\mathbf{s}_1 + \ldots + (a_n - b_n)\mathbf{s}_n,$$

but β is a linearly independent set; therefore, $a_1 = b_1, \ldots, a_n = b_n$, and the representation for $\mathbf{v}$ is unique.

THEOREM 5.2 If V is a vector space and β is a basis containing n elements, then any subset of V containing more than n elements is linearly dependent.

PROOF: Let $\beta = \{x_1, x_2, \cdots, x_n\}$ be a basis of V and let $S = \{y_1, y_2, \cdots, y_m\}$ be a subset of V with $m > n$. We claim S is linearly dependent. Consider

$$a_1 y_1 + a_2 y_2 + \cdots + a_m y_m = 0.$$

Since β is a basis, for all i, $1 \le i \le m$, there exist scalars $b_{i1}, \cdots, b_{in}$ such that

$$b_{i1}x_1 + b_{i2}x_2 + \cdots + b_{in}x_n = y_i.$$

Thus,

$$a_1(b_{11}x_1 + \cdots + b_{1n}x_n) + a_2(b_{21}x_1 + \cdots + b_{2n}x_n) + \cdots + a_m(b_{m1}x_1 + \cdots + b_{mn}x_n) = 0,$$

and after rearranging and collecting coefficients of each x_i,

$$(a_1b_{11} + \cdots + a_mb_{m1})x_1 + (a_1b_{12} + \cdots + a_mb_{m2})x_2 + \cdots + (a_1b_{1n} + \cdots + a_mb_{mn})x_n = 0.$$

Since β is a linearly independent set, the coefficients of $x_1, x_2, \cdots, x_n$ must each be zero, and

$$\begin{aligned} a_1b_{11} + a_2b_{21} + \cdots + a_mb_{m1} &= 0 \\ a_1b_{12} + a_2b_{22} + \cdots + a_mb_{m2} &= 0 \\ \vdots \qquad \vdots \qquad\qquad \vdots \quad &\quad \vdots \\ a_1b_{1n} + a_2b_{2n} + \cdots + a_mb_{mn} &= 0 \end{aligned}$$

is a system of n equations in m unknowns, $a_1, a_2, \cdots, a_m$. Since $n<m$, this system is underdetermined and has a nonzero solution; therefore, it follows that S is linearly dependent.

THEOREM 5.3 If V is a vector space with a basis β containing exactly n elements, then any basis for V contains exactly n elements.

PROOF: The proof is left as an exercise.

DEFINITION 5.2 (Dimension of a Vector Space) A vector space V is said to be of dimension n [denoted by DIM(V)] if V has a basis containing n elements. The space $\{\mathbf{0}\}$ has dimension 0.

EXAMPLE 5.4 In Example 5.2 we used the fact that we had shown in Example 2.4 that the solution set for a particular matrix equation $\mathbf{Ax} = \mathbf{0}$ formed a subspace of R^n, where $\mathbf{A}$ was a given $n \times n$ matrix. In fact, it can be shown in general that the solution set of any such matrix equation of this form is a subspace of R^n. To find a basis for the solution space of the system

$$\begin{aligned} x_1 + x_2 + 2x_3 + 3x_4 &= 0 \\ x_1 + 2x_2 + 4x_3 + 4x_4 &= 0 \\ 2x_1 + 5x_2 + 10x_3 + 9x_4 &= 0 \\ 2x_1 + 3x_2 + 6x_3 + 7x_4 &= 0 \end{aligned}$$

we first use *Derive* to **D**eclare the augmented matrix for the system and then reduce it to row echelon form using the ROW_REDUCE and Simplify commands.

$$2: \quad \text{ROW\_REDUCE} \begin{bmatrix} 1 & 1 & 2 & 3 & 0 \\ 1 & 2 & 4 & 4 & 0 \\ 2 & 5 & 10 & 9 & 0 \\ 2 & 3 & 6 & 7 & 0 \end{bmatrix}$$

$$3: \begin{bmatrix} 1 & 0 & 0 & 2 & 0 \\ 0 & 1 & 2 & 1 & 0 \\ 0 & 0 & 0 & 0 & 0 \\ 0 & 0 & 0 & 0 & 0 \end{bmatrix}$$

From statement #3 we see the solution has two arbitrary parameters since the reduced matrix has two rows of zeros. This leads to the solution $x_1 = -2b$, $x_2 = -2a - b$, $x_3 = a$, and $x_4 = b$ which may be written in general form as

$$a\begin{bmatrix} 0 \\ -2 \\ 1 \\ 0 \end{bmatrix} + b\begin{bmatrix} -2 \\ -1 \\ 0 \\ 1 \end{bmatrix}.$$

All solutions of the system are therefore contained in the SPAN(β) where

$$\beta = \left\{ \begin{bmatrix} 0 \\ -2 \\ 1 \\ 0 \end{bmatrix}, \begin{bmatrix} -2 \\ -1 \\ 0 \\ 1 \end{bmatrix} \right\},$$

and β is a basis for the solution space if we verify that the two vectors are linearly independent, which is left as a exercise.

EXAMPLE 5.5 In Exercise 1a) of Section 2.1 we showed that the set of 3×3 matrices **A** with TR(**A**) = 0 forms a subspace of $M_{n\times n}$. To find a basis for this subspace we consider the general form

$$\begin{bmatrix} p & x & y \\ u & q & z \\ v & w & r \end{bmatrix}$$

with the condition $p+q+r=0$. The following six linearly independent matrices generate arbitrary entries for the off-diagonal elements u, v, w, x, y, and z:

$$\left\{\begin{bmatrix}0&1&0\\0&0&0\\0&0&0\end{bmatrix},\begin{bmatrix}0&0&1\\0&0&0\\0&0&0\end{bmatrix},\begin{bmatrix}0&0&0\\0&0&1\\0&0&0\end{bmatrix},\begin{bmatrix}0&0&0\\1&0&0\\0&0&0\end{bmatrix},\begin{bmatrix}0&0&0\\0&0&0\\0&1&0\end{bmatrix},\begin{bmatrix}0&0&0\\0&0&0\\1&0&0\end{bmatrix}\right\}$$

The following two matrices will be used to generate 3×3 matrices satisfying the condition $p+q+r=0$:

$$\left\{\begin{bmatrix}1&0&0\\0&-1&0\\0&0&0\end{bmatrix},\begin{bmatrix}1&0&0\\0&0&0\\0&0&-1\end{bmatrix}\right\}$$

These eight matrices are linearly independent since each of the eight has one entry that is the only non-zero entry for that row-column position among the collection of eight matrices. The first six matrices clearly span the space of all 3×3 matrices with zero entries on the main diagonal. It remains to be shown that linear combinations of the last two matrices can generate all possible entries p, q, and r on the main diagonal such that $p+q+r=0$. In order to prove this, we need only show that for p, q, and r satisfying this property, there exist scalars a and b such that

$$a\begin{bmatrix}1&0&0\\0&-1&0\\0&0&0\end{bmatrix}+b\begin{bmatrix}1&0&0\\0&0&0\\0&0&-1\end{bmatrix}=\begin{bmatrix}p&0&0\\0&q&0\\0&0&r\end{bmatrix}.$$

By setting corresponding entries of the left and right sides of this equation equal to each other we obtain the equations:

$$\begin{aligned}a+b&=p\\-a&=q\\-b&=r\end{aligned}$$

This relation holds when we set $a = -q$ and $b = -r$. Since the basis has eight elements, the dimension of the space is eight.

EXAMPLE 5.6 We can use *Derive* to find a basis β for the subspace S of all 2×3 matrices **A** such that

$$\mathbf{AT} = \mathbf{T}^{\mathrm{T}}\mathbf{A}^{\mathrm{T}}$$

where

$$\mathbf{T} = \begin{bmatrix} 1 & 2 \\ 2 & 1 \\ 0 & 1 \end{bmatrix}.$$

First, we note by an argument similar to the one made in Example 2.9, S is a subspace of $M_{2\times 3}$. Next, we write an equation satisfied by the elements of S (statement #6) and establish a system of equations (statement #7) which can be solved (statement #10) to express relationships which must exist between the entries of elements **A** in S:

6: $$\begin{bmatrix} a & b & c \\ d & e & f \end{bmatrix} \cdot \begin{bmatrix} 1 & 2 \\ 2 & 1 \\ 0 & 1 \end{bmatrix} - \begin{bmatrix} 1 & 2 \\ 2 & 1 \\ 0 & 1 \end{bmatrix}` \cdot \begin{bmatrix} a & b & c \\ d & e & f \end{bmatrix}` = \begin{bmatrix} 0 & 0 \\ 0 & 0 \end{bmatrix}$$

7: $$\begin{bmatrix} 0 = 0 & 2a + b + c - d - 2e = 0 \\ -2a - b - c + d + 2e = 0 & 0 = 0 \end{bmatrix}$$

8: $$\begin{bmatrix} 2 & 1 & 1 & -1 & -2 & 0 & 0 \\ -2 & -1 & -1 & 1 & 2 & 0 & 0 \end{bmatrix}$$

9: $$\text{ROW\_REDUCE}\begin{bmatrix} 2 & 1 & 1 & -1 & -2 & 0 & 0 \\ -2 & -1 & -1 & 1 & 2 & 0 & 0 \end{bmatrix}$$

10: $$\begin{bmatrix} 1 & \frac{1}{2} & \frac{1}{2} & -\frac{1}{2} & -1 & 0 & 0 \\ 0 & 0 & 0 & 0 & 0 & 0 & 0 \end{bmatrix}$$

The system therefore has a solution $a = -\frac{1}{2}b - \frac{1}{2}c + \frac{1}{2}d + e$, where b, c, d, e, and f are all arbitrary. The general matrix that satisfies these conditions can be written as

$$\begin{bmatrix} -\frac{1}{2}b - \frac{1}{2}c + \frac{1}{2}d + e & b \\ c & d \\ e & f \end{bmatrix},$$

and S is spanned by the elements of

$$\beta = \left\{ \begin{bmatrix} -1/2 & 1 \\ 0 & 0 \\ 0 & 0 \end{bmatrix}, \begin{bmatrix} -1/2 & 0 \\ 1 & 0 \\ 0 & 0 \end{bmatrix}, \begin{bmatrix} 1/2 & 0 \\ 0 & 1 \\ 0 & 0 \end{bmatrix}, \begin{bmatrix} 1 & 0 \\ 0 & 0 \\ 1 & 0 \end{bmatrix}, \begin{bmatrix} 0 & 0 \\ 0 & 0 \\ 0 & 1 \end{bmatrix} \right\}.$$

Since each element of β has one entry that is the only non-zero value for that row-column combination, the elements of β are linearly independent. It follows that β is a basis for S and the dimension of S is five.

EXERCISES

1. Complete Example 5.4 by showing that the vectors

$$\left\{ \begin{bmatrix} 0 \\ -2 \\ 1 \\ 0 \end{bmatrix}, \begin{bmatrix} -2 \\ -1 \\ 0 \\ 2 \end{bmatrix} \right\}$$

are linearly independent.

2. Find a basis for the solution space of each of the following systems of equations:

a) $\left\{ \begin{aligned} x_1 + x_2 &= 0 \\ 3x_1 + 3x_2 &= 0 \end{aligned} \right\}$

b) $\left\{ \begin{aligned} x_1 + 2x_2 &= 0 \\ 2x_1 + x_2 &= 0 \end{aligned} \right\}$

c) $\left\{ \begin{aligned} x_1 + 2x_2 + x_3 &= 0 \\ x_1 + x_2 - x_3 &= 0 \\ 2x_1 + 3x_2 &= 0 \end{aligned} \right\}$

d) $\left\{ \begin{aligned} x_1 - x_2 + x_3 &= 0 \\ 2x_1 + x_2 - x_3 &= 0 \end{aligned} \right\}$

e) $\begin{bmatrix} 1 & 2 & 1 & 0 \\ 1 & 1 & 0 & 1 \\ 2 & 3 & 2 & 2 \end{bmatrix} \begin{bmatrix} x_1 \\ x_2 \\ x_3 \\ x_4 \end{bmatrix} = \begin{bmatrix} 0 \\ 0 \\ 0 \\ 0 \end{bmatrix}$

f)

$$\begin{bmatrix} 1 & 3 & 2 & 1 & 1 \\ 0 & 0 & 1 & 2 & -1 \end{bmatrix} \begin{bmatrix} x_1 \\ x_2 \\ x_3 \\ x_4 \\ x_5 \end{bmatrix} = \begin{bmatrix} 0 \\ 0 \end{bmatrix}$$

3. Find a basis for the subspace of all matrices **A** such that **AT** = **TA** where $\mathbf{T} = \begin{bmatrix} 1 & 1 \\ 2 & 2 \end{bmatrix}$ What is the dimension of the subspace?

4. Is the vector $\begin{bmatrix} 1 \\ 2 \\ 3 \end{bmatrix}$ in the subspace of R^3 spanned by $S = \left\{ \begin{bmatrix} 1 \\ 2 \\ 0 \end{bmatrix}, \begin{bmatrix} 2 \\ 1 \\ 0 \end{bmatrix} \right\}$? Is S a basis for some subspace of R^3? Find a vector to add to the set S so that the augmented set forms a basis for R^3.

5. Find the dimension of the subspace spanned by the polynomials $\{x^3 + x, x^2 + 1, x + 1, x^3 + x^2 + x + 1\}$. Is p(x) = $x^3 + 2x^2 + 1$ an element in this subspace?

6. A matrix $\mathbf{A} = (a_{ij})$ is said to be upper triangular if $a_{ij} = 0$ for $i > j$. Find a basis for the subspace of 3×3 upper triangular matrices.

7. Show that the dimension of the subspace of 4×4 matrices **A** with TR(**A**) = 0 is 15. Deduce that the dimension of the subspace of $n \times n$ matrices with the trace equal to zero is $n^2 - 1$.

8. A matrix is said to be skew-symmetric if $\mathbf{A} = -\mathbf{A}^{\mathrm{T}}$. Find a basis for the subspace of 3×3 skew-symmetric matrices. Deduce that the dimension of the subspace of $n \times n$ skew-symmetric matrices is $n(n-1)/2$.

9. Let

$$\mathrm{U} = \mathrm{SPAN}\left\{ \begin{bmatrix} 1 \\ 2 \\ 1 \\ 0 \end{bmatrix}, \begin{bmatrix} 1 \\ 1 \\ 2 \\ 1 \end{bmatrix}, \begin{bmatrix} 1 \\ 1 \\ 1 \\ 0 \end{bmatrix} \right\}$$

and

$$\mathrm{V} = \mathrm{SPAN}\left\{ \begin{bmatrix} 1 \\ 0 \\ 0 \\ 0 \end{bmatrix}, \begin{bmatrix} 0 \\ 1 \\ 0 \\ 0 \end{bmatrix}, \begin{bmatrix} 0 \\ 0 \\ 1 \\ 0 \end{bmatrix} \right\}$$

be subspaces of R^4. Find a basis for $U \cap V$.

10. Let

$$U = \text{SPAN}\left\{\begin{bmatrix}1 & 0\\0 & 1\end{bmatrix}, \begin{bmatrix}0 & 1\\1 & 0\end{bmatrix}\right\}$$

and

$$V = \text{SPAN}\left\{\begin{bmatrix}1 & 0\\0 & -1\end{bmatrix}, \begin{bmatrix}0 & 1\\1 & 0\end{bmatrix}\right\}$$

be subspaces of $M_{2\times 2}$. Find a basis for $U \cap V$.

11. Let $U = \text{SPAN}\left\{\begin{bmatrix}1 & 0\\0 & 0\end{bmatrix}, \begin{bmatrix}0 & 0\\0 & 1\end{bmatrix}, \begin{bmatrix}0 & 1\\1 & 0\end{bmatrix}\right\}$ and

$$V = \text{SPAN}\left\{\begin{bmatrix}1 & 0\\0 & -1\end{bmatrix}, \begin{bmatrix}0 & 1\\1 & 0\end{bmatrix}\right\}$$

be subspaces of $M_{2\times 2}$. Find a basis for $U \cap V$.

12. If β is a basis for the vector space V and K is a linearly independent subset of V with $\beta \subseteq \text{SPAN}(K)$, then K is a basis for V.

13. Prove Theorem 5.3.

14. Let K be a set of k linearly independent vectors in the vector space V, where V has dimension $n > k$. Prove that there exist n-k linearly independent vectors $\{\mathbf{x}_1, \mathbf{x}_2, \ldots, \mathbf{x}_{n-k}\} \subseteq V$ such that $K \cup \{\mathbf{x}_1, \mathbf{x}_2, \ldots, \mathbf{x}_{n-k}\}$ is a basis for V.

CHAPTER III
LINEAR TRANSFORMATIONS

Functions play an extremely important role in the study of many areas of mathematics such as calculus, where we were able to differentiate and integrate functions satisfying certain properties. Another name for a function is "transformation," and in this chapter we will study the types of transformations that are important in linear algebra: mappings from one vector space to another that preserve certain properties of vector addition and scalar multiplication. Included in our study will be a development of how these transformations are related to the matrices introduced in Chapter 1.

1. LINEAR TRANSFORMATIONS

By a tıansformation **t** from one vector space to another over the same field of scalars, we mean a function that assigns to each element in the domain space a unique element in the range space. One simple example of such a function is a matrix of order $m \times n$. Any matrix of this type can be used to transform vectors from R^n into images in R^m by performing matrix multiplication. For instance, the square matrix

$$\mathbf{A} = \begin{bmatrix} 2 & -1 \\ 0 & 3 \end{bmatrix}$$

maps vectors from R^2 into R^2 by means of matrix multiplication as follows:

$$\mathbf{A}\begin{bmatrix} 1 \\ 0 \end{bmatrix} = \begin{bmatrix} 2 \\ 0 \end{bmatrix} \qquad \mathbf{A}\begin{bmatrix} 4 \\ -1 \end{bmatrix} = \begin{bmatrix} 9 \\ -3 \end{bmatrix} \qquad \mathbf{A}\begin{bmatrix} x_1 \\ x_2 \end{bmatrix} = \begin{bmatrix} 2x_1 - x_2 \\ 3x_2 \end{bmatrix}.$$

In Theorem 3.2 of Section 1.3 we showed that **A(x + y)** = **Ax** + **Ay**, and in Theorem 3.3 of the same section we showed **A(**k**x)** = k**Ax** whenever **A** is a $m \times n$ matrix, k is a scalar, and **x** and **y** are column matrices representing vectors in R^n. It is precisely these two properties which characterize the type of function, called a linear transformation, which we will find most valuable in our study of linear algebra.

DEFINITION 1.1 (Linear Transformation) Let V and W be vector spaces over the same scalar field. A transformation $\mathbf{t}: V \to W$ is called a linear transformation if for each **x** and **y** in V and for all scalars a:

1. $\mathbf{t}(\mathbf{x}+\mathbf{y}) = \mathbf{t}(\mathbf{x}) + \mathbf{t}(\mathbf{y})$, and
2. $\mathbf{t}(a\mathbf{x}) = a\mathbf{t}(\mathbf{x})$.

EXAMPLE 1.1 In order to show that the function $\mathbf{t}: R^3 \to R^2$, defined by

$$\mathbf{t}\left(\begin{bmatrix} x_1 \\ x_2 \\ x_3 \end{bmatrix}\right) = \begin{bmatrix} x_1 + x_3 \\ x_2 + x_3 \end{bmatrix},$$

is a linear transformation, we must demonstrate that **t** satisfies both properties of Definition 1.1. The first of these properties follows since both

$$\mathbf{t}(\mathbf{x}+\mathbf{y}) = \mathbf{t}\left(\begin{bmatrix} x_1 \\ x_2 \\ x_3 \end{bmatrix} + \begin{bmatrix} y_1 \\ y_2 \\ y_3 \end{bmatrix}\right) = \mathbf{t}\left(\begin{bmatrix} x_1 + y_1 \\ x_2 + y_2 \\ x_3 + y_3 \end{bmatrix}\right) = \begin{bmatrix} x_1 + y_1 + x_3 + y_3 \\ x_2 + y_2 + x_3 + y_3 \end{bmatrix}$$

and

$$\mathbf{t}(\mathbf{x}) + \mathbf{t}(\mathbf{y}) = \mathbf{t}\left(\begin{bmatrix} x_1 \\ x_2 \\ x_3 \end{bmatrix}\right) + \mathbf{t}\left(\begin{bmatrix} y_1 \\ y_2 \\ y_3 \end{bmatrix}\right) = \begin{bmatrix} x_1 + x_3 \\ x_2 + x_3 \end{bmatrix} + \begin{bmatrix} y_1 + y_3 \\ y_2 + y_3 \end{bmatrix} = \begin{bmatrix} x_1 + y_1 + x_3 + y_3 \\ x_2 + y_2 + x_3 + y_3 \end{bmatrix}.$$

The second property also follows since

$$\mathbf{t}(a\mathbf{x}) = \mathbf{t}\left(\begin{bmatrix} ax_1 \\ ax_2 \\ ax_3 \end{bmatrix}\right) = \begin{bmatrix} ax_1 + ax_3 \\ ax_2 + ax_3 \end{bmatrix} = a\begin{bmatrix} x_1 + x_3 \\ x_2 + x_3 \end{bmatrix} = a\mathbf{t}(\mathbf{x}).$$

Linear transformations defined in this manner can also be declared and used in a *Derive* environment. To accomplish this, we use the **D**eclare and **M**atrix series of commands to input the 2×1 matrix in statement #1 below. Next, we use the **D**eclare and **F**unction series of commands to name the function "T" with input variables **x**, **y**, and **z** as the matrix defined in statement #1. (When *Derive* prompts for the function value, use the F3 function key to move a copy of the highlighted portion of the screen to the right side of the function definition. The input variables will be declared automatically.)

$$1: \quad \begin{bmatrix} x + z \\ y + z \end{bmatrix}$$

$$2: \quad T(x, y, z) := \begin{bmatrix} x + z \\ y + z \end{bmatrix}$$

The function can then be evaluated for any vector in the domain by **A**uthoring an expression such as statement #3 below and then **S**implifying the expression:

$$3: \quad T(1, 2, 3)$$

$$4: \quad \begin{bmatrix} 4 \\ 5 \end{bmatrix}$$

EXAMPLE 1.2 To show the transformation $\mathbf{t}: P^3 \to P^3$ defined by

$$\mathbf{t}\left(ax^3 + bx^2 + cx + d\right) = (a+b)x^3 + (b+c)x^2 + (c+d)x + d + a$$

is a linear transformation we again must show that **t** satisfies both properties of Definition 1.1. We accomplish this by considering only the coefficients of x^3, x^2, x, and x^0 and using *Derive*. First, we enter the vector of coefficients in statement #1 below using the **D**eclare and vecto**R** commands. Next, in statement #2, we use the **D**eclare and **F**unction commands (and the F3 command when *Derive* prompts for the function value) to enter the desired transformation represented as a vector function.

$$2: \quad T(a, b, c, d) := [a + b, b + c, c + d, d + a]$$

This formula is then used to evaluate $\mathbf{t}(p_1 + p_2)$ and both of $\mathbf{t}(p_1)$ and $\mathbf{t}(p_2)$ where

$$p_1(x) = ax^3 + bx^2 + cx + d \quad \text{and} \quad p_2(x) = px^3 + qx^2 + rx + s$$

are two arbitrary polynomials of P^3.

Next, we compute the sum of p_1 and p_2

$$p_1(x) + p_2(x) = (a + p)x^3 + (b + q)x^2 + (c + r)x + (d + s)$$

and find the transformation of this sum using *Derive*

```
3:    T(a + p, b + q, c + r, d + s)

4:    [a + b + p + q, b + c + q + r, c + d + r + s, a + d + p + s]
```

We compare this result to an expression for $\mathbf{t}(p_1) + \mathbf{t}(p_2)$

```
5:    T(a, b, c, d) + T(p, q, r, s)

6:    [a + b + p + q, b + c + q + r, c + d + r + s, a + d + p + s]
```

Since statement #4 and statement #6 are identical, it follows that $\mathbf{t}(p_1 + p_2) = \mathbf{t}(p_1) + \mathbf{t}(p_2)$.

Next, we find an expression for $q\mathbf{t}(p_1)$

```
7:    q T(a, b, c, d)

8:    [q (a + b), q (b + c), q (c + d), q (a + d)]
```

and an expression for $\mathbf{t}(q\,p_1)$

```
9:    T(q a, q b, q c, q d)

10:   [a q + b q, b q + c q, c q + d q, a q + d q]
```

Since statement #8 is equal to statement #10, $\mathbf{t}(qp_1) = q\mathbf{t}(p_1)$, and $\mathbf{t}$ satisfies the two conditions of Definition 1.1.

EXAMPLE 1.3 *Derive* can also be used to show that a transformation, such as $\mathbf{t}: P^3 \to P^3$ where $\mathbf{t}(ax^3+bx^2+cx+d)= x^3+ax^2+bx+c$, is not a linear transformation. Again, instead of using the polynomial itself, only the coefficients of x^3, x^2, x, and x^0 are used. As in Example 1.2 above, we use the **Declare** and **Function** commands together with the F3 command to define the transformation **t** in statement #2:

```
2:    T(a, b, c, d) := [1, a, b, c + d - d]
```

Next, we compute the sum of the two arbitrary polynomials p_1 and p_2 defined in Example 1.2 above and find the transformation of this sum

```
7:    T(a + p, b + q, c + r, d + s)

8:    [1, a + p, b + q, c + r]
```

Thus, $\mathbf{t}(p_1(x)+p_2(x))=x^3+(a+p)x^2+(b+q)x+c+r$. If we transform each polynomial independently and then add the result, we obtain

```
9:    T(a, b, c, d) + T(p, q, r, s)

10:   [2, a + p, b + q, c + r]
```

and $\mathbf{t}(p_1(x))+\mathbf{t}(p_2(x)) = 2x^3+(a+p)x^2+(b+q)x+c+r$. It follows that

$$\mathbf{t}(p_1(x)+p_2(x)) \neq \mathbf{t}(p_1(x))+\mathbf{t}(p_2(x)),$$

thus proving that **t** is not a linear transformation.

EXAMPLE 1.4 The function $\mathbf{t}: M_{2\times2} \to R$ defined by $\mathbf{t}(\mathbf{A}) = \mathrm{TR}(\mathbf{A})$ is a linear transformation since if **A** and **B** are be two arbitrary matrices of $M_{2\times2}$, then

$$3: \quad \mathrm{TRACE}\left(\begin{bmatrix} c & d \\ e & f \end{bmatrix} + \begin{bmatrix} g & h \\ i & j \end{bmatrix}\right)$$

```
4:    c + f + g + j
```

and

$$5: \quad \text{TRACE}\begin{bmatrix} c & d \\ e & f \end{bmatrix} + \text{TRACE}\begin{bmatrix} g & h \\ i & j \end{bmatrix}$$

$$6: \quad c + f + g + j$$

thus, $\text{TR}(\mathbf{A}+\mathbf{B}) = \text{TR}(\mathbf{A}) + \text{TR}(\mathbf{B})$. Also,

$$7: \quad a\ \text{TRACE}\begin{bmatrix} c & d \\ e & f \end{bmatrix}$$

$$8: \quad a\ (c + f)$$

$$9: \quad \text{TRACE}\left[a \begin{bmatrix} c & d \\ e & f \end{bmatrix}\right]$$

$$10: \quad a\ (c + f)$$

and $a\text{TR}(\mathbf{A}) = \text{TR}(a\mathbf{A})$; therefore, $\mathbf{t}$ satisfies the two properties of Definition 1.1.

PROPOSITION 1.1 Let V and W be vector spaces, $\mathbf{x}, \mathbf{y} \in V$ and $\mathbf{t}: V \to W$ be a linear transformation, then

a) $\mathbf{t}(\mathbf{0}) = \mathbf{0}$,

b) $\mathbf{t}(-\mathbf{x}) = -\mathbf{t}(\mathbf{x})$, and

c) $\mathbf{t}(\mathbf{x} - \mathbf{y}) = \mathbf{t}(\mathbf{x}) - \mathbf{t}(\mathbf{y})$.

PROOF: The proof of part a) is provided. The proofs of the remaining two parts are left as exercises.

Since $\mathbf{0} = 0\mathbf{v}$ whenever $\mathbf{v} \in V$ or $\mathbf{v} \in W$, we can use the second property of Definition 1.1 to obtain $\mathbf{t}(\mathbf{0}) = \mathbf{t}(0\mathbf{x}) = 0\mathbf{t}(\mathbf{x}) = \mathbf{0}$, for all $\mathbf{x} \in V$; and the proof is complete.

In Section 2.5 we learned that any vector in a vector space V with a basis β can be written as a linear combination of elements of β. Since the two properties of Definition 1.1 guarantee that images of a linear transformation preserve linear combinations, it follows that linear transformations can be completely characterized by only determining the images of all basis vectors of the domain space. For example, if $\mathbf{t}: R^2 \to R^2$ is the linear transformation such that

$$\mathbf{t}\left(\begin{bmatrix}1\\0\end{bmatrix}\right)=\begin{bmatrix}2\\1\end{bmatrix} \text{ and } \mathbf{t}\left(\begin{bmatrix}0\\1\end{bmatrix}\right)=\begin{bmatrix}3\\3\end{bmatrix},$$

then $\mathbf{t}$ maps any arbitrary vector in R^2 as follows:

$$\mathbf{t}\left(\begin{bmatrix}p\\q\end{bmatrix}\right)=\mathbf{t}\left(p\begin{bmatrix}1\\0\end{bmatrix}+q\begin{bmatrix}0\\1\end{bmatrix}\right)=p\mathbf{t}\left(\begin{bmatrix}1\\0\end{bmatrix}\right)+q\mathbf{t}\left(\begin{bmatrix}0\\1\end{bmatrix}\right)=p\begin{bmatrix}2\\1\end{bmatrix}+q\begin{bmatrix}3\\3\end{bmatrix}=\begin{bmatrix}2p+3q\\p+3q\end{bmatrix}$$

.

This leads us to the following theorem.

THEOREM 1.1 Let V be a vector space, $\beta=\{\mathbf{x}_1,\mathbf{x}_2,\cdots,\mathbf{x}_n\}$ be a basis of V, and $\mathbf{t}:V\to W$ be a linear transformation which is defined by $\mathbf{t}(\mathbf{x}_i)=\mathbf{y}_i \quad i=1,2,\cdots,n$. If $\mathbf{u}\in V$, with $\mathbf{u}=\sum_{i=1}^{n} a_i\mathbf{x}_i$, then $\mathbf{t}(\mathbf{u})=\sum_{i=1}^{n} a_i\mathbf{y}_i$.

PROOF: The proof follows immediately from the facts that $\mathbf{t}$ is linear and β is a basis, since if

$$\mathbf{u}=\sum_{i=1}^{n} a_i\mathbf{x}_i, \quad \text{then} \quad \mathbf{t}(\mathbf{u})=\mathbf{t}\left(\sum_{i=1}^{n} a_i\mathbf{x}_i\right)=\sum_{i=1}^{n} a_i\mathbf{t}(\mathbf{x}_i)=\sum_{i=1}^{n} a_i\mathbf{y}_i.$$

EXAMPLE 1.5 Let $\mathbf{t}$: $M_{2\times2} \to M_{2\times2}$ be a linear transformation satisfying

$$\mathbf{t}\left(\begin{bmatrix}0&1\\1&1\end{bmatrix}\right)=\begin{bmatrix}1&2\\1&1\end{bmatrix} \qquad \mathbf{t}\left(\begin{bmatrix}1&0\\1&1\end{bmatrix}\right)=\begin{bmatrix}1&0\\2&1\end{bmatrix}$$

$$\mathbf{t}\left(\begin{bmatrix}1&1\\0&1\end{bmatrix}\right)=\begin{bmatrix}1&0\\0&1\end{bmatrix} \qquad \mathbf{t}\left(\begin{bmatrix}1&1\\1&0\end{bmatrix}\right)=\begin{bmatrix}0&1\\1&0\end{bmatrix}.$$

We will determine if **t** is characterized by these four equations, and if so, find an expression to represent the general term

$$\mathbf{t}\left(\begin{bmatrix} p & q \\ r & s \end{bmatrix}\right).$$

First, we show **t** is defined on a basis. Since $M_{2\times 2}$ has dimension four, it is only necessary to prove

$$\beta = \left\{\begin{bmatrix} 0 & 1 \\ 1 & 1 \end{bmatrix}, \begin{bmatrix} 1 & 0 \\ 1 & 1 \end{bmatrix}, \begin{bmatrix} 1 & 1 \\ 0 & 1 \end{bmatrix}, \begin{bmatrix} 1 & 1 \\ 1 & 0 \end{bmatrix}\right\}$$

is a linearly independent set. Using *Derive*,

6: $$a \begin{bmatrix} 0 & 1 \\ 1 & 1 \end{bmatrix} + b \begin{bmatrix} 1 & 0 \\ 1 & 1 \end{bmatrix} + c \begin{bmatrix} 1 & 1 \\ 0 & 1 \end{bmatrix} + d \begin{bmatrix} 1 & 1 \\ 1 & 0 \end{bmatrix} = \begin{bmatrix} 0 & 0 \\ 0 & 0 \end{bmatrix}$$

7: $$\begin{bmatrix} b + c + d = 0 & a + c + d = 0 \\ a + b + d = 0 & a + b + c = 0 \end{bmatrix}$$

We solve this system of four equations in four unknowns using *Derive*:

9: $$\text{ROW\_REDUCE}\begin{bmatrix} 0 & 1 & 1 & 1 & 0 \\ 1 & 0 & 1 & 1 & 0 \\ 1 & 1 & 0 & 1 & 0 \\ 1 & 1 & 1 & 0 & 0 \end{bmatrix}$$

10: $$\begin{bmatrix} 1 & 0 & 0 & 0 & 0 \\ 0 & 1 & 0 & 0 & 0 \\ 0 & 0 & 1 & 0 & 0 \\ 0 & 0 & 0 & 1 & 0 \end{bmatrix}$$

Hence $a = b = c = d = 0$, and β is a linearly independent set.

To find the general form of the transformation **t**, consider

$$a\begin{bmatrix}0 & 1\\1 & 1\end{bmatrix}+b\begin{bmatrix}1 & 0\\1 & 1\end{bmatrix}+c\begin{bmatrix}1 & 1\\0 & 1\end{bmatrix}+c\begin{bmatrix}1 & 1\\1 & 0\end{bmatrix}=\begin{bmatrix}p & q\\r & s\end{bmatrix}.$$

Again, we use *Derive* to solve the resulting system:

$$12: \quad a\begin{bmatrix}0 & 1\\1 & 1\end{bmatrix}+b\begin{bmatrix}1 & 0\\1 & 1\end{bmatrix}+c\begin{bmatrix}1 & 1\\0 & 1\end{bmatrix}+d\begin{bmatrix}1 & 1\\1 & 0\end{bmatrix}=\begin{bmatrix}p & q\\r & s\end{bmatrix}$$

$$13: \quad \begin{bmatrix}b+c+d=p & a+c+d=q\\a+b+d=r & a+b+c=s\end{bmatrix}$$

Executing the ROW_REDUCE command for the augmented coefficient matrix we obtain:

$$15: \quad \begin{bmatrix}1 & 0 & 0 & 0 & -\dfrac{2p-q-r-s}{3}\\0 & 1 & 0 & 0 & \dfrac{p-2q+r+s}{3}\\0 & 0 & 1 & 0 & \dfrac{p+q-2r+s}{3}\\0 & 0 & 0 & 1 & \dfrac{p+q+r-2s}{3}\end{bmatrix}$$

From our original definition of **t** we know that

$$\mathbf{t}\left(\begin{bmatrix}p & q\\r & s\end{bmatrix}\right)=a\mathbf{t}\left(\begin{bmatrix}0 & 1\\1 & 1\end{bmatrix}\right)+b\mathbf{t}\left(\begin{bmatrix}1 & 0\\1 & 1\end{bmatrix}\right)+c\mathbf{t}\left(\begin{bmatrix}1 & 1\\0 & 1\end{bmatrix}\right)+d\mathbf{t}\left(\begin{bmatrix}1 & 1\\1 & 0\end{bmatrix}\right)$$

$$=a\begin{bmatrix}1 & 2\\1 & 1\end{bmatrix}+b\begin{bmatrix}1 & 0\\2 & 1\end{bmatrix}+c\begin{bmatrix}1 & 0\\0 & 1\end{bmatrix}+d\begin{bmatrix}0 & 1\\1 & 0\end{bmatrix}.$$

Substituting the values found in statement #15 for a, b, c, and d and simplifying, we find

$$24: \begin{bmatrix} s & -p+q+r \\ \dfrac{p-2q+4r+s}{3} & s \end{bmatrix}$$

which represents the general term $\mathbf{t}\begin{bmatrix} p & q \\ r & s \end{bmatrix}$.

EXERCISES

1. Show that the following transformations are linear:
   a) $\mathbf{t}: R^3 \to R^3$ defined by $\mathbf{t}\left(\begin{bmatrix} x_1 \\ x_2 \\ x_3 \end{bmatrix}\right) = \begin{bmatrix} x_2 \\ x_3 \\ x_1 \end{bmatrix}$.
   b) $\mathbf{t}: M_{2\times2} \to M_{2\times2}$ defined by $\mathbf{t}(\mathbf{A}) = \mathbf{A}^{\mathrm{T}}$
   c) $\mathbf{t}: M_{2\times2} \to R^2$ defined by $\mathbf{t}\left(\begin{bmatrix} x_{11} & x_{12} \\ x_{21} & x_{22} \end{bmatrix}\right) = \begin{bmatrix} x_{11}+x_{21} \\ x_{12}+x_{22} \end{bmatrix}$.
   d) $\mathbf{t}: P^3 \to R$ defined by $\mathbf{t}(p_3x^3 + p_2x^2 + p_1x + p_0) = p_0 + p_1 + p_2 + p_3$.
   e) $\mathbf{t}: R^2 \to R^2$ defined by $\mathbf{t}\left(\begin{bmatrix} x_1 \\ x_2 \end{bmatrix}\right) = \begin{bmatrix} 2x_1+3x_2 \\ x_1-2x_2 \end{bmatrix}$.

2. Let $\mathbf{t}: P^n \to P^{n-1}$ be defined by $\mathbf{t}(p(x)) = p'(x)$ where the "′" denotes differentiation. Show that **t** is a linear transformation.

3. Let $F[0,1]$ be the space of integrable functions defined on $[0,1]$. Show that the transformation $\mathbf{t}: F[0,1] \to F[0,1]$ defined by $\mathbf{t}(f(x)) = \int f(x)dx$ with the constant of integration equal to zero is a linear transformation.

4. Let $\mathbf{t}: R^2 \to R^2$ be defined by $\mathbf{t}(\mathbf{x}) = \begin{bmatrix} 1 & 1 \\ 1 & 2 \end{bmatrix}\begin{bmatrix} x_1 \\ x_2 \end{bmatrix}$. Show that **t** is a linear transformation and find $\mathbf{t}\left(\begin{bmatrix} 1 \\ 3 \end{bmatrix}\right)$.

5. Show that the following rules define a linear transformation and find the indicated transformation.
   a) Let $\mathbf{t}\left(\begin{bmatrix} 1 \\ 0 \end{bmatrix}\right) = \begin{bmatrix} 1 \\ 1 \end{bmatrix}$ and $\mathbf{t}\left(\begin{bmatrix} 0 \\ 1 \end{bmatrix}\right) = \begin{bmatrix} 2 \\ 2 \end{bmatrix}$, and find $\mathbf{t}\left(\begin{bmatrix} a \\ b \end{bmatrix}\right)$.

b) Let $\mathbf{t}\left(\begin{bmatrix}1\\1\end{bmatrix}\right)=\begin{bmatrix}2\\1\end{bmatrix}$ and $\mathbf{t}\left(\begin{bmatrix}2\\1\end{bmatrix}\right)=\begin{bmatrix}1\\1\end{bmatrix}$ and find $\mathbf{t}\left(\begin{bmatrix}a\\b\end{bmatrix}\right)$.

c) Let $\mathbf{t}\left(\begin{bmatrix}1&0\\0&0\end{bmatrix}\right)=\begin{bmatrix}1\\0\end{bmatrix}$, $\mathbf{t}\left(\begin{bmatrix}0&1\\0&0\end{bmatrix}\right)=\begin{bmatrix}1\\0\end{bmatrix}$, $\mathbf{t}\left(\begin{bmatrix}0&0\\1&0\end{bmatrix}\right)=\begin{bmatrix}0\\1\end{bmatrix}$, $\mathbf{t}\left(\begin{bmatrix}0&0\\0&1\end{bmatrix}\right)=\begin{bmatrix}0\\1\end{bmatrix}$, and find $\mathbf{t}\left(\begin{bmatrix}a&b\\c&d\end{bmatrix}\right)$.

d) Let $\mathbf{t}(1)=x^2+x$, $\mathbf{t}(x)=x+1$, $\mathbf{t}(x^2)=x^2+1$, and find $\mathbf{t}(ax^2+bx+c)$.

6. Let $\mathbf{t}: M_{2\times 2}\to M_{2\times 2}$ be defined by $\mathbf{t}\left(\begin{bmatrix}a&b\\c&d\end{bmatrix}\right)=\begin{bmatrix}a&b\\b&d\end{bmatrix}$. Is $\mathbf{t}$ a linear transformation? Is there a matrix $\mathbf{A}\in M_{2\times 2}$ such that $\mathbf{t}(\mathbf{A})=\begin{bmatrix}1&2\\2&4\end{bmatrix}$?

7. Let $\mathbf{t}: M_{3\times 3}\to M_{2\times 3}$ be defined by $\mathbf{t}\left(\begin{bmatrix}a_{11}&a_{12}&a_{13}\\a_{21}&a_{22}&a_{23}\\a_{31}&a_{32}&a_{33}\end{bmatrix}\right)=\begin{bmatrix}1&2&5\\3&4&6\end{bmatrix}\cdot\begin{bmatrix}a_{11}&a_{12}&a_{13}\\a_{21}&a_{22}&a_{23}\\a_{31}&a_{32}&a_{33}\end{bmatrix}$. Show that $\mathbf{t}$ is linear and find $\mathbf{t}\left(\begin{bmatrix}1&0&1\\0&1&0\\1&1&1\end{bmatrix}\right)$.

8. Let $\mathbf{t}: R^3\to M_{3\times 3}$ be defined by $\mathbf{t}(\mathbf{x})=\mathbf{x}\mathbf{x}^{\mathrm{T}}$. Is $\mathbf{t}$ a linear transformation? Find $\mathbf{t}\left(\begin{bmatrix}a\\b\\c\end{bmatrix}\right)$.

9. Let $\mathbf{t}: R^3\to R$ be defined by $\mathbf{t}(\mathbf{x})=\mathbf{x}^{\mathrm{T}}\mathbf{x}$. Is $\mathbf{t}$ a linear transformation? Find $\mathbf{t}\left(\begin{bmatrix}a\\b\\c\end{bmatrix}\right)$.

10. Let $\mathbf{t}: M_{2\times 2}\to M_{2\times 2}$ be defined by $\mathbf{t}(\mathbf{A})=\mathbf{A}^{\mathrm{T}}\mathbf{A}$. Is $\mathbf{t}$ a linear transformation? Find $\mathbf{t}\left(\begin{bmatrix}a&b\\c&d\end{bmatrix}\right)$.

11. Prove parts b) and c) of Proposition 1.1.

2. PROPERTIES OF LINEAR TRANSFORMATIONS

In calculus, functions were required to satisfy certain properties in order to be differentiable or integrable. As we discussed in the previous section, a special type of function, called linear transformations, plays an important role in the study of linear algebra. In fact, these functions are so important that from this point on, unless otherwise specified, we will assume that every function mentioned is a linear transformation. In this section we will examine several of the important properties of linear transformations that make them so useful in applications. Some of these properties, such as "onto" and "one-to-one," are identical to properties that characterized many of our functions in calculus, while others are unique to linear transformations. But even in cases where the property is identical to one studied in another setting, we will find that linear transformations have special characteristics that make them easier to use than more general functions.

DEFINITION 2.1 (Onto) A linear transformation $\mathbf{t}: V \to W$ is said to be onto if each $\mathbf{y} \in W$ is the image of some $\mathbf{x} \in V$.

Another way to phrase the concept of onto is to state that $\mathbf{t}$ is onto if $\mathbf{y} \in W$ implies that there exists an $\mathbf{x} \in V$ such that $\mathbf{t}(\mathbf{x}) = \mathbf{y}$.

EXAMPLE 2.1 Let $\mathbf{t}: R^2 \to R^2$ be defined by $\mathbf{t}\left(\begin{bmatrix} x_1 \\ x_2 \end{bmatrix}\right) = \begin{bmatrix} x_1 + x_2 \\ x_1 + 2x_2 \end{bmatrix}$.

In order to show $\mathbf{t}$ is onto, we let $\begin{bmatrix} a \\ b \end{bmatrix} \in R^2$ (the range space) and look for a vector $\mathbf{x} \in R^2$ (the domain space) such that $\mathbf{t}\left(\begin{bmatrix} x_1 \\ x_2 \end{bmatrix}\right) = \begin{bmatrix} a \\ b \end{bmatrix}$. But $\mathbf{x}$ exists since

$$\begin{aligned} x_1 + x_2 &= a \\ x_1 + 2x_2 &= b \end{aligned}$$

has the solution $x_1 = 2a - b$ and $x_2 = b - a$.

EXAMPLE 2.2 If $\mathbf{t}: R^2 \to R^3$ is defined by $\mathbf{t}\left(\begin{bmatrix} a \\ b \end{bmatrix}\right) = \begin{bmatrix} a \\ a+b \\ b \end{bmatrix}$, then $\mathbf{t}$ is onto if an arbitrary element $\begin{bmatrix} p & q & r \end{bmatrix}^{\mathrm{T}}$ of R^3 is the image of some vector $\begin{bmatrix} a & b \end{bmatrix}^{\mathrm{T}}$ in R^2:

$$\mathbf{t}\left(\begin{bmatrix} a \\ b \end{bmatrix}\right) = \begin{bmatrix} a \\ a+b \\ b \end{bmatrix} = \begin{bmatrix} p \\ q \\ r \end{bmatrix}.$$

By setting $p = q = r = 1$ we can see that $\mathbf{t}$ is not onto since there is not solution to the system of equations

$$\begin{aligned} a &= 1 \\ a + b &= 1 \\ b &= 1 \end{aligned}$$

and, hence, there is no vector $\begin{bmatrix} a & b \end{bmatrix}^{\mathrm{T}}$ in R^2 which maps into $\begin{bmatrix} 1 & 1 & 1 \end{bmatrix}^{\mathrm{T}}$.

EXAMPLE 2.3 Let $\mathbf{t}: R^3 \to R^2$ be defined by $\mathbf{t}\left(\begin{bmatrix} x_1 & x_2 & x_3 \end{bmatrix}^{\mathrm{T}}\right) = \begin{bmatrix} x_1 + x_2 & x_3 \end{bmatrix}^{\mathrm{T}}$. To determine if $\mathbf{t}$ is onto, we let $\begin{bmatrix} p & q \end{bmatrix}^{\mathrm{T}}$ be an arbitrary element of R^2 and seek an element $\mathbf{x} \in R^3$ such that $\mathbf{t}(\mathbf{x}) = \begin{bmatrix} p & q \end{bmatrix}^{\mathrm{T}}$, or

$$\mathbf{t}\left(\begin{bmatrix} x_1 \\ x_2 \\ x_3 \end{bmatrix}\right) = \begin{bmatrix} x_1 + x_2 \\ x_3 \end{bmatrix} = \begin{bmatrix} p \\ q \end{bmatrix}.$$

This generates a system of two equations in three unknowns which can be solved using *Derive*:

$$2: \quad \text{ROW\_REDUCE} \begin{bmatrix} 1 & 1 & 0 & p \\ 0 & 0 & 1 & q \end{bmatrix}$$

$$3: \quad \begin{bmatrix} 1 & 1 & 0 & p \\ 0 & 0 & 1 & q \end{bmatrix}$$

Thus, $x_3 = q$, $x_2 = \alpha$, and $x_1 = p - \alpha$, where α is arbitrary; and the transformation is onto.

Often when studying a linear transformation it is important to examine the set of all range vectors that are images of some domain vector. If the function is onto, this set is the entire range space, and sufficient notation already exists to study the set of images. If the function is not onto, the following definition will provide the notation necessary to examine this set.

DEFINITION 2.2 (Image of a Linear Transformation) The image of a linear transformation $\mathbf{t}{:}V \to W$, denoted by IM(**t**) is the set of all vectors of W that are the image of some vector in V:

$$\mathrm{IM}(\mathbf{t}) = \{\, \mathbf{y} \in W\!: \ \mathbf{y} = \mathbf{t}(\mathbf{x}) \text{ for some } \mathbf{x} \in V \}.$$

Note that $\mathrm{IM}(\mathbf{t}) \subseteq W$, and with this new notation we could rephrase our definition of onto by stating: **t** is onto if IM(**t**) = W.

EXAMPLE 2.4 Consider whether $[1 \quad 2 \quad 1]^{\mathrm{T}} \in \mathrm{IM}(\mathbf{t})$, where **t** is the transformation defined in Example 2.2. In order to answer this question affirmatively, we must find an $\mathbf{x} \in R^2$ such that $\mathbf{t}(\mathbf{x}) = [1 \quad 2 \quad 1]^{\mathrm{T}}$. This is equivalent to finding a solution to

$$\mathbf{t}\begin{bmatrix} x_1 \\ x_2 \end{bmatrix} = \begin{bmatrix} x_1 \\ x_1 + x_2 \\ x_2 \end{bmatrix} = \begin{bmatrix} 1 \\ 2 \\ 1 \end{bmatrix}.$$

We see that the solution pair $x_1 = 1$ and $x_2 = 1$ satisfies this equation so that $[1 \quad 2 \quad 1]^{\mathrm{T}} \in \mathrm{IM}(\mathbf{t})$. In Example 2.2 we learned that IM(**t**) $\neq R^3$. An example of a vector in R^3 which is not in IM(**t**) is $[1 \quad 2 \quad 3]^{\mathrm{T}}$. This can be seen by noting that the system of three equations in two unknowns resulting from

$$\mathbf{t}\begin{bmatrix} x_1 \\ x_2 \end{bmatrix} = \begin{bmatrix} x_1 \\ x_1 + x_2 \\ x_2 \end{bmatrix} = \begin{bmatrix} 1 \\ 2 \\ 3 \end{bmatrix}$$

has no solution since $x_1 = 1$ and $x_2 = 3$ implies that $x_1 + x_2 = 4 \neq 2$.

EXAMPLE 2.5 The transformation $\mathbf{t}: P^3 \to R^3$ defined by

$$\mathbf{t}(1) = \begin{bmatrix} 1 \\ 0 \\ 0 \end{bmatrix}, \ \mathbf{t}(x) = \begin{bmatrix} 1 \\ 1 \\ 0 \end{bmatrix}, \ \mathbf{t}(x^2) = \begin{bmatrix} 1 \\ 1 \\ 1 \end{bmatrix}, \text{ and } \mathbf{t}(x^3) = \begin{bmatrix} 0 \\ 0 \\ 0 \end{bmatrix}.$$

is onto since

$$\left\{ \begin{bmatrix} 1 \\ 0 \\ 0 \end{bmatrix}, \begin{bmatrix} 1 \\ 1 \\ 0 \end{bmatrix}, \begin{bmatrix} 1 \\ 1 \\ 1 \end{bmatrix} \right\}$$

is a basis for R^3. For example, we can use *Derive* to find a vector $p(x) \in P^3$ such that

$$\mathbf{t}(p(x)) = \begin{bmatrix} 1 \\ 2 \\ 3 \end{bmatrix}:$$

$$5: \quad a \begin{bmatrix} 1 \\ 0 \\ 0 \end{bmatrix} + b \begin{bmatrix} 1 \\ 1 \\ 0 \end{bmatrix} + c \begin{bmatrix} 1 \\ 1 \\ 1 \end{bmatrix} = \begin{bmatrix} 1 \\ 2 \\ 3 \end{bmatrix}$$

$$6: \quad \begin{bmatrix} a + b + c = 1 \\ b + c = 2 \\ c = 3 \end{bmatrix}$$

where statement #6 is a Simplification of statement #5. This system of equations can be entered as an augmented matrix and solved using *Derive* as follows:

$$8: \quad \text{ROW\_REDUCE} \begin{bmatrix} 1 & 1 & 1 & 1 \\ 0 & 1 & 1 & 2 \\ 0 & 0 & 1 & 3 \end{bmatrix}$$

$$9: \quad \begin{bmatrix} 1 & 0 & 0 & -1 \\ 0 & 1 & 0 & -1 \\ 0 & 0 & 1 & 3 \end{bmatrix}$$

Thus, $a = -1$, $b = -1$, and $c = 3$, and

$$-1\mathbf{t}(1) - 1\mathbf{t}(x) + 3\mathbf{t}(x^2) = \begin{bmatrix} 1 \\ 2 \\ 3 \end{bmatrix},$$

which implies

$$\mathbf{t}(-1 - x + 3x^2) = \begin{bmatrix} 1 \\ 2 \\ 3 \end{bmatrix}.$$

If **t** is onto, then IM(**t**) and the range space are identical, and IM(**t**) is clearly a vector space. The next two theorems show that even in cases where the IM(**t**) is a proper subset of the range space, it still satisfies all the properties of a vector space and is spanned by the set of images of the basis elements of the domain.

THEOREM 2.1 If $\mathbf{t}: V \to W$ is a linear transformation, then IM(**t**) is a subspace of W.

PROOF: The zero vector is in IM(**t**), since $\mathbf{t}(\mathbf{0}) = \mathbf{0}$. Let $\mathbf{u}, \mathbf{v} \in \mathrm{IM}(\mathbf{t})$. It follows that there exist $\mathbf{x}, \mathbf{y} \in V$ such that $\mathbf{t}(\mathbf{x}) = \mathbf{u}$ and $\mathbf{t}(\mathbf{y}) = \mathbf{v}$. Since $\mathbf{x} + \mathbf{y} \in V$ and **t** is linear, $\mathbf{t}(\mathbf{x} + \mathbf{y}) = \mathbf{t}(\mathbf{x}) + \mathbf{t}(\mathbf{y}) = \mathbf{u} + \mathbf{v}$ and $\mathbf{u} + \mathbf{v} \in \mathrm{IM}(\mathbf{t})$. Similarly $\mathbf{t}(a\mathbf{x}) = a\mathbf{t}(\mathbf{x}) = a\mathbf{u}$ and $a\mathbf{u} \in \mathrm{IM}(\mathbf{t})$. It follows by Theorem 2.2 of Chapter 2 that IM(**t**) is a subspace of W.

THEOREM 2.2 Let $\mathbf{t}: V \to W$ be a linear transformation, and $\beta = \{\mathbf{x}_1, \mathbf{x}_x, \cdots, \mathbf{x}_n\}$ be a basis for V. Then $\gamma = \{\mathbf{t}(\mathbf{x}_1), \mathbf{t}(\mathbf{x}_2), \cdots, \mathbf{t}(\mathbf{x}_n)\}$ spans IM(**t**).

PROOF: If $\mathbf{w} \in \mathrm{IM}(\mathbf{t})$, then there exists $\mathbf{x} \in V$ such that $\mathbf{t}(\mathbf{x}) = \mathbf{w}$. Let

$$\mathbf{x} = a_1\mathbf{x}_1 + a_2\mathbf{x}_2 + \cdots + a_n\mathbf{x}_n.$$

Since **t** is linear,

$$\mathbf{w} = \mathbf{t}(\mathbf{x}) = a_1\mathbf{t}(\mathbf{x}_1) + a_2\mathbf{t}(\mathbf{x}_2) + \cdots + a_n\mathbf{t}(\mathbf{x}_n),$$

and **w** is expressed as a linear combination of the elements of γ.

It is not necessarily true that γ in Theorem 2.2 is a basis for IM(**t**) since γ is not necessarily linearly independent. For example, if $\mathbf{t}: R^2 \to R^2$ is defined by $\mathbf{t}([a \quad b]^{\mathrm{T}}) = [a \quad 0]^{\mathrm{T}}$ for each $[a \quad b]^{\mathrm{T}} \in R^2$, then $\mathbf{t}([1 \quad 0]^{\mathrm{T}}) = [1 \quad 0]^{\mathrm{T}}$ and $\mathbf{t}([0 \quad 1]^{\mathrm{T}}) = [0 \quad 0]^{\mathrm{T}}$. But $[0 \quad 0]^{\mathrm{T}} = 0[1 \quad 0]^{\mathrm{T}}$; therefore, $\{[1 \quad 0]^{\mathrm{T}}, [0 \quad 0]^{\mathrm{T}}\}$ is not linearly independent and cannot be a basis. It does follow from Theorem 2.2, however, that the dimension of the image space will always be less than or equal to the dimension of the domain.

Next, we examine a property of functions (one-to-one) that describes whether all images are unique in the sense that only one domain element is mapped to each image. As we will see, linear transformations have the particularly interesting (and useful) property that if one image is unique in this sense, all images are unique.

DEFINITION 2.3 (One-to-one) A linear transformation $\mathbf{t}: V \to W$ is said to be one-to-one if $\mathbf{x} \neq \mathbf{y}$ implies $\mathbf{t}(\mathbf{x}) \neq \mathbf{t}(\mathbf{y})$.

An equivalent form of the definition for one-to-one follows from the fact the contrapositive of an implication is equivalent to the statement: The transformation **t** is one-to-one if $\mathbf{t}(\mathbf{x}) = \mathbf{t}(\mathbf{y})$ implies $\mathbf{x} = \mathbf{y}$.

EXAMPLE 2.6 The transformation $\mathbf{t}: M_{n \times n} \to M_{n \times n}$ defined by $\mathbf{t}(\mathbf{A}) = \mathbf{A}^{\mathrm{T}}$ is one-to-one since $\mathbf{A}^{\mathrm{T}} = \mathbf{B}^{\mathrm{T}}$ implies $\mathbf{A} = \mathbf{B}$.

In order to understand how the one-to-one property relates to linear transformations, we must first introduce notation describing the set of all vectors that are mapped to the zero vector.

DEFINITION 2.4 (Kernel or Null Space of a Linear Transformation) The kernel or null space of a linear transformation $\mathbf{t}:V \to W$ is the set of all vectors in V that map into the zero vector of W. In symbols we write: $\text{KER}(\mathbf{t}) = \{\mathbf{x} \in V : \mathbf{t}(\mathbf{x}) = \mathbf{0}\}$.

THEOREM 2.3 If $\mathbf{t}:V \to W$ is a linear transformation, then KER(**t**) is a subspace of V.

PROOF: The zero vector is an element of KER(**t**) since $\mathbf{t}(\mathbf{0}) = \mathbf{0}$. Let **x** and **y** be elements of KER(**t**), then $\mathbf{t}(\mathbf{x}+\mathbf{y}) = \mathbf{t}(\mathbf{x}) + \mathbf{t}(\mathbf{y}) = \mathbf{0} + \mathbf{0} = \mathbf{0}$, and $\mathbf{t}(\alpha\mathbf{x}) = \alpha\mathbf{t}(\mathbf{x}) = \alpha\mathbf{0} = \mathbf{0}$. Thus $\mathbf{x}+\mathbf{y} \in \text{KER}(\mathbf{t})$ and $\alpha\mathbf{x} \in \text{KER}(\mathbf{t})$, and by Theorem 2.2 of Chapter 2, it follows that KER(**t**) is a subspace of V.

EXAMPLE 2.7 Let $\mathbf{t}: M_{2\times2} \to M_{2\times2}$ be defined by

$$\mathbf{t}\left(\begin{bmatrix} a & b \\ c & d \end{bmatrix}\right) = \begin{bmatrix} 0 & a \\ 0 & c+d \end{bmatrix}.$$

To find a basis for the subspace KER(**t**), we consider

$$\mathbf{t}\left(\begin{bmatrix} a & b \\ c & d \end{bmatrix}\right) = \begin{bmatrix} 0 & a \\ 0 & c+d \end{bmatrix} = \begin{bmatrix} 0 & 0 \\ 0 & 0 \end{bmatrix}$$

which yields the equations

$$a = 0$$
$$c + d = 0.$$

It follows that any vector in the kernel of **t** has the form $\begin{bmatrix} 0 & b \\ -d & d \end{bmatrix}$, where b and d are arbitrary. Thus,

$$\begin{bmatrix} 0 & b \\ -d & d \end{bmatrix} = b\begin{bmatrix} 0 & 1 \\ 0 & 0 \end{bmatrix} + d\begin{bmatrix} 0 & 0 \\ -1 & 1 \end{bmatrix},$$

and $\left\{\begin{bmatrix} 0 & 1 \\ 0 & 0 \end{bmatrix}, \begin{bmatrix} 0 & 0 \\ -1 & 1 \end{bmatrix}\right\}$ is a basis for KER(**t**).

The next theorem provides us a means of simplifying the process of determining whether or not a particular linear transformation is one-to-one. Although the definition of one-to-one requires checking every vector in the range space to see if more than one domain element is mapped to it, the following argument shows that for linear transformations we need only check the zero vector in the range space. If the only element mapped to the zero vector in the range space is the zero vector in the domain space, then the linearity of the transformation can be used to show the same sort of uniqueness must also be true for all other elements of IM(**t**). This surprising result begins to demonstrate some of the nice features of linear transformations that distinguish them from the more general classes of functions we found useful in calculus. (For example, the only real number mapped to 0 by the function $f(x) = x^2$ is 0, yet f is not one-to-one since both $f(1) = 1$ and $f(-1) = 1$.)

THEOREM 2.4 If $\mathbf{t}: V \to W$ is a linear transformation, then **t** is one-to-one if and only if KER(**t**) = $\{\mathbf{0}\}$.

PROOF: Let **t** be one-to-one and $\mathbf{x} \in \text{KER}(\mathbf{t})$. By Proposition 1.1, $\mathbf{t}(\mathbf{0}) = \mathbf{0}$; therefore $\mathbf{0} \in$ KER(**t**). Since $\mathbf{x} \in \text{KER}(\mathbf{t})$, $\mathbf{t}(\mathbf{x}) = \mathbf{0}$. Hence, by the definition of one-to-one, $\mathbf{x} = \mathbf{0}$, and it follows that KER(**t**) consists of only the zero vector.

Let $\text{KER}(\mathbf{t}) = \{\mathbf{0}\}$, and choose **x** and **y** in V such that $\mathbf{t}(\mathbf{x}) = \mathbf{t}(\mathbf{y})$. From this and the linearity of **t**, $\mathbf{0} = \mathbf{t}(\mathbf{x}) - \mathbf{t}(\mathbf{y}) = \mathbf{t}(\mathbf{x} - \mathbf{y})$; thus, $\mathbf{x} - \mathbf{y} \in \text{KER}(\mathbf{t})$, and $\mathbf{x} - \mathbf{y} = \mathbf{0}$, since KER(**t**) = $\{\mathbf{0}\}$. It follows that **x** = **y**, and the proof is complete.

EXAMPLE 2.8 The transformation $\mathbf{t}: R^2 \to M_{2\times 2}$ defined by

$$\mathbf{t}\left(\begin{bmatrix} a \\ b \end{bmatrix}\right) = \begin{bmatrix} a & b \\ b & a \end{bmatrix}$$

is one-to-one since any vector $\begin{bmatrix} a & b \end{bmatrix}^{\mathrm{T}}$ mapped to the zero matrix **0** must satisfy $a = b = 0$; hence, $\mathrm{KER}(\mathbf{t}) = \{\mathbf{0}\}$.

DEFINITION 2.5 (Isomorphism, Isomorphic) A linear transformation **t**: $\mathbf{V} \to \mathbf{W}$ is said to be an isomorphism if it is both one-to-one and onto. In this case the two vector spaces **V** and **W** are said to be isomorphic.

EXAMPLE 2.9 The transformation **t** defined in Example 2.1 is an isomorphism since it is onto and the only solution to

$$\mathbf{t}\left(\begin{bmatrix} x_1 \\ x_2 \end{bmatrix}\right) = \begin{bmatrix} x_1 + x_2 \\ x_1 + 2x_2 \end{bmatrix} = \begin{bmatrix} 0 \\ 0 \end{bmatrix}$$

is $x_1 = x_2 = 0$; therefore, KER(**t**) = $\{\mathbf{0}\}$, and **t** is also one-to-one.

We have seen that for a linear transformation $\mathbf{t}: V \to W$, the image of any basis of V spans IM(V) but does not necessarily form a basis for IM(V). The next theorem provides insight into the relationship between the dimension of V and the dimension of IM(V), but first we define two terms which will help in describing this relationship.

DEFINITION 2.6 (Rank of a Linear Transformation) Let $\mathbf{t}: V \to W$ be a linear transformation. The dimension of the subspace IM(**t**) is called the rank of **t** and is noted by RK(**t**).

DEFINITION 2.7 (Nullity of a Linear Transformation) Let $\mathbf{t}: V \to W$ be a linear transformation. The dimension of the subspace KER(**t**) is called the nullity of **t** and is noted as NUL(**t**).

THEOREM 2.5 Let $\mathbf{t}: V \to W$ be a linear transformation, then

$$\mathrm{DIM}(V) = \mathrm{RK}(\mathbf{t}) + \mathrm{NUL}(\mathbf{t}).$$

PROOF: Let DIM(V) = n and let $\eta = \{\mathbf{x}_1, \mathbf{x}_2, \cdots \mathbf{x}_k\}$ be a basis for KER(**t**). Extend this basis for KER(**t**) to a basis for the space V by adding $n-k$ linearly independent vectors $\mu=\{\mathbf{y}_1,\mathbf{y}_2,\cdots,\mathbf{y}_{n-k}\}$ so that $\eta\cup\mu$ is a basis for V. [See Exercise 14 in Section 5 of Chapter 2.]

We claim $\beta=\{\mathbf{t}(\mathbf{y}_1),\mathbf{t}(\mathbf{y}_2),\cdots,\mathbf{t}(\mathbf{y}_{n-k})\}$ is a basis for IM(**t**). To show the set β is linearly independent, first let

$$a_1\mathbf{t}(\mathbf{y}_1)+a_2\mathbf{t}(\mathbf{y}_2)+\cdots+a_{n-k}\mathbf{t}(\mathbf{y}_{n-y})=\mathbf{0}.$$

Since **t** is linear

$$\mathbf{t}(a_1\mathbf{y}_1+a_2\mathbf{y}_2+\cdots+a_{n-k}\mathbf{y}_{n-k})=\mathbf{0},$$

and

$$a_1\mathbf{y}_1+a_2\mathbf{y}_2+\cdots+a_{n-k}\mathbf{y}_{n-k}\in\mathrm{KER}(\mathbf{t}).$$

Therefore, there exist coefficients $b_1,\ldots,b_k$ of $x_1,\ldots,x_k$ such that

$$a_1\mathbf{y}_1+a_2\mathbf{y}_2+\cdots+a_{n-k}\mathbf{y}_{n-k}=b_1\mathbf{x}_1+b_2\mathbf{x}_2+\cdots+b_k\mathbf{x}_k,$$

since η is a basis for KER(**t**). We may now rewrite this equation as

$$a_1\mathbf{y}_1+a_2\mathbf{y}_2+\cdots+a_{n-k}\mathbf{y}_{n-k}-b_1\mathbf{x}_1-b_2\mathbf{x}_2-\cdots-b_k\mathbf{x}_k=\mathbf{0}.$$

But $\eta\cup\mu$ is a basis for V; therefore, $a_1=a_2=\cdots=a_k=b_1=\cdots b_k=0$, which proves β is a linearly independent set.

To show the set β spans IM(**t**), first let $\mathbf{w}\in\mathrm{IM}(\mathbf{t})$. Then there exists some $\mathbf{x}\in V$ such that

$$\begin{aligned}\mathbf{w}=\mathbf{t}(\mathbf{x})&=\mathbf{t}(c_1\mathbf{y}_1+c_2\mathbf{y}_2+\cdots+c_{n-k}\mathbf{y}_{n-k}+c_1'\mathbf{x}_1+c_2'\mathbf{x}_2+\cdots+c_k'\mathbf{x}_k)\\&=c_1\mathbf{t}(\mathbf{y}_1)+c_2\mathbf{t}(\mathbf{y}_1)+\cdots+c_{n-k}\mathbf{t}(\mathbf{y}_{n-k})\end{aligned}$$

where $\mathbf{t}(\mathbf{x}_i)=\mathbf{0}$ for $i=1,2,\cdots,k$.

It follows by the definition of a basis that β is a basis for IM(**t**); hence, RK(**t**) = *n-k*, and, finally,

$$\mathrm{DIM}(V)=n=(n\text{-}k)+k=\mathrm{RK}(\mathbf{t})+\mathrm{NUL}(\mathbf{t}).$$

EXAMPLE 2.10 Let $\mathbf{t}: M_{2\times2}\to M_{2\times3}$ be defined by

$$\mathbf{t}\left(\begin{bmatrix} a & b \\ c & d \end{bmatrix}\right) = \begin{bmatrix} a+d & a+d & a+d \\ b+c & b+c & b+c \end{bmatrix}.$$

A 2×2 matrix is in KER(**t**) if $a = -d$ and $b = -c$; thus,

$$\begin{bmatrix} a & b \\ -b & -a \end{bmatrix} = a\begin{bmatrix} 1 & 0 \\ 0 & -1 \end{bmatrix} + b\begin{bmatrix} 0 & 1 \\ -1 & 0 \end{bmatrix},$$

and it follows that a basis for KER(**t**) is

$$\eta = \left\{\begin{bmatrix} 1 & 0 \\ 0 & -1 \end{bmatrix}, \begin{bmatrix} 0 & 1 \\ -1 & 0 \end{bmatrix}\right\}.$$

The vectors

$$\mathbf{t}\left(\begin{bmatrix} 1 & 0 \\ 0 & 0 \end{bmatrix}\right) = \begin{bmatrix} 1 & 1 & 1 \\ 0 & 0 & 0 \end{bmatrix} \qquad \mathbf{t}\left(\begin{bmatrix} 0 & 1 \\ 0 & 0 \end{bmatrix}\right) = \begin{bmatrix} 0 & 0 & 0 \\ 1 & 1 & 1 \end{bmatrix}$$

$$\mathbf{t}\left(\begin{bmatrix} 0 & 0 \\ 1 & 0 \end{bmatrix}\right) = \begin{bmatrix} 0 & 0 & 0 \\ 1 & 1 & 1 \end{bmatrix} \qquad \mathbf{t}\left(\begin{bmatrix} 0 & 0 \\ 0 & 1 \end{bmatrix}\right) = \begin{bmatrix} 1 & 1 & 1 \\ 0 & 0 & 0 \end{bmatrix}$$

span IM(**t**), but at most only two of them are linearly independent so that a basis for IM(**t**) is

$$\left\{\begin{bmatrix} 1 & 1 & 1 \\ 0 & 0 & 0 \end{bmatrix}, \begin{bmatrix} 0 & 0 & 0 \\ 1 & 1 & 1 \end{bmatrix}\right\}.$$

We observe that $\mathrm{DIM}(M_{2\times 2}) = \mathrm{RK}(\mathbf{t}) + \mathrm{NUL}(\mathbf{t})$.

EXAMPLE 2.11 We define the distance between two vectors in R^n as

$$d(\mathbf{x},\mathbf{y}) = \sqrt{\sum_{i=1}^{n}(x_i - y_i)^2}.$$

Let $\mathbf{t}: R^2 \to R^3$ be defined by

$$\mathbf{t}\left(\begin{bmatrix}1\\0\end{bmatrix}\right)=\begin{bmatrix}1\\2\\3\end{bmatrix} \quad \text{and} \quad \mathbf{t}\left(\begin{bmatrix}1\\1\end{bmatrix}\right)=\begin{bmatrix}2\\4\\2\end{bmatrix}.$$

It is possible to find the vector in IM(**t**) which is the element of best approximation (in the sense of being the closest with the distance measure given) to $\begin{bmatrix}0 & 1 & 2\end{bmatrix}^T$ and the vector in R^2 that maps into this element of best approximation. In order to use the results of Theorem 2.2 to determine if $\begin{bmatrix}0 & 1 & 2\end{bmatrix}^T$ is in IM(**t**), we must first show $\beta=\left\{\begin{bmatrix}1\\0\end{bmatrix},\begin{bmatrix}1\\1\end{bmatrix}\right\}$ is a basis of R^2. We know β is a linearly independent set of vectors since

$$a\begin{bmatrix}1\\0\end{bmatrix}+b\begin{bmatrix}1\\1\end{bmatrix}=\begin{bmatrix}0\\0\end{bmatrix}$$

immediately implies that $b = 0$ and $a + b = 0$, which leads to $a = b = 0$. Further, any vector $\begin{bmatrix}r & s\end{bmatrix}^T$ in R^2 can be written as a linear combination of elements of β since

$$\begin{bmatrix}r\\s\end{bmatrix}=(r-s)\begin{bmatrix}1\\0\end{bmatrix}+s\begin{bmatrix}1\\1\end{bmatrix},$$

and it follows that β is a basis for R^2. By Theorem 2.2 $\begin{bmatrix}0 & 1 & 2\end{bmatrix}^T$ is in IM(**t**) if it is in SPAN$\left(\left\{\begin{bmatrix}1 & 2 & 3\end{bmatrix}^T, \begin{bmatrix}2 & 4 & 2\end{bmatrix}^T\right\}\right)$, but

$$4:\quad a\begin{bmatrix}1\\2\\3\end{bmatrix}+b\begin{bmatrix}2\\4\\2\end{bmatrix}=\begin{bmatrix}0\\1\\2\end{bmatrix}$$

$$5:\quad \begin{bmatrix}a+2b=0\\2a+4b=1\\3a+2b=2\end{bmatrix}.$$

From this over-determined system we seek solutions for *a* and *b*:

$$7: \quad \text{ROW\_REDUCE} \begin{bmatrix} 1 & 2 & 0 \\ 2 & 4 & 1 \\ 3 & 2 & 2 \end{bmatrix}$$

$$8: \quad \begin{bmatrix} 1 & 0 & 0 \\ 0 & 1 & 0 \\ 0 & 0 & 1 \end{bmatrix}$$

The last row of statement #8 indicates there is no solution to this system. Thus, $[0 \quad 1 \quad 2]^{\mathrm{T}} \notin \mathrm{IM}(\mathbf{t})$. To find the element of best approximation, we note that for any vector $\begin{bmatrix} x \\ y \end{bmatrix}$ in R^2 :

$$\mathbf{t}\left(\begin{bmatrix} x \\ y \end{bmatrix}\right) = \mathbf{t}\left((x-y)\begin{bmatrix} 1 \\ 0 \end{bmatrix} + y\begin{bmatrix} 1 \\ 1 \end{bmatrix}\right) = (x-y)\begin{bmatrix} 1 \\ 2 \\ 3 \end{bmatrix} + y\begin{bmatrix} 2 \\ 4 \\ 2 \end{bmatrix} = \begin{bmatrix} x+y \\ 2x+2y \\ 3x-y \end{bmatrix}.$$

The distance between this vector and $[0 \quad 1 \quad 2]^{\mathrm{T}}$ is given by

$$\sqrt{(x+y-0)^2 + (2x+2y-1)^2 + (3x-y-2)^2}.$$

Using *Derive* to minimize the square of the distance:

$$9: \quad (x - y - 0)^2 + (2x + 2y - 1)^2 + (3x - y - 2)^2$$

$$10: \quad \frac{d}{dx}\left((x - y - 0)^2 + (2x + 2y - 1)^2 + (3x - y - 2)^2\right)$$

$$11: \quad \frac{d}{dy}\left((x - y - 0)^2 + (2x + 2y - 1)^2 + (3x - y - 2)^2\right)$$

$$12: \quad 28x - 16$$

$$13: \quad 12y$$

$$14: \quad x = \frac{4}{7}$$

$$15: \quad y = 0$$

where statements #12 and #13 are Simplifications of statements #10 and #11 respectively, and statements #14 and #15 are the result of solVing statements #12 and #13 (the equivalent of setting the expressions in these statements equal to zero and solving for the unknown). Therefore, the vector in IM(**t**) which is closest to $\begin{bmatrix} 0 & 1 & 2 \end{bmatrix}^T$ is

$$\mathbf{t}\begin{bmatrix} 4/7 \\ 0 \end{bmatrix} = \begin{bmatrix} 4/7 \\ 8/7 \\ 12/7 \end{bmatrix}.$$

EXERCISES

1. For the following linear transformations find
   i) A basis for IM(**t**),
   ii) A basis for KER(**t**),
   iii) NUL(**t**),
   iv) RK(**t**),
   v) Determine if the transformation is one-to-one, and
   vi) Determine if the transformation is onto.

   a) $\mathbf{t}: R^3 \to R^3$ defined by
   $$\mathbf{t}\left(\begin{bmatrix} x \\ y \\ z \end{bmatrix}\right) = \begin{bmatrix} x+y \\ 2x+2y \\ 3x+3y \end{bmatrix}$$

   b) $\mathbf{t}: M_{2\times2} \to M_{2\times2}$ defined by
   $$\mathbf{t}\left(\begin{bmatrix} a & b \\ c & d \end{bmatrix}\right) = \begin{bmatrix} a & a+b \\ a+b+c & a+b+c+d \end{bmatrix}$$

   c) $\mathbf{t}: R^2 \to M_{2\times2}$ defined by
   $$\mathbf{t}\left(\begin{bmatrix} a \\ b \end{bmatrix}\right) = \begin{bmatrix} a & 0 \\ a+b & b \end{bmatrix}$$

   d) $\mathbf{t}: M_{3\times3} \to R$ defined by $\mathbf{t}(\mathbf{A}) = \mathrm{TR}(\mathbf{A})$

   e) $\mathbf{t}: R^2 \to R^3$ defined by
   $$\mathbf{t}\left(\begin{bmatrix} a \\ b \end{bmatrix}\right) = \begin{bmatrix} a \\ a \\ b \end{bmatrix}$$

   f) $\mathbf{t}: R^3 \to R^2$ defined by
   $$\mathbf{t}\left(\begin{bmatrix} a \\ b \\ c \end{bmatrix}\right) = \begin{bmatrix} a+b \\ b+c \end{bmatrix}$$

   g) $\mathbf{t}: P^4 \to P^3$ defined by $\mathbf{t}(p(x)) = p'(x)$

2. For the following transformations find
   i) A basis for IM(**t**),
   ii) A basis for KER(**t**),
   iii) NUL(**t**),
   iv) RK(**t**),
   v) Determine if the transformation is one-to-one, and
   vi) Determine if the transformation is onto.

   a) $\mathbf{t}: R^2 \to R^3$ defined by $\mathbf{t}\left(\begin{bmatrix}1\\0\end{bmatrix}\right) = \begin{bmatrix}1\\1\\0\end{bmatrix}$ and $\mathbf{t}\left(\begin{bmatrix}0\\1\end{bmatrix}\right) = \begin{bmatrix}0\\1\\1\end{bmatrix}$

   b) $\mathbf{t}: R^2 \to M_{2\times2}$ defined by $\mathbf{t}\left(\begin{bmatrix}1\\2\end{bmatrix}\right) = \begin{bmatrix}1 & 2\\2 & 1\end{bmatrix}$ and $\mathbf{t}\left(\begin{bmatrix}1\\0\end{bmatrix}\right) = \begin{bmatrix}1 & 0\\0 & 1\end{bmatrix}$

   c) $\mathbf{t}: P^3 \to P^3$ defined by $\mathbf{t}(x^3) = x^3 + 2$, $\mathbf{t}(x^2) = x^2 + x$, $\mathbf{t}(x) = x + 1$, and $\mathbf{t}(1) = x^2 + 1$

   d) $\mathbf{t}: M_{2\times2} \to R^2$ defined by $\mathbf{t}\left(\begin{bmatrix}1 & 0\\0 & 0\end{bmatrix}\right) = \begin{bmatrix}1\\0\end{bmatrix}$, $\mathbf{t}\left(\begin{bmatrix}1 & 1\\0 & 0\end{bmatrix}\right) = \begin{bmatrix}2\\0\end{bmatrix}$, $\mathbf{t}\left(\begin{bmatrix}1 & 1\\1 & 0\end{bmatrix}\right) = \begin{bmatrix}2\\1\end{bmatrix}$, and $\mathbf{t}\left(\begin{bmatrix}1 & 1\\1 & 1\end{bmatrix}\right) = \begin{bmatrix}2\\2\end{bmatrix}$

3. Given $\mathbf{A} = \begin{bmatrix}1 & 2\\3 & 1\end{bmatrix}$ and $\mathbf{B} = \begin{bmatrix}1 & 1\\0 & 2\end{bmatrix}$ extend the set $\{\mathbf{A}, \mathbf{B}\}$ to a basis for $M_{2\times2}$.

4. Let $\mathbf{t}: R^2 \to R^4$ be defined by $\mathbf{t}\begin{bmatrix}a\\b\end{bmatrix} = \begin{bmatrix}a & 2a+b & a+2b & b\end{bmatrix}^{\mathrm{T}}$. Find the element(s) of best approximation in IM(**t**) to $\begin{bmatrix}2 & 3 & 4 & 1\end{bmatrix}^{\mathrm{T}}$. What element(s) in R^2 map into the element(s) of best approximation?

5. For the transformation in Exercise 4, find the element(s) of best approximation in IM(**t**) to $\begin{bmatrix}2 & 5 & 4 & 1\end{bmatrix}^{\mathrm{T}}$.

6. Let $\mathbf{t}: R^2 \to M_{2\times2}$ be defined by $\mathbf{t}\begin{bmatrix}a\\b\end{bmatrix} = \begin{bmatrix}a & 0\\0 & b\end{bmatrix}$. Find the element(s) of best approximation to $\begin{bmatrix}1 & 2\\3 & 4\end{bmatrix}$ where the distance between $\begin{bmatrix}x_{11} & x_{12}\\x_{21} & x_{22}\end{bmatrix}$ and $\begin{bmatrix}y_{11} & y_{12}\\y_{21} & y_{22}\end{bmatrix}$ is defined by $\sqrt{\sum_{j=1}^{2}\sum_{i=1}^{2}\left(x_{ij} - y_{ij}\right)^2}$.

7. Let $\mathbf{t}: P^{n-1} \to P^n$ be defined by $\mathbf{t}(p(x)) = \int_0^x p(t)dt$. Show that $\mathbf{t}$ is not onto, and find a basis for IM($\mathbf{t}$). Show that KER($\mathbf{t}$) = $\{\mathbf{0}\}$, and hence $\mathbf{t}$ is one-to-one.

8. Let $\mathbf{t}: V \to W$ let $\mathbf{x}, \mathbf{y} \in V$ and be linearly independent. Prove or show a counter example that $\{\mathbf{t}(\mathbf{x}), \mathbf{t}(\mathbf{y})\}$ is a linearly independent set.

9. Let $\mathbf{t}: V \to W$ and let DIM(V) be less than DIM(W). Prove or find a counter example for the following statements:

   a) **t** is onto
   b) **t** is not onto
   c) **t** is one-to-one
   d) **t** is not one-to-one.

10 Let $\mathbf{t}: V \to W$ and let DIM(V) be greater than DIM(W). Prove or find a counterexample for the following statements:

   a) **t** is onto
   b) **t** is not onto
   c) **t** is one-to-one
   d) **t** is not one-to-one.

11. Let $\mathbf{t}: R \to R$ be defined by $\mathbf{t}(x) = mx$ where m is a fixed constant. Is **t** linear? What can you say about RK(**t**)? Find a basis for IM(**t**). Find NUL(**t**). Verify that DIM(R) = RK(**t**)+ NUL(**t**).

3. COORDINATES

When we were first learning to graph points in the plane, one of the most important concepts we emphasized was of the order in which the two numbers which determined the point were listed. For example, we agreed that the point (2,3) would be different from the point (3,2) since the first value in the ordered pair would represent the number of units the point would be from the origin in the x direction, and the second number would indicate the number of units the point would be from the origin in the y direction. In our current notation representing the point (2,3) is comparable to representing a linear combination of the standard basis vectors $[1 \quad 0]^T$ and $[0 \quad 1]^T$: $(2 \quad 3)^T = 2[1 \quad 0]^T + 3[0 \quad 1]^T$. It follows that as long as we agree to always indicate the coefficient of $[1 \quad 0]^T$ first and the coefficient of $[0 \quad 1]^T$ second, the notation $(2 \quad 3)^T$ can be used as a form of shorthand to represent this linear combination. In this section we will use the principle of an ordered basis to develop an application which, among other things, will allow us to change the notation by which we represent a vector.

DEFINITION 3.1 (Ordered Basis) Let V be a finite dimensional vector space. A basis β for V is said to be ordered if the order of the elements of β is specified.

We note that an ordering of n elements is a function with domain $\{1,2,\cdots,n\}$.

EXAMPLE 3.1 Let $\sigma=\{1,\ x,\ x^2,\ x^3\}$ be an ordered basis for P^3. If $\beta=\{x,\ 1,\ x^2,\ x^3\}$ is also an ordered basis for P^3, then $\sigma\neq\beta$.

There are several vector spaces that have a particular ordered basis associated with them so frequently that they are called the "standard ordered bases" for the spaces. Included among these spaces are the following:

R^n	$\{\mathbf{e}_1,\ \mathbf{e}_2,\cdots,\ \mathbf{e}_n\}$ where $\mathbf{e}_i$ is the n dimensional column matrix with a 1 in the ith position and zeros elsewhere,
P^n	$\{1,\ x,\ x^2,\cdots,\ x^n\}$,
$M_{m\times n}$	$\{\mathbf{M}_{11},\ \mathbf{M}_{12},\cdots,\ \mathbf{M}_{mn}\}$ where $\mathbf{M}_{ij}$ is the $m\times n$ matrix with a one in the i,j position and zeros elsewhere.

Typically vectors are represented by indicating the coefficients required to represent the vector as a linear combination of vectors in a particular basis for the vector space in question. Thus by writing

$$\mathbf{x}=\begin{bmatrix}-2\\3\\1\end{bmatrix},$$

we mean

$$\mathbf{x} = -2\begin{bmatrix}1\\0\\0\end{bmatrix} + 3\begin{bmatrix}0\\1\\0\end{bmatrix} + 1\begin{bmatrix}0\\0\\1\end{bmatrix}.$$

Once a basis is fixed, each vector in the space can be represented uniquely in terms of coefficients, which, when multiplied by the basis vectors, generates the vector. This concept is formalized in the following definition.

DEFINITION 3.2 (Coordinates of a Vector) The numbers in an ordered set $\{a_1, a_2, \cdots, a_n\}$ are called the coordinates of a vector $\mathbf{x}$ with respect to an ordered basis $\beta = \{\mathbf{x}_1, \mathbf{x}_2, \cdots, \mathbf{x}_n\}$ if $\mathbf{x} = a_1\mathbf{x}_1 + a_2\mathbf{x}_2 + \cdots + a_n\mathbf{x}_n$.

EXAMPLE 3.2 Let $\{\mathbf{M}_{11}, \mathbf{M}_{12}, \mathbf{M}_{21}, \mathbf{M}_{22}\}$ be the standard ordered basis for $M_{2\times 2}$. The coordinates of

$$\mathbf{A} = \begin{bmatrix}2 & 3\\2 & 4\end{bmatrix}$$

are $\{2, 3, 2, 4\}$.

DEFINITION 3.3 (Coordinate Vector) Let V be an n dimensional vector space with ordered basis $\beta = \{\mathbf{x}_1, \mathbf{x}_2, \cdots, \mathbf{x}_n\}$. Let $\mathbf{x} \in V$ with $\mathbf{x} = \sum_{i=1}^{n} a_i\mathbf{x}_i$ then the coordinate vector of $\mathbf{x}$ with respect to β is

$$[\mathbf{x}]_\beta = \begin{pmatrix}a_1\\a_2\\\vdots\\a_n\end{pmatrix}_\beta .$$

We will adopt as standard notation the convention of placing vectors in square brackets and coordinate vectors in parentheses. For example, in R^3 with the standard basis σ, the vector

$$\mathbf{x} = \begin{bmatrix} 1 \\ 3 \\ 4 \end{bmatrix} \text{ can be expressed as } [\mathbf{x}]_\sigma = \begin{pmatrix} 1 \\ 3 \\ 4 \end{pmatrix}_\sigma .$$

EXAMPLE 3.3 If $\beta = \{x^3 + x,\ x^2 + 1,\ x + 1,\ 1\}$ is an ordered basis for P^3, then $p(x) = x^3 + 3x^2 + 2x + 4$ can be represented in terms of a coordinate vector with respect to β. Using *Derive* we write $p(x)$ in terms of the four basis vectors.

```
           3              2                              3       2
1:    a (x  + x) + b (x  + 1) + c (x + 1) + d 1 = x  + 3 x  + 2 x + 4

         3      2                            3      2
2:    a x  + b x  + x (a + c) + b + c + d = x  + 3 x  + 2 x + 4
```

Equating coefficients of powers of x, we next obtain four equations which we solve with the *Derive* commands ROW_REDUCE and Simplify.

$$4: \quad \text{ROW\_REDUCE} \begin{bmatrix} 1 & 0 & 0 & 0 & 1 \\ 0 & 1 & 0 & 0 & 3 \\ 1 & 0 & 1 & 0 & 2 \\ 0 & 1 & 1 & 1 & 4 \end{bmatrix}$$

$$5: \quad \begin{bmatrix} 1 & 0 & 0 & 0 & 1 \\ 0 & 1 & 0 & 0 & 3 \\ 0 & 0 & 1 & 0 & 1 \\ 0 & 0 & 0 & 1 & 0 \end{bmatrix}$$

Finally, we can write

$$[x^3 + 3x^2 + 2x + 4]_\beta = \begin{pmatrix} 1 \\ 3 \\ 1 \\ 0 \end{pmatrix}_\beta$$

EXAMPLE 3.4 Finding a vector from its coordinate representation is an even easier exercise. Given the ordered basis

$$\beta=\left\{\begin{bmatrix}2\\1\\1\end{bmatrix},\begin{bmatrix}1\\2\\1\end{bmatrix},\begin{bmatrix}1\\1\\2\end{bmatrix}\right\}$$

for R^3, then if

$$[\mathbf{x}]_\beta=\begin{pmatrix}1\\2\\-1\end{pmatrix},$$

$$\mathbf{x}=1\begin{bmatrix}2\\1\\1\end{bmatrix}+2\begin{bmatrix}1\\2\\1\end{bmatrix}-1\begin{bmatrix}1\\1\\2\end{bmatrix}=\begin{bmatrix}3\\4\\1\end{bmatrix}.$$

Most of our future applications using a basis will involve ordered sets of vectors; therefore, to simplify our terminology we will drop the use of the adjective "ordered" and assume all of our bases are ordered.

Frequently, we will find the need to change a vector from its coordinate representation with respect to one basis to its coordinate representation with respect to another basis. Most often this is done when we are working in a basis other than the standard basis, and we see that processing the vector in the standard basis would be more convenient. In order to develop a scheme for converting the coordinate representation of a vector from one basis to another, we let V be a vector space with bases $\beta=\{\mathbf{x}_1, \mathbf{x}_2,\cdots, \mathbf{x}_n\}$ and $\gamma=\{\mathbf{y}_1, \mathbf{y}_2,\cdots, \mathbf{y}_n\}$ and $\mathbf{x}$ be a vector represented by

$$\mathbf{x}=b_1\mathbf{x}_1 + b_2\mathbf{x}_2 +\cdots+ b_n\mathbf{x}_n$$

and

$$\mathbf{x}=c_1\mathbf{y}_1 + c_2\mathbf{y}_2 +\cdots+ c_n\mathbf{y}_n.$$

Thus, in terms of coordinate vector notation:

$$[\mathbf{x}]_\beta=\begin{pmatrix}b_1\\b_2\\\vdots\\b_n\end{pmatrix}_\beta \quad\text{and}\quad [\mathbf{x}]_\gamma=\begin{pmatrix}c_1\\c_2\\\vdots\\c_n\end{pmatrix}_\gamma.$$

To derive a relationship between $[\mathbf{x}]_\beta$ and $[\mathbf{x}]_\gamma$, we first write the elements of β as linear combinations of the elements of γ:

$$\mathbf{x}_i = \sum_{j=1}^{n} a_{ji}\mathbf{y}_j \ .$$

[Note that the order ji is chosen for the subscript variables with some knowledge of our final result.] Since

$$\mathbf{x} = b_1\mathbf{x}_1 + b_2\mathbf{x}_2 + \cdots + b_n\mathbf{x}_n,$$

it follows that

$$\begin{aligned}\mathbf{x} = {} & b_1(a_{11}\mathbf{y}_1 + a_{21}\mathbf{y}_2 + \cdots + a_{n1}\mathbf{y}_n) + \\ & b_2(a_{12}\mathbf{y}_1 + a_{22}\mathbf{y}_2 + \cdots + a_{n2}\mathbf{y}_n) + \\ & \cdots + \\ & b_n(a_{1n}\mathbf{y}_1 + a_{2n}\mathbf{y}_2 + \cdots + a_{nn}\mathbf{y}_n) \ .\end{aligned}$$

After regrouping we find

$$\begin{aligned}\mathbf{x} = {} & (b_1a_{11} + b_2a_{12} + \cdots + b_na_{1n})\mathbf{y}_1 + \\ & (b_1a_{21} + b_2a_{22} + \cdots + b_na_{2n})\mathbf{y}_2 + \\ & \cdots + \\ & (b_1a_{n1} + b_2a_{n2} + \cdots + b_na_{nn})\mathbf{y}_n \ .\end{aligned}$$

We now have two representations of the vector $\mathbf{x}$ with respect to the basis γ, but coordinate representations are unique for a given basis; therefore, it is possible to equate corresponding coefficients:

$$\begin{aligned}c_1 &= b_1a_{11} + b_2a_{21} + \cdots + b_na_{n1} \\ c_2 &= b_1a_{12} + b_2a_{22} + \cdots + b_na_{n2} \\ & \cdots \\ c_n &= b_1a_{1n} + b_2a_{2n} + \cdots + b_na_{nn}\end{aligned}$$

These equations give the desired relationship between the coordinates of any vector $\mathbf{x}$ with respect to β and γ. A more compact notation is obtained from the matrix equation:

$$\begin{pmatrix} c_1 \\ c_2 \\ \vdots \\ c_n \end{pmatrix} = \begin{bmatrix} a_{11} & a_{21} & \cdots & a_{n1} \\ a_{12} & a_{22} & \cdots & a_{n2} \\ \vdots & \vdots & \vdots & \vdots \\ a_{1n} & a_{2n} & \cdots & a_{nn} \end{bmatrix} \begin{pmatrix} b_1 \\ b_2 \\ \vdots \\ b_n \end{pmatrix}.$$

Note that the $n \times n$ matrix above is not dependent on $\mathbf{x}$; therefore, it can be used to transform any vector with a coordinate representation with respect to β into its coordinate representation with respect to γ. In the future we will use the notation $\mathbf{P}_\beta^\gamma$ to represent this transformation.

EXAMPLE 3.5 Given two bases for R^3

$$\beta = \left\{ \begin{bmatrix} 2 \\ 1 \\ 1 \end{bmatrix}, \begin{bmatrix} 1 \\ 2 \\ 1 \end{bmatrix}, \begin{bmatrix} 1 \\ 1 \\ 2 \end{bmatrix} \right\} \text{ and } \gamma = \left\{ \begin{bmatrix} 1 \\ 0 \\ 0 \end{bmatrix}, \begin{bmatrix} 1 \\ 1 \\ 0 \end{bmatrix}, \begin{bmatrix} 1 \\ 1 \\ 1 \end{bmatrix} \right\},$$

we can find $\mathbf{P}_\beta^\gamma$ by first writing each vector in β as a linear combination of vectors in γ.

$$\begin{bmatrix} 2 \\ 1 \\ 1 \end{bmatrix} = a_{11} \begin{bmatrix} 1 \\ 0 \\ 0 \end{bmatrix} + a_{21} \begin{bmatrix} 1 \\ 1 \\ 0 \end{bmatrix} + a_{31} \begin{bmatrix} 1 \\ 1 \\ 1 \end{bmatrix}$$

$$\begin{bmatrix} 1 \\ 2 \\ 1 \end{bmatrix} = a_{12} \begin{bmatrix} 1 \\ 0 \\ 0 \end{bmatrix} + a_{22} \begin{bmatrix} 1 \\ 1 \\ 0 \end{bmatrix} + a_{32} \begin{bmatrix} 1 \\ 1 \\ 1 \end{bmatrix}$$

$$\begin{bmatrix} 1 \\ 1 \\ 2 \end{bmatrix} = a_{13} \begin{bmatrix} 1 \\ 0 \\ 0 \end{bmatrix} + a_{23} \begin{bmatrix} 1 \\ 1 \\ 0 \end{bmatrix} + a_{33} \begin{bmatrix} 1 \\ 1 \\ 1 \end{bmatrix}.$$

To solve this system for the a_{ji} terms, it is necessary to solve the three systems of equations in three unknowns represented by the augmented matrices:

$$\begin{bmatrix} 1 & 1 & 1 & 2 \\ 0 & 1 & 1 & 1 \\ 0 & 0 & 1 & 1 \end{bmatrix}, \begin{bmatrix} 1 & 1 & 1 & 1 \\ 0 & 1 & 1 & 2 \\ 0 & 0 & 1 & 1 \end{bmatrix}, \text{ and } \begin{bmatrix} 1 & 1 & 1 & 1 \\ 0 & 1 & 1 & 1 \\ 0 & 0 & 1 & 2 \end{bmatrix}.$$

Since all three systems involve the same coefficients, they may be solved at the same time using *Derive*:

$$2: \quad \text{ROW\_REDUCE} \begin{bmatrix} 1 & 1 & 1 & 2 & 1 & 1 \\ 0 & 1 & 1 & 1 & 2 & 1 \\ 0 & 0 & 1 & 1 & 1 & 2 \end{bmatrix}$$

$$3: \quad \begin{bmatrix} 1 & 0 & 0 & 1 & -1 & 0 \\ 0 & 1 & 0 & 0 & 1 & -1 \\ 0 & 0 & 1 & 1 & 1 & 2 \end{bmatrix}$$

The three rightmost columns of the matrix in statement #3 represent the 3×3 matrix transformation which, when applied to the coordinate representation of a vector with respect to β, results in the coordinate representation of the same vector with respect to γ:

$$\begin{bmatrix} a_{11} & a_{21} & a_{31} \\ a_{12} & a_{22} & a_{32} \\ a_{13} & a_{23} & a_{33} \end{bmatrix} = \begin{bmatrix} 1 & -1 & 0 \\ 0 & 1 & -1 \\ 1 & 1 & 2 \end{bmatrix}.$$

To illustrate the effect of this result, first notice that if $\mathbf{x} = \begin{bmatrix} 4 & 4 & 4 \end{bmatrix}^T$, then

$$[\mathbf{x}]_\beta = \begin{pmatrix} 1 \\ 1 \\ 1 \end{pmatrix}_\beta,$$

and our 3×3 matrix transformation maps this coordinate representation as follows:

$$6: \begin{bmatrix} 1 & -1 & 0 \\ 0 & 1 & -1 \\ 1 & 1 & 2 \end{bmatrix} \cdot \begin{bmatrix} 1 \\ 1 \\ 1 \end{bmatrix}$$

$$7: \begin{bmatrix} 0 \\ 0 \\ 4 \end{bmatrix}$$

where statement #7 is the coordinate representation of $\mathbf{x}$ relative to γ, that is $[\mathbf{x}]_\gamma = \begin{pmatrix} 0 \\ 0 \\ 4 \end{pmatrix}_\gamma$.

The basic scheme used in the above example provides us an algorithm to find $\mathbf{P}_\beta^\gamma$:

1. Construct the augmented matrix $[\gamma \quad \beta]$, which is then
2. reduced to $\left[\mathbf{I} \quad \mathbf{P}_\beta^\gamma\right]$ using elementary row operations.
3. Use the transformation $[\mathbf{x}]_\gamma = \mathbf{P}_\beta^\gamma [\mathbf{x}]_\beta$ for the desired conversion.

EXAMPLE 3.6 If

$$\beta = \{x^3,\ x^3 + x^2,\ x^3 + x^2 + x,\ x^3 + x^2 + x + 1\}$$
$$\gamma = \{x^3 + x^2,\ x^2 + x,\ x + 1,\ 1\}$$

are two bases for P^3, then we can find the matrix representing the coordinate transformation $\mathbf{P}_\beta^\gamma$ by first writing the augmented matrix $[\gamma \quad \beta]$:

$$18: \begin{bmatrix} 1 & 0 & 0 & 0 & 1 & 1 & 1 & 1 \\ 1 & 1 & 0 & 0 & 0 & 1 & 1 & 1 \\ 0 & 1 & 1 & 0 & 0 & 0 & 1 & 1 \\ 0 & 0 & 1 & 1 & 0 & 0 & 0 & 1 \end{bmatrix}$$

which is formed by writing the vectors of γ and β as columns in the order in which they are listed in the bases. Next, the augmented matrix in statement #18 is reduced using elementary row operations:

$$19: \quad \text{ROW\_REDUCE}\begin{bmatrix} 1 & 0 & 0 & 0 & 1 & 1 & 1 & 1 \\ 1 & 1 & 0 & 0 & 0 & 1 & 1 & 1 \\ 0 & 1 & 1 & 0 & 0 & 0 & 1 & 1 \\ 0 & 0 & 1 & 1 & 0 & 0 & 0 & 1 \end{bmatrix}$$

$$20: \quad \begin{bmatrix} 1 & 0 & 0 & 0 & 1 & 1 & 1 & 1 \\ 0 & 1 & 0 & 0 & -1 & 0 & 0 & 0 \\ 0 & 0 & 1 & 0 & 1 & 0 & 1 & 1 \\ 0 & 0 & 0 & 1 & -1 & 0 & -1 & 0 \end{bmatrix}$$

where the four rightmost columns of statement #20 from

$$\mathbf{P}_\beta^\gamma = \begin{bmatrix} 1 & 1 & 1 & 1 \\ -1 & 0 & 0 & 0 \\ 1 & 0 & 0 & 1 \\ -1 & 0 & -1 & 0 \end{bmatrix}.$$

To transform a vector, such as x^3+1, using $\mathbf{P}_\beta^\gamma$, we must first find its coordinate representation with respect to the basis β by writing x^3+1 as a linear combination of the elements of β and Simplifying:

$$\#27: \; x^3 + 1 = a \cdot x^3 + b \cdot (x^3 + x^2) + c \cdot (x^3 + x^2 + x) + d \cdot (x^3 + x^2 + x + 1)$$

$$\#28: \; x^3 + 1 = x^3 \cdot (a + b + c + d) + x^2 \cdot (b + c + d) + x \cdot (c + d) + d$$

Next, we input the augmented matrix representing the system of four equations which results from equating corresponding coefficients on the two sides of the equal sign in statement #28 and use the *Derive* command ROW_REDUCE to obtain a solution for the system:

$$30:\quad \text{ROW\_REDUCE}\begin{bmatrix} 1 & 1 & 1 & 1 & 1 \\ 0 & 1 & 1 & 1 & 0 \\ 0 & 0 & 1 & 1 & 0 \\ 0 & 0 & 0 & 1 & 1 \end{bmatrix}$$

$$31:\quad \begin{bmatrix} 1 & 0 & 0 & 0 & 1 \\ 0 & 1 & 0 & 0 & 0 \\ 0 & 0 & 1 & 0 & -1 \\ 0 & 0 & 0 & 1 & 1 \end{bmatrix}$$

From statement #30 we see the coordinates of x^3+1 with respect to the ordered basis β are 1, 0, -1, and 1; hence,

$$1x^3+0\left(x^3+x^2\right)-1\left(x^3+x^2+x\right)+1\left(x^3+x^2+x+1\right)=x^3+1.$$

To find the coordinates of x^3+1 relative to γ, we compute $\mathbf{P}_\beta^\gamma\left[x^3+1\right]_\beta$:

$$33:\quad \begin{bmatrix} 1 & 1 & 1 & 1 \\ -1 & 0 & 0 & 0 \\ 1 & 0 & 1 & 1 \\ -1 & 0 & -1 & 0 \end{bmatrix}\cdot\begin{bmatrix} 1 \\ 0 \\ -1 \\ 1 \end{bmatrix}$$

$$34:\quad \begin{bmatrix} 1 \\ -1 \\ 1 \\ 0 \end{bmatrix}$$

$$35:\quad x^3+x^2-(x^2+x)+(x+1)$$

$$36:\quad x^3+1$$

Statement #34, which is the result of Simplifying the multiplication indicated in statement #33, yields the coordinates of x^3+1 relative to γ. Statement #35 is the result of entering these coordinates as the coefficients for the elements of the basis γ, and statement #36 is the Simplification of statement #35, confirming that the new coordinates represent the original vector x^3+1.

EXERCISES

1. Let σ be the standard ordered basis for $M_{2\times 2}$. Find the coordinate vector of $\mathbf{A} = \begin{bmatrix} -1 & 3 \\ 0 & 2 \end{bmatrix}$.

2. Let $\beta = \left\{ \begin{bmatrix} 0 & 1 \\ 1 & 1 \end{bmatrix}, \begin{bmatrix} 1 & 0 \\ 1 & 1 \end{bmatrix}, \begin{bmatrix} 1 & 1 \\ 0 & 1 \end{bmatrix}, \begin{bmatrix} 1 & 1 \\ 1 & 0 \end{bmatrix} \right\}$ be an ordered basis for $M_{2\times 2}$. Find the coordinate vector of $\mathbf{A} = \begin{bmatrix} 2 & 1 \\ 3 & -2 \end{bmatrix}$.

3. Let $\beta = \{x^3,\ x^3+x^2,\ x^3+x^2+x,\ x^3+x^2+x+1\}$ be an ordered basis for P^3. Find $[x^3]_\beta$, $[x^2+x]_\beta$, and $[x^2+1]_\beta$.

4. Let β (as defined in Exercise 3) and $\sigma = \{x^3,\ x^2,\ x,\ 1\}$ be two bases for P^3. Find $\mathbf{P}_\beta^\sigma$ and $\mathbf{P}_\sigma^\beta$, and show they are inverses.

5. Let $\beta = \left\{ \begin{bmatrix} 1 \\ 0 \end{bmatrix}, \begin{bmatrix} 1 \\ 1 \end{bmatrix} \right\}$ and $\gamma = \left\{ \begin{bmatrix} 1 \\ 2 \end{bmatrix}, \begin{bmatrix} 2 \\ 1 \end{bmatrix} \right\}$ be two bases for R^2. Find $\mathbf{P}_\beta^\gamma$ and $\mathbf{P}_\gamma^\beta$, and show that these matrices are inverses of each other. Also find $\begin{bmatrix} 4 \\ 5 \end{bmatrix}_\beta$ and $\begin{bmatrix} 4 \\ 5 \end{bmatrix}_\gamma$.

6. Let $\beta = \{\mathbf{e}_1,\ \mathbf{e}_2,\ \mathbf{e}_3\}$ and $\gamma = \{\mathbf{e}_3,\ \mathbf{e}_2,\ \mathbf{e}_1\}$ be two ordered bases for R^3. Find $\mathbf{P}_\beta^\gamma$ and $\mathbf{P}_\gamma^\beta$. Show that these matrices are inverses. Find the coordinate vectors of $\mathbf{x} = \begin{bmatrix} 2 & -1 & 3 \end{bmatrix}^T$ with respect to each of these basis and verify $[\mathbf{x}]_\beta = \mathbf{P}_\gamma^\beta [\mathbf{x}]_\gamma$.

7. Let β and γ be two bases for the finite dimensional vector space V. Show that $\mathbf{P}_\beta^\gamma$ is nonsingular.

8. Let $\beta = \left\{ \begin{bmatrix} 0 & 1 \\ 1 & 1 \end{bmatrix}, \begin{bmatrix} 1 & 0 \\ 1 & 1 \end{bmatrix}, \right.$

$\left\{\begin{bmatrix}1&1\\0&1\end{bmatrix}, \begin{bmatrix}1&1\\1&0\end{bmatrix}\right\}$ and $\gamma =$ $\left\{\begin{bmatrix}1&0\\0&0\end{bmatrix}, \begin{bmatrix}1&1\\0&0\end{bmatrix}, \begin{bmatrix}1&1\\1&0\end{bmatrix}, \begin{bmatrix}1&1\\1&1\end{bmatrix}\right\}$ be two bases for $M_{2\times 2}$. Find $\mathbf{P}_\beta^\gamma$ and $\mathbf{P}_\gamma^\beta$ and the coordinates of $\mathbf{A} = \begin{bmatrix}1&2\\3&4\end{bmatrix}$ with respect to each basis.

4. MATRIX OF A LINEAR TRANSFORMATION

Thus far we have specified linear transformations in three different ways. Some have been defined by determining the image of a general domain vector, others by providing the image of each element of a basis, and still others have been represented in terms of a matrix. In Theorems 3.2 and 3.3 of Chapter 1 we proved that matrix multiplication always satisfies the properties of a linear transformation. The question remains whether every linear transformation can be represented in terms of a matrix. In this section we prove this is the case using the concept of coordinates developed in the previous section.

DEFINITION 4.1 (Matrix of a Linear Transformation) Let V and W be finite dimensional vector spaces with respective bases $\beta=\{\mathbf{x}_1, \mathbf{x}_2, \cdots, \mathbf{x}_n\}$ and $\gamma=\{\mathbf{y}_1, \mathbf{y}_2, \cdots, \mathbf{y}_m\}$. Let $\mathbf{t}: V \to W$ be a linear transformation which is defined on β by

$$\mathbf{t}(\mathbf{x}_i) = \mathbf{w}_i \quad ; i = 1,2,\cdots,n.$$

If

$$\begin{aligned}
\mathbf{t}(\mathbf{x}_1) = \mathbf{w}_1 &= a_{11}\mathbf{y}_1 + a_{21}\mathbf{y}_2 + \cdots + a_{m1}\mathbf{y}_m \\
\mathbf{t}(\mathbf{x}_2) = \mathbf{w}_2 &= a_{12}\mathbf{y}_1 + a_{22}\mathbf{y}_2 + \cdots + a_{m2}\mathbf{y}_m \\
&\cdots \quad \cdots \quad \cdots \\
\mathbf{t}(\mathbf{x}_n) = \mathbf{w}_n &= a_{1n}\mathbf{y}_1 + a_{2n}\mathbf{y}_2 + \cdots + a_{mn}\mathbf{y}_m
\end{aligned}$$

then

$$[\mathbf{t}]_\beta^\gamma = \begin{bmatrix} a_{11} & a_{12} & \cdots & a_{1n} \\ a_{21} & a_{22} & \cdots & a_{2n} \\ \vdots & \vdots & \ddots & \vdots \\ a_{m1} & a_{m2} & \cdots & a_{mn} \end{bmatrix}$$

is the matrix of the linear transformation $\mathbf{t}:V \to W$ with respect to the bases β (for V) and γ (for W).

To see that this matrix represents the transformation $\mathbf{t}$, consider the coordinate vector $\mathbf{x}_i \in \beta$ given by $[\mathbf{x}_i]_\beta = (0 \ldots 1 \ldots 0)_\beta^{\mathrm{T}}$, where each entry is 0, except the ith position, which is 1. The matrix multiplication $[\mathbf{t}]_\beta^\gamma[\mathbf{x}_i]_\beta$ yields $(a_{1i}\ a_{2i} \ldots a_{ni})_\beta^{\mathrm{T}}$, the coordinates of $\mathbf{t}(\mathbf{x}_i) = \mathbf{w}_i$ with respect to γ. But $\mathbf{t}$ is linear; therefore,

$$\begin{aligned} \mathbf{t}(u_1\mathbf{x}_1 + u_2\mathbf{x}_2 + \ldots + u_n\mathbf{x}_n) &= u_1\mathbf{t}(\mathbf{x}_1) + u_2\mathbf{t}(\mathbf{x}_2) + \ldots + u_n\mathbf{t}(\mathbf{x}_n) \\ &= u_1\mathbf{w}_1 + u_2\mathbf{w}_2 + \ldots + u_n\mathbf{w}_n \end{aligned}$$

and a coordinate vector $(u_1\ u_2 \ldots u_n)_\beta^{\mathrm{T}}$ from V is transformed by $\mathbf{t}$ into a coordinate vector from W as follows:

$$\begin{bmatrix} a_{11} & a_{12} & \cdots & a_{1n} \\ a_{21} & a_{22} & \cdots & a_{2n} \\ \vdots & \vdots & \ddots & \vdots \\ a_{m1} & a_{m2} & \cdots & a_{mn} \end{bmatrix} \begin{pmatrix} u_1 \\ u_2 \\ \vdots \\ u_n \end{pmatrix} = \begin{pmatrix} a_{11}u_1 + a_{12}u_2 + \cdots + a_{1n}u_n \\ a_{21}u_1 + a_{22}u_2 + \cdots + a_{2n}u_n \\ \vdots \\ a_{m1}u_1 + a_{m2}u_2 + \cdots + a_{mn}u_n \end{pmatrix}.$$

If a linear transformation $\mathbf{t}:V \to W$, with respective bases β (for V) and γ (for W), is defined but its matrix representation is not known, then the following algorithm can be followed to determine the matrix:

1. Find $\mathbf{t}(\mathbf{x}_i) = \mathbf{w}_i$ for each $\mathbf{x}_i$ in β.
2. Write each $\mathbf{w}_i = a_{1i}\mathbf{y}_1 + a_{2i}\mathbf{y}_2 + \cdots + a_{mi}\mathbf{y}_m$, where $\gamma = \{\mathbf{y}_1, \mathbf{y}_2, \cdots, \mathbf{y}_m\}$.
3. Form the matrix $[\mathbf{t}]_\beta^\gamma$ by letting the coefficients a_{1i} , a_{2i} ,$\cdots$, a_{mi} become the ith column for each i.

EXAMPLE 4.1 Let $\mathbf{t}: R^3 \to R^3$ be a linear transformation defined by

$$\mathbf{t}\begin{bmatrix} x_1 \\ x_2 \\ x_3 \end{bmatrix} = \begin{bmatrix} x_1 + x_2 + x_3 \\ x_1 + x_2 \\ x_1 \end{bmatrix}.$$

Since

$$\mathbf{t}\begin{pmatrix} 1 \\ 0 \\ 0 \end{pmatrix} = \begin{pmatrix} 1 \\ 1 \\ 1 \end{pmatrix} = 1\mathbf{e}_1 + 1\mathbf{e}_2 + 1\mathbf{e}_3, \quad \mathbf{t}\begin{pmatrix} 0 \\ 1 \\ 0 \end{pmatrix} = \begin{pmatrix} 1 \\ 1 \\ 0 \end{pmatrix} = 1\mathbf{e}_1 + 1\mathbf{e}_2, \quad \text{and}$$

$$\mathbf{t}\begin{pmatrix} 0 \\ 0 \\ 1 \end{pmatrix} = \begin{pmatrix} 1 \\ 0 \\ 0 \end{pmatrix} = 1\mathbf{e}_1,$$

(where $\mathbf{e}_1$, $\mathbf{e}_2$, and $\mathbf{e}_3$ are the standard basis vectors in R^3) the matrix representation of $\mathbf{t}$ relative to the standard basis σ is

$$[\mathbf{t}]_\sigma^\sigma = \begin{bmatrix} 1 & 1 & 1 \\ 1 & 1 & 0 \\ 1 & 0 & 0 \end{bmatrix},$$

where the columns of $[\mathbf{t}]_\sigma^\sigma$ are determined by the coefficients of the images of $\mathbf{e}_1$, $\mathbf{e}_2$, and $\mathbf{e}_3$ above.

EXAMPLE 4.2 If $\mathbf{x} = [2 \;\; 3 \;\; -1]^{\mathrm{T}}$, then the coordinate vector for $\mathbf{x}$ in R^3 with the usual basis is $(2 \;\; 3 \;\; -1)^{\mathrm{T}}$, and for $\mathbf{t}$ defined in Example 4.1

$$[\mathbf{t}]_\sigma^\sigma(\mathbf{x}) = \begin{bmatrix} 1 & 1 & 1 \\ 1 & 1 & 0 \\ 1 & 0 & 0 \end{bmatrix}\begin{pmatrix} 2 \\ 3 \\ -1 \end{pmatrix} = \begin{pmatrix} 4 \\ 5 \\ 2 \end{pmatrix}.$$

It is important to keep in mind that the matrix of the linear transformation from a vector space V to a vector space W maps coordinate vectors (with respect to a particular basis for V) to coordinate vectors (with respect to a particular basis for W). Thus, the matrix representation is dependent on the particular bases chosen. In the previous two examples this was masked by the fact that the usual basis was used for R^3, since in this case the vector representation and the coordinate representation both have the same entries. The situation can become more complicated when vector spaces other than R^n are used, especially when the basis is other than the usual one. The following example illustrates.

EXAMPLE 4.3 Define the linear transformation $\mathbf{t}: M_{2\times2} \to P^3$ by

$$\mathbf{t}\left(\begin{bmatrix} a & b \\ c & d \end{bmatrix}\right) = ax^3 + bx^2 + cx + d .$$

a) To find $[\mathbf{t}]_\sigma^\sigma$ we map each coordinate vector from the usual basis for $M_{2\times2}$ to P^3 by means of **t**:

$$\mathbf{t}\left(\begin{bmatrix} 1 & 0 \\ 0 & 0 \end{bmatrix}\right) = 1x^3 + 0x^2 + 0x + 0 \qquad \mathbf{t}\left(\begin{bmatrix} 0 & 1 \\ 0 & 0 \end{bmatrix}\right) = 0x^3 + 1x^2 + 0x + 0$$

$$\mathbf{t}\left(\begin{bmatrix} 0 & 0 \\ 1 & 0 \end{bmatrix}\right) = 0x^3 + 0x^2 + 1x + 0 \qquad \mathbf{t}\left(\begin{bmatrix} 0 & 0 \\ 0 & 1 \end{bmatrix}\right) = 0x^3 + 0x^2 + 0x + 1$$

The matrix representation for **t** can now be written by taking the coefficients of the usual basis vectors x^3, x^3, x, and 1 of P^3 as columns, and the result is $[\mathbf{t}]_\sigma^\sigma = \mathbf{I}_4$.

b) If the basis for either V or W changes, then the matrix representation for **t** also changes. Consider the basis

$$\beta = \left\{ \begin{bmatrix} 0 & 1 \\ 1 & 1 \end{bmatrix}, \begin{bmatrix} 1 & 0 \\ 1 & 1 \end{bmatrix}, \begin{bmatrix} 1 & 1 \\ 0 & 1 \end{bmatrix}, \begin{bmatrix} 1 & 1 \\ 1 & 0 \end{bmatrix} \right\}$$

for $M_{2\times2}$ and the usual basis σ for P^3. To find the matrix $[\mathbf{t}]_\beta^\sigma$, we first map each of the four elements of β to P^3:

$$\mathbf{t}\left(\begin{bmatrix} 0 & 1 \\ 1 & 1 \end{bmatrix}\right) = 0x^3 + 1x^2 + 1x + 1 \qquad \mathbf{t}\left(\begin{bmatrix} 1 & 0 \\ 1 & 1 \end{bmatrix}\right) = 1x^3 + 0x^2 + 1x + 1$$

$$\mathbf{t}\left(\begin{bmatrix} 1 & 1 \\ 0 & 1 \end{bmatrix}\right) = 1x^3 + 1x^2 + 0x + 1 \qquad \mathbf{t}\left(\begin{bmatrix} 1 & 1 \\ 1 & 0 \end{bmatrix}\right) = 1x^3 + 1x^2 + 1x + 0$$

The matrix representation of the transformation **t** is therefore given by

$$[\mathbf{t}]_\beta^\sigma = \begin{bmatrix} 0 & 1 & 1 & 1 \\ 1 & 0 & 1 & 1 \\ 1 & 1 & 0 & 1 \\ 1 & 1 & 1 & 0 \end{bmatrix},$$

where the *j*th column is the coordinate vector of the image of the *j*th basis vector of β.

c) Changing the basis for W also impacts the entries for the matrix representation of the transformation **t**. Consider the basis

$$\gamma = \{x^3 + 1,\ x^2 + x,\ x,\ 1\}$$

for P^3. To find $[\mathbf{t}]_\sigma^\gamma$, we write the image of each element of the usual basis of V as a linear combination of elements of γ. For the first element of γ we obtain:

$$\mathbf{t}\left(\begin{bmatrix} 1 & 0 \\ 0 & 0 \end{bmatrix}\right) = x^3 = a(x^3 + 1) + b(x^2 + x) + cx + d = ax^3 + bx^2 + (b + c)x + (a + d)$$

which, by equating coefficients of like powers of x, generates a system of four equations in the four unknowns a, b, c, and d that can be represented by the augmented matrix:

$$\begin{bmatrix} 1 & 0 & 0 & 0 & 1 \\ 0 & 1 & 0 & 0 & 0 \\ 0 & 1 & 1 & 0 & 0 \\ 1 & 0 & 0 & 1 & 0 \end{bmatrix}.$$

Three other systems of equations are generated by following the same process for the remaining three elements of the usual basis in V. All of these systems have exactly the same coefficient matrix; therefore, the four systems can be solved simultaneously as follows:

```
2:   ROW_REDUCE [ 1 0 0 0 1 0 0 0 ]
                [ 0 1 0 0 0 1 0 0 ]
                [ 0 1 1 0 0 0 1 0 ]
                [ 1 0 0 1 0 0 0 1 ]

3:   [ 1 0 0 0  1  0 0 0 ]
     [ 0 1 0 0  0  1 0 0 ]
     [ 0 0 1 0  0 -1 1 0 ]
     [ 0 0 0 1 -1  0 0 1 ]
```

where $[\mathbf{t}]_\sigma^\gamma$ is the matrix consisting of the four rightmost columns in statement #3.

d) Finally, we seek the matrix representation for **t** when the bases for both V and W are other than the usual bases. The matrix $[\mathbf{t}]_\beta^\gamma$, where β and γ are as defined in parts b) and c) of this example, can be computed by first writing the image of each basis vector from β as a linear combination of vectors from γ. Therefore, following the pattern of part c) above, for the first element of the basis β:

$$\mathbf{t}\left(\begin{bmatrix} 0 & 1 \\ 1 & 1 \end{bmatrix}\right) = 1x^2 + 1x + 1 = a\left(x^3 + 1\right) + b\left(x^2 + x\right) + cx + d$$

$$= ax^3 + bx^2 + (b + c)x + (a + d)$$

By equating corresponding coefficients, this leads to four equations in the unknowns a, b, c, and d (with the same coefficient matrix as in part c)). Three other systems of equations, all with the same coefficient matrix, are then generated by the images of the remaining three basis vectors of β. Therefore, these four systems can be solved simultaneously:

$$\texttt{2:}\quad \texttt{ROW\_REDUCE}\begin{bmatrix} 1 & 0 & 0 & 0 & 0 & 1 & 1 & 1 \\ 0 & 1 & 0 & 0 & 1 & 0 & 1 & 1 \\ 0 & 1 & 1 & 0 & 1 & 1 & 0 & 1 \\ 1 & 0 & 0 & 1 & 1 & 1 & 1 & 0 \end{bmatrix}$$

$$\texttt{3:}\quad \begin{bmatrix} 1 & 0 & 0 & 0 & 0 & 1 & 1 & 1 \\ 0 & 1 & 0 & 0 & 1 & 0 & 1 & 1 \\ 0 & 0 & 1 & 0 & 0 & 1 & -1 & 0 \\ 0 & 0 & 0 & 1 & 1 & 0 & 0 & -1 \end{bmatrix}$$

where the matrix in statement #2 is generated in the same manner as the corresponding matrix in statement #2 of part c) above, and the four rightmost columns of statement #3 constitute $[\mathbf{t}]_\beta^\gamma$.

Although we have found four different matrix representations for the transformation $\mathbf{t}:V\to W$ in Example 4.3, the image of a vector $\mathbf{u}$ from V is the same vector in W regardless of which matrix representation is used. The following example illustrates.

EXAMPLE 4.4 Consider the transformation $\mathbf{t}: M_{2\times 2} \to P^3$ defined in Example 4.3, and let $\mathbf{u} = \begin{bmatrix} 2 & 3 \\ 1 & 0 \end{bmatrix}$.

a) If the usual bases for both V and W are used,

$$[\mathbf{t}]_\sigma^\sigma(\mathbf{u}) = \begin{bmatrix} 1 & 0 & 0 & 0 \\ 0 & 1 & 0 & 0 \\ 0 & 0 & 1 & 0 \\ 0 & 0 & 0 & 1 \end{bmatrix}\begin{pmatrix} 2 \\ 3 \\ 1 \\ 0 \end{pmatrix} = \begin{pmatrix} 2 \\ 3 \\ 1 \\ 0 \end{pmatrix} = 2x^3 + 3x^2 + x.$$

b) If the basis β defined in Example 4.3 b) is used for V and the usual basis is used for W, the vector **u** must be converted to its coordinate representation with respect to β prior to applying the matrix transformation $[\mathbf{t}]_{\beta}^{\sigma}$. Thus, using the coordinate transformation method of Section 3.3:

$$2:\quad \text{ROW\_REDUCE}\begin{bmatrix} 0 & 1 & 1 & 1 & 1 & 0 & 0 & 0 \\ 1 & 0 & 1 & 1 & 0 & 1 & 0 & 0 \\ 1 & 1 & 0 & 1 & 0 & 0 & 1 & 0 \\ 1 & 1 & 1 & 0 & 0 & 0 & 0 & 1 \end{bmatrix}$$

$$3:\quad \begin{bmatrix} 1 & 0 & 0 & 0 & -\frac{2}{3} & \frac{1}{3} & \frac{1}{3} & \frac{1}{3} \\ 0 & 1 & 0 & 0 & \frac{1}{3} & -\frac{2}{3} & \frac{1}{3} & \frac{1}{3} \\ 0 & 0 & 1 & 0 & \frac{1}{3} & \frac{1}{3} & -\frac{2}{3} & \frac{1}{3} \\ 0 & 0 & 0 & 1 & \frac{1}{3} & \frac{1}{3} & \frac{1}{3} & -\frac{2}{3} \end{bmatrix}$$

where the last four columns of statement #3 represent $\mathbf{P}_{\sigma}^{\beta}$. The vector **u** can now be written in its coordinate representation with respect to β:

$$6:\quad \begin{bmatrix} -\frac{2}{3} & \frac{1}{3} & \frac{1}{3} & \frac{1}{3} \\ \frac{1}{3} & -\frac{2}{3} & \frac{1}{3} & \frac{1}{3} \\ \frac{1}{3} & \frac{1}{3} & -\frac{2}{3} & \frac{1}{3} \\ \frac{1}{3} & \frac{1}{3} & \frac{1}{3} & -\frac{2}{3} \end{bmatrix} \cdot \begin{bmatrix} 2 \\ 3 \\ 1 \\ 0 \end{bmatrix}$$

$$7: \begin{bmatrix} 0 \\ -1 \\ 1 \\ 2 \end{bmatrix}$$

or

$$\begin{bmatrix} 2 & 3 \\ 1 & 0 \end{bmatrix} = 0\begin{bmatrix} 0 & 1 \\ 1 & 1 \end{bmatrix} - 1\begin{bmatrix} 1 & 0 \\ 1 & 1 \end{bmatrix} + 1\begin{bmatrix} 1 & 1 \\ 0 & 1 \end{bmatrix} + 2\begin{bmatrix} 1 & 1 \\ 1 & 0 \end{bmatrix}.$$

And $[\mathbf{t}]_{\beta}^{\sigma}(0\ \ {-1}\ \ 1\ \ 2)^{\mathrm{T}}$ can found as follows:

$$6: \begin{bmatrix} 0 & 1 & 1 & 1 \\ 1 & 0 & 1 & 1 \\ 1 & 1 & 0 & 1 \\ 1 & 1 & 1 & 0 \end{bmatrix} \cdot \begin{bmatrix} 0 \\ -1 \\ 1 \\ 2 \end{bmatrix}$$

$$7: \begin{bmatrix} 2 \\ 3 \\ 1 \\ 0 \end{bmatrix}$$

Thus

$$\mathbf{t}\begin{bmatrix} 2 & 3 \\ 1 & 0 \end{bmatrix} = 2x^3 + 3x^2 + x,$$

which corresponds to the image of **u** found above by means of $[\mathbf{t}]_{\sigma}^{\sigma}$.

c) In the case that the usual basis is used for V and the basis γ, defined in Example 4.3 c), is used for W, we multiply **u** by the matrix $[\mathbf{t}]_{\sigma}^{\gamma}$ found in Example 4.3c:

$$3: \begin{bmatrix} 1 & 0 & 0 & 0 \\ 0 & 1 & 0 & 0 \\ 0 & -1 & 1 & 0 \\ -1 & 0 & 0 & 1 \end{bmatrix} \cdot \begin{bmatrix} 2 \\ 3 \\ 1 \\ 0 \end{bmatrix}$$

$$4: \begin{bmatrix} 2 \\ 3 \\ -2 \\ -2 \end{bmatrix}$$

From statement #4 it follows that

$$2(x^3+1)+3(x^2+x)-2(x)-2=2x^3+3x^2+x,$$

corresponding to the result found in parts a) and b) above.

d) In the case where V has the basis β defined in Example 4.3 b), and W has the basis γ defined in Example 4.3 c), then $[\mathbf{t}]_\beta^\gamma$ is as given in Example 4.3 d). Thus, we can use the coordinate vector representation of **u** with respect to β obtained in part b) above and calculate $[\mathbf{t}]_\beta^\gamma(\mathbf{u})$:

$$3: \begin{bmatrix} 0 & 1 & 1 & 1 \\ 1 & 0 & 1 & 1 \\ 0 & 1 & -1 & 0 \\ 1 & 0 & 0 & -1 \end{bmatrix} \cdot \begin{bmatrix} 0 \\ -1 \\ 1 \\ 2 \end{bmatrix}$$

$$4: \begin{bmatrix} 2 \\ 3 \\ -2 \\ -2 \end{bmatrix}$$

which we saw in part c) above is the coordinate vector representation in γ for $2x^3+3x^2+x$, which again corresponds to the result in parts a), b), and c) above.

EXERCISES

1. Find $[\mathbf{t}]_\beta^\gamma$, where $\mathbf{t}: R^3 \to R^3$ is defined by $\mathbf{t}\left(\begin{bmatrix} x_1 \\ x_2 \\ x_3 \end{bmatrix}\right) = \begin{bmatrix} x_3 \\ x_2 + x_3 \\ x_1 + x_2 \end{bmatrix}$ and

   a) $\beta = \{\mathbf{e}_1, \mathbf{e}_2, \mathbf{e}_3\}$ and $\gamma = \{\mathbf{e}_1, \mathbf{e}_2, \mathbf{e}_3\}$

   b) $\beta = \left\{\begin{bmatrix} -1 \\ 1 \\ 1 \end{bmatrix}, \begin{bmatrix} 1 \\ -1 \\ 1 \end{bmatrix}, \begin{bmatrix} 1 \\ 1 \\ -1 \end{bmatrix}\right\}$ and $\gamma = \left\{\begin{bmatrix} 1 \\ 1 \\ 1 \end{bmatrix}, \begin{bmatrix} 1 \\ 3 \\ 0 \end{bmatrix}, \begin{bmatrix} 0 \\ 0 \\ 1 \end{bmatrix}\right\}$

   c) $\beta = \left\{\begin{bmatrix} 0 \\ 0 \\ 1 \end{bmatrix}, \begin{bmatrix} 0 \\ 1 \\ 1 \end{bmatrix}, \begin{bmatrix} 1 \\ 1 \\ 0 \end{bmatrix}\right\} = \gamma$

   d) $\beta = \left\{\begin{bmatrix} 0 \\ 2 \\ 3 \end{bmatrix}, \begin{bmatrix} 1 \\ 1 \\ 1 \end{bmatrix}, \begin{bmatrix} 1 \\ 1 \\ 0 \end{bmatrix}\right\}$ and $\gamma = \{\mathbf{e}_1, \mathbf{e}_2, \mathbf{e}_3\}$

2. Find $[\mathbf{t}]_\beta^\gamma$ where $\mathbf{t}: M_{2\times 2} \to P^3$ is defined by $\mathbf{t}\left(\begin{bmatrix} a & b \\ c & d \end{bmatrix}\right) = ax^3 + (a+b)x^2 + (c+d)x + d$ and

   a) $\beta = \left\{\begin{bmatrix} 1 & 0 \\ 0 & 0 \end{bmatrix}, \begin{bmatrix} 0 & 1 \\ 0 & 0 \end{bmatrix}, \begin{bmatrix} 0 & 0 \\ 1 & 0 \end{bmatrix}, \begin{bmatrix} 0 & 0 \\ 0 & 1 \end{bmatrix}\right\}$ and $\gamma = \{x^3, x^2, x, 1\}$

   b) $\beta = \left\{\begin{bmatrix} 0 & 1 \\ 1 & 1 \end{bmatrix}, \begin{bmatrix} 1 & 0 \\ 1 & 1 \end{bmatrix}, \begin{bmatrix} 1 & 1 \\ 0 & 1 \end{bmatrix}, \begin{bmatrix} 1 & 1 \\ 1 & 0 \end{bmatrix}\right\}$ and $\gamma = \{x^3 + 1, x^2 + 1, x + 1, 1\}$

   c) $\beta = \left\{\begin{bmatrix} 1 & 0 \\ 0 & 1 \end{bmatrix}, \begin{bmatrix} 0 & 1 \\ 1 & 0 \end{bmatrix}, \begin{bmatrix} 1 & 0 \\ 1 & 0 \end{bmatrix}, \begin{bmatrix} 0 & 1 \\ 0 & 1 \end{bmatrix}\right\}$ and $\gamma = \{x^3 + x^2, x^2 + x, x + 1, x^3 + x\}$

   d) $\beta = \left\{\begin{bmatrix} 3 & 2 \\ 1 & 0 \end{bmatrix}, \begin{bmatrix} 0 & 3 \\ 2 & 1 \end{bmatrix}, \begin{bmatrix} 1 & 0 \\ 3 & 2 \end{bmatrix}, \begin{bmatrix} 1 & 2 \\ 0 & 3 \end{bmatrix}\right\}$ and $\gamma = \{x^3, x^3 + x^2, x^3 + x^2 + x, x^3 + x^2 + x + 1\}$

3. Let $\mathbf{t}: R^3 \to R^2$ be defined by $\mathbf{t}\left(\begin{bmatrix} a \\ b \\ c \end{bmatrix}\right) = \begin{bmatrix} a+b+c \\ a+b+c \end{bmatrix}$. Find the matrix of $\mathbf{t}$ with respect to

the bases

$$\beta = \left\{ \begin{bmatrix} 0 \\ 1 \\ 1 \end{bmatrix}, \begin{bmatrix} 1 \\ 0 \\ 1 \end{bmatrix}, \begin{bmatrix} 1 \\ 1 \\ 1 \end{bmatrix} \right\} \text{ and}$$

$$\gamma = \left\{ \begin{bmatrix} 2 \\ 1 \end{bmatrix}, \begin{bmatrix} 1 \\ 2 \end{bmatrix} \right\}$$

4. Let $\mathbf{t}: R^3 \to R^1$ be defined by
$$\mathbf{t}\left(\begin{bmatrix} x_1 \\ x_2 \\ x_3 \end{bmatrix} \right) = \begin{bmatrix} x_1 & x_2 & x_3 \end{bmatrix} \begin{bmatrix} 1 \\ 2 \\ 3 \end{bmatrix}.$$
Find the matrix of **t** relative to the standard bases for R^3 and R^1.

5. Let $\mathbf{t}: R^2 \to R^4$ be defined by
$$\mathbf{t}\left(\begin{bmatrix} x_1 \\ x_2 \end{bmatrix} \right) = \begin{bmatrix} x_1 \\ x_1 + x_2 \\ x_2 \\ x_1 - x_2 \end{bmatrix}.$$
Find the matrix of **t** relative to the bases $\beta = \left\{ \begin{bmatrix} 2 \\ 1 \end{bmatrix}, \begin{bmatrix} 1 \\ 2 \end{bmatrix} \right\}$ and $\gamma =$
$$\left\{ \begin{bmatrix} 1 \\ 1 \\ 0 \\ 0 \end{bmatrix}, \begin{bmatrix} 1 \\ 1 \\ 1 \\ 0 \end{bmatrix}, \begin{bmatrix} 1 \\ 1 \\ 1 \\ 1 \end{bmatrix}, \begin{bmatrix} 0 \\ 1 \\ 1 \\ 1 \end{bmatrix} \right\}.$$

6. Let $\mathbf{t}: P^4 \to P^3$ be defined by $\mathbf{t}(p(x)) = \dfrac{d}{dx} p(x)$. Find the matrix of **t** with respect to the standard bases for P^4 and P^3.

7. Let $\mathbf{t}: M_{2\times2} \to M_{2\times2}$ be defined by $\mathbf{t}(\mathbf{A}) = \mathbf{A}^{\mathrm{T}}$. Use the standard basis for $M_{2\times2}$ and find the matrix of **t**.

8. Let $\mathbf{t}: M_{3\times3} \to R$ be defined by $\mathbf{t}(\mathbf{A}) = \mathrm{TR}(\mathbf{A})$. Find the matrix of **t** with respect to the standard basis.

9. Let the matrix of $\mathbf{t}: R^3 \to R^3$ with respect to the standard basis be $\mathbf{A} = \begin{bmatrix} 2 & 0 & 1 \\ 3 & 2 & 1 \\ 1 & -1 & 1 \end{bmatrix}$. Find an expression for the linear transformation in the form of $\mathbf{t}(\mathbf{x})$.

10. Let the matrix of $\mathbf{t}: R^3 \to R^3$ with respect to the basis
$$\beta = \left\{ \begin{bmatrix} 0 \\ 1 \\ 1 \end{bmatrix}, \begin{bmatrix} 1 \\ 0 \\ 1 \end{bmatrix}, \begin{bmatrix} 1 \\ 1 \\ 0 \end{bmatrix} \right\} \text{ be}$$
$$\mathbf{A} = \begin{bmatrix} 1 & 1 & 0 \\ 1 & 0 & 1 \\ 0 & 1 & 1 \end{bmatrix}.$$
Find an expression for $\mathbf{t}(\mathbf{x})$.

11. Let the matrix of $\mathbf{t}: P^3 \to P^3$ with respect to the basis $\{x^3 + 1,\ x^3 + x,\ x^3 + x^2,\ 2x^3\}$ be

$\mathbf{A} = \begin{bmatrix} 1 & 1 & 0 & 0 \\ 0 & 2 & 1 & 2 \\ 0 & 0 & 1 & 0 \\ 1 & -1/2 & 0 & 1 \end{bmatrix}$. Find an expression for $\mathbf{t}(p(x))$.

12. Let $\mathbf{t}: R^2 \to R^3$ be defined by $\mathbf{t}\left(\begin{bmatrix} x_1 \\ x_2 \end{bmatrix}\right) = \begin{bmatrix} x_1 + x_2 \\ x_1 - x_2 \\ 0 \end{bmatrix}$. Find the matrix of $\mathbf{t}$ with respect to the bases $\beta = \left\{\begin{bmatrix} 1 \\ 1 \end{bmatrix}, \begin{bmatrix} 1 \\ 2 \end{bmatrix}\right\}$ and $\gamma = \left\{\begin{bmatrix} 1 \\ 0 \\ 1 \end{bmatrix}, \begin{bmatrix} 1 \\ 1 \\ 0 \end{bmatrix}, \begin{bmatrix} 1 \\ 1 \\ 1 \end{bmatrix}\right\}$.

13. Let the bases be as in Example 4.3 but let $\mathbf{t}: M_{2\times 2} \to P^3$ be defined by $\mathbf{t}\left(\begin{bmatrix} a & b \\ c & d \end{bmatrix}\right) = (a+d)x^3 + (b+c)x^2 + (a+b)x + (c+d)1$. Find the matrix $[\mathbf{t}]_\beta^\gamma$.

14. Let $\mathbf{t}: R^3 \to R^3$ be defined by $\mathbf{t}\begin{bmatrix} x_1 \\ x_2 \\ x_3 \end{bmatrix} = \begin{bmatrix} x_2 + x_3 \\ x_1 + 2x_2 \\ x_2 + 2x_3 \end{bmatrix}$, and let $\beta = \left\{\begin{bmatrix} 0 \\ 1 \\ 1 \end{bmatrix}, \begin{bmatrix} 1 \\ 0 \\ 1 \end{bmatrix}, \begin{bmatrix} 1 \\ 1 \\ 0 \end{bmatrix}\right\}$ and $\gamma = \left\{\begin{bmatrix} 2 \\ 1 \\ 1 \end{bmatrix}, \begin{bmatrix} 1 \\ 2 \\ 1 \end{bmatrix}, \begin{bmatrix} 1 \\ 1 \\ 2 \end{bmatrix}\right\}$ be two bases for R^3. Find $[\mathbf{t}]_\beta^\gamma$.

5. COMPOSITION OF LINEAR TRANSFORMATIONS

Linear transformations from one vector space to another can be combined in much the same manner as any other function if the domain and range spaces are specified appropriately. The sum and difference of two linear transformations always form linear transformations (the proof is left as an exercise), but the product of two linear transformations does not necessarily even exist since the product of vectors may not be defined in a particular vector space. The concept of the composition of linear transformations is especially important. In particular, if U, V, and W are vector spaces and $\mathbf{t}: U \to V$ and $\mathbf{s}: V \to W$ are linear transformations, then the composition function $\mathbf{r}: U \to W$ exists. In this section we show $\mathbf{r}$ is also a linear transformation and establish properties associated with it.

DEFINITION 5.1 (Composition of Linear Transformations) Let U, V, and W be vector spaces, and let $\mathbf{t}_1 : U \to V$ and $\mathbf{t}_2 : V \to W$ be linear transformations. The composition of $\mathbf{t}_2$ with $\mathbf{t}_1$ is the function $\mathbf{t}_2\mathbf{t}_1 : U \to W$ defined by $\mathbf{t}_2\mathbf{t}_1(\mathbf{x}) = \mathbf{t}_2(\mathbf{t}_1(\mathbf{x}))$ for all $\mathbf{x} \in U$.

THEOREM 5.1 Let U, V, and W be vector spaces and let $\mathbf{t}_1 : U \to V$ and $\mathbf{t}_2 : V \to W$ be linear transformations. Then $\mathbf{t}_2\mathbf{t}_1 : U \to W$ is a linear transformation.

PROOF: The function $\mathbf{t}_2\mathbf{t}_1$ is defined in terms of $\mathbf{t}_1$ and $\mathbf{t}_2$, both of which are linear and therefore preserve both addition and scalar multiplication. It follows that

$$\begin{aligned}\mathbf{t}_2\mathbf{t}_1(\mathbf{x}+\mathbf{y}) &= \mathbf{t}_2(\mathbf{t}_1(\mathbf{x}+\mathbf{y})) = \mathbf{t}_2(\mathbf{t}_1(\mathbf{x})+\mathbf{t}_1(\mathbf{y})) = \mathbf{t}_2(\mathbf{t}_1(\mathbf{x}))+\mathbf{t}_2(\mathbf{t}_1(\mathbf{y}))\\ &= \mathbf{t}_2\mathbf{t}_1(\mathbf{x})+\mathbf{t}_2\mathbf{t}_1(\mathbf{y})\end{aligned}$$

and

$$\begin{aligned}\mathbf{t}_2\mathbf{t}_1(a\mathbf{x}) &= \mathbf{t}_2(\mathbf{t}_1(a\mathbf{x})) = \mathbf{t}_2(a\mathbf{t}_1(\mathbf{x})) = a\mathbf{t}_2(\mathbf{t}_1(\mathbf{x}))\\ &= a\mathbf{t}_2\mathbf{t}_1(\mathbf{x})\end{aligned}$$

hence, $\mathbf{t}_2\mathbf{t}_1$ is linear.

In the previous section we showed that every linear transformation can be represented by a matrix. The following theorem establishes that multiplication of the matrices representing two linear transformations produces the matrix of the composition of the two functions.

THEOREM 5.2 Let U, V, and W be vector spaces and $\mathbf{t}_1 : U \to V$ and $\mathbf{t}_2 : V \to W$ be linear transformations. If α, β, and γ are bases for U, V, and W respectively, then the matrix representing the transformation $\mathbf{t}_2\mathbf{t}_1$ is the matrix product $[\mathbf{t}_2]_\beta^\gamma[\mathbf{t}_1]_\alpha^\beta$.

PROOF: Let $\alpha = \{\mathbf{x}_1, \mathbf{x}_2, \cdots, \mathbf{x}_n\}$, $\beta = \{\mathbf{y}_1, \mathbf{y}_2, \cdots, \mathbf{y}_m\}$, and $\gamma = \{\mathbf{z}_1, \mathbf{z}_2, \cdots, \mathbf{z}_p\}$ be bases of U, V, and W respectively. Let

$$\mathbf{t}_1(\mathbf{x}_i) = \sum_{k=1}^{m} a_{ki}\mathbf{y}_k$$

for $i = 1,2,\ldots,n$; and

$$\mathbf{t}_2(\mathbf{y}_k) = \sum_{j=1}^{p} b_{jk} z_j$$

for $k = 1,2,\ldots,m$. By the algorithm in Section 3.4, $[\mathbf{t}_1]_\alpha^\beta = (a_{ki})$ and $[\mathbf{t}_2]_\beta^\gamma = (b_{jk})$. Using the linearity of $\mathbf{t}_1$ and $\mathbf{t}_2$ and interchanging the order of summation (which is possible since all the sums are finite), we have

$$\begin{aligned}\mathbf{t}_2\mathbf{t}_1(\mathbf{x}_i) = \mathbf{t}_2(\mathbf{t}_1(\mathbf{x}_i)) &= \mathbf{t}_2\left(\sum_{k=1}^{m} a_{ki}\mathbf{y}_k\right) = \sum_{k=1}^{m} a_{ki}\mathbf{t}_2(\mathbf{y}_k)\\ &= \sum_{k=1}^{m} a_{ki}\left(\sum_{j=1}^{p} b_{jk}\mathbf{z}_j\right) = \sum_{j=1}^{p}\left(\sum_{k=1}^{m} b_{jk}a_{ki}\right)\mathbf{z}_j\end{aligned}$$

Therefore, the coordinates of $\mathbf{t}_2\mathbf{t}_1(\mathbf{x}_i)$ are of the form $\sum_{k=1}^{m} b_{jk}a_{ki}$, $j = 1, 2,\ldots, m$; and they form the ith column of $[\mathbf{t}_2\mathbf{t}_1]_\alpha^\gamma$. But these same sums are also the result of multiplying the jth row of $[\mathbf{t}_2]_\beta^\gamma$ by the ith column of $[\mathbf{t}_1]_\alpha^\beta$ for $j = 1, 2,\ldots, m$. Thus the ith column of $[\mathbf{t}_2]_\beta^\gamma[\mathbf{t}_1]_\alpha^\beta$ equals the ith column of $[\mathbf{t}_2\mathbf{t}_1]_\alpha^\gamma$ for $i = 1, 2,\ldots, n$; and $[\mathbf{t}_2]_\beta^\gamma[\mathbf{t}_1]_\alpha^\beta = [\mathbf{t}_2\mathbf{t}_1]_\alpha^\gamma$.

EXAMPLE 5.1 Let U, V, and W be vector spaces with bases

$$\alpha = \left\{\begin{bmatrix}1\\1\\1\end{bmatrix}, \begin{bmatrix}0\\1\\1\end{bmatrix}, \begin{bmatrix}0\\0\\1\end{bmatrix}\right\}, \quad \beta = \left\{\begin{bmatrix}2\\1\end{bmatrix}, \begin{bmatrix}1\\2\end{bmatrix}\right\}, \quad \text{and} \quad \gamma = \left\{\begin{bmatrix}0\\1\\1\end{bmatrix}, \begin{bmatrix}1\\0\\1\end{bmatrix}, \begin{bmatrix}1\\1\\0\end{bmatrix}\right\}$$

respectively. Also, let $\mathbf{t}_1 : U \to V$ and $\mathbf{t}_2 : V \to W$ be defined by

$$\mathbf{t}_1\begin{bmatrix}a\\b\\c\end{bmatrix} = \begin{bmatrix}a+b\\a+c\end{bmatrix}, \quad \text{and} \quad \mathbf{t}_2\begin{bmatrix}p\\q\end{bmatrix} = \begin{bmatrix}p\\q\\p+q\end{bmatrix}$$

To find the matrix representing $\mathbf{t}_1$, we use *Derive* to perform row reductions on the matrix

$$\left[\begin{bmatrix}2\\1\end{bmatrix}\ \begin{bmatrix}1\\2\end{bmatrix}\ \mathbf{t}_1\begin{bmatrix}1\\1\\1\end{bmatrix}\ \mathbf{t}_1\begin{bmatrix}0\\1\\1\end{bmatrix}\ \mathbf{t}_1\begin{bmatrix}0\\0\\1\end{bmatrix}\right]$$

as follows:

$$2:\quad \text{ROW\_REDUCE}\begin{bmatrix}2 & 1 & 2 & 1 & 0\\ 1 & 2 & 2 & 1 & 1\end{bmatrix}$$

$$3:\quad \begin{bmatrix}1 & 0 & \frac{2}{3} & \frac{1}{3} & -\frac{1}{3}\\ 0 & 1 & \frac{2}{3} & \frac{1}{3} & \frac{2}{3}\end{bmatrix}$$

The matrix $[\mathbf{t}_1]_\alpha^\beta$ consists of the three rightmost columns of statement #3. Similarly, the matrix representing $\mathbf{t}_2$ can be obtained by using *Derive* to perform row reductions on the matrix

$$\left[\begin{bmatrix}0\\1\\1\end{bmatrix}\ \begin{bmatrix}1\\0\\1\end{bmatrix}\ \begin{bmatrix}1\\1\\0\end{bmatrix}\ \mathbf{t}_2\begin{bmatrix}2\\1\end{bmatrix}\ \mathbf{t}_2\begin{bmatrix}1\\2\end{bmatrix}\right]$$

as follows:

$$5:\quad \text{ROW\_REDUCE}\begin{bmatrix}0 & 1 & 1 & 2 & 1\\ 1 & 0 & 1 & 1 & 2\\ 1 & 1 & 0 & 3 & 3\end{bmatrix}$$

$$6:\quad \begin{bmatrix}1 & 0 & 0 & 1 & 2\\ 0 & 1 & 0 & 2 & 1\\ 0 & 0 & 1 & 0 & 0\end{bmatrix}$$

The matrix $\left[\mathbf{t}_2\right]_\beta^\gamma$ consists of the two rightmost columns of statement #6. The composition $\mathbf{t}_2\mathbf{t}_1$ maps U to W, and the matrix representing the composition can be computed by reducing

$$\left[\begin{bmatrix}0\\1\\1\end{bmatrix}\ \begin{bmatrix}1\\0\\1\end{bmatrix}\ \begin{bmatrix}1\\1\\0\end{bmatrix}\ \mathbf{t}_2\mathbf{t}_1\left(\begin{bmatrix}1\\1\\1\end{bmatrix}\right)\ \mathbf{t}_2\mathbf{t}_1\left(\begin{bmatrix}0\\1\\1\end{bmatrix}\right)\ \mathbf{t}_2\mathbf{t}_1\left(\begin{bmatrix}0\\0\\1\end{bmatrix}\right)\right]$$

where the last three columns are computed according to the rule:

$$\mathbf{t}_2\mathbf{t}_1\left(\begin{bmatrix}a\\b\\c\end{bmatrix}\right)=\mathbf{t}_2\left(\mathbf{t}_1\begin{bmatrix}a\\b\\c\end{bmatrix}\right)=\mathbf{t}_2\left(\begin{bmatrix}a+b\\a+c\end{bmatrix}\right)=\begin{bmatrix}a+b\\a+c\\2a+b+c\end{bmatrix}.$$

Using *Derive* we reduce the matrix to echelon form:

$$8:\quad \text{ROW\_REDUCE}\begin{bmatrix}0&1&1&2&1&0\\1&0&1&2&1&1\\1&1&0&4&2&1\end{bmatrix}$$

$$9:\quad \begin{bmatrix}1&0&0&2&1&1\\0&1&0&2&1&0\\0&0&1&0&0&0\end{bmatrix}$$

$$8:\quad \text{ROW\_REDUCE}\begin{bmatrix}0&1&1&2&1&0\\1&0&1&2&1&1\\1&1&0&4&2&1\end{bmatrix}$$

$$9:\quad \begin{bmatrix}1&0&0&2&1&1\\0&1&0&2&1&0\\0&0&1&0&0&0\end{bmatrix}$$

where $[\mathbf{t}_2\mathbf{t}_1]_\alpha^\gamma$ consists of the three rightmost columns of statement #9. But we also note that

$$12: \begin{bmatrix} 1 & 2 \\ 2 & 1 \\ 0 & 0 \end{bmatrix} \cdot \begin{bmatrix} \frac{2}{3} & \frac{1}{3} & -\frac{1}{3} \\ \frac{2}{3} & \frac{1}{3} & \frac{2}{3} \end{bmatrix}$$

$$13: \begin{bmatrix} 2 & 1 & 1 \\ 2 & 1 & 0 \\ 0 & 0 & 0 \end{bmatrix}$$

Thus $[\mathbf{t}_2\mathbf{t}_1]_\alpha^\gamma = [\mathbf{t}_2]_\beta^\gamma[\mathbf{t}_1]_\alpha^\beta$.

Given a linear transformation which is one-to-one and onto, an inverse function can be defined in a very natural way. The sequence of theorems following the next definition show that special conditions exist when working with linear transformations which allow us to weaken the conditions required to not only ensure the existence of the inverse function, but also guarantee its linearity as well.

DEFINITION 5.2 (Inverse of a Linear Transformation, Invertible) Let $\mathbf{t}: U \to V$ be a linear transformation that is both one-to-one and onto. If $\mathbf{t}$ is defined by the rule $\mathbf{t}(\mathbf{x}) = \mathbf{y}$, then $\mathbf{t}^{-1}: V \to U$ is defined by the rule $\mathbf{t}^{-1}(\mathbf{y}) = \mathbf{x}$. When the inverse function $\mathbf{t}^{-1}$ exists, then $\mathbf{t}$ is said to be invertible.

THEOREM 5.3 If U and V are vector spaces of equal dimension and $\mathbf{t}: U \to V$ is linear, then $\mathbf{t}$ is one-to-one if and only if it is onto.

PROOF: Recall from Theorem 2.5 that $\text{DIM}(U) = \text{RK}(\mathbf{t}) + \text{NUL}(\mathbf{t})$. First, we let $\mathbf{t}$ be one-to-one, which by Theorem 2.4 means that $\text{KER}(\mathbf{t}) = \{\mathbf{0}\}$, and $\text{NUL}(\mathbf{t}) = 0$. Thus $\text{RK}(\mathbf{t}) = \text{DIM}(U) = \text{DIM}(V)$, and $\text{IM}(\mathbf{t})$ is a subspace of V with the same dimension as V; therefore, $\text{IM}(\mathbf{t})$ must be equal to V, and it follows that $\mathbf{t}$ is onto.

Next, we let **t** be onto. This implies $\text{RK}(\mathbf{t}) = \text{DIM}(V)$, but U and V have equal dimension; therefore, $\text{DIM}(U) = \text{RK}(\mathbf{t})$, and $\text{NUL}(\mathbf{t}) = 0$. Hence, KER(**t**) = {**0**}, and **t** is one-to-one by Theorem 2.4.

We combine these ideas into the following theorem.

THEOREM 5.4 Let U and V be vector spaces of equal dimension, and $\mathbf{t}: U \to V$ be a linear transformation. Then the following three conditions are equivalent:

a.) $\mathbf{t}^{-1}$ exists.
b.) **t** is one-to-one.
c.) **t** is onto.

PROOF: The proof is left as an exercise.

THEOREM 5.5 If $\mathbf{t}: U \to V$ is a linear transformation such that $\mathbf{t}^{-1}$ exists, then $\mathbf{t}^{-1}: V \to U$ is a linear transformation.

PROOF: Let **u** and **v** be elements of V. Since **t** is onto, there exist elements **x** and **y** of U such that $\mathbf{t}(\mathbf{x}) = \mathbf{u}$ and $\mathbf{t}(\mathbf{y}) = \mathbf{v}$; and since **t** is one-to-one $\mathbf{t}^{-1}\mathbf{t}(\mathbf{z}) = \mathbf{z}$ for every element **z** in U. Thus

$$\mathbf{t}^{-1}(\mathbf{u}+\mathbf{v}) = \mathbf{t}^{-1}(\mathbf{t}(\mathbf{x})+\mathbf{t}(\mathbf{y})) = \mathbf{t}^{-1}\mathbf{t}(\mathbf{x}+\mathbf{y}) = \mathbf{x}+\mathbf{y} = \mathbf{t}^{-1}(\mathbf{u})+\mathbf{t}^{-1}(\mathbf{v})$$

and

$$\mathbf{t}^{-1}(\alpha\mathbf{u}) = \mathbf{t}^{-1}(\alpha\mathbf{t}(\mathbf{x})) = \mathbf{t}^{-1}\mathbf{t}(\alpha\mathbf{x}) = \alpha\mathbf{x} = \alpha\mathbf{t}^{-1}(\mathbf{u}),$$

and $\mathbf{t}^{-1}$ is linear.

EXAMPLE 5.2 Given $\mathbf{t}: R^2 \to R^2$ defined by

$$\mathbf{t}\left(\begin{bmatrix} a \\ b \end{bmatrix}\right) = \begin{bmatrix} a+b \\ 2a+b \end{bmatrix},$$

we can find an expression for $\mathbf{t}^{-1}$ by first considering the images of basis vectors in R^2:

$$\mathbf{t}\left(\begin{bmatrix}1\\0\end{bmatrix}\right)=\begin{bmatrix}1\\2\end{bmatrix} \text{ and } \mathbf{t}\left(\begin{bmatrix}0\\1\end{bmatrix}\right)=\begin{bmatrix}1\\1\end{bmatrix}.$$

Thus,

$$\mathbf{t}^{-1}\left(\begin{bmatrix}1\\2\end{bmatrix}\right)=\begin{bmatrix}1\\0\end{bmatrix} \text{ and } \mathbf{t}^{-1}\left(\begin{bmatrix}1\\1\end{bmatrix}\right)=\begin{bmatrix}0\\1\end{bmatrix}.$$

Next, from the matrix equation

$$\begin{bmatrix}p\\q\end{bmatrix}=a\begin{bmatrix}1\\2\end{bmatrix}+b\begin{bmatrix}1\\1\end{bmatrix},$$

we can solve for a and b using *Derive*

```
#2:  ROW_REDUCE [ 1  1  p ]
                [ 2  1  q ]

#3:  [ 1  0   q - p     ]
     [ 0  1   2·p - q   ]
```

which leads to the equation

$$\begin{bmatrix}p\\q\end{bmatrix}=(q-p)\begin{bmatrix}1\\2\end{bmatrix}+(2p-q)\begin{bmatrix}1\\1\end{bmatrix}.$$

Since $\mathbf{t}^{-1}$ is linear,

$$\begin{aligned}\mathbf{t}^{-1}\left(\begin{bmatrix}p\\q\end{bmatrix}\right)&=(q-p)\mathbf{t}^{-1}\left(\begin{bmatrix}1\\2\end{bmatrix}\right)+(2p-q)\mathbf{t}^{-1}\left(\begin{bmatrix}1\\1\end{bmatrix}\right)\\&=(q-p)\begin{bmatrix}1\\0\end{bmatrix}+(2p-q)\begin{bmatrix}0\\1\end{bmatrix}\\&=\begin{bmatrix}q-p\\2p-q\end{bmatrix}\end{aligned}$$

We confirm this result by noting

$$\mathbf{t}^{-1}\mathbf{t}\left(\begin{bmatrix} a \\ b \end{bmatrix}\right) = \mathbf{t}^{-1}\left(\begin{bmatrix} a+b \\ 2a+b \end{bmatrix}\right) = \begin{bmatrix} -(a+b)+(2a+b) \\ 2(a+b)-(2a+b) \end{bmatrix} = \begin{bmatrix} a \\ b \end{bmatrix}.$$

In Section 3.4 we showed that every linear transformation $\mathbf{t}:U \to V$ can be represented by a matrix with respect to the coordinate systems of U and V. Since these matrices map coordinate vector representations into coordinate vector representations, if n = DIM(U) and m = DIM(V), then the matrix has dimension $m \times n$. It would be natural to ask at this point whether every $m \times n$ matrix represents or induces a linear transformation from a vector space of dimension n to a vector space of dimension m, and if it does, to find a method of determining an expression for the transformation.

DEFINITION 5.3 (Transformation Induced by a Matrix) Let **A** be an $m \times n$ matrix, and let **x** be a vector in an n dimensional vector space V with coordinate representation $[\mathbf{x}]_\sigma$. The transformation $\mathbf{t}_\mathbf{A}:V \to W$ defined by $\mathbf{t}_\mathbf{A}(\mathbf{x}) = \mathbf{A}[\mathbf{x}]_\sigma$, which maps V into an m dimensional space W with standard basis, is said to be the transformation induced by the matrix **A**.

EXAMPLE 5.3 If $\mathrm{A} = \begin{bmatrix} 1 & 0 & 1 \\ 1 & 2 & -1 \end{bmatrix}$, the transformation $\mathbf{t}_\mathrm{A}:R^3 \to R^2$ induced by A is given by

$$\mathbf{t}_\mathrm{A}(\mathbf{x}) = \begin{bmatrix} 1 & 0 & 1 \\ 1 & 2 & -1 \end{bmatrix}\begin{pmatrix} x_1 \\ x_2 \\ x_3 \end{pmatrix}_\sigma = \begin{pmatrix} x_1 + x_3 \\ x_1 + 2x_2 - x_3 \end{pmatrix}_\sigma,$$

where $[\mathbf{x}]_\sigma = (x_1 \quad x_2 \quad x_3)^\mathrm{T}$.

Next, we establish a series of results which link the concept of an identity transformation to the identity matrix in a natural way. This in turn leads us to a connection between the matrix of the inverse of a linear transformation and the inverse of the matrix of the transformation.

DEFINITION 5.4 (Identity Transformation) If V is a vector space, then the transformation $\mathbf{i}:V \to V$ defined by $\mathbf{i}(\mathbf{x}) = \mathbf{x}$ for all $\mathbf{x} \in V$ is called the identity transformation.

THEOREM 5.6 The transformation $\mathbf{i}: V \to V$ is a linear transformation on the vector space V.

PROOF: The proof is left as a exercise.

LEMMA 5.1 If α is any basis for the vector space V, then $[\mathbf{i}]_\alpha^\alpha = \mathbf{I}$.

PROOF: Let $\alpha = \{\mathbf{x}_1, \mathbf{x}_2, \cdots, \mathbf{x}_n\}$. In the manner of Section 3.4, we first write the image of each basis element in its coordinate vector representation:

$$\begin{aligned} \mathbf{i}(\mathbf{x}_1) &= 1\mathbf{x}_1 + 0\mathbf{x}_2 + \cdots + 0\mathbf{x}_n \\ \mathbf{i}(\mathbf{x}_2) &= 0\mathbf{x}_1 + 1\mathbf{x}_2 + \cdots + 0\mathbf{x}_n \\ &\cdots\cdots\cdots\cdots \\ \mathbf{i}(\mathbf{x}_n) &= 0\mathbf{x}_1 + 0\mathbf{x}_2 + \cdots + 1\mathbf{x}_n. \end{aligned}$$

Next, we write the coefficients of each linear combination as the corresponding column of $[\mathbf{i}]_\alpha^\alpha$ with the result being the identity matrix $\mathbf{I}$.

THEOREM 5.7 Let U and V be vector spaces with bases $\alpha = \{\mathbf{x}_1, \mathbf{x}_2, \cdots, \mathbf{x}_n\}$ and $\beta = \{\mathbf{y}_1, \mathbf{y}_2, \cdots, \mathbf{y}_m\}$ respectively. Let $\mathbf{t}: U \to V$ be an invertible linear transformation. Then the matrix of $\mathbf{t}^{-1}$ is the inverse of the matrix of $\mathbf{t}$: $[\mathbf{t}^{-1}]_\beta^\alpha = \left([\mathbf{t}]_\alpha^\beta\right)^{-1}$.

PROOF: Since $\mathbf{t}$ is invertible, it is both one-to-one and onto. It follows from Theorem 2.4 and the fact that $\mathbf{t}$ is one-to-one that KER($\mathbf{t}$) = $\{\mathbf{0}\}$; thus, NUL($\mathbf{t}$) = 0, and RK($\mathbf{t}$) = n by Theorem 2.5. From the fact that $\mathbf{t}$ is onto we know that RK($\mathbf{t}$) = m; therefore, $m = n$. Thus

$$[\mathbf{t}^{-1}]_\beta^\alpha [\mathbf{t}]_\alpha^\beta = [\mathbf{t}^{-1}\mathbf{t}]_\alpha^\alpha = [\mathbf{i}]_\alpha^\alpha = \mathbf{I}_n = [\mathbf{i}]_\beta^\beta = [\mathbf{t}\mathbf{t}^{-1}]_\beta^\beta = [\mathbf{t}]_\alpha^\beta [\mathbf{t}^{-1}]_\beta^\alpha$$

where the third and fourth equalities follow from Lemma 5.1, the second and fifth equalities follow from the fact that $\mathbf{t}^{-1}\mathbf{t} = \mathbf{i}$, and the first and last equalities follow from Theorem 5.2.

COROLLARY 5.1 If V is a vector space with coordinate bases α and β, then the matrices of coordinate transformation are related by $\mathbf{P}_\alpha^\beta = \left(\mathbf{P}_\beta^\alpha\right)^{-1}$.

PROOF: The proof is left as an exercise.

THEOREM 5.8 If $\mathbf{A}$ is an invertible $n \times n$ matrix, then $\mathbf{A}$ induces an invertible transformation $\mathbf{t}_\mathbf{A}$ on any n dimensional vector space V, and the inverse of $\mathbf{t}_\mathbf{A}$ is the transformation induced by $\mathbf{A}^{-1}$.

PROOF: Let σ be the natural basis for V. Then the matrix relations $[\mathbf{t}_\mathbf{A}]_\sigma^\sigma = \mathbf{A}$ and $[\mathbf{t}_{\mathbf{A}^{-1}}]_\sigma^\sigma = \mathbf{A}^{-1}$ follow immediately from the definition of the transformation induced by a matrix. Since

$$[\mathbf{t}_\mathbf{A}]_\sigma^\sigma[\mathbf{t}_{\mathbf{A}^{-1}}]_\sigma^\sigma = \mathbf{A}\mathbf{A}^{-1} = \mathbf{I} = \mathbf{A}^{-1}\mathbf{A} = [\mathbf{t}_{\mathbf{A}^{-1}}]_\sigma^\sigma[\mathbf{t}_\mathbf{A}]_\sigma^\sigma$$

therefore

$$\mathbf{t}_\mathbf{A}\mathbf{t}_{\mathbf{A}^{-1}}(\mathbf{x}) = \mathbf{t}_\mathbf{I}(\mathbf{x}) = \mathbf{x} = \mathbf{t}_\mathbf{I}(\mathbf{x}) = \mathbf{t}_{\mathbf{A}^{-1}}\mathbf{t}_\mathbf{A}(\mathbf{x})$$

for all $\mathbf{x} \in V$, and $\mathbf{t}_\mathbf{A}$ is invertible with $(\mathbf{t}_\mathbf{A})^{-1} = \mathbf{t}_{\mathbf{A}^{-1}}$.

EXAMPLE 5.4 If

$$\mathbf{A} = \begin{bmatrix} 1 & 0 & 0 \\ 1 & 1 & 0 \\ 1 & 1 & 1 \end{bmatrix},$$

then $\mathbf{t}_\mathbf{A}: R^3 \to R^3$ maps an arbitrary vector

$$\mathbf{t}_\mathbf{A}\left(\begin{bmatrix} a \\ b \\ c \end{bmatrix}\right) = \begin{bmatrix} 1 & 0 & 0 \\ 1 & 1 & 0 \\ 1 & 1 & 1 \end{bmatrix}\begin{bmatrix} a \\ b \\ c \end{bmatrix} = \begin{bmatrix} a \\ a+b \\ a+b+c \end{bmatrix}.$$

Also, $\mathbf{t}_{\mathbf{A}^{-1}}: R^3 \to R^3$ can be computed by first finding $\mathbf{A}^{-1}$

$$2: \quad \begin{bmatrix} 1 & 0 & 0 \\ 1 & 1 & 0 \\ 1 & 1 & 1 \end{bmatrix}^{-1}$$

$$3: \begin{bmatrix} 1 & 0 & 0 \\ -1 & 1 & 0 \\ 0 & -1 & 1 \end{bmatrix}$$

which can then be used to find the image of an arbitrary vector

$$\mathbf{t}_{\mathbf{A}^{-1}}\left(\begin{bmatrix} p \\ q \\ r \end{bmatrix}\right) = \begin{bmatrix} 1 & 0 & 0 \\ -1 & 1 & 0 \\ 0 & -1 & 1 \end{bmatrix}\begin{pmatrix} p \\ q \\ r \end{pmatrix} = \begin{pmatrix} p \\ -p+q \\ -q+r \end{pmatrix}.$$

From this it follows that

$$\mathbf{t}_{\mathbf{A}^{-1}}\mathbf{t}_{\mathbf{A}}\left(\begin{pmatrix} a \\ b \\ c \end{pmatrix}\right) = \mathbf{t}_{\mathbf{A}^{-1}}\left(\begin{pmatrix} a \\ a+b \\ a+b+c \end{pmatrix}\right) = \begin{pmatrix} a \\ -a+(a+b) \\ -(a+b)+(a+b+c) \end{pmatrix} = \begin{pmatrix} a \\ b \\ c \end{pmatrix}$$

and similarly

$$\mathbf{t}_{\mathbf{A}}\mathbf{t}_{\mathbf{A}^{-1}}\left(\begin{pmatrix} a \\ b \\ c \end{pmatrix}\right) = \begin{pmatrix} a \\ b \\ c \end{pmatrix}.$$

thus $(\mathbf{t}_{\mathbf{A}})^{-1}$ exists and equals $\mathbf{t}_{\mathbf{A}^{-1}}$.

EXERCISES

1. Let $\alpha = \left\{\begin{bmatrix} 1 \\ 1 \end{bmatrix}, \begin{bmatrix} 1 \\ 0 \end{bmatrix}\right\}$,

   $\beta = \left\{\begin{bmatrix} 0 \\ 1 \\ 1 \end{bmatrix}, \begin{bmatrix} 1 \\ 0 \\ 1 \end{bmatrix}, \begin{bmatrix} 1 \\ 1 \\ 0 \end{bmatrix}\right\}$, and

   $\gamma = \left\{\begin{bmatrix} 1 \\ 1 \\ 0 \\ 0 \end{bmatrix}, \begin{bmatrix} 0 \\ 1 \\ 1 \\ 0 \end{bmatrix}, \begin{bmatrix} 0 \\ 0 \\ 1 \\ 1 \end{bmatrix}, \begin{bmatrix} 1 \\ 1 \\ 1 \\ 0 \end{bmatrix}\right\}$ be

   bases for R^2, R^3, and R^4 respectively.

   a) Let $\mathbf{t}: R^2 \to R^3$ be defined by $\mathbf{t}\left(\begin{bmatrix} a \\ b \end{bmatrix}\right) = \begin{bmatrix} a \\ a+b \\ b \end{bmatrix}$ and $\mathbf{s}: R^3 \to R^4$ be defined by

$\mathbf{s}\left(\begin{bmatrix} p \\ q \\ r \end{bmatrix}\right) = \begin{bmatrix} p \\ p+q \\ q+r \\ r \end{bmatrix}$. Find an expression for **st** and the matrix of **st**. Show that the product of the matrices for **s** and **t** is the same as the matrix for **st**.

b) Let $\mathbf{t}: R^2 \to R^3$ be defined by $\mathbf{t}\left(\begin{bmatrix} 1 \\ 1 \end{bmatrix}\right) = \begin{bmatrix} 2 \\ 1 \\ 0 \end{bmatrix}$, and $\mathbf{t}\left(\begin{bmatrix} 1 \\ 0 \end{bmatrix}\right) = \begin{bmatrix} 1 \\ 1 \\ 1 \end{bmatrix}$ and $\mathbf{s}: R^3 \to R^4$ be defined by $\mathbf{s}\left(\begin{bmatrix} 0 \\ 1 \\ 1 \end{bmatrix}\right) = \begin{bmatrix} 2 \\ 1 \\ 0 \\ 1 \end{bmatrix}$, $\mathbf{s}\left(\begin{bmatrix} 1 \\ 0 \\ 1 \end{bmatrix}\right) = \begin{bmatrix} 1 \\ 0 \\ 1 \\ 0 \end{bmatrix}$ and $\mathbf{s}\left(\begin{bmatrix} 1 \\ 1 \\ 0 \end{bmatrix}\right) = \begin{bmatrix} 0 \\ 1 \\ 1 \\ 1 \end{bmatrix}$. Find an expression for **st** and the matrix of **st**. Show that the product of the matrices for **s** and **t** is the same as the matrix **st**.

2. Let $\mathbf{t}: R^2 \to R^2$ be defined by $\mathbf{t}\left(\begin{bmatrix} a \\ b \end{bmatrix}\right) = \begin{bmatrix} b \\ a \end{bmatrix}$. Find an expression for $\mathbf{t}^{-1}$.

3. Let $\mathbf{t}: M_{2\times2} \to P^3$ be defined by $\mathbf{t}\left(\begin{bmatrix} a & b \\ c & d \end{bmatrix}\right) = ax^3 + (a+b)x^2 + (c-d)x - (a+d)$. Find the inverse of **t** if it exists and find the matrix representations of **t** and $\mathbf{t}^{-1}$ (if it exists).

4. Let $\mathbf{t}: M_{2\times2} \to M_{2\times2}$ be defined by $\mathbf{t}\left(\begin{bmatrix} a & b \\ c & d \end{bmatrix}\right) = \begin{bmatrix} a & b+c \\ b-c & a+d \end{bmatrix}$. If **t** has an inverse, find it. Find the matrix of **t** and the matrix of $\mathbf{t}^{-1}$ with respect to the standard basis.

5. Let $\mathbf{A} = \begin{bmatrix} 1 & 0 \\ -1 & 1 \\ 2 & 1 \end{bmatrix}$. Find an expression for $\mathbf{t}_\mathbf{A}: R^2 \to R^3$.

6. Let $\mathbf{A} = \begin{bmatrix} 1 & 1 & 0 & -1 \\ 0 & 1 & 0 & 1 \\ 1 & 0 & 1 & 0 \end{bmatrix}$. Find an expression for $\mathbf{t}_\mathbf{A}: R^4 \to R^3$.

7. Let $\mathbf{A} \begin{bmatrix} 1 & 1 & 0 \\ 2 & -1 & 1 \\ 1 & 1 & 1 \end{bmatrix}$. Find an expression for $\mathbf{t}_\mathbf{A}$. If $\mathbf{t}_\mathbf{A}^{-1}$

exists, find an expression for it and check $\mathbf{t}_{\mathbf{A}}(\mathbf{t}_{\mathbf{A}})^{-1}(\mathbf{x})$ where $\mathbf{x}$ is an arbitrary vector in R^3.

8. Let $\mathbf{A} = \begin{bmatrix} 1 & 2 & 1 \\ -1 & 1 & 1 \\ 0 & 3 & 2 \end{bmatrix}$. Find an expression for $\mathbf{t}_{\mathbf{A}}$. If $\mathbf{t}_{\mathbf{A}}^{-1}$ exists, find an expression for it and check $\mathbf{t}_{\mathbf{A}}(\mathbf{t}_{\mathbf{A}})^{-1}(\mathbf{x})$ where $\mathbf{x}$ is an arbitrary vector in R^3.

9. Let $\mathbf{t}: M_{2\times 2} \to R$ be defined by $\mathbf{t}(\mathbf{A}) = \mathrm{TR}(\mathbf{A})$. Find the matrix of $\mathbf{t}$.

10. Prove Theorem 5.4.

11. Prove Theorem 5.6.

12. Prove Corollary 5.1.

6. SIMILARITY

In Section 3.1 we motivated the definition a linear transformation by noting the mapping properties of matrix multiplication, and in Section 3.3 we showed that every linear transformation can be represented by a matrix. Example 4.3 of this chapter illustrated how this matrix representation depends on the particular bases chosen for the domain and range of the transformation. In this section we generalize the relationship between different matrix representations of a single linear transformation from a vector space V onto itself and call such matrices "similar." In later chapters we will discover several important applications of similar matrices.

Let $\mathbf{t}: V \to V$ be a linear transformation from the vector space V onto itself. If α and β are two bases for V, then we can compute $[\mathbf{t}]_\alpha^\alpha$ and $[\mathbf{t}]_\beta^\beta$ independently as indicated in Sections 3.4 and 3.5, or we can use $[\mathbf{t}]_\alpha^\alpha$ and the coordinate transformation maps $\mathbf{P}_\alpha^\beta$ and $\mathbf{P}_\beta^\alpha$ to calculate $[\mathbf{t}]_\beta^\beta$. The diagram on the following page provides an aid in visualizing the process.

To understand the diagram, first note that the basis α has been placed in the two leftmost corners of the rectangle, and the basis β has been placed in the two rightmost corners. The top and bottom sides of the rectangle indicate the transformation of a vector from a representation in one basis to another. The two sides of the rectangle indicate mappings induced by a single linear transformation $\mathbf{t}$. Note that it is possible to

$$\begin{array}{ccccc}
\alpha & \leftarrow & \mathbf{P}_\beta^\alpha & \leftarrow & \beta \\
\downarrow & & & & \downarrow \\
[\mathbf{t}]_\alpha^\alpha & & & & [\mathbf{t}]_\beta^\beta = \left(\mathbf{P}_\beta^\alpha\right)^{-1}[\mathbf{t}]_\alpha^\alpha \mathbf{P}_\beta^\alpha \\
\downarrow & & & & \downarrow \\
\alpha & \rightarrow & \mathbf{P}_\beta^{\alpha^{-1}} & \rightarrow & \beta
\end{array}$$

reach the bottom right corner from the top right corner by following two paths. The most direct path is down the right side of the rectangle which represents **t** mapping a coordinate vector with respect to β into a coordinate vector, again with respect to β. But an equivalent result can also be obtained by first mapping a coordinate vector with respect to β into its corresponding representation with respect to α. Next, the vector is transformed by **t** into an image represented in coordinate form with respect to α. Finally, the coordinate vector of the image with respect to α is mapped into its corresponding coordinate representation with respect to β. This is accomplished using the inverse of $\mathbf{P}_\beta^\alpha$ which we showed in Corollary 5.1 is equal to $\mathbf{P}_\alpha^\beta$. Examples 4.3 and 4.4 in Section 3.4 provide an illustration that the result of following these two paths is identical, and, in fact, $\left(\mathbf{P}_\beta^\alpha\right)^{-1}[\mathbf{t}]_\alpha^\alpha \mathbf{P}_\beta^\alpha\left([\mathbf{x}]_\beta\right) = [\mathbf{t}(\mathbf{x})]_\beta$.

EXAMPLE 6.1 Let $\mathbf{t}: R^3 \to R^3$ be defined by

$$\mathbf{t}(\mathbf{e}_1) = \begin{bmatrix} 1 \\ 2 \\ 3 \end{bmatrix}, \quad \mathbf{t}(\mathbf{e}_2) = \begin{bmatrix} 1 \\ 1 \\ 2 \end{bmatrix}, \quad \text{and} \quad \mathbf{t}(\mathbf{e}_3) = \begin{bmatrix} 1 \\ 1 \\ 3 \end{bmatrix}$$

(where $\mathbf{e}_1$, $\mathbf{e}_2$, and $\mathbf{e}_3$ are the three elements of the usual basis σ for R^3) and

$$\beta = \left\{ \begin{bmatrix} 2 \\ 1 \\ 1 \end{bmatrix}, \begin{bmatrix} 1 \\ 2 \\ 1 \end{bmatrix}, \begin{bmatrix} 1 \\ 1 \\ 2 \end{bmatrix} \right\}.$$

In this example the standard basis σ for R^3 plays the role of α in the diagram above. This allows us to quickly find

$$\mathbf{P}_{\beta}^{\sigma} = \begin{bmatrix} 2 & 1 & 1 \\ 1 & 2 & 1 \\ 1 & 1 & 2 \end{bmatrix},$$

where the columns of the matrix are the vectors in the basis β, and

$$[\mathbf{t}]_{\sigma}^{\sigma} = \begin{bmatrix} 1 & 1 & 1 \\ 2 & 1 & 1 \\ 3 & 2 & 1 \end{bmatrix},$$

where the columns of the matrix are the coordinate representations with respect to the usual basis of the images of the elements of σ. According to the diagram above, $[\mathbf{t}]_{\beta}^{\beta} = \left(\mathbf{P}_{\beta}^{\sigma}\right)^{-1}[\mathbf{t}]_{\sigma}^{\sigma}\mathbf{P}_{\beta}^{\sigma}$, which can be computed using *Derive*:

$$3: \quad \begin{bmatrix} 2 & 1 & 1 \\ 1 & 2 & 1 \\ 1 & 1 & 2 \end{bmatrix}^{-1} \cdot \begin{bmatrix} 1 & 1 & 1 \\ 2 & 1 & 1 \\ 3 & 2 & 3 \end{bmatrix} \cdot \begin{bmatrix} 2 & 1 & 1 \\ 1 & 2 & 1 \\ 1 & 1 & 2 \end{bmatrix}$$

$$4: \quad \begin{bmatrix} -\frac{5}{4} & -\frac{3}{4} & -1 \\ \frac{3}{4} & \frac{1}{4} & 0 \\ \frac{23}{4} & \frac{21}{4} & 6 \end{bmatrix}$$

where statement #4 is the matrix $[\mathbf{t}]_{\beta}^{\beta}$. As a check, consider the image of the vector

$$\mathbf{u} = \begin{bmatrix} 4 \\ 4 \\ 4 \end{bmatrix} = 1\begin{bmatrix} 2 \\ 1 \\ 1 \end{bmatrix} + 1\begin{bmatrix} 1 \\ 2 \\ 2 \end{bmatrix} + 1\begin{bmatrix} 1 \\ 1 \\ 2 \end{bmatrix}$$

under the transformation **t**. Either by using the definition of **t** or multiplying $[\mathbf{t}]_\sigma^\sigma[\mathbf{u}]_\sigma$, we find the image is $\left([12 \quad 16 \quad 32]_\sigma\right)^{\mathrm{T}}$. But **t(u)** can also be computed by transforming $[\mathbf{u}]_\beta$ by means of $[\mathbf{t}]_\beta^\beta$ as follows:

$$6: \quad \begin{bmatrix} -\frac{5}{4} & -\frac{3}{4} & -1 \\ \frac{3}{4} & \frac{1}{4} & 0 \\ \frac{23}{4} & \frac{21}{4} & 6 \end{bmatrix} \cdot \begin{bmatrix} 1 \\ 1 \\ 1 \end{bmatrix}$$

$$7: \quad \begin{bmatrix} -3 \\ 1 \\ 17 \end{bmatrix}$$

where statement #7 represents the image of **u** in its coordinate representation with respect to β. Converting to standard basis notation, we have $(-3 \quad 1 \quad 17)_\beta^{\mathrm{T}}$ written as

$$-3\begin{bmatrix} 2 \\ 1 \\ 1 \end{bmatrix} + 1\begin{bmatrix} 1 \\ 2 \\ 2 \end{bmatrix} + 17\begin{bmatrix} 1 \\ 1 \\ 2 \end{bmatrix} = \begin{bmatrix} 12 \\ 16 \\ 32 \end{bmatrix}_\sigma .$$

We have seen in previous sections that the matrix representation of a linear transformation from a vector space to itself with respect to the standard basis is simple to find: the columns of the matrix consist of the images of the standard basis vectors. We have also seen that it is simple to find a matrix that maps vectors from coordinate representations with respect to some basis β into their corresponding standard basis coordinate representations: the columns of the matrix consist of the vectors from β. The process outlined in the above diagram and example therefore provides us a convenient means of finding the matrix representation of a linear transformation with respect to a basis β other than the standard basis.

Next, we define a concept which includes matrix representations with respect to different bases of a linear transformation from a vector space to itself. As we will see, this concept can then be extended to a more general setting that does not even require the domain and range of the function to be of the same dimension.

DEFINITION 6.1 (Similar Matrices) If **A** and **B** are square matrices of order n, then **A** is similar to **B** whenever there exists a nonsingular matrix **P** such that $\mathbf{B} = \mathbf{P}^{-1}\mathbf{A}\mathbf{P}$.

If α and β are two bases for the same vector space V, then $[\mathbf{t}]_{\alpha}^{\alpha}$ and $[\mathbf{t}]_{\beta}^{\beta}$ are similar matrices with $[\mathbf{t}]_{\beta}^{\beta} = (\mathbf{P}_{\beta}^{\sigma})^{-1}\mathbf{A}\mathbf{P}_{\beta}^{\sigma}$ (thus $\mathbf{P}_{\beta}^{\alpha}$ plays the role of **P** in the definition). More generally, if $\mathbf{t}: U \to V$, U has bases α and β, and V has bases γ and η, then $[\mathbf{t}]_{\beta}^{\eta}$ can be computed as indicated in the following diagram:

$$
\begin{array}{lccccc}
U: & \alpha & \leftarrow & \mathbf{P}_{\beta}^{\alpha} & \leftarrow & \beta \\
 & \downarrow & & & & \downarrow \\
\mathbf{t}: & [\mathbf{t}]_{\alpha}^{\gamma} & & & & [\mathbf{t}]_{\beta}^{\eta} = \mathbf{Q}_{\gamma}^{\eta}[\mathbf{t}]_{\alpha}^{\gamma}\mathbf{P}_{\beta}^{\alpha} \\
 & \downarrow & & & & \downarrow \\
V: & \gamma & \rightarrow & \mathbf{Q}_{\gamma}^{\eta} & \rightarrow & \eta
\end{array}
$$

EXAMPLE 6.2 Let $\mathbf{t}: M_{2\times 2} \to R^3$ be defined by $t\left(\begin{bmatrix} a & b \\ c & d \end{bmatrix}\right) = \begin{bmatrix} a+d \\ 0 \\ b+c \end{bmatrix}$, $\beta = \left\{\begin{bmatrix} 2 & 1 \\ 1 & 0 \end{bmatrix}, \begin{bmatrix} 1 & 2 \\ 0 & 1 \end{bmatrix}, \begin{bmatrix} 1 & 0 \\ 2 & 1 \end{bmatrix}, \begin{bmatrix} 1 & 1 \\ 1 & 2 \end{bmatrix}\right\}$ be a basis for $M_{2\times 2}$, and $\zeta = \left\{\begin{bmatrix} 1 \\ 1 \\ 0 \end{bmatrix}, \begin{bmatrix} 0 \\ 1 \\ 1 \end{bmatrix}, \begin{bmatrix} 1 \\ 0 \\ 1 \end{bmatrix}\right\}$ be a basis for R^3. Since

$$\mathbf{t}\left(\begin{bmatrix}1 & 0\\0 & 0\end{bmatrix}\right)=\begin{bmatrix}1\\0\\0\end{bmatrix}\qquad \mathbf{t}\left(\begin{bmatrix}0 & 1\\0 & 0\end{bmatrix}\right)=\begin{bmatrix}0\\0\\1\end{bmatrix}$$

$$\mathbf{t}\left(\begin{bmatrix}0 & 0\\1 & 0\end{bmatrix}\right)=\begin{bmatrix}0\\0\\1\end{bmatrix}\qquad \mathbf{t}\left(\begin{bmatrix}0 & 0\\0 & 1\end{bmatrix}\right)=\begin{bmatrix}1\\0\\0\end{bmatrix}$$

the matrix of **t** with respect to the usual basis is given by

$$[\mathbf{t}]_{\sigma}^{\sigma}=\begin{bmatrix}1 & 0 & 0 & 1\\0 & 0 & 0 & 0\\0 & 1 & 1 & 0\end{bmatrix}.$$

Recall from Section 3.3 that for mappings of coordinate vector representations with respect to a basis other than the usual one (such as ζ for the vector space R^3 in this example) to vector representations with respect to the usual basis, the columns of the matrix are simply the vectors of the non-standard basis (in this case ζ); therefore,

$$\mathbf{Q}_{\zeta}^{\sigma}=\begin{bmatrix}1 & 0 & 1\\1 & 1 & 0\\0 & 1 & 1\end{bmatrix}.$$

Also,

$$\begin{bmatrix}2 & 1\\1 & 0\end{bmatrix}=2\mathbf{M}_{11}+1\mathbf{M}_{12}+1\mathbf{M}_{21}+0\mathbf{M}_{22}\qquad \begin{bmatrix}1 & 2\\0 & 1\end{bmatrix}=1\mathbf{M}_{11}+2\mathbf{M}_{12}+0\mathbf{M}_{21}+1\mathbf{M}_{22}$$

$$\begin{bmatrix}1 & 0\\2 & 1\end{bmatrix}=1\mathbf{M}_{11}+0\mathbf{M}_{12}+2\mathbf{M}_{21}+1\mathbf{M}_{22}\qquad \begin{bmatrix}1 & 1\\1 & 2\end{bmatrix}=1\mathbf{M}_{11}+1\mathbf{M}_{12}+1\mathbf{M}_{21}+2\mathbf{M}_{22}$$

(where $\mathbf{M}_{ij}$ is the 2×2 matrix with 1 in the ij position and 0 in the remaining positions); thus, again, the columns of the matrix which maps coordinate vector representations with respect to β into coordinate vector representations with respect to the standard basis σ for $M_{2\times 2}$ are the coefficients of the $\mathbf{M}_{ij}$, and

$$\mathbf{P}_{\beta}^{\sigma} = \begin{bmatrix} 2 & 1 & 1 & 1 \\ 1 & 2 & 0 & 1 \\ 1 & 0 & 2 & 1 \\ 0 & 1 & 1 & 2 \end{bmatrix}.$$

Using the above diagram we see that $[\mathbf{t}]_{\beta}^{\zeta} = \mathbf{Q}_{\sigma}^{\xi}[\mathbf{t}]_{\sigma}^{\sigma}\mathbf{P}_{\beta}^{\sigma} = \left[\mathbf{Q}_{\xi}^{\sigma}\right]^{-1}[\mathbf{t}]_{\sigma}^{\sigma}\mathbf{P}_{\beta}^{\varpi}$ and

$$4: \quad \begin{bmatrix} 1 & 0 & 1 \\ 1 & 1 & 0 \\ 0 & 1 & 1 \end{bmatrix}^{-1} \cdot \begin{bmatrix} 1 & 0 & 0 & 1 \\ 0 & 0 & 0 & 0 \\ 0 & 1 & 1 & 0 \end{bmatrix} \cdot \begin{bmatrix} 2 & 1 & 1 & 1 \\ 1 & 2 & 0 & 1 \\ 1 & 0 & 2 & 1 \\ 0 & 1 & 1 & 2 \end{bmatrix}$$

$$5: \quad \begin{bmatrix} 0 & 0 & 0 & \frac{1}{2} \\ 0 & 0 & 0 & -\frac{1}{2} \\ 2 & 2 & 2 & \frac{5}{2} \end{bmatrix}$$

where statement #5 is $[\mathbf{t}]_{\beta}^{\xi}$. Regardless of which matrix representation is used for **t**, the image of an arbitrary vector **u** in $M_{2\times 2}$ will be the same, although the coordinates for it depend on the particular basis in question. For example,

$$\mathbf{t}\left(\begin{bmatrix} 5 & 4 \\ 4 & 4 \end{bmatrix}\right) = \begin{bmatrix} 9 \\ 0 \\ 8 \end{bmatrix}$$

where the coordinate representations for both **u** and **t(u)** are in terms of the usual basis. But

$$\begin{bmatrix} 5 & 4 \\ 4 & 4 \end{bmatrix}_\beta = \begin{pmatrix} 1 \\ 1 \\ 1 \\ 1 \end{pmatrix};$$

therefore,

$$7: \begin{bmatrix} 0 & 0 & 0 & \frac{1}{2} \\ 0 & 0 & 0 & -\frac{1}{2} \\ 2 & 2 & 2 & \frac{5}{2} \end{bmatrix} \cdot \begin{bmatrix} 1 \\ 1 \\ 1 \\ 1 \end{bmatrix}$$

$$8: \begin{bmatrix} \frac{1}{2} \\ -\frac{1}{2} \\ \frac{17}{2} \end{bmatrix}$$

which is the coordinate vector representation of $\left(\begin{bmatrix} 9 & 0 & 8 \end{bmatrix}_\sigma\right)^T$ with respect to ζ.

EXAMPLE 6.3 Given the matrix $\mathbf{A} = \begin{bmatrix} 2 & 1 \\ 1 & 2 \\ 3 & 1 \end{bmatrix}$ and the two bases

$$\beta = \left\{ \begin{bmatrix} 2 \\ 4 \end{bmatrix}, \begin{bmatrix} -1 \\ 3 \end{bmatrix} \right\} \quad \text{and} \quad \gamma = \left\{ \begin{bmatrix} 2 \\ -1 \\ 2 \end{bmatrix}, \begin{bmatrix} 1 \\ 1 \\ 0 \end{bmatrix}, \begin{bmatrix} 2 \\ 4 \\ 1 \end{bmatrix} \right\}$$

of R^2 and R^3 respectively, we can find the matrix $[\mathbf{t_A}]_\beta^\gamma$ of the transformation $\mathbf{t}$ induced by $\mathbf{A}$. Of course the matrix representation of the transformation **t** relative to the standard basis is simply **A**. In the manner followed in Example 6.2 above we can show

$$\mathbf{P}_\beta^\sigma = \begin{bmatrix} 2 & -1 \\ 4 & 3 \end{bmatrix} \text{ and } \mathbf{Q}_\gamma^\sigma = \begin{bmatrix} 2 & 1 & 2 \\ -1 & 1 & 4 \\ 2 & 0 & 1 \end{bmatrix};$$

therefore, according to the diagram above

$$[\mathbf{t}_\mathbf{A}]_\beta^\gamma = (\mathbf{Q}_\gamma^\sigma)^{-1} \mathbf{A}\mathbf{P}_\beta^\sigma,$$

which can be computed as follows:

$$4: \quad \begin{bmatrix} 2 & 1 & 2 \\ -1 & 1 & 4 \\ 2 & 0 & 1 \end{bmatrix}^{-1} \cdot \begin{bmatrix} 2 & 1 \\ 1 & 2 \\ 3 & 1 \end{bmatrix} \cdot \begin{bmatrix} 2 & -1 \\ 4 & 3 \end{bmatrix}$$

$$5: \quad \begin{bmatrix} \frac{18}{7} & -\frac{4}{7} \\ -\frac{48}{7} & -\frac{1}{7} \\ \frac{34}{7} & \frac{8}{7} \end{bmatrix}$$

To confirm this result we calculate the coordinates of a general vector in R^2 using *Derive*:

$$9: \quad p \begin{bmatrix} 2 \\ 4 \end{bmatrix} + q \begin{bmatrix} -1 \\ 3 \end{bmatrix} = \begin{bmatrix} a \\ b \end{bmatrix}$$

and find p and q in terms of a and b

$$12: \quad \text{ROW\_REDUCE} \begin{bmatrix} 2 & -1 & a \\ 4 & 3 & b \end{bmatrix}$$

$$13: \begin{bmatrix} 1 & 0 & \dfrac{3a+b}{10} \\ 0 & 1 & \dfrac{b-2a}{5} \end{bmatrix}.$$

Any vector $\begin{bmatrix} a \\ b \end{bmatrix}$ can now be written in its coordinate vector notation with respect to β using the vector in the third column of statement #13, and its image can be computed using the matrix for $[\mathbf{t}]_\beta^\gamma$ found in statement #5 above:

$$15: \begin{bmatrix} \dfrac{18}{7} & -\dfrac{4}{7} \\ -\dfrac{48}{7} & -\dfrac{1}{7} \\ \dfrac{34}{7} & \dfrac{8}{7} \end{bmatrix} \cdot \begin{bmatrix} \dfrac{3a+b}{10} \\ \dfrac{b-2a}{5} \end{bmatrix}$$

$$16: \begin{bmatrix} \dfrac{7a+b}{7} \\ -\dfrac{14a+5b}{7} \\ \dfrac{7a+5b}{7} \end{bmatrix}$$

where the vector in statement #16 represents the coordinate vector for the image of $\begin{bmatrix} a \\ b \end{bmatrix}$ with respect to the basis γ. If we now write this coordinate vector as a linear combination of the basis vectors from γ, we have

$$\#20: \left[\frac{7\cdot a + b}{7}\right]\cdot\begin{bmatrix}2\\-1\\2\end{bmatrix} + \left[-\frac{14\cdot a + 5\cdot b}{7}\right]\cdot\begin{bmatrix}1\\1\\0\end{bmatrix} + \left[\frac{7\cdot a + 5\cdot b}{7}\right]\cdot\begin{bmatrix}2\\4\\1\end{bmatrix}$$

and finally

```
21:  [2 a + b, a + 2 b, 3 a + b]
```

which is the coordinate vector representation with respect to the usual basis of the transpose (as a space saving device) of the vector computed in statement #20 written with respect to the usual basis. This result agrees with the representation of the transformation written in terms of the usual basis:

$$\begin{bmatrix}2 & 1\\1 & 2\\3 & 1\end{bmatrix}\begin{bmatrix}a\\b\end{bmatrix} = \begin{bmatrix}2a+b\\a+2b\\3a+b\end{bmatrix}.$$

EXERCISES

1 Let $\mathbf{t}: R^2 \to R^2$ be defined by $\mathbf{t}(\mathbf{e}_1) = \begin{bmatrix}2\\3\end{bmatrix}$ and $\mathbf{t}(\mathbf{e}_2) = \begin{bmatrix}0\\4\end{bmatrix}$.
Find the matrix of $\mathbf{t}$ relative to $\beta = \left\{\begin{bmatrix}-2\\3\end{bmatrix}, \begin{bmatrix}2\\-1\end{bmatrix}\right\}$.

2. Let $\mathbf{t}: R^3 \to R^3$ be defined by $\mathbf{t}(\mathbf{e}_1) = \mathbf{e}_1$, $\mathbf{t}(\mathbf{e}_2) = \mathbf{e}_2$, and $\mathbf{t}(\mathbf{e}_3) = \mathbf{e}_3$. Find the matrix of $\mathbf{t}$ relative to

$$\beta = \left\{\begin{bmatrix}1\\2\\3\end{bmatrix}, \begin{bmatrix}-1\\-2\\3\end{bmatrix}, \begin{bmatrix}2\\2\\2\end{bmatrix}\right\}.$$

3 Let $\mathbf{t}: M_{2\times2} \to M_{2\times2}$ be defined by $\mathbf{t}\left(\begin{bmatrix}1 & 0\\0 & 0\end{bmatrix}\right) = \begin{bmatrix}1 & 2\\0 & 1\end{bmatrix}$,
$\mathbf{t}\left(\begin{bmatrix}0 & 1\\0 & 0\end{bmatrix}\right) = \begin{bmatrix}1 & 1\\1 & 1\end{bmatrix}$,
$\mathbf{t}\left(\begin{bmatrix}0 & 0\\1 & 0\end{bmatrix}\right) = \begin{bmatrix}2 & 1\\2 & 0\end{bmatrix}$, and
$\mathbf{t}\left(\begin{bmatrix}0 & 0\\0 & 1\end{bmatrix}\right) = \begin{bmatrix}0 & 1\\0 & 1\end{bmatrix}$.
Find the matrix of $\mathbf{t}$ relative to

$$\beta = \left\{\begin{bmatrix}0 & 1\\1 & 1\end{bmatrix}, \begin{bmatrix}1 & 0\\1 & 1\end{bmatrix}, \begin{bmatrix}1 & 1\\0 & 1\end{bmatrix}, \begin{bmatrix}1 & 1\\1 & 0\end{bmatrix}\right\}.$$

4. Let $\mathbf{t}: P^3 \to P^3$ be defined by $\mathbf{t}(x^3) = x^3 + x + 1$, $\mathbf{t}(x^2) = x^2$ $\mathbf{t}(x) = 2x + 3$, $\mathbf{t}(1) = 2x + 1$. Find the matrix of $\mathbf{t}$ relative to $\beta = \{x^3 + 2x^2 + 1,\ x^2 + x + 1,\ x,\ x + 2\}$.

5. Find the matrix $[\mathbf{t_A}]_\beta^\beta$ where

$$\mathbf{A} = \begin{bmatrix} 2 & 1 \\ 6 & 3 \end{bmatrix} \text{ and}$$

$$\beta = \left\{ \begin{bmatrix} 0 \\ 1 \end{bmatrix}, \begin{bmatrix} 1 \\ 0 \end{bmatrix} \right\}.$$

6. Find the matrix $[\mathbf{t_A}]_\beta^\beta$ where

$$\mathbf{A} = \begin{bmatrix} 1 & 2 & 1 \\ 0 & -1 & 3 \\ 1 & 4 & 1 \end{bmatrix} \text{ and}$$

$$\beta = \left\{ \begin{bmatrix} 1 \\ 1 \\ 1 \end{bmatrix}, \begin{bmatrix} 2 \\ 3 \\ 0 \end{bmatrix}, \begin{bmatrix} 1 \\ 0 \\ 2 \end{bmatrix} \right\}.$$

7. Find the matrix $[\mathbf{t_A}]_\beta^\beta$ where

$$\mathbf{A} = \begin{bmatrix} 3 & 1 & 2 \\ 1 & 2 & 1 \\ 1 & 1 & 2 \end{bmatrix} \text{ and}$$

$$\beta = \left\{ \begin{bmatrix} 2 \\ 1 \\ 1 \end{bmatrix}, \begin{bmatrix} 1 \\ 2 \\ 1 \end{bmatrix}, \begin{bmatrix} 1 \\ 1 \\ 2 \end{bmatrix} \right\}.$$

8. Let $\mathbf{A} \sim \mathbf{B}$ mean that $\mathbf{A}$ is similar to $\mathbf{B}$. Show that

   i. $\mathbf{A} \sim \mathbf{A}$
   ii. If $\mathbf{A} \sim \mathbf{B}$, then $\mathbf{B} \sim \mathbf{A}$
   iii. If $\mathbf{A} \sim \mathbf{B}$ and $\mathbf{B} \sim \mathbf{C}$, then $\mathbf{A} \sim \mathbf{C}$.
   (That is, show the set of all matrices similar to **A** form an equivalence relation.)

9. Show that $\begin{bmatrix} 1 & 1 \\ 3 & 2 \end{bmatrix}$ and $\begin{bmatrix} 1 & 1 \\ 2 & 1 \end{bmatrix}$ are not similar.

10. Let $\mathbf{t}: M_{2\times 2} \to R$ be defined by $\mathbf{t}(\mathbf{A}) = \mathrm{TR}(\mathbf{A})$. Let

$$\beta = \left\{ \begin{bmatrix} 0 & 1 \\ 1 & 1 \end{bmatrix}, \begin{bmatrix} 1 & 0 \\ 1 & 1 \end{bmatrix}, \begin{bmatrix} 1 & 1 \\ 0 & 1 \end{bmatrix}, \begin{bmatrix} 1 & 1 \\ 1 & 0 \end{bmatrix} \right\}$$ be a basis for $M_{2\times 2}$.

Find the matrix $[\mathbf{t}]_\beta^\sigma$ using the fact that $[\mathbf{t}]_\sigma^\sigma = [1 \;\; 0 \;\; 0 \;\; 1]$. Also, use the fact that

$$\begin{bmatrix} 3 & 3 \\ 3 & 3 \end{bmatrix}_\beta = \begin{pmatrix} 1 \\ 1 \\ 1 \\ 1 \end{pmatrix}$$

to find $\mathbf{t}\left(\begin{bmatrix} 3 & 3 \\ 3 & 3 \end{bmatrix}\right)$.

CHAPTER IV
DETERMINANTS

In previous chapters we have given many examples of functions from one vector space to another. The most important of these so far have been functions which satisfy the properties of a linear transformation. In this chapter we study a special function, called the "determinant," from the set of all square matrices to the set of real numbers. While this function does not satisfy the properties of a linear transformation, historically it has played a large role in the study of linear algebra. Although the use of determinants has diminished in recent treatments of the subject, they remain an indispensable tool in classifying matrices and other applications which will simplify our later studies.

1. DEFINITION AND COMPUTATION OF DETERMINANTS

We have already seen many applications for solving systems of equations and have noted in Section 1.6 that a system of equations has a solution whenever its coefficient matrix is invertible. In this section we seek a measure of a square matrix which will indicate if it is invertible. For 2×2 matrices this measure is easy to determine since we can use *Derive* to characterize invertible matrices:

$$3: \quad \text{ROW\_REDUCE} \begin{bmatrix} a & b & 1 & 0 \\ c & d & 0 & 1 \end{bmatrix}$$

$$4: \quad \begin{bmatrix} 1 & 0 & \dfrac{d}{a\,d - b\,c} & \dfrac{b}{b\,c - a\,d} \\ 0 & 1 & \dfrac{c}{b\,c - a\,d} & \dfrac{a}{a\,d - b\,c} \end{bmatrix}$$

It follows that the matrix $\mathbf{A} = \begin{bmatrix} a & b \\ c & d \end{bmatrix}$ is invertible whenever $ad - bc$ is not zero. If we choose this difference as a measure of **A**, called the determinant of **A**, then the measure not only indicates if the matrix is invertible, it can be used in conjunction with the information in statement #4 above to find the inverse of a matrix. This measure, and its properties related to the inverse, can be generalized to include all square matrices.

Up to this point in our study of linear algebra we have been most interested in functions which are linear. If we consider the determinant as a function from the set of all square matrices to the real numbers, then it is impossible to consider it as a linear transformation since the set of square matrices is not closed under addition. Even when the function is restricted to the set of all $n \times n$ matrices for some fixed positive integer n (which is a vector space and therefore is closed under vector addition), the determinate function is still not a linear transformation. For example, if $\mathbf{A} = \begin{bmatrix} 2 & 1 \\ 1 & 2 \end{bmatrix}$, then using the definition above for the determinant, DET(**A**) $= ad - bc = 2(2) - 1(1) = 3$, and DET(2**A**) $= 4(4) - 2(2) = 12$; hence, DET(2**A**) $\neq$ 2DET(**A**).

Although determinants do not play as large a role in the study of linear algebra as they did even a decade ago, the measure continues to be an excellent test of invertibility and remains indispensable in the study of much of the material considered in the following chapters. To begin our study of determinants we first introduce a concept which will be useful in specifying a general definition that will include all $n \times n$ square matrices.

DEFINITION 1.1 (*ij*-Minor of a Matrix) If **A** is an $n \times n$ matrix, then the *ij*- minor of **A**, denoted by α_{ij}, is the $(n\text{-}1) \times (n\text{-}1)$ matrix formed by deleting the *i*th row and *j*th column of **A**.

Using this concept of a minor we can define the determinant of a square matrix inductively by specifying the result for 1×1 and 2×2 matrices and then using the concept of a minor to allow any larger dimension square matrix to be reduced to a combination of 2×2 determinants.

DEFINITION 1.2 (Determinant of a Matrix) The following function from the set of all square matrices to the set of real numbers is called the determinant of the matrix [and noted by DET(A)].

a.) If **A** is the 1×1 matrix $\mathbf{A} = [a_{11}]$, then $\text{DET}(\mathbf{A}) = a_{11}$.

b.) If **A** is the 2×2 matrix $\mathbf{A} = \begin{bmatrix} a_{11} & a_{12} \\ a_{21} & a_{22} \end{bmatrix}$, then $\text{DET}(\mathbf{A}) = a_{11}a_{22} - a_{12}a_{21}$.

c.) If **A** is the $n\times n$ matrix $\mathbf{A} = (a_{ij})$ $i,j = 1,2,\cdots,n$, then $\text{DET}(\mathbf{A}) = \sum_{j=1}^{n}(-1)^{1+j}a_{1j}\text{DET}(\alpha_{1j})$, where α_{1j} is the $1j$- minor of **A**.

DEFINITION 1.3 (Cofactor of a Matrix Element) If $\mathbf{A} = (a_{ij})$ $i,j = 1,2,\cdots,n$, and α_{ij} is the ij minor of **A**, then the cofactor of the a_{ij} element of **A** is

$$\text{A}_{ij} = (-1)^{i+j}\text{DET}(\alpha_{ij}).$$

It follows immediately that

$$\text{DET}(\mathbf{A}) = \sum_{j=1}^{n} a_{1j}\text{A}_{1j}.$$

The following theorem provides an alternate method of evaluating the determinant of a matrix that is useful when a particular row or column of the matrix has a number of zero entries. It basically states that the determinant of a matrix can be found by finding the cofactor expansion about any row (the first part of the theorem) or column (the second part of the theorem).

THEOREM 1.1 If $\mathbf{A} = (a_{ij})$ $i,j = 1,2,\cdots,n$, then

a.) for each row i: $\text{DET}(\mathbf{A}) = \sum_{j=1}^{n} a_{ij}\text{A}_{ij}$, and

b.) for each column j: $\text{DET}(\mathbf{A}) = \sum_{i=1}^{n} a_{ij}\text{A}_{ij}$.

PROOF: The proof can be obtained by using mathematical induction. First, we find the cofactor expansion of a general 2×2 matrix about both the first and second rows and show the two expressions are equal. Next, we assume that the cofactor expansion of any row in an $(n - 1)\times(n - 1)$ matrix is equal to the determinant of the matrix and show the cofactor expansion about any row of an $n\times n$ matrix is also equal to the dterminant of the matrix. The details of the proof are left as an exercise.

EXAMPLE 1.1 According to the definition, DET(**A**) for $\mathbf{A} = \begin{bmatrix} a_{11} & a_{12} & a_{13} \\ a_{21} & a_{22} & a_{23} \\ a_{31} & a_{32} & a_{33} \end{bmatrix}$, can be evaluated by expanding about the first row of the matrix:

$$\text{DET}(\mathbf{A}) = (-1)^{1+1} a_{11}\text{DET}\begin{bmatrix} a_{22} & a_{23} \\ a_{32} & a_{33} \end{bmatrix} + (-1)^{1+2} a_{12}\text{DET}\begin{bmatrix} a_{21} & a_{23} \\ a_{31} & a_{33} \end{bmatrix} +$$

$$(-1)^{1+3} a_{13}\text{DET}\begin{bmatrix} a_{21} & a_{22} \\ a_{31} & a_{32} \end{bmatrix}$$

$$= a_{11}(a_{22}a_{33} - a_{23}a_{32}) - a_{12}(a_{21}a_{33} - a_{23}a_{31}) + a_{13}(a_{21}a_{32} - a_{22}a_{31})$$

$$= a_{11}a_{22}a_{33} - a_{11}a_{23}a_{32} - a_{12}a_{21}a_{33} + a_{12}a_{23}a_{31} + a_{13}a_{21}a_{32} - a_{13}a_{22}a_{31}$$

But Theorem 4.1 also allows DET(**A**) to be evaluated by expanding about any other row or column. For example, expansion about the third column appears as follows:

$$\text{DET}(\mathbf{A}) = (-1)^{1+3} a_{13}\text{DET}\begin{bmatrix} a_{21} & a_{22} \\ a_{31} & a_{32} \end{bmatrix} + (-1)^{2+3} a_{23}\text{DET}\begin{bmatrix} a_{11} & a_{12} \\ a_{31} & a_{32} \end{bmatrix} +$$

$$(-1)^{3+3} a_{33}\text{DET}\begin{bmatrix} a_{11} & a_{12} \\ a_{21} & a_{22} \end{bmatrix}$$

$$= a_{13}(a_{21}a_{32} - a_{31}a_{22}) - a_{23}(a_{11}a_{32} - a_{31}a_{12}) + a_{33}(a_{11}a_{22} - a_{21}a_{12})$$

$$= a_{13}a_{21}a_{32} - a_{13}a_{31}a_{22} - a_{23}a_{11}a_{32} + a_{23}a_{31}a_{12} + a_{33}a_{11}a_{22} - a_{33}a_{21}a_{12}$$

with the same results as the above expansion about the first row.

Although we will see in an example to follow that the determinant of a matrix can be found very easily using *Derive*, the manual calculation becomes very cumbersome. Often the burden of calculation can be simplified by performing basic operations on the rows or columns of the matrix prior to computing the determinant. The following theorem outlines some basic properties of determinants, including several techniques reminiscent of our elementary row operations discussed in earlier sections which can be used to accomplish this simplification process.

THEOREM 1.2 Let **A** and **B** be two square matrices of order *n*.

a) DET(**AB**) = DET(**A**)DET(**B**).

b) If **B** can be obtained from **A** by interchanging two rows (or two columns), then $\text{DET}(\mathbf{B}) = -\text{DET}(\mathbf{A})$.

c) If **A** is a square matrix of order *n*, then $\text{DET}(\mathbf{A}) = \text{DET}(\mathbf{A}^{\text{T}})$.

d) If **B** can be obtained from **A** by multiplying a row (or column) by a constant *c*, then $\text{DET}(\mathbf{B}) = c\text{DET}(\mathbf{A})$

e) If **B** can be obtained from **A** by adding a constant multiple of one row (or column) to another, then $\text{DET}(\mathbf{B}) = \text{DET}(\mathbf{A})$.

f) If two rows (or columns) of **A** are identical, then DET(**A**) = 0.

g) DET(**I**) = 1.

PROOF: The proof of most of the parts of this theorem follow either from Theorem 1.1 or from one of the previous parts of this theorem. For example:

b) To prove that the determinant of a matrix obtained by exchanging two rows of another matrix results in a determinant that is the negative of the determinant of the first matrix, we begin by considering the case where the rows are adjacent. If

$$\mathbf{A} = \begin{bmatrix} a_{11} & a_{12} & \cdots & a_{1n} \\ \vdots & \vdots & \ddots & \vdots \\ a_{i1} & a_{i2} & \cdots & a_{in} \\ a_{i+1,1} & a_{i+1,2} & \cdots & a_{i+1,n} \\ \vdots & \vdots & \ddots & \vdots \\ a_{n1} & a_{n2} & \cdots & a_{nn} \end{bmatrix}$$

and **B** is obtained by exchanging the ith and $(i + 1)$st rows of **A**

$$\mathbf{B} = \begin{bmatrix} a_{11} & a_{12} & \cdots & a_{1n} \\ \vdots & \vdots & \ddots & \vdots \\ a_{i+1,1} & a_{i+1,2} & \cdots & a_{i+1,n} \\ a_{i1} & a_{i2} & \cdots & a_{in} \\ \vdots & \vdots & \ddots & \vdots \\ a_{n1} & a_{n2} & \cdots & a_{nn} \end{bmatrix},$$

then by Theorem 1.1 we can evaluate DET(**A**) by finding the cofactor expansion about the ith row of **A** and DET(**B**) by finding the cofactor expansion about the $(i + 1)$st row of **B**. But if (α_{ij}) and (β_{ij}) are the minors of **A** and **B** respectively, then $\alpha_{ij} = \beta_{(i+1),j}$ for all j. Thus, for the cofactors, $\mathbf{A}_{ij} = -\mathbf{B}_{(i+1)j}$, and

$$\text{DET}(\mathbf{A}) = \sum_{j=1}^{n} a_{ij}\mathbf{A}_{ij} = \sum_{j=1}^{n} a_{ij}\left(-\mathbf{B}_{(i+1)j}\right) = -\sum_{j=1}^{n} b_{(i+1)j}\mathbf{B}_{(i+1)j} = -\text{DET}(\mathbf{B}).$$

This result can be extended to exchanging any two rows by noting that such an exchange can be viewed as an odd number of exchanges of adjacent rows.

f) If two rows of a matrix are identical, then exchanging them has no effect on the matrix. Yet if **A** is the matrix prior to the exchange and **B** is the matrix after the exchange, we know by part b) above that DET(**A**) = -DET(**B**), or since **A** = **B**, DET(**A**) = -DET(**A**); and it follows that DET(**A**) must be zero.

EXAMPLE 1.2 The parts of Theorem 4.2 can be illustrated using *Derive*, which recognizes the DET function in an Author command followed by the **Simplify** command.

a) $\text{DET}(\mathbf{A})\ \text{DET}(\mathbf{B}) = \text{DET}(\mathbf{AB})$:

$$3:\quad \text{DET}\begin{bmatrix} 2 & 0 & 1 \\ 0 & 1 & 1 \\ 2 & 2 & 2 \end{bmatrix} \text{DET}\begin{bmatrix} -1 & 2 & -2 \\ 3 & 4 & 2 \\ 1 & 0 & -2 \end{bmatrix}$$

$$4:\quad -64$$

$$5:\quad \text{DET}\left[\begin{bmatrix} 2 & 0 & 1 \\ 0 & 1 & 1 \\ 2 & 2 & 2 \end{bmatrix} \cdot \begin{bmatrix} -1 & 2 & -2 \\ 3 & 4 & 2 \\ 1 & 0 & -2 \end{bmatrix}\right]$$

$$6:\quad -64$$

b) Interchanging two rows (or columns) of a matrix results in the negative of the original determinant:

$$3:\quad \text{DET}\begin{bmatrix} 1 & 3 & 0 \\ -2 & 2 & 4 \\ -1 & -1 & 2 \end{bmatrix}$$

$$4:\quad 8$$

$$5:\quad \text{DET}\begin{bmatrix} -1 & -1 & 2 \\ -2 & 2 & 4 \\ 1 & 3 & 0 \end{bmatrix}$$

$$6:\quad -8$$

c) $\text{DET}(\mathbf{A}) = \text{DET}(\mathbf{A}^{\text{T}})$:

$$4:\quad \text{DET}\begin{bmatrix} 2 & 1 & 4 \\ 2 & 0 & 1 \\ 1 & 0 & 2 \end{bmatrix}$$

5: -3

$$6: \quad \text{DET} \begin{bmatrix} 2 & 2 & 1 \\ 1 & 0 & 0 \\ 4 & 1 & 2 \end{bmatrix}$$

7: -3

d) Multiplying a row (column) by a constant multiplies the determinant by the same constant:

Multiplying the second row of the first matrix in part c) above by the constant c we have

$$2: \quad \text{DET} \begin{bmatrix} 2 & 1 & 4 \\ 2c & 0 & c \\ 1 & 0 & 2 \end{bmatrix}$$

3: - 3 c

e) Adding a multiple of one row (column) to another row (column) results in a matrix with an equal determinant:

Adding three times row 1 to row 3 in the first matrix to obtain the second matrix

$$2: \quad \text{DET} \begin{bmatrix} 1 & 3 & 4 \\ 2 & 5 & 0 \\ -2 & 2 & -4 \end{bmatrix}$$

3: 60

$$7: \quad \text{DET} \begin{bmatrix} 1 & 3 & 4 \\ 2 & 5 & 0 \\ 1 & 11 & 8 \end{bmatrix}$$

8: 60

f) The determinant of a matrix with two identical columns is zero:

$$2:\quad \text{DET}\begin{bmatrix} 1 & 4 & 1 \\ 3 & 2 & 3 \\ 4 & 3 & 4 \end{bmatrix}$$

$$3:\quad 0$$

EXERCISES

1. Let $\mathbf{A} = \begin{bmatrix} 1 & 2 & 3 \\ 2 & 3 & 1 \\ 3 & 1 & 2 \end{bmatrix}$ and $\mathbf{B} = \begin{bmatrix} -1 & 3 & 4 \\ 4 & -1 & 2 \\ 0 & 2 & 1 \end{bmatrix}$. Compute the following:

   a) DET(**A**) b) DET(**B**)
   c) DET(**AB**) d) DET(**BA**)
   e) Does **AB** = **BA**?

2. Show that $\text{DET}(\mathbf{A})\text{DET}(\mathbf{A}^{-1}) = 1$, provided $\mathbf{A}^{-1}$ exists.

3. Show that if **A** and **B** are similar, then DET(**A**) = DET(**B**).

4. Construct examples to illustrate the statements in Exercises 2 and 3.

5. If $\mathbf{A} = \begin{bmatrix} 1 & 2 & 0 & 1 & 3 \\ 2 & 3 & 1 & 1 & 4 \\ 0 & 0 & 3 & 5 & 6 \\ 2 & 1 & 0 & 8 & 2 \\ 1 & 3 & 2 & 5 & 2 \end{bmatrix}$, compute

   a) A_{32} b) A_{44}
   c) A_{33}.

6. If $\mathbf{A} = \begin{bmatrix} 1 & 1 & 3 \\ 2 & 1 & 2 \\ 0 & 3 & 2 \end{bmatrix}$, then find $a_{21}A_{11} + a_{22}A_{12} + a_{23}A_{13}$.

7. For the matrix in Exercise 6, compute $\begin{bmatrix} A_{11} & A_{21} & A_{31} \\ A_{12} & A_{22} & A_{31} \\ A_{13} & A_{23} & A_{33} \end{bmatrix}$, and multiply the result by **A**.

8. Let $\mathbf{A} = \begin{bmatrix} 1 & 2 & 0 \\ -2 & 1 & 3 \\ 2 & 3 & 1 \end{bmatrix}$ and $\mathbf{B} = \begin{bmatrix} 2 & 2 & 2 \\ 3 & 2 & 1 \\ 0 & -3 & 1 \end{bmatrix}$, and compute

a) DET(**A** + **B**)
b) DET(**A**) + DET(**B**)

9. Prove the following theorems:

a) Theorem 1.1
b) Theorem 1.2

2. THE ADJOINT MATRIX

In Section 4.1 our definition of the determinant of a matrix $\mathbf{A} = \begin{bmatrix} a & b \\ c & d \end{bmatrix}$ was motivated by noticing that **A** is invertible if and only if $ad - bc \neq 0$. We therefore chose this difference to be the determinant of a 2×2 matrix. Since the determinant of a higher dimension matrix **A** is defined inductively in terms of the *ij*-minor, which is obtained from **A** by removing row *i* and column *j*, we might wonder if this test for invertibility can be generalized to higher dimension matrices. In this section we will define a matrix called the adjoint (also sometimes referred to as the adjugate matrix) in terms of the cofactors A_{ij} of the a_{ij} elements of **A**. The relationship we will be able to establish between the adjoint of a matrix **A** and the determinant of **A** will help establish a connection between invertibility and the value of the determinant of a matrix.

DEFINITION 2.1 (Adjoint of a Matrix) The adjoint of a square matrix **A** of order *n* is the matrix of order *n* comprised of the cofactors of the a_{ij} elements of **A** as follows:

$$\mathrm{ADJ}(\mathbf{A}) = \begin{bmatrix} \mathrm{A}_{11} & \mathrm{A}_{12} & \cdots & \mathrm{A}_{1n} \\ \mathrm{A}_{21} & \mathrm{A}_{22} & \cdots & \mathrm{A}_{2n} \\ \vdots & \vdots & \vdots & \vdots \\ \mathrm{A}_{n1} & \mathrm{A}_{n2} & \cdots & \mathrm{A}_{nn} \end{bmatrix}^{\mathrm{T}} = \begin{bmatrix} \mathrm{A}_{11} & \mathrm{A}_{21} & \cdots & \mathrm{A}_{n1} \\ \mathrm{A}_{12} & \mathrm{A}_{22} & \cdots & \mathrm{A}_{n2} \\ \vdots & \vdots & \vdots & \vdots \\ \mathrm{A}_{1n} & \mathrm{A}_{2n} & \cdots & \mathrm{A}_{nn} \end{bmatrix}$$

EXAMPLE 2.1 The adjoint of

$$\mathbf{A} = \begin{bmatrix} 1 & -2 & 3 \\ 3 & 0 & 2 \\ 0 & 2 & 4 \end{bmatrix}$$

can be found using *Derive*:

$$13: \quad \begin{bmatrix} \text{DET}\begin{bmatrix} 0 & 2 \\ 2 & 4 \end{bmatrix} & -\text{DET}\begin{bmatrix} 3 & 2 \\ 0 & 4 \end{bmatrix} & \text{DET}\begin{bmatrix} 3 & 0 \\ 0 & 2 \end{bmatrix} \\ -\text{DET}\begin{bmatrix} -2 & 3 \\ 2 & 4 \end{bmatrix} & \text{DET}\begin{bmatrix} 1 & 3 \\ 0 & 4 \end{bmatrix} & -\text{DET}\begin{bmatrix} 1 & -2 \\ 0 & 2 \end{bmatrix} \\ \text{DET}\begin{bmatrix} -2 & 3 \\ 0 & 2 \end{bmatrix} & -\text{DET}\begin{bmatrix} 1 & 3 \\ 3 & 2 \end{bmatrix} & \text{DET}\begin{bmatrix} 1 & -2 \\ 3 & 0 \end{bmatrix} \end{bmatrix}^{\text{`}}$$

$$14: \quad \begin{bmatrix} -4 & 14 & -4 \\ -12 & 4 & 7 \\ 6 & -2 & 6 \end{bmatrix}$$

(Notice that statement #13 is set up in the form of the middle part of the three part equation in Definition 2.1.)

Derive also has a shortcut method of calculating the adjoint of a matrix by using the **T**ransfer **L**oad **D**erive command sequence followed by entering VECTOR.MTH at the file name prompt. Among the several useful utility programs in this file is one which upon **A**uthoring the command ADJOINT **(A)** will immediately find the adjoint of the matrix **A** without going through the cumbersome exercise of explicitly setting up the determinants of each entry as we did in statement #13 above.

Next, we extend a result from Section 4.1 which connected the concepts of determinant and cofactor. This in turn leads us to a theorem which characterizes the product of a matrix **A** and its adjoint matrix.

THEOREM 2.1 Let **A** be a square matrix of order n, then

$$\sum_{k=1}^{n} a_{ik}\mathrm{A}_{jk} = \begin{cases} \mathrm{DET}(\mathbf{A}) & \text{if } i = j \\ 0 & \text{if } i \neq j \end{cases}$$

and

$$\sum_{k=1}^{n} a_{ki}\mathrm{A}_{kj} = \begin{cases} \mathrm{DET}(\mathbf{A}) & \text{if } i = j \\ 0 & \text{if } i \neq j \end{cases}.$$

PROOF: The two equations are equivalent in the sense that the first is an expansion about row i and the second is an expansion about column i. We will show that the first equation is true.

In the case that $i = j$, the summation is equal to DET(**A**) by Theorem 1.1.

If the case $i \neq j$, define a new matrix **B** equal to **A** except that $b_{jk} = a_{ik}$ for $k = 1, 2, \ldots, n$. Hence the ith and jth rows of **B** are equal, and DET(**B**) = 0 by Theorem 1.2f. Since all but the jth rows of **A** and **B** are equal, $\mathrm{A}_{jk} = \mathrm{B}_{jk}$, and

$$\sum_{k=1}^{n} a_{ik}\mathrm{A}_{jk} = \sum_{k=1}^{n} b_{jk}\mathrm{B}_{jk} = \mathrm{DET}(\mathbf{B}) = 0$$

THEOREM 2.2 If **A** is a matrix of order n, then

$$\mathbf{A}(\mathrm{ADJ}(\mathbf{A})) = (\mathrm{ADJ}(\mathbf{A}))\mathbf{A} = (\mathrm{DET}(\mathbf{A}))\,\mathbf{I}.$$

PROOF: The ij element of $\mathbf{A}\,(\mathrm{ADJ}(\mathbf{A}))$ is

$$a_{i1}\mathrm{A}_{j1} + a_{i2}\mathrm{A}_{j2} + \cdots + a_{in}\mathrm{A}_{jn},$$

which, by Theorem 2.1 is 0 for $i \neq j$ and DET(**A**) if $i = j$. The fact that **A** and ADJ(**A**) commute follows from the second part of Theorem 2.1 since the ij element of (ADJ(**A**))**A** is formed by expanding about the ith column of **A**.

EXAMPLE 2.2 When we multiply the matrix **A** of Example 2.1 by its adjoint

$$15: \begin{bmatrix} 1 & -2 & 3 \\ 3 & 0 & 2 \\ 0 & 2 & 4 \end{bmatrix} \cdot \begin{bmatrix} -4 & 14 & -4 \\ -12 & 4 & 7 \\ 6 & -2 & 6 \end{bmatrix}$$

$$16: \begin{bmatrix} 38 & 0 & 0 \\ 0 & 38 & 0 \\ 0 & 0 & 38 \end{bmatrix}$$

the result is a matrix with DET(**A**) = 38 in each of the main diagonal elements and zeros elsewhere.

We now have a means of determining if a matrix **A** is invertible based on the value of its determinant.

COROLLARY 2.1 If **A** is a square matrix of order n then

$$\mathbf{A}^{-1} = \frac{\mathrm{ADJ}(\mathbf{A})}{\mathrm{DET}(\mathbf{A})}$$

provided $\mathrm{DET}(\mathbf{A}) \neq 0$.

COROLLARY 2.2 If **A** is a square matrix of order n, then $\mathbf{A}^{-1}$ exists if and only if $\mathrm{DET}(\mathbf{A}) \neq 0$.

EXAMPLE 2.3 The inverse of the matrix **A** in Example 2.1 can be computed:

$$\mathbf{A}^{-1} = \frac{\mathrm{ADJ}(\mathbf{A})}{\mathrm{DET}(\mathbf{A})}$$

$$19: \frac{1}{38} \begin{bmatrix} -4 & 14 & -4 \\ -12 & 4 & 7 \\ 6 & -2 & 6 \end{bmatrix}$$

$$20: \begin{bmatrix} -\frac{2}{19} & \frac{7}{19} & -\frac{2}{19} \\ -\frac{6}{19} & \frac{2}{19} & \frac{7}{38} \\ \frac{3}{19} & -\frac{1}{19} & \frac{3}{19} \end{bmatrix}$$

Finally, we use the results of this section together with the properties of determinants established in Section 4.1 to establish another test for invertibility.

THEOREM 2.3 If **A** and **B** are square matrices satisfying **AB** = **I**, then **A** (and **B**) is invertible and $\mathbf{A}^{-1} = \mathbf{B}$ (and $\mathbf{B}^{-1} = \mathbf{A}$).

PROOF: Since **AB** = **I**, DET(**AB**) = DET(**I**). But DET(**AB**) = DET(**A**)·DET(**B**) by Theorem 1.2a), and DET(**I**) = 1; therefore, DET(**A**) ≠ 0, and **A** is invertible by Corollary 2.2. It follows that $\mathbf{A}^{-1}(\mathbf{AB}) = \mathbf{A}^{-1}(\mathbf{I})$ and $\mathbf{B} = \mathbf{A}^{-1}$.

EXERCISES

1. Find the adjoint of the following matrices:

a) $\begin{bmatrix} 1 & 2 \\ 2 & 3 \end{bmatrix}$ b) $\begin{bmatrix} 0 & 1 \\ 1 & 2 \end{bmatrix}$

c) $\begin{bmatrix} -2 & 6 \\ 1 & 3 \end{bmatrix}$ d) $\begin{bmatrix} 2 & 8 \\ 1 & 4 \end{bmatrix}$

2. Which of the matrices in Exercise 1 have inverses?

3. Find the adjoint of each of the following matrices:

a) $\begin{bmatrix} 0 & 3 & 2 \\ 2 & 2 & 2 \\ -2 & 1 & 4 \end{bmatrix}$

b) $\begin{bmatrix} 1 & 3 & 4 \\ 2 & 2 & 4 \\ 1 & 1 & 2 \end{bmatrix}$

4. Which of the matrices in Exercise 3 have inverses?

5. Compute $\mathbf{A}(\text{ADJ}(\mathbf{A}))$ for the matrices in Exercise 3.

6. Find the inverse of $\mathbf{A} = \begin{bmatrix} a & b \\ c & d \end{bmatrix}$ without the use of *Derive*.

7. Find the inverse of
$$\begin{bmatrix} a & b & c \\ d & e & f \\ g & h & i \end{bmatrix}$$
without the use of *Derive*.
Hint: The element in the first row and first column is
$$\frac{A_{11}}{\text{DET}(\mathbf{A})} = \frac{ei - fh}{\text{DET}(\mathbf{A})}.$$

8. Prove that
$$\text{DET}(\mathbf{A}^{-1}) = \frac{1}{\text{DET}(\mathbf{A})}.$$

9. Prove or show the following statement is false:
$$\text{TR}(\mathbf{A}^{-1}) = \frac{1}{\text{TR}(\mathbf{A})}$$

10. Prove or show the following statement is false:
$$\text{ADJ}(\text{ADJ}(\mathbf{A})) = \mathbf{A}$$

11. Prove or show the following statement is false:
$\mathbf{A} = \mathbf{A}^2 \dfrac{\text{ADJ}(\mathbf{A})}{\text{DET}(\mathbf{A})}$ provided $\text{DET}(\mathbf{A}) \neq 0$.

3. CRAMER'S RULE AND SYSTEMS OF EQUATIONS

We have already seen many applications of solving systems of equations in the previous sections of this text. In this section we develop an alternate method of solving systems of equations using determinants, called Cramer's Rule. That study will lead us to an important test for determining the dependence or independence of vectors in R^n.

Let $\mathbf{Ax} = \mathbf{b}$ be a linear system of n equations in n unknowns. One of the first methods to solve such a system we discussed is multiplying both sides of the equation by the inverse of $\mathbf{A}$. In Section 4.2 we learned that the inverse exists and equals

$$\mathbf{A}^{-1} = \frac{\text{ADJ}(\mathbf{A})}{\text{DET}(\mathbf{A})}$$

when DET(**A**) is not zero. In this case

$$\mathbf{x} = \frac{\mathrm{ADJ}(\mathbf{A})\mathbf{b}}{\mathrm{DET}(\mathbf{A})}.$$

In order to find x_i, the ith element of the vector **x**, we examine the ith row of ADJ(**A**)**b**:

$$x_i = \frac{\mathrm{A}_{1i}b_1 + \mathrm{A}_{2i}b_2 + \cdots + \mathrm{A}_{ni}b_n}{\mathrm{DET}(\mathbf{A})}.$$

The numerator on the right hand side is simply the expansion of the determinant

$$\mathrm{DET}\begin{bmatrix} a_{11} & a_{12} & \cdots & a_{1i-1} & b_1 & a_{1i+1} & \cdots & a_{1n} \\ a_{21} & a_{22} & \cdots & a_{2i-1} & b_2 & a_{2i+1} & \cdots & a_{2n} \\ \vdots & \vdots & \vdots & \vdots & \vdots & \vdots & \vdots & \vdots \\ a_{i1} & a_{i2} & \cdots & a_{ii-1} & b_i & a_{ii+1} & \cdots & a_{in} \\ \vdots & \vdots & \vdots & \vdots & \vdots & \vdots & \vdots & \vdots \\ a_{n1} & a_{n2} & \cdots & a_{ni-1} & b_n & a_{ni+1} & \cdots & a_{nn} \end{bmatrix}$$

about column i. This leads us to the following rule for solving systems of linear equations:

THEOREM 3.1 (Cramer's Rule) If $\mathbf{Ax} = \mathbf{b}$ is a system of n linear equations in n unknowns, then the ith element of the vector **x** is given by

$$x_i = \frac{\mathrm{DET}\begin{bmatrix} a_{11} & a_{12} & \cdots & a_{1(i-1)} & b_1 & a_{1(i+1)} & \cdots & a_{1n} \\ a_{21} & a_{22} & \cdots & a_{2(i-1)} & b_2 & a_{2(i+1)} & \cdots & a_{2n} \\ \vdots & \vdots & \vdots & \vdots & \vdots & \vdots & \vdots & \vdots \\ a_{i1} & a_{i2} & \cdots & a_{i(i-1)} & b_i & a_{i(i+1)} & \cdots & a_{in} \\ \vdots & \vdots & \vdots & \vdots & \vdots & \vdots & \vdots & \vdots \\ a_{n1} & a_{n2} & \cdots & a_{n(i-1)} & b_n & a_{n(i+1)} & \cdots & a_{nn} \end{bmatrix}}{\mathrm{DET}(\mathbf{A})}.$$

EXAMPLE 3.1 Cramer's Rule can be used to solve the system of equations

$$\begin{aligned} 2x_1 + 2x_2 + 4x_3 &= 5 \\ x_1 + 2x_2 - 5x_3 &= 4 \\ 3x_1 + x_2 - 3x_3 &= 5. \end{aligned}$$

First, we compute the determinant of the coefficient matrix **A** since it is used in the solution of each element of **x**:

$$2: \quad \text{DET}\begin{bmatrix} 2 & 2 & 4 \\ 1 & 2 & -5 \\ 3 & 1 & -3 \end{bmatrix}$$

$$3: \quad -46$$

Next, to solve for x_1, we find the quotient of the determinant of a new matrix formed by replacing the first column of the coefficient matrix with the vector of constants divided by the determinant of the coefficient matrix.

$$5: \quad \frac{\text{DET}\begin{bmatrix} 5 & 2 & 4 \\ 4 & 2 & -5 \\ 5 & 1 & -3 \end{bmatrix}}{-46}$$

$$6: \quad \frac{55}{46}$$

The result in statement #6 is the value for x_1. To solve for x_2 and x_3, we find similar quotients replacing the second and third columns of the coefficient matrix respectively with the constant vector. Thus

$$8: \quad \frac{\text{DET}\begin{bmatrix} 2 & 5 & 4 \\ 1 & 4 & -5 \\ 3 & 5 & -3 \end{bmatrix}}{-46}$$

$$9: \quad \frac{31}{23}$$

and

$$11: \quad \frac{\text{DET}\begin{bmatrix} 2 & 2 & 5 \\ 1 & 2 & 4 \\ 3 & 1 & 5 \end{bmatrix}}{-46}$$

$$12: \quad -\frac{1}{46}$$

yielding x_2 and x_3 respectively, and $\mathbf{x} = \begin{bmatrix} \frac{55}{46} & \frac{31}{23} & \frac{-1}{46} \end{bmatrix}^T$.

Cramer's Rule leads to the following convenient test which can be used to determine whether a system of equations has a unique solution.

THEOREM 3.2 The system of equations $\mathbf{Ax} = \mathbf{b}$ has a unique solution if $\text{DET}(\mathbf{A}) \neq 0$.

PROOF: The proof follows immediately as a consequence of Cramer's Rule.

THEOREM 3.3 The system of equations $\mathbf{Ax} = \mathbf{0}$ has a non-zero solution if and only if $\text{DET}(\mathbf{A}) = 0$.

PROOF: Let $\mathbf{C}_i$ be the matrix in Cramer's Rule with the constant vector replacing column i of the coefficient matrix $\mathbf{A}$. In this case Cramer's Rule may be written as

$$x_i = \frac{\text{DET}(\mathbf{C}_i)}{\text{DET}(\mathbf{A})}.$$

The equation

$$\text{DET}(\mathbf{A})x_i = \text{DET}(\mathbf{C}_i)$$

holds even if DET(**A**) = 0. Since $\text{DET}(\mathbf{C}_i) = 0$ for all i (every entry of the ith column of $\mathbf{C}_i$ is zero), for each i either DET(**A**) or x_i is zero. It follows that if any x_i is non-zero, then DET(**A**) = 0.

On the other hand, if DET(**A**) = 0, then **A** is not invertible by Corollary 2.2, and the augmented matrix for the system of equations **Ax** = **0** will have at least one row of zeros when reduced to row echelon form (since the rightmost column of constants in the augmented matrix is all zeros). It follows that the most general solution to the system has an arbitrary parameter; therefore, a non-zero solution exists.

Since we determine the linear independence of a set of vectors by solving a system of equations of the form **Ax** = **0**, we can use the results of Theorem 3.3 to design a test which will establish whether a set of vectors in R^n is linearly independent or linearly dependent.

THEOREM 3.4 In R^n the set of n vectors $\{\mathbf{x}_1, \mathbf{x}_2, \cdots, \mathbf{x}_n\}$ is linearly independent if $\text{DET}[\mathbf{x}_1 \quad \mathbf{x}_2 \quad \cdots \quad \mathbf{x}_n] \neq 0$, and linearly dependent if $\text{DET}[\mathbf{x}_1 \quad \mathbf{x}_2 \quad \cdots \quad \mathbf{x}_n] = 0$.

PROOF: To determine if $\{\mathbf{x}_1, \mathbf{x}_2, \cdots, \mathbf{x}_n\}$ is linearly independent or linearly dependent we consider the equation in n unknowns

$$a_1\mathbf{x}_1 + a_2\mathbf{x}_2 + \cdots + a_n\mathbf{x}_n = \mathbf{0}.$$

Since each $\mathbf{x}_i$ is an n dimensional vector, with n components, this equation can be interpreted as a system of n equations in n unknowns. By Theorem 3.2 the system has a unique solution (which therefore must be the zero solution) if

$$\text{DET}[\mathbf{x}_1 \quad \mathbf{x}_2 \quad \cdots \quad \mathbf{x}_n] \neq 0.$$

On the other hand, if

$$\text{DET}[\mathbf{x}_1 \quad \mathbf{x}_2 \quad \cdots \quad \mathbf{x}_n] = 0,$$

the system has a non zero solution by Theorem 3.3, and the vectors are linearly dependent.

EXAMPLE 3.2 The result stated in Theorem 3.4 can be used to determine if the two sets

$$S = \left\{ \begin{bmatrix} 1 \\ 2 \\ 1 \end{bmatrix}, \begin{bmatrix} -2 \\ 3 \\ 4 \end{bmatrix}, \begin{bmatrix} 0 \\ 4 \\ 1 \end{bmatrix} \right\} \quad \text{and} \quad T = \left\{ \begin{bmatrix} 1 \\ 6 \\ 4 \end{bmatrix}, \begin{bmatrix} 0 \\ 2 \\ 2 \end{bmatrix}, \begin{bmatrix} -2 \\ -3 \\ 1 \end{bmatrix} \right\}$$

are linearly independent or linearly dependent:

$$3: \quad \text{DET} \begin{bmatrix} 1 & -2 & 0 \\ 2 & 3 & 4 \\ 1 & 4 & 1 \end{bmatrix}$$

$$4: \quad -17$$

$$5: \quad \text{DET} \begin{bmatrix} 1 & 0 & -2 \\ 6 & 2 & -3 \\ 4 & 2 & 1 \end{bmatrix}$$

$$6: \quad 0$$

Thus, the set S is linearly independent while the set T is linearly dependent.

It is also possible to use determinants to find if a set of functions defined on an interval is linearly independent. The following definition and theorem provide an example.

DEFINITION 3.1 (Wronskian) The determinant

$$W(f_1, f_2, \cdots, f_n) = \text{DET} \begin{bmatrix} f_1(x) & f_2(x) & \cdots & f_n(x) \\ f_1'(x) & f_2'(x) & \cdots & f_n'(x) \\ \vdots & \vdots & \vdots & \vdots \\ f_1^{n-1}(x) & f_2^{n-1}(x) & \cdots & f_n^{n-1}(x) \end{bmatrix}$$

is called the Wronskian of the set of functions $F^{n-1}[a,b]=\{f_1(x),f_2(x),\cdots,f_n(x)\}$ which are all defined and possess at least n-1 derivatives on the interval $[a,b]$.

THEOREM 3.5 Let $F^{n-1}[a,b]=\{f_1(x),f_2(x),\cdots,f_n(x)\}$ be a set of functions defined and possessing at least n-1 derivatives on the interval $[a,b]$. If $F^{n-1}[a,b]$ is linearly dependent, then

$$\mathrm{W}(f_1,f_2,\cdots,f_n)=0$$

for all $x\in[a,b]$.

PROOF: Since $F^{n-1}[a,b]$ is linearly dependent, there exist coefficients a_1, a_2,..., a_n, not all zero, such that

$$a_1f_1(x)+a_2f_2(x)+\cdots+a_nf_n(x)=0.$$

This equation can be differentiated n-1 times yielding the system of n equations:

$$\begin{aligned}
a_1f_1(x) + a_2f_2(x) +\cdots+ a_nf_n(x) &= 0\\
a_1f_1'(x) + a_2f_2'(x) +\cdots+ a_nf_n'(x) &= 0\\
\cdots\cdots\cdots\cdots\\
a_1f_1^{n-1}(x) + a_2f_2^{n-1}(x) +\cdots+ a_nf_n^{n-1}(x) &= 0
\end{aligned}$$

Since the constants a_i; $i=1,2,\cdots,n$ are not all zero, by Theorem 3.3 the determinant of the coefficient matrix, which is $\mathrm{W}(f_1,f_2,\cdots,f_n)$, must be zero.

THEOREM 3.6 Let $F^{n-1}[a,b]=\{f_1(x),f_2(x),\cdots,f_n(x)\}$ be a set of functions defined and possessing at least n-1 derivatives on the interval $[a,b]$. If for some $x\in[a,b]$

$$\mathrm{W}(f_1,f_2,\cdots,f_n)\neq 0,$$

then $F^{n-1}[a,b]$ is a linearly independent set.

PROOF: This is the contrapositive of Theorem 3.5.

EXAMPLE 3.3 We can use the results of Theorems 3.5 and 3.6 to determine if the set of functions $\{e^{2x}, e^{-x}\}$ is linearly independent or linearly dependent on the real line. First, we evaluate the Wronskian

$$8: \quad \text{DET}\begin{bmatrix} \hat{e}^{2x} & \hat{e}^{-x} \\ 2\,\hat{e}^{2x} & -\hat{e}^{-x} \end{bmatrix}$$

$$9: \quad -3\,\hat{e}^{x}$$

where the second row of the matrix is the derivative of the first row taken column by column. (Note: In *Derive* the value e^x is entered by Authoring the statement #e^(x) or exp(x) followed by the Simplify command.) Since the function in statement #9 is non-zero for all values of x, the set of functions is linearly independent.

EXAMPLE 3.4 The set of functions $\{x+1,\ x+2,\ x+3\}$ on the real line is linearly dependent since the value of the Wronskian is zero as demonstrated by

$$11: \quad \text{DET}\begin{bmatrix} x+1 & x+2 & x+3 \\ 1 & 1 & 1 \\ 0 & 0 & 0 \end{bmatrix}$$

$$12: \quad 0$$

where the second and third rows of the matrix are the first and second derivatives of the first row taken column by column.

While the contrapositive of Theorem 3.5 (and, in fact, any theorem) is true, the converse is not. The following example provides a set of functions such that $W(f_1, f_2, \cdots, f_n) = 0$ but $F^{n-1}[a,b]$ is a linearly independent set.

EXAMPLE 3.5 The functions $f(x) = x^3$ and $g(x) = |x^3|$ are linearly independent because if p and q are two constants satisfying

$$px^3 + q|x^3| = 0,$$

then

$$p(1) + q|1| = 0$$

and

$$p(-1) + q|-1| = 0.$$

This implies both $p = q$ and $p = -q$, which is only true if $p = q = 0$, and the two functions f and g are linearly independent. On the other hand,

$$W(x^3, |x^3|) = \text{DET}\begin{bmatrix} x^3 & |x^3| \\ 3x^2 & 3x|x| \end{bmatrix} = 3x^4|x| - 3x^2|x^3| = 0;$$

therefore, the converse of Theorem 3.5 is not true.

EXERCISES

1. For the following systems of equations use Cramer's rule to find the indicated unknown

   a) Find x_2
   $$2x_1 + x_2 - x_3 = 4$$
   $$x_1 - 3x_2 + 2x_3 = 2$$
   $$x_1 + 6x_3 = 3$$

   b) Find x_3
   $$2x_1 - 3x_2 - x_3 = 0$$
   $$x_1 - x_2 + 5x_3 = 0$$
   $$4x_1 + 7x_2 + 5x_3 = 1$$

   c) Find x_1
   $$x_1 + x_2 + x_3 = 3$$
   $$x_2 + x_3 = 2$$
   $$x_3 = 1$$

   d) Find x_2
   $$x_1 + 2x_2 + 3x_3 = 4$$
   $$2x_1 + 3x_2 + 4x_3 = 1$$
   $$x_1 + 3x_2 + 5x_3 = 0$$

2. Determine if the following sets of vectors are linearly independent:

a) $\left\{\begin{bmatrix}1\\2\end{bmatrix}, \begin{bmatrix}2\\5\end{bmatrix}\right\}$

b) $\left\{\begin{bmatrix}1\\3\end{bmatrix}, \begin{bmatrix}2\\6\end{bmatrix}\right\}$

c) $\left\{\begin{bmatrix}1\\1\\2\end{bmatrix}, \begin{bmatrix}2\\1\\1\end{bmatrix}, \begin{bmatrix}1\\2\\1\end{bmatrix}\right\}$

d) $\left\{\begin{bmatrix}3\\4\\1\end{bmatrix}, \begin{bmatrix}-1\\2\\1\end{bmatrix}, \begin{bmatrix}2\\6\\2\end{bmatrix}\right\}$

3. Determine if the following systems have a non-zero solution

a) $\begin{cases} x+y=0 \\ x-y=0 \end{cases}$

b) $\begin{cases} x+2y=0 \\ 2x+4y=0 \end{cases}$

c) $\begin{cases} 2x_1+3x_2+2x_3=0 \\ 2x_1+x_2=0 \\ 2x_1+4x_2+3x_3=0 \end{cases}$

d) $\begin{cases} x+2y+2z=0 \\ 3x+4y+2z=0 \\ 4x+5y+2z=0 \end{cases}$

e) $\begin{cases} 2x+3y+z=0 \\ -2x+3y-z=0 \\ 4x+3y+5z=0 \end{cases}$

f) $\begin{cases} x+y=0 \\ y+z=0 \\ x+z=0 \end{cases}$

4. Show that the following sets of functions are linearly independent on $[-1,1]$.

a) $\{1,\ x,\ x^2,\ x^3\}$

b) $\{e^x,\ e^{2x},\ e^{3x}\}$

c) $\{\sin x,\ \cos x\}$

d) $\{1,\ \sin x,\ \cos x\}$

e) $\{\cos x,\ \cos 2x,\ \cos 3x\}$

f) $\{1,\ \sin x,\ \sin 2x\}$

5. Show that the following functions are linearly independent but that their Wronskian is zero:
$f(x)=x^3$ and $g(x)=|x^3|$.

CHAPTER V EIGENVALUES AND EIGENVECTORS

Thus far we have studied matrices from the perspective of their role as linear transformations and the resulting effect of applying them to vectors. In this chapter we examine the internal structure of matrices by studying eigenvalues, eigenvectors, canonical forms, and functions of matrices. Sometimes eigenvalues and eigenvectors are called characteristic values and characteristic vectors respectively. They play a fundamental role in the application of matrices to the solution of differential equations and in many other applications.

1. EIGENVALUES AND EIGENVECTORS

The identity matrix $\mathbf{I}_n$ has the property that $\mathbf{I}_n\mathbf{x} = \mathbf{x}$ for every n-dimensional vector $\mathbf{x}$. Other n order square matrices $\mathbf{A}$ exist such that $\mathbf{Ax} = \mathbf{x}$ for some non-zero vectors $\mathbf{x}$. For example,

$$\mathbf{A} = \begin{bmatrix} 0 & 1 \\ 1 & 0 \end{bmatrix}$$

maps any vector $\mathbf{x}$ satisfying $x_1 = x_2$ to itself. But not all n order matrices have the property that they map some non-zero vector $\mathbf{x}$ to itself. For example, the only vector the matrix $2\mathbf{I}_n$ maps to itself is the zero vector. A more interesting question is to find all the square matrices of order n that map some non-zero vector to a scalar multiple of itself. It turns out that a large important class of matrices do have this property. The vector that is mapped to a multiple of itself is called an eigenvector and the constant multiplier is called an eigenvalue.

DEFINITION 1.1 (Eigenvector, Eigenvalue) Let **A** be a matrix of order n. If **x** is a non-zero vector and λ is a number such that $\mathbf{Ax} = \lambda\mathbf{x}$, then **x** is called an eigenvector and λ is called an eigenvalue.

From this definition we obtain the relation

$$\lambda\mathbf{x} - \mathbf{Ax} = \mathbf{0}$$

or

$$(\lambda\mathbf{I} - \mathbf{A})\mathbf{x} = \mathbf{0},$$

which is an equation in the n unknown components of the vector **x**. Since the right-hand side is zero, by Theorem 3.3 of Chapter 4, this system has a solution if and only if

$$\text{DET}(\lambda\mathbf{I} - \mathbf{A}) = 0.$$

In the case that **A** is a 2×2 matrix

$$\begin{aligned}\text{DET}(\lambda\mathbf{I} - \mathbf{A}) &= \text{DET}\left(\begin{bmatrix}\lambda & 0\\ 0 & \lambda\end{bmatrix} - \begin{bmatrix}a_{11} & a_{12}\\ a_{21} & a_{22}\end{bmatrix}\right)\\ &= \text{DET}\left(\begin{bmatrix}\lambda - a_{11} & a_{12}\\ a_{21} & \lambda - a_{22}\end{bmatrix}\right)\\ &= (\lambda - a_{11})(\lambda - a_{22}) - a_{12}a_{21} = \lambda^2 - (a_{11} + a_{22})\lambda + (a_{11}a_{22} - a_{12}a_{21})\end{aligned}$$

which is a polynomial in λ of degree two. In the case that **A** is a 3×3 matrix

$$\text{DET}(\lambda\mathbf{I} - \mathbf{A}) = (\lambda - a_{11})\text{A}_{11} + a_{12}\text{A}_{12} + a_{13}\text{A}_{13}$$

which is a polynomial in λ of degree three (since A_{11} is a polynomial in λ of degree two). It follows (using a proof by mathematical induction) that DET(λ**I** - **A**) is a polynomial in λ of the same degree as the order of **A**. This polynomial plays an important role in the study of eigenvectors and eigenvalues.

DEFINITION 1.2 (Characteristic Polynomial) The polynomial

$$\mathrm{DET}(\lambda\mathbf{I}-\mathbf{A}) = \lambda^n - p_1\lambda^{n-1} - p_2\lambda^{n-2} - \cdots - p_1\lambda - p_0$$

is called the characteristic polynomial of **A**.

THEOREM 1.1 The zeros of the characteristic polynomial of **A** are the eigenvalues of **A**.

PROOF: The number λ is an eigenvalue of **A** if $\mathbf{Ax} = \lambda\mathbf{x}$, or if $(\lambda\mathbf{I}-\mathbf{A})\mathbf{x} = \mathbf{0}$, where **x** is a non-zero vector. By Theorem 3.3 of Chapter 4, the second of these two relations has a non-zero solution if and only if λ satisfies $\mathrm{DET}(\lambda\mathbf{I}-\mathbf{A}) = 0$. But $\mathrm{DET}(\lambda\mathbf{I}-\mathbf{A})$ is defined to be the characteristic polynomial of **A**, thus its zeros are the eigenvalues of **A**.

We remark that a matrix of order n has a characteristic polynomial of degree n and by the fundamental theorem of algebra has n zeros, some of which may be equal.

EXAMPLE 1.1 The eigenvalues of

$$\mathbf{A} = \begin{bmatrix} -1 & -3 & -3 \\ 0 & 2 & -1 \\ 2 & 2 & 5 \end{bmatrix}$$

can be found using *Derive*:

3: $\mathrm{DET}\left[w\begin{bmatrix} 1 & 0 & 0 \\ 0 & 1 & 0 \\ 0 & 0 & 1 \end{bmatrix} - \begin{bmatrix} -1 & -3 & -3 \\ 0 & 2 & -1 \\ 2 & 2 & 5 \end{bmatrix}\right]$

4: $w^3 - 6w^2 + 11w - 6$

5: $(w - 3)(w - 2)(w - 1)$

From statement #5 (which is found by using the Factor command on statement #4), we see the eigenvalues are 1, 2, and 3.

Given these eigenvalues of the matrix **A**, the eigenvectors of **A** can be found by solving $(\lambda\mathbf{I}-\mathbf{A})\mathbf{x}=\mathbf{0}$ for the components of **x**.

$$6: \quad \text{ROW\_REDUCE}\left[3\begin{bmatrix}1&0&0\\0&1&0\\0&0&1\end{bmatrix}-\begin{bmatrix}-1&-3&-3\\0&2&-1\\2&2&5\end{bmatrix},\begin{bmatrix}0\\0\\0\end{bmatrix}\right]$$

$$7: \quad \begin{bmatrix}1&0&0&0\\0&1&1&0\\0&0&0&0\end{bmatrix}$$

(Note how the augmented matrix representing the characteristic polynomial can be formed within the ROW_REDUCE command by first computing the coefficient matrix and then, following a comma, entering the matrix of constants.) It follows that the components of the eigenvector belonging to $\lambda=3$ are $x_3=\alpha$, $x_2=-\alpha$, and $x_1=0$; hence, the eigenvectors of **A** belonging to $\lambda=3$ are vectors of the form

$$\begin{bmatrix}0\\-\alpha\\\alpha\end{bmatrix}$$

where α is any arbitrary number. For instance, all of the following are eigenvectors belonging to $\lambda=3$:

$$\begin{bmatrix}0\\-1\\1\end{bmatrix},\quad \begin{bmatrix}0\\5\\-5\end{bmatrix},\quad \text{and} \begin{bmatrix}0\\-2\\2\end{bmatrix}.$$

As a confirmation that the product of **A** and an eigenvector of **A** is a multiple of the eigenvector, we choose an eigenvector for $\lambda=3$:

$$9: \quad \begin{bmatrix}-1&-3&-3\\0&2&-1\\2&2&5\end{bmatrix}\cdot\begin{bmatrix}0\\-1\\1\end{bmatrix}$$

$$\text{10:} \quad \begin{bmatrix} 0 \\ -3 \\ 3 \end{bmatrix}$$

and note that $\mathbf{Ax} = 3\mathbf{x}$.

By similar arguments we can show that the eigenvectors corresponding to $\lambda = 2$ have the form $[-\beta \;\; \beta \;\; 0]^{\mathrm{T}}$, and those corresponding to $\lambda = 1$ have the form $[-3\gamma \;\; \gamma \;\; \gamma]^{\mathrm{T}}$.

The following theorem establishes that a set of representative vectors chosen from the groups of eigenvectors associated with particular eigenvalues are linearly independent (and therefore, in the case of the above example, form a basis).

THEOREM 1.2 Sets of eigenvectors belonging to distinct eigenvalues are linearly independent.

PROOF: Let $\lambda_1, \lambda_2, \cdots, \lambda_p$ be distinct eigenvalues and $\mathbf{x}_1, \mathbf{x}_2, \cdots, \mathbf{x}_p$ be corresponding eigenvectors. We show $\mathbf{x}_1, \mathbf{x}_2, \cdots, \mathbf{x}_p$ are linearly independent by mathematical induction. First, $\mathbf{x}_1$, as a single vector, is linearly independent since it is a non-zero vector. Next, let $\mathbf{x}_1, \mathbf{x}_2, \cdots, \mathbf{x}_{p-1}$ be linearly independent and consider

$$a_1\mathbf{x}_1 + a_2\mathbf{x}_2 + \cdots + a_{p-1}\mathbf{x}_{p-1} + a_p\mathbf{x}_p = \mathbf{0}.$$

If we multiply this equation by $\mathbf{A}$, then

$$a_1\mathbf{Ax}_1 + a_2\mathbf{Ax}_2 + \cdots + a_{p-1}\mathbf{Ax}_{p-1} + a_p\mathbf{Ax}_p = \mathbf{0},$$

and, since $\mathbf{Ax}_i = \lambda_i\mathbf{x}_i$

$$a_1\lambda_1\mathbf{x}_1 + a_2\lambda_2\mathbf{x}_2 + \cdots + a_{p-1}\lambda_{p-1}\mathbf{x}_{p-1} + a_p\lambda_p\mathbf{x}_p = \mathbf{0}.$$

On the other hand, we can multiply our original equation by λ_p, obtaining

$$a_1\lambda_p\mathbf{x}_1 + a_2\lambda_p\mathbf{x}_2 + \cdots + a_{p-1}\lambda_p\mathbf{x}_{p-1} + a_p\lambda_p\mathbf{x}_p = \mathbf{0}.$$

If we subtract these last two equations

$$a_1(\lambda_1 - \lambda_p)\mathbf{x}_1 + a_2(\lambda_2 - \lambda_p)\mathbf{x}_2 + \cdots + a_{p-1}(\lambda_{p-1} - \lambda_p)\mathbf{x}_{p-1} + a_p(\lambda_p - \lambda_p)\mathbf{x}_p = \mathbf{0}$$

or

$$a_1(\lambda_1 - \lambda_p)\mathbf{x}_1 + a_2(\lambda_2 - \lambda_p)\mathbf{x}_2 + \cdots + a_{p-1}(\lambda_{p-1} - \lambda_p)\mathbf{x}_{p-1} = \mathbf{0}.$$

But since $\mathbf{x}_1$, $\mathbf{x}_2, \cdots$, $\mathbf{x}_{p-1}$ are linearly independent and $\lambda_i - \lambda_p \neq 0$ (the eigenvalues are distinct), $a_1 = a_2 = \cdots = a_{p-1} = 0$. Therefore, $a_p\mathbf{x}_p = \mathbf{0}$, and $a_p = 0$. It follows that the eigenvectors $\mathbf{x}_1$, $\mathbf{x}_2, \cdots$, $\mathbf{x}_p$ are linearly independent, and the proof is complete.

EXAMPLE 1.2 The eigenvectors of Example 1.1 are linearly independent since the matrix formed by taking the eigenvectors of **A** as columns has a non-zero determinant:

$$18: \quad \text{DET}\begin{bmatrix} 0 & -\beta & -3\gamma \\ -\alpha & \beta & \gamma \\ \alpha & 0 & \gamma \end{bmatrix}$$

$$19: \quad \alpha\ \beta\ \gamma$$

(which is non-zero since the parameters α, β, and γ must be non-zero to satisfy the requirement that an eigenvector cannot be the zero vector).

Next, we introduce the concept of transforming a square matrix into a matrix of the same order with non-zero entries being restricted to main diagonal elements which correspond to the eigenvalues of the matrix. This transformed diagonal matrix will prove useful in future applications.

DEFINITION 1.3 (Diagonal Matrix) A matrix **A** is said to be a diagonal matrix if $(a_{ij}) = 0$ for $i \neq j$. We use the notation

$$\begin{bmatrix} a_{11} & 0 & \cdots & 0 \\ 0 & a_{22} & \cdots & 0 \\ \vdots & \vdots & \ddots & \vdots \\ 0 & 0 & \cdots & a_{nn} \end{bmatrix} = \text{DIAG}\begin{bmatrix} a_{11} & a_{22} & \cdots & a_{nn} \end{bmatrix}.$$

THEOREM 1.3 If **A** is a matrix of order n with distinct eigenvalues $\lambda_1, \lambda_2, \cdots, \lambda_n$ and corresponding eigenvectors $\mathbf{x}_1, \mathbf{x}_2, \cdots, \mathbf{x}_n$, and **U** is the matrix $\begin{bmatrix} \mathbf{x}_1 & \mathbf{x}_2 & \cdots & \mathbf{x}_n \end{bmatrix}$, then **U** is nonsingular and

$$\mathbf{U}^{-1}\mathbf{A}\mathbf{U} = \begin{bmatrix} \lambda_1 & 0 & 0 & 0 \\ 0 & \lambda_2 & 0 & 0 \\ 0 & 0 & \ddots & 0 \\ 0 & 0 & 0 & \lambda_n \end{bmatrix}.$$

PROOF: By Theorem 1.2 the columns $\mathbf{x}_1, \mathbf{x}_2, \cdots, \mathbf{x}_n$ of **U** are linearly independent; therefore, by Theorem 3.4 of Chapter 4, DET(**U**) $\neq$ 0, and it follows from Corollary 2.2 of Chapter 4 that **U** is non-singular. Using the fact that matrix multiplication is associative,

$$\begin{aligned} \mathbf{U}^{-1}\mathbf{A}\mathbf{U} &= \mathbf{U}^{-1}\begin{bmatrix} \mathbf{A}\mathbf{x}_1 & \mathbf{A}\mathbf{x}_2 & \cdots & \mathbf{A}\mathbf{x}_n \end{bmatrix} \\ &= \mathbf{U}^{-1}\begin{bmatrix} \lambda_1\mathbf{x}_1 & \lambda_2\mathbf{x}_2 & \cdots & \lambda_n\mathbf{x}_n \end{bmatrix} \\ &= \mathbf{U}^{-1}\begin{bmatrix} \mathbf{x}_1 & \mathbf{x}_2 & \cdots & \mathbf{x}_n \end{bmatrix}\text{DIAG}\begin{bmatrix} \lambda_1 & \lambda_2 & \cdots & \lambda_n \end{bmatrix} \\ &= \mathbf{U}^{-1}\mathbf{U}\ \text{DIAG}\begin{bmatrix} \lambda_1 & \lambda_2 & \cdots & \lambda_n \end{bmatrix} \\ &= \text{DIAG}\begin{bmatrix} \lambda_1 & \lambda_2 & \cdots & \lambda_n \end{bmatrix} \end{aligned}$$

and the proof is complete.

Derive has a command, CHARPOLY(#nn) [where "#nn" is the statement number of the matrix], to compute the characteristic polynomial of a matrix **A** so that the user does not have to find and expand DET(w**I** - **A**). However, *Derive* computes $\text{DET}(\mathbf{A} - w\mathbf{I})$, and for matrices of odd order, $\text{DET}(w\mathbf{I} - \mathbf{A}) = -\text{DET}(\mathbf{A} - w\mathbf{I})$. This makes no difference when computing eigenvalues, but we will adopt the convention of finding the negative of the characteristic polynomial of matrices of odd order.

EXAMPLE 1.3 The process of computing the diagonal matrix $\mathbf{U}^{-1}\mathbf{AU}$ is called "diagonalizing" the matrix **A**. We can diagonalize the matrix

$$\mathbf{A} = \begin{bmatrix} 1 & -2 & -2 \\ 4 & 5 & 0 \\ -4 & -2 & 3 \end{bmatrix}$$

by first obtaining the characteristic polynomial of **A**:

$$2: \quad -\text{CHARPOLY}\begin{bmatrix} 1 & -2 & -2 \\ 4 & 5 & 0 \\ -4 & -2 & 3 \end{bmatrix}$$

$$3: \quad w^3 - 9w^2 + 23w - 15$$

$$4: \quad w = 1$$

$$5: \quad w = 3$$

$$6: \quad w = 5$$

and soLving for the eigenvalues shown in statements #4, #5, and #6. To find the eigenvectors, we set up

$$10: \quad \text{ROW\_REDUCE}\left[w \begin{bmatrix} 1 & 0 & 0 \\ 0 & 1 & 0 \\ 0 & 0 & 1 \end{bmatrix} - \begin{bmatrix} 1 & -2 & -2 \\ 4 & 5 & 0 \\ -4 & -2 & 3 \end{bmatrix}, \begin{bmatrix} 0 \\ 0 \\ 0 \end{bmatrix} \right]$$

and substitute the eigenvalues for w to obtain the three eigenvectors

$$\begin{bmatrix} \alpha \\ -\alpha \\ \alpha \end{bmatrix} \text{ when } w = 1; \quad \begin{bmatrix} \beta \\ -2\beta \\ \beta \end{bmatrix} \text{ when } w = 3; \quad \text{and} \quad \begin{bmatrix} 0 \\ -\gamma \\ \gamma \end{bmatrix} \text{ when } w = 5.$$

Since α, β, and γ are arbitrary, we can choose $\alpha = 1$, $\beta = 1$, and $\gamma = 1$ and substitute the corresponding eigenvectors for the columns of **U** as follows:

$$\mathbf{U} = \begin{bmatrix} 1 & 1 & 0 \\ -1 & -2 & -1 \\ 1 & 1 & 1 \end{bmatrix}.$$

The matrix **A** can now be diagonalized:

$$18: \quad \begin{bmatrix} 1 & 1 & 0 \\ -1 & -2 & -1 \\ 1 & 1 & 1 \end{bmatrix}^{-1} \cdot \begin{bmatrix} 1 & -2 & -2 \\ 4 & 5 & 0 \\ -4 & -2 & 3 \end{bmatrix} \cdot \begin{bmatrix} 1 & 1 & 0 \\ -1 & -2 & -1 \\ 1 & 1 & 1 \end{bmatrix}$$

$$19: \quad \begin{bmatrix} 1 & 0 & 0 \\ 0 & 3 & 0 \\ 0 & 0 & 5 \end{bmatrix}$$

where the elements on the main diagonal are the eigenvalues of **A**.

The following example illustrates that it is not necessary for the order of a square matrix to equal the number of its distinct eigenvalues for it to be diagonalized.

EXAMPLE 1.4 The characteristic polynomial of

$$\mathbf{A} = \begin{bmatrix} -2 & -2 & 2 \\ 4 & 5 & 0 \\ -4 & -2 & 3 \end{bmatrix}$$

can be found using *Derive*:

$$8: \quad -\ \mathrm{CHARPOLY} \begin{bmatrix} -2 & -2 & 2 \\ 4 & 4 & -2 \\ -2 & -1 & 3 \end{bmatrix}$$

$$9: \quad w^3 - 5\,w^2 + 8\,w - 4$$

$$10: \quad (w-1)(w-2)^2$$

$$11: \quad w = 1$$

Since the characteristic polynomial has a repeated root, the matrix has only two distinct eigenvalues which can be substituted for w in the expression

$$16: \quad \text{ROW\_REDUCE}\left[w \begin{bmatrix} 1 & 0 & 0 \\ 0 & 1 & 0 \\ 0 & 0 & 1 \end{bmatrix} - \begin{bmatrix} -2 & -2 & 2 \\ 4 & 4 & -2 \\ -2 & -1 & 3 \end{bmatrix}, \begin{bmatrix} 0 \\ 0 \\ 0 \end{bmatrix} \right]$$

to find the corresponding eigenvectors. We find these eigenvectors to be

$$\begin{bmatrix} 2\alpha \\ -2\alpha \\ \alpha \end{bmatrix} \text{ when } w = 1 \quad \text{and} \quad \begin{bmatrix} -\frac{\gamma}{2} + \frac{\beta}{2} \\ \beta \\ \gamma \end{bmatrix} \text{ when } w = 2.$$

The first of our three linearly independent eigenvectors can be found by letting $\alpha = 1$. The remaining two of our eigenvectors can be found by first letting $\beta = 2$ and $\gamma = 0$ and then letting $\beta = 0$ and $\gamma = 2$. The three eigenvectors

$$\begin{bmatrix} 2 \\ -2 \\ 1 \end{bmatrix}, \begin{bmatrix} -1 \\ 2 \\ 0 \end{bmatrix}, \text{ and } \begin{bmatrix} 1 \\ 0 \\ 2 \end{bmatrix}$$

can then be used to form the columns of the matrix **U**, and $\mathbf{U}^{-1}\mathbf{AU}$ again yields the eigenvalues of **A** along the main diagonal:

$$22: \quad \begin{bmatrix} 2 & -1 & 1 \\ -2 & 2 & 0 \\ 1 & 0 & 2 \end{bmatrix}^{-1} \cdot \begin{bmatrix} -2 & -2 & 2 \\ 4 & 4 & -2 \\ -2 & -1 & 3 \end{bmatrix} \cdot \begin{bmatrix} 2 & -1 & 1 \\ -2 & 2 & 0 \\ 1 & 0 & 2 \end{bmatrix}$$

$$23: \begin{bmatrix} 1 & 0 & 0 \\ 0 & 2 & 0 \\ 0 & 0 & 2 \end{bmatrix}$$

EXAMPLE 1.5 Not all matrices can be diagonalized. The characteristic polynomial of $\mathbf{A} = \begin{bmatrix} 3 & 1 \\ -1 & 1 \end{bmatrix}$ is $w^2 - 4w + 4$; therefore, the only eigenvalue of **A** is 2. From

$$9: \quad \text{ROW\_REDUCE}\left[2 \begin{bmatrix} 1 & 0 \\ 0 & 1 \end{bmatrix} - \begin{bmatrix} 3 & 1 \\ -1 & 1 \end{bmatrix}, \begin{bmatrix} 0 \\ 0 \end{bmatrix}\right]$$

$$10: \begin{bmatrix} 1 & 1 & 0 \\ 0 & 0 & 0 \end{bmatrix}$$

we find the only eigenvector of **A** has the form $\begin{bmatrix} -\alpha \\ \alpha \end{bmatrix}$. By choosing $\alpha = 1$, we obtain $\begin{bmatrix} -1 \\ 1 \end{bmatrix}$. It follows that the matrix **U** fails to exist since the single eigenvector only provides one of the two required columns.

Finally, we note that *Derive* has a pre-defined function EIGENVALUES(A,*V*) that simplifies the eigenvalues of the matrix **A** in terms of the variable *V*. Also, the utility file VECTOR.MTH described in Section 4.2 has the functions EXACT_EIGENVECTOR(A, μ) and APPROX_EIGENVECTORS(A, μ) which return an eigenvector corresponding to μ.

EXERCISES

1. Find the eigenvalues, eigenvectors, and diagonalize when possible.

   a) $\begin{bmatrix} 2 & 3 \\ 3 & 0 \end{bmatrix}$ b) $\begin{bmatrix} 3 & -16 \\ 0 & -1 \end{bmatrix}$

   c) $\begin{bmatrix} 10 & 12 \\ -6 & -8 \end{bmatrix}$ d) $\begin{bmatrix} 3 & 5 \\ 2 & 3 \end{bmatrix}$

e) $\begin{bmatrix} -7 & -13 \\ 5 & 9 \end{bmatrix}$ f) $\begin{bmatrix} 2 & 1 \\ 5 & 6 \end{bmatrix}$

2. Find the eigenvalues, eigenvectors, and diagonalize when possible.

a) $\begin{bmatrix} 11 & 6 & 8 \\ -4 & 0 & -4 \\ -7 & -5 & 4 \end{bmatrix}$

b) $\begin{bmatrix} 3 & 2 & 0 \\ 0 & 2 & 0 \\ -1 & -2 & 2 \end{bmatrix}$

c) $\begin{bmatrix} -62 & -125 & 0 \\ 33 & 65 & 1 \\ 45 & 92 & -1 \end{bmatrix}$

d) $\begin{bmatrix} 7 & 6 & 4 \\ -2 & 0 & -2 \\ -4 & -5 & -1 \end{bmatrix}$

e) $\begin{bmatrix} 11 & 24 & 1 \\ -3 & -8 & -1 \\ 12 & 25 & 1 \end{bmatrix}$

f) $\begin{bmatrix} 1 & 2 & 4 \\ 3 & 2 & 6 \\ 2 & 1 & 0 \end{bmatrix}$

3. If **A** is either an upper triangular matrix or a lower triangular matrix, show that the elements on the main diagonal are the eigenvalues of **A**.

4. Given that the eigenvalues $\lambda_1, \lambda_2, \cdots, \lambda_n$ of a matrix **A** all satisfy $|\lambda_i| < 1$ for $i = 1, 2, \cdots, n$, prove that $\text{DET}(\mathbf{I} - \mathbf{A}) \neq 0$.

5. Prove that if **A** is similar to a diagonal matrix and **B** is any matrix similar to **A**, then **B** is similar to a diagonal matrix.

6. Prove that if $\mathbf{P}^{-1}\mathbf{A}\mathbf{P} = \mathbf{D}$ where **D** is a diagonal matrix, then $\mathbf{P}^{-1}\mathbf{A}^n\mathbf{P} = \mathbf{D}^n$.

7. Use the result of Exercise 6 to find $\mathbf{A}^6$ if $\mathbf{A} = \begin{bmatrix} -1 & -1 & -3 \\ 0 & -1 & -2 \\ 0 & 1 & 1 \end{bmatrix}$. Also find a general expression for $\mathbf{A}^n$.

8. Prove that if **A** is similar to a diagonal matrix $\text{DIAG}(\lambda_1, \lambda_2, \cdots, \lambda_n)$, then $\text{DET}(\mathbf{A}) = \prod_{i=1}^{n} \lambda_i$.

2. THE CAYLEY-HAMILTON THEOREM

The fundamental importance of the characteristic polynomial of a matrix **A**, which was introduced in the previous section, is illustrated by the fact that its zeros are the eigenvalues of **A**. This polynomial plays many other important roles in the study of linear algebra. To understand some of these roles, we must first extend our concept of a polynomial by allowing the substitution of a matrix into a scalar polynomial. For example, if the matrix **A** of order n were substituted for x in the polynomial

$$p(x) = x^3 + 2x^2 + 3x + 4,$$

we would obtain the matrix

$$p(\mathbf{A}) = \mathbf{A}^3 + 2\mathbf{A}^2 + 3\mathbf{A} + 4\mathbf{I}.$$

which has the same order as **A**. With this option we will be led to a powerful result (the Cayley-Hamilton Theorem) which has many applications including new methods for calculating the inverse of a matrix, its eigenvalues, and its powers.

EXAMPLE 2.1 If $p(x) = x^3 + 2x^2 + x - 3$ and

$$\mathbf{A} = \begin{bmatrix} 1 & 2 \\ 3 & 1 \end{bmatrix},$$

then p(**A**) can be found using the **M**anage **S**ubstitute command sequence in *Derive*.

$$1: \quad P(x) := x^3 + 2x^2 + x - 3x^0$$

$$2: \quad \begin{bmatrix} 1 & 2 \\ 3 & 1 \end{bmatrix}$$

$$3: \quad P\begin{bmatrix} 1 & 2 \\ 3 & 1 \end{bmatrix} := \begin{bmatrix} 1 & 2 \\ 3 & 1 \end{bmatrix}^3 + 2\begin{bmatrix} 1 & 2 \\ 3 & 1 \end{bmatrix}^2 + \begin{bmatrix} 1 & 2 \\ 3 & 1 \end{bmatrix} - 3\begin{bmatrix} 1 & 2 \\ 3 & 1 \end{bmatrix}^0$$

$$4: \quad \begin{bmatrix} 31 & 28 \\ 42 & 31 \end{bmatrix}$$

After **D**eclaring the **F**unction p in statement #1, we **D**eclared the **M**atrix in statement #2. At the prompt requesting an expression following the **M**anage **S**ubstitute command sequence in statement #3, we entered #1 to refer to statement #1. At the prompt requesting a value, we entered #2 to refer to the matrix in statement #2. Statement #4 is obtained by **S**implifying statement #3. Note that *Derive* treats $\mathbf{A}^0$ as the identity matrix of the same order as **A**.

Recall that in Section 5.1 we learned how to find a polynomial dependent on a matrix **A** called the characteristic polynomial, and in Theorem 1.1 of the same section we proved that the zeros of this polynomial are the eigenvalues of the matrix. In light of Example 2.1 above, we might wonder what effect substituting the matrix **A** into its characteristic polynomial would have. The main result of this section, the Cayley-Hamilton Theorem, will provide the answer to this question. The adjoint of the matrix $w\mathbf{I}$ - **A** will play a key role in the proof of the Cayley-Hamilton Theorem. The following example provides some insight into properties which the adjoint satisfies that will be useful in this proof.

EXAMPLE 2.2 If

$$\mathbf{A} = \begin{bmatrix} 1 & 0 & 6 \\ 3 & 2 & 1 \\ 3 & 2 & 1 \end{bmatrix},$$

then ADJ(λ**I** - **A**) can be computed by first forming $w\mathbf{I} - \mathbf{A}$,

$$4: \quad \begin{bmatrix} w - 1 & 0 & -6 \\ -3 & w - 2 & -1 \\ -3 & -2 & w - 1 \end{bmatrix}$$

and then invoking the utility program AJOINT in the VECTOR.MTH file described in Section 4.2.

$$5: \quad \text{ADJOINT} \begin{bmatrix} w - 1 & 0 & -6 \\ -3 & w - 2 & -1 \\ -3 & -2 & w - 1 \end{bmatrix}$$

$$
6: \quad \begin{bmatrix} w^2 - 3w & 12 & 6w - 12 \\ 3w & w^2 - 2w - 17 & w + 17 \\ 3w & 2w - 2 & w^2 - 3w + 2 \end{bmatrix}
$$

Notice that this matrix has for its entries polynomials in w of degree at most two. For the purposes of proving the Cayley-Hamilton Theorem later in this section it will be useful for us to express this adjoint as a linear combination of matrices with entries corresponding to the coefficients of the different powers of w. For this example the linear combination would appear as follows:

$$
\begin{bmatrix} w^2 - 3w & 12 & 6w - 12 \\ 3w & w^2 - 2w + 7 & w + 17 \\ 3w & 2w - 2 & w^2 - 3w + 2 \end{bmatrix} =
$$

$$
w^2 \begin{bmatrix} 1 & 0 & 0 \\ 0 & 1 & 0 \\ 0 & 0 & 1 \end{bmatrix} + w \begin{bmatrix} -3 & 0 & 6 \\ 3 & -2 & 1 \\ -3 & 2 & -3 \end{bmatrix} + \begin{bmatrix} 0 & 12 & -12 \\ -6 & 19 & 17 \\ 12 & -2 & 2 \end{bmatrix}.
$$

Next, we observe another property of the ADJ(w**I** - **A**) that will be useful in the proof of the Cayley-Hamilton Theorem. The product of w**I** - **A** with ADJ(w**I** - **A**) results in a diagonal matrix with the entries along the main diagonal being polynomials in w:

$$
\begin{bmatrix} w - 1 & 0 & -6 \\ -3 & w - 2 & -1 \\ -3 & -2 & w - 1 \end{bmatrix} \cdot \begin{bmatrix} w^2 - 3w & 12 & 6w - 12 \\ 3w & w^2 - 2w - 17 & w + 17 \\ 3w & 2w - 2 & w^2 - 3w + 2 \end{bmatrix}
$$

$$
\begin{bmatrix} w^3 - 4w^2 - 15w & 0 & 0 \\ 0 & w^3 - 4w^2 - 15w & 0 \\ 0 & 0 & w^3 - 4w^2 - 15w \end{bmatrix}
$$

$$\begin{bmatrix} w-1 & 0 & -6 \\ -3 & w-2 & -1 \\ -3 & -2 & w-1 \end{bmatrix} \cdot \begin{bmatrix} w^2-3w & 12 & 6w-12 \\ 3w & w^2-2w-17 & w+17 \\ 3w & 2w-2 & w^2-3w+2 \end{bmatrix}$$

$$\begin{bmatrix} w^3-4w^2-15w & 0 & 0 \\ 0 & w^3-4w^2-15w & 0 \\ 0 & 0 & w^3-4w^2-15w \end{bmatrix}$$

Later, we will prove the polynomial appearing on the main diagonal of the matrix product of $w\mathbf{I}$ - **A** with ADJ($w\mathbf{I}$ - **A**) is always the characteristic polynomial of the matrix **A**. For the purposes of this example, we simply demonstrate this fact:

$$9: \quad -\text{CHARPOLY}\begin{bmatrix} 1 & 0 & 6 \\ 3 & 2 & 1 \\ 3 & 2 & 1 \end{bmatrix}$$

$$10: \quad w^3-4w^2-15w$$

Next, as a prelude to proving the Cayley-Hamilton Theorem we establish two results illustrated in the above example which describe ADJ($\lambda\mathbf{I}$ - **A**) and its elements in terms of polynomials in λ.

LEMMA 2.1 If **A** is a matrix of order n, then ADJ($\lambda\mathbf{I}$ - **A**) is a matrix with polynomial entries in λ of degree at most n - 1.

PROOF: The entries of ADJ($\lambda\mathbf{I}$ - **A**) are cofactors of $\lambda\mathbf{I}$ - **A**, which in turn are calculated from the determinants of the minors of $\lambda\mathbf{I}$ - **A**. These minors are matrices of order n-1 since both **I** and **A** are of order n. Also, since $\lambda\mathbf{I}$ - **A** only has entries containing λ on the main diagonal, the determinant of an ij-minor of $\lambda\mathbf{I}$ - **A** is a polynomial in λ of degree n-1 if i

$i = j$ and a polynomial in λ of degree n-2 if $i \neq j$. It follows that the entries of ADJ(λ**I** - **A**) are polynomials in λ of degree at most n-1.

LEMMA 2.2 The matrix ADJ(λ**I** - **A**) may be written as

$$\lambda^{n-1}\mathbf{B}_1 + \lambda^{n-2}\mathbf{B}_2 + \cdots + \lambda\mathbf{B}_{n-1} + \mathbf{B}_n$$

where the $\mathbf{B}_i$ are constant matrices that depend on **A**.

PROOF: The proof follows immediately from the fact that the entries of ADJ(λ**I** - **A**) are polynomials in λ of degree at most n-1.

EXAMPLE 2.3 If $p(\lambda)$ is the characteristic polynomial of

$$\mathbf{A} = \begin{bmatrix} 4 & 3 & 11 \\ 9 & 7 & 24 \\ -4 & -3 & -11 \end{bmatrix},$$

we can find $p(\mathbf{A})$ using the *Derive* command -CHARPOLY (with the negative sign chosen because **A** is of odd order).

$$2: \quad -\text{CHARPOLY}\begin{bmatrix} 4 & 3 & 11 \\ 9 & 7 & 24 \\ -4 & -3 & -11 \end{bmatrix}$$

$$3: \quad w^3 - 4\,w$$

$$4: \quad \begin{bmatrix} 4 & 3 & 11 \\ 9 & 7 & 24 \\ -4 & -3 & -11 \end{bmatrix}^3 - 4\begin{bmatrix} 4 & 3 & 11 \\ 9 & 7 & 24 \\ -4 & -3 & -11 \end{bmatrix}$$

$$5: \quad \begin{bmatrix} 0 & 0 & 0 \\ 0 & 0 & 0 \\ 0 & 0 & 0 \end{bmatrix}$$

Thus $p(\mathbf{A}) = \mathbf{0}$.

As we shall see in the next theorem, a matrix always satisfies its own characteristic polynomial. This remarkable result, with seemingly limitless applications, is known as the Cayley-Hamilton Theorem.

THEOREM 2.1 (Cayley-Hamilton) If $\mathbf{A}$ is a matrix of order n with characteristic polynomial $p(\lambda)$, then $p(\mathbf{A})=\mathbf{0}$.

PROOF: First, using Lemma 2.2, we write

$$\text{ADJ}(\lambda\mathbf{I}-\mathbf{A})=\mathbf{B}_1\lambda^{n-1}+\mathbf{B}_2\lambda^{n-2}+\cdots+\mathbf{B}_{n-1}\lambda+\mathbf{B}_n.$$

From Theorem 2.2 of Chapter 4

$$(\lambda\mathbf{I}-\mathbf{A})\text{ADJ}(\lambda\mathbf{I}-\mathbf{A})=\text{DET}(\lambda\mathbf{I}-\mathbf{A})\mathbf{I}$$

or, by Lemma 2.2 and the definition of a characteristic polynomial,

$$(\lambda\mathbf{I}-\mathbf{A})(\mathbf{B}_1\lambda^{n-1}+\mathbf{B}_2\lambda^{n-2}+\cdots+\mathbf{B}_{n-1}\lambda+\mathbf{B}_n)=p(\lambda)\mathbf{I}.$$

Expanding the left-hand side and substituting for $p(\lambda)$

$$\begin{aligned}\mathbf{B}_1\lambda^n+(\mathbf{B}_2-\mathbf{A}\mathbf{B}_1)\lambda^{n-1}+\cdots+(\mathbf{B}_{n-1}-\mathbf{A}\mathbf{B}_{n-2})\lambda^2+(\mathbf{B}_n-\mathbf{A}\mathbf{B}_{n-1})\lambda-\mathbf{A}\mathbf{B}_n\\ =(\lambda^n-p_1\lambda^{n-1}-\cdots-p_{n-2}\lambda^2-p_{n-1}\lambda-p_n)\mathbf{I}\end{aligned}$$

If we equate coefficients of equal powers of λ, we obtain

$$\begin{aligned}-\mathbf{A}\mathbf{B}_n&=-p_n\mathbf{I}\\ \mathbf{B}_n-\mathbf{A}\mathbf{B}_{n-1}&=-p_{n-1}\mathbf{I}\\ \mathbf{B}_{n-1}-\mathbf{A}\mathbf{B}_{n-2}&=-p_{n-2}\mathbf{I}\\ &\cdots\\ \mathbf{B}_2-\mathbf{A}\mathbf{B}_1&=-p_1\mathbf{I}\\ \mathbf{B}_1&=\mathbf{I}\end{aligned}$$

Next, we multiply the second of these equations by $\mathbf{A}$, the third by $\mathbf{A}^2$, and continue until the next to the last equation is multiplied by $\mathbf{A}^{n-1}$ and the last equation by $\mathbf{A}^n$.

$$-\mathbf{AB}_n = -p_n\mathbf{I}$$
$$\mathbf{AB}_n - \mathbf{A}^2\mathbf{B}_{n-1} = -p_{n-1}\mathbf{A}$$
$$\mathbf{A}^2\mathbf{B}_{n-1} - \mathbf{A}^3\mathbf{B}_{n-2} = -p_{n-2}\mathbf{A}^2$$
$$\cdots$$
$$\mathbf{A}^{n-1}\mathbf{B}_2 - \mathbf{A}^n\mathbf{B}_1 = -p_1\mathbf{A}^{n-1}$$
$$\mathbf{A}^n\mathbf{B}_1 = \mathbf{A}^n$$

Adding the left sides of these equations we obtain the zero matrix, and adding the right sides we obtain $p(\mathbf{A})$. Thus $p(\mathbf{A}) = \mathbf{0}$.

EXAMPLE 2.4 The Cayley-Hamilton Theorem can be used to compute the inverse of a matrix such as

$$\mathbf{A} = \begin{bmatrix} 1 & 2 & 1 \\ 0 & -1 & 1 \\ 3 & 3 & 2 \end{bmatrix}.$$

If

$$p(x) = x^n - p_1x^{n-1} - \cdots - p_{n-1}x - p_n$$

is the characteristic polynomial of **A**, then by the Cayley-Hamilton Theorem $p(\mathbf{A}) = 0$, and

$$\mathbf{A}^n - p_1\mathbf{A}^{n-1} - p_2\mathbf{A}^{n-2} - \cdots - p_{n-1}\mathbf{A} = p_n\mathbf{I}.$$

The matrix **A** can be factored from the left hand side of this equation, obtaining

$$\mathbf{A}\left(\mathbf{A}^{n-1} - p_1\mathbf{A}^{n-2} - \cdots - p_{n-1}\mathbf{I}\right) = p_n\mathbf{I}.$$

By result of Exercise 9 in Section 5.1, **A** is singular if $p_n = 0$. Thus, if $p_n \neq 0$,

$$\mathbf{A}^{-1} = \frac{\mathbf{A}^{n-1} - p_1\mathbf{A}^{n-2} - \cdots - p_{n-1}\mathbf{I}}{p_n}.$$

The coefficients p_1, p_2, and p_3 of the characteristic polynomial $p(x)$ for the matrix **A** in this example can be computed

$$6: \quad -\text{CHARPOLY}\begin{bmatrix} 1 & 2 & 1 \\ 0 & -1 & 1 \\ 3 & 3 & 2 \end{bmatrix}$$

$$7: \quad w^3 - 2w^2 - 7w - 4$$

and substituted into our expression for $\mathbf{A}^{-1}$:

$$5: \quad \frac{\begin{bmatrix} 1 & 2 & 1 \\ 0 & -1 & 1 \\ 3 & 3 & 2 \end{bmatrix}^2 - 2\begin{bmatrix} 1 & 2 & 1 \\ 0 & -1 & 1 \\ 3 & 3 & 2 \end{bmatrix} - 7\begin{bmatrix} 1 & 2 & 1 \\ 0 & -1 & 1 \\ 3 & 3 & 2 \end{bmatrix}^0}{4}$$

$$6: \quad \begin{bmatrix} -\frac{5}{4} & -\frac{1}{4} & \frac{3}{4} \\ \frac{3}{4} & -\frac{1}{4} & -\frac{1}{4} \\ \frac{3}{4} & \frac{3}{4} & -\frac{1}{4} \end{bmatrix}$$

EXAMPLE 2.5 Given the matrix

$$\mathbf{A} = \begin{bmatrix} 7 & 11 & 11 \\ -7 & -11 & -11 \\ 6 & 12 & 11 \end{bmatrix}$$

we can use *Derive* to find the characteristic polynomial

$$p(\lambda) = \lambda^3 - 3\lambda^2 + 2\lambda = \lambda(\lambda - 1)(\lambda - 2),$$

and thus see that $\mathbf{A}$ has the eigenvalues $\lambda = 0,\ 1,$ and 2. We can use the Cayley-Hamilton Theorem to find the corresponding eigenvectors by first noting that

$$p(\mathbf{A}) = \mathbf{A}(\mathbf{A} - 1\mathbf{I})(\mathbf{A} - 2\mathbf{I}) = \mathbf{0}.$$

Therefore, for example, each non-zero column $\mathbf{b}_i$ of

$$\mathbf{A}(\mathbf{A} - 2\mathbf{I}) = \mathbf{B} = [\mathbf{b}_1 \quad \mathbf{b}_2 \quad \mathbf{b}_3]$$

is an eigenvector corresponding to $\lambda = 1$ since

$$(1\mathbf{I} - \mathbf{A})\mathbf{b}_i = (\mathbf{A} - 1\mathbf{I})\mathbf{b}_i = \mathbf{0}.$$

We can find these three eigenvectors corresponding to $\lambda = 1$ simultaneously by computing **A(A - 2I)**:

$$6: \quad \begin{bmatrix} 7 & 15 & 15 \\ -7 & -15 & -15 \\ 6 & 12 & 11 \end{bmatrix} \left[\begin{bmatrix} 7 & 15 & 15 \\ -7 & -15 & -15 \\ 6 & 12 & 11 \end{bmatrix} - 2 \begin{bmatrix} 7 & 15 & 15 \\ -7 & -15 & -15 \\ 6 & 12 & 11 \end{bmatrix}^0 \right]$$

$$7: \quad \begin{bmatrix} 20 & 30 & 15 \\ -20 & -30 & -15 \\ 12 & 18 & 9 \end{bmatrix}$$

Each column of statement #7 is an eigenvector corresponding to $\lambda = 1$. (Since a scalar multiple of an eigenvector is itself an eigenvector, a simpler form of the vector represented in the three columns would be $[5 \ \ -5 \ \ 3]^T$.

EXAMPLE 2.6 The Cayley-Hamilton Theorem can also be used to express powers of a matrix, such as $\mathbf{A}^5$, in terms of **A** and **I**. For the matrix

$$\mathbf{A} = \begin{bmatrix} 1 & 2 \\ 1 & 3 \end{bmatrix},$$

we can use *Derive* to find the characteristic polynomial $p(\lambda) = \lambda^2 - 4\lambda + 1$. By the Cayley-Hamilton Theorem $\mathbf{A}^2 - 4\mathbf{A} + \mathbf{I} = \mathbf{0}$ or $\mathbf{A}^2 = 4\mathbf{A} - \mathbf{I}$. Thus

$$\mathbf{A}^3 = 4\mathbf{A}^2 - \mathbf{A} = 4(4\mathbf{A} - \mathbf{I}) - \mathbf{A} = 15\mathbf{A} - 4\mathbf{I}.$$

This process may be continued recursively to obtain

$$\mathbf{A}^5 = 209\mathbf{A} - 56\mathbf{I}.$$

The right hand side of this result in *Derive* is

$$5: \quad 209 \begin{bmatrix} 1 & 2 \\ 1 & 3 \end{bmatrix} - 56 \begin{bmatrix} 1 & 0 \\ 0 & 1 \end{bmatrix}$$

$$6: \quad \begin{bmatrix} 153 & 418 \\ 209 & 571 \end{bmatrix}$$

(Of course, *Derive* will also compute this result directly.)

EXERCISES

1. Express the matrix

$$\begin{bmatrix} \lambda^3 + 2\lambda^2 - 3 & \lambda^2 + 3 & \lambda + 2 \\ \lambda^2 + \lambda + 1 & \lambda^3 - 2\lambda^2 + \lambda - 1 & \lambda^2 - 4 \\ \lambda & \lambda^2 - 1 & \lambda^3 - 1 \end{bmatrix}$$

as powers of λ times constant matrices.

2. If $p(x) = x^4 + 3x^3 + x^2 - 3x + 4$, find $p(\mathbf{A})$ where

a) $\mathbf{A} = \begin{bmatrix} 1 & 2 \\ 2 & 2 \end{bmatrix}$

b) $\mathbf{A} = \begin{bmatrix} 0 & 1 & 1 \\ 3 & -1 & 2 \\ 0 & 2 & 2 \end{bmatrix}$

3. Compute $\mathrm{ADJ}(\lambda\mathbf{I} - \mathbf{A})$ for each of the matrices in Exercise 2.

4. Multiply $(\lambda\mathbf{I} - \mathbf{A})\mathrm{ADJ}(\lambda\mathbf{I} - \mathbf{A})$ for each of the matrices in Exercise 2.

5. Verify the Cayley-Hamilton Theorem for each of the matrices in Exercise 2.

6. If $p(\lambda) = \lambda^n - p_1\lambda^{n-1} - \cdots - p_{n-1}\lambda - p_n$ is the characteristic polynomial of $\mathbf{A}$, a matrix of order n, show that $\mathrm{ADJ}(\mathbf{A}) = \mathbf{A}^{n-1} + p_1\mathbf{A}^{n-2} + \cdots + p_{n-1}\mathbf{I}$.

7. Use the Cayley-Hamilton Theorem to compute $\mathbf{A}^6$, where $\mathbf{A} = \begin{bmatrix} 1 & 1 \\ 2 & 3 \end{bmatrix}$.

8. Use the Cayley-Hamilton Theorem to compute $\mathbf{A}^5$, where
$$\mathbf{A} = \begin{bmatrix} -1 & -2 & -4 \\ 5 & 7 & 11 \\ -3 & -4 & -6 \end{bmatrix}.$$

9. Use the Cayley-Hamilton Theorem to compute $\mathbf{A}^{-1}$ for the matrices in Exercises 7 and 8 if possible. If it is not possible, state why.

10. Use the Cayley-Hamilton Theorem to compute the eigenvectors of the matrix in Exercise 9.

11. For a nonsingular matrix of order 2 show that
$$\mathbf{A}^{-1} = \frac{\mathbf{A} - \mathrm{TR}(\mathbf{A})\mathbf{I}}{-\mathrm{DET}(\mathbf{A})}.$$

12. Let $\mathbf{A}$ be a matrix of order n. Show that $\mathrm{SPAN}\{\mathbf{I}, \mathbf{A}, \mathbf{A}^2 \cdots, \mathbf{A}^n\}$ is a subspace of the space of $n \times n$ matrices and that the dimension of this subspace is less than or equal to n.

13. Let
$$\mathbf{A} = \begin{bmatrix} 0 & 0 & \cdots & 0 & p_n \\ 1 & 0 & \cdots & 0 & p_{n-1} \\ 0 & 1 & \cdots & 0 & p_{n-2} \\ \vdots & \vdots & & \vdots & \vdots \\ 0 & 0 & \cdots & 1 & p_1 \end{bmatrix}.$$
Show that the characteristic polynomial of $\mathbf{A}$ is $p(\lambda) = \lambda^n - p_1\lambda^{n-1} - p_2\lambda^{n-2} - \cdots - p_1$ [Hint: Use induction and expand about the first row.]

14. Let
$$\mathbf{A} = \begin{bmatrix} 0 & 0 & 0 & -1 \\ 1 & 0 & 0 & 2 \\ 0 & 1 & 0 & 1 \\ 0 & 0 & 1 & -2 \end{bmatrix}.$$
Find $\mathbf{A}^4 + 2\mathbf{A}^3 - \mathbf{A}^2 - 2\mathbf{A} + \mathbf{I}$. Show $\mathbf{A}$ is not singular, and find $\mathbf{A}^{-1}$. Let $\mathbf{P}$ be a non-singular matrix of order 4. What is the characteristic polynomial of $\mathbf{P}^{-1}\mathbf{AP}$.

15. If $\mathbf{A} = \begin{bmatrix} 1 & 1 & 0 \\ 2 & 1 & 1 \\ 3 & 2 & 4 \end{bmatrix}$, then use $\mathbf{A}^4 + a\mathbf{A}^3 + b\mathbf{A}^2 + c\mathbf{A} + d\mathbf{I} = \mathbf{0}$ to find a, b, c, and d and thus, the characteristic polynomial of $\mathbf{A}$.

3. SPECIAL TYPES OF MATRICES

In many physical and scientific applications special types of matrices play important roles. For example, in Section 2.2 we have defined a real valued matrix **A** to be symmetric if $\mathbf{A} = \mathbf{A}^{\mathrm{T}}$. In problems involving coupled structural systems, symmetric matrices have been found to describe the physical realities of the structure. In this section we examine the properties of the eigenvalues of this and other special types of matrices. Although symmetric matrices must have real number entries, there is a corresponding property for matrices with complex number entries.

DEFINITION 3.1 (Hermitian Matrix) If **A** is a complex valued matrix, $\mathbf{A} = \left(a_{pq}\right) = \left(u_{pq} + iv_{pq}\right)$, then we define the operation $\mathbf{A}^*$ by $\mathbf{A}^* = \left(\bar{a}_{qp}\right) = \left(u_{qp} - iv_{qp}\right) = \left(\bar{a}_{pq}\right)^{\mathrm{T}}$. A matrix is said to be Hermitian if $\mathbf{A} = \mathbf{A}^*$.

EXAMPLE 3.1 If $\mathbf{A} = \begin{bmatrix} 1+2i & 2 \\ 2-3i & 2i \end{bmatrix}$, then $\mathbf{A}^* = \begin{bmatrix} 1-2i & 2+3i \\ 2 & -2i \end{bmatrix}$.

It follows immediately that every symmetric matrix is also a Hermitian matrix since in this case $\overline{a_{pq}} = a_{pq}$ for each pq. We recall that the eigenvalues of a matrix are the zeros of the characteristic polynomial of the matrix. Clearly, matrices exist which generate characteristic polynomials with real roots, complex roots, and a mixture of real and complex roots. The following pair of theorems give two classes of matrices (one of which is the set of Hermitian [and therefore symmetric] matrices) which have purely real or purely imaginary eigenvalues.

THEOREM 3.1 If **A** is either a Hermitian or symmetric matrix, then the eigenvalues of **A** are real.

PROOF: Let **A** be Hermitian so that $\mathbf{A} = \mathbf{A}^*$. Let λ be an eigenvalue of **A** and **x** be its corresponding eigenvector. Since by definition this means that $\mathbf{Ax} = \lambda\mathbf{x}$, we can take the conjugate and transpose of both sides of the equation to obtain $\mathbf{x}^*\mathbf{A}^* = \bar{\lambda}\mathbf{x}^*$. (Recall from Theorem 3.1 of Chapter 1 that $(\mathbf{Ax})^T = \mathbf{x}^T\mathbf{A}^T$.) If we multiply this equation on the right by **x**, we obtain $\mathbf{x}^*\mathbf{A}^*\mathbf{x} = \bar{\lambda}\mathbf{x}^*\mathbf{x}$. On the other hand, if we multiply $\mathbf{Ax} = \lambda\mathbf{x}$ on the left by $\mathbf{x}^*$, we obtain $\mathbf{x}^*\mathbf{Ax} = \lambda\mathbf{x}^*\mathbf{x}$. Thus

$$\bar{\lambda}\mathbf{x}^*\mathbf{x} = \mathbf{x}^*\mathbf{A}^*\mathbf{x} = \mathbf{x}^*\mathbf{Ax} = \lambda\mathbf{x}^*\mathbf{x},$$

and $\bar{\lambda} = \lambda$, which implies λ is real. Note, in accordance with the comment preceding this theorem, that a symmetric matrix is simply a special case of the Hermitian matrix, and the proof is complete.

EXAMPLE 3.2 The eigenvalues of the symmetric matrix

$$\begin{bmatrix} 2 & 4 & 2 \\ 4 & 8 & 4 \\ 2 & 4 & 2 \end{bmatrix}$$

can be found using *Derive*:

$$10: \quad \text{EIGENVALUES} \begin{bmatrix} 2 & 4 & 2 \\ 4 & 8 & 4 \\ 2 & 4 & 2 \end{bmatrix}$$

11: [w = 0, w = 12]

and the eigenvalues are 0 and 12. (This command will not give the multiplicity if any of the eigenvalues have multiplicity greater than one, as in this case. If it is desired to know if one or more of the eigenvalues has multiplicity greater than one, we would need to obtain the characteristic polynomial and factor it if possible.)

DEFINITION 3.2 (Skew-Hermitian and Skew-symmetric Matrices) A matrix **A** is said to be skew-Hermitian if $\mathbf{A}^* = -\mathbf{A}$ and skew-symmetric if the entries of **A** are real and $\mathbf{A}^T = -\mathbf{A}$.

THEOREM 3.2 If **A** is Skew-Hermitian (skew-symmetric), then the eigenvalues of **A** are pure imaginary numbers.

PROOF: The proof is similar to the proof of Theorem 3.1 and is left as a exercise.

A symmetric matrix **A** has the property that $\mathbf{A}\mathbf{A}^{\mathrm{T}} = \mathbf{A}^2$. Some matrices have the property that $\mathbf{A}\mathbf{A}^{\mathrm{T}} = \mathbf{I}_n$ so that $\mathbf{A}^{\mathrm{T}}$ acts as the multiplicative inverse of **A**. It is easy to see that the identity matrix $\mathbf{I}_n$ satisfies both properties. Later we will see other examples of the second property where **A** is not the identity. As was the case for symmetric matrices above, the eigenvalues of a matrix **A** which has its transpose as its inverse can be characterized in a useful way. Also, this type of matrix can be generalized to complex valued matrices in much the same way we generalized symmetric matrices to Hermitian matrices.

DEFINITION 3.3 (Unitary and Orthogonal Matrices) An invertible matrix **A** is said to be unitary if $\mathbf{A}^* = \mathbf{A}^{-1}$ and orthogonal if the elements of **A** are real and $\mathbf{A}^{\mathrm{T}} = \mathbf{A}^{-1}$.

THEOREM 3.3 If λ is an eigenvalue of a unitary (orthogonal) matrix, then $|\lambda| = 1$.

PROOF: Let **A** be unitary and λ be an eigenvalue of **A** with corresponding eigenvector **x**. Using the same logic as in the proof of Theorem 3.1, we obtain $\mathbf{x}^*\mathbf{A}^*\mathbf{x} = \bar{\lambda}\mathbf{x}^*\mathbf{x}$. On the other hand (see Exercise 13),

$$\mathbf{A}^{-1}\mathbf{x} = \frac{1}{\lambda}\mathbf{x},$$

or, since $\mathbf{A}^* = \mathbf{A}^{-1}$,

$$\mathbf{A}^*\mathbf{x} = \frac{1}{\lambda}\mathbf{x}.$$

Multiplying both sides of this equation on the left by $\mathbf{x}^*$, we obtain

$$\mathbf{x}^*\mathbf{A}^*\mathbf{x} = \frac{1}{\lambda}\mathbf{x}^*\mathbf{x}.$$

It follows that

$$\bar{\lambda}\mathbf{x}^*\mathbf{x} = \mathbf{x}^*\mathbf{A}^*\mathbf{x} = \frac{1}{\lambda}\mathbf{x}^*\mathbf{x},$$

and by equating the coefficients of $\mathbf{x}^*\mathbf{x}$, we have $\bar{\lambda} = \frac{1}{\lambda}$, or $\bar{\lambda}\lambda = 1$, which means $|\lambda|^2 = 1$, and thus $|\lambda| = 1$.

EXAMPLE 3.3 The matrix

$$\mathbf{A} = \begin{bmatrix} \cos t & \sin t & 0 \\ -\sin t & \cos t & 0 \\ 0 & 0 & 1 \end{bmatrix}$$

is orthogonal since $\mathbf{A}\mathbf{A}^{\mathrm{T}} = \mathbf{I}$ as is shown by

$$2: \quad \begin{bmatrix} \mathrm{COS(t)} & \mathrm{SIN(t)} & 0 \\ -\mathrm{SIN(t)} & \mathrm{COS(t)} & 0 \\ 0 & 0 & 1 \end{bmatrix} \cdot \begin{bmatrix} \mathrm{COS(t)} & \mathrm{SIN(t)} & 0 \\ -\mathrm{SIN(t)} & \mathrm{COS(t)} & 0 \\ 0 & 0 & 1 \end{bmatrix}^{'}$$

$$3: \quad \begin{bmatrix} 1 & 0 & 0 \\ 0 & 1 & 0 \\ 0 & 0 & 1 \end{bmatrix}$$

To show the eigenvalues of **A** have magnitude 1, we compute them using *Derive* and use the ABS(#nn) command to find their magnitude.

$$4: \quad \mathrm{EIGENVALUES} \begin{bmatrix} \mathrm{COS(t)} & \mathrm{SIN(t)} & 0 \\ -\mathrm{SIN(t)} & \mathrm{COS(t)} & 0 \\ 0 & 0 & 1 \end{bmatrix}$$

$$5: \quad [w = 1, w = \mathrm{COS(t)} - \hat{\imath}\,|\mathrm{SIN(t)}|, w = \mathrm{COS(t)} + \hat{\imath}\,|\mathrm{SIN(t)}|]$$

$$6: \quad |w = \mathrm{COS(t)} - \hat{\imath}\,|\mathrm{SIN(t)}||$$

$$7: \quad |w| = 1$$

$$8: \quad |w = \mathrm{COS(t)} + \hat{\imath}\,|\mathrm{SIN(t)}||$$

$$9: \quad |w| = 1$$

Closely related to orthogonal matrices is the concept of an orthogonal basis. In calculus we used the scalar or dot product of two vectors in R^2 or R^3 to determine if they were orthogonal or perpendicular. Next, we will expand on that earlier concept of a scalar or dot product by adapting it to our more general concept of the vector spaces R^n and C^n.

DEFINITION 3.4 (Scalar Product of Vectors) The scalar product of two vectors **x** and **y** in C^n (R^n) is defined by

$$\langle \mathbf{x}, \mathbf{y} \rangle = x_1\bar{y}_1 + x_2\bar{y}_2 + \cdots + x_n\bar{y}_n$$

(where $\overline{y_i}$ is replaced by y_i for vectors in R^n).

THEOREM 3.4 If $\mathbf{x}, \mathbf{y}, \mathbf{z} \in C^n$, then

a) $\langle \mathbf{x}, \mathbf{x} \rangle = \sum_{i=1}^{n} |x_i|^2 \geq 0$

b) $\overline{\langle \mathbf{x}, \mathbf{y} \rangle} = \langle \mathbf{y}, \mathbf{x} \rangle$

c) $\langle c\mathbf{x}, \mathbf{y} \rangle = c\langle \mathbf{x}, \mathbf{y} \rangle = \langle \mathbf{x}, \bar{c}\mathbf{y} \rangle$

d) $\langle \mathbf{x} + \mathbf{y}, \mathbf{z} \rangle = \langle \mathbf{x}, \mathbf{z} \rangle + \langle \mathbf{y}, \mathbf{z} \rangle$

PROOF: The proof is a straight forward application of the definition of a scalar product and is left as an exercise.

It should be noted that a very useful immediate consequence of part a) of Theorem 3.4 is the fact that $\langle \mathbf{x}, \mathbf{x} \rangle = 0$ if and only if $\mathbf{x} = \mathbf{0}$.

DEFINITION 3.5 (Length of a Vector) The length of a vector $\mathbf{x} \in C^n$ is

$$\|x\| = \sqrt{\langle \mathbf{x}, \mathbf{x} \rangle}.$$

DEFINITION 3.6 (Orthogonal Vectors) Two vectors $\mathbf{x}, \mathbf{y} \in C^n$ are said to be orthogonal if $\langle \mathbf{x}, \mathbf{y} \rangle = 0$.

Since the scalar product of the zero vector with any other vector is always zero, we consider it to be orthogonal to every vector.

DEFINITION 3.7 (Orthonormal Vectors) Two vectors $\mathbf{x},\mathbf{y} \in C^n$ are said to be orthonormal if they are orthogonal and both have length 1.

EXAMPLE 3.4 The column vectors of the matrix in Example 3.3 are orthonormal. In fact, it follows immediately from the definitions of orthogonal, unitary, and matrix multiplication that the column vectors of any orthogonal or unitary matrix are orthonormal.

THEOREM 3.5 If K = $\{\mathbf{x}_1,\mathbf{x}_2,\cdots,\mathbf{x}_k\}$ is a set of non-zero orthogonal vectors with $\langle \mathbf{x}_i,\mathbf{x}_j \rangle = 0$ for $i \neq j$, then K is linearly independent.

PROOF: Let $\mathbf{y}$ be a linear combination of elements of K equal to the zero vector:

$$\mathbf{y} = a_1\mathbf{x}_1 + a_2\mathbf{x}_2 + \cdots + a_k\mathbf{x}_k = \mathbf{0}.$$

Since $\mathbf{y} = \mathbf{0}$, $\langle \mathbf{x}_i,\mathbf{y} \rangle = 0$ for all $i = 1,2,\ldots,k$. But each $\mathbf{x}_i \neq 0$; therefore, $\langle \mathbf{x}_i,\mathbf{x}_i \rangle \neq 0$. It follows then from Theorem 3.4 that

$$\begin{aligned}\langle \mathbf{x}_i,\mathbf{y} \rangle &= \bar{a}_1\langle \mathbf{x}_i,\mathbf{x}_1 \rangle + \ldots + \bar{a}_i\langle \mathbf{x}_1,\mathbf{x}_i \rangle + \ldots + \bar{a}_k\langle \mathbf{x}_i,\mathbf{x}_i \rangle \\ &= \bar{a}_i\langle \mathbf{x}_i,\mathbf{x}_i \rangle \\ &= 0\end{aligned}$$

and $\overline{a_i} = 0$, which implies $a_i = 0$. Since i was chosen arbitrarily, it follows that $a_1 = a_2 = \cdots = a_k = 0$, and the set K is linearly independent.

DEFINITION 3.8 (Orthogonal, Orthornormal Basis) A basis $\beta = \{\mathbf{x}_1,\mathbf{x}_2,\cdots,\mathbf{x}_k\}$ of a vector space V is said to be orthogonal if the elements of β are pairwise orthogonal, that is if $\langle \mathbf{x}_i,\mathbf{x}_j \rangle = 0$ when $i \neq j$. The basis β is said to be orthonormal if it is orthogonal and the length of each element in β is 1, that is $\langle \mathbf{x}_i,\mathbf{x}_i \rangle = 1$ for all $i = 1,2,\cdots,k$.

THEOREM 3.6 (Gram-Schmidt) Let $\{\mathbf{x}_1, \mathbf{x}_2, \cdots, \mathbf{x}_k\}$ be a set of linearly independent vectors in C^n. Then there exists a set of orthogonal vectors $\{\mathbf{u}_1, \mathbf{u}_2, \cdots, \mathbf{u}_k\}$ such that $\text{SPAN}\{\mathbf{x}_1, \mathbf{x}_2, \cdots, \mathbf{x}_k\} =$ SPAN $\{\mathbf{u}_1, \mathbf{u}_2, \cdots, \mathbf{u}_k\}$.

PROOF: The proof is by an inductive construction. First, we let $\mathbf{u}_1 = \mathbf{x}_1$ and determine $\mathbf{u}_2$ so that it is both a linear combination of $\mathbf{u}_1$ and $\mathbf{x}_2$

$$\mathbf{u}_2 = \mathbf{x}_2 + a_{21}\mathbf{u}_1$$

and orthogonal to $\mathbf{u}_1$

$$\langle \mathbf{u}_2, \mathbf{u}_1 \rangle = \langle \mathbf{x}_2, \mathbf{u}_1 \rangle + a_{21}\langle \mathbf{u}_1, \mathbf{u}_1 \rangle = 0.$$

Solving for a_{21}, we find

$$a_{21} = -\frac{\langle \mathbf{x}_2, \mathbf{u}_1 \rangle}{\langle \mathbf{u}_1, \mathbf{u}_1 \rangle},$$

and substituting this result into our original expression for $\mathbf{u}_2$ above, we obtain a vector value that is both a linear combination of $\mathbf{x}_1$ and $\mathbf{u}_1$ (and hence of $\mathbf{x}_1$ and $\mathbf{x}_2$) and orthogonal to $\mathbf{u}_1$:

$$\mathbf{u}_2 = \mathbf{x}_2 - \frac{\langle \mathbf{x}_2, \mathbf{u}_1 \rangle}{\langle \mathbf{u}_1, \mathbf{u}_1 \rangle}\mathbf{u}_1.$$

Since $\mathbf{u}_1 = \mathbf{x}_1$, it follows that $\mathbf{u}_1$ and $\mathbf{u}_2$ can be written as linear combinations of $\mathbf{x}_1$ and $\mathbf{x}_2$, and $\mathbf{x}_1$ and $\mathbf{x}_2$ can be written as linear combinations of $\mathbf{u}_1$ and $\mathbf{u}_2$; thus, $\text{SPAN}\{\mathbf{x}_1, \mathbf{x}_2\} = \text{SPAN}\{\mathbf{u}_1, \mathbf{u}_2\}$. Next, we construct $\mathbf{u}_3$ so that it is a linear combination of $\mathbf{u}_2, \mathbf{u}_1$, and $\mathbf{x}_3$ (hence, a linear combination of $\mathbf{x}_1$, $\mathbf{x}_2$, and $\mathbf{x}_3$)

$$\mathbf{u}_3 = \mathbf{x}_3 + a_{31}\mathbf{u}_1 + a_{32}\mathbf{u}_2$$

and is orthogonal to $\mathbf{u}_1$ and $\mathbf{u}_2$

$$\langle \mathbf{u}_3, \mathbf{u}_1 \rangle = \langle \mathbf{x}_3, \mathbf{u}_1 \rangle + a_{31}\langle \mathbf{u}_1, \mathbf{u}_1 \rangle + a_{32}\langle \mathbf{u}_2, \mathbf{u}_1 \rangle = 0$$

and

$$\langle \mathbf{u}_3, \mathbf{u}_2 \rangle = \langle \mathbf{x}_3, \mathbf{u}_2 \rangle + a_{31} \langle \mathbf{u}_1, \mathbf{u}_2 \rangle + a_{32} \langle \mathbf{u}_2, \mathbf{u}_2 \rangle = 0.$$

Since $\langle \mathbf{u}_2, \mathbf{u}_1 \rangle = \langle \mathbf{u}_1, \mathbf{u}_2 \rangle = 0$,

$$a_{31} = -\frac{\langle \mathbf{x}_3, \mathbf{u}_1 \rangle}{\langle \mathbf{u}_1, \mathbf{u}_1 \rangle} \quad \text{and} \quad a_{32} = -\frac{\langle \mathbf{x}_3, \mathbf{u}_2 \rangle}{\langle \mathbf{u}_2, \mathbf{u}_2 \rangle},$$

and substituting in the expression for $\mathbf{u}_3$ above, we obtain

$$\mathbf{u}_3 = \mathbf{x}_3 - \frac{\langle \mathbf{x}_3, \mathbf{u}_1 \rangle}{\langle \mathbf{u}_1, \mathbf{u}_1 \rangle} \mathbf{u}_1 - \frac{\langle \mathbf{x}_3, \mathbf{u}_2 \rangle}{\langle \mathbf{u}_2, \mathbf{u}_2 \rangle} \mathbf{u}_2 .$$

Again, it follows that each of $\mathbf{u}_1$, $\mathbf{u}_2$, and $\mathbf{u}_3$ can be written as a linear combination of $\mathbf{x}_1$, $\mathbf{x}_2$, and $\mathbf{x}_3$, and each of $\mathbf{x}_1$, $\mathbf{x}_2$, and $\mathbf{x}_3$ can be written as a linear combination of $\mathbf{u}_1$, $\mathbf{u}_2$, and $\mathbf{u}_3$; thus, $\text{SPAN}\{\mathbf{x}_1, \mathbf{x}_2, \mathbf{x}_3\}$ = $\text{SPAN}\{\mathbf{u}_1, \mathbf{u}_2, \mathbf{u}_3\}$. This process can be continued so that if $\mathbf{u}_1, \mathbf{u}_2, \cdots, \mathbf{u}_{k-1}$ have been constructed, then $\mathbf{u}_k$ is defined by

$$\mathbf{u}_k = \mathbf{x}_k + a_{k1}\mathbf{u}_1 + a_{k2}\mathbf{u}_2 + \cdots + a_{kk-1}\mathbf{u}_{k-1} .$$

Taking, in turn, the scalar products of $\mathbf{u}_k$ with $\mathbf{u}_1, \mathbf{u}_2, \cdots, \mathbf{u}_{k-1}$, we obtain

$$a_{kj} = -\frac{\langle \mathbf{x}_k, \mathbf{u}_j \rangle}{\langle \mathbf{u}_j, \mathbf{u}_j \rangle}$$

so that

$$\mathbf{u}_k = \mathbf{x}_k - \frac{\langle \mathbf{x}_k, \mathbf{u}_1 \rangle}{\langle \mathbf{u}_1, \mathbf{u}_1 \rangle} \mathbf{u}_1 - \cdots - \frac{\langle \mathbf{x}_k, \mathbf{u}_k \rangle}{\langle \mathbf{u}_k, \mathbf{u}_k \rangle} \mathbf{u}_k .$$

It follows that each of $\mathbf{u}_1, \mathbf{u}_2, \ldots, \mathbf{u}_k$ can be written as a linear combination of $\mathbf{x}_1, \mathbf{x}_2, \ldots, \mathbf{x}_k$, and each of $\mathbf{x}_1, \mathbf{x}_2, \ldots, \mathbf{x}_k$ can be written as a linear combination of $\mathbf{u}_1, \mathbf{u}_2, \ldots, \mathbf{u}_k$; thus, $\text{SPAN}\{\mathbf{x}_1, \mathbf{x}_2, \ldots, \mathbf{x}_k\}$ = $\text{SPAN}\{\mathbf{u}_1, \mathbf{u}_2, \ldots, \mathbf{u}_k\}$, and the proof is complete.

It may not be immediately clear what role the linear independence of the set of vectors $\{\mathbf{x}_1, \mathbf{x}_2, \cdots, \mathbf{x}_k\}$ played in the above proof, but the condition is required in order to find the vectors $\{\mathbf{u}_1, \mathbf{u}_2, \cdots, \mathbf{u}_k\}$. For example, if $\mathbf{x}_i = \mathrm{b}_1\mathbf{x}_1 + \mathrm{b}_2\mathbf{x}_2 + \ldots + \mathrm{b}_{i-1}\mathbf{x}_{i-1}$, then defining $\mathbf{u}_i$ as $\mathbf{u}_i = \mathbf{x}_i + a_{i1}\mathbf{u}_1 + a_{i2}\mathbf{u}_2 + \cdots + a_{ii-1}\mathbf{u}_{i-1}$ would imply that $\mathbf{u}_i$ is a linear combination of $\mathbf{u}_1, \mathbf{u}_2, \cdots, \mathbf{u}_{i-1}$ (since $\mathrm{SPAN}\{\mathbf{x}_1, \mathbf{x}_2, \ldots, \mathbf{x}_{i-1}\} = \mathrm{SPAN}\{\mathbf{u}_1, \mathbf{u}_2, \ldots, \mathbf{u}_{i-1}\}$); therefore, if $j \neq i$, then

$$\begin{aligned}\langle \mathbf{u}_i, \mathbf{u}_j \rangle &= \langle \mathrm{b}_1\mathbf{u}_1 + \ldots + \mathrm{b}_j\mathbf{u}_j + \ldots + \mathrm{b}_{i-1}\mathbf{u}_{i-1}, \mathbf{u}_j \rangle \\ &= \mathrm{b}_1\langle \mathbf{u}_1, \mathbf{u}_j \rangle + \ldots + \mathrm{b}_j\langle \mathbf{u}_j, \mathbf{u}_j \rangle + \ldots + \mathrm{b}_{i-1}\langle \mathbf{u}_{i-1}, \mathbf{u}_j \rangle \\ &= \mathrm{b}_j\langle \mathbf{u}_j, \mathbf{u}_j \rangle\end{aligned}$$

and $\langle \mathbf{u}_i, \mathbf{u}_j \rangle = 0$ would mean that either $\langle \mathbf{u}_j, \mathbf{u}_j \rangle = 0$ or $\mathrm{b}_j = 0$. The first case would imply that $\mathbf{u}_j = \mathbf{0}$, and the second case would lead to $\mathbf{u}_i = \mathbf{0}$. It therefore follows that the set of vectors $\{\mathbf{x}_1, \mathbf{x}_2, \cdots, \mathbf{x}_k\}$ must be linearly independent.

EXAMPLE 3.5 Given the set

$$S = \left\{ \begin{bmatrix} 0 \\ 1 \\ 1 \end{bmatrix}, \begin{bmatrix} 1 \\ 0 \\ 1 \end{bmatrix}, \begin{bmatrix} 1 \\ 1 \\ 0 \end{bmatrix} \right\},$$

we can determine an orthogonal set that spans the same space using *Derive* to compute the required scalar products of pairs of vectors. The process we will use to find $\mathbf{u}_1$, $\mathbf{u}_2$, and $\mathbf{u}_3$ follows constructive procedure outlined in the proof of Theorem 3.6. First, we begin by letting $\mathbf{u}_1$ be the first vector in S. If $\mathbf{x}_2$ is the second vector in S, then from above

$$\mathbf{u}_2 = \mathbf{x}_2 - \frac{\langle \mathbf{x}_2, \mathbf{u}_1 \rangle}{\langle \mathbf{u}_1, \mathbf{u}_1 \rangle}\mathbf{u}_1$$

or

```
                      [1, 0, 1] · [0, 1, 1]
6:   [1, 0, 1] - ───────────────────────── [0, 1, 1]
                      [0, 1, 1] · [0, 1, 1]
```

$$7: \quad \left[1, -\frac{1}{2}, \frac{1}{2}\right]$$

[where the scalar product of a vector in statement #*n* and a vector in statement #*m* is computed in *Derive* by entering #*n*.#*m*]. Next, we let $\mathbf{x}_3$ be the third vector in *S* and note from the proof above

$$\mathbf{u}_3 = \mathbf{x}_3 - \frac{\langle \mathbf{x}_3, \mathbf{u}_1 \rangle}{\langle \mathbf{u}_1, \mathbf{u}_1 \rangle}\mathbf{u}_1 - \frac{\langle \mathbf{x}_3, \mathbf{u}_2 \rangle}{\langle \mathbf{u}_2, \mathbf{u}_2 \rangle}\mathbf{u}_2.$$

Using *Derive* we compute this vector to be $\begin{bmatrix} \frac{2}{3} & \frac{2}{3} & \frac{-2}{3} \end{bmatrix}$.

The process outlined above can also be used to find an orthonormal set of vectors with the same span as a set of linearly independent vectors with complex valued entries, but the calculations in *Derive* must be adjusted to accommodate the required complex conjugate of the second complex valued vector in a scalar product. The following example illustrates how this is accomplished.

EXAMPLE 3.6 To compute the scalar product of

$$\begin{bmatrix} 1+2i \\ -3-4i \\ 2-2i \end{bmatrix} \text{ and } \begin{bmatrix} i \\ 2-5i \\ 3+2i \end{bmatrix}$$

using *Derive*, we enter the vectors and find the complex conjugate of the second vector prior to calculating the scalar product

```
3:   [1 + 2 î, -3 - 4 î, 2 - 2 î] · CONJ [î, 2 - 5 î, 3 + 2 î]

4:   18 - 34 î
```

To close this section, we give three theorems which connect the concepts of symmetric matrices, eigenvectors, and orthonormal sets of vectors.

THEOREM 3.7 If $\mathbf{A}$ is a real symmetric matrix of order n and $\mathbf{x}_1, \mathbf{x}_2$ are any two vectors in R^n (C^n), then $\mathbf{x}_1^T \mathbf{A} \mathbf{x}_2 = \mathbf{x}_2^T \mathbf{A} \mathbf{x}_1$.

PROOF: Since $\mathbf{x}_1^T \mathbf{A} \mathbf{x}_2$ is a matrix of order 1, it is symmetric, and $\mathbf{x}_1^T \mathbf{A} \mathbf{x}_2 = (\mathbf{x}_1^T \mathbf{A} \mathbf{x}_2)^T = \mathbf{x}_2^T \mathbf{A}^T \mathbf{x}_1 = \mathbf{x}_2^T \mathbf{A} \mathbf{x}_1$.

THEOREM 3.8 If $\mathbf{A}$ is a real symmetric matrix of order n, then eigenvectors corresponding to distinct eigenvalues are orthogonal.

PROOF: Let $\lambda_1 \neq \lambda_2$ be distinct eigenvalues of $\mathbf{A}$ and let $\mathbf{A}\mathbf{x}_1 = \lambda_1 \mathbf{x}_1$ and $\mathbf{A}\mathbf{x}_2 = \lambda_2 \mathbf{x}_2$. If we left multiply the first of these relations by $\mathbf{x}_2^T$ and the second by $\mathbf{x}_1^T$, we obtain $\mathbf{x}_2^T \mathbf{A} \mathbf{x}_1 = \lambda_1 \mathbf{x}_2^T \mathbf{x}_1$ and $\mathbf{x}_1^T \mathbf{A} \mathbf{x}_2 = \lambda_2 \mathbf{x}_1^T \mathbf{x}_2$. By Theorem 3.7 the left-hand sides of these two equations are equal, so $\lambda_1 \mathbf{x}_2^T \mathbf{x}_1 = \lambda_2 \mathbf{x}_1^T \mathbf{x}_2$. Since $\mathbf{A}$ is symmetric, by Theorem 3.1 the eigenvectors are real, and $\mathbf{x}_2^T \mathbf{x}_1 = \mathbf{x}_1^T \mathbf{x}_2$; therefore, $(\lambda_1 - \lambda_2)\mathbf{x}_1^T \mathbf{x}_2 = 0$. But $\lambda_1 \neq \lambda_2$; thus, $\langle \mathbf{x}_1, \mathbf{x}_2 \rangle = \mathbf{x}_1^T \mathbf{x}_2 = 0$, and the eigenvectors are orthogonal.

The next theorem is given without proof.

THEOREM 3.9 Let $\mathbf{A}$ be a real symmetric matrix of order n, then $\mathbf{A}$ has n linearly independent eigenvectors. Further, $\mathbf{A}$ possesses n orthonormal eigenvectors.

The fact that the eigenvectors in Theorem 3.9 may be taken to be orthonormal stems from the fact that vectors may be normalized to have unit length and the fact that eigenvectors corresponding to distinct eigenvectors are orthogonal. If some of the eigenvalues have more than one eigenvector corresponding to them we may use the Gram-Schmidt process to orthogonalize them.

EXERCISES

1. Find the eigenvalues of the following matrices. Before you find them use the results of this section to determine if they are real, pure imaginary, or have magnitude 1.

a) $\begin{bmatrix} 1 & 2 & 3 \\ 2 & 0 & 4 \\ 3 & 4 & 5 \end{bmatrix}$

b) $\begin{bmatrix} 1 & 2+2i & i \\ 2-2i & 0 & 3+5i \\ -i & 3-5i & 2 \end{bmatrix}$

c) $\begin{bmatrix} \cos\vartheta & 0 & \sin\vartheta \\ 0 & 1 & 0 \\ -\sin\vartheta & 0 & \cos\vartheta \end{bmatrix}$

d) $\begin{bmatrix} 0 & 1 & -1 \\ -1 & 0 & 1 \\ 1 & -1 & 0 \end{bmatrix}$

e) $\begin{bmatrix} 1 & 2 & 1 \\ 2 & 0 & 0 \\ 1 & 0 & 1 \end{bmatrix}$

f) $\begin{bmatrix} 1 & 1 & 0 \\ 1 & 1 & 0 \\ 0 & 0 & 1 \end{bmatrix}$

2 Show that the following matrix is orthogonal and find its eigenvalues:

$$\begin{bmatrix} \frac{\sqrt{6}}{6} & \frac{\sqrt{6}}{3} & \frac{\sqrt{6}}{6} \\ \frac{4\sqrt{21}}{21} & -\frac{\sqrt{21}}{21} & -\frac{2\sqrt{21}}{21} \\ \frac{\sqrt{14}}{14} & -\frac{\sqrt{14}}{7} & \frac{3\sqrt{14}}{14} \end{bmatrix}$$

3. Prove Theorem 3.2.

4. Show that $\mathbf{A} + \mathbf{A}^{\mathrm{T}}$ has real eigenvalues.

5. Show that $\mathbf{A} - \mathbf{A}^{\mathrm{T}}$ has purely imaginary eigenvalues.

6. Show that **A** is orthogonal if and only if the rows or columns of **A** form an orthonormal set of vectors.

7. Prove Theorem 3.4.

8. Use Theorem 3.4 to prove that $\langle \mathbf{x}, \mathbf{y} + \mathbf{z} \rangle = \langle \mathbf{x}, \mathbf{y} \rangle + \langle \mathbf{x}, \mathbf{z} \rangle$.

9. Find an orthogonal set of vectors that span the same subspace in R^n as

a) $\begin{bmatrix} 2 \\ 1 \end{bmatrix}, \begin{bmatrix} 0 \\ 2 \end{bmatrix}$ b) $\begin{bmatrix} 1 \\ 1 \end{bmatrix}, \begin{bmatrix} 4 \\ 5 \end{bmatrix}$

c) $\begin{bmatrix} 3 \\ 0 \end{bmatrix}, \begin{bmatrix} 0 \\ 3 \end{bmatrix}$ d) $\begin{bmatrix} 1 \\ 1 \\ 1 \end{bmatrix}, \begin{bmatrix} 1 \\ 2 \\ 1 \end{bmatrix}$

e) $\begin{bmatrix} 1 \\ 1 \\ 0 \end{bmatrix}, \begin{bmatrix} 0 \\ 1 \\ 1 \end{bmatrix}$ f) $\begin{bmatrix} 2 \\ 0 \\ 0 \end{bmatrix}, \begin{bmatrix} 1 \\ 1 \\ 1 \end{bmatrix}$

g) $\begin{bmatrix} 1 \\ 1 \\ 0 \\ 0 \end{bmatrix}, \begin{bmatrix} 0 \\ 0 \\ 1 \\ 1 \end{bmatrix}, \begin{bmatrix} 1 \\ 0 \\ 0 \\ 1 \end{bmatrix}$ h) $\begin{bmatrix} 1 \\ 2 \\ 3 \\ 4 \end{bmatrix}, \begin{bmatrix} 0 \\ 0 \\ 2 \\ 3 \end{bmatrix}$

i) $\begin{bmatrix} 1 \\ 2 \\ 0 \\ 0 \end{bmatrix}, \begin{bmatrix} 2 \\ 1 \\ 0 \\ 0 \end{bmatrix}, \begin{bmatrix} 0 \\ 0 \\ 1 \\ 0 \end{bmatrix}$

10. Illustrate Theorem 3.4 for

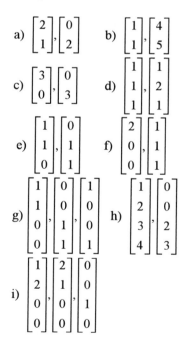

$c = 2\text{-}i,\ \mathbf{x} = \begin{bmatrix} 1-i \\ 3+2i \\ 1+3i \end{bmatrix},$

$\mathbf{y} = \begin{bmatrix} i \\ 2+i \\ 3 \end{bmatrix}$, and $\mathbf{z} = \begin{bmatrix} 2+2i \\ 2-2i \\ 3+4i \end{bmatrix}$.

11. Use the Gram-Schmidt orthogonalization process to determine whether or not $\left\{ \begin{bmatrix} 1 \\ 2 \\ 1 \end{bmatrix}, \begin{bmatrix} 2 \\ 1 \\ 2 \end{bmatrix}, \begin{bmatrix} 3 \\ 3 \\ 3 \end{bmatrix} \right\}$ is a linearly independent set of vectors in R^3.

12. Prove: A real matrix **A** of order n is symmetric if and only if $(\mathbf{Ax})^{\mathrm{T}} \mathbf{y} = \mathbf{x}^{\mathrm{T}} \mathbf{Ay}$ for all $\mathbf{x}, \mathbf{y} \in R^n$.

13. Explain how the Gram-Schmidt process can be used to construct a unitary or orthogonal matrix of order n.

14. Let λ be an eigenvalue of a nonsingular matrix **A** with eigenvector **x**, $\mathbf{Ax} = \lambda\mathbf{x}$. Prove that $\mathbf{A}^{-1}\mathbf{x} = \frac{1}{\lambda}\mathbf{x}$.

15. Prove that if **A** is orthogonally similar to a diagonal matrix then **A** is symmetric. Hint: Consider $\mathbf{Q}^{\mathrm{T}}\mathbf{AQ} = \mathrm{DIAG}[\lambda_1, \lambda_2, \cdots, \lambda_n]$ and note that the diagonal matrix is symmetric.

16. Show that if **Q** and **R** are orthogonal then **QR** is orthogonal.

17. For the following matrix **A**, find an orthonormal matrix **Q** that transforms **A** to a diagonal matrix.

a) $\mathbf{A} = \begin{bmatrix} 1 & 2 \\ 2 & 3 \end{bmatrix}$

b) $\mathbf{A} = \begin{bmatrix} 0 & 1 & 1 \\ 1 & 0 & -1 \\ 1 & -1 & 0 \end{bmatrix}$

4. BOUNDS FOR EIGENVALUES

The calculation of eigenvalues of most matrices encountered in an introductory course in linear algebra is accomplished easily enough, especially when a symbolic computer software system such as *Derive* is available to perform the basic operations. Matrices which occur in practical applications are frequently very large, and calculations to find eigenvalues become complicated to the point where the results can best be characterized as numerical approximations to the eigenvalues. In many cases it is sufficient to know the general location in the complex plane of these eigenvalues; therefore, techniques which place limits, or bounds, on the eigenvalues are all that is required. In this section we prove two theorems which effectively provide these bounds.

Thus far in our study we have used two means of describing the size of vectors. The first is related to the dimension of the vector space and consists of the number of components required to specify the vector. The second, which we usually refer to as the magnitude of the vector, translates to the length of vectors from familiar spaces such as R^2 and R^3. Thus far when discussing matrices we have only described size in terms of the number of rows and columns of the matrix, but the concept magnitude can be generalized to include matrices as well. Two of the possible ways to describe the magnitude of a matrix involve finding the maximum of the sums of the absolute values of the row (column) elements of the matrix. If **A** is a matrix of order n with $\mathbf{A} = (a_{ij})$, then we will use the following notation to simplify our discussion:

$$\mathrm{R}_i = \sum_{j=1}^{n} |a_{ij}|, \qquad \mathrm{C}_j = \sum_{i=1}^{n} |a_{ij}|$$

$$\mathrm{R} = \max_i \mathrm{R}_i, \qquad \mathrm{C} = \max_j \mathrm{C}_j .$$

THEOREM 4.1 If λ is an eigenvalue of **A**, then $|\lambda| \le \min(\mathrm{R},\mathrm{C})$

PROOF: We will prove the result for row sums only; the proof for column sums follows accordingly. Let λ be an eigenvalue of **A** and **x** be its corresponding eigenvector, $\mathbf{Ax} = \lambda\mathbf{x}$. We focus our attention on the ith component of the two sides of this equation:

$$\sum_{j=1}^{n} a_{ij}x_j = \lambda x_i .$$

Since **x** has a finite number of components, there exists an index m such that $|x_i| \le |x_m|$ for all i. Thus, using the triangle inequality

$$\left|\lambda x_m\right| = \left|\sum_{j=1}^{n} a_{mj} x_j\right| \le \sum_{j=1}^{n} \left|a_{mj}\right| \left|x_j\right| \le \sum_{j=1}^{n} \left|a_{mj}\right| \left|x_m\right|$$

Therefore,

$$\left|\lambda\right| \left|x_m\right| \le \left|x_m\right| \sum_{j=1}^{n} \left|a_{mj}\right|$$

and since $\left|x_m\right| > 0$

$$\left|\lambda\right| \le \sum_{j=1}^{n} \left|a_{mj}\right|$$

Hence,

$$\left|\lambda\right| \le \max_i \mathrm{R}_i,$$

and the proof is complete.

We recall from our previous exposure to the complex number system that $\left|(x+iy)-(a+ib)\right|$ computes the distance between the complex numbers $x + iy$ and $a + ib$. Thus, the set of all complex numbers $x + iy$ which satisfy $\left|(x+iy)-(a+ib)\right| = r$ constitutes a circle in the complex plane centered at $a+bi$ with radius r. We can now use the result established in Theorem 4.1 above to restrict the eigenvalues of a matrix **A** to be bounded by such a circle in the complex plane.

EXAMPLE 4.1 The eigenvalues of the matrix

$$\mathbf{A} = \begin{bmatrix} 1 & 2 & 3 & 1 \\ -1 & 2 & 1+2i & i \\ 1-i & 2 & 0 & 2+i \\ 1 & 2 & 1-i & 0 \end{bmatrix}$$

all lie within the boundaries of a circle centered at $0 + 0i$ in the complex plane. To see this we first compute the sums of the absolute values of the individual rows and columns:

$$\mathrm{R}_1 = 7, \quad \mathrm{R}_2 = 4+\sqrt{5}, \quad \mathrm{R}_3 = 2+\sqrt{2}+\sqrt{5}, \quad \mathrm{R}_4 = 3+\sqrt{2}$$

$$\mathrm{C}_1 = 3+\sqrt{2}, \quad \mathrm{C}_2 = 8, \quad \mathrm{C}_3 = 3+\sqrt{2}+\sqrt{5}, \quad \mathrm{C}_4 = 2+\sqrt{5}.$$

It follows that R = 7 and C = 8, and the eigenvalues of **A** lie inside the circle $|x+iy|=8$. This can be illustrated in *Derive*:

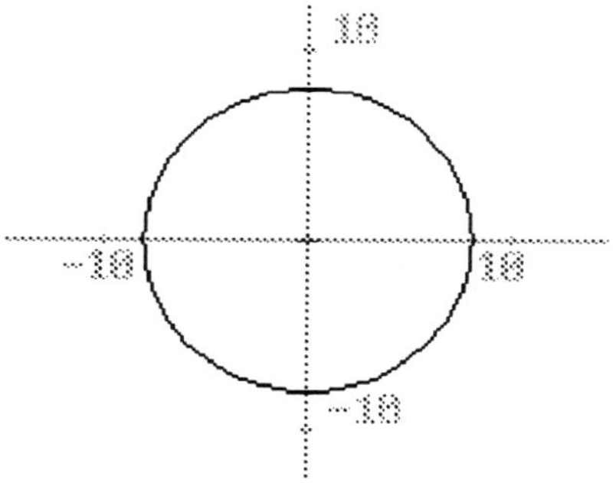

For our second theorem we define another computation of row and column elements which can be used to determine bounds on eigenvalues:

$$\mathrm{R}_i' = \sum_{\substack{j=1\\ j\neq i}}^{n} |a_{ij}| \quad \text{and} \quad \mathrm{C}_j' = \sum_{\substack{i=1\\ i\neq j}}^{n} |a_{ij}|.$$

THEOREM 4.2 (Gerschgorin) The eigenvalues of a matrix $\mathbf{A}=(a_{ij})$ lie inside the union of the disks in the complex plane

$$|\lambda - a_{ii}| \le \mathrm{R}_i' \quad \text{and} \quad |\lambda - a_{jj}| \le \mathrm{C}_j' \quad i,j=1,2,\cdots,n.$$

PROOF: We will prove the theorem for the rows of **A**. The result for columns follows since **A** and $\mathbf{A}^{\mathrm{T}}$ have the same eigenvalues. Let λ be an eigenvalue of **A** and **x** be its corresponding eigenvector, $\mathbf{Ax}=\lambda\mathbf{x}$. Focusing on the *i*th component of both sides of this equation we have

$$\sum_{j=1}^{n} a_{ij}x_j = \lambda x_i \qquad \text{for } i=1,2,\cdots,n$$

or

$$\lambda x_i - a_{ii}x_i = \sum_{\substack{j=1\\ j\neq i}}^{n} a_{ij}x_j.$$

Taking the absolute value and using the triangle inequality

$$|\lambda - a_{ii}||x_i| = \left|\sum_{\substack{j=1 \\ j\neq i}}^{n} a_{ij}x_j\right| \leq \sum_{\substack{j=1 \\ j\neq i}}^{n} |a_{ij}||x_j|$$

Since $\mathbf{x}$ has only a finite number of components, there exists an index m such that $|x_m| \geq |x_i| \quad i = 1, 2, \cdots, n$. It follows that

$$|\lambda - a_{mm}|\ |x_m| \leq |x_m| \sum_{\substack{j=1 \\ j\neq m}}^{n} |a_{mj}|.$$

and, since $x_m \neq 0$,

$$|\lambda - a_{mm}| \leq \sum_{\substack{j=1 \\ j\neq m}}^{n} |a_{mj}| = \mathrm{R}'_m$$

Thus for each eigenvalue λ there is a disk $|\lambda - a_{ii}| \leq \mathrm{R}'_i$ which contains that eigenvalue. Therefore the eigenvalues of **A** lie inside the union of all such disks. Again, the proof that the eigenvalues of **A** lie inside the union of the disks $|\lambda - a_{jj}| \leq \mathrm{C}'_j$ follows from the fact that the eigenvalues of **A** and $\mathbf{A}^{\mathrm{T}}$ are identical.

We remark that Theorem 4.2 gives a better bound of the eigenvalues of **A** than Theorem 4.1 because if $|\lambda - a_{ii}| \leq \mathrm{R}'_i$, then $|\lambda| \leq \mathrm{R}$, since $|\lambda| = |\lambda - a_{ii} + a_{ii}| \leq |\lambda - a_{ii}| + |a_{ii}| \leq \mathrm{R}'_i + |a_{ii}| = \mathrm{R}_i \leq \mathrm{R}$.

EXAMPLE 4.2 If

$$\mathbf{A} = \begin{bmatrix} -1 & -1 & -5 \\ 0 & -1 & 0 \\ 1 & 1 & 3 \end{bmatrix},$$

then we can use Gerschgorin's Theorem to find a region in the complex plane that contains the eigenvalues. First, the disks corresponding to the rows are determined:

$$|z+1| \leq 6, \quad |z+1| \leq 0, \quad \text{and} \quad |z-3| \leq 2$$

and the disks corresponding to the columns are determined:

$$|z+1|\le 1, \quad |z+1|\le 2, \text{ and } |z-3|\le 5.$$

Next, the disks are plotted for the rows and for the columns, and the intersection of the union of the row disks and the union of the column disks is shaded. Finally, the two eigenvalues $1\pm i$ and -1 are plotted:

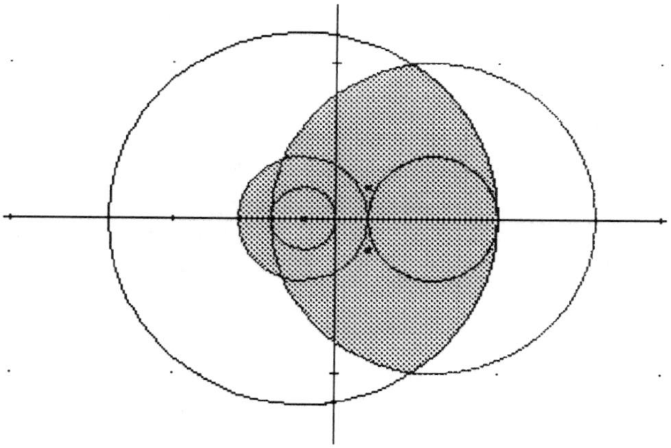

(EACH GRID MARK REPRESENTS 5 UNITS)

We note that the maximum of the row sums is 7, and the maximum of the column sums is 8. The disk with center at the origin and radius 7 encompasses almost all of the region covered by the union of all of the Gregorian disks.

We should also note that there are many other bounding theorems, but most fall between the two that have been given.

EXERCISES

1. Use Theorems 4.1 and 4.2 to find regions in the complex plane that contain the eigenvalues of the following matrices:

a) $\begin{bmatrix} 1 & 3 & 2 \\ 3 & 0 & -1 \\ 2 & -1 & 5 \end{bmatrix}$

b) $\begin{bmatrix} 1 & 2 & 3 \\ 4 & 5 & 6 \\ 7 & 8 & 9 \end{bmatrix}$

c) $\begin{bmatrix} 2 & -1 & -1 \\ 3 & 2 & -2 \\ 0 & 1 & -5 \end{bmatrix}$

2. Show that

$$\mathbf{A} = \begin{bmatrix} 8 & 1 & 1 & 0 \\ 1 & 10 & 2 & -2 \\ 0 & 1 & 5 & 3 \\ 1 & 1 & 1 & 6 \end{bmatrix}$$

is not singular. Hint: $\text{DET}(\mathbf{A}) = \prod_{i=1}^{4} \lambda_i$.

3. Prove that if **A** is a matrix with $\sum_{j=1}^{n} |a_{ij}| < |a_{ii}|$, then **A** is not singular. State the same result for columns.

4. Show that the zeros of $x^n - a_1 x^{n-1} - \cdots - a_{n-1} x - a_n$ are bounded by $\max\{|a_n|, 1 + |a_i|; i = 1, 2, \ldots, n-1\}$ and are bounded by $\max\left\{1, \sum_{i=1}^{n} |a_i|\right\}$. Hint use Exercise 13 of Section 5.2.

5. Find circles in the complex plane that contain the zeros of the polynomials:
   a) $p(x) = x^4 - 2x^3 - x^2 - x - 1$
   b) $p(x) = 2x^4 + 4x^3 - 6x^2 + 8x - 4$
   c) $p(x) = x^5 - x^4 + x^3 - x^2 + x - 1$

6. If **A** is symmetric show that the eigenvalues are contained inside the Gerschgorin disks and on the real line; hence, find intervals containing the eigenvalues of Exercise 1.

7. Let **A** be a real matrix with all of the row sums equal to 1. Show that 1 is an eigenvalue of **A**.

8. Let **A** be a real matrix with all row sums equal to 1 and all column sums equal to 1. Prove or find a counter example to the following: If λ is an eigenvalue of **A**, then $\lambda = 1$.

5. THE JORDON CANONICAL FORM

We have seen that any matrix that has a complete set of eigenvectors can be diagonalized by using a matrix **U** with columns consisting of these eigenvectors to form the product $\mathbf{U}^{-1}\mathbf{AU} = \mathbf{D}$. The benefit of forming a diagonal matrix that has similar properties to the a given matrix is the convenience associated with diagonal matrices when performing simple operations such as raising to a power, computing a square root, and evaluating other general functions. The difficulty, as pointed out in Example 1.5 of this chapter, is that not all matrices can be diagonalized. In this section we will generalize the process of diagonalizing a matrix to what is called the Jordon canonical form. We will see in the following chapters that although the Jordan canonical form is not always as convenient to work with as a diagonal matrix, it very useful for developing applications of linear algebra.

DEFINITION 5.1 (Generalized eigenvector) A nonzero vector **x** is called a generalized eigenvector, corresponding to the eigenvalue λ, of a linear transformation **t** if $(\mathbf{t} - \lambda\mathbf{i})^k \mathbf{x} = \mathbf{0}$ for some integer k.

We note that if $k = 1$ then **x** is an eigenvector, and if $k > 1$, then $(\mathbf{t} - \lambda\mathbf{i})^{k-1}\mathbf{x}$ is an eigenvector.

DEFINITION 5.2 (Set of Generalized Eigenvectors) If $\mathbf{t}: V \to V$ is a linear transformation and **x** is a generalized eigenvector corresponding to the eigenvalue λ, and if k is the smallest positive integer such that $(\lambda\mathbf{i} - \mathbf{t})^k \mathbf{x} = \mathbf{0}$, then

$$G_\lambda = \left\{(\lambda\mathbf{i} - \mathbf{t})^{k-1}\mathbf{x}, (\lambda\mathbf{i} - \mathbf{t})^{k-t}\mathbf{x}, \cdots, (\lambda\mathbf{i} - \mathbf{t})\mathbf{x}, \mathbf{x}\right\}$$

is called the set of generalized eigenvectors belonging to λ. We will also use the notation $G_\lambda = \{\mathbf{x}_{k-1}, \mathbf{x}_{k-2}, \cdots, \mathbf{x}_0\}$.

We learned in Theorem 1.2 that sets of eigenvectors belonging to distinct eigenvalues are linearly independent. The following theorem shows that sets of generalized eigenvectors satisfy the same property.

THEOREM 5.1 The members of a set of generalized eigenvectors, G_λ, are linearly independent.

PROOF: Consider the linear combination of generalized eigenvectors

$$\sum_{i=0}^{k-1} a_i (\mathbf{t} - \lambda\mathbf{i})^i \mathbf{x} = \mathbf{0}$$

If we multiply this equation by $(\mathbf{t} - \lambda\mathbf{i})^{k-1}$ we obtain $a_0 (\mathbf{t} - \lambda\mathbf{i})^{k-1} \mathbf{x} = \mathbf{0}$ so that $a_0 = 0$. If we continue in this way, we can show by induction that $a_i = 0$ for $i = 0, 1, \cdots, k-1$.

Since G_λ is linearly independent, it forms a basis for the subspace of vectors in its span. The following theorem shows that the matrix for **t** restricted to this subspace is in a form that generalizes our concept of a diagonal matrix.

THEOREM 5.2 The matrix of $\mathbf{t}: V \to W$ restricted to the subspace of V with basis $\gamma = G_\lambda$ is the $k \times k$ matrix

$$\mathbf{t}_\gamma = \begin{bmatrix} \lambda & 1 & 0 & \cdots & 0 & 0 \\ 0 & \lambda & 1 & \cdots & 0 & 0 \\ 0 & 0 & \lambda & \cdots & 0 & 0 \\ \vdots & \vdots & \vdots & \ddots & \vdots & \vdots \\ 0 & 0 & 0 & \cdots & \lambda & 1 \\ 0 & 0 & 0 & \cdots & 0 & \lambda \end{bmatrix}$$

PROOF: The entries of $\mathbf{t}_\gamma$ follow from applying the transformation **t** to each element of γ:

$$\mathbf{t}(\mathbf{x}_{k-1}) = \lambda\mathbf{x}_{k-1}$$
$$\mathbf{t}(\mathbf{x}_{k-2}) = \lambda\mathbf{x}_{k-2} + \mathbf{x}_{k-3}$$
$$\mathbf{t}(\mathbf{x}_{k-3}) = \lambda\mathbf{x}_{k-3} + \mathbf{x}_{k-4}$$
$$\cdots\cdots\cdots$$
$$\mathbf{t}(\mathbf{x}_0) = \lambda\mathbf{x}_0 + \mathbf{x}_1$$

Although a matrix in the form described in the previous theorem is not a diagonal matrix, it does have many desirable properties that make it convenient to use in applications. In fact, matrices that consist of blocks which have this form are very useful. The following definition formalizes this concept.

DEFINITION 5.3 (Jordan Canonical Form; Jordan Blocks) A matrix of order n is said to be in Jordan canonical form if it has the form

$$\mathbf{J} = \begin{bmatrix} \mathbf{J}_1 & \mathbf{0} & \cdots & \mathbf{0} \\ \mathbf{0} & \mathbf{J}_2 & \mathbf{0} & \mathbf{0} \\ \cdots & \cdots & \ddots & \cdots \\ \mathbf{0} & \mathbf{0} & \cdots & \mathbf{J}_k \end{bmatrix}$$

where each $\mathbf{J}_i$ has the form

$$\mathbf{J}_i = \begin{bmatrix} \lambda & 1 & \cdots & 0 \\ 0 & \lambda & \cdots & 0 \\ 0 & 0 & \ddots & 1 \\ 0 & 0 & \cdots & \lambda \end{bmatrix}.$$

Note that some of the matrices $\mathbf{J}_i$, which are called Jordan blocks, may be of order 1.

DEFINITION 5.4 (Canonical Basis) A set of n linearly independent generalized eigenvectors is called a canonical basis for a matrix of order n.

The next theorem is of fundamental importance and assures us that any matrix of order n can be expressed with respect to a basis of generalized eigenvectors. The proof of the existence of such a basis is beyond the scope of this book. The proof may be found in many more advanced texts of linear algebra.

THEOREM 5.3 A matrix of order n possesses a canonical basis.

EXAMPLE 5.1 If the matrix of a transformation $\mathbf{t}: R^4 \to R^4$ with respect to σ is

$$\mathbf{A} = \begin{bmatrix} 3 & 2 & 0 & -1 \\ -1 & 1 & 1 & 1 \\ 1 & 1 & 2 & 0 \\ -1 & -1 & 0 & 2 \end{bmatrix},$$

then we can find a canonical basis of generalized eigenvectors by first using *Derive* to find the characteristic polynomial is $p(\lambda) = (\lambda - 2)^4$. From this we can use the techniques of previous sections to find there is only one eigenvector, which has the form $\begin{bmatrix} -\alpha & \alpha & -\alpha & \alpha \end{bmatrix}^{\mathrm{T}}$, where α is any arbitrary number. Next, we begin the process of finding a canonical basis by multiplying candidates for a vector which will generate a set of generalized eigenvectors repeatedly by **(A** - 2**I)**. By the Cayley-Hamilton Theorem no more than four multiplications will be required before the result will be **0**. We choose as our first candidates the standard basis vectors $\mathbf{e}_1$, $\mathbf{e}_2$, $\mathbf{e}_3$, and $\mathbf{e}_4$ and write them in matrix form as the identity matrix.

7: $$\left[\begin{bmatrix} 3 & 2 & 0 & -1 \\ -1 & 1 & 1 & 1 \\ 1 & 1 & 2 & 0 \\ -1 & -1 & 0 & 2 \end{bmatrix} - 2\begin{bmatrix} 1 & 0 & 0 & 0 \\ 0 & 1 & 0 & 0 \\ 0 & 0 & 1 & 0 \\ 0 & 0 & 0 & 1 \end{bmatrix}\right] \cdot \begin{bmatrix} 1 & 0 & 0 & 0 \\ 0 & 1 & 0 & 0 \\ 0 & 0 & 1 & 0 \\ 0 & 0 & 0 & 1 \end{bmatrix}$$

8: $$\begin{bmatrix} 1 & 2 & 0 & -1 \\ -1 & -1 & 1 & 1 \\ 1 & 1 & 0 & 0 \\ -1 & -1 & 0 & 0 \end{bmatrix}$$

9: $$\left[\begin{bmatrix} 3 & 2 & 0 & -1 \\ -1 & 1 & 1 & 1 \\ 1 & 1 & 2 & 0 \\ -1 & -1 & 0 & 2 \end{bmatrix} - 2\begin{bmatrix} 1 & 0 & 0 & 0 \\ 0 & 1 & 0 & 0 \\ 0 & 0 & 1 & 0 \\ 0 & 0 & 0 & 1 \end{bmatrix}\right] \cdot \begin{bmatrix} 1 & 2 & 0 & -1 \\ -1 & -1 & 1 & 1 \\ 1 & 1 & 0 & 0 \\ -1 & -1 & 0 & 0 \end{bmatrix}$$

$$10: \begin{bmatrix} 0 & 1 & 2 & 1 \\ 0 & -1 & -1 & 0 \\ 0 & 1 & 1 & 0 \\ 0 & -1 & -1 & 0 \end{bmatrix}$$

$$11: \left[\begin{bmatrix} 3 & 2 & 0 & -1 \\ -1 & 1 & 1 & 1 \\ 1 & 1 & 2 & 0 \\ -1 & -1 & 0 & 2 \end{bmatrix} - 2 \begin{bmatrix} 1 & 0 & 0 & 0 \\ 0 & 1 & 0 & 0 \\ 0 & 0 & 1 & 0 \\ 0 & 0 & 0 & 1 \end{bmatrix}\right] \cdot \begin{bmatrix} 0 & 1 & 2 & 1 \\ 0 & -1 & -1 & 0 \\ 0 & 1 & 1 & 0 \\ 0 & -1 & -1 & 0 \end{bmatrix}$$

$$12: \begin{bmatrix} 0 & 0 & 1 & 1 \\ 0 & 0 & -1 & -1 \\ 0 & 0 & 1 & 1 \\ 0 & 0 & -1 & -1 \end{bmatrix}$$

$$13: \left[\begin{bmatrix} 3 & 2 & 0 & -1 \\ -1 & 1 & 1 & 1 \\ 1 & 1 & 2 & 0 \\ -1 & -1 & 0 & 2 \end{bmatrix} - 2 \begin{bmatrix} 1 & 0 & 0 & 0 \\ 0 & 1 & 0 & 0 \\ 0 & 0 & 1 & 0 \\ 0 & 0 & 0 & 1 \end{bmatrix}\right] \cdot \begin{bmatrix} 0 & 0 & 1 & 1 \\ 0 & 0 & -1 & -1 \\ 0 & 0 & 1 & 1 \\ 0 & 0 & -1 & -1 \end{bmatrix}$$

$$14: \begin{bmatrix} 0 & 0 & 0 & 0 \\ 0 & 0 & 0 & 0 \\ 0 & 0 & 0 & 0 \\ 0 & 0 & 0 & 0 \end{bmatrix}$$

It is evident that the last column of the matrix in statement #12 is an eigenvector since it is mapped to **0**. To obtain the corresponding set of generalized eigenvectors leading to this vector we simply follow the last column back through statements #14, 12, and 10, and 8.

$$\begin{bmatrix} 1 \\ -1 \\ 1 \\ -1 \end{bmatrix} \to \begin{bmatrix} 1 \\ 0 \\ 0 \\ 0 \end{bmatrix} \to \begin{bmatrix} -1 \\ 1 \\ 0 \\ 0 \end{bmatrix} \to \begin{bmatrix} 0 \\ 0 \\ 0 \\ 1 \end{bmatrix}$$

Thus, the Jordan canonical form of **A** with respect to this basis is obtained by creating a matrix **U** whose columns are these vectors and writing $\mathbf{U}^{-1}\mathbf{AU}=\mathbf{J}$. We perform this operation with *Derive*.

$$16: \begin{bmatrix} 1 & 1 & -1 & 0 \\ -1 & 0 & 1 & 0 \\ 1 & 0 & 0 & 0 \\ -1 & 0 & 0 & 1 \end{bmatrix}^{-1} \cdot \begin{bmatrix} 3 & 2 & 0 & -1 \\ -1 & 1 & 1 & 1 \\ 1 & 1 & 2 & 0 \\ -1 & -1 & 0 & 2 \end{bmatrix} \cdot \begin{bmatrix} 1 & 1 & -1 & 0 \\ -1 & 0 & 1 & 0 \\ 1 & 0 & 0 & 0 \\ -1 & 0 & 0 & 1 \end{bmatrix}$$

$$17: \begin{bmatrix} 2 & 1 & 0 & 0 \\ 0 & 2 & 1 & 0 \\ 0 & 0 & 2 & 1 \\ 0 & 0 & 0 & 2 \end{bmatrix}$$

We can also note that another set of generalized eigenvectors can also be found by following the third column of the matrices in statements #14, 12, and 10, and 8. Thus, sets of generalized eigenvectors are not necessarily unique for a particular matrix, but the Jordan canonical form is unique.

EXAMPLE 5.2 Techniques of previous sections show the matrix

$$\mathbf{A}=\begin{bmatrix} 4 & -2 & -4 & -6 \\ -2 & 1 & -6 & -5 \\ 1 & 3 & 10 & 7 \\ 0 & -1 & -2 & 1 \end{bmatrix}$$

has a characteristic polynomial of $p(\lambda)=(\lambda-4)^4$, and two linearly independent eigenvectors corresponding to the eigenvalue 4. We proceed as in Example 5.1 to find the generalized eigenvectors:

$$10: \left[\begin{bmatrix} 4 & -2 & -4 & -6 \\ -2 & 1 & -6 & -5 \\ 1 & 3 & 10 & 7 \\ 0 & -1 & -2 & 1 \end{bmatrix} - 4 \begin{bmatrix} 1 & 0 & 0 & 0 \\ 0 & 1 & 0 & 0 \\ 0 & 0 & 1 & 0 \\ 0 & 0 & 0 & 1 \end{bmatrix}\right] \cdot \begin{bmatrix} 1 & 0 & 0 & 0 \\ 0 & 1 & 0 & 0 \\ 0 & 0 & 1 & 0 \\ 0 & 0 & 0 & 1 \end{bmatrix}$$

11: $\begin{bmatrix} 0 & -2 & -4 & -6 \\ -2 & -3 & -6 & -5 \\ 1 & 3 & 6 & 7 \\ 0 & -1 & -2 & -3 \end{bmatrix}$

12: $\left[\begin{bmatrix} 4 & -2 & -4 & -6 \\ -2 & 1 & -6 & -5 \\ 1 & 3 & 10 & 7 \\ 0 & -1 & -2 & 1 \end{bmatrix} - 4\begin{bmatrix} 1 & 0 & 0 & 0 \\ 0 & 1 & 0 & 0 \\ 0 & 0 & 1 & 0 \\ 0 & 0 & 0 & 1 \end{bmatrix}\right] \cdot \begin{bmatrix} 0 & -2 & -4 & -6 \\ -2 & -3 & -6 & -5 \\ 1 & 3 & 6 & 7 \\ 0 & -1 & -2 & -3 \end{bmatrix}$

13: $\begin{bmatrix} 0 & 0 & 0 & 0 \\ 0 & 0 & 0 & 0 \\ 0 & 0 & 0 & 0 \\ 0 & 0 & 0 & 0 \end{bmatrix}$

Every column of the matrix in statement #11 is a eigenvector since they are all mapped into $\mathbf{0}$ by $\mathbf{A} - 4\mathbf{I}$. In this example there are two subspaces of generalized eigenvectors. To find these subspaces, we can choose any two linearly independent columns from statement #11 and follow those columns back to the original identity matrix which contained our four candidates for generating a set of generalized eigenvectors. For example, the first and second columns of statement #11 are linearly independent. When we trace them back to the identity matrix we generate the subspaces

$$\left\{\begin{bmatrix} 0 \\ -2 \\ 1 \\ 0 \end{bmatrix}, \begin{bmatrix} 1 \\ 0 \\ 0 \\ 0 \end{bmatrix}\right\} \text{ and } \left\{\begin{bmatrix} -2 \\ -3 \\ 3 \\ -1 \end{bmatrix}, \begin{bmatrix} 0 \\ 1 \\ 0 \\ 0 \end{bmatrix}\right\}.$$

We can now use these vectors as columns in a matrix which can be used to transform the matrix $\mathbf{A}$ into a matrix which consists of two Jordan blocks:

$$18: \begin{bmatrix} 0 & 1 & -2 & 0 \\ -2 & 0 & -3 & 1 \\ 1 & 0 & 3 & 0 \\ 0 & 0 & -1 & 0 \end{bmatrix}^{-1} \cdot \begin{bmatrix} 4 & -2 & -4 & -6 \\ -2 & 1 & -6 & -5 \\ 1 & 3 & 10 & 7 \\ 0 & -1 & -2 & 1 \end{bmatrix} \cdot \begin{bmatrix} 0 & 1 & -2 & 0 \\ -2 & 0 & -3 & 1 \\ 1 & 0 & 3 & 0 \\ 0 & 0 & -1 & 0 \end{bmatrix}$$

$$19: \begin{bmatrix} 4 & 1 & 0 & 0 \\ 0 & 4 & 0 & 0 \\ 0 & 0 & 4 & 1 \\ 0 & 0 & 0 & 4 \end{bmatrix}$$

EXAMPLE 5.3 For the matrix

$$\mathbf{A} = \begin{bmatrix} -4 & -2 & -1 \\ -3 & -5 & -4 \\ 10 & 10 & 8 \end{bmatrix},$$

we can find a canonical basis of generalized eigenvectors and transform **A** into its Jordan canonical form. First, we use *Derive* to find the characteristic polynomial of **A**

$$p(\lambda) = (\lambda - 3)(\lambda + 2)^2$$

and the two linearly independent eigenvectors: $\begin{bmatrix} 0 & -\alpha & 2\alpha \end{bmatrix}^T$ associated with $\lambda = 3$ and $\begin{bmatrix} -\beta & \beta & 0 \end{bmatrix}^T$ associated with $\lambda = -2$, where α and β are arbitrary. Next, we find a set of generalized eigenvectors associated with the eigenvalue -2. This time instead of using the identity matrix to provide candidates, we begin by multiplying $\mathbf{A} + 2\mathbf{I}$ by $\mathbf{A} - 3\mathbf{I}$ (since we know by the Cayley-Hamilton Theorem that $(\mathbf{A} + 2\mathbf{I})^2(\mathbf{A} - 3\mathbf{I}) = \mathbf{0}$):

$$16: \left[\begin{bmatrix} -4 & -2 & -1 \\ -3 & -5 & -4 \\ 10 & 10 & 8 \end{bmatrix} - (-2)\begin{bmatrix} 1 & 0 & 0 \\ 0 & 1 & 0 \\ 0 & 0 & 1 \end{bmatrix}\right] \cdot \begin{bmatrix} -7 & -2 & -1 \\ -3 & -8 & -4 \\ 10 & 10 & 5 \end{bmatrix}$$

$$17: \begin{bmatrix} 10 & 10 & 5 \\ -10 & -10 & -5 \\ 0 & 0 & 0 \end{bmatrix}$$

(where the last matrix in statement #16 is $\mathbf{A}-3\mathbf{I}$). By the Cayley-Hamilton Theorem we know in advance that multiplying $\mathbf{A}+2\mathbf{I}$ by the matrix in statement #17 results in the zero matrix; thus, each nonzero column of statement #17 is an eigenvector corresponding to $\lambda=-2$. We can therefore choose any of the three columns, for example column 3, to find the two generalized eigenvectors corresponding to the eigenvalue -2 :

$$\begin{bmatrix} -5 \\ 5 \\ 0 \end{bmatrix}, \begin{bmatrix} -1 \\ -4 \\ -5 \end{bmatrix}$$

Using these two vectors for the first two columns and the eigenvector corresponding to $\alpha=3$ for the eigenvalue $\lambda=3$ for the third column, we can now transform **A** into its Jordan canonical form.

$$21: \begin{bmatrix} 5 & -1 & 0 \\ -5 & -4 & -1 \\ 0 & 5 & 2 \end{bmatrix}^{-1} \cdot \begin{bmatrix} -4 & -2 & -1 \\ -3 & -5 & -4 \\ 10 & 10 & 8 \end{bmatrix} \cdot \begin{bmatrix} 5 & -1 & 0 \\ -5 & -4 & -1 \\ 0 & 5 & 2 \end{bmatrix}$$

$$22: \begin{bmatrix} -2 & 1 & 0 \\ 0 & -2 & 0 \\ 0 & 0 & 3 \end{bmatrix}$$

EXERCISES:

1. Find the Jordan canonical form of each of the following:

a) $\mathbf{A}=\begin{bmatrix} 1 & 1 & 0 \\ -3 & -2 & 1 \\ 1 & 0 & -2 \end{bmatrix}$

b) $\mathbf{A}=\begin{bmatrix} 5 & 4 & 3 \\ -12 & -10 & -8 \\ 9 & 8 & 7 \end{bmatrix}$

c) $\mathbf{A} = \begin{bmatrix} 4 & 0 & -1 & 0 \\ -1 & 6 & 3 & 1 \\ 1 & -3 & 0 & -1 \\ 1 & -3 & -3 & 2 \end{bmatrix}$

d) $\mathbf{A} = \begin{bmatrix} 1 & -1 & -2 & 0 \\ -1 & -3 & 0 & -2 \\ 1 & 7 & 3 & 3 \\ 1 & 3 & -1 & 3 \end{bmatrix}$

e) $\mathbf{A} = \begin{bmatrix} -1 & -1 & -71 & -141 \\ 1 & 0 & 104 & 208 \\ 0 & 1 & -122 & -244 \\ 0 & 0 & 64 & 127 \end{bmatrix}$

f)

$$\mathbf{A} = \begin{bmatrix} 2-i & 3-2i & 2-2i & 3-2i \\ -1+2i & -1+3i & -1+2i & -2+2i \\ 1-2i & -2i & 1-i & 3 \\ -1 & -1 & -1 & -2-i \end{bmatrix}$$

CHAPTER VI
MATRIX ANALYSIS

We have already seen applications in which matrices have been substituted into polynomials and manipulated according to the rules of matrix algebra discussed in the first chapter. (One example was in Section 5.2 when we studied the Cayley-Hamilton Theorem.) In this chapter we will examine vector and matrix norms, limits of vectors and matrices, and series and functions of matrices. Although it is not the purpose of this text to provide a detailed exposition of these topics, the material here will present a working knowledge of matrix analysis.

1. VECTOR AND MATRIX NORMS

The term "magnitude" is frequently discussed in mathematics as a measure of how one object of a certain class compares with other objects of the same kind. We commented in the first chapter that initial definitions of vectors in R^2 and R^3 usually emphasize the direction and magnitude properties of vectors in the plane and 3-space. In Section 5.3 we defined the length, or magnitude, of a vector $\mathbf{x}$ in C^n to be $\|\mathbf{x}\| = \sqrt{\langle \mathbf{x}, \mathbf{x} \rangle}$. In this section we formalize these concepts, extend them to matrices, and discuss some of their uses.

DEFINITION 1.1 (Vector Norm for R^n (C^n)) A vector norm for R^n (C^n) is a function $\|\mathbf{x}\|: R^n(C^n) \to R$ which for all vectors $\mathbf{x}, \mathbf{y} \in R^n(\text{or } C^n)$ satisfies the following three axioms:

1. $\|\mathbf{x}\| \geq 0$ and $\|\mathbf{x}\| = 0$ if and only if $\mathbf{x} = \mathbf{0}$.
2. $\|c\mathbf{x}\| = |c|\|\mathbf{x}\|$ for all scalars c.
3. $\|\mathbf{x} + \mathbf{y}\| \leq \|\mathbf{x}\| + \|\mathbf{y}\|$ for all $\mathbf{x}$, $\mathbf{y}$.

EXAMPLE 1.1 The function $\|\mathbf{x}\| = \sum_{i=1}^{n} |\mathbf{x}_i|$ defined for all $\mathbf{x} \in C^n$ is a vector norm. The first axiom of Definition 1.1 is trivially satisfied since each $|x_i| \geq 0$, and $\|\mathbf{x}\| = \mathbf{0}$ if and only if $x_i = 0$ for all i. The second axiom is likewise satisfied since

$$\|c\mathbf{x}\| = \sum_{i=1}^{n} |cx_i| = \sum_{i=1}^{n} |c||x_i| = |c| \sum_{i=1}^{n} |x_i| = |c|\|\mathbf{x}\|.$$

To show the function satisfies the third axiom, we use the triangle inequality to note:

$$\|\mathbf{x} + \mathbf{y}\| = \sum_{i=1}^{n} |x_i + y_i| \leq \sum_{i=1}^{n} (|x_i| + |y_i|) = \sum_{i=1}^{n} |x_i| + \sum_{i=1}^{n} |y_i| = \|\mathbf{x}\| + \|\mathbf{y}\|.$$

The norm function is not unique for a given vector space. In fact, there are several norms for the spaces R^n and C^n. In addition to the norm function provided in Example 1.1 above, (listed as $\|\mathbf{x}\|_S$ below) we provide two additional useful norms for $R^n(C^n)$:

1. $\|\mathbf{x}\|_S = \sum_{i=1}^{n} |x_i|$
2. $\|\mathbf{x}\|_M = \max_j |x_j|$
3. $\|\mathbf{x}\|_E = \left(\sum_{j=1}^{n} |x_j|^2 \right)^{1/2} = (\langle \mathbf{x}, \mathbf{x} \rangle)^{1/2}$

The proof that the second function is a norm is left as an exercise. In order to prove the third function is a norm we will need the following result, known as the Cauchy-Schwarz inequality:

THEOREM 1.1 (Cauchy-Schwarz Inequality) For any vectors $\mathbf{x}, \mathbf{y} \in C^n$,

$$|\langle \mathbf{x}, \mathbf{y} \rangle| \leq \sqrt{\langle \mathbf{x}, \mathbf{x} \rangle} \sqrt{\langle \mathbf{y}, \mathbf{y} \rangle}.$$

PROOF: If $\mathbf{x} = \mathbf{0}$, there is nothing to prove. Assume $\mathbf{x} \neq \mathbf{0}$, and define $\mathbf{z} = \mathbf{y} - t\mathbf{x}$, where $t = \langle \mathbf{y},\mathbf{x}\rangle / \langle \mathbf{x},\mathbf{x}\rangle$. If we compute the scalar product of $\mathbf{z}$ with itself, then

$$\langle \mathbf{z},\mathbf{z}\rangle = \langle \mathbf{z},\mathbf{y} - t\mathbf{x}\rangle = \langle \mathbf{z},\mathbf{y}\rangle - t\langle \mathbf{z},\mathbf{x}\rangle.$$

We note that $\langle \mathbf{z},\mathbf{x}\rangle = 0$, since

$$\langle \mathbf{z},\mathbf{x}\rangle = \langle \mathbf{y} - t\mathbf{x},\mathbf{x}\rangle = \langle \mathbf{y},\mathbf{x}\rangle - t\langle \mathbf{x},\mathbf{x}\rangle = \langle \mathbf{y},\mathbf{x}\rangle - \frac{\langle \mathbf{y},\mathbf{x}\rangle}{\langle \mathbf{x},\mathbf{x}\rangle}\langle \mathbf{x},\mathbf{x}\rangle.$$

Thus,

$$\langle \mathbf{z},\mathbf{z}\rangle = \langle \mathbf{z},\mathbf{y}\rangle = \langle \mathbf{y} - t\mathbf{x},\mathbf{y}\rangle = \langle \mathbf{y},\mathbf{y}\rangle - t\langle \mathbf{x},\mathbf{y}\rangle,$$

and,

$$\langle \mathbf{z},\mathbf{z}\rangle = \langle \mathbf{y},\mathbf{y}\rangle - \frac{\langle \mathbf{y},\mathbf{x}\rangle}{\langle \mathbf{x},\mathbf{x}\rangle}\langle \mathbf{x},\mathbf{y}\rangle.$$

Using the fact that $\langle \mathbf{y},\mathbf{x}\rangle = \overline{\langle \mathbf{x},\mathbf{y}\rangle}$,

$$\langle \mathbf{z},\mathbf{z}\rangle = \langle \mathbf{y},\mathbf{y}\rangle - \frac{\overline{\langle \mathbf{x},\mathbf{y}\rangle}\langle \mathbf{x},\mathbf{y}\rangle}{\langle \mathbf{x},\mathbf{x}\rangle}.$$

Noting that $\langle \mathbf{z},\mathbf{z}\rangle \geq 0$,

$$\langle \mathbf{y},\mathbf{y}\rangle \geq \frac{|\langle \mathbf{x},\mathbf{y}\rangle|^2}{\langle \mathbf{x},\mathbf{x}\rangle},$$

or

$$\langle \mathbf{x},\mathbf{x}\rangle\langle \mathbf{y},\mathbf{y}\rangle \geq |\langle \mathbf{x},\mathbf{y}\rangle|^2.$$

PROPOSITION 1.1 The function $\|\mathbf{x}\|_E$ is a vector norm.

PROOF: (To simplify notation in this proof, we use $\|\mathbf{x}\|$ in place of $\|\mathbf{x}\|_E$.) The first two axioms of Definition 1.1 follow immediately. To establish the third, note that

$$\|\mathbf{x} + \mathbf{y}\| = \langle \mathbf{x} + \mathbf{y},\mathbf{x} + \mathbf{y}\rangle = \langle \mathbf{x},\mathbf{x}\rangle + \langle \mathbf{x},\mathbf{y}\rangle + \langle \mathbf{y},\mathbf{x}\rangle + \langle \mathbf{y},\mathbf{y}\rangle,$$

and, thus

$$\|\mathbf{x}+\mathbf{y}\|^2 = \|\mathbf{x}\|^2 + \langle \mathbf{x},\mathbf{y}\rangle + \overline{\langle \mathbf{x},\mathbf{y}\rangle} + \|\mathbf{y},\mathbf{y}\|^2.$$

Since $\langle \mathbf{x},\mathbf{y}\rangle + \overline{\langle \mathbf{x},\mathbf{y}\rangle} = 2\mathrm{RE}(\langle \mathbf{x},\mathbf{y}\rangle)$, we can use the definition of the norm function and the Cauchy-Schwarz Inequality to obtain

$$\|\mathbf{x}+\mathbf{y}\|^2 = \|\mathbf{x}\|^2 + 2\mathrm{RE}(\langle \mathbf{x},\mathbf{y}\rangle) + \|\mathbf{y}\|^2 \le \|\mathbf{x}\|^2 + 2\|x\|\|y\| + \|\mathbf{y}\|^2,$$

and it follows that,

$$\|\mathbf{x}+\mathbf{y}\|^2 \le (\|\mathbf{x}\| + \|\mathbf{y}\|)^2.$$

EXAMPLE 1.2 For the vector $\mathbf{x} = [1 \quad 0 \quad 2 \quad 1 \quad -2 \quad 3]^{\mathrm{T}} \in R^6$, we note that the maximum component is 3; hence, $\|\mathbf{x}\|_{\mathrm{M}} = 3$. Also,

$$\|\mathbf{x}\|_{\mathrm{S}} = |1| + |0| + |2| + |1| + |-2| + |3| = 9$$

and

$$\|\mathbf{x}\|_{\mathrm{E}} = \left(|1|^2 + |0|^2 + |2|^2 + |1|^2 + |-2|^2 + |3|^2\right)^{1/2} = \sqrt{19}.$$

DEFINITION 1.2 (Norm of a Square Matrix) A matrix norm is a function $\|\mathbf{A}\|: M_{n\times n} \to R$ which for all matrices **A** and **B** of order n satisfies the following four axioms:

1. $\|\mathbf{A}\| \ge 0$ and $\|\mathbf{A}\| = 0$ if and only if $\mathbf{A} = \mathbf{0}$.

2. $\|c\mathbf{A}\| = |c|\|\mathbf{A}\|$

3. $\|\mathbf{AB}\| \le \|\mathbf{A}\|\|\mathbf{B}\|$

4. $\|\mathbf{A}+\mathbf{B}\| \le \|\mathbf{A}\| + \|\mathbf{B}\|$

EXAMPLE 1.3 It is straightforward argument to demonstrate that the first two properties of Definition 1.2 are satisfied by the function $\|\mathbf{A}\| = \max\limits_{j} \sum\limits_{j=1}^{n} |a_{ij}|$, and the proof is left as an exercise. To show the third property, we note

$$\|\mathbf{AB}\| = \max_i \sum_{j=1}^{n} \left| \sum_{k=1}^{n} a_{ik} b_{kj} \right| \leq \max_i \sum_{j=1}^{n} \sum_{k=1}^{n} |a_{ik} b_{kj}| \leq \max_i \sum_{j=1}^{n} \sum_{k=1}^{n} |a_{ik}| |b_{kj}|;$$

therefore,

$$\|\mathbf{AB}\| \leq \max_i \left(\sum_{k=1}^{n} \left(|a_{ik}| \sum_{j=1}^{n} |b_{kj}| \right) \right) \leq \left(\max_i \sum_{k=1}^{n} |a_{ik}| \right) \left(\max_k \sum_{j=1}^{n} |b_{kj}| \right).$$

The last two sums on the right are norms $\|\mathbf{A}\|$ and $\|\mathbf{B}\|$ respectively; therefore, $\|\mathbf{AB}\| \leq \|\mathbf{A}\| \|\mathbf{B}\|$.

To prove the fourth property, $\|\mathbf{A} + \mathbf{B}\| \leq \|\mathbf{A}\| + \|\mathbf{B}\|$, we note

$$\begin{aligned} \|\mathbf{A} + \mathbf{B}\| &= \max_i \sum_{j=1}^{n} |a_{ij} + b_{ij}| \\ &\leq \max_i \sum_{j=1}^{n} \left(|a_{ij}| + |b_{ij}| \right) \\ &\leq \max_i \sum_{j=1}^{n} |a_{ij}| + \max_i \sum_{j=1}^{n} |b_{ij}| \\ &\leq \|\mathbf{A}\| + \|\mathbf{B}\|. \end{aligned}$$

As in the case for vector norms, the matrix norm function is not unique. In addition to the norm presented in Example 1.3 above (which we label below as $\|\mathbf{A}\|_{\mathrm{R}}$), we give three additional matrix norm functions. The proofs that these functions satisfy the four axioms of Definition 1.2 are left as an exercise.

1. $\|\mathbf{A}\|_{\mathrm{R}} = \max_i \sum_{j=1}^{n} |a_{ij}|$
2. $\|\mathbf{A}\|_{\mathrm{C}} = \max_j \sum_{i=1}^{n} |a_{ij}|$
3. $\|\mathbf{A}\|_{\mathrm{E}} = \left(\sum_{j=1}^{n} \sum_{i=1}^{n} |a_{ij}|^2 \right)^{1/2}$
4. $\|\mathbf{A}\|_{\mathrm{M}} = n \max_{ij} |a_{ij}|$

EXAMPLE 1.4 If

$$\mathbf{A} = \begin{bmatrix} 1 & 2 & -4 & -2 \\ 2 & 4 & 2 & 2 \\ 3 & 3 & 0 & 3 \\ 2 & -5 & -5 & 6 \end{bmatrix},$$

we can evaluate the four matrix norms defined above.

1. The sums of the absolute values of the row elements are 9, 10, 9, and 18 respectively; therefore, $\|\mathbf{A}\|_R = 18$.
2. The sums of the absolute values of the column elements are 8, 14, 11, and 13 respectively; therefore, $\|\mathbf{A}\|_C = 14$
3. The sum of the squares of the elements of **A** is 170; therefore, $\|\mathbf{A}\|_E = \sqrt{170}$.
4. The maximum element of **A** is 6, and $n = 4$; therefore, $\|\mathbf{A}\|_M = 24$.

EXERCISES

1. For each of the vectors compute the three norms $\|\mathbf{x}\|_S$, $\|\mathbf{x}\|_M$, and $\|\mathbf{x}\|_E$.

   a) $\begin{bmatrix} 1 & -1 & 2 \end{bmatrix}^T$

   b) $\begin{bmatrix} 0 & -1 & 3 \end{bmatrix}^T$

   c) $\begin{bmatrix} 1+i & -i & 2-i \end{bmatrix}^T$

   d) $\begin{bmatrix} 0 & i & 1+2i \end{bmatrix}^T$

2. For each of the matrices compute the four norms $\|\mathbf{A}\|_R$, $\|\mathbf{A}\|_C$, $\|\mathbf{A}\|_E$, and $\|\mathbf{A}\|_M$:

   a) $\begin{bmatrix} 1 & 0 & 3 \\ 0 & 2 & 4 \\ 3 & 4 & 5 \end{bmatrix}$

   b) $\begin{bmatrix} 1 & -2 & -3 \\ 2 & 6 & 1 \\ 3 & -1 & 2 \end{bmatrix}$

   c) $\begin{bmatrix} 1+2i & 1-2i & 0 \\ i & 3i & 2 \\ 2+i & -i & 0 \end{bmatrix}$

   d) $\begin{bmatrix} 3 & i & -i \\ 1+i & 0 & 2i \\ 1 & 0 & 2-i \end{bmatrix}$

3. Show that $\|\mathbf{A}\|_E = \sqrt{\mathrm{TR}(\mathbf{A}\mathbf{A}^T)}$ if **A** has only real elements and $\|\mathbf{A}\|_E = \sqrt{\mathrm{TR}(\mathbf{A}\overline{\mathbf{A}}^T)}$ if **A** has complex elements.

4. Show that for any finite n, $\|\mathbf{A}^n\| \le \|\mathbf{A}\|^n$. (Hint: $\|\mathbf{A}^3\| = \|\mathbf{A}^2\mathbf{A}\| \le \|\mathbf{A}^2\|\|\mathbf{A}\|$ by Axiom 3 of Definition 1.2.)

5. Demonstrate the Cauchy-Schwartz inequality for the vectors

   a) $\mathbf{x} = \begin{bmatrix} 1 & 3 & 1 \end{bmatrix}^{\mathrm{T}}$, $\mathbf{y} = \begin{bmatrix} 2 & 3 & 0 \end{bmatrix}^{\mathrm{T}}$

   b) $\mathbf{x} = \begin{bmatrix} -1 & 4 & -1 \end{bmatrix}^{\mathrm{T}}$, $\mathbf{y} = \begin{bmatrix} -1 & 0 & 1 \end{bmatrix}^{\mathrm{T}}$

   c) $\mathbf{x} = \begin{bmatrix} 1+i & i & 2+i \end{bmatrix}^{\mathrm{T}}$, $\mathbf{y} = \begin{bmatrix} i & -i & 1 \end{bmatrix}^{\mathrm{T}}$

   d) $\mathbf{x} = \begin{bmatrix} 1 & i & 1-i \end{bmatrix}^{\mathrm{T}}$, $\mathbf{y} = \begin{bmatrix} 0 & 0 & 0 \end{bmatrix}^{\mathrm{T}}$

6. Compute $\|\mathbf{A}\|_{\mathrm{E}}$ by using the result of Exercise 3 above for each of the matrices in Exercise 2.

2. LIMITS OF MATRICES AND VECTORS

The study of analysis involves understanding the limiting process. We used the concept of a limit to define continuity in calculus. Limit processes were also used to define the derivative (motivated by the limit of slopes of secant lines) and the integral (motivated by the limit of areas of rectangles). Previous studies involving limit processes also considered two types of limits: limits of functions and limits of sequences. In this section we generalize the concept of limits of sequences to include matrices and vectors in order to obtain some fundamental results which we will find useful in studying applications in later sections.

DEFINITION 2.1 (Sequence of Matrices (Vectors)) By a sequence of $m \times n$ matrices (m-dimensional vectors), we mean a function mapping the positive integers into $M_{m\times n}$ (a vector space V with dimension m). We will denote the sequence by $\left(\mathbf{A}^{(k)}\right)$ or $\left(\mathbf{x}^{(k)}\right)$ with elements $\mathbf{A}^{(k)} = \left(a_{ij}(k)\right)$ or $\mathbf{x}^{(k)} = \left(x_j(k)\right)$.

EXAMPLE 2.1 If the general term of a sequence of matrices is defined by

$$\mathbf{A}^{(n)} = \begin{bmatrix} 1/n & 1/n! \\ 1/n^2 & \left(1 + 1/n\right)^n \end{bmatrix},$$

then $\mathbf{A}^{(3)}$ can be found by substituting 3 for n:

$$\mathbf{A}^{(3)} = \begin{bmatrix} 1/3 & 1/6 \\ 1/9 & 64/27 \end{bmatrix}.$$

DEFINITION 2.2 (Limit of a Sequence of Matrices or Vectors) By the limit of a sequence $\left(\mathbf{A}^{(n)}\right)$ of matrices or a sequence $\left(\mathbf{x}^{(n)}\right)$ of vectors, we mean

$$\lim_{n\to\infty} \mathbf{A}^{(n)} = \lim_{n\to\infty}\left(a_{ij}(n)\right) \text{ or } \lim_{n\to\infty} \mathbf{x}^{(n)} = \lim_{n\to\infty}\left(x_j(n)\right).$$

EXAMPLE 2.2 We can find the limit of the matrix given in Example 2.1 as follows:

$$\lim_{n\to\infty} \mathbf{A}^{(n)} = \begin{bmatrix} \lim\limits_{n\to\infty} \dfrac{1}{n} & \lim\limits_{n\to\infty} \dfrac{1}{n!} \\ \lim\limits_{n\to\infty} \dfrac{1}{n^2} & \lim\limits_{n\to\infty} \left(1+\dfrac{1}{n}\right)^n \end{bmatrix} = \begin{bmatrix} 0 & 0 \\ 0 & e \end{bmatrix}.$$

In order to determine what types matrices have the property that the sequence of consecutive powers of the matrix converge to **0**, we must first examine some important characteristics of powers of some special types of matrices.

THEOREM 2.1 Let **A** and **B** be similar matrices with $\mathbf{A} = \mathbf{U}^{-1}\mathbf{B}\mathbf{U}$, then $\mathbf{A}^m = \mathbf{U}^{-1}\mathbf{B}^m\mathbf{U}$.

PROOF: The proof is by induction on m. The theorem is true for $m = 1$. Assume it is also true for m -1: $\mathbf{A}^{m-1} = \mathbf{U}^{-1}\mathbf{B}^{m-1}\mathbf{U}$. If we left multiply both sides of this equation by **A,** we obtain

$$\mathbf{A}\mathbf{A}^{m-1} = \mathbf{A}\left(\mathbf{U}^{-1}\mathbf{B}^{m-1}\mathbf{U}\right) = \mathbf{U}^{-1}\mathbf{B}\mathbf{U}\left(\mathbf{U}^{-1}\mathbf{B}^{m-1}\mathbf{U}\right) = \mathbf{U}^{-1}\mathbf{B}^{m}\mathbf{U}$$

from which $\mathbf{A}^m = \mathbf{U}^{-1}\mathbf{B}^m\mathbf{U}$ follows immediately.

DEFINITION 2.3 (Block Diagonal Matrix) A matrix **B** of order n is said to be block diagonal if it is of the form

$$\mathbf{B} = \begin{bmatrix} \mathbf{B}_{11} & \mathbf{0} & \cdots & \mathbf{0} \\ \mathbf{0} & \mathbf{B}_{22} & \cdots & \mathbf{0} \\ \vdots & \vdots & \ddots & \vdots \\ \mathbf{0} & \mathbf{0} & \cdots & \mathbf{B}_{kk} \end{bmatrix}$$

where $\mathbf{B}_{ij}$ is of order n_i and $n_1 + n_2 + \cdots + n_k = n$.

THEOREM 2.2 If **B** is in block diagonal form, then

$$\mathbf{B}^m = \begin{bmatrix} (\mathbf{B}_{11})^m & \mathbf{0} & \cdots & \mathbf{0} \\ \mathbf{0} & (\mathbf{B}_{22})^m & \cdots & \mathbf{0} \\ \vdots & \vdots & \ddots & \vdots \\ \mathbf{0} & \mathbf{0} & \cdots & (\mathbf{B}_{kk})^m \end{bmatrix}$$

PROOF: The proof is by induction on m and is left as an exercise.

THEOREM 2.3 Let **A** be a matrix of order n, then $\lim_{n\to\infty} \mathbf{A}^n = \mathbf{0}$ if and only if **A** has eigenvalues $\lambda_1, \lambda_2, \ldots, \lambda_n$ (not necessarily distinct) which satisfy $|\lambda_i| < 1$ for i = 1, 2, ..., n.

PROOF: If $\lambda_1, \lambda_2, \ldots, \lambda_n$ are distinct, then by Theorem 1.3 of Section 5.1, **A** is similar to the diagonal matrix

$$\mathbf{D} = \mathbf{U}^{-1}\mathbf{A}\mathbf{U} = \begin{bmatrix} \lambda_1 & 0 & \cdots & 0 \\ 0 & \lambda_2 & \cdots & 0 \\ \vdots & \vdots & \ddots & \vdots \\ 0 & 0 & \cdots & \lambda_n \end{bmatrix};$$

therefore,

$$\lim_{k\to\infty} \mathbf{A}^k = \lim_{k\to\infty} \left(\left(\mathbf{U}^{-1}\right)^{-1} \mathbf{D}\mathbf{U}^{-1} \right)^k = \lim_{k\to\infty} \left(\mathbf{U}\mathbf{D}^k\mathbf{U}^{-1} \right) = \mathbf{U}\left(\lim_{k\to\infty} \mathbf{D}^k \right)\mathbf{U}^{-1}.$$

But

$$\lim_{k\to\infty} \mathbf{D}^k = \lim_{k\to\infty} \begin{bmatrix} \lambda_1 & 0 & \cdots & 0 \\ 0 & \lambda_2 & \cdots & 0 \\ \vdots & \vdots & \ddots & \vdots \\ 0 & 0 & \cdots & \lambda_n \end{bmatrix}^k = \lim_{k\to\infty} \begin{bmatrix} \lambda_1{}^k & 0 & \cdots & 0 \\ 0 & \lambda_2{}^k & \cdots & 0 \\ \vdots & \vdots & \ddots & \vdots \\ 0 & 0 & \cdots & \lambda_n{}^k \end{bmatrix}$$

by Theorem 2.2, and the rightmost limit converges to **0** if and only if $|\lambda_i| < 1$ for $i = 1, 2, \ldots, n$.

If $\lambda_1, \lambda_2, \ldots, \lambda_n$ are not distinct, then **A** is similar to a matrix

$$\mathbf{J} = \begin{bmatrix} \mathbf{J}_1 & 0 & \cdots & 0 \\ 0 & \mathbf{J}_2 & \cdots & 0 \\ \vdots & \vdots & \ddots & \vdots \\ 0 & 0 & \cdots & \mathbf{J}_m \end{bmatrix}$$

which is in Jordan canonical form with Jordan blocks $\mathbf{J}_1, \mathbf{J}_2, \cdots \mathbf{J}_m$. Thus, by Theorem 2.1, $\mathbf{A}^n = \mathbf{U}^{-1}\mathbf{J}^n\mathbf{U}$. We first note that

$$\mathbf{J}^n = \begin{bmatrix} (\mathbf{J}_1)^n & 0 & \cdots & 0 \\ 0 & (\mathbf{J}_2)^n & \cdots & 0 \\ \vdots & \vdots & \ddots & \vdots \\ 0 & 0 & \cdots & (\mathbf{J}_m)^n \end{bmatrix};$$

therefore, it suffices to focus on a single Jordon block $\mathbf{J}_i$ of order p and consider

$$(\mathbf{J}_i)^n = \begin{bmatrix} \lambda_i & 1 & \ldots & 0 & 0 \\ 0 & \lambda_i & \ldots & 0 & 0 \\ \vdots & \vdots & \ddots & \vdots & \vdots \\ 0 & 0 & \ldots & \lambda_i & 1 \\ 0 & 0 & \ldots & 0 & \lambda_i \end{bmatrix}^n.$$

To compute this matrix, we write

$$\mathbf{J}_i = \begin{bmatrix} \lambda_i & 0 & \cdots & 0 & 0 \\ 0 & \lambda_i & \cdots & 0 & 0 \\ \vdots & \vdots & \ddots & \vdots & \vdots \\ 0 & 0 & \cdots & \lambda_i & 0 \\ 0 & 0 & \cdots & 0 & \lambda_i \end{bmatrix} + \begin{bmatrix} 0 & 1 & \cdots & 0 & 0 \\ 0 & 0 & \cdots & 0 & 0 \\ \vdots & \vdots & \ddots & \vdots & \vdots \\ 0 & 0 & \cdots & 0 & 1 \\ 0 & 0 & \cdots & 0 & 0 \end{bmatrix} = \Lambda + \mathbf{H}$$

and raise $\mathbf{J}_i$ to the power n using the Binomial Theorem and the fact $\Lambda\mathbf{H} = \mathbf{H}\Lambda$ (the proof of which is left as an exercise):

$$(\mathbf{J}_i)^n = (\Lambda + \mathbf{H})^n = \Lambda^n + \binom{n}{1}\Lambda^{n-1}\mathbf{H} + \binom{n}{2}\Lambda^{n-2}\mathbf{H}^2 + \cdots + \binom{n}{p-1}\Lambda^{n-p+1}\mathbf{H}^{p-1}.$$

We recall (see Exercise 10, Section 1.3) that $\mathbf{H}^p = \mathbf{0}$ and that row i of $\mathbf{H}^k$ has $i+k$ zeros before the leading 1; therefore, after collecting terms

$$(\mathbf{J}_i)^n = \begin{bmatrix} (\lambda_i)^n & \binom{n}{1}(\lambda_i)^{n-1} & \cdots & \binom{n}{p-1}(\lambda_i)^{n-p+1} \\ 0 & (\lambda_i)^n & \cdots & \binom{n}{p-2}(\lambda_i)^{n-p+2} \\ \vdots & \vdots & \ddots & \vdots \\ 0 & 0 & \cdots & (\lambda_i)^n \end{bmatrix}.$$

In order for $\lim_{n\to\infty}(\mathbf{J}_i)^n = \mathbf{0}$, it is necessary that $|\lambda_i| < 1$. But elements of $(\mathbf{J}_i)^n$ above the main diagonal also converge to zero if $|\lambda_i| < 1$, since the ratio of a typical element $\binom{n+1}{k}(\lambda_i)^{n+1-k}$ of $(\mathbf{J}_i)^{n+1}$ to its corresponding element of $(\mathbf{J}_i)^n$ can be written as

$$\left|\frac{\dfrac{(n+1)(n)(n-1)\cdots(n-k+2)\lambda_i^{n+1-k}}{k!}}{\dfrac{(n)(n-1)\ldots(n-k+1)\lambda_i^{n-k}}{k!}}\right| = \left|\frac{n+1}{n-k+1}\lambda_i\right|,$$

and sequences with the ratio of consecutive terms eventually less than a fixed constant with magnitude less than 1 necessarily converge to zero. It follows that $\lim_{n\to\infty}\mathbf{A}^n = \mathbf{0}$ if and only if $|\lambda_i| < 1$ for each i.

THEOREM 2.4 If any norm of $\mathbf{A}$ satisfies $\|\mathbf{A}\| < 1$, then $\lim_{n\to\infty}\mathbf{A}^n = \mathbf{0}$.

PROOF: For matrix norms

$$\|\mathbf{A}^n\| \le \|\mathbf{A}^{n-1}\|\|\mathbf{A}\| \le \|\mathbf{A}^{n-2}\|\|\mathbf{A}\|^2 \le \ldots \le \|\mathbf{A}\|^n.$$

But $\|\mathbf{A}^n\| \geq 0$ and $\lim_{n\to\infty}\|\mathbf{A}\|^n = 0$; therefore, $\lim_{n\to\infty}\|\mathbf{A}^n\| = 0$, and, finally, $\lim_{n\to\infty}\mathbf{A}^n = 0$.

THEOREM 2.5 If $f(x)$ is a polynomial and if $\mathbf{Ax} = \lambda\mathbf{x}$ then $f(\mathbf{A})\mathbf{x} = f(\lambda)\mathbf{x}$.

PROOF: The proof is left as an exercise.

THEOREM 2.6 If λ is an eigenvalue of $\mathbf{A}$, then $|\lambda| \leq \|\mathbf{A}\|$.

PROOF: For each $\varepsilon > 0$, we define the matrix

$$\mathbf{B} = \frac{\mathbf{A}}{\|\mathbf{A}\| + \varepsilon},$$

and note by Definition 1.2 that the norm of $\mathbf{B}$ is

$$\|\mathbf{B}\| = \frac{\|\mathbf{A}\|}{\|\mathbf{A}\| + \varepsilon} < 1.$$

By Theorem 2.4, $\lim_{n\to\infty}\mathbf{B}^n = 0$; hence, by Theorem 2.3, the eigenvalues of $\mathbf{B}$ are all less than 1 in absolute value. Also, if λ is an eigenvalue of $\mathbf{A}$, then $\frac{\lambda}{\|\mathbf{A}\| + \varepsilon}$ is an eigenvalue of $\mathbf{B}$; therefore, $\left|\frac{\lambda}{\|\mathbf{A}\| + \varepsilon}\right| < 1$, or $|\lambda| < \|\mathbf{A}\| + \varepsilon$. Since ε is arbitrary, it follows that $|\lambda| < \|\mathbf{A}\|$.

THEOREM 2.7 The series of matrices $\mathbf{I} + \sum_{j=1}^{\infty}\mathbf{A}^j$ converges if and only if $\lim_{n\to\infty}\mathbf{A}^n = 0$. If the series does converge, its sum is $(\mathbf{I} - \mathbf{A})^{-1}$.

PROOF: Let

$$\mathbf{S}_k = \mathbf{I} + \mathbf{A} + \mathbf{A}^2 + \ldots + \mathbf{A}^k$$
$$\mathbf{AS}_k = \mathbf{A} + \mathbf{A}^2 + \ldots + \mathbf{A}^k + \mathbf{A}^{k+1}$$

Subtracting the second of these equations from the first, we obtain

$$\mathbf{S}_k - \mathbf{A}\mathbf{S}_k = (\mathbf{I} - \mathbf{A})\mathbf{S}_k = \mathbf{I} - \mathbf{A}^{k+1}$$

The inverse of **(I - A)** exists since $\text{DET}(\mathbf{I}-\mathbf{A}) \neq 0$ $[\text{DET}(\mathbf{I}-\mathbf{A}) = 0$ if and only if 1 is an eigenvalue of **A**, but since $\lim_{n\to\infty} \mathbf{A}^n = 0$, all of the eigenvalues satisfy $|\lambda| < 1]$. Thus

$$\mathbf{S}_k = (\mathbf{I} - \mathbf{A})^{-1}(\mathbf{I} - \mathbf{A}^k),$$

and

$$\lim_{k\to\infty} \mathbf{S}_k = \lim_{k\to\infty}(\mathbf{I} - \mathbf{A})^{-1}(\mathbf{I} - \mathbf{A}^k) = (\mathbf{I} - \mathbf{A})^{-1}.$$

EXERCISES

1. Find $\lim_{n\to\infty} \mathbf{x}_n$ if it exists, where

   a) $\mathbf{x}_n = \begin{bmatrix} \frac{(-1)^n}{2n+1} & \frac{1}{n} & \frac{-1}{n} \end{bmatrix}$

   b) $\mathbf{x}_n = \begin{bmatrix} (-1)^n & \sin(n\pi) & \sin^2(n) + \cos^2(n) \end{bmatrix}$

   c) $\mathbf{x}_n = \begin{bmatrix} e^{-n} & \frac{1}{n}\ln(n+1) \end{bmatrix}$

2. Find $\lim_{n\to\infty} \mathbf{A}^{(n)}$ if it exists where

   a) $\mathbf{A}^{(n)} = \begin{bmatrix} \frac{1}{n} & \frac{500}{n} \\ \frac{1}{n^2} & \frac{(-1)^n}{(-n)} \end{bmatrix}$

   b) $\mathbf{A}^{(n)} = \begin{bmatrix} (-1)^n & \frac{2}{n^4} \\ \frac{3}{n^{2n}} & (-1)^{2n+1} \end{bmatrix}$

   c) $\mathbf{A}^{(n)} = \begin{bmatrix} \left(\frac{-1}{n}\right)^2 & (-1)^{2n} + (-1)^{2n-1} \\ \frac{2n+2}{n} & \frac{2n^2+3n+1}{4n^2+2} \end{bmatrix}$

3. Prove Theorem 2.2.

4. In the proof of Theorem 2.3 we assumed $\Lambda\mathbf{H} = \mathbf{H}\Lambda$, prove that this is true.

5. Prove Theorem 2.5.

6. Use the result of Exercise 5 to show if λ is an eigenvalue of **A**, and if $f(x)$ is a polynomial, then $f(\lambda)$ is an eigenvalue of $f(\mathbf{A})$.

7. Show that if $\mathbf{A}^{(n)}$ and $\mathbf{B}^{(n)}$ are two convergent sequences of matrices of the same size then $\mathbf{A}^{(n)}+\mathbf{B}^{(n)}$ is a convergent sequence of matrices.

8. Let

$$\mathbf{A}^{(n)}=\begin{bmatrix} 2+\frac{2}{n} & \left(1+\frac{1}{n}\right)^n \\ \frac{1}{n^2} & 1+\frac{2}{n} \end{bmatrix}$$

a) Find $\lim_{n\to\infty}\mathbf{A}^{(n)}=\mathbf{A}$.

b) Find the characteristic polynomial of $\mathbf{A}^{(n)}$ and call it $p_n(\lambda)$.

c) Compute $\lim_{n\to\infty}p_n(\lambda)$

d) Find the eigenvalues of $\mathbf{A}^{(n)}$ as a function of n and call them $\lambda_1^{(n)}$ and $\lambda_2^{(n)}$

e) Let the characteristic polynomial of $\mathbf{A}$ be $p(\lambda)$.

f) Show that $\lim_{n\to\infty}p_n(\lambda)=p(\lambda)$.

g) If the eigenvalues of $\mathbf{A}$ are λ_1 and λ_2, show that $\lim_{n\to\infty}\lambda_1^{(n)}=\lambda_1$ and $\lim_{n\to\infty}\lambda_2^{(n)}=\lambda_2$.

h) Show that $\lim_{n\to\infty}\mathrm{TR}\left(\mathbf{A}^{(n)}\right)=\mathrm{TR}(\mathbf{A})$.

9. Let

$$\mathbf{A}^{(n)}=\begin{bmatrix} 2 & \frac{1}{n} \\ 0 & 2 \end{bmatrix}$$

a) Show that $\mathbf{A}^{(n)}$ is not similar to a diagonal matrix for any n even though $\lim_{n\to\infty}\mathbf{A}^{(n)}$ is a diagonal matrix.

b) If $\lim_{n\to\infty}\mathbf{A}^{(n)}=\mathbf{A}$, show that $\lim_{n\to\infty}\left(\mathbf{A}^{(n)}\right)^{-1}=\mathbf{A}^{-1}$.

10. Let

$$\mathbf{A}^{(n)}=\begin{bmatrix} \frac{1}{n} & 1+\frac{1}{n^2} \\ 1+\frac{1}{n} & \left(\frac{1}{2}\right)^n \end{bmatrix} \text{ and}$$

$$\mathbf{B}^{(n)}=\begin{bmatrix} \frac{1}{n} & 2+\frac{1}{n} \\ \frac{1}{n^2} & \left(\frac{1}{3}\right)^n \end{bmatrix}.$$

a) Show that $\mathbf{A}\pm\mathbf{B}=\lim_{n\to\infty}\left(\mathbf{A}^{(n)}\pm\mathbf{B}^{(n)}\right)$.

b) Show that $\lim_{n\to\infty}\left(\mathbf{A}^{(n)}\mathbf{B}^{(n)}\right)=\mathbf{AB}$.

11. Let $\mathbf{A}^{(n)}=\begin{bmatrix} 2-\frac{1}{n} & \frac{1}{n} \\ 1 & 3+\frac{1}{n} \end{bmatrix}$ and

$$\mathbf{B}^{(n)} = \begin{bmatrix} 2 & 2+\frac{1}{n} \\ \left(\frac{1}{2}\right)^n & \left(1+\frac{1}{n}\right)^n \end{bmatrix}$$

a) a) Show that $\mathbf{A}+\mathbf{B} = \lim_{n\to\infty}\left(\mathbf{A}^{(n)} \pm \mathbf{B}^{(n)}\right)$.

b) Show that $\lim_{n\to\infty}\left(\mathbf{A}^{(n)}\mathbf{B}^{(n)}\right) = \mathbf{AB}$.

c) Show that $\mathbf{AB}^{-1} = \lim_{n\to\infty}\left(\mathbf{A}^{(n)}\left(\mathbf{B}^{(n)}\right)^{-1}\right)$

d) Why does $\mathbf{AB}^{-1} = \lim_{n\to\infty}\left(\mathbf{A}^{(n)}\left(\mathbf{B}^{(n)}\right)^{-1}\right)$ not hold for the matrices in Exercise 10?

3. FUNCTIONS OF MATRICES

We have already worked with some simple examples of functions of matrices when studying polynomials with matrix arguments and the Cayley-Hamilton Theorem and have seen that if λ is an eigenvalue of a matrix **A**, then $p(\lambda)$ is an eigenvalue of $p(\mathbf{A})$. Functions of matrices also play an important role in the solution of linear systems of differential equations. We begin this section by stating a fundamental theorem for functions of matrices with the proof omitted.

THEOREM 3.1 If the function $f(x)$ can be expanded in a power series with circle of convergence $|x - x_0| < r$ as

$$f(x) = \sum_{k=0}^{\infty} a_k (x - x_0)^k,$$

then this series expansion holds when x is replaced by a matrix **A** whose eigenvalues lie within the circle of convergence.

This theorem permits many matrix functions to be written as infinite series:

$$e^{\mathbf{A}} = \sum_{k=0}^{\infty} \frac{1}{k!}\mathbf{A}^k$$

$$\cos(\mathbf{A}) = \sum_{k=0}^{\infty} \frac{(-1)^k}{(2k)!} \mathbf{A}^{2k}$$

$$\sin(\mathbf{A}) = \sum_{k=0}^{\infty} \frac{(-1)^k}{(2k+1)!} \mathbf{A}^{2k+1}$$

$$\ln(\mathbf{A}) = \sum_{k=1}^{\infty} \frac{(-1)^{k-1}}{k} (\mathbf{A} - \mathbf{I})^k \qquad |\lambda - 1| < 1 \text{ for all } \lambda$$

In some cases these formulas are not convenient for the computation of matrix functions. We shall concentrate on obtaining matrix functions for general matrices, examining first the case where **A** is similar to a diagonal matrix.

THEOREM 3.2 If **A** is similar to a diagonal matrix

$$\mathbf{U}^{-1}\mathbf{A}\mathbf{U} = \mathrm{DIAG}(\lambda_1, \lambda_2, \ldots, \lambda_n)$$

and if $f(x)$ possesses a power series expansion

$$f(x) = \sum_{k=0}^{\infty} a_k x^k$$

for $|x| < r$ with $|\lambda_i| < r$ for $i = 1,2,\ldots n$, then

$$f(\mathbf{A}) = \mathbf{U}\big(\mathrm{DIAG}(f(\lambda_1), f(\lambda_2), \ldots, f(\lambda_n))\big)\mathbf{U}^{-1}$$

PROOF: If all of the eigenvalues of **A** are within the circle of convergence, and if we note $\mathrm{DIAG}(\lambda_1, \lambda_2, \ldots, \lambda_n)$ by Λ, then

$$f(\Lambda) = \sum_{k=0}^{\infty} a_k \Lambda^k$$

by Theorem 3.1; therefore,

$$f(\Lambda)=\begin{bmatrix} \sum_{k=0}^{\infty} a_k \lambda_1^{\ k} & 0 & \cdots & 0 \\ 0 & \sum_{k=0}^{\infty} a_k \lambda_2^{\ k} & \cdots & 0 \\ \vdots & \vdots & \ddots & \vdots \\ 0 & 0 & \cdots & \sum_{k=0}^{\infty} a_k \lambda_n^{\ k} \end{bmatrix}$$

$$=\begin{bmatrix} f(\lambda_1) & 0 & \cdots & 0 \\ 0 & f(\lambda_2) & \cdots & 0 \\ \vdots & \vdots & \ddots & \vdots \\ 0 & 0 & \cdots & f(\lambda_n) \end{bmatrix}.$$

By Theorem 2.1, $(\mathbf{U}\Lambda\mathbf{U}^{-1})^k = \mathbf{U}\Lambda^k\mathbf{U}^{-1}$; therefore,

$$\begin{aligned} f(\mathbf{A}) = f(\mathbf{U}\Lambda\mathbf{U}^{-1}) &= \sum_{k=0}^{\infty} a_k (\mathbf{U}\Lambda\mathbf{U}^{-1})^k \\ &= \mathbf{U}\left(\sum_{k=0}^{\infty} \Lambda^k\right)\mathbf{U}^{-1} \\ &= \mathbf{U}(f(\Lambda))\mathbf{U}^{-1}. \end{aligned}$$

Since in general it is easier to operate on a diagonal matrix, we can use the results of Theorem 3.2 to calculate some simple functional values such as square roots.

EXAMPLE 3.1 Given

$$\mathbf{A} = \begin{bmatrix} -26 & -10 \\ 105 & 39 \end{bmatrix}$$

we can find $\sqrt{\mathbf{A}}$, that is find a matrix $\mathbf{B}$ such that $\mathbf{B}^2 = \mathbf{A}$.

First, we find a diagonal matrix that is similar to **A** by using *Derive* to find the eigenvalues, 9 and 4, and corresponding eigenvectors, $[-2 \quad 7]^{\mathrm{T}}$ and $[-1 \quad 3]^{\mathrm{T}}$ respectively. We can now calculate a diagonal matrix that is similar to **A**

$$14: \begin{bmatrix} -2 & -1 \\ 7 & 3 \end{bmatrix}^{-1} \begin{bmatrix} -26 & -10 \\ 105 & 39 \end{bmatrix} \cdot \begin{bmatrix} -2 & -1 \\ 7 & 3 \end{bmatrix}$$

$$15: \begin{bmatrix} 9 & 0 \\ 0 & 4 \end{bmatrix}$$

The square root of statement #15 is DIAG(3,2); therefore, by Theorem 3.2 the square root of **A** can be found by

$$17: \begin{bmatrix} -2 & -1 \\ 7 & 3 \end{bmatrix} \cdot \begin{bmatrix} 3 & 0 \\ 0 & 2 \end{bmatrix} \cdot \begin{bmatrix} -2 & -1 \\ 7 & 3 \end{bmatrix}^{-1}$$

$$18: \begin{bmatrix} -4 & -2 \\ 21 & 9 \end{bmatrix}$$

This result can be verified:

$$19: \begin{bmatrix} -4 & -2 \\ 21 & 9 \end{bmatrix}^{2}$$

$$20: \begin{bmatrix} -26 & -10 \\ 105 & 39 \end{bmatrix}$$

We note in passing that **A** has four square roots since we could have computed the square root of the diagonal matrix in statement #15 in any of the following ways:

$$\begin{bmatrix} 3 & 0 \\ 0 & 2 \end{bmatrix}, \begin{bmatrix} -3 & 0 \\ 0 & 2 \end{bmatrix}, \begin{bmatrix} 3 & 0 \\ 0 & -2 \end{bmatrix}, \begin{bmatrix} -3 & 0 \\ 0 & -2 \end{bmatrix}.$$

EXAMPLE 3.2 The concept of functions of matrices can also be used to compute the inverse of a matrix. For example, if

$$\mathbf{A} = \begin{bmatrix} 1 & -2 & -2 \\ 1 & 3 & 1 \\ -1 & 0 & 2 \end{bmatrix},$$

then we can compute the eigenvalues and eigenvectors of **A**:

$$\lambda=1,\begin{bmatrix}1\\-1\\1\end{bmatrix};\quad \lambda=2,\begin{bmatrix}0\\-1\\1\end{bmatrix};\quad \lambda=3,\begin{bmatrix}-1\\0\\1\end{bmatrix}$$

which can then be used to compute a diagonal matrix similar to **A**:

$$16:\quad \begin{bmatrix}1&0&-1\\-1&-1&0\\1&1&1\end{bmatrix}^{-1}\cdot\begin{bmatrix}1&-2&-2\\1&3&1\\-1&0&2\end{bmatrix}\cdot\begin{bmatrix}1&0&-1\\-1&-1&0\\1&1&1\end{bmatrix}$$

$$17:\quad \begin{bmatrix}1&0&0\\0&2&0\\0&0&3\end{bmatrix}$$

Using the fact that the inverse written in functional notation is $f(x)=\dfrac{1}{x}$, we note that $f(1)=1$, $f(2)=\dfrac{1}{2}$, and $f(3)=\dfrac{1}{3}$, and thus obtain

$$19:\quad \begin{bmatrix}1&0&-1\\-1&-1&0\\1&1&1\end{bmatrix}\cdot\begin{bmatrix}1&0&0\\0&\frac{1}{2}&0\\0&0&\frac{1}{3}\end{bmatrix}\cdot\begin{bmatrix}1&0&-1\\-1&-1&0\\1&1&1\end{bmatrix}^{-1}$$

$$20:\quad \begin{bmatrix}1&\frac{2}{3}&\frac{2}{3}\\-\frac{1}{2}&0&-\frac{1}{2}\\\frac{1}{2}&\frac{1}{3}&\frac{5}{6}\end{bmatrix}$$

It is easy to verify that statement #20 represents the inverse of **A**.

If a matrix **A** is similar to a matrix in Jordan canonical form, it is still possible to compute $f(\mathbf{A})$ using the same principle as the one developed in Theorem 3.2. The next two theorems give a method of computation.

THEOREM 3.3 Let **A** be a square matrix of order p which is similar to a matrix **J** consisting of a single Jordan block, $\mathbf{A} = \mathbf{UJU}^{-1}$. If $f(x)$ is a function with a power series expansion having a radius of convergence which includes the single eigenvalue λ of **A**, then

$$f(\mathbf{A}) = \mathbf{U}f(\mathbf{J})\mathbf{U}^{-1} = \mathbf{U}\begin{bmatrix} f(\lambda) & \dfrac{f'(\lambda)}{1!} & \cdots & \dfrac{f^{(p-1)}(\lambda)}{(p-1)!} \\ 0 & f(\lambda) & \cdots & \dfrac{f^{(p-2)}(\lambda)}{(p-2)!} \\ \vdots & \vdots & \ddots & \vdots \\ 0 & 0 & \cdots & f(\lambda) \end{bmatrix}\mathbf{U}^{-1}.$$

PROOF: Since λ is included in the radius of convergence for the power series expansion of f, we can expand $f(x)$ into a power series about λ:

$$f(x) = f(\lambda) + \frac{f'(\lambda)}{1!}(x-\lambda) + \frac{f''(\lambda)}{2!}(x-\lambda)^2 + \ldots + \frac{f^{(n)}(\lambda)}{n!}(x-\lambda)^n + \ldots$$

If we substitute **A** for x and $\lambda\mathbf{I}$ for λ we obtain

$$f(\mathbf{J}) = f(\lambda)\mathbf{I} + \frac{f'(\lambda)}{1!}(\mathbf{J}-\lambda\mathbf{I}) + \frac{f''(\lambda)}{2!}(\mathbf{J}-\lambda\mathbf{I})^2 + \ldots + \frac{f^{(n)}(\lambda)}{n!}(\mathbf{J}-\lambda\mathbf{I})^n + \ldots$$

But the powers of $\mathbf{J} - \lambda\mathbf{I} = \begin{bmatrix} 0 & 1 & \cdots & 0 & 0 \\ 0 & 0 & \cdots & 0 & 0 \\ \vdots & \vdots & \ddots & \vdots & \vdots \\ 0 & 0 & \cdots & 0 & 1 \\ 0 & 0 & \cdots & 0 & 0 \end{bmatrix}$ are computed in the same manner as the powers of **H** were computed in the proof of Theorem 2.4 of this chapter. Thus

$$f(\mathbf{J})=\begin{bmatrix} f(\lambda) & \dfrac{f'(\lambda)}{1!} & \cdots & \dfrac{f^{(p-1)}(\lambda)}{(p-1)!} \\ 0 & f(\lambda) & \cdots & \dfrac{f^{(p-2)}(\lambda)}{(p-2)!} \\ \vdots & \vdots & \ddots & \vdots \\ 0 & 0 & \cdots & f(\lambda) \end{bmatrix},$$

and since $f(\mathbf{A})=f(\mathbf{UJU}^{-1})=\mathbf{U}f(\mathbf{J})\mathbf{U}^{-1}$, by an argument identical to that used in the proof of Theorem 3.2, our desired result holds.

THEOREM 3.4 If **A** is similar to a matrix **J** which can be written in the Jordan canonical form

$$\mathbf{J}=\begin{bmatrix} \mathbf{J}_1 & \mathbf{0} & \cdots & \mathbf{0} \\ \mathbf{0} & \mathbf{J}_2 & \cdots & \mathbf{0} \\ \vdots & \vdots & \ddots & \vdots \\ \mathbf{0} & \mathbf{0} & \cdots & \mathbf{J}_n \end{bmatrix}$$

and if $f(x)$ possesses a power series expansion

$$f(x)=\sum_{k=0}^{\infty} a_k x^k$$

for $|x|<r$ with $|\lambda_i|<r$ for $i = 1,2,\ldots n$ with, then

$$f(\mathbf{J})=\begin{bmatrix} f(\mathbf{J}_1) & \mathbf{0} & \cdots & \mathbf{0} \\ \mathbf{0} & f(\mathbf{J}_2) & \cdots & \mathbf{0} \\ \vdots & \vdots & \ddots & \vdots \\ \mathbf{0} & \mathbf{0} & \cdots & f(\mathbf{J}_n) \end{bmatrix}.$$

PROOF: The theorem follows from arguments similar to those used in the proofs of the above theorems in this section and the fact that

$$\begin{bmatrix} \mathbf{J}_1 & \mathbf{0} & \cdots & \mathbf{0} \\ \mathbf{0} & \mathbf{J}_2 & \cdots & \mathbf{0} \\ \vdots & \vdots & \ddots & \vdots \\ \mathbf{0} & \mathbf{0} & \cdots & \mathbf{J}_n \end{bmatrix}^m = \begin{bmatrix} \mathbf{J}_1^{\,m} & \mathbf{0} & \cdots & \mathbf{0} \\ \mathbf{0} & \mathbf{J}_2^{\,m} & \cdots & \mathbf{0} \\ \vdots & \vdots & \ddots & \vdots \\ \mathbf{0} & \mathbf{0} & \cdots & \mathbf{J}_n^{\,m} \end{bmatrix}.$$

EXAMPLE 3.3 If

$$\mathbf{A} = \begin{bmatrix} 5 & 7 & 4 & 2 \\ -3 & -6 & -3 & -4 \\ 2 & 4 & 3 & 3 \\ 3 & 10 & 3 & 8 \end{bmatrix},$$

then we can find $\sqrt{\mathbf{A}}$ by first using *Derive* to find that the characteristic polynomial of **A**: $p(\lambda) = (\lambda - 4)^2(\lambda - 1)^2$. Corresponding to $\lambda = 4$, a set of generalized eigenvectors is

$$\left\{ \begin{bmatrix} 3 \\ -3 \\ 3 \\ 3 \end{bmatrix}, \begin{bmatrix} -3 \\ -5 \\ 5 \\ 8 \end{bmatrix} \right\},$$

and corresponding to $\lambda = 1$, a set of generalized eigenvectors is

$$\left\{ \begin{bmatrix} 3 \\ 0 \\ -3 \\ 0 \end{bmatrix}, \begin{bmatrix} -2 \\ 3 \\ -1 \\ -3 \end{bmatrix} \right\}.$$

From this we compute $\mathbf{J} = \mathbf{U}^{-1}\mathbf{A}\mathbf{U}$

26: $\begin{bmatrix} 3 & 2 & 3 & -2 \\ -3 & -5 & 0 & 3 \\ 3 & 5 & -3 & -1 \\ 3 & 8 & 0 & -3 \end{bmatrix}^{-1} \cdot \begin{bmatrix} 5 & 7 & 4 & 2 \\ -3 & -6 & -3 & -4 \\ 2 & 4 & 3 & 3 \\ 3 & 10 & 3 & 8 \end{bmatrix} \cdot \begin{bmatrix} 3 & 2 & 3 & -2 \\ -3 & -5 & 0 & 3 \\ 3 & 5 & -3 & -1 \\ 3 & 8 & 0 & -3 \end{bmatrix}$

27: $\begin{bmatrix} 4 & 1 & 0 & 0 \\ 0 & 4 & 0 & 0 \\ 0 & 0 & 1 & 1 \\ 0 & 0 & 0 & 1 \end{bmatrix}$

and note that **J** consists of two Jordan blocks $\mathbf{J}_1$ and $\mathbf{J}_2$. Using first Theorem 3.4 and then Theorem 3.3, we find

$$\sqrt{\mathbf{J}} = \begin{bmatrix} \sqrt{\mathbf{J}_1} & 0 \\ 0 & \sqrt{\mathbf{J}_2} \end{bmatrix} = \begin{bmatrix} \sqrt{4} & 1/2\sqrt{4} & 0 & 0 \\ 0 & \sqrt{4} & 0 & 0 \\ 0 & 0 & \sqrt{1} & 1/2\sqrt{1} \\ 0 & 0 & 0 & \sqrt{1} \end{bmatrix} = \begin{bmatrix} 2 & 1/4 & 0 & 0 \\ 0 & 2 & 0 & 0 \\ 0 & 0 & 1 & 1/2 \\ 0 & 0 & 0 & 1 \end{bmatrix}$$

which can be transformed into $\sqrt{\mathbf{A}}$:

30: $\begin{bmatrix} 3 & 2 & 3 & -2 \\ -3 & -5 & 0 & 3 \\ 3 & 5 & -3 & -1 \\ 3 & 8 & 0 & -3 \end{bmatrix} \cdot \begin{bmatrix} 2 & \frac{1}{4} & 0 & 0 \\ 0 & 2 & 0 & 0 \\ 0 & 0 & 1 & \frac{1}{2} \\ 0 & 0 & 0 & 1 \end{bmatrix} \cdot \begin{bmatrix} 3 & 2 & 3 & -2 \\ -3 & -5 & 0 & 3 \\ 3 & 5 & -3 & -1 \\ 3 & 8 & 0 & -3 \end{bmatrix}^{-1}$

$$31: \begin{bmatrix} \frac{5}{2} & \frac{11}{4} & \frac{3}{2} & \frac{3}{4} \\ -1 & -\frac{5}{4} & -1 & -\frac{5}{4} \\ \frac{1}{2} & \frac{3}{4} & \frac{3}{2} & \frac{3}{4} \\ 1 & \frac{13}{4} & 1 & \frac{13}{4} \end{bmatrix}$$

which can be easily verified as being one of the square roots of **A**.

EXAMPLE 3.4 Given the matrix $\mathbf{A} = \begin{bmatrix} 3 & 1 \\ -1 & 1 \end{bmatrix}$, we can compute sin(**A**) and cos(**A**) by first using Euler's equation $e^{it} = \cos(t) + i\sin(t)$ to find $e^{i\mathbf{A}} = \cos(\mathbf{A}) + i\sin(\mathbf{A})$, and then taking the real part and the imaginary part of this result to obtain our results. Using *Derive* we can easily find that **A** has only one eigenvalue, $\lambda = 2$, and that 2 has only one linearly independent eigenvector, $[1 \quad -1]^{\mathrm{T}}$. Thus, any vector which is not a multiple, such as $[1 \quad 0]^{\mathrm{T}}$, together with the eigenvector forms a generalized set of eigenvectors which can be used to transform **A** into its Jordan canonical form **J**:

$$13: \begin{bmatrix} 1 & 1 \\ -1 & 0 \end{bmatrix}^{-1} \cdot \begin{bmatrix} 3 & 1 \\ -1 & 1 \end{bmatrix} \cdot \begin{bmatrix} 1 & 1 \\ -1 & 0 \end{bmatrix}$$

$$14: \begin{bmatrix} 2 & 1 \\ 0 & 2 \end{bmatrix}$$

Next, using the formula given in Theorem 3.3 and letting $f(x) = e^{ix}$ and $f'(x) = ie^{ix}$, we can compute

$$e^{i\mathbf{J}} = \begin{bmatrix} e^{2i} & ie^{2i} \\ 0 & e^{2i} \end{bmatrix}.$$

By Theorem 3.3, $e^{i\mathbf{A}}$ is given by

$$17: \quad \begin{bmatrix} 1 & 1 \\ -1 & 0 \end{bmatrix} \cdot \begin{bmatrix} \hat{e}^{\hat{\imath}\,2} & \hat{\imath}\,\hat{e}^{\hat{\imath}\,2} \\ 0 & \hat{e}^{\hat{\imath}\,2} \end{bmatrix} \cdot \begin{bmatrix} 1 & 1 \\ -1 & 0 \end{bmatrix}^{-1}$$

but $\mathrm{RE}\left(e^{i\mathbf{A}}\right) = \cos(\mathbf{A})$ and $\mathrm{IM}\left(e^{i\mathbf{A}}\right) = \sin(\mathbf{A})$; hence,

$$18: \quad \mathrm{RE}\left[\begin{bmatrix} 1 & 1 \\ -1 & 0 \end{bmatrix} \cdot \begin{bmatrix} \hat{e}^{\hat{\imath}\,2} & \hat{\imath}\,\hat{e}^{\hat{\imath}\,2} \\ 0 & \hat{e}^{\hat{\imath}\,2} \end{bmatrix} \cdot \begin{bmatrix} 1 & 1 \\ -1 & 0 \end{bmatrix}^{-1}\right]$$

$$19: \quad \mathrm{IM}\left[\begin{bmatrix} 1 & 1 \\ -1 & 0 \end{bmatrix} \cdot \begin{bmatrix} \hat{e}^{\hat{\imath}\,2} & \hat{\imath}\,\hat{e}^{\hat{\imath}\,2} \\ 0 & \hat{e}^{\hat{\imath}\,2} \end{bmatrix} \cdot \begin{bmatrix} 1 & 1 \\ -1 & 0 \end{bmatrix}^{-1}\right]$$

$$20: \quad \begin{bmatrix} \mathrm{COS}(2) - \mathrm{SIN}(2) & -\mathrm{SIN}(2) \\ \mathrm{SIN}(2) & \mathrm{COS}(2) + \mathrm{SIN}(2) \end{bmatrix}$$

$$21: \quad \begin{bmatrix} \mathrm{COS}(2) + \mathrm{SIN}(2) & \mathrm{COS}(2) \\ -\mathrm{COS}(2) & \mathrm{SIN}(2) - \mathrm{COS}(2) \end{bmatrix}$$

where statement #20 is obtained by simplifying statement #18, and, hence, is cos(**A**); and statement #21 is obtained by simplifying statement #19, and, hence, is sin(**A**).

EXAMPLE 3.5 Given

$$\mathbf{A} = \begin{bmatrix} 2 & 2 & 1 \\ -1 & -2 & 0 \\ -5 & -3 & -3 \end{bmatrix}$$

we can find $e^{i\mathbf{A}}$ by first using *Derive* to find the characteristic polynomial of **A** to be $p(\lambda) = (\lambda + 1)^3$; hence, $\lambda = -1$ is the only eigenvalue, and, again using *Derive*, multiples of $\begin{bmatrix} 1 & -1 & -1 \end{bmatrix}^{\mathrm{T}}$ are the only eigenvectors. It then follows that $\begin{bmatrix}1 & -1 & -1\end{bmatrix}^T$, $\begin{bmatrix}1 & 0 & -2\end{bmatrix}^T$, and $\begin{bmatrix}0 & 0 & 1\end{bmatrix}^T$ forms a set of generalized eigenvectors which can be used to transform **A** into its Jordan canonical form

$$15:\quad \begin{bmatrix}1 & 1 & 0\\ -1 & 0 & 0\\ -1 & -2 & 1\end{bmatrix}^{-1} \cdot \begin{bmatrix}2 & 2 & 1\\ -1 & -2 & 0\\ -5 & -3 & -3\end{bmatrix} \cdot \begin{bmatrix}1 & 1 & 0\\ -1 & 0 & 0\\ -1 & -2 & 1\end{bmatrix}$$

$$16:\quad \begin{bmatrix}-1 & 1 & 0\\ 0 & -1 & 1\\ 0 & 0 & -1\end{bmatrix}$$

In this case, $f(x) = e^{tx}$, $f'(x) = te^{tx}$, and $f''(x) = t^2e^{tx}$; therefore, by Theorem 3.3

$$e^{t\mathbf{J}} = \begin{bmatrix} e^{-t} & te^{-t} & \dfrac{t^2e^{-t}}{2!} \\ 0 & e^{-t} & te^{-t} \\ 0 & 0 & e^{-t} \end{bmatrix}$$

and we obtain $e^{t\mathbf{A}}$

$$18:\quad \begin{bmatrix}1 & 1 & 0\\ -1 & 0 & 0\\ -1 & -2 & 1\end{bmatrix} \cdot \begin{bmatrix} ê^{-t} & t\,ê^{-t} & \dfrac{t^2}{2}\,ê^{-t} \\ 0 & ê^{-t} & t\,ê^{-t} \\ 0 & 0 & ê^{-t} \end{bmatrix} \cdot \begin{bmatrix}1 & 1 & 0\\ -1 & 0 & 0\\ -1 & -2 & 1\end{bmatrix}^{-1}$$

which we simplify to obtain

#19:
$$\begin{bmatrix} \hat{e}^{-t}\cdot(t^2+3\cdot t+1) & \hat{e}^{-t}\cdot\left[\dfrac{t^2}{2}+2\cdot t\right] & \hat{e}^{-t}\cdot\left[\dfrac{t^2}{2}+t\right] \\ -t\cdot\hat{e}^{-t}\cdot(t+1) & -\dfrac{\hat{e}^{-t}\cdot(t^2+2\cdot t-2)}{2} & -\dfrac{t^2\cdot\hat{e}^{-t}}{2} \\ -t\cdot\hat{e}^{-t}\cdot(t+5) & -\dfrac{t\cdot\hat{e}^{-t}\cdot(t+6)}{2} & -\dfrac{\hat{e}^{-t}\cdot(t^2+4\cdot t-2)}{2} \end{bmatrix}$$

DEFINITION 3.1 (Derivative of a Matrix) If **A** is a matrix with elements which are differentiable functions of t and $\mathbf{A}(t)=(a_{ij}(t))$, then the derivative of **A** is defined by

$$\frac{d}{dt}\mathbf{A}(t)=\left(\frac{d}{dt}a_{ij}(t)\right).$$

THEOREM 3.4 Let **A**(t) and **B**(t) be matrices for which the product **A**(t)**B**(t) is defined, then

$$\frac{d}{dt}[\mathbf{A}(t)\mathbf{B}(t)]=\dot{\mathbf{A}}(t)\mathbf{B}(t)+\mathbf{A}(t)\dot{\mathbf{B}}(t)$$

PROOF: If the product

$$\mathbf{A}(t)\mathbf{B}(t)=\sum_{k=1}^{n}a_{ik}(t)b_{kj}(t)$$

is differentiated, then

$$\frac{d}{dt}(\mathbf{A}(t)\mathbf{B}(t))=\sum_{k=1}^{n}\left[\left(\frac{d}{dt}a_{ik}(t)\right)b_{kj}(t)+a_{ik}(t)\left(\frac{d}{dt}b_{kj}(t)\right)\right]$$

from which the desired result follows.

THEOREM 3.5 The derivative with respect to t of the matrix exponential function $e^{t\mathbf{A}}$ is $\mathbf{A}e^{t\mathbf{A}}$.

PROOF: If we expand $e^{t\mathbf{A}}$ in a power series and differentiate term by term we obtain

$$e^{t\mathbf{A}} = \sum_{k=0}^{\infty} \frac{1}{k!} t^k \mathbf{A}^k,$$

from which it follows

$$\frac{d}{dt} e^{t\mathbf{A}} = \sum_{k=0}^{\infty} \frac{1}{k!} k t^{k-1} \mathbf{A}^k = \mathbf{A} \sum_{k=1}^{\infty} \frac{1}{(k-1)!} t^{k-1} \mathbf{A}^{k-1} = \mathbf{A} e^{t\mathbf{A}}.$$

THEOREM 3.6 The following differentiation formulas hold:

$$\frac{d}{dt}\cos(t\mathbf{A}) = -\mathbf{A}\sin(t\mathbf{A})$$
$$\frac{d}{dt}\sin(t\mathbf{A}) = \mathbf{A}\cos(t\mathbf{A})$$

PROOF: These formulas may be obtained by differentiating $e^{it\mathbf{A}}$.

EXERCISES

1. Complete Example 3.4.

2. Find $\sqrt{\mathbf{A}}$ if

a) $\mathbf{A} = \begin{bmatrix} 30 & 7 \\ -42 & -5 \end{bmatrix}$

b) $\mathbf{A} = \begin{bmatrix} -11 & -5 \\ 30 & 14 \end{bmatrix}$

3. Find cos(**A**) if

a) $\mathbf{A} = \begin{bmatrix} -5 & -2 \\ 13 & 5 \end{bmatrix}$

b) $\mathbf{A} = \begin{bmatrix} 7 & 3 \\ -18 & 8 \end{bmatrix}$

4. Find $e^{\mathbf{A}}$ if

a) $\mathbf{A} = \begin{bmatrix} -1 & -1 & 1 \\ -2 & 0 & -2 \\ -2 & 2 & -4 \end{bmatrix}$

b) $\mathbf{A} = \begin{bmatrix} 1 & -1 & 1 \\ -6 & -2 & 0 \\ -6 & -2 & 0 \end{bmatrix}$

5. Find $\sqrt{\mathbf{A}}$ if

a) $\mathbf{A} = \begin{bmatrix} 6 & 1 \\ -4 & 2 \end{bmatrix}$

b) $\mathbf{A} = \begin{bmatrix} -6 & 1 \\ -4 & -2 \end{bmatrix}$

6. Compute cos(t**A**) if

a) $\mathbf{A} = \begin{bmatrix} -3 & 0 & 1 \\ -2 & -1 & 1 \\ -4 & 0 & 1 \end{bmatrix}$

b) $\mathbf{A} = \begin{bmatrix} -2 & 3 & 1 \\ 4 & -8 & -4 \\ -4 & 10 & 7 \end{bmatrix}$

7. For the matrix in Exercise 6a compute sin(t**A**) and differentiate this function to obtain **A**cos(t**A**). Compare this result to the result of Exercise 6a.

8. Let $p(x) \in P^n$ show that $p(\mathbf{A}^{\mathrm{T}}) = (p(\mathbf{A}))^{\mathrm{T}}$.

9. Let $\mathbf{A} = \begin{bmatrix} 1 & 1 \\ 6 & 4 \end{bmatrix}$ and compute cos(**A**) and sin(**A**) by computing $e^{i\mathbf{A}}$. Verify that $\cos^2 \mathbf{A} + \sin^2 \mathbf{A} = \mathbf{I}$.

10. From the results in Exercise 9, find sin(2**A**) by using the identity sin(2x) = 2sin(x)cos(x) and find cos(2**A**) by using the identity cos(2x) = $\cos^2(x) - \sin^2(x)$

11. Solve Exercise 9 with $\mathbf{A} = \begin{bmatrix} 0 & 1 \\ -4 & -4 \end{bmatrix}$.

12. Compute $\sqrt{\mathbf{A}}$ where $\mathbf{A} = \begin{bmatrix} 2 & 1 & 1 & 0 \\ 4 & 5 & -3 & -1 \\ -8 & 1 & 9 & 1 \\ -15 & 2 & 1 & 10 \end{bmatrix}$.

13. Compute $e^{\mathbf{A}}$ for the matrix in Exercise 12.

14. If $\mathbf{A} = \begin{bmatrix} 1 & 10 & 4 \\ -2 & -25 & -10 \\ 5 & 60 & 24 \end{bmatrix}$, then find $\mathbf{A}^{2n}$ and $\mathbf{A}^{2n+1}$.

4. FUNCTIONS OF MATRICES - AN ALGORITHM

The computation of functions of matrices can become tedious even with the use of *Derive*. The algorithm presented in this section will usually reduce the amount of work required since it neither involves the computation of eigenvectors nor generalized eigenvectors. The procedure is based on the principle of finding a polynomial which will be equal to the desired matrix function when the matrix is substituted for the scalar argument.

We will now proceed with the development of the algorithm for finding *f*(**A**) in the special case when **A** has only eigenvalues of multiplicity one. Let *f*(**A**) have the following power series expansion:

$$f(\mathbf{A}) = a_0\mathbf{I} + a_1\mathbf{A} + a_2\mathbf{A}^2 + a_3\mathbf{A}^3 + \ldots.$$

If the characteristic polynomial of **A** is $p(\lambda) = \lambda^n - p_{n-1}\lambda^n - \ldots - p_1\lambda - p_0$, then by the Cayley-Hamilton Theorem, **A** is a zero of $p(\lambda)$; hence, $\mathbf{A}^n$ can be expressed as a linear combination of lesser powers of **A**:

$$\mathbf{A}^n = p_{n-1}\mathbf{A}^{n-1} + p_{n-2}\mathbf{A}^{n-2} + \ldots + p_1\mathbf{A} + p_0\mathbf{I}.$$

In a similar manner, any power of **A** may be expressed as a linear combination of powers of **A** which are less than n. For example, if $\mathbf{A}^2 = r_1\mathbf{A} + \mathbf{r}_0\mathbf{I}$, then

$$\begin{aligned}\mathbf{A}^3 = \mathbf{A}^2 \cdot \mathbf{A} &= (r_1\mathbf{A} + r_0\mathbf{I}) \cdot \mathbf{A} \\ &= r_1\mathbf{A}^2 + r_0\mathbf{A} \\ &= r_1\,(r_1\mathbf{A} + r_0\mathbf{I}) + r_0\mathbf{A} \\ &= (r_1^2 + r_0)\mathbf{A} + r_1r_0\mathbf{I}\end{aligned}$$

and higher powers follow similarly. Thus, we can write

$$f(\mathbf{A}) = r_{n-1}\mathbf{A}^{n-1} + r_{n-2}\mathbf{A}^{n-2} + \ldots + r_0\mathbf{I},$$

where the coefficients $r_0, r_1, \ldots, r_{n-1}$ are yet to be determined. If λ is any eigenvalue of **A** and **x** is its corresponding eigenvector, then *f*(λ) is an eigenvalue of *f*(**A**); thus, $f(\mathbf{A})\mathbf{x} = f(\lambda)\mathbf{x}$. But, also

$$\begin{aligned}f(\mathbf{A})\mathbf{x} &= (r_{n-1}\mathbf{A}^{n-1} + r_{n-2}\mathbf{A}^{n-2} + \ldots + r_0\mathbf{I})\mathbf{x} \\ &= r_{n-1}(\mathbf{A}^{n-1}\mathbf{x}) + r_{n-2}(\mathbf{A}^{n-2}\mathbf{x}) + \ldots + r_0\mathbf{x} \\ &= r_{n-1}(\lambda^{n-1}\mathbf{x}) + r_{n-2}(\lambda^{n-2}\mathbf{x}) + \ldots + r_0\mathbf{x} \\ &= (r_{n-1}\lambda^{n-1} + r_{n-2}\lambda^{n-2} + \ldots + r_0)\mathbf{x}\end{aligned}$$

and thus

$$f(\lambda) = r_{n-1}\lambda^{n-1} + r_{n-2}\lambda^{n-2} + \ldots + r_0 .$$

Since λ was an arbitrary eigenvalue, we can substitute in turn the n eigenvalues of **A** and obtain n equations for the n unknowns $r_0, r_1, \ldots, r_{n-1}$.

Another approach to finding the polynomial $f(\lambda) = r_{n-1}\lambda^{n-1} + r_{n-2}\lambda^{n-2} + \ldots + r_1\lambda + r_0$ is to realize that if $f(x)$ is an analytic function (a function that possesses derivatives of all orders) and $p(x)$ is a polynomial of degree n, then there exists an analytic function $q(x)$ and a polynomial $r(x)$ of degree less than or equal to n - 1 such that

$$f(x) = p(x)q(x) + r(x).$$

To help us determine q and r, we may re-write this expression as

$$\frac{f(x) - r(x)}{p(x)} = q(x)$$

In this form , our goal is to find an $r(x)$ so that $q(x)$ is analytic wherever $f(x)$ is analytic. To achieve this, we must choose $r(\lambda) = r_{n-1}\lambda^{n-1} + r_{n-2}\lambda^{n-2} + \ldots + r_1\lambda + r_0$ so that $f(\alpha) - r(\alpha) = 0$ whenever $p(\alpha) = 0$. In the case that $p(x)$ has n distinct zeros, we get n equations

$$\begin{aligned} r_0 + r_1\alpha_1 + r_2\alpha_1 + \cdots + r_{n-1}\alpha_1^{n-1} &= f(\alpha_1) \\ r_0 + r_1\alpha_2 + r_2\alpha_2 + \cdots + r_{n-1}\alpha_2^{n-1} &= f(\alpha_2) \\ \cdots \qquad\qquad & \quad \cdots \\ r_0 + r_1\alpha_n + r_2\alpha_n + \cdots + r_{n-1}\alpha_n^{n-1} &= f(\alpha_n) \end{aligned}$$

This $n \times n$ system may be solved for the unknown coefficients $r_0,\ r_1,\ \cdots,\ r_{n-1}$ thus yielding an $n-1$ degree polynomial that makes $q(x)$ analytic.

If an eigenvalue is of multiplicity $1 < m \le n$, we can't substitute this eigenvalue into the equation to obtain the coefficients m times since there would be no unique solution for the coefficients in the system to determine

$r_0, r_1, \ldots, r_{n-1}$. In the case of multiple roots we may differentiate $f(x) = p(x)q(x) + r(x)$ to obtain

$$f'(x) = p'(x)q(x) + p(x)q'(x) + r'(x)$$

and upon substitution of the multiple root, for example α_m, we obtain

$$f'(\alpha_m) = r'(\alpha_m)$$

since both $p(\alpha_m) = 0$ and $p'(\alpha_m) = 0$. We may continue this procedure until we exhaust the multiplicity of the root α_m.

Once $r(x)$ has been determined, we write $f(x) = p(x)q(x) + r(x)$, and substitute **A** for x and obtain

$$f(\mathbf{A}) = p(\mathbf{A})q(\mathbf{A}) + r(\mathbf{A})$$

By the Cayley-Hamilton Theorem $p(\mathbf{A}) = \mathbf{0}$ so that $f(\mathbf{A}) = r(\mathbf{A})$.

EXAMPLE 4.1 We can find $\sin(\mathbf{A})$ for

$$\mathbf{A} = \begin{bmatrix} 7 & 10 \\ -3 & -4 \end{bmatrix}$$

by first using *Derive* to determine the eigenvalues of **A** to be 1 and 2. Next, we set up the polynomial expression of degree 1 which will become $\sin(\mathbf{A})$,

$$\sin(x) = ax + b,$$

and substitute the two eigenvalues into this equation yielding the system of equations

$$\sin(1) = a1 + b$$
$$\sin(2) = a2 + b$$

This system is easily solved with *Derive*:

```
8:    ROW_REDUCE [ 1  1  SIN(1) ]
                 [ 2  1  SIN(2) ]

9:  [ 1  0    SIN(2) - SIN(1)  ]
    [ 0  1  2 SIN(1) - SIN(2)  ]
```

If we substitute these results for the coefficients in $ax + bx^0 = \sin(x)$, we obtain

```
12:  (SIN(2) - SIN(1)) [  7  10 ] + (2 SIN(1) - SIN(2)) [  7  10 ]^0
                       [ -3  -4 ]                       [ -3  -4 ]
```

which may be Simplified to

```
13:  [ 6 SIN(2) - 5 SIN(1)   10 SIN(2) - 10 SIN(1) ]  = SIN [  7  10 ]
     [ 3 SIN(1) - 3 SIN(2)    6 SIN(1) - 5 SIN(2)  ]        [ -3  -4 ]
```

EXAMPLE 4.2 Find $e^{t\mathbf{A}}$ when

$$\mathbf{A} = \begin{bmatrix} -2 & 2 & -2 \\ 1 & 3 & 2 \\ 1 & -2 & 1 \end{bmatrix}$$

Using *Derive* we find the eigenvalues of **A** to be 1, -1, and 2; hence, the eigenvalues of $t\mathbf{A}$ are t, $-t$, and $2t$. We substitute these eigenvalues into $e^x = ax^2 + bx + c$ to obtain three equations in the unknowns a, b, and c, which in this case will be functions of t.

$$e^t = at^2 + bt + c$$
$$e^{-t} = a(-t)^2 + b(-t) + c$$
$$e^{2t} = a(2t)^2 + b(2t) + c$$

This system can be solved using *Derive*

$$5: \quad \mathrm{ROW\_REDUCE}\begin{bmatrix} t^2 & t & 1 & \hat{e}^{t} \\ (-t)^2 & -t & 1 & \hat{e}^{-t} \\ (2t)^2 & 2t & 1 & \hat{e}^{2t} \end{bmatrix}$$

$$6: \quad \begin{bmatrix} 1 & 0 & 0 & \dfrac{\hat{e}^{2t}}{3t^2} - \dfrac{\hat{e}^{t}}{2t^2} + \dfrac{\hat{e}^{-t}}{6t^2} \\ 0 & 1 & 0 & \dfrac{\hat{e}^{t}}{2t} - \dfrac{\hat{e}^{-t}}{2t} \\ 0 & 0 & 1 & -\dfrac{\hat{e}^{2t}}{3} + \hat{e}^{t} + \dfrac{\hat{e}^{-t}}{3} \end{bmatrix}$$

which substituted into $ax^2 + bx + cx^0$ gives $e^{t\mathbf{A}}$ (we substitute $t\mathbf{A}$ into this expression for x).

$$9: \quad \begin{bmatrix} \hat{e}^{2t} - 2\hat{e}^{t} + 2\hat{e}^{-t} & 2\hat{e}^{2t} - 2\hat{e}^{t} & 2\hat{e}^{2t} - 4\hat{e}^{t} + 2\hat{e}^{-t} \\ \hat{e}^{2t} - \hat{e}^{t} & 2\hat{e}^{2t} - \hat{e}^{t} & 2\hat{e}^{2t} - 2\hat{e}^{t} \\ -\hat{e}^{2t} + 2\hat{e}^{t} - \hat{e}^{-t} & 2\hat{e}^{t} - 2\hat{e}^{2t} & -2\hat{e}^{2t} + 4\hat{e}^{t} - \hat{e}^{-t} \end{bmatrix}$$

EXAMPLE 4.3 We can evaluate $e^{t\mathbf{A}}$ for the matrix

$$\mathbf{A} = \begin{bmatrix} -1 & 0 & 2 \\ 1 & 1 & -4 \\ 1 & 2 & -4 \end{bmatrix}$$

by first using *Derive* to obtain the characteristic polynomial

$$p(w) = w^3 + 4w^2 + 5w + 2 = (w+2)(w+1)^2.$$

From this we see that the eigenvalue -1 has multiplicity 2. Our goal is to determine the coefficients in

$$e^x = ax^2 + bx + c$$

so that

$$e^{t\mathbf{A}} = a(t\mathbf{A})^2 + b(t\mathbf{A}) + c\mathbf{I}.$$

Since -1 is of multiplicity 2, we differentiate the above polynomial expression for e' with respect to x to obtain $e^x = 2ax + b$. After substituting the eigenvalues of $t\mathbf{A}$, which are $-t$ and $-2t$, we have a system of three equations in the three unknowns a, b, and c

$$\begin{aligned} e^{-t} &= a(-t)^2 + b(-t) + c \\ e^{-t} &= 2at + b \\ e^{-2t} &= a(-2t)^2 + b(-2t) + c \end{aligned}$$

which we can solve using *Derive*

$$12: \quad \text{ROW\_REDUCE} \begin{bmatrix} (-t)^2 & -t & 1 & \hat{e}^{-t} \\ -2t & 1 & 0 & \hat{e}^{-t} \\ (-2t)^2 & -2t & 1 & \hat{e}^{-2t} \end{bmatrix}$$

$$13: \quad \begin{bmatrix} 1 & 0 & 0 & \dfrac{\hat{e}^{-t}(t-1)}{t^2} + \dfrac{\hat{e}^{-2t}}{t^2} \\ 0 & 1 & 0 & \dfrac{\hat{e}^{-t}(3t-2)}{t} + \dfrac{2\hat{e}^{-2t}}{t} \\ 0 & 0 & 1 & 2t\hat{e}^{-t} + \hat{e}^{-2t} \end{bmatrix}$$

The last column of statement #13 provides expressions for the coefficients a, b, and c, and the polynomial form of e^{tA} is given by

$$15: \left[\frac{\hat{e}^{-t}\,(t-1)}{t^{2}} + \frac{\hat{e}^{-2\,t}}{t^{2}}\right]\left[t\begin{bmatrix} -1 & 0 & 2 \\ 1 & 1 & -4 \\ 1 & 2 & -4 \end{bmatrix}\right]^{2} +$$

$$\left[\frac{\hat{e}^{-t}\,(3\,t-2)}{t} + \frac{2\,\hat{e}^{-2\,t}}{t}\right]\left[t\begin{bmatrix} -1 & 0 & 2 \\ 1 & 1 & -4 \\ 1 & 2 & -4 \end{bmatrix}\right] +$$

$$(2\,t\,\hat{e}^{-t} + \hat{e}^{-2\,t})\left[t\begin{bmatrix} -1 & 0 & 2 \\ 1 & 1 & -4 \\ 1 & 2 & -4 \end{bmatrix}\right]^{0}$$

The simplified version of this expression will not all fit on the *Derive* screen at one time so we provide the three columns in the following three separate *Derive* statements:

$$19: \begin{bmatrix} \hat{e}^{-t}\,(2\,t-1) + 2\,\hat{e}^{-2\,t} \\ \hat{e}^{-t}\,(2-t) - 2\,\hat{e}^{-2\,t} \\ \hat{e}^{-t} - \hat{e}^{-2\,t} \end{bmatrix}$$

$$22: \begin{bmatrix} 4\,\hat{e}^{-t}\,(t-1) + 4\,\hat{e}^{-2\,t} \\ \hat{e}^{-t}\,(5-2\,t) - 4\,\hat{e}^{-2\,t} \\ 2\,\hat{e}^{-t} - 2\,\hat{e}^{-2\,t} \end{bmatrix}$$

$$25: \begin{bmatrix} 2\hat{e}^{-t}(3-2t) - 6\hat{e}^{-2t} \\ 2\hat{e}^{-t}(t-3) + 6\hat{e}^{-2t} \\ 3\hat{e}^{-2t} - 2\hat{e}^{-t} \end{bmatrix}$$

Our algorithm can also be used to compute the inverse of a function. Although this method is clearly not the most efficient means of finding a matrix inverse, the example does demonstrate the wide utility of the algorithm.

EXAMPLE 4.4 The function $f(x) = \frac{1}{x}$ can be used to compute the inverse of a matrix such as

$$\mathbf{A} = \begin{bmatrix} 1 & 2 \\ -3 & 5 \end{bmatrix}.$$

First, we find the eigenvalues of **A**

$$2: \quad \text{EIGENVALUES} \begin{bmatrix} 1 & 3 \\ -2 & 3 \end{bmatrix}$$

$$3: \quad [w = 2 - \sqrt{5}\,\hat{\imath},\ w = 2 + \sqrt{5}\,\hat{\imath}]$$

Next, we write

$$\frac{1}{x} = ax + b$$

and substitute the eigenvalues for x

$$5: \quad \frac{1}{2 - \sqrt{5}\,\hat{\imath}} = a\,(2 - \sqrt{5}\,\hat{\imath}) + b$$

$$6: \quad \frac{1}{2 + \sqrt{5}\,\hat{\imath}} = a\,(2 + \sqrt{5}\,\hat{\imath}) + b$$

This system can then be solved for a and b.

$$3: \quad \text{ROW\_REDUCE}\begin{bmatrix} 2 - \sqrt{5}\,\hat{\imath} & 1 & \dfrac{1}{2 - \sqrt{5}\,\hat{\imath}} \\ 2 + \sqrt{5}\,\hat{\imath} & 1 & \dfrac{1}{2 + \sqrt{5}\,\hat{\imath}} \end{bmatrix}$$

$$3: \quad \begin{bmatrix} 1 & 0 & -\dfrac{1}{9} \\ 0 & 1 & \dfrac{4}{9} \end{bmatrix}$$

We can now substitute the values $a = -\dfrac{1}{9}$ and $b = \dfrac{4}{9}$ into our polynomial expression for $f(x) = \dfrac{1}{x}$ to find $\mathbf{A}^{-1}$

$$11: \quad \left[-\frac{1}{9}\right]\begin{bmatrix} 1 & 3 \\ -2 & 3 \end{bmatrix} + \frac{4}{9}\begin{bmatrix} 1 & 3 \\ -2 & 3 \end{bmatrix}^0$$

$$12: \quad \begin{bmatrix} \dfrac{1}{3} & -\dfrac{1}{3} \\ \dfrac{2}{9} & \dfrac{1}{9} \end{bmatrix}$$

As a check

$$13: \quad \begin{bmatrix} \dfrac{1}{3} & -\dfrac{1}{3} \\ \dfrac{2}{9} & \dfrac{1}{9} \end{bmatrix} \cdot \begin{bmatrix} 1 & 3 \\ -2 & 3 \end{bmatrix}$$

$$14: \quad \begin{bmatrix} 1 & 0 \\ 0 & 1 \end{bmatrix}$$

EXERCISES

1. In each of the following problems let $\mathbf{A} = \begin{bmatrix} -2 & -6 \\ 3 & 7 \end{bmatrix}$ and find

   a) $e^{\mathbf{A}}$ b) $e^{t\mathbf{A}}$
   c) $\sin(\mathbf{A})$ d) $\sqrt{\mathbf{A}}$
   e) $\ln(\mathbf{A})$ f) $\mathbf{A}^{-1}$
   g) $e^{it\mathbf{A}} = \cos(t\mathbf{A}) + \sin(t\mathbf{A})$
   h) $\cos^2(t\mathbf{A}) + \sin^2(t\mathbf{A})$

2. In each of the following problems let $\mathbf{A} = \begin{bmatrix} -7 & 0 & -16 \\ -5 & 4 & -10 \\ 8 & 0 & 17 \end{bmatrix}$ and find

   a) $e^{\mathbf{A}}$ b) $e^{t\mathbf{A}}$
   c) $\sin(\mathbf{A})$ d) $\sqrt{\mathbf{A}}$
   e) $\ln(\mathbf{A})$ f) $\mathbf{A}^{-1}$
   g) $e^{it\mathbf{A}} = \cos(t\mathbf{A}) + \sin(t\mathbf{A})$
   h) $\cos^2(t\mathbf{A}) + \sin^2(t\mathbf{A})$

3. Find $e^{t\mathbf{A}}$ if

   a) $\mathbf{A} = \begin{bmatrix} -1 & -1 \\ 5 & 1 \end{bmatrix}$

   b) $\mathbf{A} = \begin{bmatrix} -5 & -1 \\ 18 & 1 \end{bmatrix}$

   c) $\mathbf{A} = \begin{bmatrix} -13 & -12 & -10 \\ 15 & -13 & -10 \\ -3 & 2 & 0 \end{bmatrix}$

   d) $\mathbf{A} = \begin{bmatrix} 4 & 3 & 2 & -3 \\ -1 & 0 & -3 & -3 \\ -2 & -2 & 1 & 4 \\ 1 & 1 & 0 & -1 \end{bmatrix}$

CHAPTER VII
APPLICATIONS

In this chapter we will consider some of the many applications of linear algebra. The sections are self contained and are not intended to be related. In this way an introduction to the topic at hand may be studied in one module.

1. LEAST SQUARES APPROXIMATION

Many times in applied settings it is necessary to find an equation which will provide an approximation function for a set of data. One of the most widely used methods of finding this equation is called the least squares approximation. There are many reasons for the popularity of this method, not the least of which is that the computation is straight forward. In addition to being uncomplicated to compute, the measure used to determine goodness of fit for the least square method also results in a curve which has the visual appearance of representing the average curve.

DEFINITION 1.1 (Scatter Diagram) A scatter diagram is a set of (data) points plotted in the coordinate plane. We will denote the points as (x_i, y_i), $i = 1, 2, \ldots, N$.

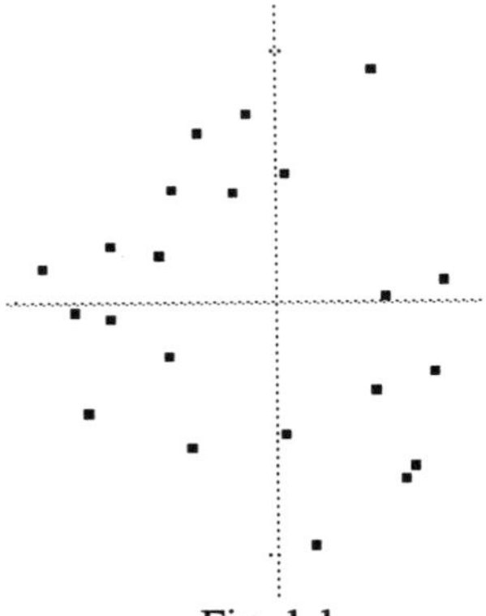

Fig. 1.1
Scatter Diagram

A scatter diagram is simply a graph of the points in the coordinate plane. If a set of data reflects a trend or satisfies some relationship, the scatter diagram often provides some insight into the types of functions which might be used to approximate the data.

DEFINITION 1.2 (Approximating Function) By an approximating function we mean a linear combination of a set of functions $\{f_1(x), f_2(x), \cdots, f_n(x)\}$. The approximating function has the form

$$\Phi(x) = a_1 f_1 + a_2 f_2 + \cdots + a_n f_n ,$$

and $\{f_1(x), f_2(x), \cdots, f_n(x)\}$ is called the approximating set.

The principle of least squares can be stated as follows: Given a set of N points (x_i, y_i), i = 1, 2, ..., N, determine the set of values $\{a_1, a_2, \cdots, a_m\}$ such that

$$\Omega(a_1, a_2, \cdots, a_m) = \sum_{j=1}^{N} \left(\sum_{i=1}^{m} a_i f_i(x_j) - y_j \right)^2$$

is a minimum over all possible choices of $\{a_1, a_2, \cdots, a_m\}$. These values can be found by using techniques of calculus. If we differentiate Ω with respect to each of the unknown coefficients a_i, , i = 1,2,...,m and set the results equal to zero, we obtain m equations in the m unknowns $\{a_1, a_2, \cdots, a_m\}$. Next, by finding

$$\frac{\partial \Omega}{\partial a_p} = \sum_{j=1}^{N} 2 \sum_{i=1}^{m} \left(a_i f_i(x_j) - y_j \right) f_p(x_j) = 0, \quad p = 1,2,\ldots,m$$

we obtain the system of m equations:

$$\begin{array}{c}
a_1 \sum_{j=1}^{N} f_1(x_j) f_1(x_j) + \cdots + a_m \sum_{j=1}^{N} f_m(x_j) f_1(x_j) = \sum_{j=1}^{N} f_1(x_j) y_j \\
a_1 \sum_{j=1}^{N} f_1(x_j) f_2(x_j) + \cdots + a_m \sum_{j=1}^{N} f_m(x_j) f_2(x_j) = \sum_{j=1}^{N} f_2(x_j) y_j \\
\vdots \qquad\qquad \vdots \qquad\qquad \vdots \qquad\qquad \vdots \\
a_1 \sum_{j=1}^{N} f_1(x_j) f_m(x_j) + \cdots + a_m \sum_{j=1}^{N} f_m(x_j) f_m(x_j) = \sum_{j=1}^{N} f_m(x_j) y_j
\end{array}$$

The matrix of this system,

$$\mathbf{A} = \begin{bmatrix} \sum_{j=1}^{N} f_1(x_j) f_1(x_j) + \cdots + \sum_{j=1}^{N} f_m(x_j) f_1 \\ \sum_{j=1}^{N} f_1(x_j) f_2(x_j) + \cdots + \sum_{j=1}^{N} f_m(x_j) f_2 \\ \vdots \qquad \vdots \qquad \vdots \\ \sum_{j=1}^{N} f_1(x_j) f_m(x_j) + \cdots + \sum_{j=1}^{N} f_m(x_j) f_m \end{bmatrix}$$

is called the normal matrix which, if it is not singular, can be used in a row reduction process to find a unique solution for $\{a_1, a_2, \cdots, a_m\}$ given the column of constants:

$$\begin{bmatrix} \sum_{j=1}^{N} f_1(x_j) y_j \\ \sum_{j=1}^{N} f_2(x_j) y_j \\ \vdots \\ \sum_{j=1}^{N} f_m(x_j) y_j \end{bmatrix}$$

One method that can be used in forming the normal matrix is to consider the matrix

$$\mathbf{M} = \begin{bmatrix} f_1(x_1) & f_1(x_2) & \cdots & f_1(x_N) \\ f_2(x_1) & f_2(x_2) & \cdots & f_2(x_N) \\ \cdots & \cdots & \ddots & \cdots \\ f_m(x_1) & f_m(x_2) & \cdots & f_m(x_N) \end{bmatrix}$$

so that $\mathbf{A} = \mathbf{M}\mathbf{M}^{\mathrm{T}}$, and the right hand side of the normal equation is $\mathbf{My}$.

EXAMPLE 1.1 The least squares approximation process can be applied to the data set

x	1	2	3	4	5	6	7	8	9	10
y	-6	-5	-2	3	10	19	30	43	58	75

using the approximating set $\{1, x, x^2\}$. First, we form the matrix **M** using *Derive*.

$$1: \quad \begin{bmatrix} 1 & 1 & 1 & 1 & 1 & 1 & 1 & 1 & 1 & 1 \\ 1 & 2 & 3 & 4 & 5 & 6 & 7 & 8 & 9 & 10 \\ 1 & 4 & 9 & 16 & 25 & 36 & 49 & 64 & 81 & 100 \end{bmatrix}$$

Next, the normal matrix is obtained by computing $\mathbf{A} = \mathbf{M}\mathbf{M}^{\mathrm{T}}$:

$$3: \quad \begin{bmatrix} 10 & 55 & 385 \\ 55 & 385 & 3025 \\ 385 & 3025 & 25333 \end{bmatrix}$$

To obtain the right hand side of the matrix equation, we first make a matrix of the y values

$$4: \quad [\,-6 \quad -5 \quad -2 \quad 3 \quad 10 \quad 19 \quad 30 \quad 43 \quad 58 \quad 75\,]$$

and then multiply statement #1 by the transpose of statement #4, which simplifies to

$$6: \quad [225,\ 1980,\ 17358]$$

The values for the unknowns a, b, and c in the linear combination $a + bx + cx^2$ of functions from the approximating set can now be computed by finding the product of $\mathbf{A}^{-1}$ with the transpose of statement #6:

$$7: \quad \begin{bmatrix} 10 & 55 & 385 \\ 55 & 385 & 3025 \\ 385 & 3025 & 25333 \end{bmatrix}^{-1} \cdot [\,225 \quad 1980 \quad 17358\,]'$$

$$8: \quad \begin{bmatrix} -5 \\ -2 \\ 1 \end{bmatrix}$$

The least squares approximation is therefore $\Phi(x) = -5 - 2x + x^2$. Of course, this equation fits the data perfectly since the y values were computed from this equation.

EXAMPLE 1.2. Given a set of data such as

X	1.36	2.14	2.76	4.40	4.99	5.85	6.89	8.25	8.50	10.09
Y	3.65	2.65	-0.20	-2.12	-1.96	0.49	3.44	2.88	0.97	-2.11

we can plot a scatter diagram and use that to help select an approximating set, which in turn can be used in conjunction with the least squares approximation method to find a function which best fits the data. A scatter diagram plot of the data appears as

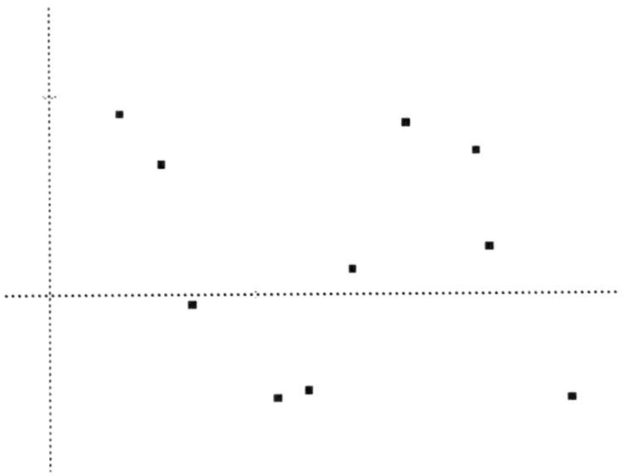

Fig. 1.2
Scatter Diagram Plot for Example 1.2

At this point in our method we need to make a wise choice of an approximating set. The arrangement of data points in the scatter diagram is reminiscent of graphs of the sine and cosine functions; therefore, we choose $\{1, \sin(x), \cos(x)\}$ for the approximating set. The approximating function will thus be a linear combination of these functions, or

$$\Phi(x) = a(1) + b\sin(x) + c\cos(x)$$

where the a, b, and c are to be determined. We will determine the matrix **M** defined by

$$\mathbf{M} = \begin{bmatrix} m_{1j} \\ m_{2j} \\ m_{3j} \end{bmatrix} \text{ where } m_{1j} = 1,\ m_{2j} = \sin(x_j),\ m_{3j} = \cos(x_j),\ j = 1, \cdots, 10.$$

The first row of **M** is just the constant vector

```
3:   [1, 1, 1, 1, 1, 1, 1, 1, 1, 1]
```

The second row of **M** can be obtained from the *Derive* statement VECTOR(SIN(ELEMENT(#1,i,1)),i,1,10,1). Here #1 refers to statement #1, which contains the table of data items listed above with the ten *X* values in the first column and the ten *Y* values in second column. The effect of the *Derive* statement is to evaluate the sine function at the ten data points (*X* values) in the above table and store the results in the vector

```
5:   [0.977864, 0.842330, 0.372399, -0.951601, -0.961712, -0.419764,
```

(Here only the first six elements of the vector appear because of space limitations.) Similarly, the third row of **M** can be obtained from the *Derive* code VECTOR(COS(ELEMENT(#1,i,1)),i,1,10,1). As above, the effect of this command is to evaluate the cosine function at the ten data points in the above table and store the results in the vector

```
7:   [0.209238, -0.538961, -0.928072, -0.307332, 0.274058, 0.907633,
```

(Again, only the first six elements of the vector appear because of space limitations.) The matrix **M** is obtained by entering the *Derive* command [#3,#5,#7]. The first five columns of **M** are as follows (*Derive* statement #8):

```
[ 1          1          1          1          1
  0.977864   0.842330   0.372399  -0.951601  -0.961712
  0.209238  -0.538961  -0.928072  -0.307332   0.274058
```

and the normal matrix $\mathbf{A} = \mathbf{M}\mathbf{M}^{\mathrm{T}}$ is given in statement #10:

$$10: \begin{bmatrix} 10 & 1.53362 & -1.33650 \\ 1.53362 & 6.00600 & -0.829608 \\ -1.33650 & -0.829608 & 3.99399 \end{bmatrix}$$

Recall that the right hand side of the normal equation is **My**. The *Derive* command VECTOR(ELEMENT(#1,i,2),i,1,10,1) selects the Y values from our data table (which has been stored as a two column matrix in *Derive* statement #1) in the form of a vector $\mathbf{y}^T$:

12: [3.65, 2.65, -0.2, -2.12, -1.96, 0.49, 3.44, 2.88, 0.97, -2.11]

The product of statement #8 (**M**) and the transpose of statement #12 ($\mathbf{y}^T$) yields:

14: [7.69, 16.1192, 2.87128]

which is the constant vector on the right hand side of the normal equation. We can now solve for a, b, and c by computing the product of $\mathbf{M}^{-1}$ and the constant vector in statement #14. The result is

$$15: \begin{bmatrix} 10 & 1.53362 & -1.33650 \\ 1.53362 & 6.00600 & -0.829608 \\ -1.33650 & -0.829608 & 3.99399 \end{bmatrix}^{-1} \cdot [7.69, 16.1192, 2.87128]$$

16: [0.544244, 2.74818, 1.47185]

It follows that our desired linear combination of functions from the approximation set is

17: 0.544244 + 2.74818 SIN(x) + 1.47185 COS(x)

This function, when graphed along with the scatter diagram, appears as

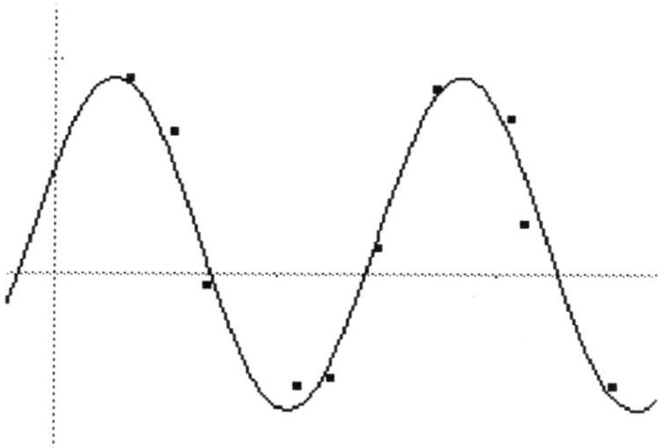

Fig. 1.3
Scatter Diagram and Graph for Example 1.2

EXAMPLE 1.3. To find a least squares approximation to the following data

x	-2.00	-1.65	-1.21	-0.53	-0.50	0.25	0.86	1.31	1.69	1.23
y	-1.52	-0.60	0.07	0.06	0.93	1.29	1.70	2.24	2.98	4.00

we begin by sketching a scatter diagram of the data

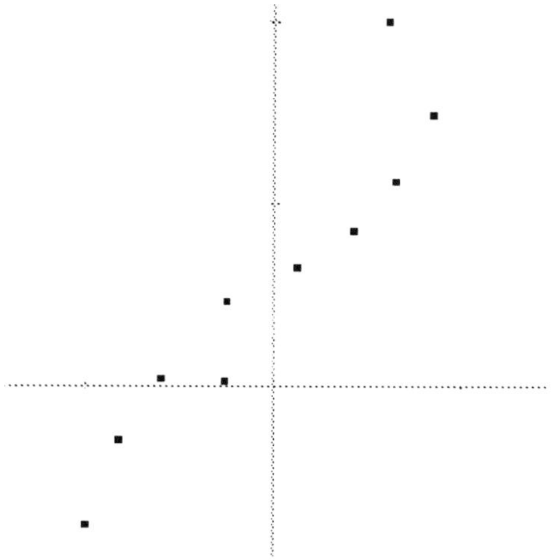

Fig. 1.4
Scatter Diagram for Example 1.3

and inputting the data from the table into a *Derive* statement in the form of a 10×2 matrix with columns consisting of the data in the rows of the table. By examination of the scatter diagram we determine that a reasonable approximation set would be $\{1, x, x^2, x^3\}$. Since the first of these functions is the constant 1, the first row of the matrix **M** can be found according to the above rule to be

```
5:   [1, 1, 1, 1, 1, 1, 1, 1, 1, 1]
```

The second row of **M** is defined in terms of the second function in the approximation set according to the *Derive* statement VECTOR(ELEMENT(#3, i, 1,), X, 1, 10, 1), which yields

```
[-2, -1.65, -1.21, -0.5, -0.53, 0.25, 0.86, 1.31, 1.69, 1.23]
```

(The #3 refers to the *Derive* statement for the matrix representing the data in the table.) The third row of **M** is defined in terms of the third function in the approximation set according to the *Derive* statement VECTOR((ELEMENT(#3, i, 1))^2, X, 1, 10, 1) , which yields

```
[4, 2.7225, 1.4641, 0.25, 0.2809, 0.0625, 0.7396, 1.71609, 2.85
```

(Here a portion of the ninth and all of the tenth elements of the third row are missing.) Finally, the fourth row of **M** is defined in terms of the fourth function in the approximation set according to the *Derive* statement VECTOR((ELEMENT(#3, i, 1))^3, X, 1, 10, 1), which yields

```
[-8, -4.49212, -1.77156, -0.125, -0.148877, 0.015625, 0.636055
```

(Here only the first seven elements are shown.) The first seven columns of the matrix **M** can then be represented as

12:

1	1	1	1	1	1	1
-2	-1.65	-1.21	-0.5	-0.53	0.25	0.86
4	2.7225	1.4641	0.25	0.2809	0.0625	0.7396
-8	-4.49212	-1.77156	-0.125	-0.148877	0.015625	0.636055

The normal matrix **A** can now be obtained by finding $\mathbf{MM}^T$:

14:
$$\begin{bmatrix} 10 & -0.55 & 15.6047 & -4.95011 \\ -0.55 & 15.6047 & -4.95011 & 39.6390 \\ 15.6047 & -4.95011 & 39.6390 & -25.9661 \\ -4.95011 & 39.6390 & -25.9661 & 119.575 \end{bmatrix}$$

As in the previous example, to obtain the right hand side of the normal equation, we extract the second column of matrix representing the data table above (which, we are assuming is in *Derive* statement #3 in the form of a 10×2 matrix) and multiply it by **M**. This results in the vector

18: [11.15, 18.1236, 12.3831, 42.5706]

Finally, the approximating function, which is a linear combination of the four functions in the approximating set, can be obtained by multiplying $\mathbf{A}^{-1}$ by the vector in statement #18 yielding the coefficients which can be used to express the approximating function as a linear combination of the four functions in the approximating set:

20: [1.16554, 1.07929, 0.0219008, 0.0512358]

21: $1.16554 + 1.07929\,x + 0.0219008\,x^2 + 0.0512358\,x^3$

A plot of the approximating function on the same set of axes with the scatter diagram would appear as follows:

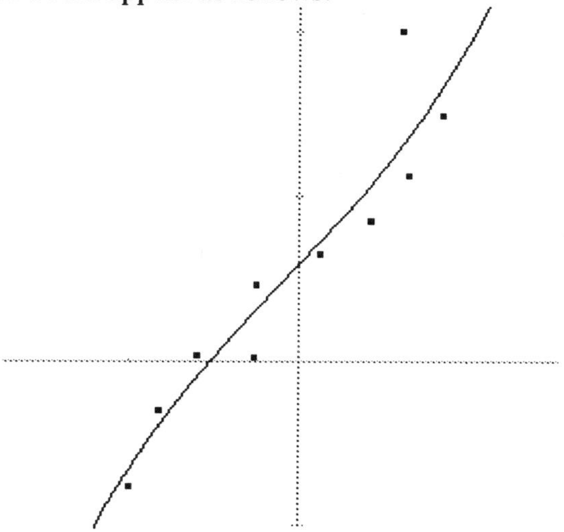

Fig. 1.5
Scatter Diagram and Plot of Example 1.3

EXERCISES

1. Find a least squares approximation to the data

x	y
-2	-10
-1	-2
0	0
1	2
2	10
3	30
4	68
5	130
6	222
7	350

using a linear combination of the elements of the set $\{1, x, x^2, x^3\}$.

2. Find a least squares approximation to the data

x	y
1.27	3.42
2.21	4.24
3.08	4.51
4.30	5.04
5.16	5.67
6.11	7.08
7.13	9.37
8.24	10.0
9.00	11.0
10.1	10.8

using a linear combination of the elements of

a) $\{1, x\}$

b) $\{1, x, \sin(x)\}$

3. Find a least squares approximation to the data

x	y
0.42	0.17
1.09	2.91
2.10	4.01
3.28	5.50
4.23	7.41
5.41	8.50
6.48	9.46
7.09	10.9
8.03	11.5
9.06	12.5

using a linear combination of

a) $\{1, x\}$

b) $\{1, x, \ln(x)\}$

4. Find the least squares approximation to the data generated with *Derive* by the command

[VECTOR(X + 1/2)
RANDOM(1), X, 1, 10, 1),
VECTOR(X^2 + X +1 +
RANDOM(1), X, 1, 10, 1)]

5. Find the least squares approximation to the data generated with *Derive* by the command

[VECTOR(X+.5
RANDOM(1),X,1,10,1),
VECTOR(X + .5 SIN(X) -.5
COS(X) +RANDOM(1), X, 1, 10,1]

x	y
-5.04217	-3.2116
-3.92021	-3.20423
-3.09074	-3.53269
-1.88611	-3.13088
-0.823750	-0.558704
-0.155396	1.26477
0.852444	3.10012
2.03087	3.07690
2.98786	3.11277
4.16079	3.47112
5.23199	5.18250

Hint: Use a linear combination of elements of the set $\{1, x, \text{Atan}(x), \sin(x), \cos(x)\}$.

2. MARKOV PROCESSES

Many physical systems and social phenomena exist in one of several states. For example, suppose two people, call them A and B, play a game tossing coins and each begins the game with three coins. Each player tosses one coin and A keeps any coin that lands heads and B keeps any coin that lands tails. After this event A can have two, three, or four coins. The players then play again with the same rules, and after this second event the number of coins A can have depends on the number A had at the start of the second round of the game. We see that, even for this relatively uncomplicated scenario, describing the situation soon becomes very complicated. In order to describe the game more precisely let us call the number of coins possessed by A states. If A has no coins, the state will be labeled S_0; if A has one coin, the state will be labeled S_1; and so on until we come to the situation where A has six coins, which is labeled S_6. In this way any possible outcome of an event may be described by one of the set of states $\{S_0, S_1, S_2, \cdots, S_6\}$. We note that the state of the game may change each time the game is played. Thus far we have described this game with a number of states and a sequence of events. The transition from one state to another is a probabilistic situation and does not depend on how many times the game has been played. Consider the following table which gives the probability of transition from the state in the left margin to the state in the top margin.

	S_0	S_1	S_2	S_3	S_4	S_5	S_6
S_0	1	0	0	0	0	0	0
S_1	1/4	1/2	1/4	0	0	0	0
S_2	0	1/4	1/2	1/4	0	0	0
S_3	0	0	1/4	1/2	1/4	0	0
S_4	0	0	0	1/4	1/2	1/4	0
S_5	0	0	0	0	1/4	1/2	1/4
S_6	0	0	0	0	0	0	1

The probabilities are computed independently of the number of times the game has been played and depend only on the state of the game and on the state the game might enter in the next transition.

DEFINITION 2.1 (Markov Chain) A Markov chain is a sequence of events within a system which may be in any one of a finite number of states $\{S_1, S_2, \cdots, S_n\}$ at any given point in the sequence. The system may change from state S_i to state S_j as a result of an event in the sequence. The system changes from S_i to S_j with probability P_{ij} which depends only on the two states S_i and S_j.

The above definition assumes the Markov property that given the current state, the probability of any event in the future is independent of the past.

DEFINITION 2.2 (Transition Matrix) The transition matrix of a Markov chain is the matrix

$$\mathbf{P} = \left(P_{ij}\right)$$

where P_{ij} is the probability defined in Definition 2.1.

We remark that the row sums of a transition matrix are all 1 since the sum of the probabilities of changing from state S_i to state S_j, $j = 1, 2, \cdots, n$, is 1.

EXAMPLE 2.1 The transition matrix for the Markov process described in the opening paragraph of this section is the 7×7 matrix

$$\mathbf{P} = \begin{bmatrix} 1 & 0 & 0 & 0 & 0 & 0 & 0 \\ 1/4 & 1/2 & 1/4 & 0 & 0 & 0 & 0 \\ 0 & 1/4 & 1/2 & 1/4 & 0 & 0 & 0 \\ 0 & 0 & 1/4 & 1/2 & 1/4 & 0 & 0 \\ 0 & 0 & 0 & 1/4 & 1/2 & 1/4 & \\ 0 & 0 & 0 & 0 & 1/4 & 1/2 & 1/4 \\ 0 & 0 & 0 & 0 & 0 & 1/4 & 1 \end{bmatrix}$$

EXAMPLE 2.2 For the system with three states S_1, S_2, and S_3. defined by the following table

	S_1	S_2	S_3
S_1	0.1	0.7	0.2
S_2	0.3	0.7	0
S_3	0	1	0

the transition matrix is

$$\mathbf{P} = \begin{bmatrix} 0.1 & 0.7 & 0.2 \\ 0.3 & 0.7 & 0 \\ 0 & 1 & 0 \end{bmatrix}$$

EXAMPLE 2.3 If the process described in Example 2.1 is in state S_1, we can find the probability that it will be in state S_2 in two transitions by computing the sum of all possible sequences of states leading from state S_1 to state S_2 in two transitions.

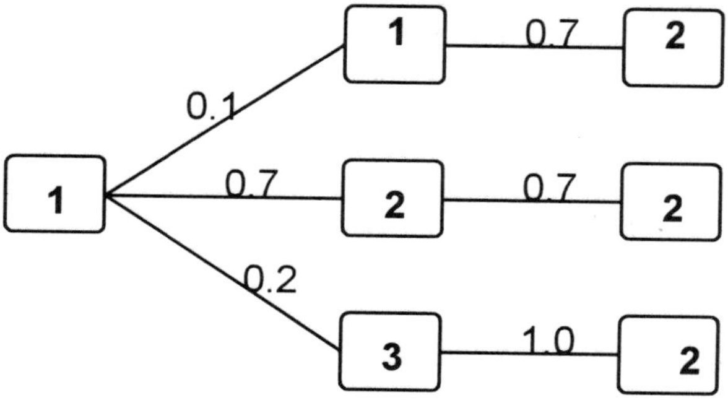

The probability is given by

$$P_{11}P_{12} + P_{12}P_{22} + P_{13}P_{32} =$$
$$(0.1)(0.7) + (0.7)(0.7) + (0.2)(1.0) = 0.76$$

We also notice that the above equation is exactly the same calculation required to find the (1,2) element of $\mathbf{P}^2$.

$$\#1: \quad \begin{bmatrix} 0.1 & 0.7 & 0.2 \\ 0.3 & 0.7 & 0 \\ 0 & 1 & 0 \end{bmatrix}$$

$$\#2: \quad \begin{bmatrix} 0.1 & 0.7 & 0.2 \\ 0.3 & 0.7 & 0 \\ 0 & 1 & 0 \end{bmatrix} \cdot \begin{bmatrix} 0.1 & 0.7 & 0.2 \\ 0.3 & 0.7 & 0 \\ 0 & 1 & 0 \end{bmatrix}$$

#3: Notation := Decimal

$$\#4: \quad \begin{bmatrix} 0.22 & 0.76 & 0.02 \\ 0.24 & 0.7 & 0.06 \\ 0.3 & 0.7 & 0 \end{bmatrix}$$

EXAMPLE 2.4 For the system in Examples 2.2 and 2.3 we can find the probability that the system will be in state S_2 after 10 transitions by computing **P** to the tenth power:

$$\#5: \quad \begin{bmatrix} 0.1 & 0.7 & 0.2 \\ 0.3 & 0.7 & 0 \\ 0 & 1 & 0 \end{bmatrix}^{10}$$

$$\#6: \quad \begin{bmatrix} 0.23809533 & 0.71428518 & 0.047619478 \\ 0.23809526 & 0.71428586 & 0.047618870 \\ 0.23809435 & 0.71428609 & 0.047619552 \end{bmatrix}$$

From this we can make the following probability statements:

$$P(S_2 \text{ in 10 transitions}) \approx 0.714$$

Note that this probability is not dependent on the starting state since all the entries in the second column of $\mathbf{P}^{10}$ are approximately equal. We also observe that

$$P(S_1 \text{ in 10 transitions}) \approx 0.238$$

and

$$P(S_2 \text{ in 10 transitions}) \approx 0.048.$$

DEFINITION 2.3 (Probability Vector or State Vector) A row vector $\mathbf{p} = \begin{bmatrix} p_1 & p_1 & \cdots & p_n \end{bmatrix}$ is said to be a probability vector if $p_i \geq 0 \; i = 1,2,\cdots,n$ and if $\sum_{i=1}^{n} p_i = 1$. A probability vector is also called a state vector.

We observe that each row of a transition matrix is a probability vector. Further we observe, as a consequence of Theorem 4.1 in Chapter V, that all of the eigenvalues lie inside or on the unit circle of the complex plane.

Since a Markov chain describes a sequence of events, it is convenient to relate these events to an index set say $I = \{t_0, t_1, t_2, t_3, \cdots\}$ to denote how many transitions the system has undergone. (Here t_0 indicates the system in its initial condition.) With this indexing we will use the vector $\mathbf{p}(t_i)$ to indicate the probability that the system is in a given state at the transition i. Thus, if

$$\mathbf{p}(t_i) = \begin{bmatrix} p_1(t_i) & p_2(t_i) & \cdots & p_n(t_i) \end{bmatrix},$$

then $p_k(t_i)$ is the probability that the system is in state S_k at transition i. If it is clear from the context, we also write $\mathbf{p}(t_i)$ as

$$\mathbf{p}(t_i) = \begin{bmatrix} p_1 & p_2 & \cdots & p_n \end{bmatrix}.$$

With this notation we see that

$$\mathbf{p}(t_1) = \mathbf{p}(t_0)\mathbf{P}$$

since

$$p_i(t_1) = \sum_{k=1}^{n} p_k(t_0) P_{ki}.$$

Similarly,

$$\mathbf{p}(t_2) = \mathbf{p}(t_1)\mathbf{P} = (\mathbf{p}(t_0)\mathbf{P})\mathbf{P} = \mathbf{p}(t_0)\mathbf{P}^2,$$

and generally

$$\mathbf{p}(t_m) = \mathbf{p}(t_0)\mathbf{P}^m.$$

DEFINITION 2.4 (Regular Markov Chain) A Markov chain with transition matrix **P** is said to be regular if for some n, $\mathbf{P}^n$ has all positive entries.

The next theorem, which is proved in many probability texts, will be stated here without proof.

THEOREM 2.1 If **P** is the transition matrix of a regular Markov process, then

$$\lim_{n\to\infty} \mathbf{P}^n = \mathbf{T},$$

where each row of **T** is the solution of

$$\begin{bmatrix} p_1 & p_2 & \cdots & p_n \end{bmatrix}\mathbf{P} = \begin{bmatrix} p_1 & p_2 & \cdots & p_n \end{bmatrix}$$

satisfying $\sum_{i=1}^{n} p_i = 1$.

THEOREM 2.2 If $\mathbf{p}(t_0)\mathbf{P}^k = \mathbf{p}(t_k)$, then $\lim_{k\to\infty} \mathbf{p}(t_k) = \mathbf{p}(t_0)\mathbf{T}$.

PROOF: The proof follows immediately from the fact that $\lim_{n\to\infty} \mathbf{P}^n = \mathbf{T}$.

EXAMPLE 2.5 We can find $\lim_{n\to\infty} \mathbf{P}^n$, where **P** is the transition matrix of Example 2.2, by first solving

$$\begin{bmatrix} x & y & z \end{bmatrix}\begin{bmatrix} 0.1 & 0.7 & 0.2 \\ 0.3 & 0.7 & 0 \\ 0 & 1 & 0 \end{bmatrix} = \begin{bmatrix} x & y & z \end{bmatrix}$$

subject to the condition $x+y+z=1$. Using *Derive*, we find

$$3:\quad [\,x\ \ y\ \ z\,]\cdot\begin{bmatrix} 0.1 & 0.7 & 0.2 \\ 0.3 & 0.7 & 0 \\ 0 & 1 & 0 \end{bmatrix} = [\,x\ \ y\ \ z\,]$$

$$4:\quad \left[\frac{x}{10}+\frac{3\,y}{10}=x\quad \frac{7\,x}{10}+\frac{7\,y}{10}+z=y\quad \frac{x}{5}=z\right]$$

where statement #4 is the Simplification of statement #3. Next, we soLve statement #4, which assigns an arbitrary parameter to x, and then we impose the condition that the sum of x, y, and z must equal 1:

$$5:\quad \left[x=@2,\ y=3\,@2,\ z=\frac{@2}{5}\right]$$

$$6:\quad a+3\,a+\frac{a}{5}=1$$

$$7:\quad a=\frac{5}{21}$$

$$8:\quad \left[x=\frac{5}{21},\ y=3\,\frac{5}{21},\ z=\frac{\frac{5}{21}}{5}\right]$$

The solution of statement #6, which is given in statement #7, is then substituted into statement #4 to obtain statement #8.

$$9:\quad \left[x=\frac{5}{21},\ y=\frac{5}{7},\ z=\frac{1}{21}\right]$$

$$10:\quad [x=0.23809523,\ y=0.71428571,\ z=0.047619047]$$

Statements #9 and #10 are simplifications of statement #8. The required limit is the 3×3 matrix with each row having the elements indicated by statement #10, which can be compared with Example 2.4.

We can also find the limit by considering $\mathbf{xP} = \mathbf{x}$ or $\mathbf{x}(\mathbf{P} - \mathbf{I}) = \mathbf{0}$, which can be solved by using the *Derive* command

$$\text{ROW\_REDUCE}(\mathbf{P}^{\mathrm{T}} - \mathbf{I}, \mathbf{0}).$$

EXAMPLE 2.6 A salesman travels between London, New York, and Tokyo changing towns with approximately the following probabilities. If he is in London, he will stay in London with a probability of 0.1, go to New York with a probability of 0.4, and go Tokyo with a probability of 0.5. If the salesman is in New York, he will stay there with a probability of 0.3 and go to London and Tokyo with probabilities of 0.5 and 0.2 respectively. If he is in Tokyo, he will stay there with a probability of 0.2 and go to New York with a probability of 0.3 and to London with a probability of 0.5. His boss has not been in contact with him in a long time and wishes to call him. We can use a table of transition probabilities to determine the order she should call each of the cities in order to reach him with the fewest number of calls.

	LONDON	NEW YORK	TOKYO
LONDON	0.1	0.4	0.5
NEW YORK	0.5	0.3	0.2
TOKYO	0.5	0.3	0.2

First , we enter the transition matrix into *Derive* and solve $(\mathbf{P}^{\mathrm{T}} - \mathbf{I})\mathbf{x} = \mathbf{0}$:

$$5: \quad \text{ROW\_REDUCE}\left(\begin{bmatrix} 0.1 & 0.4 & 0.5 \\ 0.5 & 0.3 & 0.2 \\ 0.5 & 0.3 & 0.2 \end{bmatrix}' - \begin{bmatrix} 1 & 0 & 0 \\ 0 & 1 & 0 \\ 0 & 0 & 1 \end{bmatrix}, \begin{bmatrix} 0 \\ 0 \\ 0 \end{bmatrix}\right)$$

$$6: \quad \begin{bmatrix} 1 & 0 & -\dfrac{50}{43} & 0 \\ 0 & 1 & -\dfrac{47}{43} & 0 \\ 0 & 0 & 0 & 0 \end{bmatrix}$$

The desired probability vector thus has the form

$$\begin{bmatrix} \frac{50}{43}\alpha & \frac{47}{43}\alpha & \alpha \end{bmatrix}$$

where the sum of the elements is one.

$$7: \quad \frac{50}{43} a + \frac{47}{43} a + a = 1$$

$$8: \quad a = \frac{43}{140}$$

This value can then be substituted into the probability vector as follows.

$$9: \quad \left[\frac{50}{43} a, \frac{47}{43} a, a\right]$$

$$10: \quad \left[\frac{50}{43} \frac{43}{140}, \frac{47}{43} \frac{43}{140}, \frac{43}{140}\right]$$

$$11: \quad \left[\frac{5}{14}, \frac{47}{140}, \frac{43}{140}\right]$$

12: [0.35714285, 0.33571428, 0.30714285]

Each row of the limit matrix is therefore as statement #12. This limiting vector gives the equilibrium probabilities; therefore, and the salesman is in London with a probability of 0.357, New York with a probability of 0.336, and Tokyo with a probability of 0.307.

A second type of Markov process which has interesting applications is called an absorbing Markov process.

DEFINITION 2.5 (Absorbing State) A state S is said to be absorbing if the probability of remaining in S once it is obtained is one.

EXAMPLE 2.7 Consider the Markov process with states and transition probabilities given in the following table:

	S_1	S_2	S_3	S_4
S_1	0.5	0.2	0.3	0
S_2	0	1	0	0
S_3	0	0	1	0
S_4	0.5	0	0	0.5

The transition matrix is given by

$$\mathbf{P}' = \begin{bmatrix} 0.5 & 0.2 & 0.3 & 0 \\ 0 & 1 & 0 & 0 \\ 0 & 0 & 1 & 0 \\ 0.5 & 0 & 0 & 0.5 \end{bmatrix}$$

and states S_2 and S_3 are absorbing states. It will be convenient to rewrite this matrix placing the absorbing states in the upper left hand portion of the matrix. This is simply a matter of renaming the states and the process will not be changed. Thus we will use the transition matrix

$$\mathbf{P} = \begin{bmatrix} 1 & 0 & 0 & 0 \\ 0 & 1 & 0 & 0 \\ 0.2 & 0.3 & 0.5 & 0 \\ 0 & 0 & 0.5 & 0.5 \end{bmatrix}$$

At this point we can ask what the probability would be for the system to be in each of the absorbing states after a large number of trials. In order to understand what is occurring, we raise **P** to a high power, for example 10, and examine the result

$$2: \begin{bmatrix} 1 & 0 & 0 & 0 \\ 0 & 1 & 0 & 0 \\ 0.3 & 0.2 & 0.5 & 0 \\ 0 & 0 & 0.5 & 0.5 \end{bmatrix}^{10}$$

$$3: \begin{bmatrix} 1 & 0 & 0 & 0 \\ 0 & 1 & 0 & 0 \\ 0.59941406 & 0.39960937 & 9.765625\ 10^{-4} & 0 \\ 0.59355468 & 0.39570312 & 0.009765625 & 9.765625\ 10^{-4} \end{bmatrix}$$

We observe that the probability of the system beginning in either of the original states S_1 or S_4 being in the absorbing state S_2 is approximately 0.6 and being in the absorbing state S_3 is approximately 0.4.

Next, we examine, from an analytical standpoint, the transition matrix with absorbing states representing a system satisfying the assumption that there is a path to an absorbing state from each non-absorbing state. In this case, as in the example above, we write the $n \times n$ transition matrix with m absorbing states in the form

$$\mathbf{P} = \begin{bmatrix} \mathbf{I} & \mathbf{0} \\ \mathbf{N} & \mathbf{Q} \end{bmatrix}$$

where $\mathbf{N}$ is an $(n-m)\times m$ submatrix component and $\mathbf{Q}$ is an $(n-m)\times(n-m)$ submatrix. Using this form we can compute powers of $\mathbf{P}$:

$$\mathbf{P}^2 = \begin{bmatrix} \mathbf{I} & \mathbf{0} \\ \mathbf{N}+\mathbf{QN} & \mathbf{Q}^2 \end{bmatrix} = \begin{bmatrix} \mathbf{I} & \mathbf{0} \\ (\mathbf{I}-\mathbf{Q})\mathbf{N} & \mathbf{Q}^2 \end{bmatrix}$$

$$\mathbf{P}^3 = \begin{bmatrix} \mathbf{I} & \mathbf{0} \\ (\mathbf{I}+\mathbf{Q}+\mathbf{Q}^2)\mathbf{N} & \mathbf{Q}^3 \end{bmatrix}.$$

and more generally,

$$\mathbf{P}^n = \begin{bmatrix} \mathbf{I} & \mathbf{0} \\ \left(\sum_{i=0}^{n-1} \mathbf{Q}^i\right)\mathbf{N} & \mathbf{Q}^n \end{bmatrix}.$$

Taking the limit as $n \to \infty$, we find

$$\lim_{n\to\infty} \mathbf{P}^n = \begin{bmatrix} \mathbf{I} & \mathbf{0} \\ (\mathbf{I}-\mathbf{Q})^{-1}\mathbf{N} & \mathbf{0} \end{bmatrix}$$

since $\lim_{n\to\infty} \sum_{i=0}^{\infty} \mathbf{Q}^i = (\mathbf{I}-\mathbf{Q})^{-1}$ and $\lim_{n\to\infty} \mathbf{Q}^n = \mathbf{0}$ (see Theorem 2.7 in Chapter VI). Although we have not shown that the eigenvalues of $\mathbf{Q}$ are less than one in magnitude, the fact that $\lim_{n\to\infty} \mathbf{Q}^n = \mathbf{0}$ can be seen from probability considerations. Since there is a path from each non-absorbing state to an absorbing state and since the states associated with the sub matrix $\mathbf{Q}$ are all non-absorbing states, the system has probability zero of remaining in a non-absorbing state indefinitely. This gives the following theorem.

THEOREM 2.3 If

$$\mathbf{P} = \begin{bmatrix} \mathbf{I} & \mathbf{0} \\ \mathbf{N} & \mathbf{Q} \end{bmatrix}$$

is the transition matrix of an absorbing Markov process, then

$$\lim_{n\to\infty} \mathbf{P}^n = \begin{bmatrix} \mathbf{I} & \mathbf{0} \\ (\mathbf{I}-\mathbf{Q})^{-1}\mathbf{N} & \mathbf{0} \end{bmatrix}.$$

Further $(\mathbf{I}-\mathbf{Q})^{-1}$ gives the expected number of passages through each non-absorbing state.

Next, we establish a routine to determine the expected number of visits to state S_j . If X_{ij} is the number of visits to state S_j given that the system starts in state S_i , then

$$X_{ij} = I_0 + I_1 + I_2 + \cdots$$

where

$$I_k = \begin{cases} 1 & \text{If the system is in } S_j \text{ at time } k \\ 0 & \text{If the system is not in } S_j \text{ at time } k \end{cases}$$

If E(K) is the expected value of the random variable K, then

$$\mathrm{E}\left(X_{ij}\right)=\sum_{k=0}^{\infty}\mathrm{E}(I_k)=\sum_{k=0}^{\infty}\left[P^k\right]_{ij}$$

where $\left[P^k\right]_{ij}=P\left(\text{System is in state } S_j \text{ at time } k \middle| \text{System is in } S_i \text{ at time } 0\right)$. Thus, when restricted to the non-absorbing states,

$$\left[(\mathbf{I}-\mathbf{Q})^{-1}\right]_{ij}=\left[\sum_{k=0}^{\infty}\mathbf{Q}^k\right]_{ij}=\mathrm{E}\left(\text{number of visits to state } S_j \mid \text{system starts in } S_i\right).$$

EXAMPLE 2.8 Consider a simple situation, often called a gamblers ruin, where two players A and B have 2 and 3 gambling chits respectively with which to play a game where the probability that A wins is p and the probability that B wins is $1 - p$. If A wins B pays A a chit and if B wins A pays B a chit. They continue to play until one player has all of the chits. The game can be considered as a Markov process where the states are the number of chits held by A. The possible states are 0, 1, 2, 3, 4, and 5. The states 0 (B has all the chits) and 5 (A has all the chits) are absorbing states. The transition matrix for this Markov process is

$$\mathbf{P}'=\begin{bmatrix}1&0&0&0&0&0\\p&0&1-p&0&0&0\\0&p&0&1-p&0&0\\0&0&p&0&1-p&0\\0&0&0&p&0&1-p\\0&0&0&0&0&1\end{bmatrix}.$$

where each row and column represents the corresponding state. Following the model discussed prior to Theorem 2.3, we rearrange the matrix so that the absorbing states appear in the upper left hand corner.

$$\mathbf{P}=\begin{bmatrix}1&0&0&0&0&0\\0&1&0&0&0&0\\0&0&0&1-p&0&p\\0&0&p&0&1-p&0\\0&1-p&0&p&0&0\\p&0&1-p&0&0&0\end{bmatrix}$$

We note that this is a similarity transformation and enter this matrix into *Derive*

$$\#1: \begin{bmatrix} 1 & 0 & 0 & 0 & 0 & 0 \\ 0 & 1 & 0 & 0 & 0 & 0 \\ 0 & 0 & 0 & 1-p & 0 & p \\ 0 & 0 & p & 0 & 1-p & 0 \\ 0 & 1-p & 0 & p & 0 & 0 \\ p & 0 & 1-p & 0 & 0 & 0 \end{bmatrix}$$

Using the notation above we determine the matrices **Q** and **N**, extracting **Q** from statement #1 by the *Derive* command

VECTOR(VECTOR(ELEMENT(#1, i, j) , j, 3, 6), i, 3, 6)

resulting in

$$\#3: \begin{bmatrix} 0 & 1-p & 0 & p \\ p & 0 & 1-p & 0 \\ 0 & p & 0 & 0 \\ 1-p & 0 & 0 & 0 \end{bmatrix}$$

Similarly, the matrix **N** may be extracted by the command

VECTOR(VECTOR(ELEMENT(#1, i, j), j, 1, 2), i, 3, 6).

yielding

$$\#5: \begin{bmatrix} 0 & 0 \\ 0 & 0 \\ 0 & 1-p \\ p & 0 \end{bmatrix}$$

We next form $(\mathbf{I}-\mathbf{Q})^{-1}\mathbf{N}$ to compute the probabilities of going from state 3 to state 0 and from state 3 to state 5. Row 2 of this product (the product is contained in *Derive* statement #7, which is omitted here) can be extracted by the command

VECTOR(ELEMENT(#7, 2, j), j, 1, 2)

resulting in

$$\#10: \left[\frac{p^3}{p^4 - 2p^3 + 4p^2 - 3p + 1}, \frac{(p-1)^2 (p^2 - p + 1)}{p^4 - 2p^3 + 4p^2 - 3p + 1}\right]$$

The first column provides the probability that A wins. In books devoted to probability a common exercise would be to determine analytically the probability of starting in state i and being absorbed in state 5 as

$$\frac{1-\left(\frac{1-p}{p}\right)^i}{1-\left(\frac{1-p}{p}\right)^5}.$$

if $p \neq 1/2$ and $i/5$ if $p = 1/2$. We may simplify this expression, noting that the probability that A wins is equivalent to the system being in state 2 (i = 2) and obtain the result in statement #10 from statement #12 as statement #13:

$$\#12: \frac{1 - \left[\frac{1-p}{p}\right]^2}{1 - \left[\frac{1-p}{p}\right]^5}$$

:

$$\#13: \frac{p^3}{p^4 - 2p^3 + 4p^2 - 3p + 1}$$

We can also use *Derive* to show that the sum of the elements in statement #10 is 1. If a graph of the first element in statement #10 is drawn, the probability of A winning the game as a function of p will be illustrated.

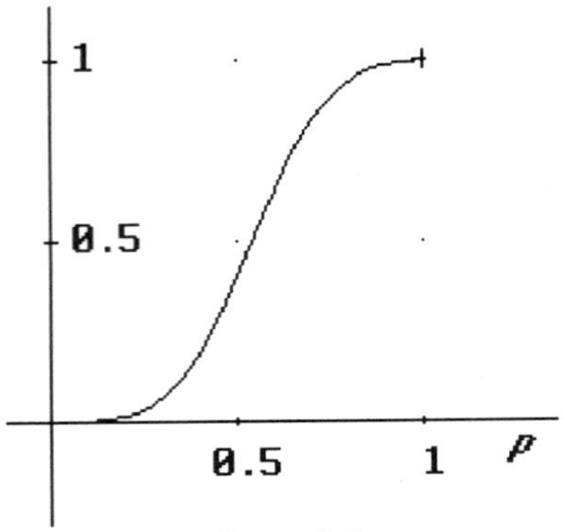

Figure 2.1

We observe from this graph that A has a less than 0.5 probability of winning even when the probability that A wins each event is 0.5. This is because A has 2 chits to start the game while B had 3. In fact the probability that A will win the game if $p = 0.5$ is 0.4.

Finally, we examine the expected number of times the game is in each state before absorption. To do this we need $(\mathbf{I}-\mathbf{Q})^{-1}$ which is given in statement #19. The element $\left((\mathbf{I}-\mathbf{Q})^{-1}\right)_{ij}$ gives the expected number of times the system is in state j given that it started in state i.

#17: $$\left[\begin{bmatrix} 1 & 0 & 0 & 0 \\ 0 & 1 & 0 & 0 \\ 0 & 0 & 1 & 0 \\ 0 & 0 & 0 & 1 \end{bmatrix} - \begin{bmatrix} 0 & 1-0.5 & 0 & 0.5 \\ 0.5 & 0 & 1-0.5 & 0 \\ 0 & 0.5 & 0 & 0 \\ 1-0.5 & 0 & 0 & 0 \end{bmatrix}\right]^{-1}$$

#18: Notation := Decimal

#19: $$\begin{bmatrix} 2.4 & 1.6 & 0.8 & 1.2 \\ 1.6 & 2.4 & 1.2 & 0.8 \\ 0.8 & 1.2 & 1.6 & 0.4 \\ 1.2 & 0.8 & 0.4 & 1.6 \end{bmatrix}$$

The interpretation of this matrix is as follows: If the system starts in state 2, it will on the average be in state 1, 1.6 times; state 2, 2.4 times; state 3, 1.2 times; and state 4, 0.8 times (counting the original time, before absorption).

EXERCISES

1. Given the transition matrix
$$\mathbf{P} = \begin{bmatrix} 0.4 & 0.6 \\ 0.2 & 0.8 \end{bmatrix}$$
show that it defines a regular Markov process and calculate $\mathbf{P}^{10}$ and $\lim_{n\to\infty} \mathbf{P}^n$.

2. Given the transition matrix
$$\mathbf{P} = \begin{bmatrix} 0.2 & 0.3 & 0.5 \\ 0.1 & 0.2 & 0.7 \\ 0 & 0.1 & 0.9 \end{bmatrix}$$
show that it defines a regular Markov process and calculate $\mathbf{P}^{10}$ and $\lim_{n\to\infty} \mathbf{P}^n$.

3. Given the transition matrix
$$\mathbf{P} = \begin{bmatrix} 0.2 & 0.2 & 0.5 & 0.1 \\ 0 & 0 & 1 & 0 \\ 0.1 & 0.8 & 0.1 & 0 \\ 0.4 & 0.4 & 0.1 & 0.1 \end{bmatrix}$$
show that it defines a regular Markov process and calculate $\mathbf{P}^{10}$ and $\lim_{n\to\infty} \mathbf{P}^n$.

4. There are two boxes each containing 3 balls. In the two boxes there are 3 green balls and 3 red balls. An event is said to take place when a ball is drawn at random from box A and placed in box B and a ball is then drawn from box B (which now contains 4 balls) at random and placed in box A. Show that the transition matrix is for this event is
$$\mathbf{P} = \begin{bmatrix} \frac{3}{12} & \frac{9}{12} & 0 & 0 \\ \frac{1}{12} & \frac{4}{12} & \frac{4}{12} & 0 \\ 0 & \frac{4}{12} & \frac{7}{12} & \frac{1}{12} \\ 0 & 0 & \frac{9}{12} & \frac{3}{12} \end{bmatrix}$$
where the states are the number of green balls in box A. Row 1 represents the state that there are 0 green balls in box A, row 2 represents the state that there is 1 green ball in box A, etc. What are the equilibrium probabilities $\left(\lim_{n\to\infty} \mathbf{P}^n\right)$ for each state?

5. In a particular viewing area there 4 popular television channels. Each hour the viewers consider changing channels and they change according to the probabilities given in the following table:

	A	B	C	D
A	0.4	0.3	0.2	0.1
B	0.2	0.2	0.4	0.2
C	0.3	0.3	0.1	0.3
D	0.3	0.3	0.3	0.1

Find the equilibrium probabilties. If there was a program on channel A at 1400 hours which drew 91% of the possible viewers with the remainder split equally between the other 3 stations, what is the distribution of the viewers at 1800 hours and at 2000 hours?

6. Two players A and B match coins in such a way that one or the other wins one coin each time they play with equal probability. If each have two coins when they begin, write a transition matrix to describe the game. What is the probability of each of them winning? How many times would you expect them to play the game before one of them wins? What if A has 3 coins and B has 1? What if A has one coin and B has 3?

7. Given the transition matrix

$$\mathbf{P} = \begin{bmatrix} 1 & 0 & 0 & 0 & 0 & 0 \\ 0 & 1 & 0 & 0 & 0 & 0 \\ 0 & 0 & 1 & 0 & 0 & 0 \\ 0 & 0 & 0 & 1 & 0 & 0 \\ 0.1 & 0.1 & 0 & 0.1 & 0.2 & 0.5 \\ 0.1 & 0.1 & 0.1 & 0 & 0.5 & 0.2 \end{bmatrix}$$

How many absorbing states does the process have? Find the matrix **N**. Find the matrix **Q**. Find the matrix $(\mathbf{I}-\mathbf{Q})^{-1}$ and interpret its meaning. Find $(\mathbf{I}-\mathbf{Q})^{-1}\mathbf{N}$ and interpret its meaning.

8. Given a system with states S_1, S_2, S_3 and S_4 where S_1 is absorbing. Let p_{ij} be the probability of passing from state S_i to state S_j. Further let $p_{12} = 0.2$, $p_{32} = 0.5$, $p_{43} = 1.0$, $p_{23} = p$, and $p_{34} = q$. Find values for p and q. Describe the process.

9. A prison has 5 cells C_1, C_2, C_3, C_4, and C_5. A prisoner is placed in cell C_5 and the next day he draws a card marked with a 1, 2, 3, or 4 sending him to the corresponding cell. If he draws cell C_1 he is set free immediately. If he draws cell C_2 he goes to cell C_5 the next day with probability 1. If he chooses cell C_3, the next day he goes to cell C_2 or C_4 with equal probability. If he chooses cell C_4, the next day he goes to C_2 or C_3 with equal probabilities of 0.25 or to cell C_5 with probability 0.5. From cell C_5 the process is repeated until he chooses C_1 and is free. How long does he expect to stay in prison?

3. DIFFERENCE EQUATIONS

Difference equations are the discrete equivalent to differential equations. In fact in the limiting sense, difference equations become differential equations. They are also known in some settings as recurrence equations. Our definition of a difference equation will be developed from some rather simple concepts, but the applications which follow from these concepts are varied and interesting.

DEFINITION 3.1 (Homogeneous Difference Equation with Constant Coefficients) A homogeneous difference equation with constant coefficients is a relation defined on the non-negative integers recursively between the successive values of the relation according to the following rule (which is called the general difference equation):

$$y(k+1) = a_0 y(k) + a_1 y(k-1) + \cdots + a_n y(k-n),$$

where $a_0, a_1, \cdots, a_n$ are constants.

DEFINITION 3.2 (Solution of a Difference Equation) By the solution of a difference equation, we mean a tabulation of a set of values or a relation defined on the positive integers that satisfies the recursive relation of the general difference equation. By a particular solution of a difference equation, we mean a solution that satisfies specified initial conditions.

EXAMPLE 3.1 To find the solution of the difference equation $y(k+2) = y(k+1) + 2y(k)$ with initial conditions $y(0) = 1$ and $y(1) = 2$, we first tabulate the values generated by the recursive relation:

k	0	1	2	3	4	5	...
$y(k)$	1	2	4	8	16	32	...

and notice that the solution gives powers of 2.

The general difference equation which appears in Definition 3.1 can be written using matrix notation. If we assume the initial conditions are $y(n), y(n-1), \cdots, y(0)$, then we can write

$$[y(n)\quad y(n-1)\quad \cdots \quad y(0)]\begin{bmatrix} a_0 & 1 & 0 & \cdots & 0 \\ a_1 & 0 & 1 & \cdots & 0 \\ \cdots & \cdots & \cdots & \cdots & \cdots \\ a_{n-1} & 0 & 0 & \cdots & 1 \\ a_n & 0 & 0 & \cdots & 0 \end{bmatrix} = [y(n+1)\quad y(n)\quad \cdots \quad y(1)]$$

where $a_0, a_1, \cdots, a_n$ are the coefficients from the general difference equation in the form of Definition 3.1. This can be rewritten in the shorthand notation

$$\mathbf{y}(0)\mathbf{A} = \mathbf{y}(1).$$

Using the recurrence property of the difference equation, it follows that

$$\mathbf{y}(2) = \mathbf{y}(1)\mathbf{A} = \mathbf{y}(0)\mathbf{A}^2,$$

and in general

$$\mathbf{y}(n) = \mathbf{y}(n-1)\mathbf{A} = \mathbf{y}(0)\mathbf{A}^n.$$

DEFINITION 3.3 (Recurrence Matrix) The matrix **A** in the above relation is called the recurrence matrix.

EXAMPLE 3.2 We can now represent the difference equation for Example 3.1 in terms of its recurrence matrix

$$[y(1)\quad y(0)]\begin{bmatrix} 1 & 1 \\ 2 & 0 \end{bmatrix} = [y(2)\quad y(1)]$$

and in general

$$[y(n)\quad y(n-1)]\begin{bmatrix} 1 & 1 \\ 2 & 0 \end{bmatrix} = [y(n+1)\quad y(n)]$$

or

$$[y(1)\quad y(0)]\begin{bmatrix} 1 & 1 \\ 2 & 0 \end{bmatrix}^n = [y(n+1)\quad y(n)] \quad n = 0,1,2,\cdots.$$

We may substitute the initial conditions and obtain

$$[2 \quad 1]\begin{bmatrix} 1 & 1 \\ 2 & 0 \end{bmatrix}^n = [y(n+1) \quad y(n)] \quad n = 0,1,2,\cdots,$$

and in particular for $n = 5$

$$3: \quad [\,2 \quad 1\,] \cdot \begin{bmatrix} 1 & 1 \\ 2 & 0 \end{bmatrix}^5$$

$$4: \quad [\,64 \quad 32\,]$$

We notice that the columns of statement #4 yield the values 2^6 and 2^5.

If we can diagonalize or find the Jordan canonical form of **A** in

$$\mathbf{y}(n-1) = \mathbf{y}(n)\mathbf{A}$$

by finding a matrix **K** such that

$$\mathbf{K}^{-1}\mathbf{A}\mathbf{K} = \mathbf{C},$$

then a closed form solution to the difference equation would have the general solution

$$\mathbf{y}(0)\mathbf{K}\mathbf{C}^n\mathbf{K}^{-1} = \mathbf{y}(n).$$

EXAMPLE 3.3 We can use the Jordan canonical form technique described in the paragraph above to find the general solution of the difference equation of Example 3.1. The eigenvectors of **A** can be used to form the matrix

$$\mathbf{K} = \begin{bmatrix} 1 & 1 \\ -2 & 1 \end{bmatrix}$$

so that

$$\mathbf{K}^{-1}\mathbf{A}\mathbf{K} = \begin{bmatrix} -1 & 0 \\ 0 & 2 \end{bmatrix}.$$

The general solution of the difference equation is thus given by

$$13: \quad [\,2 \quad 1\,] \cdot \begin{bmatrix} 1 & 1 \\ -2 & 1 \end{bmatrix} \cdot \begin{bmatrix} -1 & 0 \\ 0 & 2 \end{bmatrix}^{n} \cdot \begin{bmatrix} 1 & 1 \\ -2 & 1 \end{bmatrix}^{-1}$$

$$14: \quad [\,2^{n+1} \quad 2^{n}\,]$$

EXAMPLE 3.4 The Fibonacci number sequence is described by the difference equation

$$y(n+2) = y(n+1) + y(n)$$

with the initial conditions $y(0) = 0$ and $y(1) = 1$. The general solution of the difference equation with recurrence matrix

$$\mathbf{A} = \begin{bmatrix} 1 & 1 \\ 1 & 0 \end{bmatrix}$$

is given by

$$3: \quad [\,0 \quad 1\,] \cdot \begin{bmatrix} 1 & 1 \\ 1 & 0 \end{bmatrix}^{n} \cdot$$

We will diagonalize the recurrence matrix by first finding the matrix of eigenvectors

$$\mathbf{K} = \begin{bmatrix} 1 & 1 \\ -\left(\sqrt{5}+1\right)/2 & \left(\sqrt{5}-1\right)/2 \end{bmatrix}$$

so that

$$\mathbf{C} = \mathbf{K}^{-1}\mathbf{A}\mathbf{K}$$

is given by

$$12: \begin{bmatrix} \frac{1}{2} - \frac{\sqrt{5}}{2} & 0 \\ 0 & \frac{\sqrt{5}}{2} + \frac{1}{2} \end{bmatrix}$$

Next, we form

$$\begin{bmatrix} y(n+1) & y(n) \end{bmatrix} = \begin{bmatrix} 1 & 0 \end{bmatrix} \mathbf{K}\mathbf{C}^n\mathbf{K}^{-1},$$

where **K** and **C** are defined as above. In order to find a particular term in the Fibonacci sequence we simply substitute appropriately for n. For example, in order to find $y(100)$, the one hundredth term in the sequence, we compute $\begin{bmatrix} 1 & 0 \end{bmatrix} \mathbf{K}\mathbf{C}^{99}\mathbf{K}^{-1}$:

23: [354224848179261915075 218922995834555169026]

The first component of statement #23 is $y(100)$ and the second component is $y(99)$.

EXAMPLE 3.5 The difference equation

$$y(k+3) = y(k+2) + y(k+1) - y(k)$$

with initial conditions $y(2) = 5$, $y(1) = 3$, and $y(0) = 1$ can be represented in matrix form by

$$\begin{bmatrix} y(k+2) & y(k+1) & y(k) \end{bmatrix} \begin{bmatrix} 1 & 1 & 0 \\ 1 & 0 & 1 \\ -1 & 0 & 0 \end{bmatrix} = \begin{bmatrix} y(k+3) & y(k+2) & y(k+1) \end{bmatrix},$$

and the general solution is given by

$$\begin{bmatrix} 5 & 3 & 1 \end{bmatrix} \begin{bmatrix} 1 & 1 & 0 \\ 1 & 0 & 1 \\ -1 & 0 & 0 \end{bmatrix}^n = \begin{bmatrix} y(n+2) & y(n+1) & y(n) \end{bmatrix}.$$

By using *Derive* we find that the recurrence matrix is not diagonalizable, but instead is similar to a matrix in Jordan canonical form.

$$23: \begin{bmatrix} 1 & 0 & 1 \\ 0 & 1 & -2 \\ -1 & 1 & 1 \end{bmatrix}^{-1} \cdot \begin{bmatrix} 1 & 1 & 0 \\ 1 & 0 & 1 \\ -1 & 0 & 0 \end{bmatrix} \cdot \begin{bmatrix} 1 & 0 & 1 \\ 0 & 1 & -2 \\ -1 & 1 & 1 \end{bmatrix}$$

$$24: \begin{bmatrix} 1 & 1 & 0 \\ 0 & 1 & 0 \\ 0 & 0 & -1 \end{bmatrix}$$

We find by the methods of Section 6.3 that

$$\begin{bmatrix} 1 & 1 & 0 \\ 1 & 0 & 1 \\ -1 & 0 & 0 \end{bmatrix}^n = \begin{bmatrix} 1 & 0 & 1 \\ 0 & 1 & -2 \\ -1 & 1 & 1 \end{bmatrix} \begin{bmatrix} 1 & n & 0 \\ 0 & 1 & 0 \\ 0 & 0 & (-1)^n \end{bmatrix} \begin{bmatrix} 1 & 0 & 1 \\ 0 & 1 & -2 \\ -1 & 1 & 1 \end{bmatrix}^{-1}$$

We apply the right hand side to the matrix consisting of initial conditions

$$8: \begin{bmatrix} 5 & 3 & 1 \end{bmatrix} \cdot \left[\begin{bmatrix} 1 & 0 & 1 \\ 0 & 1 & -2 \\ -1 & 1 & 1 \end{bmatrix} \cdot \begin{bmatrix} 1 & n & 0 \\ 0 & 1 & 0 \\ 0 & 0 & (-1)^n \end{bmatrix} \cdot \begin{bmatrix} 1 & 0 & 1 \\ 0 & 1 & -2 \\ -1 & 1 & 1 \end{bmatrix}^{-1} \right]$$

$$9: \begin{bmatrix} 2n + 5 & 2n + 3 & 2n + 1 \end{bmatrix}$$

where statement #9 is statement #8 simplified. The solution given in statement #9 is $[y(n+2) \quad y(n+1) \quad y(n)]$.

EXAMPLE 3.6 To solve the difference equation $y(k+2) = 4y(k+1) - 4y(k)$ with the initial conditions $y(0) = b$ and $y(1) = a$, we first find the recurrence matrix

$$\mathbf{R} = \begin{bmatrix} 4 & 1 \\ -4 & 0 \end{bmatrix},$$

and then transform **R** into its Jordan canonical form

$$\begin{bmatrix} 1 & 0 \\ -2 & 1 \end{bmatrix}^{-1} \begin{bmatrix} 4 & 1 \\ -4 & 0 \end{bmatrix} \begin{bmatrix} 1 & 0 \\ -2 & 1 \end{bmatrix} = \begin{bmatrix} 2 & 1 \\ 0 & 2 \end{bmatrix}.$$

Applying the methods of Section 6.3, we find

$$\begin{bmatrix} 2 & 1 \\ 0 & 2 \end{bmatrix}^{n} = \begin{bmatrix} 2^n & n2^{n-1} \\ 0 & 2^n \end{bmatrix},$$

and it follows that the solution of the difference equation with the initial conditions $\begin{bmatrix} a & b \end{bmatrix}$ is given by

$$23: \quad [\, a \quad b \,] \cdot \begin{bmatrix} 1 & 0 \\ -2 & 1 \end{bmatrix} \cdot \begin{bmatrix} 2^n & n\, 2^{n-1} \\ 0 & 2^n \end{bmatrix} \cdot \begin{bmatrix} 1 & 0 \\ -2 & 1 \end{bmatrix}^{-1}$$

$$24: \quad \left[\, 2^n\, (a\,(n+1) - 2\,b\,n) \quad 2^{n-1}\, (a\,n + 2\,b\,(1-n)) \,\right]$$

In particular, if $a = 3$ and $b = 1$, then the solution is given by

$$26: \quad \left[\, 2^n\, (n+3) \quad 2^{n-1}\, (n+2) \,\right]$$

or

$$y(n) = 2^{n-1}(n+2).$$

EXAMPLE 3.7 We can describe the difference equation which computes the mean of the previous three values in a number sequence by the recurrence relation

$$y(k+3) = \frac{y(k+2) + y(k+1) + y(k)}{3}.$$

In matrix form with initial conditions $y(0) = a$, $y(1) = b$, and $y(2) = c$, this recurrence relation is represented by

$$\begin{bmatrix} a & b & c \end{bmatrix} \begin{bmatrix} 1/3 & 1 & 0 \\ 1/3 & 0 & 1 \\ 1/3 & 0 & 0 \end{bmatrix} = \begin{bmatrix} y(n+2) & y(n+1) & y(n) \end{bmatrix}.$$

We leave finding the general solution of this difference equation as an exercise.

EXERCISES:

1. Find the solution of the difference equation $y(k+2) = y(k+1) + 2y(k)$ with initial conditions $y(0) = 0$ and $y(1) = 1$.

2. Find the solution of the difference equation $y(n+2) = y(n+1) - 2y(n)$ with initial conditions $y(0) = 1$ and $y(1) = 1$.

3. Find the solution of the difference equation $y(n+2) = y(n+1) + y(n)$ with initial conditions $y(0) = 0$ and $y(1) = -1$.

4. A sequence of numbers $\{y(n)\}$, $n = 1, 2, 3, \ldots$, is determined by $y(n+2) = \dfrac{y(n+1) + y(n)}{2}$, where $y(1) = 1$ and $y(2) = 2$. Find a general expression for $y(n+1)$ and $\lim_{n\to\infty} y(n)$ if the limit exists.

5. If an amount 1 is invested at 6% compounded annually, find the difference equation to express the value of the investment an the end of the next year. Find the general solution of the difference equation.

6. If the next number in a sequence is determined by the average of the previous three terms, find the difference equation to express the general term of the sequence. Find the general term of the sequence. Find the limit of the general term. (Complete Example 3.7)

7. Solve the difference equation $y(n+3) = -4y(n+2) + 5y(n+1) - 2y(n)$ with initial conditions $y(0) = 0$, $y(1) = 1$, and $y(2) = 1$.

8. Solve the difference equation $y(n+3) = 6y(n+2) - 12y(n+1) + 8y(n)$ with initial conditions $y(0) = 1$, $y(1) = 2$, and $y(2) = 3$.

9. Solve the difference equation of Exercise 8 with initial conditions $[y(2) \quad y(1) \quad y(0)] = [a \quad b \quad c]$.

10. Given the difference equation $y(n+2) = py(n+1) + qy(n)$ with $p + q = 1$, and initial conditions $[y(1) \quad y(0)] = [a \quad b]$, where $a + b = 1$, find $\lim_{n\to\infty} y(n)$ for $p = 1/4$, $p = 1/2$, and $p = 3/4$.

4. LINEAR SYSTEMS OF DIFFERENTIAL EQUATIONS WITH CONSTANT COEFFICIENTS

Many physical problems of engineering and physics involve linear systems of differential equations with constant coefficients. An example of such a system is

$$\begin{aligned} \dot{x}_1 &= 2x_1 + 3x_2 - 2x_3 \\ \dot{x}_2 &= 4x_1 - x_2 + 2x_3 \\ \dot{x}_3 &= 4x_1 + 3x_2 - x_3 \end{aligned}$$

This system involves three unknown dependent variables, x_1, x_2, and x_3, an independent variable t, and derivatives with respect to t, noted here with a dot over the dependent variables. This system may be written in matrix notation as

$$\begin{bmatrix} \dot{x}_1 \\ \dot{x}_2 \\ \dot{x}_3 \end{bmatrix} = \begin{bmatrix} 2 & 3 & -2 \\ 4 & -1 & 2 \\ 4 & 3 & -1 \end{bmatrix} \begin{bmatrix} x_1 \\ x_2 \\ x_3 \end{bmatrix}.$$

or $\dot{\mathbf{x}} = \mathbf{A}\mathbf{x}$ where

$$\mathbf{A} = \begin{bmatrix} 2 & 3 & -2 \\ 4 & -1 & 2 \\ 4 & 3 & -1 \end{bmatrix}.$$

A system such as this is said to be a homogeneous linear system with constant coefficients. If the system has the form $\dot{\mathbf{x}} = \mathbf{A}\mathbf{x} + \mathbf{b}$, where the vector $\mathbf{b}$ is a function of the independent variable t, then the system is called a nonhomogeneous system with constant coefficients.

We will first concentrate on homogeneous systems since the solution of the nonhomogeneous system depends on the solution of the homogeneous system. We learned in Theorem 3.5 of Chapter VI that the derivative of the matrix exponential function $e^{t\mathbf{A}}$ is $\mathbf{A}e^{t\mathbf{A}}$. This gives some insight into the solution of the homogeneous system of equations $\dot{\mathbf{x}} = \mathbf{A}\mathbf{x}$ since $e^{t\mathbf{A}}$ is a solution of the matrix equation $\dot{\mathbf{X}} = \mathbf{A}\mathbf{X}$, and each column of $e^{t\mathbf{A}}$ is a solution of the differential equation.

We omit the proof of the following theorem.

THEOREM 4.1 The dimension of the solution space of $\dot{\mathbf{x}} = \mathbf{A}\mathbf{x}$, where $\mathbf{A}$ is an $n \times n$ matrix is n.

Next, we provide a way to find the general solution of a homogeneous system of differential equations.

THEOREM 4.2 If $e^{t\mathbf{A}} = \mathbf{U} = \begin{bmatrix} \mathbf{u}_1 & \mathbf{u}_2 & \cdots & \mathbf{u}_n \end{bmatrix}$ then,

$$\mathbf{x} = c_1\mathbf{u}_1 + c_2\mathbf{u}_2 + \cdots + c_n\mathbf{u}_n$$

is the general solution of $\dot{\mathbf{x}} = \mathbf{A}\mathbf{x}$.

PROOF: Since each column of $\mathbf{U}$ is a solution of $\dot{\mathbf{x}} = \mathbf{A}\mathbf{x}$ and $\{\mathbf{u}_1, \mathbf{u}_2, \ldots, \mathbf{u}_n\}$ is a linearly independent set because $\mathrm{DET}\left(e^{\mathbf{A}}\right) \neq 0$, the columns of $\mathbf{U}$ form a basis for the space of solutions. Hence any solution may be written as a linear combination of the columns of $\mathbf{U}$.

EXAMPLE 4.1 To determine the general solution of $\dot{\mathbf{x}} = \mathbf{A}\mathbf{x}$, where

$$\mathbf{A} = \begin{bmatrix} -13 & -28 \\ 6 & 13 \end{bmatrix},$$

we first find the matrix exponential function by the method given in Section 6.3. Using *Derive*, we find the eigenvalues to be 1 and -1 and the respective eigenvectors to be $\begin{bmatrix} 2 \\ -1 \end{bmatrix}$ and $\begin{bmatrix} 7 \\ -3 \end{bmatrix}$. The resulting matrix of eigenvectors is therefore

$$\mathbf{K} = \begin{bmatrix} 2 & 7 \\ -1 & -3 \end{bmatrix}$$

so that

$$\mathbf{K}^{-1}\mathbf{A}\mathbf{K} = \begin{bmatrix} 1 & 0 \\ 0 & -1 \end{bmatrix},$$

and

$$e^{t\mathbf{A}} = \begin{bmatrix} 2 & 7 \\ -1 & 3 \end{bmatrix} \begin{bmatrix} e^t & 0 \\ 0 & e^{-t} \end{bmatrix} \begin{bmatrix} 2 & 7 \\ -1 & 3 \end{bmatrix}^{-1} = \begin{bmatrix} 7e^{-t} - 6e^t & 14e^{-t} - 14e^t \\ 3e^t - 3e^{-t} & 7e^t - 6e^{-t} \end{bmatrix}.$$

It follows by Theorem 4.2 that the general solution is given by

$$\mathbf{x} = c_1 \begin{bmatrix} 7e^{-t} - 6e^t \\ 3e^t - 3e^{-t} \end{bmatrix} + c_2 \begin{bmatrix} 14e^{-t} - 14e^t \\ 7e^t - 6e^{-t} \end{bmatrix}.$$

It is left as a exercise to verify that $\dot{\mathbf{x}} = \mathbf{Ax}$.

EXAMPLE 4.2 To determine the general solution of $\dot{\mathbf{x}} = \mathbf{Ax}$, where

$$\mathbf{A} = \begin{bmatrix} 1 & 0 & 0 \\ -1 & 1 & 1 \\ 0 & 0 & 1 \end{bmatrix}$$

we again use *Derive* to find that **A** has only one eigenvalue, namely 1, and only two linearly independent eigenvectors, examples of which are $[1 \ \ 0 \ \ 1]^{\mathrm{T}}$ and $[0 \ \ 1 \ \ 0]^{\mathrm{T}}$. We can use the techniques of Section 5.5 to see that $\{[0 \ \ 1 \ \ 0]^{\mathrm{T}}, [0 \ \ 0 \ \ 1]^{\mathrm{T}}\}$ forms a set of generalized eigenvectors; therefore, the Jordan form of **A** is

$$\begin{bmatrix} 0 & 0 & 1 \\ 1 & 0 & 0 \\ 0 & 1 & 1 \end{bmatrix}^{-1} \begin{bmatrix} 1 & 0 & 0 \\ -1 & 1 & 1 \\ 0 & 0 & 1 \end{bmatrix} \begin{bmatrix} 0 & 0 & 1 \\ 1 & 0 & 0 \\ 0 & 1 & 1 \end{bmatrix} = \begin{bmatrix} 1 & 1 & 0 \\ 0 & 1 & 0 \\ 0 & 0 & 1 \end{bmatrix},$$

and

$$e^{t\mathbf{A}} = \begin{bmatrix} 0 & 0 & 1 \\ -1 & 1 & 1 \\ 0 & 1 & 1 \end{bmatrix} \begin{bmatrix} e^t & te^t & 0 \\ 0 & e^t & 0 \\ 0 & 0 & e^t \end{bmatrix} \begin{bmatrix} 0 & 0 & 1 \\ -1 & 1 & 1 \\ 0 & 1 & 1 \end{bmatrix}^{-1} = \begin{bmatrix} e^t & 0 & 0 \\ -te^t & e^t & te^t \\ 0 & 0 & e^t \end{bmatrix}.$$

Hence, by Theorem 4.2, the general solution is given by

$$\mathbf{x} = c_1\begin{bmatrix} e^t \\ -te^t \\ 0 \end{bmatrix} + c_2\begin{bmatrix} 0 \\ e^t \\ 0 \end{bmatrix} + c_3\begin{bmatrix} 0 \\ te^t \\ e^t \end{bmatrix}.$$

A higher order differential equation with constant coefficients may be written as a first order system with constant coefficients by using suitable substitutions.

EXAMPLE 4.3 The differential equation

$$\frac{d^n y}{dx^n} + a_{n-1}\frac{d^{n-1}y}{dx^{n-1}} + \cdots + a_1\frac{dy}{dx} + a_0 y = 0$$

can be written as a first order system by first making the substitutions $u_1 = y,\ u_2 = \dfrac{dy}{dx},\ u_3 = \dfrac{d^2y}{dx^2}, \cdots, u_n = \dfrac{d^{n-1}y}{dx^{n-1}}$. With these substitutions $u_1' = u_2,\ u_2' = u_3, \cdots, u_{n-1}' = u_n,\ u_n' = -a_{n-1}u_n - a_{n-2}u_{n-1} - \cdots - a_1u_2 - a_0u_1$. The system can be written in matrix form

$$\begin{bmatrix} u_1' \\ u_2' \\ \vdots \\ u_n' \end{bmatrix} = \begin{bmatrix} 0 & 1 & 0 & \cdots & 0 \\ 0 & 0 & 1 & \cdots & 0 \\ \cdots & \cdots & \cdots & \ddots & \cdots \\ -a_0 & -a_1 & -a_2 & \cdots & -a_{n-1} \end{bmatrix} \begin{bmatrix} u_1 \\ u_2 \\ \vdots \\ u_n \end{bmatrix}.$$

EXAMPLE 4.4 The differential equation $y''' + 2y'' - 3y' + 2y = 0$ can be written as a first order system by first making the substitutions $u_1 = y$, $u_2 = y'$, and $u_3 = y''$. It follows that $u_1' = y' = u_2$, $u_2' = y'' = u_3$, and $u_3' = y''' = -2y + 3y' - 2y'' = -2u_1 + 3u_2 - 2u_3$, and thus,

$$\begin{bmatrix} u_1' \\ u_2' \\ u_3' \end{bmatrix} = \begin{bmatrix} 0 & 1 & 0 \\ 0 & 0 & 1 \\ -2 & 3 & -2 \end{bmatrix} \begin{bmatrix} u_1 \\ u_2 \\ u_3 \end{bmatrix}.$$

We may also use the algorithm of Section 6.4 to compute the matrix exponential function.

EXAMPLE 4.5 In order to apply the algorithm of Section 6.4 to the matrix

$$\mathbf{A} = \begin{bmatrix} -1 & 0 & -1 \\ -3 & -2 & 2 \\ 1 & 0 & -3 \end{bmatrix}$$

we first find the eigenvalues of **A**:

$$2:\quad \text{EIGENVALUES}\begin{bmatrix} -1 & 0 & -1 \\ -3 & -2 & 2 \\ 1 & 0 & -3 \end{bmatrix}$$

$$3:\quad [w = -2]$$

Next, we set e^x equal to a general quadratic expression and differentiate twice to create the system of equations:

$$e^x = ax^2 + bx + c$$

$$e^x = 2ax + b$$

$$e^x = 2a$$

where x will assume the eigenvalue of $t\mathbf{A}$, namely $-2t$. We use *Derive* to solve this system for the coefficients a, b, and c:

$$\#6:\quad \text{ROW\_REDUCE}\begin{bmatrix} (-2\cdot t)^2 & -2\cdot t & 1 & \hat{e}^{-2\cdot t} \\ 2\cdot(-2\cdot t) & 1 & 0 & \hat{e}^{-2\cdot t} \\ 2 & 0 & 0 & \hat{e}^{-2\cdot t} \end{bmatrix}$$

$$\#7:\quad \begin{bmatrix} 1 & 0 & 0 & \dfrac{\hat{e}^{-2\cdot t}}{2} \\ 0 & 1 & 0 & \hat{e}^{-2\cdot t}\cdot(2\cdot t + 1) \\ 0 & 0 & 1 & \hat{e}^{-2\cdot t}\cdot(2\cdot t^2 + 2\cdot t + 1) \end{bmatrix}$$

The last column of statement #7 is the solution for a, b, and c. After substituting $t\mathbf{A}$ for x, $e^{-2x}/2$ for a, $e^{2t}(2t+1)$ for b, and $e^{-2t}(2t^2+2t+1)$ for c. The final result, after simplification is

$$\#10: \begin{bmatrix} \hat{e}^{-2\cdot t}\cdot(t+1) & 0 & -t\cdot\hat{e}^{-2\cdot t} \\ -\dfrac{t\cdot\hat{e}^{-2\cdot t}\cdot(t+6)}{2} & \hat{e}^{-2\cdot t} & \dfrac{t\cdot\hat{e}^{-2\cdot t}\cdot(t+4)}{2} \\ t\cdot\hat{e}^{-2\cdot t} & 0 & \hat{e}^{-2\cdot t}\cdot(1-t) \end{bmatrix}$$

The general solution is

$$\#14: c1\cdot\begin{bmatrix} \hat{e}^{-2\cdot t}\cdot(t+1) \\ -\dfrac{t\cdot\hat{e}^{-2\cdot t}\cdot(t+6)}{2} \\ t\cdot\hat{e}^{-2\cdot t} \end{bmatrix} + c2\cdot\begin{bmatrix} 0 \\ \hat{e}^{-2\cdot t} \\ 0 \end{bmatrix} +$$

$$c3\cdot\begin{bmatrix} -t\cdot\hat{e}^{-2\cdot t} \\ \dfrac{t\cdot\hat{e}^{-2\cdot t}\cdot(t+4)}{2} \\ \hat{e}^{-2\cdot t}\cdot(1-t) \end{bmatrix}$$

We will now consider the case of the nonhomogeneous linear system with constant coefficients. A system of this type has the form

$$\dot{\mathbf{x}} = \mathbf{A}\mathbf{x} + \mathbf{b}$$

where the elements of $\mathbf{b}$ are functions of t.

THEOREM 4.3 Let $e^{t\mathbf{A}} = [\mathbf{u}_1 \quad \mathbf{u}_2 \quad \cdots \quad \mathbf{u}_n]$ so that

$$\mathbf{u} = c_1\mathbf{u}_1 + c_2\mathbf{u}_2 + \cdots + c_n\mathbf{u}_n$$

is the general solution of $\dot{\mathbf{x}} = \mathbf{A}\mathbf{x}$. Let $\mathbf{p}$ be any particular solution of $\dot{\mathbf{x}} = \mathbf{A}\mathbf{x} + \mathbf{b}$. Then the general solution of this nonhomogeneous equation has the form

$$\mathbf{u} = c_1\mathbf{u}_1 + c_2\mathbf{u}_2 + \cdots + c_n\mathbf{u}_n + \mathbf{p}.$$

PROOF: The expression $\mathbf{u} = c_1\mathbf{u}_1 + c_2\mathbf{u}_2 + \cdots + c_n\mathbf{u}_n + \mathbf{p}$ is a solution since $\dot{\mathbf{p}} = \mathbf{A}\mathbf{p} + \mathbf{b}$ and $\mathbf{u}_j = \mathbf{A}\mathbf{u}_j$ for $j = 1, 2, \cdots, n$ and

$$\begin{aligned}\frac{d}{dt}(c_1\mathbf{u}_1 + c_2\mathbf{u}_2 + \cdots + c_n\mathbf{u}_n + \mathbf{p}) &= \sum_{i=1}^{n} c_i \frac{d}{dt}\mathbf{u}_j + \frac{d}{dt}\mathbf{p} \\ &= \sum_{i=1}^{n} c_i \mathbf{A}\mathbf{u}_i + \mathbf{A}\mathbf{p} + \mathbf{b} \\ &= \mathbf{A}\left(\sum_{i=1}^{n} c_i\mathbf{u}_i + \mathbf{p}\right) + \mathbf{b}\end{aligned}$$

Hence, $c_1\mathbf{u}_1 + c_2\mathbf{u}_2 + \cdots + c_n\mathbf{u}_n + \mathbf{p}$ is a solution of the nonhomogeneous equation $\dot{\mathbf{x}} = \mathbf{A}\mathbf{x} + \mathbf{b}$.

Next, let $\mathbf{u}$ be any solution of $\dot{\mathbf{x}} = \mathbf{A}\mathbf{x} + \mathbf{b}$and consider $\mathbf{u} - \mathbf{p}$:

$$\frac{d}{dt}(\mathbf{u} - \mathbf{p}) = \dot{\mathbf{u}} - \dot{\mathbf{p}} = \mathbf{A}\mathbf{u} + \mathbf{b} - (\mathbf{A}\mathbf{p} + \mathbf{b}) = \mathbf{A}\mathbf{u} - \mathbf{A}\mathbf{p} = \mathbf{A}(\mathbf{u} - \mathbf{p}).$$

Thus $\mathbf{u} - \mathbf{p}$ is a solution of $\dot{\mathbf{x}} = \mathbf{A}\mathbf{x}$ so that

$$\mathbf{u} - \mathbf{p} = c_1\mathbf{u}_1 + c_2\mathbf{u}_2 + \cdots + c_n\mathbf{u}_n;$$

and, consequently,

$$\mathbf{u} = c_1\mathbf{u}_1 + c_2\mathbf{u}_2 + \cdots + c_n\mathbf{u}_n + \mathbf{p}.$$

Next we present a method which finds a particular solution $\mathbf{p}$ for a linear system of differential equations. The method is called variation of parameters and is based on the method of variation of parameters from the study of ordinary differential equations. In this method we will attempt to find a solution of $\dot{\mathbf{x}} = \mathbf{A}\mathbf{x} + \mathbf{b}$ in the form of

$$\mathbf{p} = e^{t\mathbf{A}}\mathbf{u}.$$

If we substitute this expression into the system of differential equations, we obtain

$$\frac{d}{dt}\left(e^{t\mathbf{A}}\mathbf{u}\right) = \mathbf{A}e^{t\mathbf{A}}\mathbf{u} + \mathbf{b}.$$

Upon performing the indicated differentiating, this equation becomes

$$\mathbf{A}e^{t\mathbf{A}}\mathbf{u} + \mathbf{e}^{t\mathbf{A}}\dot{\mathbf{u}} = \mathbf{A}\left(e^{t\mathbf{A}}\mathbf{u}\right) + \mathbf{b}.$$

Subtracting $\mathbf{A}e^{t\mathbf{A}}\mathbf{u}$ from both sides we obtain $e^{t\mathbf{A}}\dot{\mathbf{u}} = \mathbf{b}$, but $e^{t\mathbf{A}}$ is not singular and $\left(e^{t\mathbf{A}}\right)^{-1} = e^{-t\mathbf{A}}$; therefore, $\dot{\mathbf{u}} = e^{-t\mathbf{A}}\mathbf{b}$. Integrating both sides of this equation

$$\mathbf{u} = \int e^{-t\mathbf{A}}\mathbf{b}dt.$$

Hence, the particular solution is

$$\mathbf{p} = e^{t\mathbf{A}}\int e^{-t\mathbf{A}}\mathbf{b}dt.$$

EXAMPLE 4.6 To solve the nonhomogeneous system of differential equations

$$\dot{\mathbf{x}} = \mathbf{A}\mathbf{x} + \mathbf{b}$$

where

$$\mathbf{A} = \begin{bmatrix} -2 & 1 \\ 0 & -1 \end{bmatrix} \text{ and } \mathbf{b} = \begin{bmatrix} t \\ 1 \end{bmatrix}.$$

we use *Derive* to find $e^{t\mathbf{A}}$

$$10: \begin{bmatrix} \hat{e}^{-2t} & \hat{e}^{-t} - \hat{e}^{-2t} \\ 0 & \hat{e}^{-t} \end{bmatrix}$$

Next, we form $\left(e^{t\mathbf{A}}\right)^{-1} = e^{-t\mathbf{A}}$, and the product $e^{-t\mathbf{A}}\mathbf{b}$

$$12: \quad \begin{bmatrix} \hat{e}^{-2\,(-t)} & \hat{e}^{-\,-t} - \hat{e}^{-2\,(-t)} \\ 0 & \hat{e}^{-\,-t} \end{bmatrix}$$

$$13: \quad \begin{bmatrix} \hat{e}^{-2\,(-t)} & \hat{e}^{-\,-t} - \hat{e}^{-2\,(-t)} \\ 0 & \hat{e}^{-\,-t} \end{bmatrix} \cdot \begin{bmatrix} t \\ 1 \end{bmatrix}$$

$$14: \quad \begin{bmatrix} \hat{e}^{2\,t}\,(t - 1) + \hat{e}^{t} \\ \hat{e}^{t} \end{bmatrix}$$

and we integrate $e^{-t\mathbf{A}}\mathbf{b}$

$$15: \quad \int \begin{bmatrix} \hat{e}^{2\,t}\,(t - 1) + \hat{e}^{t} \\ \hat{e}^{t} \end{bmatrix} dt$$

$$16: \quad \begin{bmatrix} \hat{e}^{2\,t}\left[\dfrac{t}{2} - \dfrac{3}{4}\right] + \hat{e}^{t} \\ \hat{e}^{t} \end{bmatrix}$$

The result of the integration is given in statement #16. Finally, the particular solution **p** is

$$\mathbf{p} = e^{t\mathbf{A}} \int e^{-t\mathbf{A}}\mathbf{b}\,dt$$

$$17: \quad \begin{bmatrix} \hat{e}^{-2\,t} & \hat{e}^{-t} - \hat{e}^{-2\,t} \\ 0 & \hat{e}^{-t} \end{bmatrix} \cdot \begin{bmatrix} \hat{e}^{2\,t}\left[\dfrac{t}{2} - \dfrac{3}{4}\right] + \hat{e}^{t} \\ \hat{e}^{t} \end{bmatrix}$$

$$18: \begin{bmatrix} \dfrac{t}{2} + \dfrac{1}{4} \\ 1 \end{bmatrix}$$

As a check, we show that $\dot{\mathbf{p}} - \mathbf{Ap} = \mathbf{b}$

$$21: \frac{d}{dt}\begin{bmatrix} \dfrac{t}{2} + \dfrac{1}{4} \\ 1 \end{bmatrix} - \begin{bmatrix} -2 & 1 \\ 0 & -1 \end{bmatrix} \cdot \begin{bmatrix} \dfrac{t}{2} + \dfrac{1}{4} \\ 1 \end{bmatrix}$$

$$22: \begin{bmatrix} t \\ 1 \end{bmatrix}$$

EXAMPLE 4.7 The differential equation $y''' + 2y'' + y' + 2y = \sin t$ can be changed by first making the substitutions $u_1 = y$, $u_2 = y'$, and $u_3 = y''$. With these substitutions $\dot{u}_1 = u_2$, $\dot{u}_2 = u_3$, and $\dot{u}_3 = -2y - y' - 2y'' + \sin t = -2u_1 - u_2 - 2u_3 + \sin t$. The first order system can thus be written as

$$\begin{bmatrix} \dot{u}_1 \\ \dot{u}_2 \\ \dot{u}_3 \end{bmatrix} = \begin{bmatrix} 0 & 1 & 0 \\ 0 & 0 & 1 \\ -2 & -1 & -2 \end{bmatrix} \begin{bmatrix} u_1 \\ u_2 \\ u_3 \end{bmatrix} + \begin{bmatrix} 0 \\ 0 \\ \sin t \end{bmatrix}$$

Next, the matrix $e^{t\mathbf{A}}$ can be found using *Derive*, and the matrix $e^{t\mathbf{A}}\int e^{-t\mathbf{A}}\mathbf{b}\,dt$ is given in statement #22:

$$\#22: \begin{bmatrix} \dfrac{(14-5\ t)\ \mathrm{SIN}(t)}{50} - \dfrac{(5\ t+1)\ \mathrm{COS}(t)}{25} \\ \dfrac{(4-5\ t)\ \mathrm{COS}(t)}{50} + \left[\dfrac{t}{5} - \dfrac{3}{50}\right] \mathrm{SIN}(t) \\ \dfrac{\mathrm{COS}(t)^3}{10} + \mathrm{COS}(t) \left[\dfrac{10\ t-3}{50} - \dfrac{\mathrm{SIN}(t)^2}{10}\right] + \left[\dfrac{t}{10} + \dfrac{3}{25}\right] \mathrm{SIN}(t) \end{bmatrix}$$

We leave as an exercise the verification that $\dot{\mathbf{p}} - \mathbf{Ap} = \mathbf{b}$.

EXERCISES

1. Write in matrix form:

   a) $\begin{cases} \dot{x}_1 = 2x_1 + 3x_2 \\ \dot{x}_2 = -3x_1 + x_2 \end{cases}$

   b) $\begin{cases} \dot{x}_1 = x_2 \\ \dot{x}_2 = x_1 \end{cases}$

   c) $\begin{cases} \dot{x}_1 = x_2 + x_3 + \cos t \\ \dot{x}_2 = x_1 + x_3 + \sin t \\ \dot{x}_3 = x_1 + x_2 + 1 \end{cases}$

   d) $\begin{cases} \ddot{x}_1 + \dot{x}_2 + x_1 + x_2 = \cos t \\ \ddot{x}_2 + \dot{x}_1 + \dot{x}_2 + x_2 = \sin t \end{cases}$

2. Find the general solution of $\dot{\mathbf{x}} = \mathbf{A}\mathbf{x}$ where

   a) $\mathbf{A} = \begin{bmatrix} 1 & 3 \\ -2 & -4 \end{bmatrix}$

   b) $\mathbf{A} = \begin{bmatrix} -7 & -10 \\ 5 & 7 \end{bmatrix}$

   c) $\mathbf{A} = \begin{bmatrix} -9 & -13 \\ 5 & 7 \end{bmatrix}$

   d) $\mathbf{A} = \begin{bmatrix} -3 & -4 \\ 1 & 1 \end{bmatrix}$

3. Find the general solution of $\dot{\mathbf{x}} = \mathbf{A}\mathbf{x}$ where

   a) $\mathbf{A} = \begin{bmatrix} -2 & -4 & -1 \\ 3 & 5 & 1 \\ 2 & 2 & 3 \end{bmatrix}$

   b) $\mathbf{A} = \begin{bmatrix} -3 & -4 & 0 \\ 2 & 3 & -1 \\ 1 & 2 & -1 \end{bmatrix}$

   c) $\mathbf{A} = \begin{bmatrix} 1 & 0 & 4 \\ 0 & 1 & -3 \\ 3 & 4 & 1 \end{bmatrix}$

   d) $\mathbf{A} = \begin{bmatrix} 7 & 6 & 10 \\ -7 & -6 & -10 \\ -3 & -2 & -5 \end{bmatrix}$

4. Find a particular solution for $\dot{\mathbf{x}} = \mathbf{A}\mathbf{x} + \mathbf{b}$ where $\mathbf{A}$ is as in Exercise 2 and $\mathbf{b}$ is given by

   a) $\mathbf{b} = \begin{bmatrix} 0 \\ 1 \end{bmatrix}$ b) $\mathbf{b} = \begin{bmatrix} \sin t \\ \cos t \end{bmatrix}$

   c) $\mathbf{b} = \begin{bmatrix} 1 \\ t \end{bmatrix}$ d) $\mathbf{b} = \begin{bmatrix} e^t \\ e^{-t} \end{bmatrix}$

5. Find a particular solution for $\mathbf{x} = \mathbf{A}\mathbf{x} + \mathbf{b}$ where $\mathbf{A}$ is as in Exercise 3 and $\mathbf{b}$ is given by

   a) $\mathbf{b} = \begin{bmatrix} 1 \\ t \\ t^2 \end{bmatrix}$ b) $\mathbf{b} = \begin{bmatrix} 1 \\ 0 \\ \sin t \end{bmatrix}$

   c) $\mathbf{b} = \begin{bmatrix} 1 \\ 1 \\ 1 \end{bmatrix}$ d) $\mathbf{b} = \begin{bmatrix} \cos t \\ 1 \\ \sin t \end{bmatrix}$

6. Transform the differential equation $\ddot{y} - 3\dot{y} + 2y = 0$ to a first order system and find the general solution. Show that the second component of the solution is the derivative of the first component. Explain.

7. Finish Example 4.7 by verifying $\dot{\mathbf{p}} - \mathbf{A}\mathbf{p} = \mathbf{b}$.

ANSWERS TO SELECTED EXERCISES

SECTION 1.2 ◆ PAGE 16

1. a) $\begin{bmatrix} 0 & 2 \\ 2 & 8 \end{bmatrix}$ b) $\begin{bmatrix} 2 & 2 \\ 4 & 0 \end{bmatrix}$ c) $\begin{bmatrix} 1 & 6 \\ 7 & 20 \end{bmatrix}$ d) $\begin{bmatrix} 4 & 8 \\ 8 & 8 \end{bmatrix}$

   e) $\begin{bmatrix} -1 & -2 \\ -3 & -4 \end{bmatrix}$ f) $\begin{bmatrix} 1 & 0 \\ 1 & -4 \end{bmatrix}$ g) $\begin{bmatrix} 0 & -2 \\ -2 & -8 \end{bmatrix}$ h) $\begin{bmatrix} -3 & -6 \\ -9 & -12 \end{bmatrix}$

2. a) **-A-B** b) $-\alpha\mathbf{A}$ c) $(-\mathbf{A})^{\mathrm{T}}$

   d) $-(\mathbf{A}+\mathbf{B}) = \begin{bmatrix} -6 & 7 & 1 & -2 \\ -4 & 0 & 2 & 1 \end{bmatrix}$; $-5\mathbf{A} = \begin{bmatrix} -15 & 10 & -30 & -10 \\ 0 & 5 & 35 & -40 \end{bmatrix}$;

   $$-\mathbf{A}^{\mathrm{T}} = \begin{bmatrix} -3 & 0 \\ 2 & 1 \\ -6 & 7 \\ -2 & -8 \end{bmatrix}$$

3. $\mathbf{X} = \begin{bmatrix} 0 & -3 & -1 \\ 2 & 4 & 6 \end{bmatrix}$

4. $\begin{bmatrix} 2 & 5 \\ 5 & 8 \end{bmatrix}$

5. The sum does not exist since the transpose of a 2×3 matrix is a 3×2 matrix and can not be added to a 2×3.

6. $\begin{bmatrix} -1 & 6 \\ 7 & 11 \end{bmatrix}$

SECTION 1.3 ◆ PAGE 25

1. a) $\begin{bmatrix} 3 & 1 & 3 & 2 & 2 \\ 1 & 2 & 2 & 0 & 1 \\ 1 & -3 & -1 & 2 & 0 \\ 6 & 2 & 6 & 4 & 4 \end{bmatrix}$ b) $\begin{bmatrix} 2 & 4 & 11 \\ 12 & 0 & 15 \end{bmatrix}$ c) Not defined

   d) $\begin{bmatrix} 8 & -1 & 2 & 13 \end{bmatrix}^{\mathrm{T}}$ e) Not defined f) $\begin{bmatrix} 42 & -50 & 21 & 32 & -6 \\ 12 & -7 & 11 & -36 & 20 \end{bmatrix}$

2. $\begin{bmatrix} x+2y+3z \\ 2x-y+2z \\ 2x+3y+z \end{bmatrix}$ 3. $\begin{bmatrix} 0 & 0 \\ 0 & 0 \end{bmatrix}$

4. $(\mathbf{AB})^T = \mathbf{B}^T\mathbf{A}^T = \begin{bmatrix} 0 & 4 & 2 \\ 0 & 2 & 1 \\ 1 & 2 & 0 \\ 1 & 6 & 2 \end{bmatrix}$ while $\mathbf{A}^T\mathbf{B}^T$ is not defined

SECTION 1.4 • PAGE 32

1. a) Does not exist b) Does not exist c) $\begin{bmatrix} 1/8 & 3/16 \\ -1/8 & 5/16 \end{bmatrix}$

d) Does not exist e) $\begin{bmatrix} 1/2 & -1/8 & -1/4 \\ -1/2 & 5/8 & 1/4 \\ 1/2 & 1/8 & -3/4 \end{bmatrix}$ f) Does not exist

g) $\frac{1}{329}\begin{bmatrix} -77 & 25 & -28 \\ 63 & 18 & -7 \\ 14 & 4 & 35 \end{bmatrix}$ h) $\frac{1}{1513}\begin{bmatrix} -21 & -18 & 245 & -41 \\ 390 & -98 & -11 & 113 \\ -264 & 206 & 54 & 133 \\ -41 & 181 & -26 & -8 \end{bmatrix}$

i) $\frac{1}{680}\begin{bmatrix} 32 & 334 & -674 & 784 & 250 \\ -88 & 144 & -144 & 224 & 120 \\ 120 & -830 & 1170 & -1480 & -210 \\ 4 & 63 & 107 & -72 & -75 \\ -8 & 44 & -44 & 144 & -20 \end{bmatrix}$

2. $(\mathbf{AB})^{-1} = \mathbf{B}^{-1}\mathbf{A}^{-1} = \frac{1}{3}\begin{bmatrix} 13 & -10 \\ -1 & 1 \end{bmatrix}$ 3. $(\mathbf{A}^T)^{-1} = (\mathbf{A}^{-1})^T = \frac{1}{2}\begin{bmatrix} 3 & -3 & 1 \\ 1 & 1 & -1 \\ -3 & 1 & 1 \end{bmatrix}$

4. $\mathbf{X} = \begin{bmatrix} 1 & 1 & 1 \\ 1 & 3 & 5 \\ 0 & -1 & -2 \end{bmatrix}$

SECTION 1.5 ◆PAGE 40

1. $\begin{bmatrix} 1 & 3 & 3 \\ 0 & -1 & 0 \\ 0 & -8 & -7 \end{bmatrix}$ All of the entries of column 1 below the first element are 0.

$$\begin{bmatrix} 1 & 0 & 0 \\ -1 & 1 & 0 \\ 0 & 0 & 1 \end{bmatrix}\begin{bmatrix} 1 & 0 & 0 \\ 0 & 1 & 0 \\ -3 & 0 & 1 \end{bmatrix}$$

2. $\begin{bmatrix} 1 & 0 & 0 \\ 1 & 1 & 0 \\ 3 & 0 & 1 \end{bmatrix}$

3. $\mathbf{E} = \begin{bmatrix} 0 & 1 & 0 \\ 0 & 0 & 1 \\ 1 & 0 & 0 \end{bmatrix}, \quad \mathbf{E}^{-1} = \begin{bmatrix} 0 & 0 & 1 \\ 1 & 0 & 0 \\ 0 & 1 & 0 \end{bmatrix}$

4. $\mathbf{E} = \begin{bmatrix} 1 & 0 \\ -1 & 1 \end{bmatrix}$, and $x = 2$.

5. By interchanging columns 3 and 1 and then interchanging columns 1 and 2 we obtain

$$\mathbf{E} = \begin{bmatrix} 0 & 1 & 0 \\ 1 & 0 & 0 \\ 0 & 0 & 1 \end{bmatrix}\begin{bmatrix} 0 & 0 & 1 \\ 0 & 1 & 0 \\ 1 & 0 & 0 \end{bmatrix} = \begin{bmatrix} 0 & 1 & 0 \\ 0 & 0 & 1 \\ 1 & 0 & 0 \end{bmatrix}, \ \mathbf{E}^{-1} = \begin{bmatrix} 0 & 0 & 1 \\ 0 & 1 & 0 \\ 1 & 0 & 0 \end{bmatrix}\begin{bmatrix} 0 & 1 & 0 \\ 1 & 0 & 0 \\ 0 & 0 & 1 \end{bmatrix} = \begin{bmatrix} 0 & 0 & 1 \\ 1 & 0 & 0 \\ 0 & 1 & 0 \end{bmatrix}$$

Note that the inverse is obtained by taking the interchanges in reverse order.

6.

$$\begin{bmatrix} 1 & 0 & 0 & 0 \\ 0 & 1 & 0 & 0 \\ 0 & 0 & 1 & 0 \\ 0 & 0 & 0 & 1/2 \end{bmatrix}\begin{bmatrix} 1 & 0 & 0 & 0 \\ 0 & 1 & 0 & 0 \\ 0 & -1 & 1 & 0 \\ 0 & -1 & 0 & 1 \end{bmatrix}\begin{bmatrix} 1 & 0 & 0 & 0 \\ 0 & 1/3 & 0 & 0 \\ 0 & 0 & 1 & 0 \\ 0 & 0 & 0 & 1 \end{bmatrix}\begin{bmatrix} 1 & 0 & 0 & 0 \\ -1 & 1 & 0 & 0 \\ 0 & 0 & 1 & 0 \\ -2 & 0 & 0 & 1 \end{bmatrix}\begin{bmatrix} 1/2 & 0 & 0 & 0 \\ 0 & 1 & 0 & 0 \\ 0 & 0 & 1 & 0 \\ 0 & 0 & 0 & 1 \end{bmatrix}\begin{bmatrix} 2 & 4 & 6 & 2 \\ 1 & 5 & 3 & 4 \\ 0 & 1 & 1 & 4 \\ 2 & 5 & 6 & 5 \end{bmatrix} =$$

$$\begin{bmatrix} 1 & 2 & 3 & 1 \\ 0 & 1 & 0 & 1 \\ 0 & 0 & 1 & 3 \\ 0 & 0 & 0 & 1 \end{bmatrix}$$

$$\begin{bmatrix}2&0&0&0\\0&1&0&0\\0&0&1&0\\0&0&0&1\end{bmatrix}\begin{bmatrix}1&0&0&0\\1&1&0&0\\0&0&1&0\\2&0&0&1\end{bmatrix}\begin{bmatrix}1&0&0&0\\0&3&0&0\\0&0&1&0\\0&0&0&1\end{bmatrix}\begin{bmatrix}1&0&0&0\\0&1&0&0\\0&1&1&0\\0&1&0&1\end{bmatrix}\begin{bmatrix}1&0&0&0\\0&1&0&0\\0&0&1&0\\0&0&0&2\end{bmatrix}\begin{bmatrix}1&2&3&1\\0&1&0&1\\0&0&1&3\\0&0&0&1\end{bmatrix}=\mathbf{A}$$

$$\begin{bmatrix}2&0&0&0\\1&3&0&0\\0&1&1&0\\2&1&0&2\end{bmatrix}\begin{bmatrix}1&2&3&1\\0&1&0&1\\0&0&1&3\\0&0&0&1\end{bmatrix}=\mathbf{A}$$

7.

$$\begin{bmatrix}3&0&0&0\\1&2&0&0\\4&2&2&0\\0&0&1&1\end{bmatrix}\begin{bmatrix}1&2&4&3\\0&1&0&3\\0&0&1&3\\0&0&0&1\end{bmatrix}=\mathbf{A}$$

SECTION 1.6 • PAGE 52

1. a) $x=-2,\quad y=2$ b) $x=2,\quad y=-1$ c) No solution

2. a) $x=21,\quad y=69,\quad z=-43$ b) No solution c) $x=0,\quad y=0,\quad z=1$

3. a) $\left\{\begin{matrix}x+2y=4\\3x+4y=5\end{matrix}\right\}$ $x=-3,\quad y=7/2$.

   b) $\left\{\begin{matrix}x+3y+5z=7\\2x+4y+6z=8\\3x+5y+7z=9\end{matrix}\right\}$ $z=\alpha$ where α is arbitrary,

   $y=3-2\alpha$, and $x=-2+\alpha$.

   c) $\left\{\begin{matrix}x+y+2z=3\\2x+2y+3z=5\\3x+3y+4z=8\end{matrix}\right\}$ No solution.

4. Set up $\begin{bmatrix}2&3&2&1&4\\4&1&8&2&7\end{bmatrix}$ and reduce to $\begin{bmatrix}1&0&11/5&1/2&17/10\\0&1&-4/5&0&1/5\end{bmatrix}$ giving the solutions: a) $x=11/5,\quad y=-4/5$ b) $x=1/2\quad y=0$ c) $x=17/10,\quad y=1/5$.

8. The matrix factors so the system may be written as:

$$\begin{bmatrix} 2 & 0 & 0 & 0 \\ 1 & 3 & 0 & 0 \\ 0 & 1 & 1 & 0 \\ 2 & 1 & 0 & 2 \end{bmatrix}\begin{bmatrix} 1 & 2 & 3 & 1 \\ 0 & 1 & 0 & 1 \\ 0 & 0 & 1 & 3 \\ 0 & 0 & 0 & 1 \end{bmatrix}\begin{bmatrix} x_1 \\ x_2 \\ x_3 \\ x_4 \end{bmatrix} = \begin{bmatrix} 2 \\ 2 \\ 1 \\ 3 \end{bmatrix}$$

set

$$\begin{bmatrix} 1 & 2 & 3 & 1 \\ 0 & 1 & 0 & 1 \\ 0 & 0 & 1 & 3 \\ 0 & 0 & 0 & 1 \end{bmatrix}\begin{bmatrix} x_1 \\ x_2 \\ x_3 \\ x_4 \end{bmatrix} = \begin{bmatrix} z_1 \\ z_2 \\ z_3 \\ z_4 \end{bmatrix}$$

and solve

$$\begin{bmatrix} 2 & 0 & 0 & 0 \\ 1 & 3 & 0 & 0 \\ 0 & 1 & 1 & 0 \\ 2 & 1 & 0 & 2 \end{bmatrix}\begin{bmatrix} z_1 \\ z_2 \\ z_3 \\ z_4 \end{bmatrix} = \begin{bmatrix} 2 \\ 2 \\ 1 \\ 3 \end{bmatrix}$$

to obtain $z_1 = 1$, $z_2 = 1/3$, $z_3 = 2/3$, and $z_4 = 1/3$. Thus

$$\begin{bmatrix} 1 & 2 & 3 & 1 \\ 0 & 1 & 0 & 1 \\ 0 & 0 & 1 & 3 \\ 0 & 0 & 0 & 1 \end{bmatrix}\begin{bmatrix} x_1 \\ x_2 \\ x_3 \\ x_4 \end{bmatrix} = \begin{bmatrix} 1 \\ 1/3 \\ 2/3 \\ 1/3 \end{bmatrix}$$

giving $x_1 = 5/3$, $x_2 = 0$, $x_3 = -1/3$, and $x_4 = 1/3$.

9. $x_1 = 143/3$, $x_2 = -49/3$, $x_3 = -10$, and $x_4 = 3$.

SECTION 1.7 ◆ PAGE 61

1. a) $x = 1$, $y = 0$ b) No solution c) $y = \alpha$(arbitrary), $x = 2 + \alpha$
   d) $x = -2$, $y = 3$, $z = 2$
   e) $z = \alpha$ (arbitrary), $y = -1/3 - 1/3\,\alpha$, $x = 5/3 + 2/3\,\alpha$
   f) No solution g) $x = -1$, $y = -2$, $z = 8$, and $w = -3$
   h) No solution i) No solution
   j) $z = \alpha$ (arbitrary), $y = -13/17 + 8/17\,\alpha$, and $x = 11/17 + 5/17\,\alpha$
   k) $w = \alpha$ (arbitrary), $y = -3 + 4\alpha$, and $x = 5/2 + 3/2\,\alpha$
   l) No solution

2.
$$\begin{bmatrix} 1 & 0 & 0 & 1 \\ 0 & 1 & 0 & 2 \\ 0 & 0 & 1 & -4 \end{bmatrix}$$

3. Reduce $\begin{bmatrix} 1 & 2 & 3 & 8 \\ 3 & 1 & 1 & 1 \end{bmatrix}$ to $\begin{bmatrix} 1 & 0 & -1/5 & -6/5 \\ 0 & 1 & 8/5 & 23/5 \end{bmatrix}$ and obtain the solutions
a) $x = -1/5, \quad y = 8/5$ and b) $x = -6/5, \quad y = 23/5$

4. $4 - 4\xi$ must equal zero (use elementary matrices) in which case $\xi = 1$. In this case $y = \alpha$ (arbitrary) and $x = 1 - 3\alpha$.

5. The vector form is: $[x \quad y \quad z] = [2 \quad 1 \quad 0] + t[1 \quad -2 \quad 1]$.

6. There is no solution to the pair of equations.

7. The line common to all three planes is
$[x \quad y \quad z] = [3/4 \quad 1/2 \quad 0] + t[1/4 \quad 1/2 \quad 1]$

8. The two equations have no common points.

9. $(-71/42 \quad -83/42 \quad -5/42)$

10. The general solution is: $x_7 = \alpha, \quad x_6 = 1 - 2\alpha, \quad x_5 = \beta, \quad x_4 = 1 - 3\alpha - 2\beta,$
$x_2 = \gamma, \quad x_1 = 2 - \alpha - 2\gamma$

SECTION 2.1 • PAGE 73

5. The most general 2×2 matrix is $\begin{bmatrix} a & b \\ c & d \end{bmatrix}$. Set up the equation
$\begin{bmatrix} 0 & 1 \\ 1 & 0 \end{bmatrix}\begin{bmatrix} a & b \\ c & d \end{bmatrix} = \begin{bmatrix} a & b \\ c & d \end{bmatrix}\begin{bmatrix} 0 & 1 \\ 1 & 0 \end{bmatrix}$, which implies $a = d$ and $b = c$ so the most general matrix which commutes with the given matrix is $\begin{bmatrix} a & b \\ b & a \end{bmatrix}$. We must go on to show that a matrix of this form satisfies the axioms for a vector space.

6. No matrix commutes with the given matrix. Thus the set is empty and is therefore not a vector space.

7. There are no such matrices since **AT** is a 2×3 and $\mathbf{T}^T\mathbf{A}^T$ is a 3×2 so that the two matrices cannot be equal. The matrix **B** can not be a member of this set since it is empty.

8. The set of 3×1 matrices of the form $\begin{bmatrix} -2a & 0 & a \end{bmatrix}^T$ where a is arbitrary satisfies the condition. It must be shown that matrices of this form satisfy the axioms of a vector space.

9. There is no matrix **Y** which satisfies this condition so that Y is the empty set and does not form a vector space.

10. No. Axiom 6 is not satisfied. 11. Yes. 12. Yes.

13. Yes. 14. No. In fact, F does not contain the zero function.

SECTION 2.2 ◆ PAGE 83

1. c) The set contains only the matrix $\begin{bmatrix} 0 & 0 & 0 \end{bmatrix}$ and is a subspace.
   d) The set contains matrices of the form $\begin{bmatrix} \frac{-2\beta - \alpha}{3} & \beta & \alpha \end{bmatrix}$ where α and β are arbitrary. We must show that the set satisfies the conditions of Theorem 2.2.
   e) Matrices of the form $\begin{bmatrix} a & b \\ b & \frac{2a-3b}{2} \end{bmatrix}$, where a and b are arbitrary satisfy the condition. We must show that matrices if this type satisfy Theorem 2.2.

2. a) The set does not contain the zero matrix.
   b) The only matrix that satisfies this condition is $\begin{bmatrix} 1/2 & 1/2 & 1/2 \end{bmatrix}$. The set does not contain the zero, or is not closed with respect to addition or multiplication by a scalar.
   c) Matrices which satisfy this condition have the form $\begin{bmatrix} \frac{1-2a-2b}{3} & b & a \end{bmatrix}$ where a and b are arbitrary but nonzero.
   d) The set does not include the zero vector (function).

SECTION 2.3 ◆ PAGE 91

1. b) $a(x^2 + x) + b(x+1) + c(x^2 + 1) = 0$ implies $(a+c)x^2 + (a+b)x + b + c = 0$ which, in turn implies, $a = 0$, $b = 0$, and

$c = 0$. Which means the vectors are linearly independent.

5. $a(x^3 + x^2) + bx + c(x^2 + x) + d = x^3 + 2x^2 + 3x + 4$ implies
$ax^3 + (a + c)x^2 + (b + c)x + d = x^3 + 2x^2 + 3x + 4$ which implies
$a = 1,\ a + c = 2,\ a + b = 3,$ and $d = 4$. Thus $a = 1,\ b = 2,\ c = 1,$ and $d = 4$.

6. In the representation
$$a\begin{bmatrix}1 & 0\\0 & 0\end{bmatrix} + b\begin{bmatrix}0 & 1\\0 & 0\end{bmatrix} + c\begin{bmatrix}0 & 0\\1 & 0\end{bmatrix} + d\begin{bmatrix}0 & 0\\0 & 1\end{bmatrix} + e\begin{bmatrix}1 & 1\\1 & 1\end{bmatrix} = \begin{bmatrix}1 & 2\\3 & 4\end{bmatrix}$$
$a = 1 - \alpha,\ b = 2 - \alpha,\ c = 3 - \alpha,\ d = 4 - \alpha$ and $e = \alpha$ where α is arbitrary.
The representation is not unique.

SECTION 2.4 ◆ PAGE 100

1. Yes

2. Yes. In $a\begin{bmatrix}2 & 1\\1 & 1\end{bmatrix} + b\begin{bmatrix}2 & 2\\1 & 1\end{bmatrix} + c\begin{bmatrix}2 & 2\\2 & 1\end{bmatrix} + d\begin{bmatrix}2 & 2\\2 & 2\end{bmatrix} = \begin{bmatrix}1 & 2\\1 & 3\end{bmatrix}$ $a = -1,\ b = 1,$
$c = -2$, and $d = 5/2$.

3. Yes. $0(x^3 + 1) - 1(x^2 + 1) + 1(x + 1) + 1(x^3 + x^2 + x + 1) = x^3 + 2x + 1$

4. Yes. In $a\begin{bmatrix}1\\2\\3\end{bmatrix} + b\begin{bmatrix}0\\0\\1\end{bmatrix} = \begin{bmatrix}1\\2\\1\end{bmatrix}$ $a = 1$ and $b = -2$

5. The most general vector in R^2 is $\begin{bmatrix}p\\q\end{bmatrix}$ solve $a\begin{bmatrix}\pi\\e\end{bmatrix} + b\begin{bmatrix}1\\1\end{bmatrix} = \begin{bmatrix}p\\q\end{bmatrix}$ for a and b
in terms of p and q and find $a = \dfrac{p - q}{\pi - e}$ and $b = \dfrac{ep - \pi q}{e - \pi}$.

6. The most general matrix contained in the set is $\begin{bmatrix}p & q\\r & -p\end{bmatrix}$ and
$$p\begin{bmatrix}1 & 0\\0 & -1\end{bmatrix} + q\begin{bmatrix}0 & 1\\0 & 0\end{bmatrix} + r\begin{bmatrix}0 & 0\\1 & 0\end{bmatrix} = \begin{bmatrix}p & q\\r & -p\end{bmatrix}$$

7. The most general symmetric matrix in $M_{2\times2}$ is $\begin{bmatrix}p & q\\q & r\end{bmatrix}$ and

$$p\begin{bmatrix}1 & 0\\0 & 0\end{bmatrix}+q\begin{bmatrix}0 & 1\\1 & 0\end{bmatrix}+r\begin{bmatrix}0 & 0\\0 & 1\end{bmatrix}=\begin{bmatrix}p & q\\q & r\end{bmatrix}$$

8. $\begin{bmatrix}a+b+2c\\a+2c\\0\end{bmatrix}$ where a, b, and c are arbitrary.

9. Vectors of the form $ax^2+bx+a+b=\text{SPAN}(S)$. There are many choices x^2+x+2 and x^2+1 are in SPAN(S) and x^2+x is not.

10. It is easy to show that any element in SPAN(S) has the form $\begin{bmatrix}p & q\\q & r\end{bmatrix}$ where p, q, and r are arbitrary. Solve for a, b, and c in $a\begin{bmatrix}1 & 1\\1 & 0\end{bmatrix}+b\begin{bmatrix}0 & 1\\1 & 1\end{bmatrix}+c\begin{bmatrix}0 & 2\\2 & 0\end{bmatrix}=\begin{bmatrix}p & q\\q & r\end{bmatrix}$ to obtain $a=p$, $b=r$, and $c=-\dfrac{p-q+r}{2}$.

SECTION 2.5 • PAGE 109

1. $a\begin{bmatrix}0\\-2\\1\\0\end{bmatrix}+b\begin{bmatrix}-2\\-1\\0\\2\end{bmatrix}=\begin{bmatrix}0\\0\\0\\0\end{bmatrix}$ implies $a=0$ and $b=0$.

2. a) $\begin{bmatrix}1\\-1\end{bmatrix}$ b) The only solution is $x_1=0$ and $x_2=0$. c) $\begin{bmatrix}3\\-2\\1\end{bmatrix}$

d) $\begin{bmatrix}0\\1\\1\end{bmatrix}$ e) $\begin{bmatrix}-3\\2\\-1\\1\end{bmatrix}$ f) $\left\{\begin{bmatrix}-3\\0\\1\\0\\1\end{bmatrix},\begin{bmatrix}3\\0\\-2\\1\\0\end{bmatrix},\begin{bmatrix}-3\\1\\0\\0\\0\end{bmatrix}\right\}$

3. $\left\{\begin{bmatrix}1 & 0\\0 & 1\end{bmatrix},\begin{bmatrix}-1 & 1\\2 & 0\end{bmatrix}\right\}$

4. No. Yes. One such vector is $\begin{bmatrix}0\\0\\1\end{bmatrix}$.

5. The first three vectors are linearly independent, but all four vectors are not. The dimension is therefore 3. Yes.

9. A basis for $U \cap V$ is $\left\{ \begin{bmatrix} 1 \\ 0 \\ 1 \\ 0 \end{bmatrix}, \begin{bmatrix} 0 \\ 1 \\ 0 \\ 0 \end{bmatrix} \right\}$.

10. A basis is $\left\{ \begin{bmatrix} 0 & 1 \\ 1 & 0 \end{bmatrix} \right\}$

11. A basis is $\left\{ \begin{bmatrix} 1 & 0 \\ 0 & -1 \end{bmatrix}, \begin{bmatrix} 0 & 1 \\ 1 & 0 \end{bmatrix} \right\}$

SECTION 3.1 ◆ PAGE 121

4. $\begin{bmatrix} 4 \\ 7 \end{bmatrix}$

5. a) $\mathbf{t}\begin{bmatrix} a \\ b \end{bmatrix} = \begin{bmatrix} a+2b \\ a+2b \end{bmatrix}$ b) $\mathbf{t}\begin{bmatrix} a \\ b \end{bmatrix} = \begin{bmatrix} 3b-a \\ b \end{bmatrix}$

c) $\mathbf{t}\begin{bmatrix} a & b \\ c & d \end{bmatrix} = \begin{bmatrix} a+b \\ c+d \end{bmatrix}$ d) $\mathbf{t}(ax^2+bx+c) = (a+c)x^2 + (b+c)x + (a+b)1$

6. Yes $\begin{bmatrix} 1 & 2 \\ c & 4 \end{bmatrix}$ where c is arbitrary.

7. $\begin{bmatrix} 6 & 7 & 6 \\ 9 & 10 & 9 \end{bmatrix}$

8. **t** is not linear. $\begin{bmatrix} a^2 & ab & ac \\ ab & b^2 & bc \\ ac & bc & c^2 \end{bmatrix}$

9. **t** is not linear. $a^2+b^2+c^2$

10. **t** is not linear. $\begin{bmatrix} a^2+c^2 & ab+cd \\ ab+cd & b^2+d^2 \end{bmatrix}$

SECTION 3.2 ◆ PAGE 136

1. a) i) $\begin{bmatrix} 1 \\ 2 \\ 3 \end{bmatrix}$ ii) $\left\{ \begin{bmatrix} -1 \\ 1 \\ 0 \end{bmatrix}, \begin{bmatrix} 0 \\ 0 \\ 1 \end{bmatrix} \right\}$ iii) 2 iv) 1

v) Not one to one vi) Not onto

b) i) $\left\{\begin{bmatrix}1 & 1\\1 & 1\end{bmatrix},\begin{bmatrix}0 & 1\\1 & 1\end{bmatrix},\begin{bmatrix}0 & 0\\1 & 1\end{bmatrix},\begin{bmatrix}0 & 0\\0 & 1\end{bmatrix}\right\}$ ii) KER($\mathbf{t}$) = $\mathbf{0}$ iii) 0

iv) 4 v) yes; one-to-one vi) yes; onto

c) i) $\left\{\begin{bmatrix}1 & 0\\1 & 0\end{bmatrix},\begin{bmatrix}0 & 0\\1 & 1\end{bmatrix}\right\}$ ii) KER($\mathbf{t}$) = $\mathbf{0}$ iii) 0

iv) 2 v) yes; one-to-one vi) Not onto

d) i) $\{1\}$ ii) $\left\{\begin{bmatrix}0&1&0\\0&0&0\\0&0&0\end{bmatrix},\begin{bmatrix}0&0&1\\0&0&0\\0&0&0\end{bmatrix},\begin{bmatrix}0&0&0\\1&0&0\\0&0&0\end{bmatrix},\begin{bmatrix}0&0&0\\0&0&1\\0&0&0\end{bmatrix},\begin{bmatrix}0&0&0\\0&0&0\\1&0&0\end{bmatrix},\begin{bmatrix}0&0&0\\0&0&0\\0&1&0\end{bmatrix}\right\}$

iii) 6 iv) 1 v) Not one-to-one vi) yes; onto

e) i) $\left\{\begin{bmatrix}1\\1\\0\end{bmatrix},\begin{bmatrix}0\\0\\1\end{bmatrix}\right\}$ ii) KER($\mathbf{t}$) = $\mathbf{0}$. iii) 0

iv) 2 v) Yes; one-to-one vi) Not onto

f) i) $\left\{\begin{bmatrix}1\\0\end{bmatrix},\begin{bmatrix}0\\1\end{bmatrix}\right\}$ ii) $\begin{bmatrix}1\\-1\\1\end{bmatrix}$ iii) 1

iv) 2 v) Not one-to-one vi) yes; onto

g) i) $\{x^3, x^2, x, 1\}$ ii) KER($\mathbf{t}$) = 1 iii) 1

iv) 4 v) Not one-to-one vi) Yes; onto

2. a) i) $\left\{\begin{bmatrix}1\\1\\0\end{bmatrix},\begin{bmatrix}0\\1\\1\end{bmatrix}\right\}$ ii) KER($\mathbf{t}$) = $\mathbf{0}$ iii) 0

iv) 2 v) $\mathbf{t}$ is one-to-one vi) $\mathbf{t}$ is not onto

b) i) $\left\{\begin{bmatrix}1 & 2\\2 & 1\end{bmatrix},\begin{bmatrix}1 & 0\\0 & 1\end{bmatrix}\right\}$ ii) KER($\mathbf{t}$) = $\mathbf{0}$ iii) 0

iv) 2 v) $\mathbf{t}$ is one to one vi) $\mathbf{t}$ is not onto

c) i) The vectors x^2+2, x^2+x, $x+1$, and x^2+1 span IM(**t**) but are not linearly independent, howver x^2+2, x^2+x, $x+1$ are linearly independent and form a basis for IM(**t**)

ii) KER(**t**) = **0** iii) 0 iv) 3

v) **t** is one to one vi) **t** is not onto.

d) i) $\left\{\begin{bmatrix}1\\0\end{bmatrix},\begin{bmatrix}2\\1\end{bmatrix}\right\}$ ii) $\left\{\begin{bmatrix}1 & -1\\0 & 0\end{bmatrix},\begin{bmatrix}0 & 0\\1 & -1\end{bmatrix}\right\}$ iii) 2

iv) 2 v) **t** is not one to one vi) **t** is onto

3. Add $\left\{\begin{bmatrix}1 & 0\\0 & 0\end{bmatrix},\begin{bmatrix}0 & 1\\0 & 0\end{bmatrix}\right\}$ Note that there many choices.

4. $\begin{bmatrix}6/5 & 18/5 & 18/5 & 6/5\end{bmatrix}^T$, $\begin{bmatrix}6/5 & 6/5\end{bmatrix}^T$

5. The element itself which is $\mathbf{t}\begin{bmatrix}2\\1\end{bmatrix}$

6. $\begin{bmatrix}1 & 0\\0 & 4\end{bmatrix}$

7. If the basis for P^{n-1} is taken to be $\{1, x, x^2, \cdots, x^{n-1}\}$ there is no element that maps into 1. A basis for IM(**t**) is $\{x, x^2, \cdots, x^n\}$. KER(**t**) = 0 since $\int_0^x 0\,dx = 0$.

SECTION 3.3 ◆ PAGE 149

1. $(-1 \quad 3 \quad 0 \quad 2)^T$

2. $(-2/3 \quad 1/3 \quad -5/3 \quad 10/3)^T$

3. $\begin{pmatrix}1\\0\\0\\0\end{pmatrix},\begin{pmatrix}-1\\0\\1\\0\end{pmatrix}$, and $\begin{pmatrix}-1\\1\\-1\\1\end{pmatrix}$

4. $\mathbf{P}^{\sigma}_{\beta} = \begin{bmatrix}1 & -1 & 0 & 0\\0 & 1 & -1 & 0\\0 & 0 & 1 & -1\\0 & 0 & 0 & 1\end{bmatrix}$ and $\mathbf{P}^{\beta}_{\sigma} = \begin{bmatrix}1 & 1 & 1 & 1\\0 & 1 & 1 & 1\\0 & 0 & 1 & 1\\0 & 0 & 0 & 1\end{bmatrix}$.
The product of these two matrices is the identity.

5. $\mathbf{P}_{\gamma}^{\beta} = \begin{bmatrix} -1 & 1 \\ 2 & 1 \end{bmatrix}$, $\mathbf{P}_{\beta}^{\gamma} = \begin{bmatrix} -1/3 & 1/3 \\ 2/3 & 1/3 \end{bmatrix}$. The product of these two matrices is the identity. $\begin{bmatrix} 4 \\ 5 \end{bmatrix}_{\beta} = \begin{pmatrix} -1 \\ 5 \end{pmatrix}$ $\begin{bmatrix} 4 \\ 5 \end{bmatrix}_{\gamma} = \begin{pmatrix} 2 \\ 1 \end{pmatrix}$ Also note $\begin{bmatrix} -1 & 1 \\ 2 & 1 \end{bmatrix}\begin{pmatrix} 2 \\ 1 \end{pmatrix} = \begin{pmatrix} -1 \\ 5 \end{pmatrix}$ and $\begin{bmatrix} -1/3 & 1/3 \\ 2/3 & 1/3 \end{bmatrix}\begin{pmatrix} -1 \\ 5 \end{pmatrix} = \begin{pmatrix} 2 \\ 1 \end{pmatrix}$.

6. $\mathbf{P}_{\gamma}^{\beta} = \mathbf{P}_{\beta}^{\gamma} = \begin{bmatrix} 0 & 0 & 1 \\ 0 & 1 & 0 \\ 1 & 0 & 0 \end{bmatrix}$, $\begin{bmatrix} 2 \\ -1 \\ 3 \end{bmatrix}_{\beta} = \begin{pmatrix} 2 \\ -1 \\ 3 \end{pmatrix}$, $\begin{bmatrix} 2 \\ -1 \\ 3 \end{bmatrix}_{\gamma} = \begin{pmatrix} 3 \\ -1 \\ 2 \end{pmatrix}$

8. $\mathbf{P}_{\beta}^{\gamma} = \begin{bmatrix} -1 & 1 & 0 & 0 \\ 0 & -1 & 1 & 0 \\ 0 & 0 & -1 & 1 \\ 1 & 1 & 1 & 0 \end{bmatrix}$ $\mathbf{A}_{\beta} = \begin{pmatrix} 7/3 \\ 4/3 \\ 1/3 \\ -2/3 \end{pmatrix}$ $\mathbf{A}_{\gamma} = \begin{pmatrix} -1 \\ -1 \\ -1 \\ 4 \end{pmatrix}$ Note $\mathbf{P}_{\beta}^{\gamma}\mathbf{A}_{\beta} = \mathbf{A}_{\gamma}$

SECTION 3.4 • PAGE 160

1. a) $\begin{bmatrix} 0 & 0 & 1 \\ 0 & 1 & 1 \\ 1 & 1 & 0 \end{bmatrix}$ b) $\frac{1}{2}\begin{bmatrix} -5 & 3 & 3 \\ 3 & -1 & -1 \\ 5 & -3 & 1 \end{bmatrix}$ c) $\begin{bmatrix} -1 & -1 & 2 \\ 1 & 2 & 0 \\ 0 & 0 & 1 \end{bmatrix}$ d) $\begin{bmatrix} 0 & 1 & 1 \\ 2 & 1 & 1 \\ 3 & 1 & 0 \end{bmatrix}$

2. a) $\begin{bmatrix} 1 & 0 & 0 & 0 \\ 1 & 1 & 0 & 0 \\ 0 & 0 & 1 & 1 \\ 0 & 0 & 0 & 1 \end{bmatrix}$ b) $\begin{bmatrix} 0 & 1 & 1 & 1 \\ 1 & 1 & 2 & 2 \\ 2 & 2 & 1 & 1 \\ -2 & -3 & -3 & -4 \end{bmatrix}$

c) $\begin{bmatrix} 1 & 0 & 1/2 & 1/2 \\ 0 & 1 & 1/2 & 1/2 \\ 1 & 0 & 0 & 1 \\ 0 & 0 & 1/2 & -1/2 \end{bmatrix}$ d) $\begin{bmatrix} -2 & -3 & 0 & -2 \\ 4 & 0 & -4 & 0 \\ 1 & 2 & 3 & 0 \\ 0 & 1 & 2 & 3 \end{bmatrix}$

3. $\begin{bmatrix} 2/3 & 2/3 & 1 \\ 2/3 & 2/3 & 1 \end{bmatrix}$ 4. $\begin{bmatrix} 1 & 2 & 3 \end{bmatrix}$ 5. $\begin{bmatrix} 2 & 1 \\ 0 & 3 \\ 0 & -3 \\ 1 & 2 \end{bmatrix}$

6. $\begin{bmatrix} 4 & 0 & 0 & 0 & 0 \\ 0 & 3 & 0 & 0 & 0 \\ 0 & 0 & 2 & 0 & 0 \\ 0 & 0 & 0 & 1 & 0 \end{bmatrix}$

7. $\begin{bmatrix} 1 & 0 & 0 & 0 \\ 0 & 0 & 1 & 0 \\ 0 & 1 & 0 & 0 \\ 0 & 0 & 0 & 1 \end{bmatrix}$

8. $\begin{bmatrix} 1 & 0 & 0 & 1 \end{bmatrix}$

9. $\mathbf{t}\begin{bmatrix} x \\ y \\ z \end{bmatrix} = \begin{bmatrix} 2x+z \\ 3x+2y+z \\ x-y+z \end{bmatrix}$

10. $\mathbf{t}\begin{bmatrix} x \\ y \\ z \end{bmatrix} = \begin{bmatrix} x+y \\ x+z \\ y+z \end{bmatrix}$

11. $\mathbf{t}(ax^3+bx^2+cx+d) =$
$(2a+c-d)x^3+bx^2+(-a+2b+2c+3d)x+a-b$

12. $\begin{bmatrix} 2 & 4 \\ 2 & 3 \\ -2 & -4 \end{bmatrix}$

13. a) $\begin{bmatrix} 1 & 0 & 0 & 1 \\ 0 & 1 & 1 & 0 \\ 1 & 1 & 0 & 0 \\ 0 & 0 & 1 & 1 \end{bmatrix}$ b) $\begin{bmatrix} 1 & 2 & 2 & 1 \\ 2 & 1 & 1 & 2 \\ 1 & 1 & 2 & 2 \\ 2 & 2 & 1 & 1 \end{bmatrix}$

c) $\begin{bmatrix} 1 & 0 & 0 & 1 \\ 0 & 1 & 1 & 0 \\ 1 & 0 & -1 & 0 \\ -1 & 0 & 1 & 0 \end{bmatrix}$ d) $\begin{bmatrix} 1 & 2 & 2 & 1 \\ 2 & 1 & 1 & 2 \\ -1 & 0 & 1 & 0 \\ 1 & 0 & -1 & 0 \end{bmatrix}$

14. $\frac{1}{4}\begin{bmatrix} 1 & 0 & -1 \\ 1 & 0 & 7 \\ 5 & 1 & -1 \end{bmatrix}$

SECTION 3.5 • PAGE 173

1. a) $\mathbf{st}\begin{bmatrix} a \\ b \end{bmatrix} = \begin{bmatrix} a \\ 2a+b \\ a+2b \\ b \end{bmatrix}$ $[\mathbf{st}]_\alpha^\gamma = \begin{bmatrix} 1 & 1 \\ 2 & 1 \\ 1 & 0 \\ 0 & 0 \end{bmatrix}$ $[\mathbf{t}]_\alpha^\beta = \begin{bmatrix} 1 & 0 \\ 0 & 0 \\ 1 & 1 \end{bmatrix}$

$[\mathbf{s}]_\beta^\gamma = \begin{bmatrix} 0 & 1 & 1 \\ 1 & 0 & 1 \\ 1 & 1 & 0 \\ 0 & 0 & 0 \end{bmatrix}$ $\begin{bmatrix} 0 & 1 & 1 \\ 1 & 0 & 1 \\ 1 & 1 & 0 \\ 0 & 0 & 0 \end{bmatrix}\begin{bmatrix} 1 & 0 \\ 0 & 0 \\ 1 & 1 \end{bmatrix} = \begin{bmatrix} 1 & 1 \\ 2 & 1 \\ 1 & 0 \\ 0 & 0 \end{bmatrix}$

b) $\mathbf{t}\begin{bmatrix} a \\ b \end{bmatrix} = \begin{bmatrix} a+b \\ a \\ a-b \end{bmatrix}$ $\qquad$ $\mathbf{s}\begin{bmatrix} x \\ y \\ z \end{bmatrix} = \begin{bmatrix} -\dfrac{x-y-3z}{2} \\ y \\ x \\ y \end{bmatrix}$

$$\mathbf{st}\begin{bmatrix} a \\ b \end{bmatrix} = \begin{bmatrix} \dfrac{3a-4b}{2} \\ a \\ a+b \\ a \end{bmatrix} \qquad [\mathbf{st}]_{\alpha}^{\gamma} = \begin{bmatrix} 0 & 1 \\ 3/2 & -1/2 \\ 1 & 1 \\ -1/2 & 1/2 \end{bmatrix}$$

$$[\mathbf{t}]_{\alpha}^{\beta} = \frac{1}{2}\begin{bmatrix} -1 & 1 \\ 1 & 1 \\ 3 & 1 \end{bmatrix} \qquad [\mathbf{s}]_{\beta}^{\gamma} = \begin{bmatrix} 2 & -1 & 1 \\ -1 & -1 & 1 \\ 1 & 0 & 1 \\ 0 & 2 & -1 \end{bmatrix}$$

$$\begin{bmatrix} 2 & -1 & 1 \\ -1 & -1 & 1 \\ 1 & 0 & 1 \\ 0 & 2 & -1 \end{bmatrix} \frac{1}{2}\begin{bmatrix} -1 & 1 \\ 1 & 1 \\ 3 & 1 \end{bmatrix} = \begin{bmatrix} 0 & 1 \\ 3/2 & -1/2 \\ 1 & 1 \\ -1/2 & 1/2 \end{bmatrix}$$

2. $\mathbf{t}^{-1}\begin{bmatrix} x \\ y \end{bmatrix} = \begin{bmatrix} y \\ x \end{bmatrix}$

3. $\mathbf{t}^{-1}\left(px^3 + qx^2 + rx + s\right) = \begin{bmatrix} p & -p+q \\ -p+r-s & -p-s \end{bmatrix}$

$$[\mathbf{t}]_{\sigma}^{\sigma} = \begin{bmatrix} 1 & 1 & 0 & -1 \\ 0 & 1 & 0 & 0 \\ 0 & 0 & 1 & 0 \\ 0 & 0 & -1 & -1 \end{bmatrix} \qquad [\mathbf{t}^{-1}]_{\sigma}^{\sigma} = \begin{bmatrix} 1 & -1 & -1 & -1 \\ 0 & 1 & 0 & 0 \\ 0 & 0 & 1 & 0 \\ 0 & 0 & -1 & -1 \end{bmatrix}$$

4. $\mathbf{t}^{-1}\begin{bmatrix} p & q \\ r & s \end{bmatrix} = \begin{bmatrix} p & \dfrac{q+r}{2} \\ \dfrac{q-r}{2} & s-p \end{bmatrix}$ $\qquad$ $[\mathbf{t}]_{\sigma}^{\sigma} = \begin{bmatrix} 1 & 0 & 0 & 0 \\ 0 & 1 & 1 & 0 \\ 0 & 1 & -1 & 0 \\ 1 & 0 & 0 & 1 \end{bmatrix}$

$$[\mathbf{t}^{-1}]_{\sigma}^{\sigma} = \begin{bmatrix} 1 & 0 & 0 & 0 \\ 0 & 1/2 & 1/2 & 0 \\ 0 & 1/2 & -1/2 & 0 \\ -1 & 0 & 0 & 1 \end{bmatrix}$$

5. $\mathbf{t}_{\mathbf{A}}\begin{bmatrix} x \\ y \end{bmatrix} = \begin{bmatrix} x \\ -x+y \\ 2x+y \end{bmatrix}$

6. $\mathbf{t}_{\mathbf{A}}\begin{bmatrix} x \\ y \\ z \\ w \end{bmatrix} = \begin{bmatrix} x+y-w \\ y+w \\ x+z \end{bmatrix}$

7. $\mathbf{t}_{\mathbf{A}}\begin{bmatrix} x \\ y \\ z \end{bmatrix} = \begin{bmatrix} x+y \\ 2x-y+z \\ x+y+z \end{bmatrix}$ $\quad \mathbf{t}_{\mathbf{A}^{-1}}\begin{bmatrix} x \\ y \\ z \end{bmatrix} = \begin{bmatrix} \dfrac{2x+y-z}{3} \\ \dfrac{x-y+z}{3} \\ -x+z \end{bmatrix}$

8. $\mathbf{t}_{\mathbf{A}}\begin{bmatrix} x \\ y \\ z \end{bmatrix} = \begin{bmatrix} x+2y+z \\ -x+y+z \\ 3y+2z \end{bmatrix}$ $\quad \mathbf{t}_{\mathbf{A}}^{-1}$ does not exist.

9. $\begin{bmatrix} 1 & 0 & 0 & 1 \end{bmatrix}$

SECTION 3.6 ◆ PAGE 185

1. $\begin{bmatrix} 2 & 2 \\ 0 & 4 \end{bmatrix}$

2. $\mathbf{I}$

3. $\dfrac{1}{3}\begin{bmatrix} 2 & 2 & 4 & 1 \\ 2 & -1 & -2 & 1 \\ 2 & 5 & 7 & 4 \\ 5 & 5 & 1 & 7 \end{bmatrix}$

4. $\dfrac{1}{2}\begin{bmatrix} 2 & 0 & 0 & 0 \\ 0 & 2 & 0 & 0 \\ 5 & 3 & 1 & 7 \\ 1 & 1 & 3 & 5 \end{bmatrix}$

5. $\begin{bmatrix} 3 & 6 \\ 1 & 2 \end{bmatrix}$

6. $\begin{bmatrix} 2 & -18 & 15 \\ 0 & 5 & -3 \\ 2 & 16 & -6 \end{bmatrix}$

7. $\dfrac{1}{4}\begin{bmatrix} 17 & 10 & 13 \\ 1 & 6 & 1 \\ 1 & 2 & 5 \end{bmatrix}$

10. $\begin{bmatrix} 1 & 2 & 2 & 1 \end{bmatrix}$ $\quad \begin{bmatrix} 1 & 2 & 2 & 1 \end{bmatrix}\begin{bmatrix} 1 \\ 1 \\ 1 \\ 1 \end{bmatrix} = [6]$

SECTION 4.1 • PAGE 195

1. a) -18 b) 25 c) -450 d) -450

5. a) -42 b) 27 c) 33

6. 0

7. $\begin{bmatrix} -4 & 7 & -1 \\ -4 & 2 & 4 \\ 6 & -3 & -1 \end{bmatrix}$ $\begin{bmatrix} 10 & 0 & 0 \\ 0 & 10 & 0 \\ 0 & 0 & 10 \end{bmatrix}$

8. a) 30 b) -6

SECTION 4.2 • PAGE 200

1. a) $\begin{bmatrix} 3 & -2 \\ -2 & 1 \end{bmatrix}$ b) $\begin{bmatrix} 2 & -1 \\ -1 & 0 \end{bmatrix}$ c) $\begin{bmatrix} 3 & -6 \\ -1 & -2 \end{bmatrix}$ d) $\begin{bmatrix} 4 & -8 \\ -1 & 2 \end{bmatrix}$

2. a, b, and c have inverses.

3. a) $\begin{bmatrix} 6 & -10 & 2 \\ -12 & 4 & 4 \\ 6 & -6 & -6 \end{bmatrix}$ b) $\begin{bmatrix} 0 & -2 & 4 \\ 0 & -2 & 4 \\ 0 & 2 & -4 \end{bmatrix}$

4. a) has an inverse b) has no inverse

5. a) $\begin{bmatrix} -24 & 0 & 0 \\ 0 & -24 & 0 \\ 0 & 0 & -24 \end{bmatrix}$ b) $\begin{bmatrix} 0 & 0 & 0 \\ 0 & 0 & 0 \\ 0 & 0 & 0 \end{bmatrix}$

6. $\dfrac{1}{ad-bc}\begin{bmatrix} d & -b \\ -c & a \end{bmatrix}$

7. $\dfrac{1}{\text{DET}(\mathbf{A})}\begin{bmatrix} ei-fh & ch-ib & bf-ce \\ fg-di & ai-cg & cd-af \\ dh-eg & bg-ah & ae-bd \end{bmatrix}$

SECTION 4.3 • PAGE 209

1. a) $x_2 = 5/43$ b) $x_3 = -1/136$ c) $x_1 = 1$ d) no solution

2. a) L.I.; $\text{DET}(\mathbf{A}) = 1$ b) L.D.; $\text{DET}(\mathbf{A}) = 0$
   c) L.I.; $\text{DET}(\mathbf{A}) = 4$ d) L.D.; $\text{DET}(\mathbf{A}) = 0$

3. a) no, DET(**A**) = -2 b) yes, DET(**A**) = 0 c) yes, DET(**A**) = 0
   d) yes, DET(**A**) = 0 e) no, DET(**A**) = 36 f) no, DET(**A**) = 2

SECTION 5.1 • PAGE 221

1. a) Eigenvalues $\{1-\sqrt{10}, 1+\sqrt{10}\}$;

   Eigenvectors $1-\sqrt{10}$, $\begin{bmatrix} \frac{1}{3}-\frac{\sqrt{10}}{3} \\ 1 \end{bmatrix}$ and $1+\sqrt{10}$, $\begin{bmatrix} \frac{1}{3}+\frac{\sqrt{10}}{3} \\ 1 \end{bmatrix}$

   $$\begin{bmatrix} \frac{1}{3}-\frac{\sqrt{10}}{3} & \frac{1}{3}+\frac{\sqrt{10}}{3} \\ 1 & 1 \end{bmatrix} \begin{bmatrix} 2 & 3 \\ 3 & 0 \end{bmatrix} \begin{bmatrix} \frac{1}{3}-\frac{\sqrt{10}}{3} & \frac{1}{3}+\frac{\sqrt{10}}{3} \\ 1 & 1 \end{bmatrix} = \begin{bmatrix} 1-\sqrt{10} & 0 \\ 0 & 1+\sqrt{10} \end{bmatrix}$$

   b) $$\begin{bmatrix} 1 & 4 \\ 0 & 1 \end{bmatrix}^{-1} \begin{bmatrix} 3 & -16 \\ 0 & -1 \end{bmatrix} \begin{bmatrix} 1 & 4 \\ 0 & 1 \end{bmatrix} = \begin{bmatrix} 3 & 0 \\ 0 & -1 \end{bmatrix}$$

   c) $$\begin{bmatrix} -1 & -2 \\ 1 & 1 \end{bmatrix}^{-1} \begin{bmatrix} 10 & 12 \\ -6 & -8 \end{bmatrix} \begin{bmatrix} -1 & -2 \\ 1 & 1 \end{bmatrix} = \begin{bmatrix} -2 & 0 \\ 0 & 4 \end{bmatrix}$$

   d) $$\begin{bmatrix} -\sqrt{10} & \sqrt{10} \\ 2 & 2 \end{bmatrix}^{-1} \begin{bmatrix} 3 & 5 \\ 2 & 3 \end{bmatrix} \begin{bmatrix} -\sqrt{10} & \sqrt{10} \\ 2 & 2 \end{bmatrix} = \begin{bmatrix} 3-\sqrt{10} & 0 \\ 0 & 3+\sqrt{10} \end{bmatrix}$$

   e) $$\begin{bmatrix} -8-i & -8+i \\ 5 & 5 \end{bmatrix}^{-1} \begin{bmatrix} -7 & -13 \\ 5 & 9 \end{bmatrix} \begin{bmatrix} -8-i & -8+i \\ 5 & 5 \end{bmatrix} = \begin{bmatrix} 1-i & 0 \\ 0 & 1+i \end{bmatrix}$$

   f) $$\begin{bmatrix} -1 & 1 \\ 1 & 5 \end{bmatrix}^{-1} \begin{bmatrix} 2 & 1 \\ 5 & 6 \end{bmatrix} \begin{bmatrix} -1 & 1 \\ 1 & 5 \end{bmatrix} = \begin{bmatrix} 1 & 0 \\ 0 & 7 \end{bmatrix}$$

2. a)

   $$\begin{bmatrix} 23 & -4+8\sqrt{2}i & -4-8\sqrt{2}i \\ -32 & 2-4\sqrt{2}i & 2+4\sqrt{2}i \\ 1 & 9 & 9 \end{bmatrix}^{-1} \begin{bmatrix} 11 & 6 & 8 \\ -4 & 0 & -4 \\ -7 & -5 & 4 \end{bmatrix} \begin{bmatrix} 23 & -4+8\sqrt{2}i & -4-8\sqrt{2}i \\ -32 & 2-4\sqrt{2}i & 2+4\sqrt{2}i \\ 1 & 9 & 9 \end{bmatrix} =$$

   $$\begin{bmatrix} 3 & 0 & 0 \\ 0 & 6-4\sqrt{2}i & 0 \\ 0 & 0 & 6-4\sqrt{2}i \end{bmatrix}$$

b) There are two eigenvalues 3 and 2. There are 2 linearly independent eigenvectors belonging to the eigenvalue 2, and one belonging to 3.

$$\begin{bmatrix} -2 & 0 & -1 \\ 1 & 0 & 0 \\ 0 & 1 & 1 \end{bmatrix}^{-1} \begin{bmatrix} 3 & 2 & 0 \\ 0 & 2 & 0 \\ -1 & -2 & 2 \end{bmatrix} \begin{bmatrix} -2 & 0 & -1 \\ 1 & 0 & 0 \\ 0 & 1 & 1 \end{bmatrix} = \begin{bmatrix} 2 & 0 & 0 \\ 0 & 2 & 0 \\ 0 & 0 & 3 \end{bmatrix}$$

c)

$$\begin{bmatrix} 25 & 125 & 125 \\ -12 & -64+2i & -64-2i \\ -21 & -89+2i & -89-2i \end{bmatrix}^{-1} \begin{bmatrix} -62 & -125 & 0 \\ 33 & 65 & 1 \\ 45 & 92 & -1 \end{bmatrix} \begin{bmatrix} 25 & 125 & 125 \\ -12 & -64+2i & -64-2i \\ -21 & -89+2i & -89-2i \end{bmatrix} =$$

$$\begin{bmatrix} -2 & 0 & 0 \\ 0 & 2-2i & 0 \\ 0 & 0 & 2+2i \end{bmatrix}$$

d)

$$\begin{bmatrix} -4 & -2 & -1 \\ 2 & 1 & 0 \\ 3 & 1 & 1 \end{bmatrix}^{-1} \begin{bmatrix} 7 & 6 & 4 \\ -2 & 0 & -2 \\ -4 & -5 & -1 \end{bmatrix} \begin{bmatrix} -4 & -2 & -1 \\ 2 & 1 & 0 \\ 3 & 1 & 1 \end{bmatrix} = \begin{bmatrix} 1 & 0 & 0 \\ 0 & 2 & 0 \\ 0 & 0 & 3 \end{bmatrix}$$

e)

$$\begin{bmatrix} 7 & 55 & 55 \\ -3 & -25-2\sqrt{5} & -25+2\sqrt{5} \\ 9 & 50-7\sqrt{5} & -50+7\sqrt{5} \end{bmatrix}^{-1} \begin{bmatrix} 11 & 24 & 1 \\ -3 & -8 & -1 \\ 12 & 25 & 1 \end{bmatrix} \begin{bmatrix} 7 & 55 & 55 \\ -3 & -25-2\sqrt{5} & -25+2\sqrt{5} \\ 9 & 50-7\sqrt{5} & -50+7\sqrt{5} \end{bmatrix} =$$

$$\begin{bmatrix} 2 & 0 & 0 \\ 0 & 1-\sqrt{5} & 0 \\ 0 & 0 & 1+\sqrt{5} \end{bmatrix}$$

f)

$$\begin{bmatrix} 1 & 4 & 4 \\ -3 & 6 & 6 \\ 1 & -2-3\sqrt{2} & -2+3\sqrt{2} \end{bmatrix}^{-1} \begin{bmatrix} 1 & 2 & 4 \\ 3 & 2 & 6 \\ 2 & 1 & 0 \end{bmatrix} \begin{bmatrix} 1 & 4 & 4 \\ -3 & 6 & 6 \\ 1 & -2-3\sqrt{2} & -2+3\sqrt{2} \end{bmatrix} =$$

$$\begin{bmatrix} -1 & 0 & 0 \\ 0 & 2-3\sqrt{2} & 0 \\ 0 & 0 & 2+3\sqrt{2} \end{bmatrix}$$

7. $\mathbf{A}^6 = \begin{bmatrix} 1 & -1 & 2 \\ 0 & -1 & 0 \\ 0 & 0 & -1 \end{bmatrix}$

$$\mathbf{A}^n = \begin{bmatrix} 1 & 5 & 5 \\ 0 & 4+2i & 4-2i \\ 0 & -3+i & -3-i \end{bmatrix} \begin{bmatrix} (-1)^n & 0 & 0 \\ 0 & (-1)^{-\frac{n}{2}} & 0 \\ 0 & 0 & (-1)^{\frac{n}{2}} \end{bmatrix} \begin{bmatrix} 1 & 5 & 5 \\ 0 & 4+2i & 4-2i \\ 0 & -3+i & -3-i \end{bmatrix}^{-1}$$

$$\mathbf{A}^{2n+1} = \begin{bmatrix} -1 & -1 & 3 \\ 0 & -1 & -2 \\ 0 & 1 & 1 \end{bmatrix}, \quad \mathbf{A}^{2(n+1)} = \begin{bmatrix} 1 & -1 & 2 \\ 0 & -1 & 0 \\ 0 & 0 & -1 \end{bmatrix}, \quad \mathbf{A}^{2n+3} = \begin{bmatrix} -1 & 2 & 1 \\ 0 & 1 & 2 \\ 0 & -1 & -1 \end{bmatrix},$$

$$\mathbf{A}^{2(n+2)} = \begin{bmatrix} 1 & 0 & 0 \\ 0 & 1 & 0 \\ 0 & 0 & 1 \end{bmatrix} \quad \text{for } n = 0,1,2,\cdots.$$

SECTION 5.2 ◆ PAGE 232

1. $\lambda^3 \begin{bmatrix} 1 & 0 & 0 \\ 0 & 1 & 0 \\ 0 & 0 & 1 \end{bmatrix} + \lambda^2 \begin{bmatrix} 2 & 1 & 0 \\ 1 & -2 & 1 \\ 0 & 1 & 0 \end{bmatrix} + \lambda \begin{bmatrix} 0 & 0 & 1 \\ 1 & 1 & 0 \\ 1 & 0 & 0 \end{bmatrix} + \begin{bmatrix} -3 & 3 & 2 \\ 1 & -1 & -4 \\ 0 & -1 & -1 \end{bmatrix}$

2. a) $\begin{bmatrix} 118 & 144 \\ 144 & 190 \end{bmatrix}$ b) $\begin{bmatrix} 46 & 47 & 89 \\ 57 & 83 & 136 \\ 84 & 94 & 182 \end{bmatrix}$

3. a) $\begin{bmatrix} \lambda-2 & 2 \\ 2 & \lambda-1 \end{bmatrix}$ b) $\begin{bmatrix} \lambda^3-\lambda-6 & \lambda & \lambda+3 \\ 3\lambda-6 & \lambda^2-2\lambda & 2\lambda+3 \\ 6 & 2\lambda & \lambda^2+\lambda-3 \end{bmatrix}$

4. a) $\begin{bmatrix} \lambda^2-3\lambda-2 & 0 \\ 0 & \lambda^2-3\lambda-2 \end{bmatrix}$ b) $\begin{bmatrix} \lambda^3-\lambda^2-9\lambda & 0 & 0 \\ 0 & \lambda^3-\lambda^2-9\lambda & 0 \\ 0 & 0 & \lambda^3-\lambda^2-9\lambda \end{bmatrix}$

7. The characteristic polynomial is $p(\lambda) = \lambda^2 - 4\lambda + 1$. If $x^2 - 4x + 1 = 0$ then $x^2 = 4x - 1$ so that $x^3 = 4x^2 - x = 4(4x-1) - x = 15x - 4$ continue in this

way until $x^6 = 780x - 209$ which implies

$$\mathbf{A}^6 = 708\mathbf{A} - 209\mathbf{I} = \begin{bmatrix} 571 & 780 \\ 1560 & 2131 \end{bmatrix}.$$

8. The characteristic polynomial is $\lambda^3 - \lambda$. Thus by the Cayley-Hamilton Theorem $\mathbf{A}^3 - \mathbf{A} = \mathbf{0}$. This equation implies $\mathbf{A}^3 = \mathbf{A}$. Hence $\mathbf{A}^5 = \mathbf{A}^3 = \mathbf{A}$.

9. For the matrix of exercise 7 the characteristic polynomial is $p(\lambda) = \lambda^2 - 4\lambda - 1$ so that $\mathbf{A}^2 - 4\mathbf{A} + \mathbf{I} = \mathbf{0}$ which implies $\mathbf{A}^2 - 4\mathbf{A} = -\mathbf{I}$ or $\mathbf{A}(\mathbf{A} - 4\mathbf{I}) = -\mathbf{I}$. Hence, $-(\mathbf{A} - 4\mathbf{I}) = \mathbf{A}^{-1}$ and

$$-\left(\begin{bmatrix} 1 & 1 \\ 2 & 3 \end{bmatrix} - 4\begin{bmatrix} 1 & 0 \\ 0 & 1 \end{bmatrix}\right) = \begin{bmatrix} 3 & -1 \\ -2 & 1 \end{bmatrix} = \mathbf{A}^{-1}.$$ The matrix in exercise 8 has no inverse since the characteristic polynomial is $w^3 - w$. By the Cayley-Hamilton Theorem $\mathbf{A}^3 - \mathbf{A} + 0\mathbf{I} = \mathbf{0}$, which implies $\mathbf{A}(\mathbf{A}^2 - \mathbf{I}) = 0\mathbf{I}$. From this we see the matrix is singular.

10. The characteristic polynomial of $\mathbf{A}$ is $p(w) = w(w-1)(w+1)$. Thus, by the Cayley-Hamilton Theorem $\mathbf{A}(\mathbf{A} - \mathbf{I})(\mathbf{A} + \mathbf{I}) = \mathbf{0}$. Each column of

$$(\mathbf{A} - \mathbf{I})(\mathbf{A} + \mathbf{I}) = \begin{bmatrix} 2 & 4 & 6 \\ -8 & -12 & -4 \\ 1 & 2 & 3 \end{bmatrix}$$

is an eigenvector corresponding to $w = 0$ since by the Cayley-Hamilton Theorem $(\mathbf{A} - 0\mathbf{I})[(\mathbf{A} - \mathbf{I})(\mathbf{A} + \mathbf{I})] = \mathbf{0}$. Each column of

$$\mathbf{A}(\mathbf{A} - \mathbf{I}) = \begin{bmatrix} 4 & 6 & 10 \\ -8 & -12 & -20 \\ 4 & 6 & 10 \end{bmatrix}$$

is an eigenvector corresponding to $w = 1$ since $(\mathbf{A} + 1\mathbf{I})[\mathbf{A}(\mathbf{A} - \mathbf{I})] = \mathbf{0}$. Each column of

$$\mathbf{A}(\mathbf{A} + \mathbf{I}) = \begin{bmatrix} 2 & 2 & 2 \\ 2 & 2 & 2 \\ -2 & -2 & -2 \end{bmatrix}$$

is an eigenvector corresponding to $w = -1$ since $(\mathbf{A} - 1\mathbf{I})[\mathbf{A}(\mathbf{A} + \mathbf{I})] = \mathbf{0}$

14. The characteristic polynomial is $p(w) = w^4 + 2w^3 - w^2 - 2w + 1$ so by the Cayley-Hamilton Theorem $p(\mathbf{A}) = \mathbf{0}$. Thus, $\mathbf{A}(\mathbf{A}^3 + 2\mathbf{A} - \mathbf{A} - 2\mathbf{I}) = -\mathbf{I}$ and

$$\mathbf{A}^{-1} = -(\mathbf{A}+2\mathbf{A}-\mathbf{A}-2\mathbf{I}) = \begin{bmatrix} 2 & 1 & 0 & 0 \\ 1 & 0 & 1 & 0 \\ -2 & 0 & 0 & 1 \\ -1 & 0 & 0 & 0 \end{bmatrix}$$

15. $a=-6,\ b=5,\ c=3$.

SECTION 5.3 ◆ PAGE 244

1. a) Eigenvalues are real and approximately equal to $\{-0.59847, 8.86124, -2.26277\}$
   b) Eigenvalues are real and approximately equal to $\{0.427555, 7.90092, -5.32874\}$
   c) Eigenvalues have magnitude 1 $\{1, \cos\vartheta + i|\sin\vartheta|, \cos\vartheta - i|\sin\vartheta|\}$
   d) Eigenvalues are purely imaginary $\{0, \sqrt{3}i, -\sqrt{3}i\}$
   e) Eigenvalues are real and approximately equal to $\{0.806063, -1.70927, 2.90321\}$

2. Multiply $\mathbf{AA}^{\mathrm{T}} = \mathbf{I}$ Eigenvalues are approximately $\{-1, 0.99590+0.0903831i, 0.99590-0.0903831i\}$ Note that they have magnitude 1.

8. a) One set is $\left\{\begin{bmatrix}2\\1\end{bmatrix}, \begin{bmatrix}2\\-4\end{bmatrix}\right\}$ b) One set is $\left\{\begin{bmatrix}1\\1\end{bmatrix}, \begin{bmatrix}1\\-1\end{bmatrix}\right\}$

   c) One set is $\left\{\begin{bmatrix}3\\0\end{bmatrix}, \begin{bmatrix}0\\3\end{bmatrix}\right\}$ d) One set is $\left\{\begin{bmatrix}1\\1\\1\end{bmatrix}, \begin{bmatrix}1/4\\-1/2\\1/4\end{bmatrix}\right\}$

   e) One set is $\left\{\begin{bmatrix}1\\1\\0\end{bmatrix}, \begin{bmatrix}1\\-1\\-2\end{bmatrix}\right\}$ f) One set is $\left\{\begin{bmatrix}2\\0\\0\end{bmatrix}, \begin{bmatrix}0\\-2\\-2\end{bmatrix}\right\}$

   g) One set is $\left\{\begin{bmatrix}1\\1\\0\\0\end{bmatrix}, \begin{bmatrix}0\\0\\1\\1\end{bmatrix}, \begin{bmatrix}-1\\1\\1\\-1\end{bmatrix}\right\}$ h) One set is $\left\{\begin{bmatrix}1\\2\\0\\0\end{bmatrix}, \begin{bmatrix}-3/2\\3/4\\0\\0\end{bmatrix}, \begin{bmatrix}0\\0\\1\\0\end{bmatrix}\right\}$

10. Applying the orthogonalization process to the first vectors gives the set

$$\left\{\begin{bmatrix}1\\2\\1\end{bmatrix},\begin{bmatrix}-1\\1\\-1\end{bmatrix}\right\}$$

Applying the orthogonalization process again to

$$\begin{bmatrix}3\\3\\3\end{bmatrix}+a\begin{bmatrix}1\\2\\1\end{bmatrix}+b\begin{bmatrix}-1\\1\\-1\end{bmatrix}$$ gives $a=-2$ and $b=1$. The resulting sum is $\begin{bmatrix}0\\0\\0\end{bmatrix}$.

16. $\begin{bmatrix}\sqrt{\frac{1}{2}-\frac{\sqrt{5}}{10}}\\ \sqrt{\frac{1}{2}+\frac{\sqrt{5}}{10}}\end{bmatrix}$ and $\begin{bmatrix}\sqrt{\frac{1}{2}+\frac{\sqrt{5}}{10}}\\ -\sqrt{\frac{1}{2}-\frac{\sqrt{5}}{10}}\end{bmatrix}$ are eigenvectors corresponding to $2+\sqrt{5}$ and $2-\sqrt{5}$ respectively. Also,

$$\begin{bmatrix}\sqrt{\frac{1}{2}-\frac{\sqrt{5}}{10}} & \sqrt{\frac{1}{2}+\frac{\sqrt{5}}{10}}\\ \sqrt{\frac{1}{2}+\frac{\sqrt{5}}{10}} & -\sqrt{\frac{1}{2}-\frac{\sqrt{5}}{10}}\end{bmatrix}^T\begin{bmatrix}1&2\\2&3\end{bmatrix}\begin{bmatrix}\sqrt{\frac{1}{2}-\frac{\sqrt{5}}{10}} & \sqrt{\frac{1}{2}+\frac{\sqrt{5}}{10}}\\ \sqrt{\frac{1}{2}+\frac{\sqrt{5}}{10}} & -\sqrt{\frac{1}{2}-\frac{\sqrt{5}}{10}}\end{bmatrix}=$$

$$\begin{bmatrix}2+\sqrt{5} & 0\\ 0 & 2-\sqrt{5}\end{bmatrix}$$

17. If

$$\mathbf{Q}=\begin{bmatrix}\sqrt{2}/2 & \sqrt{6}/6 & \sqrt{3}/3\\ 0 & \sqrt{6}/3 & -\sqrt{3}/3\\ \sqrt{2}/2 & -\sqrt{6}/6 & -\sqrt{3}/3\end{bmatrix},\text{ then }\mathbf{Q}^T\mathbf{AQ}=\begin{bmatrix}1&0&0\\0&1&0\\0&0&-2\end{bmatrix}.$$

SECTION 5.4 ◆ PAGE 251

1. a) $|\lambda|\le 8$ and $|\lambda-1|\le 5\cup|\lambda|\le 4\cup|\lambda-5|\le 3$
   b) $|\lambda|\le 18$ and $\{|\lambda-1|\le 5\cup|\lambda-5|\le 10\cup|\lambda-9|\le 15\}\cap$
   $\{|\lambda-1|\le 11\cup|\lambda-5|\le 10\cup|\lambda-9|\le 9\}$
   c) $|\lambda|\le 8$ and $\{|\lambda-2|\le 2\cup|\lambda-2|\le 5\cup|\lambda+5|\le 1\}\cap$
   $\{|\lambda-2|\le 3\cup|\lambda-2|\le 2\cup|\lambda+5|\le 3\}$

2. The eigenvalues lie interior to the union of the circles

$$|\lambda-8|\le 2,\ |\lambda-10|\le 5,\ |\lambda-5|\le 4, \text{ and } |\lambda-6|\le 3$$

none of which include the origin. Thus, no eigenvalue can be zero.

5. a) $|z-2|\le 1 \cup |z|\le 2$ where $z=x+iy$.
   b) $|z-2|\le 9$ where $z=x+iy$ includes all of the roots.
   c) $|z-1|\le 4$ where $z=x+iy$ includes all of the roots.

SECTION 5.5 • PAGE 261

1. $$\begin{bmatrix}1&1&0\\-2&-1&1\\1&0&0\end{bmatrix}^{-1}\begin{bmatrix}1&1&0\\-3&-2&-1\\1&0&-2\end{bmatrix}\begin{bmatrix}1&1&0\\-2&-1&1\\1&0&0\end{bmatrix}=\begin{bmatrix}-1&1&0\\0&-1&1\\0&0&-1\end{bmatrix}$$

2. $$\begin{bmatrix}1&-6&3\\-3&12&-12\\3&-6&9\end{bmatrix}^{-1}\begin{bmatrix}5&4&3\\-12&-10&-8\\9&8&7\end{bmatrix}\begin{bmatrix}1&-6&3\\-3&12&-12\\3&-6&9\end{bmatrix}=\begin{bmatrix}2&0&0\\0&0&1\\0&0&0\end{bmatrix}$$

3. $$\begin{bmatrix}1&1&0&0\\0&-1&1&0\\1&1&-1&0\\-2&1&-1&1\end{bmatrix}^{-1}\begin{bmatrix}4&0&-1&0\\-1&6&3&1\\1&-3&0&-1\\1&-3&-3&2\end{bmatrix}\begin{bmatrix}1&1&0&0\\0&-1&1&0\\1&1&-1&0\\-2&1&-1&1\end{bmatrix}=\begin{bmatrix}3&0&0&0\\0&3&1&0\\0&0&3&1\\0&0&0&3\end{bmatrix}$$

4. $$\begin{bmatrix}-4&-4&4&-4\\4&0&-4&8\\0&4&4&-8\\-8&0&4&-8\end{bmatrix}^{-1}\begin{bmatrix}1&-1&-2&0\\-1&-3&0&-2\\1&7&3&3\\1&3&-1&3\end{bmatrix}\begin{bmatrix}-4&-4&4&-4\\4&0&-4&8\\0&4&4&-8\\-8&0&4&-8\end{bmatrix}=\begin{bmatrix}2&1&0&0\\0&2&0&0\\0&0&0&1\\0&0&0&0\end{bmatrix}$$

5. Let **U** be the matrix

$$\begin{bmatrix}233+736\,\hat{\imath} & -368+564\,\hat{\imath} & 233-736\,\hat{\imath} & -368-564\,\hat{\imath}\\ -435-966\,\hat{\imath} & 483-832\,\hat{\imath} & -435+966\,\hat{\imath} & 483+832\,\hat{\imath}\\ 519+1048\,\hat{\imath} & -524+976\,\hat{\imath} & 519-1048\,\hat{\imath} & -524-976\,\hat{\imath}\\ -272-528\,\hat{\imath} & 256-504\,\hat{\imath} & -272+528\,\hat{\imath} & 256+504\,\hat{\imath}\end{bmatrix}$$

then

$$\mathbf{U}^{-1}\mathbf{AU} = \begin{bmatrix} 1-2i & 1 & 0 & 0 \\ 0 & 1-2i & 0 & 0 \\ 0 & 0 & 1+2i & 1 \\ 0 & 0 & 0 & 1+2i \end{bmatrix}$$

6.

$$\begin{bmatrix} -4 & 4+4i & -8 & -4-8i \\ 0 & -4 & 8 & 4+8i \\ 4 & -4i & -16 & -16i \\ 0 & 0 & 8 & -4+8i \end{bmatrix} \begin{bmatrix} 2-i & 3-2i & 2-2i & 3-2i \\ -1+2i & -1+3i & -1+2i & -2+2i \\ 1-2i & -2i & 1-i & 3 \\ -1 & -1 & -1 & -2-i \end{bmatrix} \begin{bmatrix} -4 & 4+4i & -8 & -4-8i \\ 0 & -4 & 8 & 4+8i \\ 4 & -4i & -16 & -16i \\ 0 & 0 & 8 & -4+8i \end{bmatrix} =$$

$$\begin{bmatrix} i & 1 & 0 & 0 \\ 0 & i & 0 & 0 \\ 0 & 0 & -i & 1 \\ 0 & 0 & 0 & -i \end{bmatrix}$$

SECTION 6.1 • PAGE 268

1. a) $\|\mathbf{x}\|_S = 4$ $\quad \|\mathbf{x}\|_M = 2$ $\quad \|\mathbf{x}\|_E = \sqrt{6}$
   b) $\|\mathbf{x}\|_S = 4$ $\quad \|\mathbf{x}\|_M = 3$ $\quad \|\mathbf{x}\|_E = \sqrt{10}$
   c) $\|\mathbf{x}\|_S = \sqrt{2} + 1 + \sqrt{5} \approx 4.65028$ $\quad \|\mathbf{x}\|_M = \sqrt{5}$ $\quad \|\mathbf{x}\|_E = 2\sqrt{2}$
   d) $\|\mathbf{x}\|_S = 1 + \sqrt{5}$ $\quad \|\mathbf{x}\|_M = \sqrt{5}$ $\quad \|\mathbf{x}\|_E = \sqrt{6}$

2. a) $\|\mathbf{A}\|_R = 12$ $\quad \|\mathbf{A}\|_C = 12$ $\quad \|\mathbf{A}\|_E = \sqrt{80}$ $\quad \|\mathbf{A}\|_M = 15$
   b) $\|\mathbf{A}\|_R = 9$ $\quad \|\mathbf{A}\|_C = 9$ $\quad \|\mathbf{A}\|_E = \sqrt{69}$ $\quad \|\mathbf{A}\|_M = 18$
   c) $\|\mathbf{A}\|_R = 6$ $\quad \|\mathbf{A}\|_C = 4 + \sqrt{5}$ $\quad \|\mathbf{A}\|_E = \sqrt{29}$ $\quad \|\mathbf{A}\|_M = 9$
   d) $\|\mathbf{A}\|_R = 5$ $\quad \|\mathbf{A}\|_C = 4 + \sqrt{2}$ $\quad \|\mathbf{A}\|_E = \sqrt{23}$ $\quad \|\mathbf{A}\|_M = 9$

SECTION 6.2 • PAGE 275

1. a) $\begin{bmatrix} 0 & 0 & 0 \end{bmatrix}$ $\quad$ b) Does not exist $\quad$ c) $\begin{bmatrix} 0 & 0 \end{bmatrix}$

2. a) $\begin{bmatrix} 0 & 0 \\ 0 & 0 \end{bmatrix}$ $\quad$ b) Does not exist $\quad$ c) $\begin{bmatrix} 0 & 0 \\ 2 & 1/2 \end{bmatrix}$

8. a) $\begin{bmatrix} 2 & e \\ 0 & 1 \end{bmatrix}$ b) $p_n(w) - \dfrac{\left(\dfrac{n+1}{n}\right)^n}{n^2} - \dfrac{4w}{n} + \dfrac{6}{n} + \dfrac{4}{n^2} + w^2 - 3w + 2$

c) $p(w) = w^2 - 3w + 2$ d) $w_n = \dfrac{\pm\sqrt{4\left(\dfrac{n+1}{n}\right)^n + n^2}}{2n} + \dfrac{3n+4}{2n}$

f) $\lim\limits_{n\to\infty} p_n(w) = \lim\limits_{n\to\infty} \dfrac{\left(\dfrac{n+1}{n}\right)^n}{n^2} - \dfrac{4w}{n} + \dfrac{6}{n} + \dfrac{4}{n^2} + w^2 - 3w + 2 = p(w)$

g) $\lim\limits_{n\to\infty} w_n = \lim\limits_{n\to\infty} \dfrac{\pm\sqrt{4\left(\dfrac{n+1}{n}\right)^n + n^2}}{2n} + \dfrac{3n+4}{2n} = 2,1$ 2 for the + and 1 for the -

h) $\mathrm{TR}\left(\mathbf{A}^{(n)}\right) = \dfrac{4}{n} + 3$

9) a) $\begin{bmatrix} 1/n & 0 \\ 0 & 1 \end{bmatrix}^{-1} \begin{bmatrix} 2 & 1/n \\ 0 & 2 \end{bmatrix} \begin{bmatrix} 1/n & 0 \\ 0 & 1 \end{bmatrix} = \begin{bmatrix} 2 & 1 \\ 0 & 2 \end{bmatrix}$ which is not similar to a diagonal matrix.

b) $\left(\mathbf{A}^{(n)}\right)^{-1} = \begin{bmatrix} 1/2 & -1/4n \\ 0 & 1/2 \end{bmatrix}$

SECTION 6.3 ◆ PAGE 290

2) a) $\sqrt{\mathbf{A}} = \begin{bmatrix} 6 & 1 \\ -6 & 1 \end{bmatrix}$ b) $\sqrt{\mathbf{A}} = \begin{bmatrix} 4+3i & -2+i \\ 12-6i & 6-2i \end{bmatrix}$

3) a) $\cos(\mathbf{A}) = \dfrac{e(e^2+1)}{2} \begin{bmatrix} 1 & 0 \\ 0 & 1 \end{bmatrix}$

b) $\cos(\mathbf{A})_{11} = e^{\frac{\sqrt{215}}{2}} \left(\dfrac{\cos\left(\dfrac{15}{2}\right)}{2} + \dfrac{\sqrt{215}\sin\left(\dfrac{15}{2}\right)}{430} \right) +$

$e^{\frac{-\sqrt{215}}{2}} \left(\dfrac{\cos\left(\dfrac{15}{2}\right)}{2} - \dfrac{13\sqrt{215}\sin\left(\dfrac{15}{2}\right)}{430} \right)$

$$\cos(\mathbf{A})_{12} = -\frac{3\sqrt{215}e^{\frac{\sqrt{215}}{2}}\sin\left(\frac{15}{2}\right)}{215} \qquad \cos(\mathbf{A})_{21} = \frac{18\sqrt{215}e^{\frac{\sqrt{215}}{2}}\sin\left(\frac{15}{2}\right)}{215}$$

$$\cos(\mathbf{A})_{22} = e^{\frac{\sqrt{215}}{2}}\left(\frac{\cos\left(\frac{15}{2}\right)}{2} - \frac{\sqrt{215}\sin\left(\frac{15}{2}\right)}{430}\right) +$$

$$e^{\frac{-\sqrt{215}}{2}}\left(\frac{\cos\left(\frac{15}{2}\right)}{2} - \frac{13\sqrt{215}\sin\left(\frac{15}{2}\right)}{430}\right)$$

4) a) $$e^{\mathbf{A}} = \begin{bmatrix} e^{-1} & -e^{-2}(e-1) & e^{-2}(e-1) \\ -e^{-2}(e-1) & e^{-2}(2e-1) & -2e^{-2}(e-1) \\ -e^{-2}(e-1) & 2e^{-2}(e-1) & -e^{-2}(2e-3) \end{bmatrix}$$

b) $$e^{\mathbf{A}} = \begin{bmatrix} e & 1-e & e-1 \\ 2e^{-2}(1-e^{3}) & e^{-2}(2e^{3}-3e^{2}+2) & -e^{-2}(2e^{3}-3e^{2}+1) \\ 2e^{-2}(1-e^{3}) & 2e^{-2}(e^{3}-2e^{2}+1) & -e^{-2}(2e^{3}-4e^{2}+1) \end{bmatrix}$$

5) a) $$\sqrt{\mathbf{A}} = \begin{bmatrix} 5/2 & 1/4 \\ -1 & 3/2 \end{bmatrix}$$ b) $$\sqrt{\mathbf{A}} = \begin{bmatrix} \frac{5i}{2} & -\frac{i}{4} \\ i & \frac{3i}{2} \end{bmatrix}$$

6) a) $$\cos(t\mathbf{A}) = \begin{bmatrix} \cos t - 2t\sin t & 0 & t\sin t \\ -2t\sin t & \cos t & t\sin t \\ -4t\sin t & 0 & \cos t + 2t\sin t \end{bmatrix}$$

b) $$\cos(t\mathbf{A}) = \begin{bmatrix} \cos t + 2t\sin t & 4t\sin t & 4t\sin t \\ -2t\sin t & \cos t - 4t\sin t & -4t\sin t \\ t\sin t & 2t\sin t & \cos t + 2t\sin t \end{bmatrix}$$

7) $$\cos(t\mathbf{A}) = \begin{bmatrix} -2\cos t - \sin t & 0 & t\cos t \\ -2t\sin t & \sin t & t\cos t \\ -4t\cos t & 0 & -\sin t + 2\cos t \end{bmatrix}$$

9) $$\mathrm{RE}(e^{i\mathbf{A}}) = \begin{bmatrix} 3\cos 2 - 2\cos 3 & 3\cos 2 - 3\cos 3 \\ 2\cos 3 - 2\cos 2 & 3\cos 3 - 2\cos 2 \end{bmatrix} = \cos(\mathbf{A})$$

$$\mathrm{IM}\left(e^{i\mathbf{A}}\right)=\begin{bmatrix} 2\sin 3-3\sin 2 & 3\sin 3+3\sin 2 \\ -2\sin 3-2\sin 2 & -3\sin 3-2\sin 2 \end{bmatrix}=\sin(\mathbf{A})$$

10) $$\sin(2\mathbf{A})=\begin{bmatrix} 2\sin 6+3\sin 4 & 3\sin 6+3\sin 4 \\ -2\sin 6-2\sin 4 & -3\sin 6-2\sin 4 \end{bmatrix}$$

$$\cos(2\mathbf{A})=\begin{bmatrix} -4\cos^2 3+6\cos^2 2-1 & 6\cos^2 2-6\cos^2 3 \\ 4\cos^2 3-4\cos^2 2 & 6\cos^2 3-4\cos^2 2-1 \end{bmatrix}$$

11) $$\sin(2\mathbf{A})=\begin{bmatrix} -\sin 4+8\cos^2 2-4 & 4\cos^2 2-2 \\ 8-16\cos^2 2 & -\sin 4-8\cos^2 2+4 \end{bmatrix}$$

$$\cos(2\mathbf{A})=\begin{bmatrix} 4\sin 4+2\cos^2 2-1 & 2\sin 4 \\ -8\sin 4 & -4\sin 4+2\cos^2 2-1 \end{bmatrix}$$

12) $$\sqrt{\mathbf{A}}=\begin{bmatrix} 3/2 & 1/4 & 1/4 & 0 \\ 2/3 & 9/4 & -7/12 & -1/6 \\ -5/3 & 1/4 & 37/12 & 1/6 \\ -19/6 & 1/2 & 1/3 & 19/6 \end{bmatrix}$$

13) $$e^{\mathbf{A}}=\begin{bmatrix} -e^4 & e^4 & e^4 & 0 \\ e^4\left(2e^5-3\right) & 2e^4 & 2e^4 & -e^9 \\ -e^4\left(2e^5+1\right) & e^4 & e^4 & e^9 \\ -e^4\left(3e^5+2\right) & 2e^4 & e^4\left(2-e^5\right) & 2e^9 \end{bmatrix}$$

14) $$\mathbf{A}^{2n}=\begin{bmatrix} 1 & 0 & 0 \\ -2 & 5 & 2 \\ 5 & -10 & -4 \end{bmatrix} \qquad \mathbf{A}^{2n+1}=\mathbf{A}$$

SECTION 6.4 ◆ PAGE 301

1) a) $e^{\mathbf{A}}=\begin{bmatrix} 2e-e^4 & 2e-2e^4 \\ e^4-e & 2e^4-e \end{bmatrix}$ b) $e^{t\mathbf{A}}=\begin{bmatrix} 2e^t-e^{4t} & 2e^t-2e^{4t} \\ e^{4t}-e^t & 2e^{4t}-e^t \end{bmatrix}$

c) $\sin(\mathbf{A})=\begin{bmatrix} 2\sin(1)-\sin(4) & 2\sin(1)-2\sin(4) \\ \sin(4)-\sin(1) & 2\sin(4)-\sin(1) \end{bmatrix}$

d) $\sqrt{\mathbf{A}}=\begin{bmatrix} 0 & -2 \\ 1 & 3 \end{bmatrix}$ e) $\ln(\mathbf{A})=\begin{bmatrix} -2\ln 2 & -4\ln 2 \\ 2\ln 2 & 4\ln 2 \end{bmatrix}$

f) $\mathbf{A}^{-1} = \begin{bmatrix} 7/4 & 3/2 \\ -3/4 & -1/2 \end{bmatrix}$

g) $\cos(\mathbf{A}) = \begin{bmatrix} 2\cos(t) - \cos(4t) & 2\cos(t) - 2\cos(4t) \\ \cos(4t) - \cos(t) & 2\cos(4t) - \cos(t) \end{bmatrix}$ h) **I**

$\sin(\mathbf{A}) = \begin{bmatrix} 2\sin(t) - \sin(4t) & 2\sin(t) - 2\sin(4t) \\ \sin(4t) - \sin(t) & 2\sin(4t) - \sin(t) \end{bmatrix}$

2) a) Set $t = 1$ in 2 b)

b) $e^{t\mathbf{A}} = \begin{bmatrix} 2e^{t} - e^{9t} & 0 & 2e^{t} - 2e^{9t} \\ e^{4t} - e^{9t} & e^{4t} & 2e^{4t} - 2e^{9t} \\ -e^{t} + e^{9t} & 0 & -e^{t} + 2e^{9t} \end{bmatrix}$

c) $\sin(\mathbf{A}) = \begin{bmatrix} 2\sin(1) - \sin(9) & 0 & 2\sin(1) - 2\sin(9) \\ \sin(4) - \sin(9) & \sin(4) & 2\sin(4) - 2\sin(9) \\ \sin(9) - \sin(1) & 0 & 2\sin(9) - \sin(1) \end{bmatrix}$

d) $\sqrt{\mathbf{A}} = \begin{bmatrix} -1 & 0 & -4 \\ -1 & 2 & -2 \\ 2 & 0 & 5 \end{bmatrix}$

e) $\ln(\mathbf{A}) = \begin{bmatrix} -2\ln(3) & 0 & -4\ln(3) \\ -2\ln\left(\frac{3}{2}\right) & 2\ln(2) & -4\ln\left(\frac{3}{2}\right) \\ 2\ln(3) & 0 & 4\ln(3) \end{bmatrix}$

f) $\mathbf{A}^{-1} = \begin{bmatrix} 17/9 & 0 & 16/9 \\ 5/36 & 1/4 & 5/18 \\ -8/9 & 0 & -7/9 \end{bmatrix}$

$\cos(t\mathbf{A}) = \begin{bmatrix} 2\cos(t) - \cos(9t) & 0 & 2\cos(t) - 2\cos(9t) \\ \cos(4t) - \cos(9t) & \cos(4t) & 2\cos(4t) - 2\cos(9t) \\ \cos(9t) - \cos(t) & 0 & 2\cos(9t) - \cos(t) \end{bmatrix}$ h) **I**

$\ldots \sin(9t) \quad 0 \quad 2\sin(t) - 2\sin(9t)$

$\ldots) \quad \sin(4t) \quad 2\sin(4t) - 2\sin(9t)$

$0 \quad 2\sin(9t) - \sin(t)$

$\frac{-\sin(2t)}{2}$

$\cos(2t) + \frac{\sin(2t)}{2}$

b) $e^{tA} = e^{-2t}\begin{bmatrix} \cos(3t)-\sin(3t) & -\dfrac{\sin(3t)}{3} \\ 6\sin(3t) & \cos(3t)+\sin(3t) \end{bmatrix}$

c)

$$e^{-2t}\begin{bmatrix} \frac{\cos(2t)}{4}-\frac{3\sin(2t)}{2}+\frac{3}{4} & -\left(\frac{\cos(2t)}{2}+\frac{\sin(2t)}{2}-\frac{1}{2}\right) & \frac{1}{4}-\frac{\cos(2t)}{4} \\ \frac{9\cos(2t)}{4}+5\sin(2t)-\frac{9}{4} & \frac{5\cos(2t)}{2}+\frac{\sin(2t)}{2}-\frac{3}{2} & \frac{3\cos(2t)}{4}-\frac{\sin(2t)}{2}-\frac{3}{4} \\ -\left(\frac{21\cos(2t)}{4}+\frac{11\sin(2t)}{2}-\frac{21}{4}\right) & -\left(\frac{7\cos(2t)}{2}-\frac{\sin(2t)}{2}-\frac{7}{2}\right) & -\left(\frac{3\cos(2t)}{4}-\sin(2t)-\frac{7}{4}\right) \end{bmatrix}$$

d) $$e^{tA} = e^{t}\begin{bmatrix} -\frac{t^2-6t-2}{2} & \frac{6t-t^2}{2} & \frac{t^3-9t^2+12t}{2} & \frac{t^3-6t^2-9t}{3} \\ \frac{t^2-2t}{2} & \frac{t^2-2t+2}{2} & -\frac{t^3-3t^2+18t}{6} & -\frac{t^3+9t}{3} \\ -2t & -2t & t^2+1 & 2t^2+4t \\ t & t & -\frac{t^2}{2} & -\left(t^2+2t-1\right) \end{bmatrix}$$

SECTION 7.1 ◆ PAGE 312

1. $0(1)+1(x)+0(x^2)+1(x^3)$

2. a) $1.68946+0.95222x$ b) $1.37656+0.994249x+0.843605\sin x$

3. a) $0.937975+1.3452x$ b) $1.24946+0.901179x+1.43945\ln x$

6. $0.567224+0.884102x+0.401164$ Atan $x+1.08362\sin x+0.918856\cos x$

SECTION 7.2 ◆ PAGE 329

1. $\begin{bmatrix} 0.25 & 0.75 \\ 0.25 & 0.75 \end{bmatrix}$

2. $\mathbf{P}^2$ has no zero entries. $\dfrac{1}{70}\begin{bmatrix} 1 & 8 & 61 \\ 1 & 8 & 61 \\ 1 & 8 & 61 \end{bmatrix}$

3.

$$\begin{bmatrix} 0.2 & 0.2 & 0.5 & 0.1 \\ 0 & 0 & 1 & 0 \\ 0.1 & 0.8 & 0.1 & 0 \\ 0.4 & 0.4 & 0.1 & 0.1 \end{bmatrix}^{10}$$

$$\begin{bmatrix} 0.0699846 & 0.449437 & 0.473470 & 0.00710716 \\ 0.0789385 & 0.532659 & 0.382230 & 0.00617152 \\ 0.0564793 & 0.324040 & 0.610969 & 0.00851100 \\ 0.0616257 & 0.371766 & 0.558628 & 0.00797941 \end{bmatrix}$$

Each row of the limit matrix is $\begin{bmatrix} \frac{45}{673} & \frac{283}{673} & \frac{340}{673} & \frac{5}{673} \end{bmatrix}$

4. Each row of the limit matrix is $\begin{bmatrix} \frac{1}{20} & \frac{9}{20} & \frac{9}{20} & \frac{1}{20} \end{bmatrix}$

5. At 1800 hours the distribution is $[0.3030 \quad 0.2727 \quad 0.2477 \quad 0.1765]$
At 2000 hours the distribution is $[0.3030 \quad 0.2727 \quad 0.2475 \quad 0.1768]$

6.

$$\mathbf{P} = \begin{bmatrix} 1 & 0 & 0 & 0 & 0 \\ 0 & 1 & 0 & 0 & 0 \\ 1/2 & 0 & 0 & 1/2 & 0 \\ 0 & 0 & 1/2 & 0 & 1/2 \\ 0 & 1/2 & 0 & 1/2 & 0 \end{bmatrix}, \quad (\mathbf{I}-\mathbf{Q})^{-1} = \begin{bmatrix} 1/2 & 1 & 1/2 \\ 1 & 2 & 1 \\ 1/2 & 1 & 3/2 \end{bmatrix},$$

$$(\mathbf{I}-\mathbf{Q})^{-1}\mathbf{N} = \begin{bmatrix} 3/4 & 1/4 \\ 1/2 & 1/2 \\ 1/4 & 3/4 \end{bmatrix}$$

7. 4 absorbing states

$$\mathbf{N} = \begin{bmatrix} 0.1 & 0.1 & 0 & 0.1 \\ 0.1 & 0.1 & 0.1 & 0 \end{bmatrix}, \quad \mathbf{Q} = \begin{bmatrix} 0.2 & 0.5 \\ 0.5 & 0.2 \end{bmatrix}, \quad (\mathbf{I}-\mathbf{Q})^{-1} = \frac{1}{39}\begin{bmatrix} 80 & 50 \\ 50 & 80 \end{bmatrix},$$

$$(\mathbf{I}-\mathbf{Q})^{-1}\mathbf{N} = \begin{bmatrix} 1/3 & 1/3 & 5/39 & 8/39 \\ 1/3 & 1/3 & 8/39 & 5/39 \end{bmatrix}$$

8. $p = 0.6$ and $q = 0.1$. The transition matrix is

$$\mathbf{P} = \begin{bmatrix} 1 & 0 & 0 & 0 \\ 0.2 & 0 & 0.6 & 0.2 \\ 0 & 0.5 & 0.4 & 0.1 \\ 0 & 0 & 1 & 0 \end{bmatrix}, \ (\mathbf{I}-\mathbf{Q})^{-1} = \begin{bmatrix} 5 & 8 & 9/5 \\ 5 & 10 & 2 \\ 5 & 10 & 3 \end{bmatrix}, \ \mathbf{N} = \begin{bmatrix} 0.2 \\ 0 \\ 0 \end{bmatrix}.$$

9. The transition matrix for the process is

$$\mathbf{P} = \begin{bmatrix} 1 & 0 & 0 & 0 & 0 \\ 0 & 0 & 0 & 0 & 1 \\ 0 & 0.5 & 0 & 0.5 & 0 \\ 0 & 0.25 & 0.25 & 0 & 0.5 \\ 0.25 & 0.25 & 0.25 & 0.25 & 0 \end{bmatrix}, \ (\mathbf{I}-\mathbf{Q})^{-1} = \frac{1}{7}\begin{bmatrix} 22 & 10 & 12 & 28 \\ 20 & 18 & 16 & 28 \\ 18 & 12 & 20 & 28 \\ 15 & 10 & 12 & 28 \end{bmatrix}$$

The expected number of days in each cell, given that he started in cell 5 is the sum $\frac{15+10+12+28}{7} = \frac{65}{7} = 9.29$

SECTION 7.3 • PAGE 338

1. $$\begin{bmatrix} y(n+1) & y(n) \end{bmatrix} = \begin{bmatrix} 1 & 0 \end{bmatrix} \begin{bmatrix} 1 & 1 \\ -2 & 1 \end{bmatrix} \begin{bmatrix} (-1)^n & 0 \\ 0 & 2^n \end{bmatrix} \begin{bmatrix} 1 & 1 \\ -2 & 1 \end{bmatrix}^{-1}.$$

$$y(n) = \frac{2^n}{3} - \frac{(-1)^n}{3}$$

2. $$\begin{bmatrix} y(n+1) & y(n) \end{bmatrix} =$$

$$\begin{bmatrix} 1 & 1 \end{bmatrix} \begin{bmatrix} 1 & 1 \\ \frac{-1+\sqrt{7}i}{2} & \frac{-1-\sqrt{7}i}{2} \end{bmatrix} \begin{bmatrix} \left(\frac{1+\sqrt{7}i}{2}\right)^n & 0 \\ 0 & \left(\frac{1-\sqrt{7}i}{2}\right)^n \end{bmatrix} \begin{bmatrix} 1 & 1 \\ \frac{-1+\sqrt{7}i}{2} & \frac{-1-\sqrt{7}i}{2} \end{bmatrix}^{-1}$$

3. $$\begin{bmatrix} y(n+1) & y(n) \end{bmatrix} = \begin{bmatrix} -1 & 0 \end{bmatrix} \begin{bmatrix} 2 & 2 \\ -\sqrt{5}-1 & \sqrt{5}-1 \end{bmatrix} \begin{bmatrix} \frac{1-\sqrt{5}}{2} & 0 \\ 0 & \frac{1+\sqrt{5}}{2} \end{bmatrix} \begin{bmatrix} 2 & 2 \\ -\sqrt{5}-1 & \sqrt{5}-1 \end{bmatrix}^{-1}$$

4. $$y(n) = \frac{5}{3} - \frac{2^{1-n}(-1)^n}{3}, \quad \lim_{n\to\infty} y(n) = \frac{5}{3}.$$

5. $y(n+1)=1.06y(n)$ with $y(0)=0$ and $y(1)=1$. In matrix form

$$\begin{bmatrix} y(n+1) & y(n) \end{bmatrix} = \begin{bmatrix} y(n) & y(n-1) \end{bmatrix} \begin{bmatrix} 1.06 & 1 \\ 0 & 0 \end{bmatrix}^n$$

6. The difference equation is given by $y(n+3)=\frac{1}{3}\left(y(n+2)+y(n+1)+y(n)\right)$

The recurrence matrix is

$$\begin{bmatrix} 1/3 & 1 & 0 \\ 1/3 & 0 & 1 \\ 1/3 & 0 & 0 \end{bmatrix}$$

The general solution is found by

$$\begin{bmatrix} y(n+2) & y(n+1) & y(n) \end{bmatrix} = \begin{bmatrix} a & b & c \end{bmatrix} \mathbf{UDU}^{-1}$$

where

$$\mathbf{U} = \begin{bmatrix} 3 & 3 & 3 \\ 2 & -2-\sqrt{2}i & -2+\sqrt{2}i \\ 1 & -1+\sqrt{2}i & -1-\sqrt{2}i \end{bmatrix} \text{ and } \mathbf{D} = \begin{bmatrix} 1 & 0 & 0 \\ 0 & -\frac{1}{3}-\frac{\sqrt{2}i}{3} & 0 \\ 0 & 0 & -\frac{1}{3}+\frac{\sqrt{2}i}{3} \end{bmatrix}$$

$$\lim_{n\to\infty} y(n) = \frac{3a+2b+c}{6}$$

7. The recurrence matrix is

$$\mathbf{A} = \begin{bmatrix} 4 & 1 & 0 \\ -5 & 0 & 1 \\ 2 & 0 & 0 \end{bmatrix}$$

The matrix is placed into Jordan form by

$$\begin{bmatrix} 1 & 0 & 1 \\ -3 & 1 & -2 \\ 2 & -2 & 1 \end{bmatrix} \mathbf{A} \begin{bmatrix} 1 & 0 & 1 \\ -3 & 1 & -2 \\ 2 & -2 & 1 \end{bmatrix}^{-1} = \begin{bmatrix} 1 & 1 & 0 \\ 0 & 1 & 0 \\ 0 & 0 & 2 \end{bmatrix}$$

$$\begin{bmatrix} y(n+3) & y(n+2) & y(n+1) \end{bmatrix} =$$

$$\begin{bmatrix} 1 & 1 & 0 \end{bmatrix} \begin{bmatrix} 1 & 0 & 1 \\ -3 & 1 & -2 \\ 2 & -2 & 1 \end{bmatrix} \begin{bmatrix} 1 & n & 0 \\ 0 & 1 & 0 \\ 0 & 0 & 2^n \end{bmatrix} \begin{bmatrix} 1 & 0 & 1 \\ -3 & 1 & -2 \\ 2 & -2 & 1 \end{bmatrix}^{-1} =$$

$$\begin{bmatrix} -2^{n+2}+2n+5 & -2^{n+1}+2n+3 & -2^n+2n+1 \end{bmatrix}$$

Note that the Jordan form raised to the n power is

$$\begin{bmatrix} 1 & n & 0 \\ 0 & 1 & 0 \\ 0 & 0 & 2^n \end{bmatrix}$$

8. The recurrence matrix is

$$\mathbf{A} = \begin{bmatrix} 6 & 1 & 0 \\ -12 & 0 & 1 \\ 8 & 0 & 0 \end{bmatrix}$$

If $\mathbf{U} = \begin{bmatrix} 1 & 0 & 0 \\ -4 & 1 & 0 \\ 4 & -2 & 1 \end{bmatrix}$, then

$$\mathbf{U}^{-1}\mathbf{A}\mathbf{U} = \begin{bmatrix} 2 & 1 & 0 \\ 0 & 2 & 1 \\ 0 & 0 & 2 \end{bmatrix}$$

and

$$\mathbf{J}^n = \begin{bmatrix} 2^n & n2^{n-1} & \dfrac{n(n-1)2^{n-2}}{2} \\ 0 & 2^n & n2^{n-1} \\ 0 & 0 & 2^n \end{bmatrix};$$

thus,

$$\begin{aligned} &\left[y(n+2) \quad y(n+1) \quad y(n)\right] = \left[3 \quad 2 \quad 1\right]\mathbf{U}\mathbf{J}^n\mathbf{U}^{-1} = \\ &\left[-2^{n-1}\left(n^2+3n-6\right) \quad -2^{n-2}\left(n^2+n-8\right) \quad -2^{n-3}\left(n^2-n-8\right)\right] \end{aligned}$$

9. $$y(n) = 2^{n-3}\left(an(n-1) - 4\left(bn(n-2) - c\left(n^2-3n+2\right)\right)\right)$$

10.

$$p = \frac{1}{4}, \lim_{n\to\infty} y(n) = \frac{a+3}{7}$$

$$p = \frac{1}{2}, \lim_{n\to\infty} y(n) = \frac{a+1}{3}$$

$$p = \frac{3}{4}, \lim_{n\to\infty} y(n) = \frac{3a+1}{5}$$

SECTION 7.4 ◆ PAGE 349

1. a) $\begin{bmatrix}\dot{x}_1\\ \dot{x}_2\end{bmatrix}=\begin{bmatrix}2 & 3\\ -3 & 1\end{bmatrix}\begin{bmatrix}x_1\\ x_2\end{bmatrix}$ b) $\begin{bmatrix}\dot{x}_1\\ \dot{x}_2\end{bmatrix}=\begin{bmatrix}0 & 1\\ 1 & 0\end{bmatrix}\begin{bmatrix}x_1\\ x_2\end{bmatrix}$

   c) $\begin{bmatrix}\dot{x}_1\\ \dot{x}_2\\ \dot{x}_3\end{bmatrix}=\begin{bmatrix}0 & 1 & 1\\ 1 & 0 & 1\\ 1 & 1 & 0\end{bmatrix}\begin{bmatrix}x_1\\ x_2\\ x_3\end{bmatrix}+\begin{bmatrix}\cos t\\ \sin t\\ 1\end{bmatrix}$

   d) Let $u_1=x_1$, $u_2=\dot{x}_1$, $u_3=x_2$, and $u_4=\dot{x}_2$ With these substitutions the system becomes

$$\begin{bmatrix}\dot{u}_1\\ \dot{u}_2\\ \dot{u}_3\\ \dot{u}_4\end{bmatrix}=\begin{bmatrix}0 & 1 & 0 & 0\\ -1 & 0 & -1 & -1\\ 0 & 0 & 0 & 1\\ 0 & -1 & -1 & -1\end{bmatrix}\begin{bmatrix}u_1\\ u_2\\ u_3\\ u_4\end{bmatrix}+\begin{bmatrix}0\\ \sin t\\ 0\\ \cos t\end{bmatrix}$$

2. a) $\begin{bmatrix}x_1\\ x_2\end{bmatrix}=c_1\begin{bmatrix}3e^{-t}-2e^{-2t}\\ 2e^{-2t}-2e^{-t}\end{bmatrix}+c_2\begin{bmatrix}3e^{-t}-3e^{-2t}\\ 3e^{-2t}-2e^{-t}\end{bmatrix}$

   b) $\begin{bmatrix}x_1\\ x_2\end{bmatrix}=c_1\begin{bmatrix}\cos t-7\sin t\\ 5\sin t\end{bmatrix}+c_2\begin{bmatrix}-10\sin t\\ \cos t+7\sin t\end{bmatrix}$

   c) $\begin{bmatrix}x_1\\ x_2\end{bmatrix}=c_1e^{-t}\begin{bmatrix}\cos t-8\sin t\\ 5\sin t\end{bmatrix}+c_2e^{-t}\begin{bmatrix}-13\sin t\\ \cos t+8\sin t\end{bmatrix}$

   d) $\begin{bmatrix}x_1\\ x_2\end{bmatrix}=c_1e^{-t}\begin{bmatrix}1-2t\\ t\end{bmatrix}+c_2e^{-t}\begin{bmatrix}-4t\\ 2t+1\end{bmatrix}$

3. a) $\begin{bmatrix}x_1\\ x_2\\ x_3\end{bmatrix}=c_1\begin{bmatrix}-e^{3t}-e^{2t}+3e^{t}\\ e^{3t}+e^{2t}-2e^{t}\\ e^{3t}-e^{t}\end{bmatrix}+c_2\begin{bmatrix}-e^{3t}-2e^{2t}+3e^{t}\\ e^{3t}+2e^{2t}-2e^{t}\\ e^{3t}-e^{t}\end{bmatrix}+c_3\begin{bmatrix}-e^{3t}+e^{2t}\\ e^{3t}-e^{2t}\\ e^{3t}\end{bmatrix}$

   b)

$$\begin{bmatrix}x_1\\ x_2\\ x_3\end{bmatrix}=c_1\begin{bmatrix}e^{-t}-2\sin t\\ \frac{1}{2}\left(-e^{-t}+\cos t+3\sin t\right)\\ \sin t\end{bmatrix}+c_2\begin{bmatrix}-4\sin t\\ \cos t+3\sin t\\ 2\sin t\end{bmatrix}+c_3\begin{bmatrix}2e^{-t}-2\cos t+2\sin t\\ -e^{-t}+\cos t-2\sin t\\ \cos t-\sin t\end{bmatrix}$$

   c) $\begin{bmatrix}x_1\\ x_2\\ x_3\end{bmatrix}=c_1e^{t}\begin{bmatrix}6t^2+1\\ -\dfrac{9t^2}{2}\\ 3t\end{bmatrix}+c_2e^{t}\begin{bmatrix}8t^2\\ -6t^2+1\\ 4t\end{bmatrix}+c_3e^{t}\begin{bmatrix}4t\\ -3t\\ 1\end{bmatrix}$

d)

$$\begin{bmatrix} x_1 \\ x_2 \\ x_3 \end{bmatrix} = c_1 \begin{bmatrix} e^{-2t}(5\sin t - \cos t) + 2 \\ e^{-2t}(\cos t - 5\sin t) - 1 \\ e^{-2t}\dfrac{4\cos t - 7\sin t}{5} - \dfrac{4}{5} \end{bmatrix} + c_2 \begin{bmatrix} e^{-2t}(2\sin t - 2\cos t) + 2 \\ e^{-2t}(2\cos t - 2\sin t) - 1 \\ e^{-2t}\dfrac{4\cos t - 2\sin t}{5} - \dfrac{4}{5} \end{bmatrix} +$$

$$c_2 \begin{bmatrix} 10e^{-2t}\sin t \\ -10e^{-2t\sin t} \\ e^{-2t}(\cos t - 3\sin t) \end{bmatrix}$$

4 a) $\mathbf{p} = \begin{bmatrix} \dfrac{3}{2} \\ -\dfrac{1}{2} \end{bmatrix}$ b) $\mathbf{p} = \begin{bmatrix} 7t\cos t - (9t+7)\sin t \\ \left(\dfrac{7t}{2} + 3\right)\sin t - 2t\cos t \end{bmatrix}$

c) $\mathbf{p} = \begin{bmatrix} \dfrac{6-13t}{2} \\ \dfrac{3(3t-1)}{2} \end{bmatrix}$ d) $\mathbf{p} = \begin{bmatrix} -2t^2e^t \\ \dfrac{e^t}{4} + e^t(t^2+t) \end{bmatrix}$

5. a) $\mathbf{p} = \begin{bmatrix} \dfrac{18t^2+210t+511}{108} \\ \dfrac{18t^2+102t+295}{108} \\ -\dfrac{9t^2-12t-40}{27} \end{bmatrix}$ b) $\mathbf{p} = \begin{bmatrix} -(t+1)\cos t + (2-t)\sin t - 1 \\ \left(t+\dfrac{1}{2}\right)\cos t + \left(\dfrac{t}{2} - \dfrac{3}{2}\right)\sin t + 1 \\ \dfrac{t\cos t}{2} + \left(\dfrac{t-1}{2}\right)\sin t + 1 \end{bmatrix}$

c) $\mathbf{p} = \begin{bmatrix} -25 \\ 17 \\ 6 \end{bmatrix}$ d) $\mathbf{p} = \begin{bmatrix} -\cos t + \dfrac{15\sin t}{4} + 2t - \dfrac{2}{5} \\ \cos t - \dfrac{11\sin t}{4} - t + \dfrac{2}{5} \\ \dfrac{3\cos t}{8} - \dfrac{7\sin t}{8} - \dfrac{4t}{5} + \dfrac{6}{25} \end{bmatrix}$

6. Let $u_1 = y$ and $u_2 = \dot{y}$. With these substitutions $\dot{u}_1 = u_2$ and $\dot{u}_2 = -2u_1 + 3u_2$. Then the first order system is

$$\begin{bmatrix} \dot{u}_1 \\ \dot{u}_2 \end{bmatrix} = \begin{bmatrix} 0 & 1 \\ -2 & 3 \end{bmatrix} \begin{bmatrix} u_1 \\ u_2 \end{bmatrix}$$

The general solution is

$$\begin{bmatrix} u_1 \\ u_2 \end{bmatrix} = c_1 \begin{bmatrix} 2e^t - e^{2t} \\ 2e^t - 2e^{2t} \end{bmatrix} + c_2 \begin{bmatrix} e^{2t} - e^t \\ 2e^{2t} - e^t \end{bmatrix} = \begin{bmatrix} y \\ \dot{y} \end{bmatrix}$$

SYMBOLS

$\mathbf{t}^{-1}$	Inverse transformation, 167
$\mathbf{t}_{\mathbf{A}}$	Transformation induced by the matrix **A**, 170
$\mathbf{i}$	Identity transformation, 179
$\mathbf{A} \sim \mathbf{B}$	**A** is similar to **B**, 186
α_{ij}	Minor of the matrix **A**, 188
DET(**A**)	Determinant of the matrix **A**, 189, 212
$\mathbf{A}_{ij}$	Cofactor of the matrix **A**, 189
ADJ(**A**)	Adjoint of the matrix **A**, 196
$W(f_1, f_2, \ldots, f_n)$	Wronskian of the set of functions $\{f_1, f_2, \ldots, f_n\}$, 206
$\mathrm{DIAG}(a_{11} \ldots a_{nn})$	Diagonal matrix, 217
$\mathbf{A}^*$	$(\bar{a}_{qp})$ for the complex valued matrix (a_{pq}), 234
C^n	Ordered n-tuples of complex numbers, 238, 263
$\langle \mathbf{x}, \mathbf{y} \rangle$	Scalar product of two vectors, 238
$\Vert\mathbf{x}\Vert$	Length of a vector or vector norm, 238, 264
R_i	$\sum_{j=1}^{n} \lvert a_{ij} \rvert$, for the matrix (a_{ij}), 247
C_j	$\sum_{i=1}^{n} \lvert a_{ij} \rvert$, for the matrix (a_{ij}), 247
R	$\max_i \mathrm{R}_i$, 247
C	$\max_j \mathrm{C}_j$, 247
G_λ	Set of generalized eigenvectors belonging to λ, 253
$\Vert\mathbf{x}\Vert_{\mathrm{S}}$	$\sum_{i=1}^{n} \lvert x_i \rvert$, 264
$\Vert\mathbf{x}\Vert_{\mathrm{M}}$	$\max_j \lvert x_j \rvert$, 264
$\Vert\mathbf{x}\Vert_{\mathrm{E}}$	$\left(\sum_{j=1}^{n} \lvert x_j \rvert^2 \right)^{1/2}$, 264
$\Vert\mathbf{A}\Vert$	Norm of a square matrix **A**, 266
$\Vert\mathbf{A}\Vert_{\mathrm{R}}$	$\max_i \sum_{j=1}^{n} \lvert a_{ij} \rvert$, 267
$\Vert\mathbf{A}\Vert_{\mathrm{C}}$	$\max_j \sum_{i=1}^{n} \lvert a_{ij} \rvert$, 267

$\|\mathbf{A}\|_E$	$\left(\sum_{j=1}^{n}\sum_{i=1}^{n}\|a_{ij}\|^2\right)^{1/2}$, 267
$\|\mathbf{A}\|_M$	$n \max_{ij}\|a_{ij}\|$, 267
$\left(\mathbf{A}^{(n)}\right)$	Sequence of matrices $\mathbf{A}^{(1)}, \mathbf{A}^{(2)}, \ldots, \mathbf{A}^{(k)}, \ldots$, 270
$\mathbf{J}$	Matrix in Jordan canonical form, 272
Λ	DIAG (λ_i,..., λ_i), 272, 278
$f(\mathbf{A})$	Function of a matrix, 277, 282
$\sqrt{\mathbf{A}}$	Square root of a matrix, 284
$e^{\mathbf{A}}$	Exponential function of a matrix, 286, 339
$\dot{\mathbf{x}}$	Derivative of the vector **x**, 339

INDEX

I

J

K

L

M

N

O

P

R

S

T

U

V

W

Mathematical Activities with Computer Algebra: a photocopiable resource book

Etchells T, Hunter M, Monaghan J, Pozzi S, Rothery A

This photocopiable resource book is the first of a new generation of support materials for computer algebra. Designed to be used with any computer algebra system, the authors go beyond mere button pressing and show how to harness the power of computer algebra systems for educational purposes. Concepts are illustrated, techniques and methods presented, and modelling and applications are explained. Appendices give overviews of DERIVE, Maple, Mathematica, Theorist (Math Plus) and the new TI-92 calculator.

Activity Worksheets, Help Sheets and Teaching Notes cover a wide range of mathematical topics at school and college level.

Topics covered include; functions and graphs, differentiation, integration, sequences and series, vectors and matrices, mechanics, trigonometry, numerical methods.

Activities include: Multiplying factors; Equation of a tangent; Taxing functions; The tile factory; Function and derivative - visualisation; The approximate derivative function; Sketching graphs; Pollution and population; Max cone; Optimising transport costs; Area under a curve; Enclosed areas; A function whose derivative is itself; Wine glass design; The limit of a sequence; Visualising Taylor approximations; Visualising matrix transformations; Blood groups; Circular motion; Swing safety; No turning back; Modelling the sine function; Solving equations with tangents.

Chartwell-Bratt, ISBN 0-86238-405-2, 1995

Teaching Mathematics with DERIVE Josef Boehm (ed)

Proceedings of the 1992 Conference on the Didactics of Computer Algebra

Chartwell-Bratt, 298 pages, ISBN 0-86238-319-6, 1993

DERIVE in Education: Opportunities and Strategies

H Heugl, B Kutzler (eds)

Proceedings of the 1993 Conference on the Didactics of Computer Algebra

Chartwell-Bratt, 302 pages, ISBN 0-86238-351-X, 1994

DERIVE-based Investigations for Post-16 Core Mathematics, 2nd Ed

A J Watkins

Practical investigations using DERIVE. Extensively trialled.

Chartwell-Bratt, 102 pages, ISBN 0-86238-312-9, 1993

Mathematics with Excel David Sjostrand

Makes good use of Excel's graphical features to illustrate and help visualisation of important mathematical concepts. Based on Excel v5 but usable with earlier versions and other spreadsheets. Also shows how to link Excel with DERIVE.

Chartwell-Bratt, 260 pages, ISBN 0-86238-361-7, 1994

Modelling with Spreadsheets Andrew Rothery

Usable with any spreadsheet. Explains the principles of modelling and spreadsheets. "Optimisation" is central theme. Clear and accessible.

Chartwell-Bratt, 63 pages, ISBN 0-86238-258-0, 1989

Technology in Mathematics Teaching
- a bridge between teaching and learning
Edited by Leone Burton and Barbara Jaworski

Blackboard and chalk are no longer the sole technology available to the mathematics teacher or tutor. In many classrooms, students might be expected to learn using computers, calculators, film, television, video and many other media. However, very often technology is introduced into mathematics classrooms without due consideration of its role, or its impact on learning and teaching.

This book addresses issues raised by the introduction of technology into the teaching and learning of mathematics. It uses the metaphor of technology acting as a 'bridge' between the teacher's planning and the learner's developing understanding.

Chapters address the learning of mathematics at every level, primary to tertiary. The technologies discussed are substantially those of the computer and the calculator but reference is also made to others, including video and film. Whether dealing with general issues, or the specifics of, for example, using a particular piece of computer software, authors keep as a main focus the mathematics learning and teaching environment.

The book is divided into six sections: Setting the Scene; Why Technology; Using Calculators; How may technology support school algebra?; Advanced Mathematics - Some Perspectives; Innovative Uses of Technology.

Chartwell-Bratt, 496 pages, ISBN 0-86238-401-X, 1995

Discovering Geometry with a Computer
- using Cabri-Geometre Heinz Schumann and David Green

This book provides a wide ranging discussion of geometrical investigation aided by a computer. Although the book begins with an introduction to one particular software package - Cabri-Geometre - to which it refers throughout, most of the activities suggested will be of interest to users of other software packages such as Geometer's Sketchpad and Geometry Inventor.

The topics covered in depth are: Learning geometry through interactive construction; Creating macros; Discovering theorems; Loci; Symmetry; Geometrical microworld design; Isoperimetric problems; Transformations; Twenty problems to investigate. Contains over 900 geometrical diagrams and hundreds of ideas for investigation are to be found throughout its pages.

Associated with the book is a disk (MS-DOS or Macintosh formats) containing over 400 Cabri-Geometre figures and macros designed to illustrate the contents of the book and to aid personal exploration and extension.

Chartwell-Bratt, 282 pages, ISBN 0-86238-373-0, 1995